Women in Relationships with Bisexual Men

Women in Relationships with Bisexual Men

Bi Men By Women

Maria Pallotta-Chiarolli

co-researched with
Sara Lubowitz

LEXINGTON BOOKS
Lanham • Boulder • New York • London

Published by Lexington Books
An imprint of The Rowman & Littlefield Publishing Group, Inc.
4501 Forbes Boulevard, Suite 200, Lanham, Maryland 20706
www.rowman.com

Unit A, Whitacre Mews, 26-34 Stannary Street, London SE11 4AB

Copyright © 2016 by Lexington Books

All rights reserved. No part of this book may be reproduced in any form or by any electronic or mechanical means, including information storage and retrieval systems, without written permission from the publisher, except by a reviewer who may quote passages in a review.

British Library Cataloguing in Publication Information Available

Library of Congress Control Number: 2015952401
ISBN: 978-0-7391-3457-3 (cloth : alk. paper)
ISBN: 978-1-4985-3005-7 (pbk. : alk. paper)
ISBN: 978-0-7391-3459-7 (electronic)

∞™ The paper used in this publication meets the minimum requirements of American National Standard for Information Sciences—Permanence of Paper for Printed Library Materials, ANSI/NISO Z39.48-1992.

Printed in the United States of America

From Maria:

*To Mr and Mrs Queer...
from Mardi Gras to Sublime Point...
he was the Dancing Queen and the English Patient
she was the Lilith and the Naomi (no me, name me, know me)
I thank you all*

From Sara:

*To my late mother Susan Thomas for the love she gave me from the time I was born to the time that she died. She made me, me.
Thanks Mum.
And to Mark, you know why.
And to my two girls who are great*

Contents

Acknowledgments ix

PART I: INTRODUCTION 1

1 "Outside Belonging": An Introduction to the Women,
  their Men, and the Research 3

2 "Border Women and Their Border Men": Some Theories,
  Definitions, and Debates Framing the Research 41

3 "You know, the old Kinsey scale": Women Talk about
  their Partners' Bisexualities 71

4 "I Have A Sexuality Too": Women Discussing
  their Own Sexualities 93

PART II: THE JOURNEYS 125

5 "Starting Out Knowing": Negotiating the Beginning of the
  Relationship 127

6 "Changing Course Midstream": From Closet to Confrontation 151

7 "We've Arrived Where We Started and Know the Place for
  the First Time": Women Reflecting on 'Staying the Course'
  or 'Splitting Up' 193

PART III: MAPPING THE LANDSCAPE 211

8 "New Rules, No Rules, Old Rules or Our Rules":
  Women Designing MOREs with their Partners 213

9 "The Problem Is That He's A Man, Not That He's Bisexual": Women Discussing Masculinity, Misogyny, Privilege, and Power	235
10 "What Do We Tell The Kids?": Women Talk about Bisexual Fathers	259
11 "Spreading Disease With the Greatest of Ease": Negotiating Sexual Health Issues	295

PART IV: BORDER DWELLING AS OUTSIDERS BELONGING — 321

12 "Minute by Minute Maneuvering": Navigating the Heteroworld	323
13 "Ewww, Girl Germs": Women's Experiences and Perceptions of Homonormativity	375
14 "The Priest Told Him to Marry Me and He'd Go Straight": Bordering Religion and Spirituality in MOREs	395
15 "It's A Matter of Family Honor and Shame": Negotiating Ethnic and Racial Identities and Community Codes	415
16 "When Your Relationship Isn't Recognized by Relationship Services": Misrepresentations and Erasures in Health Services	437

PART V: NOT JUST BELONGING BUT BLOOMING IN THE BORDERLANDS — 471

17 "A Door that hasn't been Opened": Women's Final Words for Future Women	473
References	489
Index	525
About the Author	541

Acknowledgments

This book would not have been possible without the women who lived and loved, laughed and cried, and then laughed and cried again as they opened their hearts and minds and their worlds to us. In particular, we honour the women who have died since the project, including Alice and her partner Paul, Brenda and Soulla (pseudonyms), and Brenda's partner Edward (pseudonym).

We also wish to honour the supportive bisexual men in these women's lives, and send our heartfelt hope for peace and consolation to those men who wreaked havoc in women's lives. We know the world which forced you to hurt yourself, and thus hurt those who loved you, and we hope this book is a step in shifting that devastating heteropatriarchal and biphobic framework.

Our huge thanks and respect to Fritz Klein (1932–2006) who initiated, inspired, and encouraged so many of us with his intellect, wit and passion. We wish you were alive to read this book as one of many legacies to your work.

Other Australian colleagues who have supported us with their conversation, research and activism include Graham McKay, Kirsten McLean, Wayne Roberts, Glen Vassallo, and Michael Wynter. We also send our appreciation and admiration to all the Bisexual Groups in the world, and their leaders such as Meg John Barker, Sheela Lambert, Robyn Ochs and Ron Suresha, whose activism and passion have nourished us along this journey.

To the patient and unwaveringly supportive publishers at Lexington Books, who allowed deadlines to come and go: Michael Sisskin, Jana Hodges-Kluck, Joseph Parry, and Brighid Stone. And to Anita Singh and crew at Deanta Global Publishing Services for patiently and meticulously checking the text, creating the index and converting the manuscript into a book!

Maria also wishes to thank Adrian Kelly from Transcripts Plus, Agnes Lichtor and Rebecca Sion for sensitive transcription of the interviews. And to Rob Chiarolli for patiently doing fiddly manuscript formatting. Finally, to Dr. Elyse Warner, who took the time to cast the last editorial/pruning eye over this manuscript. Your fresh approach was the last much needed pit-stop!

A special thank you goes to Bryan Mooney who discovered Edward Burne-Jones' "Garden of Pan" with Maria at the National Gallery of Victoria.

Maria sends huge bacis to her family and friends, her family of friends, and her friends in family; to all her loved ones for patience, love, support, food and fun.

This project was begun with a Deakin University Faculty Grant at a time when Australian universities had not increasingly become corporatized technocratic Kafkaesque places. This book has increasingly been slowed down over the years and much of it was written between midnight and 3am when those hours could not be found during the day. I thank those leaders and colleagues in my university and others who have had the courage and conviction to maintain the focus on education, not on bureaucratisation. In particular, I wish to honor Teresa Capetola, Professor Raewyn Connell, Matthew Ebden, Dr. Jess Heerde, Shalika Hegde, Professor Wayne Martino, Professor Baden Offord and Professor Bob Pease. I also wish to honour my PhD students, past and present, for the challenges, camaraderie and passion to make academia socially useful.

Finally, as this book enters its final stages of launching into the world to hopefully do some queering good, Maria is mourning the death of David Bowie (1947–2016). She sends her deep love and gratitude to her "sexy-smart starman" who landed in her life in 1972 when she was a 12 year-old alien, queering/clearing her vision of genders, sexualities, colonialism and cultures, and initiating a lifelong "loving the alien" in herself and others.

Part I

INTRODUCTION

Chapter 1

"Outside Belonging"
An Introduction to the Women, their Men, and the Research

> This is the first time I've been able to talk to anybody. I need to do this . . . and the prospect of having a whole lot of information about other women who have been in similar situations is really great for me. (Gerry)

> Having lived with Gennaro I see all the little nastiness that he faces, the confusions in the world, all these preconceptions that people have. I notice that it really cuts him, like badly. Whatever I can do to prevent that I am wanting to do. (Lizz)

> I think it's important to acknowledge what I've gone through. My journey was a very painful experience on lots of levels. (Nirupa)

The above quotes are from three out of 78 Australian women who participated in this research project, having been or currently in a relationship with a bisexual man. They provide a small but powerful insight into the many reasons why women wanted to participate in this project, as well as giving us a glimpse into lives, intimacies, relationships and families that span the gamut from extremely oppressive to extremely liberating. The women are culturally and geographically diverse, ranging from the ages of 19 to 65. They are in monogamous, open, and polyamorous relationships with bisexual-identifying and/or bisexual-behaving men. Some of these women are mothers, some are grandmothers. Some identify as bisexual or lesbian, some as heterosexual, while others refuse to categorize their own sexualities. Some women entered the relationship never imagining their partners would one day 'come out' or be 'found out' to be bisexual, and thus began mapping a terrain they found alien and terrifying. Some women entered the relationship knowing their partners were bisexual and began to navigate their journey through both exhilarating and exhausting territory. Indeed, a partner's 'disclosure' or 'discovery' raised issues of closeting and coming out for the women themselves in relation to 'who to tell' such as their children, families, friends, and work colleagues. For other women, being in a relationship with a bisexual man meant navigating a route through sometimes converging, sometimes conflicting communities, such as straight friendships, gay communities, and ethnic and religious communities.

In this book, some women express much anger and grief over having their lives turned upside down by the betrayal and deception of their husbands. Other women feel strong and confident, adamantly stating that they would never be in a relationship with a heterosexual man after having experienced greater emotional depth, sexual intimacy, and equitable gender relations with a bisexual man. Indeed, some women are not concerned with the way their partners perform their sexuality, but are very concerned if their partners perform their masculinity in traditional patriarchal or misogynist ways. Some women found their own sexualities and femininities shutting down or being repressed and dismissed, while others found their sexualities and femininities flourishing and freed to explore and expand.

Some women found themselves dealing with STIs and HIV/AIDS, and/or a range of mental and emotional health issues, and subsequent associations with a range of health and counselling services. Other women were already living with chronic illnesses and disabilities. And there were some women who described themselves as physically, emotionally and mentally healthy and happy with their lives and relationships.

Given the above overview of the range of women's experiences and perspectives, Probyn's term, "outside belonging" or "inbetween categories of specificity" (1996: 9), is applicable to the women in our research and their bisexual male partners. These relationships provide insights into the border existences, boundary demarcations, devastating oppressions, exhilarating affirmations, and innovative negotiations of the women and their partners in order to construct or dismantle, maintain or regain healthy sexual, emotional, and social relationships. Their mixed-orientation relationships will from now on be abbreviated as MOREs in this book because the customary acronym MOMs limits these relationships only to mixed-orientation marriages. MOREs are not only 'outside' gendernormative and heteronormative constructs of heterosexual identity and heterosexual relationships, but also 'belonging' in the sense that they may 'pass' as 'normal' heterosexual couples. They are also 'outside' the homonormative constructs of gay identity and gay community in Australia while simultaneously 'belonging' due to their partners' and sometimes their own same-sex attractions and relationships. Thus, interestingly, the acronym MORE symbolically represents this being on the borders and beyond, outside and inside, and always something more, something else, something in excess (Derrida, 1981).

The questions that will be addressed in this book include:

- How, when and why is the man's bisexuality disclosed or discovered?
- How do these relationships work and where do they flounder?
- How do the men and women in these relationships negotiate and establish "new rules" and boundaries in order to construct and maintain their relationships?
- How do they deal with issues such as social, community, and familial ostracism, or the silence about their relationships within these networks?
- What would they like to see in popular culture and the media about their relationships?
- What are the experiences of the women in accessing health services and community services?
- What do these women's experiences tell us about early-twenty-first century constructions and understandings of intimate relationships, sex and love; sociocultural representations and categorizations of gender and sexuality; and the impact of class, rural/urban settings, ethnicity, Indigeneity, religion and education on interpersonal relationships?

This book is thus an attempt to explore very underresearched but, as we shall read, overstereotyped and sensationalized areas of human relationships. As Heath writes, relationships involving bisexual people are either "excluded from the research or the people involved in those relationships treated as if they hold an identity they have not chosen and might not accept" (2010: 119). Bostwick & Hequembourg call this "epistemic injustice," divided into "testimonial injustice" wherein a bisexual's voice and perspectives are given less credibility; and "hermeneutical injustice" wherein the limitations of current knowledge prevent bisexual voices and perspectives from being understood (2014: 490; see also Klesse, 2011; Ripley et al. 2011). Indeed, bisexual men and their relationships were not studied systematically until the 1980s, in the midst of a heightened concern about men who had sex with men and women (MSMW) being a threat to otherwise 'low-risk populations' for HIV transmission. Thus, this book will develop the broader pioneering work undertaken by researchers and activists such as Buxton (1991, 2001, 2004a, b; 2006a, b, c, d; 2007, 2011) & Gochros (1989) within an Australian context. Indeed, Buxton provides the "working definition" of bisexuality which frames our research:

> bisexual persons are sexually, emotionally, and erotically attracted to both men and women, usually in varying degrees that may fluctuate over time; and may or may not have sex with partners of both genders, in the same time period or over time; and self-identify as bisexual. Like homosexuality and heterosexuality,

bisexuality is multidimensional, involving sexual fantasies, emotional and social attractions, sexual desires, and pleasurable lovemaking (2006c: 109–110; see also Kort, 2014a).

This book will also illustrate how the relationships, lifestyles and sexual health issues of women and their bisexual male partners have been subjected to one or more of the following forms of "bisexual erasure," "bi-negativity," "biphobia," or "monosexism" (Barker & Langdridge, 2012; Barker et al. 2012) in most research, popular culture, and textually:

- *Underrepresentation*: a lack of visibility, data and analysis rendering certain relationship forms nonexistent. For example, very rarely do we read positive stories about a bisexually active man's strategies of negotiating his sexual practices and intimate relationships with his female and male partners;
- *Misrepresentation*: stereotypes, media and popular culture constructions, societal presumptions and prejudices about bisexual men. For example, that bisexual men are AIDS carriers; are secretly engaging in sexual relations with men; identify as bisexual rather than heterosexual or gay; and that all their women partners are unaware of the men's sexuality;
- *Outdated representation*: knowledge and research lacks updating and revision. For example, we need to acknowledge and understand emerging terms such as "sexual fluidity," "heteroflexibility," "homoflexibility" and "straight men with gay interests" (Kort, 2014a); "girlfags" (Hardy, 2012) and "femantasy" (Simpson, 2006) in the articulation of the diversity of sexual desires. We also need to update our awareness and understanding of the impact of increasing media coverage of partnering possibilities, such as polyamory, that disrupt the gay/straight and monogamist/promiscuous binaries;
- *Homogenized representation*: where the diversity within groups, subcultures and categories such as sexual categories is not presented. For example, very rarely do we read of class, ethnicity, disability, geographical location, gendered expectations and other factors that influence a woman's decisions and negotiations in relation to a bisexual man. Finally, we need to adopt decolonizing practices and explore precolonial and non-Western constructions of MOREs, reclaiming cultural pasts and incorporating contemporary postcolonial MOREs (see Low & Pallotta-Chiarolli, 2015). For example, in Japan, "fujoshi" are "naughty or rotten girls" who write and read Boys Love manga; "fudanshi" are "rotten boys," heterosexual men who read Boys Love manga or are sexual/loving partners of "fujoshi"; and "bishonen" or androgynous "beautiful boys" are traditional masculine representations in Japanese pre-Western history (Bauer, 2013; Levi et al. 2010; McLelland et al. 2015).

Summaries of the project have already been published (Pallotta-Chiarolli, 2014, 2015; Pallotta-Chiarolli & Lubowitz, 2003) while excerpts from some interviews were used in Pallotta-Chiarolli (2010a).We specifically wanted to interview Australian women because although women's perspectives on their bisexual partners and their MOREs had been somewhat represented in international research, many Australian women stated they felt overwhelmingly isolated, invisible, unrepresentable and deliberately ignored, sometimes by their own male partners, often by families, friends, health services, and more broadly in Australian media, popular culture and research.

> Many famous [Australian] women are married to men who have sex with men, but it's never ever spoken about and there is such a stigma around it. And that terrible terrible thing [where sometimes the men suicide] ... because he had been caught in the toilets with a man. But what happened to his wife and whether she knew or not was never, ever discussed. She was just completely invisible. (Sara)

We were also mindful of needing to investigate what bisexual men had written about themselves and their women partners. In his overview of the available research and literature on bisexual men, Steinman (2011) found that bisexual men were less likely than bisexual women to publicly and analytically articulate their experiences. Beemyn reflected on how bisexual men continue to be "a notable absence and a contested presence" in research and literature (2011: 390). Thus, accessing the few but highly significant and groundbreaking anthologies that provided biographical narratives and first-person insights was important (Beemyn & Steinman, 2001a, b; Klein & Schwartz, 2001; Ochs & Williams, 2014; Suresha & Chvany, 2005). Beemyn (2011) recalls the difficulty in finding a publisher, an experience I faced when trying to find an Australian publisher. Indeed, I was told by a couple of publishers (both male, white and straight-identifying) that whilst they were willing to publish the 'known' negative facets of **MORES** as these would have a readership, the kinky/queer/feminist/positive perspectives on bisexual men were "unbelievable" and would not find a readership. On the other hand, assumed lack of readership was demonstrated by several international publishers, who believed a book on Australian MOREs would hold limited international interest.

Another issue of which we were mindful was that although there has been an increasing amount of research on bisexuality since 2011, recent scholarship has attempted to move bisexuality to the center of queer theory "for theorizing bisexuality vis-a-vis abstract systems" and "for grasping bisexuality as a politically infused identity" (Steinman, 2011: 402). While very significant, this work tends to limit the ability to understand bisexuality as an everyday "lived experience," particularly in relation to the bisexual men and their partners who do not identify with or align themselves with queer and/or sex-positive activist communities. Steinman's view resonates with many women in our research who for various reasons did not see themselves and their partners as members of or supported by LGBTQ communities (see Chapter 13). Similarly, as Buxton writes in relation to straight wives of bisexual men and heteroworld, "their heterosexuality is now an 'issue'—not a privilege" (2011: 542; see chapter 12).

I have structured the chapters so that each provides our research findings and also documents and directs readers to further definitional, theoretical and empirical work to date, including some pertinent media, popular culture and literary texts that the research participants referred to. This structure also honors one of their major recommendations: that this work be made available as a valuable resource for educators, health workers, families, and wider communities and society. Thus, what may appear to be scattered and meandering material of various genres and styles, interwoven with the voices of the participants themselves, is actually a deliberate attempt to follow branches and threads that ultimately contextualise and interweave the sociocultural, health, educational, interpersonal and personal lives of the research participants, and those who contest, connect and collaborate with them in various social settings.

"WE DON'T FIT ANYWHERE"

> We don't fit anywhere ... we're a minority group, whereas in actual fact we're probably the majority group. It's just that people don't identify with being bisexual, they just identify as being either gay or heterosexual. (Nina)

> I would like other women to know that if you're not being hurt and if you're not being corrupted and if you're not being coerced, then it is actually possible to maintain a relationship with a bisexual man. He's bi, he's not gay, and that's the difference. (Monica)

In their research into queer Maori history, Aspin & Hutchings discuss "a striking example of a heterosexual veneer being applied to our history" by Western colonial constructions of sexual duality (2006: 229). They explore the Te Arawa love story of Tutanekai and Hinemoa, and how contemporary storytellers have omitted Tutanekai's male companion called Tiki. Mention is made of Tiki in the *Dictionary of the Maori Language,* first compiled in 1832 by the missionary Herbert Williams, as the takatapui of Tutanekai, a takatapui being "an intimate companion of the same sex." In the following, Te Awekotuku's rendition reveals how much of precolonial history has been filtered through colonial heteromonogamism:

> This word [takatapui] is associated with one of the most romantic, glamorized, man-woman love stories of the Maori world, . . . Tutanekai, with his flute and his favorite intimate friend, his hoa takatapui, Tiki, and Hinemoa, the determined, valorous, superbly athletic woman—my ancestress—who took the initiative herself, swam the midnight water of the lake to reach him, and interestingly, consciously and deliberately masqueraded as a man, as a warrior, to lure him to her arms. Isn't that another, intriguing way of looking at this story? And isn't that a way which we, our community and tradition, have been denied? (Te Awekotuku, 1991: 37; see also Te Awekotuku, 2001).

As Aspin & Hutchings add, "we can be sure that the relationships that existed between these three people were sanctioned and celebrated within the whanau, hapu and iwi to which they belonged" (2006: 230).

The English painter, Edward Burne-Jones, seems to evoke a similar narrative of Hinemoa, Tutanekai and Tiki in his painting *The Garden of Pan* (1886–1887), reprinted on the cover of this book. A man and a woman, both naked, sit intimately together, gazing across a stream to Pan, who is sitting on a rock playing his flute while looking out at the viewer. In ancient Greek religion and mythology, Pan is the god of the wild and companion of the nymphs. He is also connected to fertility, is famous for his sexual powers, and is the archetype of male sexual virility. There is also a myth of Pan learning masturbation from his father, Hermes, and teaching the habit to shepherds.

Given these representations of Pan, gaze again at the cover of this book. How do we read the expressions and bodily stances of the man and woman towards Pan in Burne-Jones' painting? Is she holding the man back from Pan or is she as drawn to him as her partner? Indeed, is she offering her partner to Pan? Is the man drawn to Pan or wary of him? Is he slightly in front of his partner in order to hold her back from sexual temptation? The possibilities of these multiple interpretations will become evident in the lived experiences of the women in this research.

Thus, here we have two mythologies represented in text and art from both precolonial and colonial contexts which problematize sexual binaries and monogamies. Indeed, the term 'takatapui' has taken on renewed significance in an era of decolonizing practices among Maori sexual minorities. It "allows for a fluidity within sexual orientation that is located within a Maori paradigm" (Aspin & Hutchings, 2006: 231; see also Kahaleole & Kauanui, 1996).

Similar to the multiple interpretations made available in "The Garden of Pan" and the Te Arawa story, contemporary bisexuality forces into the foreground the reality that it is not always possible to tell the entirety of a person's sexual and romantic desires, behaviors and intimate relationships based on heterocolonialist, monosexist presumptions about the correlation of sexual orientation with the current or publicly acknowledged sexual partner.

These absences, erasures, and "exclusion by inclusion" (Pallotta-Chiarolli, 2010a, b; 2015a; see also Martin & Pallotta-Chiarolli, 2009; Pallotta-Chiarolli & Martin, 2009) into gay or straight categories of identity and relationship leave some relationships and families feeling silenced and invisibilized, even within sociocultural and health settings that purport to espouse a sexual diversity framework. Thus, it was an imperative of this research to ask women about the history of their relationships with their partners, as well as about their partner's known histories before and after the relationship. Our aim was to incorporate the multiplicity of encounters, contexts and time spans that would make bisexuality visible in its shifting and varying permutations.

In relation to the increasing sociocultural legitimation of gay and lesbian identities and families, there appears to have developed what could be defined as a homonormative hierarchy based on what is constructed as the dominant or central-within-the-marginal homosexual group: usually white, middle-class, monogamously coupled, exclusively homosexual relationships and families (Cover, 2010; Klesse, 2007). I wish to state clearly here that our intention is not to position homonormativity alongside heteronormativity in terms of power within the wider society, but to consider difference, power and hierarchy within the nonheterosexual margin as a consequence, reflection, and emulation of the workings of heteronormative hierarchical discourses within the wider society (Pallotta-Chiarolli, 2010a). For example, some advocates of same-sex marriages and families assimilate to and perpetuate what Hidalgo et al. (2008) define as "the dyadic imaginary." Riggs uses the term "domestication" to describe how gays and lesbians accept "the terms for belonging offered to us by the state" (2007: 191). Klesse refers to the delineation between "Good Homosexuals" and "Dangerous Queers" as being the machinations of heteronormativity with which some gays and lesbians are complicit (2007: 11). Indeed, the title of Ocean's (2008) paper succinctly summarizes the disruptive potential of including bisexuality, particularly in its nonmonogamous forms, being feared by many same-sex marriage activists: "Bisexuals are Bad for the Same-Sex Marriage Business." Thus, what Ritchie & Barker (2006) call "mononormativity" involves the formation of new boundaries and borders between "the legitimate [heterosexual monogamous nuclear families] and the about-to-be legitimate [homosexual monogamous nuclear families] from those relationships and sexual practices which become more intensively inscribed as illegible [bisexual, multisexual, multipartnered families]" (Baird, 2007: 167). The risk of normalization, domestication or sanction is that it may "ultimately serve to further enshrine the existing forms of kinship that are available (and recognized) under a heteropatriarchy, rather than creating a space for new ways of understanding ourselves and our relationships with other people" (2007: 191; see also Bertone & Pallotta-Chiarolli, 2014; O'Brien, 2007). Thus, while there is a growing body of debate, research and activism addressing same-sex marriages and gay and lesbian families, multisexual, "queerly mixed" or MORE families have not been explored to any significant extent, particularly in relation to health, education and popular culture (Galupo, 2008; Marsh, 2011; Pallotta-Chiarolli, 2011). MOREs, particularly nonmonogamous and polyamorous ones, are in the precarious position of lacking visibility and legitimation just as Indigenous, ethnic and gay/lesbian families have experienced at various points in history (Attali, 2005).

I wish to state clearly that this book is not intended to undermine, displace or negate the significance and necessity of gay and lesbian research, activism and education campaigns to end homophobia and homonegativity. Nor is it meant to undermine, displace or negate the significance of recognizing, affirming and celebrating same-sex marriages and families in political, legal, educational, health, religious and sociocultural systems and structures (Marsh, 2011). Indeed, my own previous research and activism have been positioned within promoting sexual diversity education and health largely in relation to gay and lesbian children and same-sex families (eg Martino & Pallotta-Chiarolli, 2003; Pallotta-Chiarolli, 2005a; 2015a). This book is also not intended to undermine, displace, or negate heterosexual relationships and families. Heterosexuality and monogamy should continue to be affirmed and celebrated, but should not be privileged or constructed as the only form of sexuality or relationship/family worthy of validation and attention within our political, legal, educational, health, religious and sociocultural systems and structures.

Finally, this book is not intended to place bisexual men and their partners, relationships, families and communities on a pedestal proclaiming their perfection. This would be another form of discrimination and devaluation via simplistic representation, fetishism and trivialization, thereby reducing bisexuality to the level of 'trendification' and exoticization for the salacious entertainment of the heteronormative Center. It would also ignore and silence the realities of oppression and repression that some women are confronted with in their relationships with their bisexual male partners, thereby replicating the very patriarchal systems of isolation and misogyny these women are already dealing with in their relationships and externally within health, community and wider social settings.

Rather, this book is about broadening, interrogating and adding to ongoing debates and activism regarding sexual diversity, relationship diversity and family diversity. In this way, our work as health researchers, policy makers and educators, and our lives as families, friends, neighbors and community members of MOREs, do not merely assimilate or accommodate to the parameters still being set by a heteronormative Center, but transforms the very way we conceptualize, converse and take action.

I will now provide an overview and analysis of our research methods and processes. I hope that this will encourage further research that addresses the limitations of our own, and further extends the parameters of queer investigation and theorization into sexualities, families and relationships.

"PASSIONATE SOCIOLOGY AND QUEER COYOTES"

> From doing this research, I feel like there is a community of women that I belong to. One that I hadn't really thought about much before, and I'm sure within that community there's as many variations as in every community. (Katie)

This research raises significant questions in regard to accessing women who remain largely hidden, and acknowledging and honoring their concerns about representation, accessibility and voice. In this book, I have chosen to quote at length from their interviews, given the women's strong desire to be heard and to speak for themselves in the safe and yet empowering space of this research and ensuing text. By foregrounding the voices, perspectives, and experiences of women in MOREs, it will make visible the "non-normative intimacies" (Roseneil & Budgeon, 2004: 138) usually concealed in our communities due to mononormativity, biphobia, polyphobia, and misogyny. As Rich writes:

> The pattern of the carpet is a surface. When we look closely, or when we become weavers, we learn of the tiny multiple threads unseen in the overall pattern, the knots on the underside of the carpet (1979: 187).

For example, the populist self-help genre, which often involves counselors and writers who themselves have been in MOREs, has been known to delimit these relationships by defining them as "straight/gay marriages," such as in the example below from the newsletters of Bonnie Kaye:

> I never dignify them by calling them something chic like mixed orientation marriages. To me mixed orientation is Jewish/Catholic or white/black where people know up front before marriage what the obstacles are. Straight/gay marriages are more like Alice in Wonderland marriages. Distorted at best. . . . If anything, call them what I call them, mismarriages, meaning a mistaken marriage (2008: 115).

What seems to be missed by self-help writers and counselors such as Kaye is the fact that "Jewish/Catholic" and "white/black" marriages have all been called "mismarriages" and stigmatized as "distorted" and "mistaken" at various points in history. Indeed, this has been done by counselors such as herself who could not perceive or did not want to fathom the positive realities of many mixed marriages. Likewise, they did not attribute many of the "obstacles" these relationships faced, including partners not being "up front before marriage," to the very external prescriptions and discriminations perpetuated by "experts" such as herself.

In relation to Kaye's comment about the "Alice in Wonderland" illusion of these marriages as viable and valid, a research participant, Nicole, wanted our research to provide some insights into this very question: "It would make a very interesting book to look at the collision between the reality and the fantasy." Grace & Benson (2000) assert that queer research entails building a knowledge base where description, interpretation and analysis lead to critical dialogue and "resist-stances," a term they coined to describe direct actions informed and enacted in the intersection of the lived experience and the research. Likewise, Hill (1995) coined the term "fugitive knowledge," produced as an integral part of demonstrating and acknowledging the authority, dignity and integrity of queer persons, or persons such as the women in our research, who have felt their dignity and authority being invisibilized, undermined or overdetermined in research, policy, and action. As Erera writes, researchers "need to keep clear the distinctions between the institutionalized family, the ideology of the family, and the lives of actual families" such as women and their MORE families (2002: 2). She states that "there is far too much emphasis on the supposed deficits and problems with diverse families, and insufficient attention to their strengths" (2002: 213). Indeed, Erera finds that many of the problems these families experience are due to factors outside the family itself, "imposed by a social environment that does not accept or support them" (2002: 217; see also Pallotta-Chiarolli, 2006; 2010a, b). What will become very apparent in the following chapters when women discuss the ways their partners concealed their bisexuality are the machinations of heteronormative sociocultural systems of discrimination and ostracism that framed the fears and self-and-other deceptions of bisexual men to the detriment of themselves, their partners, and their families. Thus, although this research documents the deficits and problems many women experience in relationships with bisexual men, it will also move beyond this prescriptive, biphobic representation to consider the strengths and abilities these women and their partners display. It will also provide many examples where being in a relationship with a bisexual man is not constructed by women as an issue for problematization and pathologization. Indeed, they consider their external sociocultural environments, including health services, to be highly problematic in their insistence on problematizing and pathologizing their MOREs, as well as being the very prescriptive societal frameworks which determine and steer the behaviors of betrayal, abuse and deception in their bisexual partners (Elia, 2010).

Thus, rather than constructing women in MOREs solely as passive and ignorant "wounded identities" always at risk, "a crucial counter-narrative" is made available that highlights the pleasure, agency and power many women experience in these relationships (Rasmussen, 2004: 456). What needs to be highlighted are the factors supporting women's pleasure, power and agency, and the factors that are detrimental to these three attributes, which thereby affect women's health and wellbeing, and the health and wellbeing of their relationship and family.

Given the sensitivity and secrecy surrounding these issues for many women and their partners, and therefore the difficulty in accessing participants, a variety of recruitment methods were used. Mindful of what Savin-Williams calls "clinical traps" wherein research recruitment and analysis flounder if they do not allow for the fact that "sexual behavior, sexual attraction, and sexual identity questions do not always solicit similar populations" (2008: 135–136), we worked on the premise of self-identification and self-ascription by our research participants, even if this appeared to create so-called contradictions and incongruences of identity. As Albury found in her research on heterosexualities:

> A more disciplined researcher might dismiss respondents who expressed more than one 'strong' identity as 'noise in the data', or impossible "data unicorns" (Jesdale, 2013) . . . I have chosen to accept that some people might, indeed, choose to identify strongly with these different categories (2015: 651).

Recruitment flyers, e-mails, press releases, and information were sent to any known support groups for women with gay and bisexual partners as well as groups for gay and bisexual married men, women's health services, community services, gay men's services, HIV/AIDS services, multicultural services, and bisexual social and support groups. We tried to ensure that a range of social and support sites were accessed so we would have a wide gamut of experiences and perspectives ranging from very problematic to very positive. We did not want to replicate the existing norm of negative research and writing about the oppression of women in relationships with gay-identifying men, within which the category of bisexual was often subsumed. However, we still wanted to tell those stories where they were relevant to our research, such as men who identified as gay but loved and were sexual with their female partners, because they were valid and common. We also did not want to set up a new norm of glorifying MOREs by only interviewing straight, bisexual and queer women in highly satisfactory or kinky/queer/polyamorous/BDSM relationships, as this would again silence the oppression some women were experiencing from their partners. However, women in these highly satisfying and/or kinky/queer/polyamorous/BDSM relationships had stories we wanted to tell because they were also valid and common. So mostly we relied on who came forward, with the only parameter being that the research participant identified as a woman and identified her partner as bisexual, whether that meant in identity and/or behavior. In hindsight, we acknowledge a major limitation in our language and strategies of recruitment was the failure to access transgendered MTF women and bisexual FTM partners.

A snowball sampling strategy was easily established as individuals known to us or who had participated in the research introduced other possible participants, who then informed others of our work, who then would contact us. Friends in certain networks, communities and organizations would direct potential participants to us or direct us to possible participants. Bisexual men would tell their women partners about the project. E-mail and Internet list members would recommend participating in the research to others. Snowball sampling was thus effective as it is a "method that is suited to studies that focus on a sensitive issue or private matter" (Kowalewski, 1988: 214–215). This was especially pertinent as issues of trust and confidentiality were important to the women. Above all, the priority in qualitative research is to "protect the well-being of participants" (Mann & Stewart, 2000: 63). Thus, we approached this research with the deepest respect for the women and their families, and we have undertaken this research in the hope that this material will help other women struggling with similar issues and create, as Katie says at the beginning of this section, a sense of *"community."*

As stated earlier in this chapter, this book will foreground women's narratives, vignettes, and voices in what at times may be considered laboriously lengthy quotes and stories. This method is in keeping with what Game & Metcalfe (1996) call "passionate sociology" which challenges modernist masculinist academic knowledge as "something dispassionate and disembodied, a product of the mind rather than the heart, body or soul" (1996: 4; see also Altork, 1995; hooks, 1994; Letherby, 2003; Livholts, 2012). "Passionate sociology" also asks that we consider the accessibility of our research. Again, this was an issue for our research participants. Their powerful, emotive and insightful voices, and the use of narrative and anecdote as accessible ways of knowing, are border research methods, as they border the poetic and the academic, the analysis and the story. Thus, this research is a work of passionate sociology because it is "concerned with the sharp and specific experiences of life; not seeking to dissolve these experiences in the pursuit of idealized abstraction, it wants to *feel* them" (1996: 5). We are researchers who are also women, mothers and in relationships with men, and with Sara married to a bisexual man for over 15 years. We endeavored to represent the data "so that the humanness of these experiences is not lost . . . [and] must have the power to give the reader a [greater] sense of what it is that was experienced . . . than does the presentation of facts and information"

(Goodfellow, 1998). Barker & Langdridge write that as researchers and writers, we need to be aware of "the potential for violence in the act of representation" (2010: 763). Thus, we need to engage in research methodologies that are "reflexive, cautious and considerate of issues of accountability to participants, and of how it may be read by the wider world" (2010: 763; see also Barker et al. 2012).

"Passionate sociology" is also about empowerment and agency, as it aims to "unsilence the silenced" (Le Compte, 1993). By encouraging the women to tell their stories, this research constructs them as agents who uncover, keep covered, and discover in order to challenge the "limits [and costs] of the sayable." (Butler, 2004: xvii). Through 'uncovering' aspects of their lives, the women assist research and the empowering of other women in their situations, while simultaneously our role as researchers is to maintain a 'cover' for them in order not to harm the women, their partners and families within their everyday worlds. Situated on the border of uncovering and covering is 'discovering', not only by the readers but also by participants about themselves and about others. Protected and strategic unsilencing allows participants to discover an empowering impetus and a growing confidence to continue to find ways of being agents in the negotiation of the tensions surrounding the issues of stigma and marginality in their lives, and to challenge the silence and denial regarding their locations within health services, the wider society and their communities of significant others. Thus, this research is committed to the feminist research ethos that emphasizes "participant empowerment" and "emancipatory research" (Yip, 2008: 7; see also Barker et al. 2012). For example, at regular points throughout the years of this research, some women kept in contact, began their own projects and Internet sites, undertook new life directions or new ways of seeing their lives as part of their activist, social and support objectives.

This discussion about 'passionate sociology' raises the question in regard to 'rightness' and 'wrongness', moral universality or relativity in regard to whether we should accept the participants' versions of the truth, and thereby see our role as one of describer, or challenge them and thereby disrupt their evocations of their lived realities. In presenting the rationalizations and justifications of a person, we could be seen to be accepting these rationalizations and justifications. We could be accused of presenting a one-sided and distorted view, particularly as our purpose was not to interview the male partners and consider their perspectives on the same issues. It was not the purpose of this research to match or compare the women's perspectives with those of their partners. Certainly, future couples research with both bisexual men and their partners discussing their interconnected lives would be very useful. We contend that our research is not presenting a distorted view of reality, but is presenting a view of the particular reality that engages each research participant. In his pioneering studies of "deviance," Becker writes that "we [do not] know to what extent ordinary members of conventional society actually share, to some degree, the perspectives of deviant groups" (1973: 174). This comment is particularly pertinent to many of our research participants who may appear within their everyday worlds to be part of heterosexual couples in conventional heterosexual families, and then are revealed in this research to be bisexual and/or in multisexual and polyamorous families.

In summary, "passionate sociologists" working with people in the borderlands become a catalyst for border crossings: by empowering the border dwellers wishing to cross "la frontera" (the border) and by raising the awareness of those in the mainland of the existence and experiences of border dwellers (Anzaldua, 1987a). The role of these researchers can be described as what Valadez & Elsbree call "queer coyotes," serving as "mediators" in these queer border crossings (2005: 175; see also Naples, 2004). In this research, we perceived our role to be that of "queer coyote" researchers as we fulfilled and continue to fulfill four characteristics of border crossing research as set out by Valadez & Elsbree:

- operating in "secreto": being secretive and protective of the research participants while simultaneously using the research process to help them move forward and cross borders;
- knowing "los codigos": knowing the codes of both the border zone and Center, and thus teaching, explaining and working with the codes of each to the other such as relaying the needs of the women to health services as well as conveying the existence of useful health services to the women;
- having "la facultad": reading different situations and contexts quickly and accurately; seeing into the deeper realities below the surface such as understanding the wider heteronormative framings, often interwoven with particular cultural and religious framings, within which the male partners experienced oppression and then became complicit in the oppression of their female partners;
- expressing sincere "compromiso": having a commitment toward social transformation, social justice and the politics of recognition (2005: 176–177; see also Pallotta-Chiarolli & Pease, 2014).

"I FEEL REALLY COMFORTABLE IN HAVING SHARED IT"

I felt coming here was going to bring it all up again for me . . . . [now] I feel really comfortable in having shared it . . . because there are ears out there that need to hear what I say, and if I can save someone going through what I've been through, then I've made a difference. (Mary)

Interviews were conducted by Sara and myself with the original intent of recruiting 50 participants. We later decided to keep the project open as some women were still requesting to be involved after finding out about our research. The interviews took place wherever it was convenient and comfortable for the women. This included their homes, university and health service offices, parks, shopping centers, and cafes, and their workplaces. Some women preferred audio-recorded phone interviews, and a few chose to e-mail their written responses to us. These latter responses ranged from one-line answers to several paragraphs. In some interviews, children were present and, as small children will unselfconsciously do, they provided welcome interludes, unwanted interruptions or impetus for further discussion! In some interviews, the male partners were present, as requested and desired by the women. At times, the men participated in the conversations and for the purposes of this research their comments have been included, as requested by their women partners. For example, Krystle wanted her husband Greg to participate as he also had questions he was hoping the interview would answer. The following is an example of a partner in the background as the interview is being conducted over the phone. Joanne is discussing what fears some people have if bisexuality becomes more accepted: "It's those bisexuals needing to increase their ranks! [Ben's voice is heard in the background] Yeah, Ben says the evil bisexual army marches on. [Laughing]" (Joanne). Below is an example of a partner being present during the interview and the camaraderie between the couple, as well as the camaraderie between the research(ed) couple and the researcher, with whom they shared an Adelaide Italian migrant community and heritage:

Yvonne: I mean, we talk about it [whether to have outside partners of the opposite sex].

Robert: We shout about it as well.

Yvonne: We shout, yes, we argue about it too.

Robert: Yvonne hits me. [Laughing]

Yvonne: [Laughing]. I don't do that.

Robert: Oh, really? . . . Well, it [our relationship] seems to work. I think it works.

Yvonne: You just like me because I've got big tits and I'm curvy.

Robert: She's cuddly. She's cuddly, she's cuddly. [hugging and kissing Yvonne]

Yvonne: I'll tell you something really funny. He loves Italian women and I said, "Oh, Maria's got long hair" and he goes "Ohhhhhhhhh" and I'm like—

Maria: [Interrupting] And look at the state of my long hair!

Robert: It's okay.

Yvonne: Yeah, like, keep it in your pants, boy! He likes curvy women, Italian women you know.

Robert: Well, Yvonne will say to me, "Look, look, but you can't touch" and I'm like, "Yeah, okay."

Yvonne: Yeah, but only when I say you can look.

Robert: Yeah. [Laughing] Like the woman in the supermarket, remember? . . . You were standing there telling me, "Robert, check her out, you missed it."

Maria: Oh, see? You're a bloody tease, Yvonne. Like, you're teasing him on and then you go "Nooooo."

Yvonne: Yeah, absolutely! [Laughing].

Most of the semistructured interviews lasted two hours or longer, and the participants were given their transcripts to edit, veto, and add to in any way they wished. The women were also given the option of choosing pseudonyms, and many did. Some of the women wrote accompanying letters, others sent in poems, while some maintained phone and e-mail contact for years and occasionally met up with the researchers. Mindful of not initiating unwanted new contact or bring back to the present issues and lived experiences that may have been archived in the past, a final attempt was made to connect with each participant and check on their names/pseudonyms and permissions, and inform them of the publication date.

Some women chose to share their transcripts with their partners while others chose to participate in the research without their partners' knowledge. Other women made their partners aware that the interview was a space for them to independently, privately and safely discuss a whole range of issues without needing to consider or accommodate the perspectives and concerns of their partners:

> The last time we had an argument about this project was only a week ago. I think Darren is very threatened by the fact that I'm on the phone here right now. But I've told him, "Bugger off, I'm doing it." I said, "Look it's nothing that really concerns you. It's something that I want to do." . . . He's mostly concerned that I'm going to revisit areas that drag up all these feelings and then I'm going to be [pausing] difficult, yeah, for the next couple of days and that's made him feel very insecure. (Sherry)

Thus, for many women, the interview was a therapeutic space, a space for saying what had for so long remained unsaid, unsayable, or edited for the comfortable consumption of partners, families, friends and health service providers. Some women did express concerns that the research was positioning them as speaking on behalf of their partner, or having their partner "known" according to what they as women partners knew or wanted "known":

> I think I'm conscious of the way that through me Tony's being researched and his sexual behaviour. I think this has been really important research to do, but I suppose it does pose a bit of a problem for me, in my mind, how can that be avoided where his sexual activity, his values, his history, his personal experiences, have been brought up through me, when he really had no control . . . I think it is murky, but I think this research is really valid, definitely. (Katie)

Many women clearly explained they were using the research project to gain support for themselves as well as enjoying being part of a larger support network, a space wherein a form of community of shared experiences and insights was being constructed via the conduit role of the research and researcher:

> Well, it wasn't entirely altruistic that I decided to participate. I thought every time I talk to someone who knew about my experience, I feel better somehow. . . . but also I thought if this is going to be published in some way, other people out there who don't have some sort of support network may buy the book and may think, "Ah ha, somebody else has gone through it and they've survived." (Jane)

Some women used the research space as the only place they were prepared to be public about the relationship:

> I don't really want to be labeled as Maura the woman partner of some bi. There are people that I am not out about my relationship . . . I don't want the questions and finger pointing. (Maura)

Others saw the research space as another place where they could be public as they refused to stay in the closet because of their partners:

> I know it sounds weird, but I didn't want to be in his closet. It is his closet and it is of his own devising. So, here I am and I don't actually care what people think of me and that's when I got in touch with you, and when you suggested being interviewed, I thought, "Yeah, I'd love that, I want to be out. I don't care," and that's why I'll be happy to go under my own name for this. . . . He married a loud mouth. He knew I was a loud mouth [Laughing]. (Monica)

Occasionally, women told us they had informed their adolescent and adult children that they would be part of this project and while most of their children were supportive and encouraging, a few women did encounter resistance:

> Andrew [the son] didn't really want me to come today. I don't think he actually knows where I am today. I said, "I'm going to Deakin for a meeting," but I don't think he twigged, but when you first sent me the info and he saw it, he said, "Well, you're not doing that, are you?" and I said, "Well, actually I am. It's actually something I'd enjoy doing and it would be actually something that I'd love reading when it's all done." (Steph)

As discussed in the long and strong history of feminist research methods (eg Oakley, 1981; Fonow & Cook, 1991; Letherby, 2003), and has already been evident in the examples provided above from the transcripts, the interviews are better described as conversations and connections with exchanges involving much camaraderie and shared laughter, grieving and shared sadness, anger and contentment, shared confidences particularly in relation to intimate or sexual details, languid pauses of reflection, conversational "sidetracks," information on resources, and questions asked of us as interviewers about our own lives as women in relationships with men, and about our lives as mothers. As Oakley writes, "personal involvement," subjective bias, and influence over the participants is unavoidable (1981: 58). Indeed, Sara and I experienced a whole gamut of emotions in each interview, and often turned to each other afterwards to vent our distress, "anger, resentment, fatigue, indignation, annoyance, aggravation, outrage, and irritation" (Blee, 2003: 22); voice our awe and admiration for the strength many women displayed; or reminisce about an interview with laughter, not at the expense of the woman or as part of put-down humor, but as part of celebrating the joys and happy experiences the women had shared with us. Thus, the interview created "a transformative space, which changes both the interviewer and interviewee" (Heckert, 2005: 110).

The friendly and equitable nature of the research relationship was often evident when the women would initiate discussions about the research terms and methods, or confidently respond to any queries we had about the way they felt about our research and ourselves as researchers. Indeed, these women positioned themselves as the experts and superior to us the researchers due to their firsthand insights and experiences. Here is an example of a participant critiquing the research and encouraging us to clarify our questions and terms:

> *Jude:* I would just encourage you to keep open about the definitions of bisexuality as you go through your work. And my partner and I had quite a conversation around your working titles like the "new rules or no rules" and what that might mean.

Maria: Yeah? Tell us, tell us, and be absolutely blunt.

Jude: Well, I was thinking that maybe you meant, you know, that people have assumptions that if there's a bisexual relationship then there's no rules at all, when in fact maybe it's about different rules ... Another issue was what you mean by "bisexually active," you know, because my partner's not having sex with men, but if he was looking at porn or fantasizing about men, then is that bisexually active?

In particular, the women loved talking to Sara as she had convened and facilitated the Women Partners of Bisexual Men support group at ACON (AIDS Council of New South Wales) and had produced several resources (e.g. Lubowitz, 1995a, b; 1997). Likewise, the women considered my long-standing public participation, activism and publications in feminist, educational, multicultural and queer communities as important in why they felt comfortable disclosing intimate personal and relationship details. It was known that I had been working on a novel for adolescents and young adults which included the theme of bisexual relationships. Set within a multicultural multisexual Australia, the publication of *Love You Two* was met with widespread support from Australian and international poly and bi groups, and indeed was co-winner of the 2010 Lambda Literary Awards in the Bisexual Fiction category (Pallotta-Chiarolli, 2008). It was also known that since 1999, I had been developing a project about the schooling experiences of bisexual adolescents and children from polyamorous families (Pallotta-Chiarolli, 2010a, b, 2011; 2015a; Pallotta-Chiarolli et al. 2013). Some of the women did tell us how important it was for them to do some research of their own about us, thereby checking our credibility before agreeing to be our research participants: "Your reputation preceded you... they [a bisexual network] sent me an email just explaining that you had done a lot of work and that I should contact you. So I Googled you" (Sharae).

> I had actually heard your name, Sara, before and I had met you before at a Bi conference very briefly so I knew that you were a real person who had some interest in bisexuality, and I'd read something of Maria's, so I knew that she also had some experience ... Cause I often find there are a lot of people who want to meet bisexual gals or boys and they are doing it out of a complete ignorance about where they are going with it which can sometimes be very difficult to deal with. So I thought, well, these women have a clue. (Lizz)

Other women commented on how Sara and I came across as approachable: "it's [the research] going to be something from actual women, not from some professor that's sat behind a computer that thinks they know" (Lesley).

"I DON'T KNOW IF I WILL EVER TIRE OF TELLING MY STORY"

I don't know if I will ever tire of telling my story. It is very cathartic to talk about it. (Marissa)

At the end of this chapter, I have provided a table with the demographic information research participants disclosed about themselves, their partners, and families. This always includes the name of the woman (a pseudonym unless an interviewee wanted their real name used). This name is then positioned underneath each quote and within the discussion. In this way, the reader is able to refer back to Table 1 to become informed, contextualize, and understand other facets in the woman's life. Via this system, I want readers to get to know the women as three-dimensional, within a range of settings and contexts, and with names that you will meet again and again as you journey through this book.

The following chapter 2, will provide a theoretical and historical overview of bisexuality and its insider/outsider/no-sider positionings, and how these theories are useful in understanding the social and interpersonal locations of women in relationships with bisexual men. Chapter 2 will also provide a more detailed exploration of research with bisexual men and MORES, and how these terms are being defined and utilized in this research.

Chapter 3 onwards will address specific themes the women raised. Chapters 3 and 4 will present women's perspectives and experiences in exploring and understanding their partners' and their own sexual landscapes, categories and experiences.

Chapters 5 and 6 will present the various 'journeys' of the relationships the women undertook such as 'started out knowing': embarking on the relationship knowing their partners were bisexual. Other women found that while travelling along one journey, some form of disclosure or discovery of their partners' bisexuality led them or forced them to 'change course midstream': from closet to confrontation, the terrain and directions ahead were unplanned for and often completely unknown. Chapter 7 presents the hindsight perspectives and reflections of women who look back at the journey from a position of 'arrival' within the relationship or post-divorce, whether it be 'to arrive where they started' with much more understanding and peace, or arriving in a place and space completely different to their point of departure.

Chapters 8 to 11 will explore the ways the women and their partners 'mapped the landscape' they found themselves traversing in their relationships' journeys. It may also have required, demanded or imposed on women the mapping, re-mapping and unmapping of relationship rules: 'new rules, no rules, or his and her rules' in the quest to navigate the shifting boundaries of freedom and responsibility. Other women wanted to discuss the patriarchal power of masculine privilege and misogyny that impacted upon their relationship landscape and journey more than their partner's bisexuality: "the problem is that he's a man, not that he's bisexual." Chapter 10 will engage with the question 'What do we tell the kids?' as this was a dominant concern for many women in the landscaping of family to benefit their children or to minimize the harm done to their children. In Chapter 11, women discuss the ever-present concern of STIs and HIV/AIDS and how they found themselves having to or wanting to map these issues, or journeying in ways that debunked the mainstream stereotype that bisexual men are "spreading disease with the greatest of ease."

Chapters 12 to 16 take us out of the landscaping of the relationships themselves into the locating of the women and their relationships as 'border-dwelling' and 'outside belonging' of various external worlds and communities. The issue of 'minute by minute maneuvering' prevailed for all women as they navigated the heteronormative world of families, workplaces, communities, media and society. However, they also had to navigate the 'ewww, girl germs' homonormative spaces of gay men's communities. While the bisexual man might be able to draw upon the gay community to give shape to, legitimize, and support recognition and acceptance of same-sex desire, these same communities often serve to delegitimize and problematize his marriage and his love and desire for his female partner: "What both scripts [heteronormative and homonormative] seem to agree on is that the two do not or should not coexist—not in one person or in one life" (Swan & Benack, 2012: 52). The significance of religion was also an issue many women wished to discuss: from women who reported "the priest told him to marry me and he'd go straight" to the women who discarded conventional religious beliefs as being irrelevant or oppressive in their desire to travel forward positively with their partners. Ethnic community codes also required negotiation and relocation for many women, some of whom felt forced to make or endure decisions based on constructions of "it's a matter of family honor and shame." Finally, another significant 'world' to be navigated and mapped was that of health settings and services, such as women reporting how "your relationship isn't recognized by relationship counselling," thereby encountering systemic and institutional misrepresentations and erasures.

The final chapter 17 takes us forward through 'a door that hasn't been opened' on the journey to map out a future place not only of 'belonging in the borderlands' but also of blooming there. The women provide some final words for other women in the recognition, affirmation and understanding of sexual and relationship diversity.

In the last few lines of D.H. Lawrence's novel *Women in Love*, first published in 1920, Birkin tries to tell the woman he loves, Ursula, how he also loved Gerald, who has been killed and for whom Birkin is grieving deeply:

> "I don't believe it," she said. "It's an obstinacy, a theory, a perversity . . . You can't have two kinds of love. Why should you!" "It seems as if I can't," he said "yet I wanted it."
> "You can't have it, because it's false, impossible," she said. "I don't believe that," he answered.

And there the novel ends, devoid of the "two kinds of love" which flourished in the precolonial Te Arawa story, and denying the multiple possibilities suggested in the colonial era's *The Garden of Pan*. But in a decolonizing world of intermixture, fluidity and multiplicity is where this book begins, with the women's voices as travel guides.

Chapter 1

Table 1.1 Research Participants, their Partners and Demographics

Name	Age	Location	Cultural Identity/ Background	Religious Identity/ Background	Relationship Status	Sexual Identity/ Preferences	Employment/ Education	Children	Health/ STIs/HIV
Alice	65	Sydney	Both Anglo-Australian	Both Agnostic	Married for 40 years	Heterosexual monogamous	Retired Lawyer	3 adult children, one is a lesbian; 3 grandchildren	None
Paul	64					Bisexual nonmonogamous	Retired Lawyer		
Anne	37	Melbourne	Both Anglo-Australian	Both have Baptist evangelical backgrounds	Both previously married, together 8 years	Bisexual poly	Masseur	None	None
Peter	40					Bicurious poly and 2 long-term female partners	Musician; sound and studio technician	Two teenagers from previous marriage	
Annette	27	Melbourne	Both Anglo-Australian	Both agnostic	10 years together	Pansexual poly in a relationship with a woman	Postgraduate student and part-time tutor	None	None
John	27					Bisexual monogamous			Agoraphobia
Antonietta	55	Adelaide	Italian	Catholic	Separated after 10 years but chose not to divorce	Heterosexual	Sales	2 children, 1 grandson	None
Bill	55		Anglo-Australian	Catholic		Gay	Sales	None	
Ava	27	Inner city Melbourne	Greek-American	Agnostic/Wiccan	7 years together	Bisexual polyamorous	Music editor/ magazine editor	None	None
Unnamed			Western European and Eastern European Jewish	Agnostic		Shifts between bisexual and hetero/poly	Software Designer		
Barb	44	Melbourne	Spanish-Irish	Catholic	26 years together, married	Heterosexual	Social Worker and Fitness Leadership	1 daughter, 11 and 1 son, 7	None
Andrew	47		Anglo-Australian	Atheist		Bisexual monogamous	Environmental Scientist		

"Outside Belonging"

Name	Age	Location	Ethnicity	Religion	Relationship	Sexuality	Occupation	Children	Health
Beth	37	Rural Tasmania	Anglo-Australian	Lapsed Presbyterian	10 years together unmarried, now separated	Heterosexual	Secretary	None	None
Unnamed						Gay	Business owner		
Brenda	62	Rural Victoria	Scottish	Both Presbyterian	Married for 40 years	Heterosexual	Retired nurse	1 son, 33 and 1 daughter, 35	None
Edward	65		Anglo-Australian			Bisexual nonmonogamous	Farmer		
Christine	38	Perth	Chinese	Catholic	Divorced from previous marriage, married 3 years	Both bisexual nonmongamous	Both own and run Arts/Crafts Business	1 child, 4 years old	None
Un-named			Anglo-American	Atheist					
Deanna	29	Melbourne	Italian-Australian	Catholic	Together for 2 years, now apart	Bisexual	Dancer, multimedia artist, dance teacher	None	Genital Herpes contracted from partner
Dave			Jewish	Jewish		Bisexual-heterosexual	Dancer		Genital Herpes
Erin	36	Adelaide	Both Anglo-Australian	Atheist	Divorced after 10 years together, 6 of them married. Now both have male partners	Heterosexual	Web developer; IT	None	None
Shane	36			Conservative Lutheran background		Gay	Disabilities Carer		

Continued

Table 1.1 Research Participants, their Partners and Demographics *(Continued)*

Name	Age	Location	Cultural Identity/ Background	Religious Identity/ Background	Relationship Status	Sexual Identity/ Preferences	Employment/ Education	Children	Health/ STIs/HIV
Evelyn Primary partner plus secondary partner	49	Sydney	German-English	Agnostic	Divorced from 1st husband after 5 years; has had 3 bisexual male partners including 3 years with the latest one as well as heterosexual primary partner	Heterosexual polyamorous Bisexual polyamorous secondary partner who has a woman as his primary partner	Journalist in children's magazines	None	None
Fay	62	Melbourne	Both Anglo-Australian	Both Uniting Church but with born-again Christian backgrounds	Married 32 years	Heterosexual	Minister's Wife, Nurse	3: gay son, a daughter and a foster son	None
Bill	62					Gay	Minister, Nurse		Manic depression
Felicity	49	Melbourne	Both English	Anglican	Married for 23 years, now separated	Heterosexual	Music teacher	3: a daughter, 22, and 2 sons, 20 and 16	None
Michael	55			Church of England		Bisexual celibate	Minister		
Gerry	52	Outer Melbourne suburbs	Both English	Unspecified	Previously married for 17 years; together with Simon for 16 years	Heterosexual	Primary school teacher	1 daughter in her 30s and a grandson	HIV negative
Simon						Bisexual	Unemployed	Simon has children in late teens from previous marriage	HIV positive
Gloria	35	Adelaide	Both Italian	Both lapsed Catholic	Married 10 years, together 20 years	Both bisexual polyamorous	Secondary school teacher	2: boy 8 and girl 5	None
Sam	36						Retail sales manager		

Name	Age	Location	Ethnicity	Religion	Relationship	Sexuality	Occupation	Children	Health
Hannah	55	Melbourne	English-Scottish	Both Presbyterian	Married 35 years, now divorcing	Lesbian	HIV/STI educator and counselor	3: daughters 30 and 26, and son 26	None
Dean						Gay	Health educator		
Heather	40	Outer Melbourne suburbs	English-Australian	Unspecified	Married 17 years, together 23	Heterosexual	Nurse	3: son 12 and twin boy/girl 10	Crabs contracted from partner
Ian	40		Scottish			Gay	Outreach team coordinator for people with intellectual disabilities		Gonorrhea
Helena	50	Melbourne	Both Anglo-Australian	Muslim convert from Christian/spiritualist	Divorced after 26 years together	Heterosexual	Secondary school art teacher	3: 2 boys 25 and 10 and girl 23	None
Tom	53			Muslim convert from Anglican since 1970s		Ambiguous/asexual	International trade relations		
Jacinta	34	Sydney	Both Anglo-Australian	Both spiritual/agnostic	Married 15 years	Bisexual polyamorous	Both in Management of a Wealth Education company	3: 2 girls and a boy	None
Corey						Bisexual polyamorous			
Jane	55	Sydney North Shore	Both Anglo-Australian	Both Presbyterian	Married 30 years	Heterosexual	Secondary School Teacher	2: boy and girl in late 20s	Breast cancer
Rob						Bisexual	Business Owner		HIV positive
Jean	53	Adelaide	Both English	Both agnostic	Married 35 years	Heterosexual	Own a retail business together	3 adult children, 3 grandchildren	Chronic fatigue
Anthony	53					Bisexual			None

Continued

Table 1.1 Research Participants, their Partners and Demographics (Continued)

Name	Age	Location	Cultural Identity/ Background	Religious Identity/ Background	Relationship Status	Sexual Identity/ Preferences	Employment/ Education	Children	Health/ STIs/HIV
Jeanette	61	Sydney North Shore	Both Pakeha New Zealander	Both strict Presbyterian backgrounds, atheist now	32 years married and now divorced for 2 years	Heterosexual	Art Gallery Information Officer	2: daughter 34, son 28	Heart condition and depression; genital warts and pubic lice from partner
Maurice	60					Bisexual	TV director		Genital warts and pubic lice
Jenna	46	Perth	Anglo-Australian	nonreligious (spiritual)	Married 3 years, together over 10 years	Bicurious	Education	2: boy and girl in late teens	None
Jack	43		European - Australian	nonreligious (spiritual)		Bisexual	Education	3: 2 boys, 1 girl mid teens	
Jess	36	Sydney Eastern Suburbs	Both Pakeha New Zealander	Both Christian	Married for 6 years, divorced and now less remarried	Heterosexual	Both in Sales and Marketing	1 son; and now 1 daughter with new partner	None
Anton						Gay/bisexual			
Joanne	26	Inner city Brisbane	Polish-Scottish	Both Pagan	4 years together	Both bisexual polyamorous	Human services university student	None	None
Ben	27		Anglo-Australian				Medieval History student and teacher/actor		
Jolene	44	Remote North-West Queensland	Anglo-Celtic	Anglican	7 years together	Bisexual	Lecturer in Nursing	1 daughter from previous relationship, 14; and he has a 21 year old son and 26 year old daughter from a previous relationship	None
Charlie	49		Welsh	Atheist		Bisexual	Federal government position		

Name	Age	Location	Ethnicity	Religion	Relationship	Sexuality	Occupation	Children	Health
Josie	33	Melbourne	Both Anglo-Australian	Both Atheist	Married 12 years, now separated	Heterosexual	Teacher	2: 9 and 7 years old	None
Dean	38					Bisexual	Civil Engineer		Depression and suicidal
Jude	33	Canberra	Dutch	Both atheist	4 months together	Bisexual	Community Health Worker	None	None
Unnamed	32		Anglo-Australian			Bisexual	Counsellor	2 children, 6 and 7, from previous marriage	
Kaitlin	54	Rural coastal Victoria	Both Anglo-Celtic	Both Uniting Church	Married 22 years, divorced 5 years	Heterosexual	Uniting Church Minister	2: son 22 and daughter 20	HIV indeterminate
Ross	52					Gay	Teacher/Librarian		None
Katie	25	Inner city Melbourne	Anglo-Australian	Agnostic	8 years together	Heterosexual	Community Development Officer in Youth Housing	None	None
Joe	26		Maltese	Strong Catholic background, now agnostic		Bisexual	Social Worker and Community Activist in Sustainability and Poverty		
Kirsten	36	Sydney	Both Anglo-Saxon	Both spiritual but not organized religion	Married 5 years	Both bisexual polyamorous	Stay at home Mum/graphic designer	3 year old son	None
Cris	31						Internet security specialist		
Kristina	30	Melbourne	Both Anglo-Australian	Both Atheist	Previously married for 8 months, 5 years with Mark	Heterosexual	Housing support worker	1 daughter	None
Mark	37					Prefers no label	Infant school teacher		IV drug user

Continued

Table 1.1 Research Participants, their Partners and Demographics *(Continued)*

Name	Age	Location	Cultural Identity/ Background	Religious Identity/ Background	Relationship Status	Sexual Identity/ Preferences	Employment/ Education	Children	Health/ STIs/HIV
Krystle	46	Rural South Australia	Scottish	Both Lutheran	Married 26 years	Heterosexual	Adult education lecturer	3 boys: 23, 22 and 20	None
Greg	46		Anglo-Australian			Bisexual	Musician/ secondary school music teacher		
Lauren	19	Adelaide	Irish	Both atheist	7 months together	Heterosexual	Biotechnology University student	None	Genital Warts contracted from partner
Adam	25		American			Bisexual	Behavioural Science University student		Genital warts
Leanne	42	Perth	Anglo-Australian	Buddhist	11 years together	Bicurious	Life coach and Reiki masseur/ University Humanities Student	3 children from previous relationship but Lew is father to the youngest since he was 3: 24, 19, 15	None
Lew	34		Croatian	Nonpractising Catholic		Bisexual	National Sales manager in Industrial Products		
Lesley	34	Regional North Queensland	Both Anglo-Australian	Both Christian	20 years together, 14 married	Heterosexual	Stay at home mother/pastry cook	6 children: 13, 11, 8 year old twins, 7 and 6	None
Gary	36					Bisexual	Ambulance Officer/ Paramedic		Agoraphobia
Lilith	33	Inner city Sydney	Egyptian	Spiritual	10 years together	Heterosexual polyamorous	University tutor and researcher	None	None
Adam	32		English	Atheist		Bisexual nonmonogamous	IT software and systems designer		

"Outside Belonging" 33

Name	Age	Location	Ethnicity	Religion	Relationship	Sexuality	Occupation	Children	Health
Lisa	37	Sydney	Anglo-Saxon	Uniting Church	14 years together, divorced for 4 years	Heterosexual	Nurse/Midwife	1 son, 10	None
Dean			Ghanian	Unspecified		Bisexual	Unspecified		
Lizette	34	Rural New South wales	Scottish	Not practising Catholic	Together 13 years, married 11 years, separated 2 years	Heterosexual	Nurse	2: son from previous marriage and daughter from this marriage	Panic attacks/anxiety disorder
Rod						Gay			
Lizz	24	Inner city Sydney	Czech	Both atheist	Together 3.5 years	Both queer polyamorous	Healthcare researcher	None	None
Gennaro	30		Italian				IT software designer		
Loredana	52	Inner city Sydney	Italian	Nominal Catholic	Married 30 years	Heterosexual	Adult education teacher	Son 25; daughter 21	Multiple sclerosis, in a wheelchair
Peter	51		Anglo-Australian	Strong Catholic		Prefers no label	Environmental management in Asian countries		None
Louisa	38	Inner city Melbourne	Both Anglo-Australian	Both atheist	4 years together	Heterosexual	Community development worker in drugs and alcohol; sex worker	3 children from previous relationship: 2 sons: 21 and 10, and 1 daughter, 6	None
Lawrence	30					Bisexual	Architect		
Luna	33	Melbourne	Both Anglo-Australian	Both agnostic	10 years together, separated for 5 years	Bisexual	Aged Care carer	Son 13 and daughter, 12 from previous relationship	HIV positive
Neil	34					Bisexual	Supermarket shelf-stacking/cleaning; sex worker		HIV positive, speed and heroin addictions
Maria	40	Inner city Sydney	Both Anglo-Australian	Both Christian	20 years together	Heterosexual	Childcare worker	3: 13, 10 and 5	Panic attacks
Unnamed	42					Bisexual	Engineer		Chlamydia

Continued

Table 1.1 Research Participants, their Partners and Demographics *(Continued)*

Name	Age	Location	Cultural Identity/ Background	Religious Identity/ Background	Relationship Status	Sexual Identity/ Preferences	Employment/ Education	Children	Health/ STIs/HIV
Marissa	47	Melbourne	Italian	Both agnostic	Married 19 years, separated 3 months	Heterosexual	Midwife	4 children: 15, 14, 12, 8. He has a 21 year old from a previous relationship	None
Murray	50		English			Bisexual	Employment Agency Officer		
Mary	49	Sydney	Irish	Catholic/ Buddhist	Together 10 years from ages 17 to 29. He died of AIDS in 1994	Heterosexual	Architect	1 son, 29	None
James (deceased)						Bisexual	Was in aircraft maintenance and department store displays		Died of AIDS
Maura	36	Sydney	Irish	Catholic	10.5 years together, separated 5 years	Bisexual	Teacher's Aid and Interpreter	1 girl, 10	None
James	36					Bisexual			
Maz	30	Regional New South Wales	Anglo-Australian	Non-practising Christian	Married 6 years, now divorced	Heterosexual with bisexual tendencies	Property Management	1 son from a previous relationship	Depression and suicidal
Un-named	30		Indigenous	Atheist		Bisexual	IT maintenance		None
Monica	31	Sydney	Both Anglo-Australian	Atheist	Married 8 years	Heterosexual	Film Production	3: daughter 5, and twins, 2	In remission from uterine cancer
Martin	31			Protestant		Bisexual	Arts Lawyer		Clinical depression

"Outside Belonging" 35

Name	Age	Location	Ethnicity	Religion	Relationship	Sexuality	Occupation	Children	Health
Naomi	40	Adelaide	Italian	Both spiritual	9 years together	Heterosexual polyamorous with a heterosexual husband of 14 years	Secondary school Teacher	Daughter, 13 and son, 10, from relationship with husband	Genital herpes, not contracted from either partner but passed on to both partners with their consent
Andrew	39		English			Bisexual nonmonogamous			Genital herpes
Nicole	47	Inner city Melbourne	Anglo-Chinese	Non-practising Catholic	24 years together	Heterosexual	University administration	32 year old son from previous relationship adopted by partner	None
Un-named	57		English			Bisexual polyamorous	Secondary school teacher		
Nina	45	Rural Victoria	Both Anglo-Australian	None specified	2 years together	Bisexual	Nurse	1 son, 15, from previous relationship	None
Un-named						Gay	Building Construction Supervisor		
Nirupa	45	Inner city Sydney	Russian	Jewish/Buddhist/ Osho	5 years together	Bisexual polyamorous	Sex Therapist	None	None
Un-named			South African Afrikaaner	Jewish		Bisexual	Family Therapist		
Pat	37	Sydney	Both Greek	Both Greek Orthodox	12 years married, now separated	Heterosexual	Factory trainer/ supervisor	None	None
Un-named						Gay			
Paula	47	Sydney	Both Anglo-Australian	Christian	Divorced	Heterosexual	School counsellor	3 boys: 24, 21 and 16	None
Graham				Catholic		Gay			
Rachel	38	Sydney	English	Both atheist	10 years together, married for 5	Heterosexual with bisexual tendencies	Marketing	1 daughter	None
Un-named			Anglo-Australian			Bisexual	Hairdresser		

Continued

Table 1.1 Research Participants, their Partners and Demographics *(Continued)*

Name	Age	Location	Cultural Identity/ Background	Religious Identity/ Background	Relationship Status	Sexual Identity/ Preferences	Employment/ Education	Children	Health/ STIs/HIV
Raven	45	Melbourne	Both Anglo-Saxon	Christian Brethren background	12 years together	Prefers no labels	Commonwealth Public servant/ Writer	Nigel has teenage daughter	None
Nigel	45			Atheist		Bisexual	Commonwealth Public Servant		
Rose	29	Inner city Melbourne	Russian/Hungarian	Jewish pagan	7.5 years together and 4 years with a woman, also Jewish	Bisexual polyamorous	Both magazine editors	None	None
Tovi		Sydney				Bisexual polyamorous but only with other bisexual men and women			
Rosemary	27	Regional New South Wales	Italian-Irish	Both Catholic backgrounds, now atheist	4 years married	Heterosexual	Nurse	2 pre-school boys	None
Jack	28		Anglo-Australian			Gay	Stay at home father/ photographer		
Sally	39	Adelaide	Both Anglo-Australian	Catholic	Married 17 years	Heterosexual	Business analyst	2 daughters, 14 and 7	None
Michael	38			Anglican		Sexually fluid between sexual, bisexual, homosexual	Business management		
Sara	37	Inner city Sydney	South African English and Jewish heritage	Both atheists	16 years together, 15 married	Heterosexual	Health promotion worker and researcher	Daughter 5	None
Mark	47		Anglo-Australian			Bisexual	Orchestra Musician		
Scarlett	44	Melbourne	Anglo-Australian	"Retired Catholic"	Married 15 years	Heterosexual	Psychologist/ Family Therapist	3 daughters: 22, 21 and 18	None
Harry	44		English	Agnostic		Bisexual	State politics		

Name	Age	Location	Ethnicity	Religion	Relationship	Sexuality	Occupation	Children	Illness
Sharae	38	Outer Melbourne suburbs	Both Anglo-Australian	Pagan	Married 10 years, 12 together	Heterosexual	Stay-at-home mother, writer, website manager	2 daughters, 15 year old from previous marriage, and 11 year old	None
Michael	37			Atheist		Bisexual	Computer technician		
Sascha	28	Sydney	Both Anglo-Australian	None specified	1.5 years together, then sexual friends for 8 years	Lesbian	University Health Promotion student	None	None
James	28					Gay			
Shelley	27	Rural Western Australia	Anglo-Scottish	Both born again Christian backgrounds, now atheist	10 years together	Bisexual	Stay at home mother	Son, 5; daughter, 6	None
Phil	28		Anglo-Polish			Bisexual	Butcher in supermarket chain		
Sherry	32	Darwin	Indigenous-Chinese	Both Catholic	11 years together	Bisexual	Office Administrator	2: daughter 10 and son 8	None
Darren	33		Irish			Bisexual	Air surveillance operator in airforce		
Simone	54	Rural New South Wales	Irish-English	From Catholic to Pentecostal	5.5 years together	Bisexual	Counsellor with the unemployed	1 daughter, 28, and 3 grandsons	None
Luke	42		Pakeha New Zealander	Spiritual		Bisexual	Tradesman/Photographer		
Soulla	44	Sydney	Greek	Greek Orthodox	Married 17 years	Heterosexual	Factory worker	2 daughters, 15 and 13	Breast cancer
Keith	50		Anglo-Australian	Converted to Greek orthodox		Bisexual	Factory floor supervisor		None

Continued

Table 1.1 Research Participants, their Partners and Demographics *(Continued)*

Name	Age	Location	Cultural Identity/ Background	Religious Identity/ Background	Relationship Status	Sexual Identity/ Preferences	Employment/ Education	Children	Health/ STIs/HIV
Steph	47	Melbourne	Anglo-Saxon	Both Church of England	25 years married, now separated	Prefers no labels	Outdoor educator in primary schools	2: daughter 21 and son, 18	None
David	50		English			Gay	Business Manager in Asia		
Sue	38	Melbourne	Both Anglo-Australian	Both Church of England	19 years married, separated for 1.5 years	Heterosexual	Medical pathologist	2: daughter, 6 and son, 2	None
John	39					Sexually fluctuates	Accountant and Software Management		
Susanna	28	Regional New South Wales	Celtic-Australian	Church of Christ background, now Buddhist	5 years together, ended 2.5 years ago	Heterosexual	Graphic designer	1 daughter, 4	None
Un-named	38					Sexually shifts between bisexual and heterosexual			
Suzette	36	Inner city Sydney	English	Buddhist	18 months	Bisexual	Artist	2 children from previous marriage: 10 and 9	Chronic fatigue
George	37		Pakeha New Zealander			Bisexual polyamorous	Computer technician		None
Sylvia	47	Melbourne	English-Jewish	Atheist	Married 12 years, now divorced	Heterosexual	Receptionist	2 boys, 21 and 19; older daughter died at 1 year old, would now be 23	None
Larry	44		Jewish descent	Catholic		Prefers no labels	Restaurant owner		

38 *Chapter 1*

Name	Age	Location	Ethnicity	Religion	Relationship	Sexuality	Occupation	Children	Health
Tamara	30	Canberra	Indigenous	Both Catholic	2 years	Bisexual	Paralegal	Deceased child from previous relationship	In recovery from previous nervous breakdown
Un-named	40		Maltese			Bisexual	Intelligence Officer, Department of Defence		None
Temptress	26	Sydney	Portuguese	Catholic	1.5 years defacto	Bisexual nonmonogamous	Office Administrator	None	Genital fungal infection from partner
Fernando			Argentinian	Catholic		No label, non-monogamous	Musician		Genital fungal infections
Vicky	43	Rural ACT	Both Anglo-Australian	Catholic	Married 24 years	Heterosexual	Receptionist in family service station business	3 boys: 23, 19 and 16	None
Mike	45						Mechanic in family service station business		
Yvonne	30	Adelaide	Italian	Catholic	14 months, Robert previously married	Heterosexual	Sales and marketing	Robert has 9 year old daughter from previous marriage	None
Robert	35		Scottish	Protestant		Bisexual	Cleaner and taxi-driver		

Chapter 2

"Border Women and Their Border Men"

Some Theories, Definitions, and Debates Framing the Research

> The world isn't heterosexual or homosexual, it's lotsasexuals.
> —Wendy, 15. (in Pallotta-Chiarolli, 2010a: 3)

This chapter will situate the research within ongoing queer, feminist, sociological definitions, debates, research and activism in regard to bisexual masculinities and MOREs. It is an overview of the theories and terms I use 'in making sense' of participants' perceptions and lived experiences. I will provide some theoretical and discursive tools with which MOREs can be situated, understood and articulated, but without reducing their multiplicity to simplistic, dichotomous and homogenizing caricatures. Throughout the subsequent chapters, through an immersion in the empirical data and the women's lives, it will become apparent that they undertake three strategies in their encounters with others about their bisexual partners and MOREs:

- strategies of passing: "getting the glass slipper to fit" (George, 1992) through *normalization*: silence, erasure, absence, mimicry and assimilation in relation to a range of socio-cultural settings;
- strategies of bordering: "haciendo caras/making faces" (Anzaldua, 1990) through *negotiation*: balancing, weaving, maneuvering between the various worlds and communities they inhabit;
- strategies of polluting: being "the stranger, the undecidable" (Bauman, 1988–1989) through *noncompliance*: personal agency, resistance and politicization by letting people know about their bisexual partners. It must be stated here that "polluting" is used as a positive term of strength, agency and empowerment, rather than implying negative, insidious, harmful or underhanded machinations (Douglas, 1966).

These three strategies are framed and impacted upon by three interweaving social processes of positioning which will be evident in each chapter:

- social ascription: being what external society and its systems, such as a health system, demand from a woman, her partner and their family;
- community acknowledgement: being what a woman's significant others positively affirm or negatively discourage, such as in an extended family, workplace community, gay and lesbian community, and ethnic community;
- personal agency: being what a woman, her partner and/or family actually do despite the regulations and oppressions from both the wider society and one's communities.

"WHOSE TRUTH? WHOSE REALITY?": THEORIZING BIFURCATION AND BORDERDWELLING

In Bartlett's play, *Cock,* the bisexual character John says the following when both the woman and man he loves come together over dinner:

> "I know it's weird but I'm trying to work out how to handle this, who to be, because I'm two different people with the two of you when you're separate and now I'm in the middle and no one" (2013: 71).

His situation reflects Western discourses which have embedded in them dichotomous logics of 'either/or' that tend to force relationships and identity-formations, and the organizations and systems that dis/service them, into bifurcated categories (Gibian, 1992). However, the reality of contemporary relationships and identifications is not dichotomous but fluid, transitory, fragmented, episodic. As John says later, "maybe it's not a switch, one way or the other, maybe it's more like a stew, complicated things bubbling up" (Bartlett, 2013: 86). Dichotomous logics of "either/or" establish destructive potentialities or actually do damage to people's lived realities, including those of bisexual men and their women partners. Scarduzio & Geist-Martin refer to "fractured" identities, highly pertinent to MOREs as their fractures can be viewed as experiences wherein "identities collide, contradict, and slip as individuals struggle to communicate an identity that fits" these il/logics of bifurcation (2008: 374). In the words of bisexual singer/songwriter Tom Robinson, bisexual men and their partners and families are "simply trying to live a both/and life in an either/or world" (in Bennett, 1992: 205).

The logics I utilize in this book to describe and interpret the social relations and identifications of women and their bisexual male partners without dichotomous reduction and distortion can be defined by the French term "metissage" and the Spanish term "mestizaje." Both these terms mean mixture and multiplicity, or as so aptly translated by some of the bisexual young people in my previous research, "being messy" (Pallotta-Chiarolli, 2010a: 29). Mestizaje, or borderland theory, has been amplified and adopted by Latina/Chicana-American feminists of diverse sexualities to define identity as being in process, multiplaced and shifting (eg Anzaldua, 1987a, b; Lugones, 1994; Molina,1994; Moraga, 1981). Mestizaje persons often find themselves challenging and being challenged by the discourses and ideologies of what is binarily constructed as the powerful Center, such as the heteronormative Center that requires men and women to be in monogamous heterosexual relationships, and the power-challenging Margins, such as the homonormative sexual duality Margin which requires men and women to be in monogamous homosexual relationships. This hierarchical dualism has constructed a borderland within which mestizaje persons such as bisexual men, their women partners and their families, attempt to weave and live their "multiple threads" by inhabiting "multiple lifeworlds" (Cope & Kalantzis, 1995), such as those of extended family, communities, workplaces, schools and health services. This book will present what can healthily eventuate when these multiple weavings are made possible, and what harm eventuates when they are made impossible.

Foucault's (1986) construct of heterotopia also acknowledges how several incompatible complexities, contradictions and disidentifications can coexist and blur within one space, as in the multiple-within space of a MORE. Indeed, heterotopic sites facilitate acts of resistance and transgression:

> Living as we did—on the edge—we developed a particular way of seeing reality. We looked both from the outside in and from the inside out. We focused our attention on the center as well as on the margin . . . We understood both. . . . a mode of seeing unknown to most of our oppressors that sustained us (hooks in Trinh, 1990a: 341).

The women and their partners in this book voluntarily or reluctantly inhabit heterotopic locations within, between and beyond the binary hierarchy of lifelong marital monogamy and noncommitted, nonmonogamous sexual encounters; and the hierarchical duality of heterosexuality/homosexuality.

Unlike Zipkin who believes labels are "a necessary step to take before we get to the place where we don't need them anymore" (1992: 72), mestizaje theory does not argue for the need to do away with all frameworks, boundaries, identities and truths. This absolute unfixedness would only be the polar extreme of absolute fixedness, becoming another form of regimentation and oppression (Weeks, 1987). After all, most of the participants in this research intentionally ascribe themselves, their partners and their relationships with labels such as "heterosexual," "bisexual," "polyamorous," and "queer." Thus, the intention of this book is not to argue for the "impossibility of identity" (Dowsett, 1997: 274). Rather, the argument put forward is the impossibility for MOREs and the individuals in these relationships to fit neatly into singular, fixed definitions; and the simultaneous impossibility of doing away with the effects of identity categories and definitions altogether. The problem is not that there is no truth, but that there is "too much truth" that powerful discourses conceal (Derrida, 1981: 105). It is those borderzones of "too much truth," constructed as 'unreal' or negated in dichotomous discursive boundaries, which will be explored in this book in relation to MOREs.

The notion of the "something else besides" as found in Bhabha's work in relation to postcolonial diasporic cultures is pertinent to MOREs: "There is a sense of disorientation, a disturbance of direction, in the 'beyond': an exploratory, restless movement . . . here and there, on all sides" (1994: 1). In this study, MOREs inhabit the "something else besides," aptly the something more, between heterosexual and homosexual, monogamy and promiscuity, monosexuality and bisexuality, "normal" marriage and "abnormal" relationship, from where they "incite border dialogues, to encourage boundary crossings" (Angelides & Bird, 1995: 4).

In Derridean deconstruction, 'difference' is defined as hybrid, fluid and multiple rather than just a point of comparison and contrast between two fixed polarities. It also means:

- "difference beyond": What differences do women in relationships with bisexual men experience that challenge or go beyond mainstream understandings and constructions of 'different' relationships?
- "difference as excess" or "a point beyond which language and explanation cannot proceed": How do queerly mixed relationships illustrate limitations and absences in language and discourse? Will this book struggle in discussing and explaining MORE experiences within a language and discursive framework that does not allow for them?
- "difference within": How do the mixtures and differences among and between queerly mixed relationships problematize any attempt at homogenizing and generalizing these relationships?
- "difference against": how do the lives and loves described in this book disrupt and question conventional assumptions and accepted silences in relation to mixed sexualities in relationships? (Burbules, 1997: 106–108).

As stated in chapter 1, representations of bisexual men in film and popular culture will also be discussed in this book to explore cultural mis/constructions of Derridean 'difference': "the bisexual as outlaw: breaking all laws of identification and commitment" (Vicari, 2011: 8). In *Sunday, Bloody*

Sunday (1971), Bob Alcon is a metissage borderdweller: a young man romantically and sexually involved with a young woman, Alex, and an older man, Dr. Hersch. They both constitute separate complete worlds which Bob visits "the way a spaceman traveller might visit different planets, planets which are connected through Bob" (2011: 9–10). His two partners are living in two separate worlds of heteronormativity and homonormativity, yet they know about each other's existence. Indeed, they are depicted as connected via the metaphor of using the same telephone switchboard exchange, suggesting they share the same world of mononormativity, which Bob eventually escapes by leaving both of them to go to America. However, what is left open in the film is whether he will find anything "different" there.

Another film which explores the multiple worlds and multiple antilinear possibilities of a bisexual life is the Brazilian film *Possible Loves* (2001). Its repetitions of the same man's romantic moments are different according to differently gendered partners. The director, Sandra Wernick, cuts back and forth between them rather than letting each one play out individually. As one of the characters says regarding sexual preferences, "we must consider every possibility, no prejudices." Indeed the film, even by its very title *Possible Loves,* plays upon the openness of bisexuality and its multiple possibilities and intricacies, thereby questioning the singularity and simplicity inherent in many monosexual narratives of the one great love in life.

"OUTSIDE BELONGING": SOCIAL, COMMUNITY AND AGENTIC POSITIONING

Women and their bisexual male partners are faced with the inability of carrying one's multiple realities into all one's sites of existence at all times. In being 'at home' within 'homelessness', and 'homeless' within 'home', they locate/situate themselves elsewhere—that is, everywhere and nowhere. 'I use my bisexual wits to cross boundaries, crack codes, and bring back a store of secret information that society would like to use to keep us *all* in thrall . . . home is not a place, but a process' (Queen, 1991: 20–21). Each home-site is an equally complex product of the ever-shifting geography of social relations present and past. For those who have been displaced from some original place of possible physical, social and emotional belonging, such as women who began in a "home" of being married to a heterosexual man who later identifies and behaves bisexually, "home" is "neither here nor there" but is "*both* here *and* there—an amalgam, a pastiche, a performance . . . [of] roles and relationships of both belonging and foreignness"(Bammer, 1992: xix).

Likewise, women with bisexual male partners may remain silent when their realities are either ignored or subsumed into the gay, lesbian, or straight categories. Indeed, many of the women in this research could identify with the following description of borderdwelling by Trinh:

> But every place she went they pushed her to the other side and that other side pushed her to the other side of the other side of the other side, kept in the shadows of the other (1990b: 328).

As introduced earlier in this chapter, three interweaving social processes of positioning will be explored throughout this book:

(a) "They Say, Therefore I Should Be"

Social ascription refers to the labels and classifications imposed on one by the powerful central discourses within a society as upheld by institutions such as the media, religion, education and the law: "The barracks stands by the church stands by the schoolroom . . . surveillance depends [upon them] for its strategies of objectification, normalization and discipline" (Bhabha, 1990: 86).

(b) "They Say, Therefore I Must Be"

In a society that has despised and devalued certain groups, it is necessary and desirable for members of those groups to adhere to one another, acknowledge community membership and identification, and celebrate a common culture, heritage, and experience. This grouping is usually referred to as a "community." Rigid conformity and uniformity become internally coercive as a means of resisting external social coercion (Udis-Kessler, 1990). Difficulties and contradictions will manifest themselves within that "imagined community" (Anderson, 1983) in relation to how it will present itself to the wider society, and how it will deal with internal differences: "Mestizas belong even where 'their own people' deny it" (Phelan, 1994: 66).

(c) "I Say, Therefore I Am"

Whether within the wider society or a community, constructions of social relations with no room for personal agency but only for "social puppets on fine, flexible wires dancing across stages not of their own making" are problematic (Boden, 1990: 193). People are, and always have been, active agents in the constitution of their unfolding social worlds and the recognition of themselves within it (Butler, 1993; Pallotta-Chiarolli & Pease, 2014):

> I did it, and I didn't die. I didn't even languish. Quite the contrary—I flourished. And with every fresh act of daring against the taboo, I blossomed more. Instead of hiding all scrunched up in my fearful skin, clinging to it, I began to slough it

off and stand up straight, clear and clean, my strong new skin gleaming in the sunlight (Johnson, 1987: 9).

Thus, being on the borders allows for agency in relation to action, identity and community allegiance. A mestizaje construction of agency transcends both "thoroughgoing determinism and unqualified freedom, while preserving all possibilities between these extremes" (Cohen, 1987: 285). Passing, bordering, and polluting (normalization, negotiation and noncompliance) happen simultaneously and in interwoven ways. Being located in the borderland involves a straddling of various identifications and social groups, drawing the best from each into a personal behavioral and interpersonal system, and remaining detached enough to be able to critique and challenge these very locations and groupings. Being located in the borderland means acknowledging that while one is actively pursuing this metissage personal agency, choosing from the sexual, interpersonal, political, legal, economic, social and cultural options available to one at a particular historical, economic, political time, there are external forces and discourses from both power-challenging minority communities and the powerful Center of the wider society constantly trying to pinpoint, locate, fixate, label, construct and ascribe an identity that is acceptable and useful to them (Pallotta-Chiarolli & Pease, 2014).

As examined in later chapters, there are particular circumstances that tend to influence the level and nature of agency of women in MOREs, whether this agency be predisclosure or postdisclosure of their partner's bisexuality. They need to have:

- access to knowledge of their social, gendered and sexual locations, including health promotion programs, textual resources and resource persons;
- the modes of articulating and utilizing this knowledge, including the possibilities of financially supporting various individual and couple desires and goals such as travel, education, maintaining various households, caring for children;
- the means of disseminating this knowledge to others such as their support networks, their children, coworkers, and others who validate and respect their knowledge.

"OUTSIDE BELONGING": STRATEGIES OF PASSING (NORMALIZATION), BORDERING (NEGOTIATION), AND POLLUTING (NONCOMPLIANCE)

The following description is very applicable to the shifts and unfixedness inherent in the lives of multiplaced/denied-a-place persons such as women

48   *Chapter 2*

in MOREs who have travelled out of the range of simple sociocultural allegiances, boundaries and reclamations:

> She has this fear that she has no names that she has many names that she doesn't know her names She has this fear that she's an image . . . She has this fear that if she digs into herself she won't find anyone (Anzaldua, 1987a: 43).

Passing and Normalization

Passing and normalization are two strategies that will become very evident in many bisexual men in relation to their partners, the external society and some communities; in some of the lesbian and bisexual women partners in relation to society and certain communities; and in some of the heterosexual women partners about their male partners in relation to society and some communities. We will also poignantly hear from some women who passed to themselves by denying or repressing the awareness or suspicion that their partners were not heterosexual, as well as how their partners tried to pass as straight to themselves and indeed got married in order not to confront their bisexuality:

> When was the first time I noticed I had the gift of making myself invisible? . . . It was a self I erased myself, or was it that I was being erased? I don't know. The only thing I know was that I was still there. I knew that I was there, but nobody saw me (Lizarraga, 1993: 32).

Kroeger provides a succinct definition of 'passing':

> Passing involves erasing details or certain aspects of a given life in order to move past perceived, suspected, or actual barriers to achieve desired ends. . . . and the way society rewards and personalizes people when they do (2003: 8).

Anzaldua discusses the metaphor 'haciendo caras' as a performance strategy and points out both its ascribed and agentic elements:

> *haciendo caras*, "making faces" means to put on a face . . . Some of us are forced to acquire the ability, like a chameleon, to change color when the dangers are many and the options few . . . These masking roles exact a toll . . . After years of wearing masks we may become just a series of roles, the constellated self limping along with its broken limbs . . . Between the masks we've internalized, one on top of another, are our interfaces . . . from which we can thrust out and crack the masks . . . . We begin to acquire the agency of making our own *caras* (Anzaldua, 1990a: xv–xvi).

The "emotion work" (Hochschild, 1983) involved in self-presentation, role performance and the manipulation of external appearance through constructing our "interface" can lead to stress. Hence, Hochschild calls for a "healthy false self," which enables discretion and safety while allowing the emergence of the "true self" when there is minimal danger (1983: 195). Of course, the whole dichotomous construction of 'true' and 'false,' 'inner' and 'acted' selves can be problematized as drawing upon essentialist discourses of an authentic self removed from sociopolitical and sociocultural contextualization. The participants and their partners in our research are social performers who know the lines in the 'dominant' drama of heterosexuality and heteromonogamous family, and are able to "take license with the play, acting it in a variety of styles, substituting lines and switching characters"(Cohen & Taylor, 1976: 64). This script manipulation means mestizaje persons monitor their own performance, such as script switching, script evasion and juxtaposition. Swan & Benack discuss how when a 'queer man' confronts the conflict between his marriage and his same-sex desire, he finds himself in an "unscripted space" (2012: 50). This can be very troubling for these men and their partners due to the insidious power of two cultural discourses: *the orientation script* which constructs an essentialist fixed view of sexual desire; and *the monogamy script* which includes the belief that: "When people are in love, they want to have sex only with their beloved" (2012: 53). Swan & Benack conclude that it is evidence of the power of socially defined scripts that "they struggle, often desperately, to find a way to make sense of their feelings in terms of these dominant cultural narratives" (2012: 55) constructing terms such as "one woman short of gay" or "just a good buddy with benefits" (2012: 56; see also Kort, 2014b). The queer spouse's same-sex desire has to mean that:

> he loves his wife less than he (and she) thought he did; his acting on that desire has to be a move away from the marriage. Conversely, his love for his wife and commitment to the marriage have to be a force that undermines the importance and validity of his same-sex desire. The scripts do not allow for even the possibility of a good resolution that includes all the parts, a way of integrating all of these desires into one meaningful, understandable, harmonious life (2012: 59–60).

In the following chapters, the above major concealment/passing strategies will be evident in women in MOREs, their partners and families. Richardson (1985) provides the following summary of these passing strategies:

- withdrawing: giving up a part of one's identity in a given interpersonal, social or community context;
- compartmentalizing: placing every role into a different "airtight cubicle" in order to have the best of all worlds (Richardson, 1985: 73);

- cloaking: appearing to be "conventional, legitimate" which they both are and aren't (Richardson, 1985: 74). Examples of this camouflage are using words like "dad's best friend" or "family friend" to describe a husband's male partner;
- fictionalizing: creating stories for deception, omission, constructing gaps and filling in gaps with creations and fantasies.

Bordering and Negotiation

The prohibited and forbidden, such as bisexuals, are in a constant state of transition, the inhabitants of the borderlands of which Anzaldua writes: "This is my home/ this thin edge of/ barbwire" (1987a: 3). She utilizes the term *nepantla* to theorize this liminality and borderdwelling (in Anzaldua & Keating, 2002: 1). They are "threshold people" who develop what Anzaldua describes as a "perspective from the cracks" (in Keating, 2005: 2). *Nepantla* is a zone of possibility, where *nepantleras* are exposed to new perspectives and knowledge "and where you question the basic ideas, tenets, and identities inherited from your family, your education, and your different cultures" (Azaldua and Keating, 2002: 547–48). In some situations in this book, women in MOREs become *nepantleras*, facilitating crossings and negotiations for their partners and themselves: "Contraries meet and mate and I work best at the limits of all categories" (Trinh, 1991: 53).

Pollution and Non-Compliance

'Polluting' is used as a metaphor of strength, agency and empowerment, and is not intended to imply negative, insidious or harmful machinations (Douglas, 1966). Indeed, it is only through polluting existing and residual systems and structures via noncompliance and innovation that emergent and empowering systems and structures can evolve (Pallotta-Chiarolli & Pease, 2014).

> I am an act of kneading, uniting and joining that not only has produced both a creature of darkness and a creature of light, but also a creature that questions the definitions of light and dark and gives them new meanings (Anzaldua, 1987a: 80–81).

MOREs are the excess, unable to be fixed and incorporated within heterocoupledom or homocoupledom. Therefore, they find their supposed "impurity and defilement" produce "endless efforts to dam up, resist, rebuild the old partitions, to blame what could no longer be thought without confusion, to blame difference *as* wrongful confusion!" (Derrida in Kamuf, 1991: 256–57; see also Derrida, 1981). This seepage of "edge identities" (Bersten, 2008: 25) is evident even in monogamous MOREs, wherein many couples seek ways of creating a "bisexual display" (Hartman-Linck, 2014) as part of everyday life such as creating visual and visible nonheterosexual space in the home and voicing one's bisexuality in public spaces, thereby attempting to avoid their bimonogamy being subsumed or invisibilized into hetero- or homomonogamy. Barker (2015) refers to "mindful bi-furiosity" in order to claim bisexual marginalization as a site of resistance.

Bauman uses the Derridean definition of the "undecidable" to represent any identity that "calls the bluff of the opposition" (1990: 145; see also Derrida, 1981). This is similar to Simmel's (1971) theory of the "stranger" who has the agentic characteristics of mobility and freedom from convention, thereby challenging a group's or institution's "thinking as usual" (Schutz, 1944: 501). These metaphors aptly apply to women and their bisexual partners in MOREs as they are "that third element which should not be. The true hybrids, the monsters: not just unclassified, but unclassifiable" (Bauman, 1990: 148–49). In order to maintain their semblance/illusion of "order or structure," societies and their institutions endeavor to alleviate the "stranger that threatens the stability and coherence" of that social order. This is accomplished by "suppressing and excluding any individual or group that comes to symbolize disorder or ambivalence" (Marotta, 2002: 38; see also Marotta, in press). However, any push for purity only reproduces pollutants who, in this way, are agents in the reconstitution of the social order.

> You say my name is ambivalence? Think of me as Shiva, a many-armed and legged body with one foot on brown soil, one on white, one in straight society, one in the gay world, the man's world, the women's, . . . A sort of spider woman hanging by one thin strand of web. Who, me confused? Ambivalent? Not so. Only your labels split me (Anzaldua, 1987a: 205).

"TO BE OR NOT, OR BOTH OR NEITHER": DEFINING, DENYING AND QUEERING BISEXUALITY AND 'LIMBO MEN'

The research in this book is framed by a growing body of queer scholarship on bisexuality (e.g., Alexander & D'Onofrio, 2010; Anderlini-D'Onofrio, 2004; Dodge & Sandfort, 2007; Fox, 2004; McLean, 2003; Pallotta-Chiarolli, 2015a). For some theorists, bisexuality is considered to be an inclusive term that defines immense possibilities, whether they are acted upon or not (Angelides, 2006; Diamond, 2008, 2009; Halperin, 2009; Wark, 1997). For example, Orlando (1991) claims that the denial of bisexuality creates an absurd and endless parade of obfuscating terms, as is seen with Kaye's (2008) terms "straight gay men and limbo men." Orlando offers the following: "lesbians with 'boy toys,'" lesbians and gay men who "sports-fuck" with the opposite sex, and the parade of acronyms such as MSWM and MSWMW

(1991: 229). Phellas & Coxon use the term "queer bisexuality" to explain that "bisexuality and queerness are not mutually exclusive. Rather, bisexual constitutes one realm of queerness" (in Phellas, 2012: 243). Angelides believes it is in this very fluidity that the subversive, and perhaps politically productive, possibilities of bisexuality lie: "I aim, therefore, to situate bisexuality in fragmented and fluid spaces; that is, in subject-positions without rigid borders"(1995: 38). For example, the men and sometimes the women in our research are sexual borderdwellers because they:

- do not identify as gay, lesbian, or heterosexual;
- do identify as bisexual;
- do behave bisexually while adopting a gay, lesbian, or heterosexual label;
- do use broader and more inclusive terms such as "sexually flexible," "sexually fluid," "heteroflexible" or "straight with gay interests";
- do dismiss sexual labelling altogether.

Borrowing from the 'one-drop theory' of race in which a dominant White culture once viewed anyone with even a portion of Black genetic ancestry as Black, Anderson refers to the "one-time rule of homosexuality": "one same-sex sexual experience is equated with a homosexual orientation in masculine peer culture, ruling out the possibility of men engaging in recreational same-sex sex without being homosexualized by their behavior" (2008: 105; see also Corley & Kort, 2006; Kort, 2014a). For example, Reisen et al. (2010) report that almost one tenth of the men who identified as straight in a population-based sample in New York City reported having sexual intercourse with only men in the previous year. Other researchers such as Ward refute the "One-drop theory" by referring to "white hetero-masculine logics" that sex with men goes by other names such as "experimentation," "jokes," "games," "masculinity-enhancing" and "paradoxically, a means of inoculating oneself against authentic gayness" (2015: 25, 27). Ward (2015) labels this "hetero-exceptionalism".

In the Klein Sexual Orientation Grid, sexual orientation is a multivariate concept comprised of three variables which directly describe the sexual self (attraction, fantasy, and behavior); three which describe aspects considered crucial to the composition of sexual orientation (emotional preference, social preference, and heterosexual or homosexual lifestyle); and also the variable of self-identification (Klein et al. 1985; see also Klein, 1993; Savin-Williams, 2005; 2008).

Boulton et al. (1989) identified six patterns of bisexuality:

- transitional (as part of the process of 'coming out' as gay);
- unique (almost exclusively homosexual or heterosexual with occasional deviations);

- serial (alternating patterns of exclusive hetero- and homosexuality);
- concurrent-straight (predominantly heterosexual with some homosexual contacts);
- concurrentgay (predominantly homosexual with some heterosexual contacts);
- concurrent-contact (large numbers of homosexual and heterosexual contacts

Meyer (2010) observes at least nine different types of bisexuality coalesced around three themes. The first group comprises:

- *situational bisexuality* where heterosexuals engage in same-sex behavior given extenuating restrictive circumstances, such as being incarcerated in a same-sex prison;
- *transitional bisexuality* where the goal is to bridge an identity change from heterosexual to homosexual;
- *chic bisexuality* (or *heteroflexibility*) where same-sex behavior is used as a means of cultivating social acceptance, such as being part of a swingers group or girls being sexual with each other to please a boyfriend. "Trendy bisexuality" is very popular in some youth cultures and is distinctly tied to heteronormativity because the individual eventually defers to powerful heterosexual norms (Diamond, 2005).

The above bisexualities occur within a temporary liminal space, and the end result is an identity as heterosexual or homosexual. In the second set of situations identified by Meyer (2010), individuals know their desire and behavior are bisexual, but they refuse to accept bisexuality as an identity category. Alternatively, because heteronormativity establishes bisexual identity as a debatable construct, they do not adopt this as a label:

- *historic bisexuality* where an individual's sexual history includes behaviors and/or fantasies contrary to their current sexual identification (e.g., a man claiming a heterosexual identity while having a history of sexual encounters with other men);
- *technical bisexuality* where an individual has sex with men and women but prefers to be identified as heterosexual, lesbian or gay;
- *cop-out bisexuality* where individuals want the "best of both worlds" without having to commit themselves to a particular partner or lifestyle. This form of bisexuality is most frequently associated with individuals participating in swinger culture (deVisser & McDonald, 2007).

In a third grouping by Meyer (2010), bisexuality can be defined by the relational choices an individual makes with respect to romantic attachments:

- *sequential bisexuality* where an individual creates serially monogamist consecutive relationships with different sexes over time such that at any one point they are involved with only one sex. Their sexual identity is based on the sex of their current romantic partner;
- *concurrent bisexuality* where an individual maintains relationships with both sexes at the same time, therefore being nonmonogamous or polyamorous;
- *experimental bisexuality* where an individual tests relationships with more than one sex at a time to see which sex appeals to them the most. The individual is not necessarily invested in identity labels, but rather sees sex as a form of play and pleasure outside the construct of identity.

Specifically acknowledging the diversity within the category of bisexual masculinities, Buchbinder and Waddell (1992) outline three classes of male bisexuals: petrotropic bisexuality, mainly active with women; homotropic bisexuality, mainly active with men; and ambitropic bisexuality, engaged in partial sexual activity with both men and women (see also Jones, 2000). Likewise, in their Internet research, Dodge & Rosenberger referred to the "typologies" of male bisexual behavior including "men in transition," "experimenters," "opportunity-driven men," and "men with dual involvement" (2012: 16). Lastly, based on his research, Malcolm (2000) explains how for many men, having sex with men is devoid of any meaning other than direct sexual satisfaction. This behavior does not "imply pathology nor does it require complex symbolic explanations or differential identity labelling" (2000: 266). He "tentatively identifies" four distinct types of behaviorally bisexual men:

- "adventurers": heterosexual men whose homosexual behavior is most likely opportunistic;
- "avoiders" who report an onset of homosexual feelings in early or pre-adolescence which were ignored;
- "repressors" who experience homosexual feelings from mid-adolescence but do not incorporate this into their developing sexual schemas until much later in life, usually after being in long-term heterosexual relationships;
- "defensives" who identify as heterosexual or bisexual while their reported sexual and emotional feelings are homosexual, and who are likely to continue with their marriages (2000: 291).

Malcolm also refers to true "dualists" (2001: 293), the "middle ground of this landscape" who identify and behave as bisexual (2000: 292). In his research, 88.5% of this last group of men remained within their marital relationships. Indeed, the bisexually identified men tend to report "a primacy of intimacy and attachment" to their heterosexual relationships and seek out sexual contact with men for "a specific type of sexual satisfaction that they associate with men and masculinity" (2000: 294).

As has become apparent from the above lists of labels, no matter what definitions and judgments of bisexuality are applied, there are as many ways to classify and categorize bisexuality as there are manifestations of bisexuality. Nevertheless, there are certain spatial models within which bisexuality is positioned:

- the conflict (either/or) models: bisexuality as largely transitional, anxious fence-sitters "torn between two worlds" (Moore & Norris, 2005; Zinik, 1985);
- the synthesis (both/and) models: bisexual orientation as "the best of both worlds," these polar worlds remain unchallenged and fixed (Klein, 1993; Moore & Norris, 2005);
- the Kinseyan continuum of sexuality based on binary opposition: heterosexuality and homosexuality at opposite ends. Bisexuality falls in the middle, sometimes as an incompletion, a split, or halves rather than a whole (Kinsey et al., 1948, 1953);
- the monosexual to multisexual model which places homosexuality and heterosexuality at one end of a continuum as monosexist gender-linked choices of sexual partner, and bisexuality at the other as nonmonosexist non-gender-specific (Barker, 2013; Ross & Paul, 1992);
- the mestizaje models that insist the very power of what is defined as bisexuality is its unclassifiability and multiplicity, its being everywhere and elsewhere and nowhere (Angelides, 2001; Wark, 1997).

While the conflict model accurately predicts higher levels of conflict, coercion and confusion for bisexual individuals, as will be evident in some of the bisexual male partners in this book, it is important not to assume that this is linked to underlying pathology. Instead, the links between individual conflict and external ascriptions and coercions need to be acknowledged and addressed, as exemplified in the men who did not disclose to their women partners until circumstance or discovery forced disclosure. Indeed, this identity conflict, or legitimation crisis, refers to "the problem of the multiply defined self whose definitions have become incompatible" (Baumeister et al. 1985: 408). However, this identity conflict can also be compartmentalized into personal sexual identity and social sexual identity. For example, Moore & Norris found that despite higher levels of sexuality conflict in the external world, 85% of bisexuals in their research "experienced their sexual identity in a fairly cohesive manner" (2005: 23; see also Diamond, 2009). In an earlier study, Boulton & Fitzpatrick (1993) reported that over 90% of men who were asked how they personally viewed bisexuality indicated that it was natural, normal and common. The findings from Rostosky et al's study also revealed 11 positive aspects of a bisexual identity such as "living authentically and honestly, exploring sexuality and relationships, developing empathy for others, forging strong connections to others and to the larger community and engaging in social justice activism" (2010: 140). However, these self-ascriptive views contrasted dramatically with their quite clear views of the societal meaning of their bisexuality as problematic and negative. The lack of social sexual identity validation may at least partially account for the higher rates of psychological distress and substance abuse that have been documented in samples of bisexual-identified adults, as will be discussed further in chapter 16.

Given this discussion about the multiple ways of defining and positioning bisexuality, and when considering how the term is used or not used by our participants and their partners, I align myself with Halperin who does not even "purport to say what *bisexuality* really means or try to indicate how it should be understood." He contents himself with "merely noting . . . the word signifies different things to different people. Even more important, it keeps getting used in different ways, or to refer to different things" and proceeds to list 13 different definitions of bisexual people, all of which will be evident in this book (2009: 452).

I realize as I write within this second decade of the twenty-first century, I am also on the border of emerging sexual identities and concepts which challenge bisexuality as well as heterosexuality and homosexuality. For example, as presented in chapter 1, Albury introduces the term "identity-plus" to define how multiple sexual orientations might coexist within heterosexuality: "To identify as strongly heterosexual *and* strongly bi-curious *and* strongly bisexual may signal a strategic desire to be recognized as nonnormatively sexual in a way that defies standard categories" (2015: 662). Autumn (2013) introduces the concepts of pansexuality and pomosexuality, the latter being the "queer erotic reality beyond the boundaries of gender, separatism, and essentialist notions of sexual orientation" (Queen & Schimel cited in Autumn, 2013: 333). As research and theory become more trans* inclusive (the exclusion of transgenderism has been addressed in the first chapter as a significant limitation in this book) and communities come to accept the concepts of sexual fluidity, choice and nonbinary living, there will be more insight into pansexuality and pomosexuality. Meanwhile, we are still having to address the sometimes scholarly and general societal residualism that persists in claiming:

> Bisexuality . . . is an out-and-out fraud, . . . as rational as one declaring that a man can at the same time have cancer and perfect health . . . Nobody can dance at two different weddings at the same time (Bergler, 1956: 80–81).

If it may be a relief to think this view was held in the 1950s, it is then doubly concerning to find how many people, including academics, scientists, counsellors and activists, still hold this view, as will be discussed further in chapter 3.

As introduced in chapter 1, Bonnie Kaye's perspectives are based on supporting women who have experienced deceptive and distressing relationships of betrayal and abuse with their nonheterosexual partners, and indeed her work within the self-help genre has given encouragement and support to many women. However, her frameworks, like those of Jeffreys (1999), are simultaneously problematic for they construct no borderspace for the acknowledgment of the reality of bisexual diversities; and the understanding that it is possible, indeed a reality, for women and their partners to negotiate positive nonpatriarchal relationships with bisexual men.

> Bisexuality is an excuse. For gay men it is an illusion, creating a picture that allows them to fit into the straight world. For their straight wives it is a delusion, creating a justification for keeping the marriage together (Kaye, 2000: 147).

Kaye assigns labels such as "straight gay husbands" and "limbo men," an insidious form of bifurcated logics premised on the existence of heterosexual and homosexual "worlds" between which there is an unbridgeable chasm rather than a borderland where women and their partners can create positive ways of living, loving and lusting. Nevertheless, she conflates these contradictions when she defines "straight gay husbands," adhering to the "one-time rule of homosexuality" (Anderson, 2008: 105):

> If you look like a duck, walk like a duck, act like a duck, but have sex with a goose, are you still a duck or are you a goose? I say you're a goose. . . . So, to simplify your confusion, let me say this—STRAIGHT MEN DON'T HAVE GAY SEX. You can call it whatever makes you feel better, but I still call it *gay*—all the way (2008: 73).

She blatantly dismisses the Kinsey scale and proposes a dichotomous one of her own.

> The scale has two levels:
> 1. Heterosexual. This is a man who craves sex only with a woman because these are the only sexual feelings that arouse him.
> 2. It's for all the other men who desire penis on any level, incidentally, occasionally, every blue moon, just out of curiosity, or in a fantasy.
>
> Think of all the anguish this new scale will take away from people who are intellectualizing about where they stand on the Kinsey scale. . . . Why does something this simple have to become so complicated? (Kaye, 2008: 155–156).

Kaye provides the following as universal examples of men's statements where they endeavor to refute what she perceives as the reality of being "gay," without considering these statements as actually very viable if one acknowledges the bisexual borderland between straight and gay. This will become very apparent in this book where the following are actually described by women as being experienced by their bisexual partners (see also Kort, 2014a):

1. I'm not gay, but I like looking at gay pornography as part of a full pornographic fantasy show.
2. I'm not gay, but sometimes I call gay sex lines because the way they talk stimulates me sexually.
3. I'm not gay, but when I was younger, before I met you, I had a one-time sexual encounter with a man, but I only let him perform oral sex on me.
4. I'm not gay, but there are times I think that I am bisexual because I look at guys and find them sexually appealing. I would never act on it though.
5. I'm not gay, but sometimes the thought of anal penetration turns me on.
6. I'm not gay, but when I was in college, we would all get stoned/drunk and have big orgies where everyone was having sex with everyone.
7. I'm not gay, but I have a fantasy about both of us having sex with another man. (2003: unnumbered)

Without awareness that it is oppressive surveillance and restrictive definitions such as hers that create the context within which some men may play out their deceptive scenarios with other men or feel coerced to "choose to be gay," Kaye then also constructs a universal unquestionable category of "limbo women" who also exist in this "No Zone" with their partners (2003: unnumbered).

THE REPRESENTATIONS AND REPORTING OF BISEXUAL MEN IN RESEARCH

As discussed in chapter 1, bisexuality and bisexual men reside on the borders of sexuality research (Heath, 2005). Indeed, researchers into male bisexualities are often marginalized and have difficulty establishing a stable career trajectory based on grants and institutional support (see Dodge, 2014 for a personal account). Hudson (2013) has published the most comprehensive literature review on married men who have sex with men and finds that the most basic questions that motivate and gain major funding in both quantitative and qualitative gay and lesbian research, such as "how many?" and "who are they," remain unanswered and underresearched in relation to bisexual-identifying and bisexual-behaving people (see also

Pallotta-Chiarolli, 2006b). The exact number of bisexual men is difficult to determine for two main reasons. First, due to the label itself being stigmatized, many men may feel coerced to identify as either heterosexual or homosexual in research. Second, the figures vary depending upon whether the research has been conducted using sexual identity and/or sexual behavior as the defining criteria (Dodge & Rosenberger, 2012; Fox 2004; Malebranche et al. 2010; Schrimshaw et al. 2013b). Eisner (2013) states that male bisexuality usually appears in only three research contexts: medical, sexual and denial. The medical institution is "a normalizing agent, deciding which behavior is normal and which should be corrected" and much of the research about bisexual men and sex has been in relation to STI/HIV transmission (Eisner, 2013: 206).

Of particular interest have been recent scientific studies and media reports of those studies aimed at disproving the existence of male bisexuality (Carey, 2005; Erickson-Schroth & Mitchell, 2009). Bailey and his team sought to scientifically disprove the existence of male bisexuality by reducing male bisexual identity to patterns of sexual arousal (see Eisner, 2013). Reiger et al. (2005) examined physiological sexual arousal and function among self-identified bisexual men, but only in a controlled clinical setting with limited investigation into other factors influencing these areas of sexuality. The hypothesis behind the study was that bisexual men do not exist and that those who claim to be bisexual are either straight and pretending to be more open than they are, or gay and in denial. The original study did not prove what it set out to establish and yet the sensationalist media reporting of the study assisted in its construction as scientific fact. The results of the study indicate that the genital arousal of bisexual men in penile circumference looks very similar to that of heterosexual and homosexual men, therefore most of the self-identified bisexuals were aroused just as proportionately by either men or women instead of equally by both, leading Carey (2005) and others reporting the study in the media to conclude that the bisexual men were either "straight, gay or lying." This subsequently became the title of an article appearing in the *New York Times* on July 5, 2005 (Carey, 2005). The researcher, Bailey, is also known to have said that homosexuality is a big evolutionary mistake, coauthoring an article defending heterosexual eugenics "or a parent's right to abort gay fetuses, if it were possible to predict" (Eisner, 2013: 204). Even before his controversial study about bisexual men, Bailey had made remarks that no bisexual men exist and all women are actually bisexual. He had even used the expression 'gay, straight or lying,' several times. As Eisner concludes, Bailey's study of bisexual men

> perpetuates the patriarchal values of science ... by presuming that white heterosexual men have the authority on bisexual men, ... by perpetuating a

hierarchical dynamic of the researched as the objective observer and bisexual men as the objectified raw material (2013: 215).

In response to the study, the heads of the American Institute of Bisexuality (AIB) funded additional research by Bailey and his team. The second study published in 2011 was undertaken using the very same methods but this time found that bisexual men actually do exist. Eisner argues that while it appears that the AIB did well in finding scientific proof of the existence of bisexual men, by funding another similar study it reinforced the medicalization of bisexual men "as a species to be studied and dissected," and also reinforced the methods of the previous study by reusing them, thereby also reinforcing the results of the previous study (2013: 215). Eisner also compares media reactions to both studies and finds that while *The New York Times* did publish the follow-up, "it wasn't half as popular as the original article. . . . It also didn't get picked up as much by other press and media" (2013: 217). She cites Simpson who wrote that the first study "told people—straight and gay—what they wanted to hear and what common sense tells them to be the case. The second study, he says, got the result they [AIB] wanted but I fear they're wasting their money and merely encouraging more gay science" (in Eisner, 2013: 217; see also Tuller, 2011 for another research example). Simpson, Eisner and others conclude that the AIB

> would have done better to fund research actually discussing bisexual men, their identities and their lives. . . . Particular attention should be paid to marginalized groups of bisexual men, such as bi- trans and intersex men, bi-men of color, disabled and chronically ill bi-men (Eisner, 2013: 218).

Interestingly, the original research actually showed that most of the men, including those who identified as heterosexual and homosexual, were somewhat aroused by their nonpreferred sex, even if that arousal was not as great as the arousal to their preferred sex, suggesting that most men may possess a certain capacity for bisexual arousal. However, rather than deducing that most men are bisexual, Rieger et al. concluded "it remains to be shown that male bisexuality exists" (2005: 581).

This denial of bisexuality in men has been criticized by some writers, social commentators and other researchers. For example, in an essay entitled "*Curiouser And Curiouser: The Strange 'Disappearance' Of Male Bisexuality,*" Simpson queries a range of curious heteropatriarchal gendered contradictions such as between the "commonness of female bisexuality and the 'non-existence' of the male variety"; and that "bi guys are freaks and liars" while female bisexuality is "natural and as true as it is wonderful and real and . . . hot!" (2006: pages unnumbered). Schnarrs et al. critique physiological studies as they "sought to determine what bisexual men find attractive (or arousing) in men and women without trying to understand what these men feel is desirable in sexual partners of both genders" (2012: 248). As Vicari queries, "If an orientation is a complicated nexus of cultural identification, experience and the willingness to self label, then how could it be reduced to a simple physiological response?" (2011: 21).

Rosenthal et al. (2011) also critique past research which does not find bisexual genital arousal patterns among bisexual men, as these studies may have been affected by recruitment techniques. For example, bisexual men needed only to identify as bisexual and to self-report bisexual attractions (see for example Rieger et al., 2005). Thus, the bisexual samples may have been populated by men who had never or rarely behaved bisexually and perhaps identified as bisexual for reasons other than strong arousal to both sexes. For example, some men identify as bisexual not because they show bisexual arousal but because they have distinct personalities that open them to a variety of sexual experiences, including sexual experiences with the less preferred sex. On average, the bisexual men in their own research sample had distinctly bisexual patterns of both genital and subjective arousal: "That is, their arousal responses to their less arousing sex tended to be higher than those of homosexual and heterosexual men" (2011: 113).

Lippa's (2012) research with bisexual men's and women's sexual attraction to photographed male and female 'swimsuit models' who varied in attractiveness showed that bisexual men and women showed bisexual patterns of attraction and viewing times to photo models, which strongly distinguished them from same-sex heterosexual and homosexual participants (see also Cerny & Jansen, 2011; Ebsworth & Lalumiere, 2012). In another study conducted by Reiger & Savin-Williams (2012), the pupil dilation of 325 men and women of various sexual orientations to male and female erotic stimuli was studied. They found that self-reported sexual orientation corresponded with pupil dilation. They concur with Rosenthal et al. (2011) as bisexual men displayed bisexual pupil dilation patterns consistent with the finding that bisexual men show bisexual genital arousal. They also agree that more stringent recruitment methods, such as through websites that cater towards men who seek sexual relations with both men and women, produce self-reported bisexual men who show a bisexual arousal pattern.

This scientific research provides, although it should not have been necessary, a kind of "existence proof" (Lippa, 2012) of what Klein stated so succinctly twenty years earlier: "Can human beings love both men and women at the same time? They can if they can" (1993: 6). Indeed, the available sociological evidence suggests bisexual men are more numerous if we take into account not only identifying as bisexual but behaving bisexually throughout the life span. For example, in the United States, the Center for Disease

Control and Prevention's National Center for Health Statistics found that 6% of young men in their late teens and early twenties reported at least one same-sex encounter (Mosher et al. 2005). They also found that 1.8% of men aged eighteen to forty-four gave their sexual preference as bisexual. The San Francisco Human Rights Commission (2011) report on data from the 2002 National Survey of Family Growth which found that 1.8% of men identify as bisexual and about 6% of men reported attractions to both women and men. In large national studies, behavioral bisexuality among men has been found to be between 0.7% and 5.8% in the general U.S. population, while numbers of self-identified bisexual men in these samples are often smaller (Laumann et al. 1994; Reece et al., 2010). In general, self-identified bisexual individuals also report high rates of bisexual behaviors (Dodge et al. 2008; Stokes et al. 1993; 1996). Longitudinal studies have demonstrated that bisexual identity remains stable for many self-identified bisexual individuals (Weinberg et al., 1994; 2001). However, fluidity and fluctuations in self-identity have also been found to occur, particularly among women (Diamond, 2003, 2008; Diamond & Butterworth, 2008). Jeffries (2011) believes that research findings which show behaviorally bisexual men have a larger number of partners than homosexual or heterosexual men might be attributed to several major factors including that having multiple partners may be one way that men assert themselves as bisexual in a society that denigrates bisexuality. It may also reflect "reverse causation": as men have more partners over time, their likelihood of having sex with both men and women may increase. Also, men who have had more partners are likely to have relatively liberal attitudes toward sexuality, which may justify opposite- and same-sex partnering within a short time period.

THE REPRESENTATIONS AND REPORTING OF MOREs IN RESEARCH

Research on MOREs as dichotomous straight/gay relationships reached a peak during the 1980s. Prior to this, the first studies of gay married men or their wives were clinical in nature, appearing in 1969 (Imielinsky, 1969; Buxton, 2006a, c, d). The studies often focused on closeted or troubled gay husbands or their wives (Hatterer, 1970; 1974). After the American Psychiatric Association removed homosexuality from the *Diagnostic and Statistical Manual of Mental Disorders* in 1973, several nonclinical studies appeared. This research examined gay husbands' struggles with their own negative views of homosexuality, acceptance of being gay, and integration of their homosexual orientation with their roles as spouses in heterosexual marriages and as fathers (see Buxton, 1999, 2001, 2006a, b, d). In only two studies were openly gay/straight couples described as enjoying satisfying relationships and were termed "the new couple" (Nahas & Turley, 1979). The other early study that challenged prevailing notions of all same-sex attracted men feeling coerced to marry women in order to conceal their sexuality was conducted by Latham & White (1978). They found many of the men expressed strong desires for a family and children and had established a meaningful and satisfying relationship with the spouse to be. When asked if they had married in an attempt to change their sexual orientation, all of the male respondents answered in the negative. Latham & White (1978) recommend that before therapists working with MOREs impose certain assumptions and prescriptive responses, they need to consider the following factors for purposes of assessment and treatment planning, depending on whether the women had control over the decisions and whether they and their partners agreed upon them. These factors, to be discussed again in later chapters, include:

- What were the initial reasons for marrying?
- Are sexual relations within the marriage being maintained?
- Would the heterosexual partner be allowed to experiment outside the marriage, if desired, equally to what the same-sex attracted partner would do rather than creating a sexual "double standard"?
- What is the degree of open communication in the relationship?
- What are the couple's abilities to establish certain "ground" rules for the relationship? (1978: 208; see also Suresha & Chvany, 2005).

In the 1980s, with the development of the *Klein Sexual Orientation Grid* (Klein et al. 1985), several researchers examined the experiences of married bisexual spouses, mostly husbands, and bisexual/gay-heterosexual couples (Kohn & Matusow, 1980; Wolf, 1985). The mid- to late 1980s saw the first studies of heterosexual wives in MOREs (Hays & Samuels, 1989; Gochros, 1989) followed by a handful of books in the 1990s, two on gay–straight relationships (Whitehead, 1997; Whitney, 1990) and one on heterosexual wives and husbands of gay, lesbian or bisexual spouses (Buxton, 1991). In the early twenty-first century, one report appeared on wives of gay husbands (Grever, 2001) and two on marriages that continued after disclosure (Buxton, 2001, 2004a, b). All told, literature about MOREs was minimal, especially empirical data about bisexual-heterosexual couples. Moreover, in most research on gay and bisexual spouses, data gathered from bisexual participants was included with those from gay men, thereby hiding specific characteristics of each orientation.

Jorm et al. (2002) found a strong increase in research reports on women of homosexual partners from the beginning of the 1990s to the early 2000s, which suggests a greater willingness by women to engage in this research. Rust (2000) notes that many of these projects were based on research participants who were in therapy or support groups seeking help adjusting to the newly revealed sexual orientation of the nonheterosexual partner, thereby generating data and conclusions based largely on the problematization of these relationships. The research and publications were also increasing at the same time as increasing knowledge of HIV/AIDS transmission was generating fear "of those who kept one foot in the gay world and the other foot in the heterosexual world" (Rust, 2000: 293). Another simultaneous factor was the increase in gay activism and visibility that was "beginning to reach the homes of people who had married to deny or conceal their gayness or bisexuality" (Rust, 2000: 293). Research on MOREs was framed by theorists such as Weeks (1998) discussing how families of choice, the varied patterns of domestic involvement, sexual intimacy, and mutual responsibilities, were increasingly displacing traditional patterns of marriage and family and required rigorous research. For example, Page (2004) found that 33% of her bisexual sample was involved in a polyamorous relationship, while 54% considered this type of relationship ideal (in Weitzman, 2006). Buxton's (2006b) role as director of the Straight Spouse Network, her research and other research studies (Pallotta-Chiarolli and Lubowitz, 2003; Pallotta-Chiarolli, 2010a, 2013, 2014) conclude that many heterosexual partners do not necessarily want a relationship to end if a partner identifies as gay, lesbian or bisexual. There may be a strong bond that both partners do not wish to break, and they come to see themselves as life partners in a MORE that deconstructs and broadens the meaning of marriage, interrogates the binarily constructed heterosexual/homosexual divide, and challenges gendernormative roles in relationships.

Very early studies such as Nahas & Turley (1979) found women who are happy living in MOREs have several things in common. As will become apparent through many of the women's stories discussed in chapters 5, 6 and 7, they appear to be women whose fulfillment in life does not depend on conventional notions of marriage and motherhood; were not dependent on their partners for contentment in social and business affairs; feel personally and professionally equal to men; are less bothered if their husbands are with men and more bothered if they are with other women; and do not consider monogamy to be necessary for a successful relationship. These women are less concerned with "maintaining appearances and upholding tradition" than with "achieving one-to-one compatibility" and consider their relationship, "not as a poor compromise, but with enthusiasm and flexibility" (Nahas & Turley, 1979: 21–22; see also Malone, 1980). Hence, self-ascription far outweighed the significance of social ascription and the approval of significant others.

One of the studies that heralded the research studies of the 1990s and early twenty-first century was the study of gay men and straight women in intimate relationships by Whitney (1990). She found that many women deliberately chose gay-identifying men as partners and coparents due to their broader and nonnormative constructions and performances of masculinity. Although Whitney used the term 'gay' to define the men, she did find that 64% of the men said that although their sexual attraction to men was stronger, they had also experienced satisfying sexual relationships with women. However, of these, only 22% actually identified themselves as bisexual. Most men agreed that decisions about commitment were based on more than sexual preference, and that there are many different factors that enter into a decision about which course of life or relationship to pursue. For 68% of the respondents, the most important issue was love for the individual person, regardless of gender.

For 50% of the men, the benefits of being in a relationship with a woman outweighed the negatives as they considered their personal needs and priorities, and operationalized normative constructs of gender roles:

> the desire to have children, the attraction of a traditional lifestyle, the need to have a close, permanent companion, and the belief that strong, emotional attachments were preferable to strong, erotic attachments. Some men reported feeling emotionally fulfilled with women even though their primary sexual attraction was for men." (Whitney, 1990: 35).

For 36% of the men, women were seen as deeper and more reflective, men as more superficial, and women were more willing to make commitments; were more open about sharing their feelings and less judgmental when the men expressed deeply felt doubts and fears. Women were more willing to make sacrifices for the sake of their relationships, and more often shared interests in common with the men. Compared with gay men, women were less concerned with physical appearance, sexual performance and age.

Whitney's (1990) study with women is in direct contrast to Atwood's (1998) later study which also provided a profile on wives who marry bisexual men. Again, sociocultural constructs of gendered roles were evident. The majority of them "were willing to hang in there even as their self esteem got used" (1998: 19). They tended to accept the blame, believed they could change circumstances, used denial as a primary coping strategy, hated to fail and refused to give up on their partners, saw divorce as a defeat, saw themselves as martyrs, worried about what other people thought, struggled with saying 'no' and setting meaningful limits, and were impressed by the charm and superficial traits in the men. Atwood concluded that the women "are conditioned to be accepting of male moral transgressions" such as having sexual problems and spending more unnecessary time away from home than most husbands (1998: 20).

Over ten years later, Pearcey & Olson (2009) surveyed 90 heterosexual women who were married or partnered with gay or bisexual men. The two most important factors in the decision to marry or partner for nearly a quarter of the women related to the treatment they received from these males in addition to the attitudes and values these men portrayed. Approximately 11% knew of their partners' gay or bisexual tendencies prior to the marriage or partnership. 46% of the married respondents had divorced, and 17% remained married to their husbands. The wives who discovered their partners' bisexuality expressed feeling anger (22%), resentment (20%), less attractive (16%), understanding (11%), and relief due to 'problem identification' (13%).

What is also significant and in line with the previously discussed issue of the misrepresentation of bisexual men in research is the number of studies which used the category 'gay' to represent all men who were same-sex attracted and in marriages with women. This "exclusion by inclusion" (Pallotta-Chiarolli & Martin, 2009) remains problematic as in this chapter, I am referring to some studies which say they are about gay married men, and yet which at times indicate that some of these men chose to behave bisexually, discussed their relationships with their female partners as primary, loving and sexually satisfying, or even identified as bisexual. Where research does differentiate between gay and bisexual married men, the findings mostly reveal important variations. In Australia, Malcolm (2002) compared "ever-married" and "never-married" behaviorally bisexual men and found those who identified as "gay/homosexual" in the "ever-married" category showed higher levels of life stress than those who identified as "bisexual". In Buxton's (2001) study of MORES, 59% of the heterosexually married gay men sought counseling or therapy to cope with disclosure of their sexual orientation as compared to 16% of the married bisexual men. Higgins (2002) researched the experience of previously married gay men in Australia and their reasons for marriage to see whether same-sex attracted men who marry are in fact bisexual rather than exclusively gay. He found that most of the men he surveyed currently self-identified as "gay," and there was no significant difference between the two groups on their ratings of the degree to which their sexual desires/erotic fantasies, sexual behaviors, or emotional attachments are heterosexual or homosexual. Thus, his research suggests a different conclusion: that bisexuality is not a sufficient explanation for marriage in same-sex attracted men (see also Higgins, 2006).

Higgins (2002) also found that the two most frequent reasons for marriage were that it seemed "natural," and the desire for children and family life. Multiple other studies have also indicated individuals married in order to fulfil societal or familial expectations, or because it was the "natural" or "normal" thing to do (Coleman, 1982; Corley & Kort, 2006; Kays & Yarhouse, 2010; Yarhouse et al. 2003). Higgins (2002) argues that the cognitive dissonance aroused by the inconsistency of married men's erotic desires for men and their marriage to women are resolved initially by adopting attitudes consistent with public behaviors (i.e., their heterosexual marriage). Cognitive dissonance increases, however, when, after having successfully suppressed their erotic desires for other men for a period of months/years after marrying, they increasingly seek out sexual contact with other men. Higgins also found that marriages generally occurred when the respondents were young, suggesting that they are entering these marriages before they gain the relevant life experiences to help them resolve their concerns over their sexual identity and erotic object choice. However, the degree of bisexuality may explain differences within the group of same-sex-attracted men. Yarhouse et al. (2003) found that sexual minority spouses reported a decrease in their same-sex attractions and an increase in their opposite-sex attractions from before marriage to the time of the study.

At times, authors or researchers themselves cast negative or problematic judgments about the men in their research. For example, Leddick's (2003) collection of autobiographical accounts of 39 men subsumes all the men into the gay married men category, even as some of the men discussed how to establish new configurations of family relationships that expand the options available. What is also of interest is their differences in experiences and decisions based on age. Leddick refers to the "The Hidden Generation" who were over 60 and usually remained closeted as within their younger temporal context of overt legal, medical and sociocultural surveillant homophobia, there had been no place for men to live together and no concept of having a happy life outside their marriage to women. Likewise, social ascension, social status and a wealthy lifestyle were paramount and thus not to be jeopardized by coming out as gay into a world that did not affirm, let alone recognize, gay identities and relationships. Thus, they kept their relationships with men outside the marriage rigidly concealed, constructing a dichotomy between their married heterosexual lives and their 'real' gay lives. The "Confused Generation" were in their 50s and also wanted the pleasures that come with status, often immersing themselves in demanding jobs and activities to keep themselves from thinking about their sexual preference. Indeed, they were often not fully aware of their sexual predilection, and often maintained self-deception until later in life. However, once they understood their sexuality, they left their marriages and "adapted more honestly to a gay lifestyle" (2003: 3). This was also the main movement of the "Out and About Generation" in their 40s: "most would create lives for themselves in the gay community and make no attempt at even partial closeting in professional and social worlds" (2002: 3). On the other hand, Leddick grapples with the more fluid and diverse border-crossings and borderdwellings of what he calls the "Guilt-Free Generation." These men were in their 30s and Leddick concludes that they often had difficulty coming to terms with being gay as they lost heteroprivilege, thereby implying that this was why they remained in their relationships with women. However, the younger men were more likely to call themselves bisexual as shifting sociocultural norms allowed for this blending and bordering of straight and gay worlds. His summation undermines these men who stated they did not want to leave the straight world for the gay world as they "say they are truly bisexual and some married simply because they wanted to" (2003: 3). Overall, these men had successful careers, felt less called upon to defend gay rights and fight for acceptance, and had greater freedom in how they would construct their sexual, relationship and family lives.

A study which challenged prevailing notions of bisexual men in MOREs being unable to remain monogamous was Edser & Shea's (2002) study of bisexual men in monogamous marriages. They were all still attracted to males, and the majority of them married for love and still loved their wives very much, with the key variable being the degree of homosexuality. The researchers concluded that the men in this sample seem to be psychologically stable, not under inordinate stress, and the majority of their marriages appeared to be in relatively good condition. The study shows respondents' marriages were anything but brief with 5–9 years (45%), 10–19 years (20%), and 20 plus years (25%). Therefore, "we might find it difficult to accept the veracity of the equation: bisexual married man = inevitable divorce" (2002: 27). Almost half of the men stopped having sex with males before marriage, 23% at the time of, and 30% after marriage. Thus, for bisexual men "who find heterosexual sex to be satisfying and not repugnant, monogamous marriage is a viable life-option" (Edser & Shea, 2002: 7). Importantly, the researchers conceded that their own assumptions and hypothesis had been challenged as they had "anticipated a higher degree of dissonance than what was observed" (2002: 21).

In the research, those with healthy MOREs are referred to by some counsellors as "resilient couples" where they report mutual satisfaction and do not experience themselves as at-risk for marital dissolution (Yarhouse & Pawlowski, 2003). However, the term 'resilient' indicates a default position based on heteronormative external ascriptions that these relationships are normally meant to fail and confront overwhelming obstacles. Research needs to address how for some couples, being in MOREs was perceived as a default and normal position from the beginning. For the men who did experience confusion and dissonance in Edser & Shea's (2002) study, "a little" and "somewhat" describe the amount of confusion, while "a little" describes the levels of anxiety. "A little" guilt was also demonstrated such as fantasizing sexually about other men while having intercourse with one's wife, but "checking out" other men was considered an easy and harmless expression "during the course of the day's events" (2002: 22). Another interesting finding was the men "overwhelmingly" dismissing the following as reasons for marrying: to have children, to avoid the gay or bisexual label, to avoid loneliness, because of family pressure, and because of societal pressure. Indeed, 80% had disclosed to their wives to some degree, and 65% of the wives fell in the 'tolerant,' 'understanding,' or 'accepting' categories. Fifty percent of the bisexual men reported their marriages as being "excellent" and "very good," while a further 30% described them as being "workable." They rated their communication with their partners very highly and appreciated their ability to talk about the sexuality issue with their wives. They also concluded that "a healthy and active sex life with one's wife is a solid indicator of the way a man might judge his marriage" (2002: 24). Thus, as will also become evident in this book, marriage, indeed monogamous marriage, can be a viable state for some bisexual men who have lower Kinsey Profiles. Sixty percent of Edser & Shea's (2002) cohort could be labeled Straight Leaning bisexuals while about 40% experienced a change in sexual orientation in marriage in the Straight direction, 40% experienced No Change and 20% in the Gay direction (see also Jones, 2000).

One of the most comprehensive studies of bisexual men, which combines both quantitative research and autobiography, is by John Barrington (1981), a highly visible bisexual man in the United Kingdom. When Smith meets with Barrington with a view to writing his biography, he recalls being told the following: "that he was happily married, had been for 30 years, had two daughters and one grandchild" (1997: 2). The autobiography does document the above as well as Barrington's various relationships with men, his arrests for dealing in gay pornography, and his lifelong noncompliance to simplistic expectations and labels. Indeed, in a diary note from 1990, Barrington wrote in his quantitative researcher's style: "For 350 nights each year for 30 years I have shared a midnight bath with my wife and we have both slept naked together. We made love very approximately 7000 times, more than three times as often as I made love with men. How do I sexually define myself?" (in Smith, 1997: 110). Smith discusses how from January 1956, John regarded himself as three different people: first, the respected married man; second, an artist, draftsman and publisher, celebrity hunter, philanthropist and the researcher/writer of one of the first books on men who are sexually attracted to other men called *Sexual Alternatives for Men* (Barrington, 1981). The third self was a "promiscuous" gay pornographer unscrupulous in business, morals and pleasure seeking. Barrington described one of his days in 1957 when the three selves and the three worlds came together, and how his "straight married father" perfomativity enhanced the meeting of young men:

> I, my wife, her younger sister were walking along the promenade at Richmond beside the Thames. Me, wheeling the big double pram, camera around my neck of course. We met a real discovery, Don, 5ft 9in athletic, Australian, well-tanned, crew-cut beach boy and merchant seaman, handsome and unattached. . . . The normality of my appearance, my expensive cameras, the laughing happy babies disarmed young men who otherwise would never have accepted the cards I gave them (in Smith, 1997: 131).

Perhaps the most outstanding single factor that comes out of Barrington's bisexual case histories is their dispelling of many of the pseudopsychological myths of the time. For example, he found that a very high proportion of these men came from large and very happy families, and none had a feminine upbringing, excessive mother love or maternal domination. Nearly all acquired from an outside family influence an interest in the male sex at a very early age, implying that individuals acquire homosexual interests and homosexual acts as part of healthy childhood development. Another important discussion, although problematic in the trivialization implied by the word "hobby," is Barrington's finding that women partners of bisexual men are more adaptable to a "new male arrival than they are to another female . . . provided she loses nothing sexually, socially or financially from her husband's hobby" (1981: 133). Barrington also dispelled long-held myths by presenting his findings that a bisexual man's fulfilling sex life with his wife may be enhanced rather than eroded by his same-sex sex life. He does provide two sexual reasons for why many bisexual men say they desire sexual contact with men, particularly if these practices are abhorrent to or not desired by their wives: the desire for oral sex as both recipient and giver, including with ejaculation in the mouth; and anal sex as both recipient and giver. Another point that he raises is how many men and their wives establish threesomes or some form of polyamorous relationship with the husband's male partner(s).

More recently, researchers into polyamory are constructing new terms to describe the various relationship forms and feelings that arise in satisfying nonmonogamous MOREs (eg Anapol, 2012; Barker & Langdrige, 2011). Compersion is "the joy at seeing one's partners happily in love with others" (Sheff, 2014: 20). "Metamor" or an OSO, (other significant other), is the partner of a partner with whom there is no sexual connection. "Polyaffectivity" is a term Sheff uses for emotionally intimate polyrelationships which are nonsexual, who see each other as family members; and the "polyamorous possibility" is what Sheff calls the mindset which acknowledges the potential to love multiple partners at the same time (2014: 21).

CONCLUSION

The first two chapters have provided an introduction to the research questions and participants, research methods, the theories and definitions of the terms used in this work, and an historical overview of the literature and empirical data to date. We now begin to explore and understand the specific experiences of the women and their bisexual partners in our own research.

Chapter 3

"You know, the old Kinsey scale"
Women Talk about their Partners' Bisexualities

> Well, my interpretation of what he says to me is that he is attracted equally to men and women. I think he realizes that there are degrees. You know, the old Kinsey scale. (Jane)

In this chapter, we will be discussing men's bisexualities according to the three facets discussed in chapter 2:

- what men say they are sexually,
- what men actually do sexually;
- what women partners say men are based on their partners' sexual practices, stated sexual identities and their own interpretations.

This triage is evident in Jane's comment above in regard to her partner's attractions: her "interpretation" of what he says and feels which are aligned with what he does. In many cases, however, identity and practice were not always aligned for the men, and indeed, what women concluded as their partners' sexual identities based on what they said and did were not always aligned with what their partners self-ascribed, particularly if their partners felt coerced to adopt an identity based on sexual binary. For example, Felicity stated that her husband said that she was "tying him down to say he was one thing or another." What becomes apparent throughout these discussions, however, is the applicability of what Jane calls *"the old Kinsey scale"* as men, and sometimes the women, meandered and maneuvered along the Kinsey and, indeed, the Klein scale, according to factors such as age, circumstance, opportunity, and relationship status (see also Kort, 2014a). Also useful, albeit more rigid, is Bleiberg et al.'s (2005) five-stage layer-cake model of bisexual identity development. Layer one involves socialization into the heterosexual world and developing a heterosexual identity. Layer two involves experiencing homosexual feelings, thoughts and behaviors. Layer three is the acceptance of homosexual attraction while maintaining a heterosexual identity. Layer four involves the integration and assimilation of heterosexual and homosexual identities, with layer five being identification as bisexual.

Increasingly, in both the media and research, there is an attention to Kinsey/Klein scales of sexual continuum for men's sexualities, although Phellas & Coxon comment on how "Two straight identified men kissing one another on the lips without it being staged as simply a comic moment is a rare sight" in the media (in Phellas, 2012: 200). With the film *The Dallas Buyers Club* (2013) and the real character it was based on, one of the key questions has been: Was Ron Woodroof actually bisexual? He may have been bisexual, he may have been heterosexual with occasional sex with other men, he may have been gay with occasional sex with women. Wickman (2014) concludes "Whatever the case may be . . . [the director Bortn] gave Woodroof's story a somewhat neater and simpler trajectory than it had in reality." In *Shame* (2011), Michael Fassbender plays a predominantly heterosexual 'sex addict' hitting rock bottom when he enters a gay club, depicted in salacious sleaziness, for a back room tryst with a male stranger. "That explicit representations such as these are still configured in such alarming alarmist extremes suggests that male bisexuality still provokes deep anxiety, even within films, that otherwise offer formative or at least sympathetic portraits of queer characters" (Phellas & Coxon in Phellas, 2012: 243).

Thus, far from being "overpowering and charismatic personalities who silence all quibbles by conscripting everyone in sight into one enormous nonstop orgy" such as in *The Rocky Horror Picture Show* (1975) and *Interview With A Vampire* (1994) and their branding of "predatory super human bisexual men," actual bisexual men have "admitted to very human size doubts and second guesses" and dealing with rejection when it comes to exploring and enjoying their variegated sexual desires (Vicari, 2011: 19–20). For example, in the road movie *Y Tu Mama Tambien* (2001), two close friends, Julio and Tenoch, are teenage boys who discover and explore their sexual attraction to each other in a threesome with a married woman in her late twenties. A discomfort then sets in as they return to Mexico City. They stop seeing each other until a chance encounter in a coffee shop a year later. Amidst the awkwardness, they exchange information about new girlfriends as if assuring each other of their heterosexualities, and the narrator reveals they will never see each other again. In *Chuck & Buck* (2001), two childhood friends who were sex-playmates meet up again as adults and have to navigate that Chuck now identifies as straight and Buck as gay. The film explores the fear of exposure some heterosexual men experience when they have had previous sexual relations with another man. Buck's behavior becomes increasingly erratic and obsessive and by the end of the film, they have had sex and then part ways until Buck is invited to Chuck's wedding and sexual binary peace is restored. What is absent in these representations is a language that supports the theory that people can be heteroflexible, homoflexible and bisexual over time, place and space. Kort (2014b) talks about *13 Minutes or So* (2013), an award-winning film that dramatizes heteroflexibility as "sweet, endearing and [it] illustrates how complicated all of this really is . . . for many straight men who occasionally have sex with other men given the right situation or circumstance, and not necessarily based on any attraction towards men as a whole." While heteroflexible men are ostracized for "turning gay," Kort points out the double standard at play when a gay man comes out as homoflexible: He is applauded as it aligns with heterosexuality:

> I was telling a straight friend that as I get older, I find myself noticing women in sexual ways more than I ever have before. This straight friend high-fived me! He didn't say, "Ew, that's STRAIGHT!" (2014b: pages unnumbered).

Given the above discussion of the limitations of classification in sexual labelling, a necessary problematic in this chapter is that I am also constructing arbitrary categories of sexual identity in order to provide a structure within which to explore the Kinsey/Klein scales of sexual attraction, practice and identification in men, according to or as reported by their women partners. These are:

1. Men who identify as *bisexual*
2. Men who identify as *gay*
3. Men who identify as *heterosexual*
4. Men who identify as *queer, something else, or dismiss labelling* altogether

"ESSENTIALLY IT HAS BEEN A BISEXUAL IDENTIFICATION"

> Essentially it has been a bisexual identification, but at other times, he's been more comfortable identifying himself as deviant or disobedient. (Katie)

In this section, I present women discussing their partners as being "essentially" bisexual. However, as with Katie, there was much slippage and shift in sexual identity labels, indeed a playfulness (Lugones, 1990) and parodying of labels, given that the identity of bisexual is itself problematic, "deviant or disobedient" for many in both the heterosexual and homosexual worlds (as discussed further in chapters 12 and 13). Other women saw bisexuality as a clear and unproblematic category within which there were varying degrees of sexual attraction and simultaneous or sequential sexual action with men and women: "His last serious partner before me was a man. Since we've been together, he hasn't slept with a man" (Kirsten).

> Martin has described himself as bisexual. He appears to be equally attracted to both men and women. . . . it's always struck me as really amusing but he really likes voluptuous, rubinesque women. I lost about twenty-five kilos and he was always saying, "You're too skinny." . . . But then the blokes that he's attracted to are just the opposite . . . just so different to me that I really believe he must be right in the middle of a Kinsey continuum. (Monica)

Sara's partner was aware of his bisexual attractions as a child before bisexual behaviors and identification: "he says he can remember being a tiny child on Manly Beach, and finding it pleasurable to look at both the men and the women on the beach" (Sara). This is theorized by Comeau as the "label-first" sequence or the "identity-centered pattern" of sexual development (2012: 332). In other words, these men solidify a bisexual identity and self-label as bisexual before engaging in sex with more than one gender. This cognitive exploration of sexuality has been documented in other studies on bisexuals and illustrates how attraction and desire are a critical dimension of identity development before sexual activity commences (Rust, 2000, 2001).

Most women in our research identified their partners as having more desire for women than for men, and/or being sexually active with only them as their primary partner/female partner/life partner: "my husband, bisexual, likes to be with a man now and then. He likes to be with me as a woman all the time" (Lesley).

> He does describe himself as bisexual . . . It means to him that he would like to continue to have a relationship with me but also finds it exciting to have a sexual relationship with men, and finds it impossible not to do that in fact now. . . . He tells me he has no inclination to live with a male. . . . [and] certainly not other women, no. (Gerry)

In Naomi's situation, her partner identified as bisexual in attractions even if he had never had sex with a woman before her, leading her to remain cautious that she was just "a sexual experiment":

> It's bloody flattering I guess, "No you are more than enough," but when he is in his other moods he will go, "Are you kidding? More than one of you? Ra ra ra all day and bloody periods, sharing the bathroom and shoving each other out of the way at the mirror." . . . He does porn shops and their backrooms where you watch a video and he might have sex as well. He finds it really interesting because he gets more propositions when he is in a straight video place than a gay one . . . When we first set up, the first four months I kept myself really cool,

I thought this is probably a sexual experiment with a woman going on here for him and that's OK, I will take what I want out of it cause I fancy him but I am going to have to deal with him being gay. He kept telling me, "No, no, it's going to be a lot longer than this," and that was terrifying for him cause he has never felt this strongly for anyone, . . . I keep telling him "If you want to have sex with a woman you go for it." He flirts with women, he has women as friends, but when it gets to that point he just doesn't . . . but with guys it's like [clicks fingers] instant yes. (Naomi)

Some women believed most men (and women) were bisexual to some degree: "I say to everybody 85% of people are bisexual and the other 15% lie. [Laughing]" (Sharae). Other women were aware of their partners' same-sex attraction and their discomfort with identifying that and exploring it, due to years of socially enforced repression and shame: "I can definitely understand in society, that it's horrible [to be bisexual]. . . . so many jokes . . . and he thought "Oh I can never show my true colors" (Maz). They encouraged their partners to acknowledge their bisexuality, embrace it as an identity and explore it:

I believe in that Kinsey continuum, because we're all at different stages in our life. . . . And I think he's in closet denial and I think that comes out in his behavior, the angry person. (Lisa)

As Joseph writes, many sexually fluid men have lived within a "discursive silence," and a "cognitive leap" is required to move from "an expression of an action you have engaged in to actually finding words for it" (1997: 138).

I think Pete had been a bit homophobic, or at least very distancing himself from the parts of himself that homosexually need to be nurtured. . . . because he's still uncomfortable with it a bit, and I would be more than delighted if somebody he could develop a really loving, close, nurturing long-term relationship with came along. . . . he hasn't made that leap yet, and I would love to see him make it. . . . He's now much softer, much more willing to engage on topics of male/male sexuality and what his experience is. (Anne)

There were many women like Anne who wanted their partners to stop feeling ashamed and inadequate. However, some were also worried that there was a fine line between their partners identifying/behaving as bisexual, and then moving further into being gay and away from them as women. Indeed, even though their partners stated they were bisexual, there were some women who worried that their partners were actually gay and found it difficult to accept or understand bisexuality. Ross (1983) refers to the "defense theory" whereby the self-label of bisexual may be used by some men as a defense of semiacceptability for those most uncomfortable or anxious about their homosexuality:

> Is he really gay but just quite doesn't know how to work that out for himself? Do people just progressively go into identifying as bisexual and then eventually coming out gay? (Scarlett)
>
> With a straight man you know you're what they want whereas with a bisexual man, I'm always guessing in my head if he's going to change his mind. (Lauren)

Some women believed that the way their partners had sex with them, such as enjoying anal penetration as both inserter and recipient, exemplified how tenuous the "thin line" between being bi and gay actually was, even though their partners clearly stated they were bisexual, and even though their own sexual pleasure with other women was never seen as meaning they could be lesbian:

> He loves getting fucked up the arse. . . . [and] for me it's been great sex with him. I mean, for me he's my perfect partner. . . . He loves fucking me when I lie down on my tummy. That's how he fucks men. That's his favorite position, and I get scared because I'm thinking I need to find out ASAP whether he's bi or gay, . . . they say that bisexuality is such a thin line, hey, to being gay, so I'm scared to actually lose my man to being gay. . . . With me [becoming a lesbian], no, it's really funny, I tell him that won't happen. (Temptress)

Yvonne discussed how she queries her partner's self-identification as bisexual as to her it means an equal and confident desire for all sexual acts with both men and women, whereas he is "quite specific" about the types of sexual acts that he engages in "with men and everything else grosses him out." For many men such as Yvonne's partner, oral sex was engaged in much more than anal sex. This may be a sexual desire and/or it may be linked to heteropatriarchy which is "absolutely premised on the refusal of the anus on the part of men" (Joseph, 1997: 142; see also Ward, 2015).

> I don't think he's comfortable with what he does, because he comes home from a sex venue and he drinks enough Listerine [mouthwash] to probably get him pissed. . . . and locks the bathroom door. We never lock the bathroom door and he'll scrub in the shower almost like a rape victim kind of a mentality. (Yvonne)

Yvonne's description of her partner's cleansing rituals after sex with men brings to mind King's notion that:

> sometimes they feel so dirty and so guilty when they return home that they feel like they have to get clean by being intimate with their girlfriends or wives.

They intensify the lovemaking to compensate for what they did an hour earlier (2004: 55).

Indeed, frequenting sex workers, beats and other sex-on-premises venues is common for men who are not comfortable publicly acknowledging their bisexuality, whether it be to themselves, to their female partners, or to the wider society. Coon writes about the culture of beats she learned about through her husband:

> A beat provides a quick and anonymous means for a man who wants to be sexually stimulated by another man to do so without any disruption to their daily routine. . . . It's free, discreet and there aren't any worries about anyone getting jealous and telling your wife or your girlfriend what you are doing. . . . This covert culture is so widespread that there are even websites dedicated to guys posting when and where they will be, so that other guys can be there at the same time. Recently I also discovered that there are [Grindr] applications you can get for your smart phones and devices that offer a network for gay, bi or curious guys wanting to connect with other guys (2012: 163, 165).

She also provides Australian examples of bisexual men frequenting beats:

> This issue was brought to the public's attention in 1997 when NSW Supreme Court Judge David Yeldham gassed himself in the family car rather than face the Police Royal Commission (and his family) about the double life he was living. He was caught out visiting public beats, yet he appeared to be living a heterosexual life as a married man raising a family. More recently NSW Labour MP, David Campbell was filmed leaving a gay sex sauna in May 2010. He resigned over this public outing of his secret life (2012: 166).

Scrimshaw et al.'s (2013) study with nondisclosing bisexual men found that 74% reported meeting a male partner in a sexual venue (e.g., bar or club, park) in the past year. Strategies to reduce the risk of discovery while seeking male partners included: avoiding certain venues, meeting partners on the Internet, and having sex at the partner's place. Given the critical importance of concealment from their female partners, these men also preferred venues that have potential nonsexual uses or were not exclusively gay-focused so that they could use this as a cover story if they were discovered there. For example, the US Senator Larry Craig was caught in a public toilet but said he was there to use the toilet, even though several men came forward to say they had sex with him (Blank, 2012).

There has been research into what bisexually behaving and/or identifying men desire and do with men and women. Bisexual men's behaviors are often summarized as "having sex with both men and women," without specifying what *sex* may be for these individuals (Sandfort & Dodge, 2009). Schnarrs et al. (2012) found that traditional gender role performance and the participants' own socialization into roles as men influenced what men found socially, emotionally and sexually attractive in men and women. Most likely informed by notions of heteronormativity, heteropatriarchy and gendernormativity, men indicated they were attracted to a traditional masculine personality, demeanor or attributes such as boldness or confidence, specifically indicating that feminine or effeminate men were not attractive. A masculine body that was muscled, strong and looked manly attracted them to other men, particularly abdominal muscles, the chest and the penis. Similar themes emerged concerning attraction to women associated with idealized femininity, specifically to women's breasts and buttocks. Sexually, the men in Schnarrs et al. (2012) mostly reported only engaging in anal sexual behaviors with male sexual partners and would not consider engaging in these same behaviors with female sexual partners. Oral sex behaviors were similar for both genders, and reasons for not performing oral sex on male or female partners were based on personal preferences such as the appearance of their male partner, their degree of sexual attraction, while some did not like performing oral sex on women because they find women's genitals unattractive. Participants indicated they experienced more emotional connections with women, which is perhaps an outcome of gendered expectations of women as being more emotionally available, nurturing and caregiving, than men (Connell, 2002, 2005). Nevertheless, they felt men "were better at understanding them," experienced connections with other men as friendship and that this type of connection allowed them to "be themselves" in front of men in ways they might not be able to be with women (2012: 257). As a character in Brant's novel explains:

> As men we understand male desire. . . . How many women know what our balls can endure or the sensations we get from them? Two men can explore without inhibition. They can enjoy their bodies in ways most women would find distasteful. It's different because there's no feminine protocol to fret over (2006: 178–179).

Zimmerman (2012) lists studies which indicate that men and women view the purpose of extradyadic sex differently, with men commonly seeking secondary partners to fill sexual needs, whereas women seek secondary partners to fill emotional connection and autonomy needs. Furthermore, studies find men are more likely than women to cognitively separate sex from love, and tend to value sexual variety and novelty whereas women usually value security in a relationship. Participants in Schnarrs et al. (2012) modified dominant sexual scripts by engaging in sex with men. However, they were constrained by these same dominant gendered sexual scripts in that sex with men was often limited with regard to emotional connection; sexual positions were given gendered labels (e.g., receptive anal sex as the 'female' role); and sex with women represented 'normal' behavior and allowed for emotional closeness. For example, behaviors relating to intimacy or closeness such as kissing and caressing were often reserved for women. In his work with African-American men "on the down-low" (DL), meaning having sex with men while in relationships with women, Boykin (2005) discusses how many men see a sexual encounter with a man as "a means of getting a quick sexual high and that's it . . . relationships should be pursued only with women" (2005: 170; see also King, 2004). Kort (2012a, 2014a) refers to some men who are "homo-sexual and hetero-emotional": have sexual interest in men but never have romantic interest in them so they partner with women, fall in romantic love and are able to have sex with them, keeping their sexual fantasies about men in their heads and sometimes engaging in them as well.

> He says he is [physically attracted to me]and I feel that he is, but not because of the female package that I come in but because of what's inside, your personality and that kind of stuff. (Rosemary)

It must be pointed out that there are alternatives to these gendernormative discourses in relation to male and female partners within particular communities and contexts, such as in polyamorous communities, where heteropatriarchal norms and expectations around women's sexualities have been defied (Sheff, 2005). Beye's autobiography of his bisexual relationships discusses the assertive sexuality of his first wife who knew he was bisexual:

> of my sexual education at home, I had learned that women were not aroused by the sight of men, nor were they willing to respond to men's aggressive actions but rather waited, quite passively, for the male's arrival and entry. Mary was not like this; . . . it was a revelation to me, Mary's continuing surge of sexual desire matching my own... Monday, Mary and I met again at the drug store, where she told me that she had spent Saturday night with her casual boyfriend. 'I just wanted to be sure that I knew what I was doing,' she said with a laugh. 'Yes, you and I had a great night of sex but, you know, forsaking all others as the marriage service says. I just wanted to comparison shop.' I smiled but I was scandalised. Obviously the irony of my adhering to the double standard for males and females did not strike me (2012: 91–94).

He also reflects on the gendernormative differences in his sexual behaviours and feelings with men and women:

> The first great discovery of heterosexual intercourse from a veteran of the active role in homosexual anal intercourse was delight at the easy entry. . . . The

missionary position allowed me to feel my control of her body through my legs and pelvis. It was my show. I was a god, an emperor and king after all those years on my knees, staring at a guy's pubic hair as I went up and down on him or if I was penetrating my partner, more often than not, confronted with shoulder blades or when face-to-face, having to manage the logistics of balance and stance . . . For the first time in my life I understood that a woman's a mystery. By this I mean I have complete familiarity with a male's erotic responses because I myself was a male. . . . he will discover that he can never finally sense her response to his presence or to his actions because there is no true analogue to his own bodily responses, not even massaging the clitoris (2012: 91–95).

In Brant's novel, the theories and debates presented in this section are explored via conversations during group sex between three married men, such as the following:

"I have a theory," Tim said. . . . "I think bisexuality is nature's way to provide straight men with an alternative sexual release" . . . . "No matter how you explain it," James said, "it's part of human nature. Has been down through the ages. Men used to go off into the woods together when their wives were tired of having babies. History is full of it.". . . "Now it's called perversion," [David said] (Brant, 2006: 122).

"IT'S KIND OF A GREAT MYSTERY"

The thing that I've noticed about the gay men that I ever had sex with... It's almost like they are not confronting that desire [for women] . . . It's kind of a great mystery. It strikes me as really bizarre like you go to one of the leather dance parties and one of my obviously very female friends will get picked up by this guy who's the big leather daddy from hell. . . . they will acknowledge it [their desire for women and having sex with women] only to the point where they will go, "Oh I was really pissed" or "I was really out of it and I am really sorry that it happened." (Lizz)

Many women expressed the same intrigue or frustration as Lizz with men who identified as gay and yet were having sexual and loving relationships with women, particularly if they then tried to deny, excuse or felt ashamed of these opposite-sex behaviors and attractions: "he's always said he's gay but if he was gay, well, how come the sex that we had was so good, and he would say it was good too" (Jess). This was particularly significant for women in long-term relationships with men identifying as gay:

He says to me, "I still love you and no one I have ever met, I've never ever felt the same way as I have about you" and that just tears me apart . . . He said that he came to a point when he finally accepted that he was in fact gay. . . . And that was a huge confusion to me. (Erin)

Erin's words echo those of the wife in the film *Change of Heart* (1998), whose husband says he is gay and had desires for men before he met her but then fell in love with her, has loved her deeply and completely for 20 years, until he falls in love with a man. A similar narrative occurs in *Boulevard* (2014) with Robin Williams in his last film before suiciding as the husband, Nolan, whose desire for men is awakened when he almost runs over a young man, Leo (Roberts 2015).

There were also women in our research who were comfortable with bisexual men but would not want to be in relationships with men who identified as gay, partly because it was likely these men were hiding their attractions to women from other gay men, including male partners:

> I would definitely walk away [if he was gay]. In fact, one of my flat mates is attracted to a homosexual man, who has a tendency to be with women, and I said to her the other day, "Don't you dare, because all you'll ever be is a hole for him to fuck." . . . I'm afraid of all the shit that comes with it. The fact that they're not free to communicate [their desires for women], that they're not free to be themselves [to other gay men]. (Deanna)

For Jean, being gay was defined by certain sexual acts which she also defined as what 'normal' people do not do, even though her partner insisted his sexual practices did not define his sexual identity: "he kept on saying, 'I'm not gay.' And I kept on saying, 'If you stick your cock up a bloke's arse, you're gay. Normal people don't do that'" (Jean). This linking of sexual behavior to sexual identity is counteracted by some married gay-identifying men such as Leavitt who has been monogamously married to a woman for 25 years:

> In my use of the word "gay," I refer to the orientation of sexual preference, not the act or frequency of sexual contact with other men. As a result, with this definition, I can say definitively that I am gay, and I am married to a woman. . . . somebody piped up, "You have got to be the gayest straight man I have ever met." Yeah, that pretty much sums it up in a single sentence. . . . I'm still physically attracted to other men. I don't *want* to give that up. I'm not trying to be straight (2006: 6–9).

Another mystery and issue of frustration for some women was the experience of their partners leaping from one end of the Kinsey/Klein scale to the polar opposite, whereby a partner would change from heterosexual to gay in identity and accompanying performances, behaviors and embodiment: "Rod's as gay as gay now. You know, like he just evolved" (Lizette).

> Why does this happen? Why after ten years, why can they suddenly turn the other way, when they've been in love and in a happy heterosexual relationship? (Beth)

I felt like he was very much turning into somebody else, and that this wasn't the person that I knew and that I was in love with. He was changing his physical appearance very much. Getting tips in his hair, the gelling of the hair. Went out and finally got the earring that he always said he wanted, but he's always been really quite conservative. He became quite obsessive about his diet and not eating junk and working out a lot more. And worrying about body hair. Getting me to pluck any hairs from his back, and this has gone on to greater levels now where he waxes and trims his leg hair and plucks his eyebrows. . . . It was only what I would describe as an adolescence re-visited, really. (Sue)

There were also women who pressured or expected their partners to make a decision about being either heterosexual or homosexual as being bisexual was not considered a viable or secure identity or behavioral option:

He comes back at me that I forced him to make a decision, because I did tell him that I didn't want him to be giving me some sort of false sense of security and then in five years' time tell me, "Oh, look, I've got it all wrong, I'm really gay." So probably about three weeks after he was saying he was bisexual he said he was homosexual. (Hannah)

For some women, biological essentialism or changes over the life course were seen as providing some answers to this 'evolution':

I think it happened at the change of life. . . . and it's as though they've got a lot of the hormones, but they haven't all kicked in, and then suddenly at fifty, they all kick in where they should have kicked in at puberty. (Jean)

Kaye (2002) also provides a biological essentialist explanation to how younger men can be sexually aroused by women even if they are gay but eventually need to come out:

In late adolescence, young adulthood up to about 30's, a guy is driven by raging hormones and need for release—basically he could "do it" with anything or anyone just to get off. As time goes on, and they are not as driven biologically, they have to supplement the drive with . . . male fantasies [which] become prevalent . . . and eventually even the male fantasies are no longer able to make him perform. That is usually the "crisis" that leads them to actively fool around.

What is not discussed here is which differences or possibilities might be evident if a man was able to openly communicate and act upon his desire for men as well as his ongoing desire for his female partner, so that rather than sublimating same-sex attraction into fantasy or secret sex with men, as necessitated by the sociocultural adherence to monogamy and monosexuality, men and women were able to negotiate workable and shifting arrangements to cater for shifting desires. For example, in an early study, Coleman (1982) reported how sexual problems occurred in 61% of the straight–gay marriages in his research, such as erectile difficulty, low frequency of sexual activity and low sexual desire, while there were a number of relationships where there seemed to be satisfactory sexual activity and no reported sexual dysfunctions. Approximately 93% of the men had engaged in sexual activity with other males outside of their marital relationship, varying from a single incident to sexual encounters at least once a week, but 64% of these men decided to remain married with only 15% of these admitting they would probably eventually leave their wives to pursue same-sex relationships.

Kaye (2003) provides what she calls the "Gay Husband Check List" which even includes a man calling himself bisexual unquestionably means he is gay:

1. You have a normal sexual appetite, but your mate thinks you have excessive sexual needs.
2. There is a decline of sexual activity early in your marriage.
3. Your husband is repulsed by normal sexual activity.
4. Your mate admits to having had more than two homosexual encounters.
5. Your husband reveals he's bisexual.
6. Your partner visits gay bars claiming he's there only to hang out with his gay friend(s).
7. Your mate watches porno movies with gay male scenes.
8. Your mate makes continual homophobic comments.
9. Your partner's ego appears to be boosted by compliments from gay men.

Again, while not denying that some of the above may be due to a partner's homosexuality, not allowing for other factors to be responsible such as age, relationship dynamics, men having friends of diverse sexualities, diverse constructions of masculinity, and assuming a generalizable understanding of what constitutes "normal sexual appetite" and "normal sexual activity," is very problematic. In the following, Kaye reveals the paranoia and doubts that she believes all women will experience with a gay partner and not with a straight partner. What does not get addressed here, indeed gets completely denied, is the reality that a straight partner may also be having sex with his partner while fantasizing about other women, accessing straight porn and other equivalent behaviors that Kaye problematizes in same-sex-attracted men:

> I would always have to wonder if he is turned on by me or by fantasizing about men when he is with me just so he can sexually perform. I would think about that during every sexual encounter, taking away the possible pleasure ... The truth is, women who have straight husbands never have to spend time thinking about this issue (2008: 197).

This lack of critique of heterosexual men's sexual desires, fantasies, and behaviors away from or while they are having sex with their female partners is even further entrenched when Kaye refers to popular cultural images and texts of how straight men behave when they are in love with women. Thus, she utilizes misogynist, reductionist, and illusory mainstream media images as the measurement for women to evaluate their partners' ways of loving:

> One of my online support group members . . . told me that she was going to rent some romantic videos for the evening to see how straight men act. . . . I think this is probably one of the best ways to get some reality in check. Compare the actions of your husband to those of a man in love with a woman in a movie. Trust me, he's not thinking about men when he's kissing the leading lady. If you can't be a leading lady in your relationship, then you are cheating yourself out of your right as a woman (Kaye, 2003).

What remains unproblematized here are the following potential scenarios: that the man in the movie may be fantasizing or desiring other women; that the actor may actually be bisexual or gay in real life "performing" the role of a straight man; and that a woman can be "a leading lady" if she is in a relationship with a man who also desires sex or loving relationships with men. Indeed, in our research, there were women who did accept that their partners had always been gay and this identity could sit comfortably interwoven with a healthy, loving and sexual long-term relationship:

> Dean was a gay man, always. My mother used to say to me, "He's a wonderful man. He never looks at another woman." And I thought that was so cute, I loved that, because I've got someone who won't leave me for another woman. (Hannah)

"HE WILL BE STRAIGHT FOR THE REST OF HIS LIFE"

> Paul says he will be straight for the rest of his life . . . But he will have sex with both of us [her and her bisexual husband]. We relate to him as a co-parent and equal partner in the family... Love and intimacy are the satisfaction- sex is just for fun. . . . For every guy who identifies as gay but occasionally sleeps with a woman, there is one who identifies as straight but makes the occasional exception with a man. Maybe one day they will all identify as bi. (Jacinta)

As Jacinta explains about her polyamorous relationship with Paul and her bisexual husband, some women were in relationships with men who identified as heterosexual but, due to circumstance or context, had sexual attractions and/or experiences with other men. Joseph believes that a main reason why some men may identify as straight is because they are married: "it is as basic as that" (1997: 128). Thus, one's public position in known and normative social structures such as marriage becomes one's identity while the private self may behave differently, and be vulnerable to public shaming if revealed. A character in Brant's novel, Jorge, says:

> Funny thing about straight guys, . . . They're curious about other men, but most would fight to the death before admitting it. Bet we'd be surprised how many stick something long and round up their ass when their wives are out shopping (2006: 179).

According to the Center for Disease Control, more than 3 million men who self-identify as straight secretly have sex with other men (Kort, 2007). Stewart et al. (2000) found that those who identified as heterosexual in a short demographic questionnaire later explained that they did not necessarily rule out sexual experiences with other men. They preferred a "case-by-case approach" to potential sexual partners rather than adopting preset categories of who could or could not be a sexual partner. For some men, it was "an experience to experience," while others described themselves as unsure, self-questioning and in process (2000: 417). Rather than interpret these responses as marks of uncertainty, instability and confusion, Stewart et al. (2000) suggest that while some men may select a sexual identity of heterosexual as it is a "convenient (or habitual response to) social identity," interpersonal and emotional qualities may become more significant within their private sexual relationships.

Anderson constructed the term "inclusive masculinity" to describe heterosexual-identifying men who were comfortable sleeping with, hugging, dancing and being sexual in some way with other men: "Upon learning that I was gay, four men immediately informed me that they once had sex with a man. Second, a woman's presence was not required for these men to engage in same-sex sex" (2008: 110). In total, 40% of the self-identified heterosexual men said they once engaged in, or continue to engage in, some form of same-sex sex. Leanne recalls trying to chat about this with heterosexual-identifying friends:

> We were saying men enjoy oral sex and they wouldn't mind who was giving it to them if they were blindfolded and one of the young girls said to her boyfriend, "Oh you wouldn't," and he said, "Yeah I probably would," and she got really cross. (Leanne)

In a later study, Anderson describes those men subscribing to "orthodox masculinity" requiring the "good cause scenario": a woman's sexual presence and possibly her request for same-sex sexual behaviors by men in "switches and trains" behaviors (2009: 148):

Same-sex sex is largely seen as a way of sharing "conquests" with "brothers," mutually reassuring each other of their heterosexual desirability. It is also a way to get and give pleasure from men, although the subjective desire for men remains stigmatized (Anderson, 2008: 111).

Kort (2013, 2014a) also discusses straight men who enjoy "cuckolding": their female partners being what Ley (2009) calls "hot wives" having sex with other men, either in front of them, nearby or with their knowledge about when and where it occurs. They're often sexually aroused by feeling humiliated that their female partners are being pleased by another man whom they see as more potent and better endowed. Other men enjoy being sexual with another man's female partner in front of him, or at least with his knowledge. Sometimes they engage in sexual behavior with the man, but only in the presence of the female partner. Also of interest and potentially linked to not using the label 'bisexual' is the "near-total absence of voluntary discussion" among some men about receiving or giving anal sex (Anderson, 2008: 112). This leads Anderson to wonder whether future labelling of sexuality may be determined more by sexual practice such as being the inserter or recipient in anal sex rather than the gender of one's partner.

The media plays a very important role in reducing cultural homohysteria among heterosexual men. For example, Greg Araki's films often depict the tentative attempts of straight males to realise their bisexual potential. The British television show for adolescents, *Skins* (2007–2013), frequently portrays straight high-school boys behaving in ways that "would likely shock men of older generations." In one episode, the leading heterosexual character decides to give his best gay male friend a blow job. "There was no justification for it. Nor was his heterosexuality questioned. It was, rather, just something to do while on holiday" (Anderson, 2009: 150). The Internet has also been influential in breaking down homophobic sex-gender binaries and boundaries, with many sites that ask for, cater for, allow for sexual fluidity and multiplicity in practice and desire in all its permutations, rather than focus on sexual identity (Benn, 2012). Taormino (2008) invites us to "Take a brief scroll through one day's worth of 'Men Seeking Men' posts on New York City's *Craigslist*, with its dozens of listings like 'Str8 Guy Needs Great Cocksucker' or 'Handsome Masculine Married Irish Guy Seeks One or Two Hung Married Irish Buddies Who Want Head and Maybe More.'" She lists some of the reasons why heterosexual men "get it on" with other men: for anonymous, no-strings-attached sex; to explore homoerotic desire without a gay identity or relationship; or to fulfill a fantasy, including one of dominance and submission: "I believe male-to-male sex is more about the act, more about animalistic expression and lust" (Jenna). Corley & Kort concur, reporting that in their clinical experiences, some reasons heterosexual-identifying men give for having sex with men include wanting to increase their sexual high through increased risk or intensity or

> as part of curiosity, a sexual ritual, drug/sex ritual, or a fetish . . . sex with men is usually inexpensive, convenient and can be managed in a variety of anonymous ways such as obtaining a massage with a 'happy ending,' sexual encounters in steam rooms, restrooms, rest stops, or by hooking up with someone via the Internet (2006: 169).

> He'd go to places around Oxford Street and there would be holes that you put your penis through, and big mattresses where everybody would be sleeping on them, and that it was just purely sex for sex's sake and he said that he really enjoyed it, . . . and it took a little while for me to get used to not making it horrific and not getting appalled by it, because it's just not what I do. (Mary)

> I found out about glory holes and I was so upset. I didn't realize that men did this to themselves. It was just like "My God, you must think nothing of yourselves to do that." (Annette)

More recently, Kort (2012b) has created *Straight Guise*, a website about straight men having sex with men, where he reports that straight men with a higher sex drive tend to be more willing to be sexual with other men. Thus, in discussing sexualities, it may not be about sexual orientation as much as it is about sexual drive, behavior and specific fetishes such as "for male feet or even a penis fetish . . . They are not interested in looking up at the man, they are not interested in his pleasure" (2012c: page unnumbered). Thus, Kort (2013, 2014a) provides the top five reasons heterosexual men engage in sexual behavior with other men as being sexual abuse history leading to homosexual imprinting, sexual addiction, fetishism, sexual fantasies such as anal penetration, and availability and opportunity. Kort also refers to "Narcissism" whereby straight men use sex with men to be worshipped and adored. For some of these men, being sexual with another woman is 'cheating' on one's spouse; being sexual with another male is not (see also Denes et al, 2015).

In her work on white straight men who have sex with men, Ward (2015) indentified various scripts of "hetero-exceptionalism" to "protect and justify the homosexual behavior of heterosexuals": "necessary "such as under coercion during "institutional hazing" to prove one's endurance and resilience; "homosocial" where "dude-sex" is "not-gay" friendly encounters with "normal, average guys"; and "accidental" where it occurs while intoxicated or other unplanned circumstances (2015: 98–99, 128).

In Schneider & Schneider's (1990) survey, husbands who had sexual relationships with men viewed their behavior as an addiction and learned to take responsibility to avoid situations where they might act on their addiction. In turn, their wives, understanding their husbands' extramarital sexual activity was an addiction and not a choice, and therefore it could be cured, accepted and worked with their husbands as they participated in addiction programs. Kort (2012b) discusses how straight men will have sex with other men in their addiction to "heighten their arousal by doing something shameful and taboo . . . But when the sexual behavior is over, he will drop into shame, despair, depression, remorse and guilt for having engaged in his obsessions and compulsions." Unlike some therapists who want to pathologize these men, treat them for sexual addiction, or 'cure them' of homosexuality, Kort approaches his clients by unpacking some of the cultural baggage that contributes to this phenomenon: "They are working through issues of father hunger, lack of touch from other males, and the need for contact with other men on deeper levels that women enjoy with each other" (Kort, 2012b). He discusses how the actor John Travolta has been lambasted in the media about his sexual touching, harassment and demands on his masseurs, with speculation he might be gay: "if we are going to speculate about men's sexuality, we deserve the same room and understanding that women have around sexual fluidity . . . and they don't 'turn gay'" (Kort, 2012a).

In the light of Kort's discussions, there were women in our research whose partners identified as heterosexual but were secretly having relationships with men:

> I really don't like talking about sexuality in these terms [identity and labels], because it almost goes against what it is that I subscribe to myself. . . . I think that it's [his sexuality] more about a state of humanity, a state of the heart, than it is about a state of what their genitals like to spend their time doing . . . I have a problem with the climate that we're in now that creates a certain type of behavior that then perpetuates on top of the women . . . because they don't tell the truth, because they hide. (Deanna)

The internet, chat lines, mobile phones and the increasing proliferation of sexual imageries has made it much easier for otherwise heterosexual men to discreetly explore their "bi-curiousness" which Simpson (2006) defines as "a recent, erotic paddling-pool coinage which attempts to avoid the plunge-pool identity of 'bisexual.'" He believes there are increasing numbers of 'bi-curious' men, especially those under 35 (see also Anderson et al, 2015; McCormack et al, 2015). They are a generation of men who have grown up with frank discussions of homosexuality in the media and the commodification of masculinity via metrosexuality:

> glossy, glamorous images of male desirability rammed down their throats, on billboards, magazines, films, pop music, TV and even and especially on the playing field . . . Anyone claiming that men simply don't have a bisexual responsiveness should be made to watch the porn consumed by straight men

today. . . . young, attractive, smooth, worked out, metrosexual men that the camera lingers over much more than in the past (2006: pages unnumbered).

Simpson (2006) quips about how 'bi-curious' men express a very strong desire to try oral sex with a man, "most men would suck their own penis if they could, but most can't, so have to 'phone a friend'. Or rather a stranger." Often these heterosexual 'bi-curious' and/or sexually adventurous men have had these fantasies for a long time before acting on them, and haven't spoken to anyone, "especially sex researchers," about them.

So far we have discussed heterosexual men who are heteroflexible, bi-curious or bisexual-behaving. In this research, there were also women whose partners had been bisexual and then became heterosexual. This was of concern to some women who had been attracted to their partners because of their bisexuality and sexual adventurousness, and found that 'becoming heterosexual' meant becoming more gendernormative and heteronormative:

He changed. When we first got together, he considered himself to be quite bi, but now he's considered himself as very heterosexual. Which is why I really didn't want to stay with him. (Susanna)

Other women were comfortable with and understood their partners' shifting bi-to-hetero identities according to shifting contexts, circumstances and passions in life:

When I met him, he was one of Australia's premier bi activists actually. It was kind of funny, because back in the States, at university, we had all these little brochures and pamphlets, and one of them was about dispelling bi myths and it was actually co-written by my partner and his other partner and so then I came over here and it's like, "It's you. You wrote it. See, you're famous." . . . . and I think that's part of why he doesn't identify [as bi] any more. I think he got very heavily into the activism and politics of it, and got burnt out on it very quickly. And now he chooses to spend most of his relationship energy with women and so he doesn't necessarily feel that it's accurate to identify as bi. And because he doesn't have the political activity any more, he doesn't feel like taking the identity just for political reasons either. (Ava)

"THERE'S A LOT OF SHADES OF GRAY"

I don't see it as anything is absolute 100% anything. I see life as a continuum. And that's probably because of where I'm at, really comfortable with my bisexuality . . . There's a lot of shades of gray between black and white. (Nina)

As Nina describes, there were many women who questioned fixed and absolute sexual categories altogether, whether in their partners, themselves, or both. They spoke about sexual continuums, sexual fluidity and the confusion and difficulty their partners and/or themselves experienced when trying to position sexual desires and behaviors within categories based on sexual orientation, thereby queering the whole notion of sexual labelling (Heckert, 2005): "what he used to say often was how much he was different from everyone and that he just loved that. . . . he just didn't want to fit in" (Kristina). They often resisted conventional heterosexuality as it excluded same-sex possibilities but also resisted a gay identity because it was "an undesirable limitation" (Stewart et al. 2000: 418). Thus, they adopted a border position that questions and subverts potential social limitations of being known as gay, bisexual or straight: "he's not sure what his sexuality is. . . . I understand it's complex, he actually says that he's celibate" (Felicity).

> when you say gay, lesbian or bi, they mean so many different things to so many different people and it's a bit like using a word and you know a meaning for yourself, but other people have their own meanings to it. . . . It's funny because it's [sexual labels] something that we [her partner and herself] haven't really talked about in ages. We've kind of moved on. [Laughing]. (Leanne)

Some of the women used the term "queer": "there are a lot of young guys who to me look very much like they fit in to the category of queer" (Lizz). While some women reported how freeing this queerification or release from labelling could be, other women reported how the inability to have a label could be fraught with confusion and stress in a world of what Raven calls "entrenchment" in two-dimensionality. In the following, Sally believes her partner's queer fluctuation between labels is indicative of deep self-hatred and confusion:

> [He identifies as] asexual at the moment, but it fluctuates between homosexuality, bisexual and having no interests in anybody. . . . he's had no sexual experience with another male at all . . . he's got lots of scared issues I think of identifying one way or the other. . . . I don't think at the moment he feels comfortable in his own skin. (Sally)

The problematization of fixed binary sexual orientations was accentuated when coupled with the gender binary, as in the experiences of Lilith and Louisa who found that being sexually involved with transgender people led to further queerification of sexual identity systems:

> Sometimes it's like we're too queer for the queer. But there's so many relationships out there like us that just don't fit the labels. . . . I've seen people not know

what to make of it when we gave a party and both Adam and I enjoy male strippers and there's my partner Adam nuzzling into the leather and silver-studded crotch-piece on this Tom of Finland cartoon come to life dressed as a police officer and the boys are urging him on to remove the uniform piece by piece and turn the baton onto and into Adam. And then Adam lies collapsed from exhaustion on the table, and I'm there force-feeding him creamy chunks of apple pie and trying to have my own private moments in the bathroom with the stripper and his partner who's a pre-op transsexual with great breasts and a great cock. Later, when everyone's left, over coffee and chocolate cake, we sit and chat, recounting the thrill of things we did like Adam licking a policeman's boots while his hands were handcuffed behind him, and I was pretending to penetrate him with the baton. And then we do the domestics or cuddle in our pajamas like your everyday Mr and Mrs Queer. (Lilith)

The pre-op trannies would have a boyfriend, but the boyfriend had a girlfriend. And that to me is he wanted anal sex, he wanted the male side, so he'd use a tranny, . . . Yeah, the girlfriends knew, and hated it. . . . the trannies, they are just devastated, and I find it really sad, because they so desperately want to be this woman that he's in a relationship with, but if this tranny was that woman, then he would be in a relationship with another tranny or another man, and trying to get that across to them is really hard. (Louisa)

CONCLUSION

In this chapter, I have explored the mestizaje realities of bisexuality, homoflexibility and heteroflexibility, as well as the Derridean space of being "beyond labels." We have seen men and their partners endeavoring to exercise personal agency, selecting and determining necessary or desired sexual labels from the constructions available, or attempting to devise alternative sexual labels for themselves. Baumeister (2004) uses the term "erotic plasticity" to refer to the extent to which the sex drive can be constrained by social, cultural and situational factors, with high plasticity entailing the capacity to change and adapt. As strangers (Bauman, 1992) questioning the unquestionable and taken-for-grantedness (Schutz, 1944) of sexual identity classification systems, Butler's position reflects and supports many of our research participants' border-zone positioning of "outside belonging" or "inbetween categories of specificity" (Probyn, 1996: 9): "I'm permanently troubled by identity categories, consider them to be invariable stumble-blocks, and understand them, even promote them, as sites of necessary trouble" (1991: 14).

Chapter 4

"I Have A Sexuality Too"

Women Discussing their Own Sexualities

> We've been concerned with not making his sexuality the only sexuality in the relationship. . . . I have a sexuality too, and my sexuality is being overlooked and ignored. And I like my sexuality. It changes and develops. (Katie)

In this chapter, we will be exploring how women perceived and experienced their own sexualities in relation to or independent of their partners' bisexualities. As Katie states so clearly, external heteropatriarchal perceptions and representations of the opposite-sex relationship, which may then be internalized, tend to consider the man's sexuality as the master signifier of the sexuality of the woman, indeed of the relationship itself. It is important to consider the impact of the man's bisexuality and sexual relationships on his partner's sexual identity, sexual confidence and sexual relationships. It is also important to consider dominant misogynist constructions of female sexuality and sexual expression with which the women may have entered the relationship, and if and how these shifted independently or in conjunction with negotiating sexual intimacy with their partners. There also needs to be space for those women who entered the relationship as queer, polyamorous and/or feminist women, already having explored their sexual desires and indeed, actively selecting a bisexual male partner or encouraging their male partners to queerify their sexualities and the relationship. In one of the earliest studies of women in MOREs, Gochros found that they are:

> well-educated, professional woman in a high socio-economic status, . . . who had at least average interest in heterosexuality, who was well able to attract heterosexual men, who rated herself and appeared highly self-confident and assertive, . . . [and] an emphasis on non-sexism in choice of mate and self-rated sexual naivety at marriage. How different that naivety was from that of other

newly-weds, particularly in the era in which most of these women had married, is questionable (1989: 40).

Gochros was thus challenging the stereotype or assumption that women who marry bisexual men differ from other women in having low self-esteem and assertiveness, lack of attractiveness, and latent lesbian or bisexual desires.

The main themes to be explored in this chapter are:

1. Women experience *sexual inadequacy and unsatisfactory sexual relationships* with their partners, particularly with partners who had not previously disclosed their bisexuality or who upheld strong patriarchal notions of gendered sexualities; and how sometimes there were consequent ramifications for future relationships with other men.
2. Women experience *a new kind of sexual confidence*, and the permission and space in the relationship to explore, expand and enjoy their sexualities.
3. Women enter the relationship as queer feminists, and continue *to negotiate and affirm their own nonnormative and/or nonheterosexual sexualities* within the context of the relationship.

"WE'D NEVER WORN OUT THE MIDDLE OF THE BED EVER"

> We'd never worn out the middle of the bed ever. We both slept on the edge of the bed, and I know when I decided I'd stay in the marriage, well, if it's a marriage without sex, so be it and I'll look at the other positive things that the marriage has. . . . it's twenty-six years almost since we've even had intercourse. (Fay)

Like Fay, many women in our research had experienced or were experiencing an absence of sexual intimacy, feelings of sexual inadequacy and/or unsatisfactory sexual relationships with their partners: "I questioned my sexuality and what was I doing wrong. . . . I blamed myself" (Pat). These feelings were particularly evident in women with partners who had not disclosed their bisexuality and, upon disclosure or discovery, women were left feeling relief at having some answers to why their sexual intimacy had always felt uncomfortable, fake or insufficient. They were also left feeling grief, anger and loss at the time wasted in not having had a wonderful sexual relationship with a man they loved:

> I do care and feel for Dave, but by the same token, I'm fucked off. What's happened to my sexuality? I can't see it. I've just completely put it under the covers, and I'm only 29, and instead of taking off cruising along and developing your sexuality, educating yourself . . . all of a sudden, at a really vital time of life you find that you've got no air. (Deanna)

Not much sexual intimacy and as the years went by I just felt unattractive. And the resentment now is that I had lots of offers, you know, when I was younger, and I chose to ignore them because I thought I was doing the right thing. And I've said all this to him, in anger. ... At one stage he said in our younger years when we were first married that I was like a nymphomaniac, and really I could never see that. ... I consider myself a virgin, absolutely, even though I've had two children, because I've never slept with anybody else, and I chose that, but I thought I was doing what he was doing [being monogamous and having very little sex]. I was not given a choice. (Loredana)

Like Fay earlier, some women rationalized that what they had gained from the marriage due to their partners' positive qualities, often nonpatriarchal, had more than compensated for a lack of sexual intimacy:

On the one hand you've got a relationship and a marriage which most people don't have. It's the most wonderful marriage you could possibly ask for. ... I went through thinking about marriage. What is it? It's a partnership, it's support, it's love. Okay, well, I've got all that. How important is the sexual side? And then I thought, well, it's not, I suppose, in the big picture, but if he would have been a more demonstrative, hugging, kissing person, maybe there might have been something there, but to have none of that either was really quite difficult. (Sally)

There is very little sex between us and at first I found it difficult to accept Keith made love to me because he loved me emotionally but he wasn't really lusting after me. But then, that early lust stuff seems to die in most marriages anyway. At least, I've always had the physical affection, kisses, cuddles, a great sensitive person to talk to. (Soulla)

According to Kaye, women like Sally and Soulla fit into the category of "women with limited sexual experience." They think that their sexual relationship with their husband was satisfactory or satisfying because they have not experienced "real sex" and "real true passion" (Kaye, 2001). In a heightened glorification of heterosexual relationships, she writes: "Women aren't made to feel as if making love is an imposition, or that their sex drive is abnormal. Straight men don't continually look for excuses why they won't have sex with their wives, and if they can't have sex they are not looking to place the blame with their wives" (2008: 191). However, as Gochros points out, it is not only MOREs that need to address issues of sexual dissatisfaction. "After all, the rush of how-to sex manuals, the vast amounts of money and time spent on sex therapy and counselling ... started with and remains mainly focused on the sexual problems of exclusively straight couples" (1989: 175). As the bisexual men in Brant's novel discuss:

"Yeah, we're oddities," said Jake. "Straight men are the lucky ones. No complications. No hang-ups."

"Not all of 'um. Not according to some of the women I know," said James. "You hear complaints all the time. Wham, bam, thank-you ma'am. They're called minutemen and jerks. . . . He's so proud of his dick, he thinks all he has to do to make a woman happy is stick it in there and pump it a few times." (2006: 265).

Klaar (2012) also found that in many cases, the sex life of the couple had long since ceased to exist and the participants had adjusted to this. When they finally knew why, "the women understood on one level that it had nothing to do with them. But, on another level, they felt that they had been made unwitting partners in a sham" (2012: 112).

> Is it right to say that I love Bill when I've never experienced the full relationship that it could have been had he been heterosexual? You know, I just love him for the person that he is, for his honesty and his integrity and his compassion and his sensitivity. (Fay)

Kaye (2003) discusses the quandary some of these women have when they come across as complaining about "great" marriages and "great" guys who

> are there raising the family with you. They are helping to support your financial needs or at least sharing in them. They are taking part in the social activities that you have decided are important. They are doing lots for you—and how do you show your appreciation? By badgering them with little innuendos and questioning looks . . . on the issue of sex.

Other women in our research, however, had indeed experienced a good sexual relationship with their partners who also desired having sex with men. Some women described how the marriage had provided a love, affection and security they had never experienced as a child:

> my dad, he's like a very typical Italian strong male, and has never told me that he loves me, never shown me affection and sometimes I question whether I'm in this relationship because I'm seeking that sort of affection. . . . my partner's always hugging me, always holds my hands and is always very affectionate. (Yvonne)

In an early study, Hatterer (1974) identified how women in MOREs felt inadequate in many areas of their gender and erotic identifications, and the links to abusive upbringings. Thus, for some women, an abusive childhood coupled with a lack of sexual experience and confidence with men led to the marriage:

I was from an abusive family, and I suppose meeting Ian, he was just a very good friend of mine, and when he turned it into something sexual, I was actually quite surprised, and I didn't even give myself a choice whether that's what I wanted. I didn't want to hurt his feelings. I wasn't actually sexually attracted to him at all. And when he decided he loved me, I just said, "Oh, okay, I love you too," but I don't think I did . . . Well, I don't even know if I know what love is. But, I adore him . . . I feel like, yes, I accepted Ian into my life because he wasn't a threat to me . . . Look, it [sex] was perfect when it was happening but it was once a month, and I felt very deprived in that area. I felt, "What's wrong with me?" or "What's wrong with him?" (Heather)

A third group of women were those who had experienced abusive childhoods which then led to abusive relationships with previous heterosexual partners, and/or who had rebelled against this by breaking the rules of a chaste femininity. In Temptress's case, although she chose Fernando as a partner because of his safe and gentle sexuality, she found that this was also not as satisfying as she had experienced in her rebellious past:

Oh, ex-husband I was raped fully all the time, up the arse, in the vagina, completely raped. Ripped off my nipple. . . . it was a wild thing for him, because I'm the wild child. You walk in the door and you see Temptress, you know, the party chick. It's actually very bad for me, because I'm very vulnerable because of my upbringing, because of my parents, bashing, bashing, bashing. And my Dad said, "If you tell anyone I'll kill you as well as mother." So, it was like for years, shut up, shut up. Be the good girl, be the little girl. And I had my first sexual experience when I was fifteen, and from then on it was just like, full blast. Really wild experiences. That's why when I come to Fernando I want someone to teach me some new stuff, and that's where the relationship sometimes dies. Because I get bored. (Temptress)

For Suzette, abuse and lack of sexual intimacy and fulfilment in her previous marriage to a heterosexual man was *"baggage"* she had to deal with in her current relationship with a bisexual man:

[Not having sex] was his way I think of showing me how much he detested me and, you know, "So disgusting I can't even touch you." He pushed me around quite a few times. . . . So, that holding back of physical intimacy brings some issues to the fore with me and if things start slowing down [with the current bisexual partner] in that regard I start going, "Oh, my God, he hates me, he doesn't love me any more. He thinks I'm disgusting." . . . I've had depression for many, many years and medication for that. I still have a lot of self-worth and self-confidence issues which I deal with. (Suzette)

For other women, disclosure or discovery of a partner's bisexuality provided answers for and relief from an unsatisfactory sexual relationship while also opening up new issues on how to proceed with sexual intimacy in the future. Issues around shifting sexual behaviors and mismatched sexual desires came to the fore:

> He used to be quite demanding of me and disappointed if things didn't happen. I used to dread bedtime and I don't dread that anymore. . . . I suppose it's taken the pressure off our sex life—that was always a big wedge between us. And he's also more relaxed himself. I feel that we're closer . . . [but] I'm wondering if he still fancies me, because I'm used to him being more aggressive—not violent—but assertive. For example if we were in the kitchen making coffee, he used to be very physical—like, groping and grabbing. He doesn't do that any more. And I don't know if that's partly because he's getting that somewhere else, or if it's just that he's realized I've never really liked it. I was always telling him that. So it's opened up more issues that I suppose we still have to resolve. (Maria)

As discussed by Kort (2014a) & Benn (2012), some women's lack of interest in certain forms of sexual play was perceived to be responsible for their partners going outside the marriage to have sex with men:

> The implication is that I wasn't sexually adequate. . . . He says that he'd obviously tried various things, like the leather skirt and the occasional asking me to dress up and whip him or tie him up. And I'd been happy to do that on an occasional basis, but obviously from my responses, he said, "Look, I knew you weren't into it." (Gerry)

> He was sexually not happy. He wanted to sleep with men. It was as simple as that. When you're not sexually happy, you begin to become sexually dysfunctional . . . he said the reason why he was suffering from premature ejaculation was because of what it was that I was doing in bed, apparently. "You're not doing this right, you're not doing that." Now I look back, I was so naïve, hey, and couldn't see what was going on. (Deanna)

Lubowitz (1997) found that some women who had in the past been coerced to engage in sexual practices that they did not feel comfortable with would have feelings of anger at their partner. They would also have feelings of helplessness because they could not compete with other men, even if they adopted sexual practices that simulate what their partners may be experiencing with men:

> He wanted anal sex all the time, and I just wasn't interested, both recipient and active, yeah . . . . and he would masturbate the whole time talking about having sex with men. (Louisa)

In his "how-to manual," Benn (2012) provides a step-by-step guide for men who wish to explore "meaningful male-only sex lives while still being in heterosexual relationships—but there are dangers and consequences." Writing as a "very happily" married man and an "equally happy" man in a "series of gay male-to-male relationships" for more than 40 years (2012: 7), Benn guides the reader from understanding the "reasons" why they wish to have sex with men, predominantly based on deficits in their current straight sexual life, and the "allure of the gay lifestyle." He provides practical information on where and how to meet men, such as "sourcing sex" from the Internet and "cruising the beats," what health issues to be aware of and how to "play safe," and becoming informed about "gay sexuality" such as what to wear, including underwear, and how gay bars, saunas and group sex work. Benn also provides warnings of possible ramifications of "secret male sexual friendships" ranging from the personal, such as experiencing guilt reactions, to the familial and social, such as being outed and being blackmailed. Apart from the complex problematics of condoning sexual infidelity and deception of women partners, Benn's book has also been criticized for its constant reference to "slow death by loneliness" and how sexless or sexually dissatisfying marriages with women are "to blame" for men seeking sex with men. When he does encourage men to communicate with their women partners about their sexual desires and concerns, he does so respectfully and gently, unlike the affronting language he uses when referring to women's menstrual weeks as "sexless wastelands" (2012: 36) and "Period Privacy" (2012: 34); women's "hang-ups about placing a penis inside their mouth" (2012: 35); "nightgowns for her and pajamas for him . . . wife is a controller . . . the wife has turned into his mother" (2012: 33) and " he sees himself as merely a cog in *her* wheel, to do *her* bidding whenever *she* so desires" (2012: 46). These statements are misogynist and justify bipatriarchal behaviors, as will be further explored in chapter 9. As King writes,

> Nothing will make a brother who likes to have sex with other brothers stop . . . Men will lie and say it's the woman's fault. Some brothers complained about their ladies being boring in bed or getting fat. They complained about women not allowing them to go in really deeply when they had sex or about the kids waking up in the middle of the night. . . . They're also searching for motivations and excuses for living this double life (2004: 47–48).

Buxton (2006c) found issues of inadequacy and insecurity in women arising in her research after bisexual partners had come out. However, once heterosexual spouses understand bisexuality, and if their partners still desire them sexually and provide sexual pleasure, they do not feel quite as sexually rejected. Others feel they must prove that they are better sexual partners to their bisexual spouses than any potential or actual outside lover. For other women, there was a sense of anxiety that it was their nonnormative femininity or their propensity to appear or perform in more masculine ways that had initially attracted a bisexual man to them. This meant they were to blame for the failed relationship:

> I started to get really sort of messed up because like, all of my life, people always called me a bit of a tomboy . . . all of a sudden, it's just like, "Wow, is Dave only attracted to me because I'm sort of not feminine? Petite man?" . . . But, then, it's like, I'm a woman who doesn't like lace. I'm a woman who'd rather play basketball. . . . So, what it did for kicking out my sexual identity, it's full-on. . . . my silver cord that runs through my being is woman and she took a beating . . . and if I find myself attracted to a man now, the first thing I think about is, "Am I not feminine enough?" I even give myself the word "masculine." (Deanna)

Gochros (1989) also found that women sometimes wondered if they had driven their husbands to homosexuality because of their so-called masculine traits (see also Yarhouse & Pawlowski, 2003). In the film *Possible Loves* (2001), Julia cuts her hair short and begins to dress boyishly when she is enraged and embittered after Carlos leaves her for Pedro. It's "as if she could no longer be a woman now that Carlos has revealed that he also loves a man" (Vicari, 2011: 148):

> I remember in the first month or so kept looking in the mirror going, "God, I must look like a man. There must be something about me that's masculine and I can't see it." . . . when we did have sex it was almost like it was such a relief to find that he still found me attractive, but then thoughts would happen afterwards, "So what did he have to think about to make that happen?" . . . so they're the sorts of things that gnaw at you. Like a gradual erosion. (Sally)

Other issues the women raised in relation to nonnormative aesthetics of femininity were in relation to body image and disability. For some women, not measuring up to mainstream constructions of female beauty and body made them blame themselves for their partners' lack of sexual interest:

> After I had my son, the sex basically stopped, and I feel like I have an amazing sex drive and I was becoming insecure, it was always related to self-esteem, body image . . . He never had a problem with me being a big woman, and I think African men don't, they like big women. But he would now say things about my weight, "I don't find you attractive any more." (Lisa)

> My sexuality has really been affected, my self-esteem, . . . because of MS [Multiple Sclerosis]. I've also had a colostomy. So my bowels stopped working a couple of years ago. Now, it's interesting that I've been reading—and I

believe this—that the bowel is the organ in your body which is most affected by emotional upheaval. I thought, "Yes, exactly." (Loredana)

For some women in our research, feelings of sexual inferiority were linked to having their female sexuality and gendered expression of their heterosexuality rejected or made to feel inferior or inadequate when compared to a man's body, sexuality and masculinity, what a man can do sexually which her partner craved and which she felt she could not provide: "there was the insecurity: I'm a woman, I'm never going to be a man so how and what am I meant to do? . . . I was never going to satisfy that side of it for him" (Maz). In Catherine Breillat's powerful and yet problematic film *Anatomy of Hell* (2004), the gay-identifying man whom the female protagonist pays to have sex with her actively voices disgust of her body, particularly her flesh and genitals. She tells him to pull out her bloodied tampon. Wordlessly, he obeys and holds it up in fascination. Commenting on how men are afraid of the impurity of menstrual blood, she steeps the tampon in a glass of water, turning the water a hazy reddish colour and then offers the glass to him: "Don't we drink the blood of our enemies?" she asks. After they have sex, his penis is covered in her blood and he returns to his former disgust. He takes his money reluctantly and leaves, but remains haunted by her. He returns wanting to begin all over again, encounters her on the cliffs and pushes her off the edge into the ocean. I concur with Vicari who concludes,

> Breillat reinforces this [sex/gender] dualistic thinking in her very pessimism. Instead of imagining that male bisexuality could truly represent the growth of feeling and response in a man, she forces the man into the role of killer in order to justify the woman's original futility and oppression (2011: 227).

> He wasn't into my body. Like, I was fucking him. He wasn't necessarily fucking me. Like, there was a lot of anal play, a lot of me giving him head. Really not a lot of straight up sort of heterosexual sex. He wasn't sort of going, "Oh, my God, you've got the most amazing body. What fantastic tits you've got," this sort of stuff. I think I was a big blow up doll for him. (Sascha)

Other women expressed this feeling of feminine failure as being unable to compete with a man in gaining and keeping their partners sexually attracted to them:

> It's quite damaging. I know all the sort of logic now, but at the time, you just think, "Well, I'm just a loser. I can't compete with a man," and I always thought to myself if he was having an affair with a woman, I'd be really upset and I'd go through quite a lot of the same feelings, but I'd still have this sense of, "Well, you're having an affair with a woman because there's something wrong with

our relationship. Therefore, if we work on the problems in our relationship, you won't need to have the affair and you can come back to me." . . . and when your partner tells you that they're batting for the other team, there's just nothing you can do about it. (Erin)

The various ways these women felt "inadequate" or adopted mental, emotional and sexual strategies and "logics" to accommodate or compensate for the lack of satisfying and confident sexual intimacy suggest they are what Kaye (2008) calls "Limbo women" in "Sexual Limbo":

> No diet, no breast implant, no sexy clothes, no new hair style, no new approaches to sexual satisfaction is going to move their husbands into the straight zone. Eventually, they admit defeat.

However, for some "Limbo women," another issue that required acknowledgment was how broader heteropatriarchal societal norms around women's expression and assertions of their sexualities also framed their "Sexual Limbo," their interpersonal frustrations and insecurities. For example, Nicole discussed the positives and negatives of sharing her husband with a man who also lives with them. And, while the lack of sexual intimacy is a pertinent issue, Nicole also rationalized and considered it from various perspectives, including the broader issue of the societal myths and cultural discourses surrounding long-term sexual relationships with which she was raised:

> I suspect that no relationship lasts in the same way forever, it can't. ... It's like the whole marriage myth, it's a pretense, it's a fairy land sort of thing. And, look, I'm sure there are people who have a genuine long-term, affectionate relationship . . . my parents went through a very difficult time, and they split up when I was sixteen, their relationship was just horrid and I thought, "Oh, I'm not going to let that happen to me." And then I looked around, and all the other couples were all screaming at one another. Nothing worked. There were no happy couples, no happy families. . . . I was very cynical about relationships, so I was very surprised that I actually agreed to marry this guy because initially I refused when he asked me because I just didn't believe in the idea of marriage. . . . so a lot of women, because they tie sex and love together, go, "Am I missing out? Is this normal? I'm not getting the affection I need, but what do I need?" (Nicole)

Hence, the heteronormative and heteropatriarchal societal and familial frameworks had already constructed and enforced gendernormative femininity and compulsory marriage for women, within which marrying their partners without interrogating his sexuality or exploring their own sexuality had occurred:

At the same time that I was courting with Dean, at school in teenage years, I was quite attracted to other women. I never thought anything of it, that I could do anything about it, and it was something that I just put aside. I wouldn't know who to talk to about it. So, I was quite isolated . . . The thing was you got married, and there was no question you could do anything else, and I didn't really struggle with that, although, when I look back on my life, I now know that not being heterosexual had a lot to do with how I felt. There wasn't really any evidence of any kind of sex education. . . . In a way what happened [with her partner disclosing first], I suppose it was a relief we both felt like that. And, yes, we were able to discuss that together. It was all a bit hazy, it was all very complicated and messy . . . I was a woman who was attracted to women who lived in the suburbs. I didn't have any political outlook, I didn't have any kind of opinion. I suppose I'm like a lot of other women I talk to who feel that they're in love with the person, not the sex, who then become quite isolated if something happens. (Hannah)

My mother was always paranoid about what her friends would think so when I left home I had to take my single bed with me in case one of her friends went to my flat, went into my bedroom, saw that I had a double bed, and concluded that I was having sex. . . . it's all about you've got to maintain your reputation in the community and the thing that used to bug me was she wasn't interested really in it for my sake, she was actually worried about what they'd think of her. And my father's mother used to hang the underwear on the line inside pillow cases. So one thing was that I was reacting against basing your life on what the neighbors will think. (Jacinta)

I would never put myself in a box with a label. I had come from a very sheltered background, sexually repressed . . . If we had been brought up in a sexually positive society, to feel connected with our bodies, to masturbate, by the time we reached adolescence then we would be able to say to another, come into my sexual zone. To be able to say no, to know where sexual boundaries are. For most of us we've never had that so all the boundaries get confused. (Nirupa)

Some women discussed the long-lasting effects or consequent ramifications of having experienced sexual inadequacy or sexual betrayal in their MOREs, particularly on future relationships with other men. For example, some women cope by developing their own extramarital personal lives even if it goes against their core set of values and morals:

We married and I couldn't believe it [the lack of sexual passion]. I mean, I suppose because I'd had relationships, been fairly free, I was instantly devastated. So, it set up a pretty terrible pattern. I can remember saying to my husband when we were away on our honeymoon, "God, I've had more pleasure from my set of knives than you," horrible things to say, but God, I just always felt so frozen out... ...I did [have outside sexual partners]. . . . we had somebody [a partner of her husband's] come and stay with us who was an Indonesian, and he came on to me and I was amazed. . . . there was no way I was going to resist this. . . . Anyway, it [the affair] went on for about ten years, off and on. I actually became pregnant at some point with him. He was pretty worried by it, obviously the baby's going to pop out brown. And so I had an abortion, but it was pretty amazing to have, you know, good sex . . . And I had one sort of dalliance with my acupuncturist. And, then, I did fall for somebody that was very brief but intense, because it was very physical. . . . but I really just felt like I couldn't go on with the marriage, and these other men supported me. I mean, they said things like "Every human being has the right to be happy." (Helena)

Other women "jump right into sexual relationships" after the relationship is over in order to prove to themselves "that they are normal at least in bed" (Kaye, 2004: 45). Some women are too scared and scarred to start a relationship with a new man, or find themselves constructing high expectations to avoid finding themselves in the same predicaments:

Well, I've still got the last of Maurice's comments in my head about how hopeless I was [sexually]. . . . I used to think that other women did something magic in bed that I didn't . . . Why would I trust another man? I said to the doctor, "You know, if I met another man, I'd have to make sure he liked me." Well, she fell about laughing. And I said, "Well, you have so long been sexually rejected. I wasn't ever made to feel sexy but that's okay. I mean, at the age of sixty, I might have another ten years in me." (Jeannette)

I think that [the relationship] set me up to fail in subsequent encounters with men. I had a period of three and-a-half years of celibacy because I was shit scared. . . . Now, I often think will I ever have a long-term relationship again. I've actually had about three what I would call flings in the last two years, and I ended them all, and I don't know whether that's a trust issue or whether it's the fact that I don't want things to go wrong five years down the track. I know that I don't want to get married again. And part of me thinks that I'm okay on my own, but the sex bit is what I miss, and probably what I've always missed. That nurturing, that love and affection that someone gives you. . . . when I met him I felt madly in love. And I've never felt that way again. Yeah, there's times when I've said to myself I'm fucked in the head as far as relationships go. (Lisa)

If I ever meet anybody, I'll have the big list, "Are you gay, are you bi? Are you an alcoholic? Are you a drug taker?" and I'll have a private investigator. I mean, I'm still finding things out that I didn't know about him. (Lizette)

I went off on like sexual binges, picking up guys just to go to bed with them. Anywhere, parties, a pub. I'd have to have a lot to drink and then I'd just go to bed with them. Young guys, half my age, anything. Like, I must be a woman. It was like I was trying to prove that I was still attractive. And people tell me I'm stunning, but I had no concept of that, absolutely none. (Mary)

Other women discuss the relief and thrill rather than fear in discovering sexual intimacy and pleasure with another man:

I had a couple of really short-term, really just sex.... It was so good to feel attractive and to know that I could enjoy sex and that the person I could be with would enjoy sex and it was such a great ego boost ... it just gave me this enormous injection of life... Because feeling frightened to have sex is just awful. (Erin)

Apart from being wary about beginning a new relationship with a new man, the women found that sometimes telling a potential new partner about their past partner made the new men back away, or acted as a barrier to the further development of the relationship:

I was crying out to tell someone and I told him, and he walked away from the table. So, for me the experience, "Well, this isn't spoken about, like, wow, I better shut up." (Mary)

In the following, Erin talks about the processes she undertook as she eventually established a new long-term relationship, from not telling her first partner to telling her next partner immediately:

He knew that I'd split up from my husband, but he didn't know why, and I was always afraid to tell why, because I just thought he won't want to go near me if he knows. ... Safe sex is a reason, it's a stereotype, and it's part of homophobia, that people who have same sex relationships are dirty.... and so when I met Scott I was terrified of telling him. It was like the second night that we went out and I just didn't know where this relationship was going, but I just thought to myself if this is going anywhere I need to tell him, because I want this relationship to be based on truth from the beginning and he needs to know why that's so important to me. I was just trembling like a leaf, and he just said, "Erin, why were you so frightened to tell me? It's got nothing to do with me." (Erin)

"IT'S FABULOUS, SCINTILLATING ... I HAVE BECOME VERY LUCKY"

It's [sex with her husband] fabulous, scintillating. ... We had a week on Magnetic Island, just the two of us three weeks ago, and we probably had sex three or four times a day, every day for a week. You know, basically after so long, that it can still be exciting, it can still be satisfying, it can still be varied. I have become very lucky. (Jolene)

A second strong theme to arise out of the research in regard to women's sexualities was women experiencing a new kind of sexual confidence, and the permission and space in the relationship to explore, expand and enjoy their sexualities. Sometimes this wasn't pursued till after the relationship had ended. Nevertheless, all these women, like Jolene above, attributed their newly found active sex drive to having been through a *"fabulous, scintillating"* relationship with bisexual men. They believed this relationship allowed for, encouraged or enforced different ways of thinking in relation to women's sexualities as strong, active and to be fully enjoyed: "we've got a pretty passionate and wild sex life. And we watch porn and that sort of stuff and we sometimes go to sex shops together" (Yvonne); "we began to swing (what is good for the goose is good for the gander lol) . . . Outdoor sex is awesome" (Jenna).

> Well I'll walk in the door and I've got rose petals from my car to the door there or the bath's on with candles lit. It's very much a two way relationship, I've always been a spoiler and now I find that I'm spoilt too. (Simone)

In the following, Jean talks about how her husband went off to explore his sexuality and brought home new sexual techniques and attire which directly increased her pleasures and explorations:

> We've always had a great sex life . . . but when Anthony went to England a few years ago, I remember thinking at the time, "Hello, hello, hello, where have you learnt this?" . . . like rather than entering me or fondling me with hands as he used to, he began running his penis along me and set me on fire. Because it was getting the spot. . . . he bought a little leather g-string, the penis hung out but the balls were enclosed. (Jean)

Dominant constructions of feminine sexuality limit women's sexual autonomy. "Women are encouraged to see their bodies as passive and the objects of male desire. They are therefore constrained from exercising their own bodily appetites which are often constructed as being unnatural or as unseemly" (Ryan, 2000: 93–94; see also Ziegler et al. 2014). In Cohen's (2013) semibiography, *Confessions of a Bisexual Husband,* we follow the marriage of Gabrielle and Marco after 15 years and two children together. Within the roller-coaster of near-divorces and marital resuscitations, disastrous and delicious nonmonogamous sexual experimentations, we track Marco encouraging Gabrielle to become more sexually adventurous and her increasing sexual assertiveness and independence in group sex, such as sharing male partners at a beach beat. In parallel, Marco becomes increasingly scared and aroused with his "vision of Gabrielle the Sexual Conqueror" (2013: pages unnumbered). He arrives at an acceptance of living in the liminal space of no return to how she was and not knowing who she will become:

> I want to lock her down; close it off; buy a chastity belt . . . [scared] that I'll no longer measure up. But if we lock things down, we'll go back to stagnating and we all know how that story ends . . . Which means here we stay: risking it all in the hype that we'll continue to discover we are each other's perfect partner (2013: pages unnumbered).

In Brant's tragic novel about a group of married male friends who find sexual pleasure with each other, their discussions about women's sexual desires and what men desire from a woman reveal their limited framework within panopticonic gendernormative and heteronormative thinking regarding "macho" masculinities and what to "look for in a wife." It also presents provocative glimpses into the reality that their wives would actually be interested in breaking out of those heteropatriarchal frameworks but are also reluctant to suggest certain sexual practices for fear of being considered "queer" or "non-feminine." Indeed, after the men's sexual relationships are discovered, some of the wives admit to understanding and indeed desiring sex with some of the men themselves, or being sexual in ways that the men are sexual:

> "Ever thought about asking your wife to strap on a dildo?" James asked.
> Jake turned his head. "You kidding!... Be great though."
> Jorge laughed. "Ah, a woman who takes pleasure in ramming her man with a dildo. Where does one find a woman like that? . . . "
> "I think we choose the woman we want to marry for her feminine slant," said Jorge. "Her sexual prowess is secondary. I've always believed a woman with a man's sexual perspective probably lacks the important things we look for in a wife. We want to protect them, to cherish the softer nuances they bring to our lives. Balance is her appeal. The dominatrix with a dildo most likely has no balance at all." . . .
> "Maybe we don't know our wives as well as we should, their deep down, darkest little secrets." [said David] . . .
> "My wife's pretty adventurous. I bet she'd strap on a dildo." [said James].
> "Would you want her to?" Tim wanted to know.
> James thought for a moment and then looked up. "Yeah. I would." . . .
> "Anyway, how would you bring it up? Linda would think I was turning queer."
> James put in. "Wives want macho husbands. . . .

"We get turned on looking at another man's anus. I doubt many women do." (Brant, 2006: 120–121)

This fictional account illustrates the work of sex counselors such as Kort (2014a) regarding how many men are too afraid to ask their female partners for sexual acts such as being anal penetrators out of fear they might be gay or bisexual or that their partners might think or discover this.

A small number of men in Schnarr et al.'s (2012) research did report receptive anal sex with women, colloquially known as 'pegging', as acceptable, thereby modifying normative sexual scripts. In our research, some women report empowering nonnormative sexual explorations and pleasures. Their experiences resonate with Weeks' concept of "democratic autonomy" (1995: 66) which suggests that sexual freedom can only be realized in conditions of mutuality, when an individual's ability to seek and obtain the pleasures and emotional satisfactions desired are reliant upon the reciprocal recognition of the other. Thus, a relationship with a bisexual man was seen by some of these women as involving their sexual empowerment alongside or in mutual recognition of his own. Also of interest is the way these interpersonal mutual recognitions and encouragements are situated within a shared heteropatriarchal system which seeks to oppress and invisibilize both of them (Ryan, 2000). For example, where women are able to assert their sexual desires, this is meaningless outside the recognition and acceptance, indeed approval, of these desires by male partners who may be complicit with or privileged by this system. As a way forward, Ryan (2000) proposes that respect for women in their sexual individuality and diversity therefore implies seeking to eliminate institutionalized, heteropatriarchal, gendered and sexual discrimination and domination. It appears that with some bisexual men who themselves are actively seeking this noncompliance, women are able to experience sexual empowerment.

For the women in fulfilling relationships with bisexual men, exploring their sexualities was considered part of the meshing of feminist politics/sexualities and queer politics/sexualities in a relationship or sexual explorations that they believed they could establish with bisexual men, who, as discussed in chapter 9, were also challenging heteropatriarchal masculinities, heteronormative relationships and misogynist expectations of women (Ziegler et al. 2014):

> We went online and looked for bisexual men to have threesomes with us. On some sort of level the new found honesty between Mick and myself was a turn on. Threesomes were fun and exciting at the time and in some weird way it seemed to bring Mick and I closer together. (Marissa)

When he first told me about being bisexual, I got a bit more understanding and I started to realize that I had a thing for girls because I remembered that my first kiss was with a girl and I had actually blocked that out. So I thought, I'll give it a whirl. It was just a very opening sort of experience really. (Maz)

Diamond (2008; 2009) found that women's sexuality is fundamentally more fluid than men's, permitting greater variability in its development and expression over the life course. She describes three main ways that sexual fluidity is expressed: "nonexclusivity in attractions" (i.e., the capacity to find all genders sexually attractive), "changes in attractions" (i.e., suddenly becoming romantically involved with a woman after a lifetime dating men), and the capacity to become attracted to 'the person and not the gender'" (i.e., a partner's sex is irrelevant) (Diamond, 2009; see also Rostosky, 2010). Whether this is biological or more socially permitted for women than for men remains a point of ongoing research and debate.

I'd had sex with women plenty of times. But I'd always been a bit embarrassed about telling other partners because I saw it as non-conventional behavior. I found it very easy to talk to Charlie about it because he's so open about his sexuality and he subsequently encouraged me to explore that further ... For me it was liberating and refreshing to be able to truly open myself in a relationship without feeling condemnation and turn out the drawers and say "Okay, well, this is what's in the dark recesses of my mind." (Jolene)

I didn't necessarily identify as a lesbian, but I lived as a lesbian in that I was in a long-term relationship for five years with a woman, and I didn't think of men as people that I would necessarily have sex with, and now I have a boyfriend, I don't identify myself as bisexual. . . . I guess one of the reasons I started having sex with men is because . . . that sort of joke about lesbian bed death. I felt like saying, it's not lesbian bed death, it's fucking long-term relationship bed death. But, there was this fear that maybe it was the absence of a male sexual energy, a male sex drive that was stopping the dynamic. Like, I remembered having male lovers when I was really young and just thinking, geez man, they want to fuck all the time, a predatory sexuality that I would react to. My girlfriend was really pretty and really little and I mean, she can be predatory, but she couldn't do that fuck and throw me over the table like push my hair down and grab and fuck. Like, she couldn't do the rough trade thing which I find really sexy at times. . . . [With the second bisexual boyfriend] I just got really attached to him and he was living with two dykes. I ended up fucking the whole household. (Sascha)

Just as Sascha above desired to explore her sexuality with men after coming from a lesbian community, likewise, the growing queerifying of gay communities means that an increasing number of gay-identifying men may seek out a "mixed-queer" way of living and loving with feminist women, who also are seeking freedom from traditional gendered social and sexual roles. Or perhaps it is becoming more "okay" to say so, given that these relationships have always existed and been documented in research (Nahas & Tyler, 1979; Whitney, 1990).

Gaining sexual confidence and assertiveness after the breakdown of a relationship with a bisexual man was also a common theme for some women. Although this has been discussed in the previous section of this chapter, what is pertinent for this section is how women acknowledged that despite the difficulties of being in an unsatisfactory relationship with a bisexual man, the very being in a nongendernormative relationship had allowed for questions and possibilities to open up regarding their own sexualities which they were then able to pursue post-relationship. These may never have surfaced in a heteronormative relationship: "my maturing about sex now, and I find it immensely more pleasurable and important than I did in the past" (Josie).

> I started questioning my own sexuality, and he also kept challenging me, "You think this way for a certain reason" or "You fall into your parents' thinking this way" and so there was sort of this constant "I've got to stop just accepting things. I've got to really look at this." After this relationship ended, I actually rang a friend of mine and I talked to her and I ended up having a relationship with her and then there were other ones . . . now I have actually made contact with a chap who has Klinefelter's Syndrome. It's where they've got an extra "x" chromosome which means he identifies very strongly with his feminine side, although he identifies as being straight. He really enjoys cross-dressing. . . . he has very, very fine features but he definitely looks like a man. (Nina)

> I want a man mate. I can look like a slut and wear sexy clothes, be a slut, be normal, and there's part of them that just thinks Sylvia's great. She's not the most beautiful girl, it doesn't matter. But they want to be with me. So, that's what I look for, and I've only received that really very recently and I know I've found it . . . He is a cool cat. I know I can be odd, but he's faced his nemesis. . . . so there's that goodwill to say anything and everything that you choose. You don't have to protect the person. Women are brought up to protect. (Sylvia)

> It's interesting that the woman I am now involved with is very androgynous, she's got a very masculine body, flat chest, tall, and a deep voice. I think part of exploring myself was having lots of sexual experimentation, but ultimately I have to come to a point where sex is going to be nurturing and the relationship is going to lead to a depth of love and commitment. I do feel that my sexuality is heterosexual, but a lot of the same issues around commitment and intimacy come up no matter what gender you are with. (Nirupa)

In this section, women have presented what Julz describes as "that gut-level tug we feel toward these men that we rarely, if ever, feel with straight men," that "sense of being understood by bi men in a way that most monosexuals can't . . . a sense of possibility and potential" (2005: 217). Another common theme, particularly for bisexual women, is how they are often misunderstood by straight men, and the old myth of the "hot bi babe" rears its ugly head. Fahs discusses "public performative bisexuality" or "barsexuality" as the pressure on women to perform as bisexual for male spectatorship and pleasure (2009: 437). "Most bi women are not hypersexual, perfectly manicured porn chicks, dying to have someone 'watch'. . . . Bi men usually understand that we want to get it on with other women for the same or similar reasons as theirs" (Julz, 2005: 217). Thus, what some of the women in this research found with bisexual men was a potential "space" for "authentic female sexuality," including bisexuality, "outside of patriarchal fantasy" wherein "the rules are clear, either choose a man for a sexual partner or choose a woman with a man's approval" (Fahs, 2009: 447). These issues come to the fore in the comedy *Humpday* (2009) in which two straight men, Ben and Andrew, struggle to have sex together, including anal sex, as part of a "mutual dare" for a porn movie artfest competition. Their attempts to have sex are prolonged by lengthy discussions and frequent analyzing of how to approach the experience. Ben finally suggests they call off the project, and the two laugh at the ridiculousness of the situation. This awkwardness is in direct contrast to the lesbian lover of a bisexual female character who is comfortable with one of the men as her lover's lover. In the beginning of a threesome, for which the male partner is very enthusiastic, the lesbian lover introduces a dildo, intimating it will be used on all three of them, to which he hypocritically and stereotypically replies that "one cock is enough" and can they try sex "the conventional way." They refuse and he leaves.

It is fitting to end this section with Julz' summation: "In bi men, women like me find fellow transgressors who don't color inside the lines and who share our glee in believing that those lines may exist for the sole purpose of our delight in violating them" (2005: 220); and to follow it with an excerpt from a short story by Pritchard that demonstrates the kinds of deterritorialized sex/gender play and pleasure, and democratic autonomy and mutuality possible (Ryan, 2000; Weeks, 1995). Pritchard's story is about a polyamorous threesome wherein the two bisexual men encourage the woman to explore her penetrator pleasures:

> He unsnaps various straps and fits the harness around her loins, a pink silicone dildo poking through it. . . . She starts fucking me hard . . . I am whining and moaning in a high-pitched voice . . . She is breathing fast. "Fuck you," she enunciates. "I've got you—I'm fucking you. I don't give a shit about your pleasure." . . . Then she starts to come, and pushes it suddenly really hard all the way to the bottom. We both cry out, and she starts pounding me there,

squealing, babbling, pushing her clit against the rough leather on the inside of the harness. Her orgasm is louder than any I've gotten out of her before (1999: 207).

"I WANT MY CAKE AND TO EAT IT TOO"

> If it really comes down to the nuts and bolts, I'd say that I was bisexual. Sitting on a fence. [Laughing] That's what a lot of people say, "Make up your mind. You can't have it both ways." But, yeah, I want my cake and to eat it too. (Christine)

The third major theme was how significant the relationship with a bisexual man was for women who entered the relationship as queer feminists, and who continued to negotiate and affirm their own nonnormative, consensual nonmonogamous, polyamorous and/or nonheterosexual sexualities within the context of the relationship. This differs from women in the previous section of this chapter who discovered, explored or acknowledged their own queer sexualities for the first time within the context of the relationship. Ziegler et al. summarize the available research which shows women have a greater need "for novel stimuli in order to maintain sexual arousal," thereby meaning that women in monogamous relationships find their sexual desires diminishing while those in polyamorous relationships report "high sexual satisfaction" and the opportunity to explore their multifaceted desires (2014: 5). Ziegler et al. (2014) also point out that polyamorous relationships mean a woman feels less sexual pressure to fulfil all her partner's sexual needs as she is no longer solely responsible:

> I want to have my freedom, I want to be able to have sex with whoever and have openness in a relationship, and I want to construct and control that world, and I want it to be much larger than what the world actually is prepared to offer me.... I don't give myself a label. I certainly for many years now have not been able to come at heterosexual. I spent a period of time with the label lesbian. I've never been able to adopt the bisexual label because visually on the page, it's an ugly word I think, and just the category thing puts me off. I've talked to you before about the human that I want people to become, and that frees us from those categories. (Raven)

Brooks & Quina believe that for "a more complete picture of women's sexuality, unlabeled women must be included in research on sexual minority women, and allowing study participants to choose multiple labels, supply their own labels, or choose no label may help women with greater perceived fluidity better represent themselves in such research" (2009: 1042; see also Albury, 2015). Even among those in our research who have consciously chosen not to label themselves, including Raven above, a variety of reasons exist: personal ones such as believing that one's emotional connections and sexual behaviors do not fit any of the available categories; political reasons such as taking a stand against the heteropatriarchal sex/gender system that endorses monogamy, jealousy and men's ownership of women; and the psychological benefits of an unlabeled status such as a sense of freedom or personal agency and authenticity:

> The way I have it set up is that I have a primary relationship and then other relationships. . . . The amount of control that men will have over where a woman goes and how much time she spends doing anything else other than being totally focused on them, you know, because they're jealous, I think that is appalling. I'm deeply offended by that . . . straight men are so willing to project their jealousy on to women and use it to control women, to make themselves feel slightly safer. (Anne)

> Well, originally I thought I was heterosexual and then I thought, well, I'm bisexual, but now we've [she and her partner] sort of decided I'm pan sexual, so that sort of just makes it easier. (Annette)

Thus, many women discussed their bisexual and/or queer feminist histories and how these meant they were drawn toward bisexual and/or queer straight men in order to continue to live out their own sexual realities and desires:

> Well, I was fifteen years-of-age. I started fondling with my friend at home, and I was, "Yeah, I like this." . . . Nineteen, twenty, I met this woman and it just started. We spent three years together. Meanwhile, we'd go out to nightclubs and go look for men. And I just felt comfortable with that, and I never questioned who I was or was confused. It was like, "I need a dick," that sort of thing. . . . I like the soft, quiet one, the sensual woman, the woman with the nails. The woman who can wear heels, the most elegant thing, the woman that walks in the room and everyone looks. She's not pretty, she's not beautiful. She's just different. Feminine, with a brain, that's about it. Someone that I can talk to and be my best mate at the same time, that we can also share men together. (Temptress)

> My first love was so traditional, absolutely stunning in some ways, alright in bed and in some ways hopeless. He had failed high school, he wanted me to fail high school, get married, have kids. He was very possessive and for a little while I thought that was a lot of fun, but you can't go anywhere, do anything . . . Then he made out with my best friend behind my back, and that really hurt. . . . He said that he was doing it to basically show me that it was over. So after that I decided, "Right, that's it, I am never going to get into that kind of relationship again." By that point I was doing a lot of feminist reading about women as sexual property so that began to influence me a lot and I decided, "Right, I am going to be a sexually liberated woman and have lots of different guys and

have a career and be independent and be really strong and I am going to buy an apartment in the city." . . . I started going out with other guys and they were horrible, they were all sort of like replicas of my first boyfriend, . . . and every one had their own sexist stereotypes but then I met my hetero partner . . . and I began to test him out . . . like "I am going to have 500 boyfriends, I am going to be in love with all of them" and he'd go "Fantastic, can I live next door and be one of them?" And I was like, "This guy's not threatened." I found out that he had come out of a very traditional relationship. She would just treat him badly, she was screwing around behind his back, and she dumped him. We just began to talk through all this stuff and we just went on from there. . . . . And then I fell in love about ten years later with my bisexual partner. . . . I'm in two ordinary great relationships, if you know what I mean by that supposed contradiction. . . . I am and have always been sexually feminist. There has been a straight guy who I stopped seeing and he is just like, "Why why why?" and I just basically said "Look sexually you are great when you fuck but I actually need a lot of oral sex and you have got this squeamish attitude," and he said, "No other woman has said that." I said "Maybe they don't want to have it, maybe they can't tell you cos they're not assertive, maybe you never asked what they liked." If I have my period I let men know. I will remove pads and tampons in front of a man. I will not run off to the bathroom and I will not hide anything. It's like if this is going to turn you off then just go. . . . What it does do being polyamorous is you don't get taken for granted and you have to be safe sexually and then careful with anniversaries and birthdays and special days and it's good because the other people are like that with you. My partners have both said to me if they ever detect that I am doing favorites they would let me know about it. They don't want to hear about any argument I have had with the other person. . . . It does take a lot of work. Cause you are not only responsible for one relationship, you are responsible for another. You are not only worried about sexual health with one person but also anybody outside of that. (Naomi)

Many of these queer women talk about how they then teach or encourage their male partners to further explore their own queer desires but in queer feminist nonpatriarchal ways. In the following, Temptress challenges her partner's assumption that if she is having sex with another woman, he has the right to automatically participate and indeed take over:

We'd gone to a swingers club, and I was with her [making love to a woman they met there] and then suddenly he just took her, and I just stood back and was like, "What are you doing, Fernando? That's not how it goes." I was so upset at him . . . And I was always telling him, "Don't invade me . . . . I'm not bringing any girl home, I'm not doing anything, until you give me what I've given you [freedom to have separate relationships with men], so now you sit there and you watch." So, now we're okay, we've had a whole year and-a-half of full-on, to swingers, to BDSM clubs, to fetish clubs, to sleeping with my best mate. (Temptress)

Women also discussed how they challenge and teach their bisexual partners how to address their jealousy over their polyamorous relationships with women and other men:

> I don't want to put any restrictions at all on other people's behavior, who sleeps with who, when, doesn't bother me in the slightest. . . . It does bother Pete. I've had to fight quite a lot harder for my freedom, to insist on my right to follow what I feel I want to follow in the situations I want to follow. (Anne)

> Greg's sort of like "How much do you still love me?" . . . all I know is that when I'm with Jen and I have sex with her something clicks in my head and some chemical or something comes back into alignment and I feel better. And I've noticed Greg's starting to pick that up too and he's starting to see I'm getting something from that [relationship with Jen] I bring back into the relationship with him. (Annette)

In the following, Jacinta discusses how she initiated the conversations that assisted her partner Corey in coming to the realization of his bisexual desires and acting upon them:

> I said that's how I actually want our relationship to be [open, bisexual and polyamorous] and so we put the whole of the past relationship to bed, gave up any expectations we had of each other, and just listened and explored with the other person what's going on and really got it sorted. . . . and it's like have you got any fantasies that we haven't fulfilled. . . . And at the end of a two week period, Corey decided he would be bisexual and so we started out . . . And during that period of time it's amazing actually because I'd always been the one who ran our social calendar. I came home one night to find that he found all these internet sites like meeting places and he placed ads and we were getting responses and it was just like he'd totally taken responsibility for causing this to happen and when I saw that, I was like I don't care what it takes, I'm supporting this 100% because it's motivating to him that he's willing to actually go out and cause the relationships to come into existence. (Jacinta)

A heteronormative misogynist sex/gender system also colors how some women are much more reluctant to report that they desire sexual relations with a bisexual man than men reporting their desire for sexual relations with bisexual women (Confer & Cloud, 2011). It also sets up a shared concealment or passing to the external world with their queer partners, and interestingly could also be a means of enhancing one's experience. First, when a sexual secret is shared by those involved in the secret activity, it has the effect of creating a bond or building cohesion between them. Second, concealment adds excitement to one's sexual activity and makes one's experiences within the subculture important, creating a "sense of distinctiveness" (Stiles & Clark, 2011: 186).

In our research, there were women of diverse sexualities, including heterosexual, who were what are known as "girlfags" (see Hardy, 2012; Julz, 2005; Lambert, 2010): women who enjoy watching men have sex with men, and/or participating, and who also enjoy genderplay with their partners. O'Rourke (2005) argues for a queer heterosexuality theory within which "girlfags" can be located, the "quirkily heterosexual" (Grosz, 1995: 4).

> We have these little jokes where I tell him [my partner] that I'm going to have to teach him to give head properly. . . . I'll be doing my thing [with the men] and I'll say [to my partner], "Now, you've got to do it this way. So, you've just got to get the angle right," and it does spice it up to that extent, you know, where you can have some more fun thrown in, especially after fifteen years . . . one of my favorite stories, my husband tells it to everybody now, he went to sleep and the next morning, normal thing, rolled over to give me a kiss, and I went "Oh, cock breath." And we just lay there and laughed and laughed and laughed. (Lesley)

Girlfags in film are rare. In the comedy films, *Eating Out 1* (2004) and *Eating Out 2* (2006), the characters Gwen and Tiffani are girlfags. They enjoy having bisexual boyfriends and engaging in MMF threesomes with them. These women are portrayed as sexually confident and assertive, although Tiffani is given stereotypical 'skank' qualities. Girlfag music is also rare. Peaches is a Canadian electronic musician and performance artist whose songs are noted for disregarding traditional gender norms, and for their use of sexually explicit lyrics. In "Two Guys for Every Girl," a gender subversion of the Beach Boys' song, "Two Girls for Every Boy," she sings about desiring to see men have oral sex with each other and then taking her place as the centre of their attention and their director in a threesome.

Temptress's reminiscence below is an example of the kind of BDSM girlfag experiences with bisexual men increasingly being explored in fiction, such as in Schechter's (2013) novel, *House of Sable Locks,* albeit with none of the non-consensual and murderous elements of the story! Indeed, this steampunk novel has submissive and dominant bisexual men enjoying the sadistic administrations of both human and automaton/cyborg women and men in a brothel owned by Madame, where different rooms and floors offer different scenarios of "pleasures and torments" (2013:6).

> I gave him a gift for his birthday, it was a whole month of me being a mistress and him being my slave, so every day I give him an assignment. He sometimes had to cook, wear a little apron naked . . . on the third last day, right before his birthday, I got a man. I tied him [my partner] up. I blindfolded him. Didn't say

anything. The man did everything to him. And he [my partner] was giving head jobs and whatever, and then when the fucking started I got underneath and got him to fuck me and the guy to fuck him behind. And, on the birthday day, I took him blindfolded to my mistress and we were his mistresses and he was our slave, and dildos up the arse, non-stop, full-on. Had a stiffy all the way . . . he loved it. (Temptress)

Thus, many women in MOREs provide responses to the question posed by Beasley: "how might a transgressive heterosexuality be conceptualized?" (2010: 208). For example, the sex instruction videos *Bend Over Boyfriend* (1998) and *Tristan Taormino's Ultimate Guide to Anal Sex for Women 2* (2000) teach women how to give their male partners anal pleasure, in particular through 'pegging', anal intercourse with strap-ons or dildos (Kort, 2014a). The following are excerpts from a letter Lilith wrote to us on her returned transcript. She wanted to add more detail to her statements in the interview about being a girlfag and how having sex with Adam was a "genderfuck and sexual label fuck."

I often look at him and think in loving him, what am I? I'm straight and yet in loving him, in fucking him, in sharing girlie secrets and taking the same men to bed at the same time, am I a gay man, or a gay man-woman? . . . I remember the first time I knew I wanted to fuck him. He was lying stomach down under a tree in the park. I was checking out his butt squeezed into these tight blue jeans and as I did that, another feeling took over in me, "I want to, I can, spread those cheeks, I need to feel him inside with my fingers, slide my cunt over his butt, use my vibrator to fuck him." I got so hot and I lowered myself onto him, and began to grind. I remember how he arched his head back. He pushed back with his butt. In my mind, and later he told me in his mind, I was fucking him. All that rubbing made me come right there in the park. We went home, and I licked his man-pussy and fucked him with fingers and a vibrator and my pussy grinding between his butt-cheeks while I'm imagining I'm a man-woman fucking him, and I kept coming so hard and so did he, and he was fucked, as he was used to by men and which I'd enjoyed watching so many times, but later he told me he enjoyed having me as a woman fucking him. And in the very doing this from that time on, fucking each other and mutual pussy-licking, it was like we were both gay men, both straight women, both lesbians, both straight men. And where did our "woman" and "man" selves begin and end? It was like we were fucking with gender and it turns me on so much. And we knew we were now all of our selves but something else as well . . . we love beat sex together as well. It started in that same park which is where he also used to go go-karting, soccer-playing, tadpole-catching when he was a child and then it later became the beat-sex cruising paradise of his adolescence. Now he takes me his female partner there to have sex with guys. The first time wasn't planned. He showed me his favorite beat-spots and reminisced about the boys, the older men, and the neighbors he had sex with there. We sat on this grassy mound and just perved on the busy thoroughfare of men walking around us. Finally, it all got too much. We were so horny. So we decided to find a very secluded spot in the bushes where we wouldn't be seen. I mean, a woman at a beat? We didn't want to horrify and disturb anyone or be caught as a woman with my pants down trespassing on this male-to-male zone. Anyway, we thought we couldn't be seen. But I happened to look up and saw this guy watching us. I froze with fear and guilt. I was about to straighten up when I noticed the guy was smiling as his hand snaked down to the crotch of his own jeans. I smiled back. Adam began to fumble at his jeans around his ankles and mumbled something about why I just stood there holding my dress up around my upper thighs instead of escaping, and then the guy came up and began kissing me. Then he stroked Adam's bare arm and said, "I found you exciting. I've never allowed myself to find a woman exciting. I'd come to beats more often if I knew women came. I'm gay but I want to have sex with you both." I remember thinking it's like I'm forbidden fruit out here. And we all had a hot amazing time. Later, as Adam and I made our way out, all dizzy and euphoric, he hugged me and said, "I can't take you anywhere. You upset everything, break all the rules." . . . I have been asked by straight guys, "Why a fucking bisexual?" They can't see why I can't even stand the thought of having sex with them after making love with Adam. The straight men who wince or back off during sex if they see or feel that I'm about to do something fags do. How do I tell them it's partly what they've said, "Fucking bisexual." There is something about a man who wants to be penetrated, the way he understands the painful pleasure, the way he spreads his legs and waits, anticipates, begs to be fucked, the way his stomach muscles move as he lifts his legs and you push against him. There is something about sliding over and into this man's body and knowing the meanings and signals of his moans, his pants, his sighs, his frowns, the way he bites his lower lip. And knowing what it's like to thrust, to grunt, to see someone beneath you taking you in, your power and your vulnerability in needing to do this to him. There is something about being inside a man, his soft warm flesh, his tight sphincter wrapped around you, his prostate swelling like a giant clitoris and becoming as hard as hot stone just as he comes; and listening to the girlie squeals of ecstatic agony, feeling his shudders of sheer bliss, and knowing you know what it's like, the power of vulnerability, the power of surrender. Welcome to the queer bedroom. . . . Sometimes I dress Adam in drag and do his make-up before we go out and then I take him home and fuck him. I remember how he sent a photo to his mum of himself dressed in a floral Laura Ashley frock. She phoned back and subtly asked him about me. Finally, she admitted why: "I thought she might be a man after all." Adam laughed. "Sometimes in bed she does me over like one." His Mum was embarrassed. "I had thought she was a real woman, but then I thought she's too real woman-looking, what with all that hair and make-up and those sexy clothes, I thought she might be a man after all, and you're both pulling one over me." (Lilith)

The queer bedroom as a stage for gender subversions and bisexual performances is seen in the film *Stage Beauty* (2004). It was inspired by the seventeenth-century English actor who was particularly famous for his portrayal of female characters before women were allowed to perform on stage. When Charles II bans men from playing female roles, Kynaston loses the attention of his bisexual lover, the Duke of Buckingham, who will only have sex with him from behind on a theatre stage, and only if Kynaston wears a long blonde woman's wig. Kynaston also loses the acceptance of London society which starts to circulate rumors about their association, although until then, society ladies liked having sex with him, while he is still in female attire, in a carriage around Hyde Park. Finally, Kynaston loses all sense of a fixed gender as having gone through a long and strenuous training since boyhood to play female roles, he is unable to perform a normative masculinity. He queries whether he is "a man in woman's form, or is it the other way round?" With Maria, his dresser and aspiring actress, who models her portrayals of women on stage on his portrayals of women, he explores his gender. In a scene of erotic intimacy, she adopts various positions beneath, on top while he is face downward, and next to his body, asking him if he is the man or the woman. With different positions, he gives different genders. When she asks, "So who are you now?" he replies, "I don't know" but they are both delighted about that gender ambiguity.

Another form of queer straight girlfag erotics, the 'hot wife' and her 'cuckold', is explored in a book aptly titled *Insatiable Wives* (Ley, 2009; see also Kort, 2014a). As explained in chapter 3, the term 'hot wife' refers to a woman who has sex with men other than her partner with the husband's consent. In most cases the partners take a vicarious pleasure in watching or engaging with their female partners and the other males, or enjoy watching, hearing or knowing about their female partners' adventures. A further subgrouping is 'cuckolding' in which emphasis is placed upon the sexual humiliation of the male partner restricted to a passive or subordinated role. This may involve submissive bisexuality in what is known as 'cream-pies' where the cuckolded husband performs oral sex on his wife after she has had unprotected sex with her lover. He is thus forced to consume her lover's semen from her vagina. Ley is critical of the pathologizing of such sexual play: It is the "fear of female sexuality that drives the need to approach the hot wife phenomenon from the core assumption that it is innately pathological or unhealthy or rooted in negative feelings or experiences" (2009: 179). He found the "forced" bisexuality of submitting to dominant wives and their wives' lovers to be extremely arousing for many men due explicitly to the taboo nature of the behavior violating both the homosexuality taboo as well as heterosexpatriarchy.

I have always had problems with someone who believes that women don't like men's bodies and don't enjoy watching men together. For me it's like I find a man's body very aesthetically interesting so when you have got two men's bodies or three men's bodies and they're doing what you tell them to do to each other and to you, it's really beautiful, such a turn-on! . . . One thing that my bi partner has said is that I come a lot more and a lot faster than all the guys he's had sex with. And I do, I am very multi-orgasmic. I find some of the gay guys get a bit shocked. In bed afterwards, you close your eyes and you're drifting off and you hear them talking to each other: "God, women come really quick don't they? It's easy to make love to women." I am like "Guys, I'm listening." But I like that sort of discussion and humor and safety. . . . I find now that I tend to have more and more sex with gay or bisexual men rather than straight men . . . because of a different kind of pro-feminist vibe with these guys cos they actually respect you more, will be more sexual and sensual, and get really dirty like enjoy licking cocktails, that's mixing pussy juice and cum in your vagina. I turn down straight men because some of them I just don't want their attitudes or they're not perverted enough. (Naomi)

Another term to attempt to describe these queer imaginings and pleasures in women is what Simpson (2006) has coined "femantasy," to define women's sexual interests in "boy on boy action" as spectators and/or participants. In the following, Jolene discusses what she finds arousing, intriguing and unarousing in watching her partner having sex with men:

[Toilets] are not a place that I would want to have sex in. It's dirty, it's noisy, it's unsafe, it doesn't turn me on, but I found the acts themselves erotically satisfying, yes, arousing, just as you would watching a film. . . . I was anxious. I didn't want to get caught. I was curious, watching how he operated with men. You know, for guys trying to pick up a woman, they don't pull their willy out and wave it and say, "Here, look what I've got." It's a very different approach. . . . part of the pleasure for him is knowing that somebody's watching anyway . . . Oh, yes, we have [shared partners]. One of the guys was very gay, and found that he was uncomfortable with me. He was quite happy for me to watch, but he didn't want me to touch. (Jolene)

Simpson believes that although the media tries to deny or obliterate it with constant attention to "girl-on-girl action," it's just a matter of time before "the straightest of straight men might soon find themselves having to at least flirt in bicuriousness, just to lay women" (2006: see website). In the film *Splendor* (1999), we see a woman express her "femantasy" to her two male partners. Even though the three of them do make love and set up a long-term relationship as a polyfidelitous triad, replete with twin babies, the men are presented as engaging sexually with the woman, not with each other, even though there is a growing "bi-affectionate" emotional intimacy between them. Interestingly, *Splendor*, by gay-identifying director Greg Araki, was an homage to the actor Kathleen Robertson, whom he had previously cast as a lesbian in his earlier film, *Nowhere* (1997), and with whom he had a relationship for two years.

It stands to reason that with the growing shifts in cultural and interpersonal acknowledgments of homoerotics and homosex between men, "erotic plasticity" (Baumeister, 2004) will become more evident in men. What is also interesting is how many critics of "femantasy" are not as stridently critical of cultural representations of "straight men's girl-on-girl fantasies." McLelland questions the "incredulous 'Why?'" around women's enjoyment of male-on-male fellatio, anal intercourse, and other sexual acts and romantic expressions when "few people react with surprise to the fact that male pornography is full of 'lesbian sex'" (2006; see also Bauer, 2013; Levi et al. 2010; McLelland et al. 2015). Another criticism is that in being girlfags and femantasists, women are only objectifying men as men have done women: "Is it essentially male and/or dehumanizing?" (Meyer, 2013: 64). Indeed, as the photographer of erotic male nudes Sarah Kent comments, "To admit to sexual reponses and interests despised in the opposite sex is difficult" (Kent & Morreau, 1990: 75).

"Femantasy" is very evident in three fiction genres, written predominantly by heterosexual females and proliferating via the Internet. First, slash fiction and its subbranches, slashart and slashvidding (visuals cut and pasted from video-clips such as YouTube) often rewrite and reinscribe mainstream heterosexual male characters and storylines into same-sex and bisexual characterizations and storylines (Bauer, 2013; Cicioni, 1998; Jenkins et al. 1998). For example, the "Kirk/Spock" stories based on the *Star Trek* characters remain an important slash fiction fandom, while new slash fandoms have grown around other television shows, movies, and books with sci-fi or action adventure roots. Second, slash-like "femantasy" fiction is written in various Japanese 'anime' or 'manga' fandoms including cartoons, comics, videogames and fine art, and is referred to as "shounen-ai," "yaoi" or BL ("boys love") for homoerotic and homoromantic relationships between male characters (Bauer, 2013; Levi et al. 2010; McLelland et al. 2015; Zanghellini, 2009). These genres are differentiated from "gei comi," which is by gay men for gay men (Mizoguchi, 2003). As Japanese "yaoi" gained popularity in the United States, American women artists began creating original English-language manga for female readers featuring beautiful male-male couples referred to as "American yaoi" (Bauer, 2013; Levi et al. 2010; Wood, 2006).

Globally, the "yaoi" fandom is viewed by many cultural analysts as a "refuge" from mainstream misogynistic culture (Suzuki, 1999; Thorn, 2004). However, it is also telling that from a heteropatriarchal perspective, it has been criticized as allowing girls to avoid adult (read: heterocentric and heteropatriarchal) female sexuality as it creates and explores greater fluidity in perceptions of gender and sexuality, thereby rejecting "socially mandated" gender roles (Bauer, 2013; Meyer, 2010; Nagaike, 2015). Hashimoto (2007) has called "yaoi" a form of empowering "female fetishism," often written by women who cannot enjoy "conventional pornography, which had been made for men." Thus, Boys' Love manga provides the "imaginative resources to re-think, reconfigure, and take control" over socially ascribed notions of adult heterosexual femininity (Martin, 2012: 374).

The third fiction genre is the m/m/f ménage or m/m soft-porn novels written by heterosexual women. A well-known example is author Cat Grant (2008–2013) who writes erotic romance novels about gay and bisexual military men, athletes, gym-goers, corporates and politicians. Her *Courtland Chronicles* erotica series follows twenty years in the lives of Eric, Nick and Ally as they move from gay and straight relationships to a bisexual polyamorous relationship.

Overall, the various genres of "femantasy" highlight that as women have gained greater economic power and queer feminist understandings and assertiveness over their sexual desires, commercial demand for the sexualization of men, including "boy on boy action," may correlate despite "patriarchal opprobrium" (Kent & Morreau, 1990: 1) over this "cross-voyeurism" of "fujoshi," a Japanese word meaning "naughty girls" (Bauer, 2013: 1; Meyer, 2010), or reversal of the power hierarchy: male as active sexual scrutiniser, woman as the passive object of sexual scrutiny. Some men and feminists, such as those who critique "femantasy" genres, may think this is degrading, and certainly "yaoi" and other pornography exploiting men is subject to feminist criticisms: the depictions of male rape and pedophilia; the objectification of human beings via sexual caricatures; the creation of unrealistic sexual and physical expectations; and the consequent negative body images and interpersonal abusive expressions (Mizoguchi, 2003). Both slash fiction and the yaoi genre lack empirical research into women's motivations and desires, as well as their rewards from constructing and consuming these genres and their subsequent and/or intended "commodity, controversy, and culture" (Levi et al. 2010; McLelland et al. 2015). For example, Davies writes how women create online girlfag communities, where they "constantly discuss the characters in the most loving and explicit ways" (2005: 199).

In summary, the experiences of the women in this section contradict Kaye's advice to those who think that joining in on their husband's sexual lifestyle may help their marriage, which is "don't do it . . . You now visualise your partner for life wrapped in the arms of another man. Some women cannot picture what goes on past that point, but even this limited image is enough to bring on a feeling of heart break and revulsion" (2000: 40).

CONCLUSION

As a conclusion to this chapter, I will present some excerpts from an autobiography by Coon (2012) which encapsulates the three types of women's sexualities apparent in our research, and how women may journey from one type or stage to another. She begins as a woman in section one, lacking sexual confidence and experience. This is exacerbated by her traumatic discovery of her husband having sex with men and her compliance to normative social ascriptions regarding women's sexual passivity:

> sex just didn't do it for me. . . . As for oral sex [giving and receiving], what on earth were they thinking there? That was just hideous. . . . As for masturbating, no thank you. I'd rather go without altogether than ever touch myself like that down there. . . . Then there was the horror of my husband masturbating. . . . I thought I was happy living in my naive, little unsexed world (2012: 89).

After the discovery of her husband's sexual affairs with men, she gradually becomes one of the women in the second section in this chapter where their partners have been the *nepantleros* (Anzaldua, 2002), opening up negotiations for their female sexual journeys and various ways of border-living as a sexually self-ascriptive woman. With his encouragement and the environment of love and liberation she finds herself at first reluctantly within, she begins to explore her sexuality and seeks to educate herself away from her fears and disgust with sexual pleasures:

> When Andrew explained to me that there were strap-on dildos that I could wear to perform like a man, I was mortified. . . . It was many months after Andrew had asked me about getting a strap-on dildo that I decided it was time to conquer my fear. . . . the things you do for love. . . . It truly was a horrible experience. Buying it was one thing, wearing it was another (2012: 142–143).

> Our sex life was improving as I was finally beginning to feel comfortable with making love to Andrew using my imitation penis without the full-blown guilt afterward . . . I still had this dreaded feeling when it came to using any other toys. . . . I was sick of my ridiculous behaviour and decided to overcome this anti-toy dilemma of mine with a great idea. I'd heard of a sensuality boutique in Melbourne . . . that specialised in creating a comfortable environment for women to shop in for adult toys. I'd decided to ask them if I could work there as a sales assistant for a couple of hours a week free of charge so that I could conquer my fear of adult toys (2012: 151).

> I loved what was happening to me. I was feeling different. Every night at home I was initiating sexual interludes with my husband. I was stunned by how aroused and wet I always was or could become quite quickly. . . . everyday, ordinary

people that came to buy some extraordinary toys, magazines or other products, I discovered just how normal using sex toys was. It had all been demystified (2012: 153–152).

Finally she arrives at a stage where she could easily be one of the women in the third section of this chapter: a queer heterofeminist actively seeking sexual pleasure and subverting sex/gender norms with her partner. She has now become the "stranger" questioning the unquestionable social rules of women's heterosexuality. Hence, she is also a "homecomer," agentically coming home to her sexual desires and possibilities:

> I would rush home, eager to get my hands on my husband. . . . I even asked him to start masturbating in front of me. . . . I knew I could do anything with my husband when I started pleasuring myself in front of him. . . . Then it hit me, in a nice gentle kind of way this time—the realization that I had accomplished the goal I had set for myself in the first place . . . I was a liberated woman, a sexually liberated woman (2012: 156–158).

> I had come across a cruising club in Melbourne that opened its doors once a month for a women's only night. Jackpot! What a brilliant way to get a look at the real goings on behind closed doors. I had to go and check it out. Andrew thought it was a brilliant idea . . . experience the sensation of being with a woman . . . This was where the men played hard core. . . . For the first time in nearly twelve years I understood what it was like for a man wanting to have sex with a man purely for the sexual pleasure of it (2012: 179–189).

Part II

THE JOURNEYS

Chapter 5

"Starting Out Knowing"

Negotiating the Beginning of the Relationship

> When you're starting out knowing your partner's bisexual, it's so different to the stereotypes of discovering it much later through getting a sexual disease or checking his gay porn on the computer or going through his text messages. What about those of us who knew from the start and jumped for joy about it? What about those of us who didn't care, or were bi ourselves? (Lilith)

Like Lilith, many women in our research were aware of their partner's bisexuality before the relationship or from its early days. They believed this had a major influence on what types of tensions, if any, were experienced and how they were addressed by both the women and their partners. Our findings greatly support existing studies which confirm that, overall, "starting out knowing," or early communication and disclosure, tend to prevent more distressful situations further along in the relationship (see Kays & Yarhouse, 2010; Yarhouse et al. 2003). Pearcey & Olson (2009) found that approximately 11% of heterosexual women in their study knew of their partners' gay or bisexual tendencies prior to the marriage or partnership, and the two most important factors in the decision to marry or partner related to the treatment they received from these men in addition to the attitudes and values these men portrayed. Many women in previous research suggested that they simply accepted the bisexuality as part of their partner's persona (see Auerback & Moser, 1987; Miller et al. 2007). Indeed, part of the persona they respected and were drawn to in their partners was their total disclosure, as this was evidence of them being "politically committed bisexual men, who saw it as important in making a statement about who they were and the kind of lifestyle they wish to have" (Boulton & Fitzpatrick, 1993: 93). In Li et al.'s (2013) study, bisexual participants agreed that support from a partner specifically for bisexual identity has a positive impact on one's mental health.

There have been very few films in which a woman expresses her "break with traditional patriarchy by knowingly becoming involved with a bisexual male. Even fewer in which a woman does this without simultaneously courting humiliation, disaster and death" (Vicari, 2011: 220). For example, *Victim* (1961) has the bisexual husband being blackmailed over his affair with a young man who suicides. Although strongly challenging the criminalization and public stigmatization of homosexuality in the 1960s, the wife, Laura, is portrayed as experiencing disillusionment and disappointment that his promise to refrain from sex with men hasn't been upheld: "I was young and conceited I suppose. I thought marriage would make you content. I was wrong. That impulse is still there." Melville replies, "There hasn't been a day that I haven't thanked God for you" to which she replies, "Melville, I'm not a lifeboat for you to cling to. I'm a woman, and I want to be loved for myself." When he decides to go public through the courts about the blackmail, "to draw attention to the faults in the existing law," he asks Laura to leave: "I can just get through it to the end if I know you're not here to face the final humiliations . . . If you can bear to [come back] afterwards when it's all over . . . I'm going to need you so desperately." Throughout the film, the emphasis has been on her love for him, their honesty in his bisexuality before marriage, and we are left at the end of the film with the feeling Laura will return: "I feel very strong." Melville asks: "Strong enough?" to which she replies "I think so" before she walks out.

Another film, *De-Lovely* (2004), is also significant because after a cinematic history of married bisexual men being portrayed as deceitful adulterers, this Cole Porter biopic is the first mainstream film in which a bisexual man actually tells his wife, before they are married, about his intention to keep having relationships with men. Nevertheless, some of the situations faced in the film have his wife confronting her own initial acceptance as she experiences societal humiliation, thereby asking him to maintain his discretion in order to respect her public standing as his wife. A more recent film, *Mysteries of Pittsburgh* (2008), has a girlfriend knowing and accepting her partner is bisexual, but not accepting his cheating.

Some personal written accounts are exploring women who knowingly entered into relationships with bisexual men. In his autobiography, Beye talks about the shared sense of social outsiderhood due to their disruption of gendernormative and heteronormative sexual codes:

> If I was the town's notorious cock-sucker, she had to contend with her reputation as an easy lay. . . . she was willing to give the idea of marriage—ludicrous, crazy as it was—a try, so long as I passed the test in the basics (2012: 89–90).

"Humiliation, disaster and death" (Vicari, 2011: 220) are thus themes most prevalent in both fictional and nonfictional accounts of women entering relationships with men who they know are bisexual. In her biography of her father, Alicia Abbott traces the journey of the relationship between her father and mother, beginning when they met at a party "and [when] my father told my mother he was bisexual, she answered, 'That means you can love all of humanity instead of just half of it'" (2013: 3). She explains how her mother

> never got hung up on his boy crushes like his other girlfriends had. . . . my mother picked out the young men my father could never attract on his own. Men who'd never consider a gay encounter but who'd be up for a drunken three-way. . . . Sometimes my mum would dress in men's clothing when they went out. Dad said she made a cute boy. . . . my mum suggested they marry. "Landlords won't hassle us so much," she reasoned. "We'll be able to stock the kitchen and house with wedding presents, my parents will give us more money. Other than that, our life won't really change." (2013: 4).

But only a few months after their wedding, "their life did change":

> my mum seemed to grow restless and bored with the gay scene, just as my dad was growing bored with the domestic scene at home. Four months into the marriage, my father learned about a disturbance in New York's Greenwich Village, which was The Stonewall (2013: 5).

This precipitates his growing desire to immerse himself in gay activism and gay lifestyles in places such as San Francisco. Her father begins to describe life with his wife and his daughter as "a tired duty which rotted into an unbearable feeling of being trapped, oppressed and sucked dry" (2013: 14).

In his novel, *The Two Hotel Francforts,* Leavitt (2013) presents two couples during World War Two. They are in transit in Portugal after fleeing France and waiting for a ship to New York when the male partners begin a sexual relationship. Iris advises the protagonist not to tell his wife Jolene about the relationship between him and her husband: "My husband and I have no secrets from each other . . . it's you who's doing the thing that will surely kill her" (2013: 136). She explains why she won't "forbid" him from seeing Edward: "I'm not stupid, I know my own limits" (2013: 137). She also explains the internal machinations of the relationship:

> I don't know what he told you about the men, it's true that I slept with them but not, as he seems to have convinced himself, because I wanted to, it was because he wanted me to, which isn't to say there weren't a few times when I thought, "Iris, you might as well enjoy yourself, you deserve to" . . . Have you ever noticed that when we're walking down the street, the four of us, and

it's too narrow to go two abreast, I always walk behind Edward? Well, do you know why? It's because if I went ahead of him there'd be the chance that when I turned my head he'd be gone. . . . I love him, I can't bear the idea of losing him no matter what it costs me. I'm not what I appear, I'm not indomitable, if anything, I'm weak, embarrassingly weak (2013: 138-139).

Our research showed that even if "starting out knowing," there were often issues that surfaced or remained that required addressing. Thus, equating knowing, initial or early disclosure as completely or significantly reducing stresses or tensions is a simplistic conclusion that could create problems, particularly if it constructs a false assumption that all will be well and discounts the power of both external and internal factors that impact on the health of the relationship. Indeed, this can be compared to straight couples or gay couples who begin relationships that appear to be highly compatible, only to find that tensions and stressors surface later. What is required is an awareness of the contexts and various factors that came into play at the beginning of the relationship, as well as along the way. For example, Pearcey & Olson (2009) found that by the time they had collected their survey data with women partners, and despite early disclosure and acceptance, 46% of the married respondents had divorced, 17% remained married, and 12% were legally separated.

In this chapter, I explore the various contexts and consequences of initial or early disclosure on women and their bisexual partners. Five major themes became apparent:

1. Many women *initiated their partner's disclosure* with their own honesty and communication about their own bisexuality, or their openness toward nonheteronormative relationship and family forms such as polyamory.
2. Many women were *actively seeking and/or attracted to bisexual men* and thereby did not consider a man's bisexuality as something to be problematized or pathologized.
3. Many women entered into the relationship because they had been in previously dysfunctional heteromonogamist relationships with men who displayed heteropatriarchal constructions of masculinity. Therefore, they *welcomed the differences in the performances of masculinity and the relationship options* their bisexual partners brought into the relationships.
4. Many women had been 'warned' by their partners of their bisexuality before the relationship began, or in its early days, but this disclosure was not taken seriously, or its potential ramifications misunderstood or ignored. Therefore, as the years unfolded, *problems arose* that had not been addressed, had not been carefully negotiated, or had not been expected. These difficulties created distress, required much work, and *led to the possible cessation of the relationship*.

5. Many women had been told by their partners of their bisexuality before the relationship began, or in its early days and, as the years unfolded, *issues did arise that required further negotiation, which led to a greater openness and flourishing of the relationship.*

Overall, however, it is important to state at this point that not one woman whose partner had disclosed his bisexuality at the beginning or in the early days of the relationship regretted or resented having been told so early. They were often relieved and thankful and, in spite of the problematic situations they faced later, usually maintained strong respect and affection for their partners for not having deceived them. Indeed, where the relationships flourished and grew richer, the women directly attributed this to the initial laying of a foundation of honesty and communication upon which they could build a stronger relationship.

"IT JUST BECOMES PART OF THE FABRIC OF YOUR RELATIONSHIP"

Right from the beginning I think we both had a sense that we were from diverse sexualities. . . . I was so attracted to him, and so I told him then he told me that he'd been attracted to me and hadn't planned to do anything about it. So, yeah, I very much initiated our coming together and we've both been really honest about what we bring to the relationship and what we want from it. I think that it's quite different to start a relationship with those sorts of issues being on the table than to have them perhaps raised later on, because it just becomes part of the fabric of your relationship. (Jude)

Several women in the research initiated the disclosure of their partner's bisexuality, and often initiated the relationship and what they wanted from the relationship by disclosing their own sexual and relationship histories. Indeed, women like Jude spoke of their partners' initial hesitation to become involved with a new woman due to their own histories of having hurt women in the past by either disclosure or deception. Thus, they had internalized external social messages about the inevitable failure of any relationship with a woman:

I was like, "I'm divorced, I'm bi, I've gone through this and this and this.". . . I picked him up. I took him home. And a week into it, I said, "Can we have this relationship? . . . Let's just be truthful with each other, respect each other." (Temptress)

He was a good country bumpkin and he didn't experiment very far at that time and then when we met up and I told him of the sorts of things I was doing, as

I was with students and musicians and people slept with everyone and there weren't labels around . . . he felt that he actually wanted to take up some of those opportunities. (Raven)

Sometimes, the women were focused on finding male friends with whom to disclose their own bisexuality. It was only after this had occurred that they found the men also had their own bisexual desires and/or histories to disclose. This could lead to increasing depth and intimacy in the relationship:

> He actually was renting a place, and he was comfortable with having two lesbians living together with him . . . And because he was pretty open about it, I decided, "Okay, there's something I've got to tell you" and so came out, . . . he started to realize, too, that, well, yeah, he kind of liked being with a man too. . . . And so that's how we started to explore our sexuality together. (Christine)

> When we first met, we didn't like each other because he was working far too many hours and when he's a stressed little puppy he's not a very nice sort of person, especially when he's playing the gay boy, and because he'd just come out of a relationship with this other guy. . . . we got together and we really just needed to talk to each other a lot, because we realized, "Hang on, this is someone I can have a relationship with, a friendship, whatever." And I'd had a string of male partners who I hadn't really been able to express the bisexual side with. . . . We're lucky in that we entered into our long-term life relationship knowing what the situation was. We haven't had the rules changed. (Kirsten)

> I am not monogamous, I don't intend to live in a nuclear family unit, I practice BDSM and that is a major part of my lifestyle both socially and in the bedroom . . . We actually met on the creation of a float for the Mardi Gras Parade. . . . I guess the thing that attracted us at the time was not just that we were both bisexual, but that we were also both kind of looking for different ways of living. (Lizz)

Other women who were heterosexual but wishing to explore polyamorous, nonmonogamous and other nonnormative relationships also spoke about disclosing their relationship needs to bisexual men with the view of developing nonnormative intimacies with them:

> I knew from the beginning that he was definitely also not the monogamous type. . . . He doesn't mind that I'm going out with someone else . . . And his primary relationship is with a woman. (Evelyn)

Some women were already in social contexts where they were meeting gay men, knowing that some of the men who "were gay" were actually bisexual. Within those social circles, there was conversation and flirtation with the idea of having a relationship with a bisexual man as it could be "interesting." Once some women became very aware of mutual attractions and closeness, they exercised control and felt empowered enough to ask for clarification of the current state of the relationship and what the future would hold for them:

> I went to gay clubs and I knew lots of Mark's friends were gay. I knew that he was bi. And one of my friends was very keen on him and she'd be saying that that could be quite interesting . . . Anyway, we got on really, really well, and I used to go out with him and his boyfriend and his boyfriend was a dancer and so he was performing at night sometimes, and Mark and I went to clubs and pubs and theatre but he kept on asking to come in for coffee, and he was very, very close to me . . . And I just decided one night that I should actually ask him whether he was interested in me because it seemed to be so obvious that he was, and he said no, the thought had never even crossed his mind so it was a really kind of embarrassing situation. So, I left it for about a week and then he said he thought that was quite a good idea, actually. And we went out with each other while his boyfriend was away overseas touring, and him and his boyfriend split up. . . . And eventually I said to him, "You know, I'm either going to move in with you or I'm going to go to America and see my ex-boyfriend and do other things. I'm not going to hang around here. Either you're serious about this or you're not," so I kind of pushed him into making a decision. (Sara)

Even if both partners were in socially and sexually alternative circles where bisexuality, polyamory and BDSM were approved, there could still be misunderstandings that required clarification. Indeed, like Sara suggested, it was often the women who instigated discussion and decision-making from their partners around these concerns in order not to have their emotions and other facets of their lives disrupted or derailed:

> Well, somebody had organized a bi and poly social gathering, evening of drinks. We [male partner and I] started going out after that, probably on a weekly basis. It was a gradual process . . . for both him and for me it was a huge decision, because I have two children, so I just don't have myself to consider . . . and so I had to know where I stood and I said to him, "I want to start this relationship with complete understanding of each other. You tell me everything, and I'll tell you everything." He told me he had a BDSM mistress, which was fine by me, and it slowly became more apparent it wasn't just the BDSM, it was for a relationship. So, that's something I had to think about and deal with. She's about 50. She's a very intelligent woman. And she's really nice. I'm friends with her as well. (Suzette)

"I LOVE HIS GAY SIDE"

It was lust at first sight for me and I caught his eye. We clicked instantly and were lip locked by midnight. . . . I love his gay side and I love it when he plays or simply spends time with his gay friends. We don't take each other for granted and I know the joy of loving another human completely. We are the best of friends, always . . . I think it has been beneficial that we came out so early on to each other because it set a level of honesty and trust for us, and it is just a normal part of our relationship. (Shelley)

Several women in our research were specifically seeking a bisexual man for a relationship, or were open to relationships with bisexual men. They believed being bisexual, or as Shelley says, having "a gay side" was a positive attribute of their personality and partnering:

His bisexuality is one of the components that make him the man I fell deeply in love with when we were in our early twenties and through these 40 years, there was no way I was going to leave him unless I was unhappy with him. (Alice)

The active seeking or total endorsement of a bisexual man was enhanced by observing potential partners' sexualities and participating in their sociosexual behaviors and cultures before or early in the relationship:

I met him on the dance floor at a gay rave. We just turned around and bumped into each other. He was with a whole lot of guys and they had their shirts off and looked to be in that gay scene. So I was quite surprised that he showed any interest in me. . . . But we just kind of clicked. We moved in together a few months later after going to lots of parties together. (Rachel)

He was Mr. Fucking Insanely Good Looking, the absolute darling of the gay scene, but he'd been gay from such a young age, from 17 to when I met him at 28 and he'd been in a relationship with another man for 10 years, and he wanted to have sex with women, because he felt like he never gave heterosexuality a chance. . . . I can't even remember how we became lovers. We were just very, very close and one night got really trashed and slept with each other. (Sascha)

For Simone, this observation and participation was played out via online profiles and chats, wherein they immediately displayed the content of their offline lives:

We met online in an over 40's chat room and he was looking for a relationship with an older woman. We met, he came up the Friday for a cup of coffee, stayed for the weekend, and we've been together ever since. And the reason why we were so connected, both of us had a heavy spiritual, creative and sensual/sexual content in our profile. We've both had complicated relationships in the past, both of us let us be the people that we are, there's a total commitment to each other . . . We also meditate together to have some tantric practices that brings us closer. . . . We watch each other's backs. He's my supporter, I'm his. We complement each other. He's a very laid back kind of person, I'm this intense doer. We slot in, we're like jigsaw puzzle pieces. (Simone)

"I WAS NOT HAPPY WITH MEN"

The big thing for me was that I was not happy with men. Like, I wanted to be in a relationship but it's sort of like, you'd meet a guy and he'd want to have sex and if they wanted it, well, okay, there you go. And, consequently, I thought it [the sex] was okay, but it was never really 100% for me . . . the thing that I absolutely loved about Darren was that when I met him and we clicked and we became more and more intimate, he didn't want to have sex. There was no pressure there. He was happy just to hold my hand. He was happy just for a peck on the cheek, for a cuddle. . . . I kind of had suspicions and a lot of the people we were hanging out with thought he was gay . . . He thought he was doing such a good job of hiding it, too, which is really funny and I don't think I really cared either. I mean, he was a wonderful guy. . . . We actually had a conversation about him seeing men before we got engaged, and I was the only woman he'd ever been with. It was all very slow. It all happened as and when he was ready and by then I think I was well and truly ready. (Sherry)

Sherry provides an example of women who spoke about not wanting a man who pressured them to have unwanted or unsatisfying sex, and took their time to develop strong intimate and emotional connections. Continuing the two previous themes of women in relationships with bisexual men because of wanting a nonheteronormative life and/or a nonheteropatriarchal partner, many women clearly stated that they discussed their partner's bisexuality at the beginning of a relationship as a way of avoiding the distress of a dysfunctional relationship with a heterosexual man, and avoiding a mainstream monogamous life that they had already been through:

After the death of my son and the break-up of my relationship I fell into a million pieces and had a nervous breakdown. My partner picked up every one of those pieces and put them back together, patiently and slowly. (Tamara)

We were in Papua New Guinea. I was struggling to unshackle myself from a very unhappy marriage, and my present partner could see that I was unhappy and gradually got my trust until we became lovers . . . knowing that he was bisexual, knowing that he was having sex with men. (Jolene)

Thus, with a bisexual husband came the promise, which was kept or otherwise, of a far more fulfilling, equitable and exploratory life. Sometimes, as in the case of Helena it was the promise of a more "exotic" life:

> I met my husband through this [Islamic] spiritual exercise, and so he was a bit of a relief . . . there was just this feeling of a certain kind of security. . . . just this sort of caring and the laughter and the fun, and he'd ring me up at midnight and say, "I'm off to the supermarket. Do you want to come?" or, "Let's walk through the park." . . . this acknowledgement that I was worth having around, . . . and he had all the airs and graces of someone who, you know, knew how to do it and had the wherewithal to do it. . . . yeah, [travelling and living in Asia] we had drivers and he had a wonderful house full of antiques and Afghan hounds and, you know, all the props. (Helena)

Nina's example is of a woman who did not consider sex to be the most significant facet of a relationship and enjoyed the other dimensions of what she shared with her partner:

> I was actually in the relationship for a couple of months and still didn't realize he was gay until he actually rang me one morning and was very distressed on the phone. He kept saying, "Look, I'm gay. This is going nowhere." And I said, "So what? What do you want me to do about it?" It didn't worry me. In fact there were things that we shared on an emotional level that I've never shared with any man before. I wasn't really fussed one way or the other because I'd never actually enjoyed sex with my ex-husband. (Nina)

Heterosexual women already living polyamorous or nonmonogamous lives, or wanting a more casual relationship, also spoke about wanting a bisexual man as a partner to avoid some of the heteronormative, misogynist and patriarchal expectations and performances of previous men:

> Most of the guys I met before my bi partner were heterosexual, they were cheating on their wives, and I didn't want to buy into that, . . . And just things like boundaries. Safe sex all the time . . . But a lot of the straight guys I met couldn't handle this stuff. (Naomi)

> I had come out of a messy relationship, my ex-husband had been very volatile. I thought Lew was very cute and very young so thought this would just be some fun but three weeks later the "L word" [Love]came up but I was embroiled in sale of house, running a business, raising my kids, and just wanted a playmate but 11 years later, we're still together. I feel very lucky. (Leanne)

"I SORT OF THOUGHT, WELL, IT'S OKAY, IT'LL WORK OUT"

> Well, we were engaged, and I knew there was no way he was going to be faithful to me. . . . I sort of thought, "Well, it's okay, it'll work out." . . . But, I guess I just didn't realize. (Helena)

Several women like Helena discussed how their partners' early disclosure about their bisexuality meant they had initially believed they would be able to negotiate and navigate their way through any concern, only to find that the reality of the situation led to overwhelming complexities. Other women had believed there would be no ramifications but later could not comprehend their ignorance over such matters:

> We met each other when I was about 15 and Anton was 16, and got married when we were about 22, and we were married for about 6 years. I thought what an absolute dickhead getting yourself into this situation. And it's not like Anton had never told me, but he said, "No, no, I still love you and I still want to get married and have children." I think at the time that was what he really wanted, probably because he couldn't ever imagine living another life then either, because it was repressed, a very small place we grew up in. (Jess)

Other women believed their partners when they were told their same-sex relationships were a "*thing of the past*" and wouldn't reoccur, even if, as Yvonne explained, they knew that their partners' past relationships with women had broken up because of ongoing deception over same-sex relationships:

> It was probably two months in I reckon and he said as a young teenager, he used to keep these notebooks to write absolutely everything in them and he goes, "Oh, I just need to show you something" and he pulls out this wad of notebooks and he's turned to one and shown me this thing like when he went and gave head, just talking about experiences that he'd had with guys, and they were really graphic and I was like, "Okay, what's the story?" He goes, "Oh, it's just stuff that I did when I was younger," and I was thinking, "Okay, well, everybody experiments," and it didn't worry me too much at the time . . . and he was like, "You can leave me now if you want." But I must say, honestly, I was under the impression that he didn't really do that stuff any more. Well, he told me that he had still sort of done it. That was part of the reason why his marriage had separated . . . . So, I was a little bit ignorant. A little bit naïve I think the word is. (Yvonne)

Barb related how her partner, Andrew, had told her of his early experiences with other men and how she had believed she would be able to handle any eventuality as she was "very open sexually," something her partner had also admired in her.

> He said at the time, "I don't know where this will lead," and all along he's said, "I feel I'm bisexual." . . . When we met, I would think of myself as being very open sexually and Andrew says that about me too . . . And we were obviously

very young and I was very happy to have sex with him . . . And he used to say then, "You are so uninhibited about sex" and he'd tell me all these tales of girls he'd been with who weren't uninhibited about sex, and pretty soon after we started going out together, he told me of a few homosexual experiences he'd had in the form of him being about 13 or 14, going to stay at a friend's house in the country, and the friend's dad came into Andrew in the night, and Andrew woke up and he was fellating him, and Andrew, when he told me, didn't say, "Oh, it was awful" or "It was disturbing" . . . Then also he referred to something that happened once when he was hitchhiking. . . . I think a guy picked him up and suggested that Andrew give him head. And I've never been quite sure about whether the guy forced him or Andrew just did it . . . and once again, even though no other guys I'd ever talked to had told me anything like that, I don't remember, "Oh, that's awful" or "I wonder if he's gay or bisexual." I don't know why, but I just accepted that. (Barb)

The women would also consider the quality of their relationship, indeed the quality of the partner, to be evidence of how any issue regarding his bisexuality would be insignificant or easily managed: "I just thought, 'Well here's this guy who's a great lover, and he's choosing to be with me now and I'm female, so to me there is no issue'" (Barb). Even as behaviors and suspicions began to surface during the relationship, women would explain them away and feel proud of their ongoing openness. Indeed, they began to deny the fact that their partners had told them of their attractions and experiences with men:

In a way I look back and I mean it's a long time to be together, 26 years and I think well maybe I did not want to face it [his bisexuality]. . . . through the Internet he joined a bi men's group and he just said to me, "I've joined a men's group." And I said, "That's great." I mean, I go away for weekends with girls but I remember my friends were going, "He's joined a men's group? Who does that?" and I'm saying "Why not, what's the problem with that?" (Barb)

Hence, the common situation of their partners beginning to have affairs with men and eventually disclosing these would occur within these relationships. This means there had been two times of disclosure: one at the beginning of the relationship which had been discounted or rationalized away; and one later in the relationship when the partner discloses his ongoing secret intimacies with men. Often, it felt as if the disclosure had occurred for the first time, replete with deception and hurt:

He looks back and says that he would dream about men and he liked to look at pictures of guys and that he's tried to repress it or tried to think, "Well, I can just jerk off to a picture of a guy, and that will be all right, I don't need to actually have sex," but it got harder and harder for him to keep a lid on that . . . he just blurted out, "I can no longer hide my feelings about men," and then it was like, snap, he was his old self again, and he hugged me and I said to him, "It's an enormous relief to me to know that that's what it is," and he said at that time, "I don't want to leave you, I love what we've got but I've been having sex with men for two years. I will do that until the day I die. I know there's no way I can go back." (Barb)

Yes, I decided to stay on and just see how things would go . . . And then one Friday night we were going out after work, and so I said, "Oh, I'll go home and get you some clothes to get changed in and then come in and pick you up." And so I went to his place and on his bedside table, right near the cupboard was this receipt and it's for a box of condoms and it's like, "Hang on a minute, I'm on the pill now. What are you buying condoms for?" And I absolutely lost it and that's when he said to me that he'd still been going to the beats, and I was absolutely devastated. (Yvonne)

Sometimes the women felt they had not been told about the depth of sexual intimacy their partners were engaging in with other men. Thus, there was a feeling of deception and degradation of their trust and relationship based on a continuum of sexual intimacy that their partners were not always clear about. Helena talked about three "discoveries" that convinced her that her husband was not being honest about the quantity and depth of his relationships with other men. The discoveries, such as the third one for Helena being a "gay porn publication," also discomfited women as it made them aware that they were not as comfortable with their partner's bisexuality as they thought they were:

A letter came. I thought it was from a dear friend, an older lady, and I opened it, assuming it was to us, and it was from this guy, and so I was pretty blown away by this, and confronted him. . . . He was devastated, obviously, that by now, I'd had this information because he said he'd never had this sort of full-on sort of sexual contact, [but] the letter said, "I miss not seeing you in the shower." So, it obviously wasn't chats over cups of tea and cucumber sandwiches . . . I was cleaning out his cupboard and I found a box of condoms that was open and there were three left . . . He said, "Oh, I'd forgotten about that. It was a joke." Somebody had given them to him. . . . Then, the next time I was in his clothing sorting it out, and there was a plastic bag with a book in it, and turns out it's quite a beautifully photographed gay porn publication. . . . and he said, "This guy was going back to Indonesia and he didn't want to take it because customs is pretty heavy duty there." And I thought, "Fuck, what's this guy doing?" (Helena)

Often the second disclosure revealed the shame and other reasons that had led to the secrecy of the same-sex intimacies in ways that had not been discussed in the first disclosure, where the discourse of 'it'll be alright' or 'it will pass,' or being caught in the throes of New Relationship Energy (NRE) or lust, had foreclosed or undermined the importance of having deeper discussions regarding the shifting temporal contexts of the same-sex attractions, such as past and present experiences and feelings, and potential ramifications for the future. The second disclosure also often precipitated major negative shifts in the relationship even if it had temporarily appeared to relieve the tensions of deception. This is because the second disclosure often occurred at a major turning point in a man's life in regard to how much and how often he would pursue his relationships with other men, thereby meaning he was also instigating shifts in his relationship with his female partner that she would have to confront in ways that hadn't been warranted before. Thus, what also often began to seep in to a relationship was a sense of ambiguity, a not knowing, even though the relationship had begun within a framework of clarity and knowing. This sense of other lives and loves lurking around the relationship often became too much to bear:

> he's going out and having sex with other men, there's an increased danger – it sounds awful—of him meeting someone he will really click with, . . . Now, he says it's just sex, but because I am such an emotional, romantic sort of person, I suppose it's hard for me to wrap my head around that you could go on for years and years with these people not meaning any more to you . . . . My husband is just this enigma, he's got some other agenda going on. I've tried to get him to be honest with me, but he won't. I think because he feels then he's pinned down. (Barb)

Sometimes, this insecurity was realized where a partner did fall in love with another man to the point of wanting to leave the relationship, despite the depth of honesty and love, and the negotiations of nonmonogamy and polyamory:

> He went away [with his male partner] and he wrote to me, "Oh, God, I just love him, I'm totally committed," and I knew it. They had been always completely open about their situation, and loved one another. In fact, they brought tears to my eyes, the way they cared about one another. (Helena)

Shifting contexts such as geographical locations and work situations, and the opportunities afforded by these new circumstances, often precipitated events that led to the second disclosure. At this point, both of the partners were more prepared and aware of the kinds of concerns that needed to have been discussed years before, as it now proved too late. When work transfers led Jess and her partner to Sydney, feelings surfaced which eventually led to the end of their marriage:

Coming to Sydney was a big turning point in our relationship... [At first] we had a fantastic, probably the best part of our relationship, the most care-free, the most enjoyable, and I think it's, you know, leaving home and starting out on your own and being who you want to be without any pressure from family... Met some gay people during that time who we became quite good friends with, which I think was important in Anton's side of things. You see people living in a whole lot of different ways... I think that was what kind of slapped Anton in the face.... it brought all these feelings to the surface. (Jess)

The combination of moving to a big city and having a partner disclose his wanting to come out and end the marriage also opened Jess's eyes to her own sense of self. It made her have to "grow up" in regard to how she was going to live her life, and what she wished to maintain of her connection to her partner:

I was pregnant at the time.... If I knew where he was at and what he was thinking, at least I could make my own decisions on what to do. Sometimes I felt sorry for me, and I just didn't want to know what was going on... I think the biggest thing for me was the fact that the nest that I had built just fell out of the tree. Everything I thought that I had put into life that would get me through the long-term all of a sudden wasn't there, and that's because I was putting my efforts into Anton and not into me. And, much as it's a horrible way to learn a lesson, I'm really, really, glad that I learnt that lesson at 30 and not 50 or 60. (Jess)

Part of Jess's acceptance was feeling grateful that he had been honest enough to tell her early so that she had years to develop her own life, cultivate a friendship with him based on his honesty and communication, and have a child together. Ultimately, Jess believes the shift in geographical, economic and sociocultural location had basically "fast-tracked" what she believed was inevitable:

I think it would have taken longer to get to the same outcome. Fast-tracked it all. And I think that's just because it's [Sydney] such a gay city and because Anton knew on the inside how he was, he would have gravitated towards that anyway. (Jess)

In some situations, the women would "freak out" upon early disclosure. However, blaming their adverse reactions on ignorance, they decided to continue in the relationship:

I think it was about 3 months after the relationship started when he told me and my reaction was to just freak out because I had never heard of somebody liking both sexes. So I felt like I had lived a very sheltered life... I did [want to stay together] because I thought there seemed to be such a strong connection so I thought this guy really loves me because he has turned around and said, "I've been such an idiot and I have feelings for you." (Maz)

Even if the bisexuality had been accepted, if this was followed by early disclosure of relationship needs such as nonmonogamy which were directly in contrast to the value of monogamy the women had, some women still persisted with the relationship. This was despite potentially destructive patterns already being set up, patterns which would eventually destroy the relationship and almost destroy the woman:

> Monogamy didn't really get discussed until another 3 months to the engagement . . . . he voiced what he wanted, so it was like it was his journey and I was just there to witness it. He wanted to not have a monogamous relationship, and that was pretty devastating. I actually indulged it, and we had a few experiences, which at the time it was good, it made me grow but I realised I still didn't want it . . . we nearly split up [around our first anniversary] and that was over the open relationship issues, it just became such a huge thing for him that it just seemed to overtake and he just couldn't live like we were anymore. . . . During the crap couple of months, I attempted suicide, the possibility of losing my husband was just unbearable. My whole world had become focused on him. I also started having an affair with my best friend's husband. (Maz)

Eventually, Maz's husband "initiated the separation," not for a man, but for another woman who was also bisexual and shared his values: "he has what he wants basically."

Some women were also aware that their partner's previous relationships with women had ended over their relationships with men, but felt that establishing rules for nonmonogamy would prevent their own relationship from breaking down:

> His wife had left him thinking he would leave her for another man eventually, and at that time, he was in a fairly casual sort of relationship with a guy, but enough so that they were going overseas together, having holidays together. . . . So, we met, and initially there was fairly open and frank discussion about sexual relationships, and there was no hiding the fact that he liked guys and he'd had relationships with guys, and expected to continue to do that, but the initial explanation was that if there was a partner that he particularly liked then it was a matter of not just one person, but that we share that relationship. Initially, I had no problems if he wanted to do that. (Nicole)

Once again, shifting circumstances such as Nicole no longer wanting to continue with the agreement on nonmonogamy, external factors such as "the AIDS period" where her male partner did not want to involve her in any threesome due to the risk of spreading HIV to her, and the usual normative shifts in life, led to the deterioration of the relationship. Nevertheless, Nicole remains married to her partner:

> Everybody says "You're mad, leave him." It's just that I do see a lot of people who do leave their marriages and who are by themselves, and mostly coping okay but mostly no happier or sadder than I am. So I guess I can't think of a good enough reason to leave. (Nicole)

Mitigating circumstances and lack of agreement over other issues such as whether to have children and the amount of attention and energy the partner required for external partners, were issues which prevented a short-term relationship, based on early disclosure and complete understanding in regard to bisexuality and nonmonogamy, from ever developing into a long-term relationship:

> I was in my mid-thirties when we had a relationship and I wanted to settle down and have a child and he wanted to have a child as well, but he knew that he couldn't make that emotional commitment. . . . If I had been able to accept a more relaxed framework around a relationship then it would have worked. At the same time he had a boyfriend who was HIV-positive, they weren't having sex anymore, but he was playing the father role. So he'd do things like borrow my spare mattress for his lover to sleep on the floor . . . . The lover would be very jealous of me, there were a lot of mixed messages and my partner didn't want to end his relationship with his boyfriend because he was going through so much. I could really understand his situation. It was a very traumatic time . . . . There was a whole lot of unclarity. (Nirupa)

"IT'S JUST PART OF THE SCENERY NOW"

> He still has casual sex with guys. . . . and I have no doubt whatsoever that he will come home. He's always been fairly fickle I think where guys are concerned and no one has lasted sexually longer than 2 or 3 months . . . it's just part of the scenery now. (Sherry)

Sherry explains how they have reached a point of balance where her partner's bisexuality is "just part of the scenery," based partly on having had the history of seeing and understanding her partner's particularities when it comes to his relationships and intimacies with men. Thus, Sherry feels she can speak from a place of lived experience and proven reality, rather than a place of ignorant fear and speculation of the future. Many women in our research talked about the ongoing negotiations and/or concerns that arose which required sorting. Nevertheless, like Sherry, they went on to establish long-term, flourishing and fulfilling relationships, where the bisexuality of the partner was just a component of the relationship, and usually a positive one. For example, Brenda's story follows the trends in previous stories except that being together was the unalterable bottom line; and honesty, communication and negotiation, established as ground rules from the beginning of the relationship, were adhered to throughout. These factors led to a marriage that lasted 50 years until Edward's death:

> I didn't know anything about homosexuality at all . . . We went out together and then when I showed any affection to him he said, "No." I called him "Darling" and he said, "No, no, don't ever do that again." . . . We got engaged and then he kept saying, "There's something I have to tell you." . . . And I couldn't work out what it was. And he kept sort of putting it off . . . And I went to work one day and a doctor said, "Oh, that Edward, he was wandering around someone's block in the middle of the night and they got the police out, he's gay," and I thought, "What is he talking about, he's a big mouth." So I didn't say anything. And then Edward told me. I said, "What does that mean?" So he said, "Well, look, I don't know whether it's going to stay with me" . . . he said he loved me so we had sex, and he then said, "Well, I don't know if we should get married," and I said, "Oh, well, perhaps we love each other enough, it'll go away." And he said, "Well, perhaps it will." . . . And we got married . . . when he was ever late home, I'd say to him, "Where have you been?" and he was very honest and he'd tell me if he met anyone. . . . Now, I must admit I don't know how I'd cope if I'd been married 20 years or more and then got told he'd been leading this double life. (Brenda)

Likewise, Sherry's story depicts a series of "ups and downs" despite "clicking" together:

> When I first met him I hated him. I thought he was flamboyant. He was outrageous. I thought he was arrogant. We met at church. We were both members of the choir . . . and actually, he didn't like me either. He thought I was stuck up, arrogant, reserved . . . But we ended up talking, and we clicked. Like, I could almost hear the click and I guess I knew then that this person was going to have a big impact upon my life. It was far and away the most comfortable and most I'd enjoyed being with someone ever. It was like coming home. . . . . He had told me he felt like this for men and that he would never ever do it again. And I believed him, as you do I guess. It was amazing after a lot of heartache and a lot of tears and frustration and ups and downs and wondering just what the hell we'd done with our lives, we got married, and I honestly thought that being such a firm believer in serial monogamy that yeah, if I was the one he was with at the time, then he wouldn't do it with anyone else. (Sherry)

Sherry gave examples of the kinds of deceits that tested the quality and endurance of the relationship. These were also occurring within a framework of a gradual gaining of knowledge and insight into sexual diversity:

> It was just so different adjusting to being a wife and a mother and he would disappear at 10 o'clock at night and say, "Well, I'm going to go for a walk along the beach." I'd go, "Oh, I'd love that, let's go." He goes, "Oh, no, no, no. I need time by myself" and I'd be feeling really put out by this and eventually I just became really worried as he was doing this like two or three times a week and then he'd go shopping and he'd just disappear and you wouldn't see him. He'd say, "Oh, I've got to go to the toilet" and he'd go to the toilet for twenty minutes and it was like, "Oh, I needed to use a cubicle and there was a guy in there reading the paper." I had three years of that and then you get these phone calls and he would sort of like be whispering and huddling and laughing and, "Oh, yeah, that was just my friend from Sydney. We were talking about his boyfriend." I'd say, "Oh, yeah, okay, no problems." And one day we saw a show called "Sex Genes." We discussed the possibility of homosexuality being hereditary and one of the studies in there was a guy who had almost the exact same background as Darren. He'd had the Catholic upbringing, he'd gone to Catholic boys schools, he was a very religious bloke. He married her very quickly. They had all these kids. They had a wonderful life and then about ten years later he just snapped. He couldn't take the strain anymore and he said, "Well, I'm really gay. I'm off and out of here. Bye." And they showed him in a gay bar somewhere shooting pool . . . I sat there thinking, "Holy, freak me out," because I was identifying on Darren's behalf. So I fronted him and I said, "Is this how you feel?" It took him a couple of days to say, "Yeah." (Sherry)

Hence, this discussion precipitated the second disclosure of his current attractions and uncertainty of what the future might bring if these attractions were not given vent. It also gave Sherry the opportunity to consider what she valued and could be flexible with. Thus, a time of experimentation followed within which they both tried different ways of staying in the relationship with various amounts of freedom:

> I thought, "Okay, well, I've been married for three years with two kids. I really love this guy. I want this to work. If it's going to take some of the pressure off him—and I know he loves me—then I don't have a problem with him going out and seeing other guys, because I know that it's me that he loves and I'm his wife. The others are just sex." It took a while for me to get my head around that. And it was incredible for eight months. He felt free, he felt happy, he was going out and about. And after a while, that wasn't enough for me. I needed reaffirmation that I was still 100% hunky dory attractive to other people and I said, "Well, if it's okay for you, then I want to be able to do it as well." So we tried that and he absolutely loathed every minute of it. But he wasn't going to

say anything because of what he was doing. He was just going to shut up and put up. But I didn't really like it anyway. I didn't want anyone else, I wanted him, and the sex was just a temporary thing anyway. An attempt to patch the inferiority thing. (Sherry)

A relocation to outer suburban Sydney from Darwin led to further sexual experimentation, exploration and tests of the endurance and feasibility of the relationship:

We were in Sydney maybe only six weeks and he choofed off to Mardi Gras and didn't come home for four days. He just rang and I was so insecure because I was living in a brand new place. I didn't know anyone and I was really afraid that he was going to run off and I'd never see him again. . . . So it was a very hard year. And my kids were getting older. I wanted to do more than just sit around home, and I went to college. He went out and pursued all the alternative relationships and all sorts of sex and that's when I had my relationship with a woman. It kind of ended when Darren decided he wanted to get back together again and have a family. Well, for me that was always going to be the end goal anyway, and at this point he'd had enough of the gay life. (Sherry)

Katie also talks about the early fears and questions she faced when her partner Joe came out. She acknowledges how many of those early fears and questions were due to mainstream misrepresentations of bisexual men, as well as mainstream assumptions about compulsory, rather than chosen, monogamy being essential to a relationship:

Joe's my first serious relationship . . . I met him when I was seventeen, which is really young. . . . when we first got together, as far as I knew, Joe identified as straight. I think it was about six months into the relationship, he talked about how occasionally he felt attracted to men... Nine months into the relationship, it all came to a head, and we actually broke up for a month, where he felt that he might be gay, and he needed to take some time out to sort out how he was feeling. . . . I had grown up with all those popular myths, that bisexual people were deviant, had over-developed sex drives, lah da da da da. So I think I realized that with my experience with Joe, immediately some of those myths were being broken down. . . . [and] I grew up with ideas of what a relationship between a man and a woman should be. . . . I think I assumed monogamy. We have, you know, decided on that, and maintained that, but I kind of realized that it's an assumption that I made. (Katie)

Indeed, Katie believes that being in a relationship with a bisexual man has taught her to grow through the questioning and erosion of these norms. In the early days after disclosure, particularly when Joe went to counseling and they broke up, she had reached the opposite point to where she began when he first disclosed: from the negative stereotypes that meant the relationship was doomed, to growing and understanding how misleading these stereotypes and assumptions were. Now she couldn't understand why a relationship with a bisexual man couldn't work:

> It's really very bizarre that someone's maleness or femaleness is just so crucial to people when they're choosing a partner, aside from compassion or sensitivity or common interests or anything. . . . when we broke up I couldn't quite see how his bisexuality meant that we couldn't be together. I was quite devastated. (Katie)

And like the other women, Katie agrees that early disclosure rather than years of deception and the likelihood of finding out through an STI, was a major factor that led to the relationship developing into something "really healthy and really positive." An important facet of early disclosure was that from the beginning, the woman had agency over what she would do or not do, accept or not accept, and this feeling of being empowered made all the difference:

> I think going into a relationship knowing someone identifies as bisexual you come from a position where you felt very in control and that you'd made a decision. . . . I think at every stage I really felt like I had an ability to leave, an ability to ask any question I wanted to and not be frightened of asking them, and knowing that the other person is going to answer any question. (Katie)

For some women, there was no early or later time of doubt or fear. It was more a journey of ongoing discovery, discussion and exploration they welcomed. Part of the comfort of undertaking this journey was that they were already part of social networks where sexual diversity and genderplay were considered fun and part of eroticism. What is also significant is the dominant role the woman could take in this "unfolding," by asking questions, setting up hypothetical scenarios for her partner to consider, and seeking and enjoying her equal pleasure throughout the journey:

> I didn't ask him about his sexuality at first, not until 2 months later, and Lew was very shy about it as unsure of the response. But then he got more and more comfortable and we both checked out guys. . . . but he had never experimented, he didn't classify himself as bi or anything like that. But if I took my nightie off which was all satin, he would find that quite erotic and he would put it on. Or we went to the gay clubs, and he thought the drag queens were quite erotic, . . . I guess we've always talked about a lot of the supposedly taboo things. I'm just curious anyway just by nature, I've worked in newspapers so

I have a journalistic type mind and so I always ask lots of completely random questions and I guess we just trusted each other enough to open up and I would say, "Oh did you get aroused by that?" and he'd say "Yeah," and I'd say "What do you think that means?" and he would say "Umm not sure" so it was just an unfolding over time. Throughout those discussions, I'd ask "How far would you go? Would you want to explore that?" and "Let's do that together." . . . he found a house share and the guy who owned the house was a gay guy so there was an incident between them then. He told me it may happen and straight after it happened he rang me and we talked at length about it. (Sherry)

For some women, the assumption after early disclosure was that the relationship would never be more than friendship. Once the intensity of the feelings between them was acknowledged and led to a more serious relationship, some women would begin to experience the "fears and insecurities" that needed to be worked through:

When he told me that he was bisexual, I didn't care, we were just friends, and then one night all of a sudden he said he wanted to kiss me but he thought it would ruin the relationship and then we sort of talked about it for a minute and we kissed and it took a few days to set in my head that it was going in that direction . . . then I thought that it would just be a really short relationship. I didn't think it would go anywhere . . . the more serious the relationship got, the more I noticed it was starting to bother me . . . and you know when you meet someone new, it's all really exciting, and then after that sort of wears off, I started thinking, "Okay, well, now I'm dating a bisexual man," and then I started thinking about all the other implications. So it was just sort of adjusting to the new feelings towards him. . . . It's mostly fears and a bit of insecurities, that he needs something that I can't give him. He just tries to reassure me. . . . he's not going to do anything that would hurt me . . . I think that it could be a really good long-term relationship. (Lauren)

Some women met their partners when their partners believed they were gay. Thus, the early disclosure became one of bisexuality after having "been gay." This also led to caution and a pragmatic attitude of having "no delusions" that the relationship would ever be more than a sexual friendship or a short-term experimental relationship:

When I met Jack, his description of himself was just "gay." . . . We were friends for a few months and then it was a very spontaneous thing that just happened one night and even at the time we still didn't consider ourselves boyfriend/girlfriend. We just sort of considered that we were friends that did have sex and we were completely on the understanding that there were certainly no delusions involved . . . I mean, there are a whole lot of girls out there that just sort of believe that they can just sort of change them and that's that, and everything would be fine. I never had that. (Rosemary)

Women like Rosemary continued to protect themselves with this "no delusions" approach even as the relationship intensified, including having children together. Indeed, having known about and understood a partner's sexual desires and sexual history made it easier for the women to again exercise control over any situations that arose and their own feelings and goals. It also allowed them to take into strong consideration their partner's possible fears and concerns as the relationship developed, such as being "conscious of trapping" and making sure their partners had the "freedom option":

> We both wanted children. That was a big deal, and even when I was pregnant with the eldest one, I sort of held off and thought, "Well, I'll wait and see how he feels when the baby comes." I was sort of very conscious of trapping, I guess. I hadn't any doubt about how committed he was to the relationship and the child but I still wanted to really give him the freedom option and I was more than prepared to have a baby on my own. I just didn't want to smother him, stopping him from living the life that he wanted to live, so I just sort of gave him the widest scope but within not a very long period of time after the baby had come, it was apparent that he didn't want to go anywhere, and that's how it has been since. . . . I mean, certainly I worry that he's missing out. I say it to him, that I don't want him to one day turn around and go, "Oh, my God, what have I been doing with my life?" (Rosemary)

CONCLUSION

In this chapter, we have met women who began relationships with men who they knew to be "outside belonging" (Probyn, 1996) the polarities of heterosexual and homosexual identities, communities and relationships. By embarking on MOREs with these 'stranger/homecomer' men, the women themselves became strangers to the traditional social constructions of hetero-relationships. What followed was the women either becoming homecomers to their own agency in developing successful self-ascriptive relationships in this borderzone or "third space" (Bhabha, 1990); or experiencing further trauma and alienation living on the "thin edge of barbed wire" (Anzaldua, 1987a: 75) in relation to societal approval and community acknowledgment, leading to MOREs floundering due to a variety of reasons, not always related to the men's sexualities.

In summary, what prevails in all the discussions and examples in this chapter are the following factors: early disclosure is unanimously preferred to deception and later disclosure either through discovery or confession; and early disclosure does not necessarily guarantee the smooth progress of the relationship (Suresha & Chvany, 2005). Other mitigating factors include (a) the kinds of assumptions and beliefs both the women and their partners have about bisexuality and monogamy; (b) how open the women and their partners are to sexual and relationship exploration, experimentation and testing the endurance of the relationship in order to arrive, or not arrive, at a place of feasibility and flexibility; (c) the social networks and milieus the women and their partners are already part of which provide an encouraging, approving and knowledgeable context within which to establish, experiment and/or just enjoy the relationship from its onset; and (d) the confidence, control, assertiveness, independence, flexibility and sense of empowerment the women have in determining, deciding and responding to the early disclosure and any ongoing or ensuing sexual and relationship adventures and journeys.

Health services are increasingly contacted by younger women who are contemplating a long-term relationship with a man who has informed them of his bisexuality, and the focus relates to the permanency of the relationship rather than the way they feel about his bisexuality. Thus, it is hoped that as young men are growing up in sociocultural situations and contexts that permit more of this discussion and openness about sexual fluidity, they will become a generation who do not find themselves in distressing and often desperate situations, as described by many women partners of older adult bisexual men in this book. Ripley et al found that many bisexual men felt confident enough to publicly identify as bisexual at ages 13–15, with half of the men waiting until around 18 years of age to come out; this nevertheless highlights "bisexual men's growing confidence and the increased social acceptance of bisexuality today" (2011: 202; see also McCormack et al. 2014, 2015).

Indeed, my hope is that our kind of research, and the dissemination of its findings and recommendations, is part of the journey toward service provision and sociocultural shifts that mean such erasures, constraints and deceptions with self and others may no longer be required.

Chapter 6

"Changing Course Midstream"
From Closet to Confrontation

> I had no idea what was going on in his head. My head was like totally scrambled. I'd been like a chicken that was blindfolded while he was changing course midstream. (Mary)

In the previous chapter, we explored the influence of early disclosure on women and their partners and the development of their relationships. In this chapter, we will hear from women who did not "start out knowing" about their partner's bisexuality. Through disclosure or discovery at some point along the way, they found their partners, themselves and their relationships "changing course midstream." As one of Buxton's participants said, "The unimaginable had happened. . . . It was like trying to stand on water. Everything was in waves. There was no solid ground anywhere" (1991: 19). The women found themselves in limbo or on a border, torn in many directions as they struggled to connect or extricate the past from the present in order to set off on a new future. This change of direction either required a renavigation of a new course for the relationship or eventually led to the end of the relationship, despite the many facets of life they had built together. The following excerpt from a poem sent by Steph conveys this "changing course":

> I, a companion for many miles
> Now trudge burdened,
> Along a separate path,
> Alone.
>
> —Steph

Gochros (1989) lists the number of ways official disclosures/discoveries might occur. Given in the order usually, not always, from least stressful to most stressful, they are as follows:

1. He voluntarily tells.
2. He tells when pressured by his female partner's questions.
3. The female partner discovers incriminating evidence like a love note or gay pornography, confronts him, and he then reveals his same-sex desires or activities.
4. He tells when forced to because of an arrest, job dismissal or STI.
5. The female partner is told by another person, sometimes the male partner's lover, and he then 'voluntarily' tells her.
6. The female partner is told in the presence of another person, usually a professional, after years of denying it, or she receives confirmation of her suspicions, but he never admits anything.
7. The female partner discovers him in a homosexual act.

It needs to be stated that discovery is a qualitatively different experience to disclosure. Although disclosure can lead to feelings of shock, anger, disappointment and confusion, discovery can shake the very foundation of trust and intimacy in the relationship. Indeed, Yarhouse & Pawlowski (2003) found that discovery is much more difficult for a marriage than disclosure.

Many films about bisexual men in MOREs are premised on the disclosure/discovery plot device for conflict, melodrama and tragedy; or the male protagonist's secret bisexuality is part of a larger theme or trajectory of deception and betrayal, and their negative repercussions. *Inside Daisy Clover* (1965) explores the corruption of innocence, the superficiality and pretenses of Hollywood. Charismatic bisexual heartthrob actor Wade is deceptive, traitorous, narcissistic and his female partners suffer. When he abandons the "new Hollywood sensation" Daisy so soon after marrying her, she has a major breakdown. Resonating with Goffman's (1963) front stage (public self) and back stage (private/real self) theory of stigma management, their producer Raymond says to her:

> All the good women and all the good men never could put Wade together again. They take him to heart, they take him to bed. . . . Then one day they wake up alone. She [my wife] didn't stand a chance. I told Millora what would happen, it happened. She cut her wrists . . . Thousands of girls keep watching him in dark movie houses, go home, they dream about him in dark little bedrooms. Thousands of wives wish their husbands were exactly like him. . . . You can't help admiring the man.

Wade returns, handsome as ever, saying, "Won't you join me back in the limelight, little lady of pain?" However, the finale has Daisy burning down the beachhouse she has been isolated in by Raymond to recover, and running away from her Hollywood life of deception and facades: "someone declared war," she says.

In *Cabaret* (1972), the wealthy and cultured bisexual Maximillian seduces both Sally and Brian, without either knowing of the other, and then abandons them both. Indeed, Liza Minelli was later married to the bisexual entertainer and songwriter Peter Allen, who died of AIDS. In *Total Eclipse* (1995), based on the love story between the poets Rimbaud and Verlaine, the latter falls passionately in love with Rimbaud, while trying to continue his love for his long-suffering wife, Mathilde. She is suspicious of Rimbaud from the beginning, and Verlaine becomes emotionally and physically abusive until Mathilde eventually divorces him. Indeed, the young Rimbaud acts as sadistically to Verlaine as does Verlaine to his young wife, whom he eventually deserts. The destructive, implosive and yet passionate relationship between the poets is often contrasted against the more peaceful albeit more staid relationship between Verlaine and Mathilde. This is quite different to films such as *Brokeback Mountain* (2005) where the sympathetic and empathic focus is on the love story between Jack and Ennis, obscuring the other stories about love, family and the heartache of discovery or disclosure experienced by their wives (Carpenter, 2005).

The holding of secrets or Communication Privacy Management (CPM) theory (Petronio, 2002; Petronio, 2010) is very pertinent to the issue of disclosure/discovery. It offers a framework for understanding what types of information are considered private and the rules individuals follow to regulate their private information. It has three main assumptions regarding information ownership and control: that tension exists between the desire to disclose and conceal private information; that individuals perceive themselves as having ownership of their private information; and that individuals use a system of privacy rules to create and maintain boundaries around their private information. Only recently has the issue of privacy been addressed within the context of behaviorally-bisexual men (e.g., Munoz-Laboy et al., 2009). These studies reported that privacy issues, including viewing the topic of sexuality as a private, personal issue; the cultural importance of keeping sexual matters private; or not identifying as bisexual, were reasons for nondisclosure of their same-sex behaviors. In line with Kroeger's (2003) theory of agentic passing, Persson & Richards argue that nondisclosure can provide "protection and peace of mind" and give individuals "a sense of control" while disclosure could "open up an unknown and irrevocable terrain of contentions, unpredictability, fears, scrutiny, unspoken concerns or unresponsiveness, effects that amplified feelings of difference rather than provided therapeutic release" (2008: 76). Vangelisti (1994) identified three categories of secrets, all of which are pertinent to MOREs: taboo secrets, rule violations, and conventional secrets. Taboo secrets, if disclosed, would bring stigma to the bisexual man. Rule violations refer to activities that break rules established and enforced by one's family or partner; and conventional secrets refer to content regarded as no one's business outside the family or relationship. Cloven & Roloff (1993) discuss the "chilling effect," whereby partners withhold information from each other due to the perceived partner's disapproval. When Easterling et al. asked why participants kept a personal secret from a romantic partner, "to avoid hurting the partner" was the top reason reported by almost 40% of the respondents, with "it would alter our relationship" and "I feel so ashamed for what I did" reported by 18% and 11% of the respondents, respectively (2012: 206). Schrimshaw et al.'s (2014) study found that bisexual men offered a number of privacy rules to justify their nondisclosure, including: their same-sex behaviors were their own business; others had no reason to know; the topic of sexual behavior was too personal; they were private people in general; and it was inappropriate to discuss same-sex behavior in many contexts.

As introduced in chapter 2, "emotional labor" or "emotion management" strategies are greatly applied by bisexual men in order to prevent disclosure/discovery (Hochschild, 1983). These techniques entail two forms of acting: "surface acting" such as changing the external appearance or adopting a strategy of pretense in order to give the impression of a particular feeling; and "deep acting" which involves working on one's inner feelings in order to alter them or exchange them for other feelings. In this way, one or both of two desired outcomes or "exchange values" and "use values" may be achieved: "pain avoidance" and "advantage-seeking" (1983: 36). However, Hochschild also points to inherent dangers in these forms of "emotion work" or socially ascriptive performances. First, at some crucial points in life, such as when a bisexual man's "surface acting" is revealed and he can no longer maintain the "deep acting" required to present a public heterosexual self, the fusion or estrangement between the "true self" and "acted self" will be tested. Second, the "false self," which is a "sociocentric, other-directed self," may set itself up as the "real self" so one's "inner self" never emerges, such as when even after discovery of one's secret sexual relations with other men, the bisexual partner will continue to deny his emotional and behavioral realities (1983: 136). Grever recounts her own feelings of duality experienced during her excessive stress after her partner's disclosure/discovery: "I felt almost like two people. A stranger who inhabited my dragging body and a detached observer watching the whole drama with dark fascination" (2001: 101).

Anderson (2012) has developed the "dyadic dissonance theory" to describe the cognitive dissonance between what individuals want emotionally and what is wanted somatically, such as sexual desires. In desiring but not wanting to cheat, men set out to rectify their dissonance through pornography, visualizing themselves having sex with someone else while having sex with their partner, and/or flirting with others online. Eventually, however, these imagined/cyber forms of extradyadic sex may not be enough. Anderson's research suggests that at that point, cheating, or the avoidance of disclosure, might actually help save relationships, such as not having to "deal with social shame and stigma" and the loss of their partners by "admitting publicly that they are not monogamous" and/or bisexual (2012: 15).

Buxton (2006a, d) documents the coping processes women partners undergo in navigating these shifting heterotopic spaces (Foucault, 1986). This involves proceeding through common stages from initial trauma to eventual transformation after there has been either and/or "disclosure" or "discovery," the latter including evidence such as "gay-related Websites, . . . telephone numbers on matchbooks from gay bars, or semen stains on underwear in the laundry basket" (2006a: 111). Disclosure/discovery may occur at any point in a relationship, with three main times being early when the couple has a newborn or small children; during a midlife crisis or after a parent's death; or later when the couple become 'empty nesters.' Disclosure/discovery is usually followed by one of three trajectories. About a third of the couples break up quickly, because the bisexual partner has a lover or wants to live as 'a gay person' in the gay community, or the heterosexual partner cannot tolerate deception, an affair, nonmonogamy, or homosexual behavior (Buxton, 2001, 2004a, b). Another third stay together for two or three years to sort out alternatives, deciding finally to separate. The final third commit themselves to redefining the marriage so they can stay together. Of this third group, about half determine after about three years that separation is best for their relationship, and the remaining half stay married for three or more years. In both cases, the couples form strong bonds that last even if the marriage does not. Coleman (1982) found that after disclosure/discovery, 55% of the men decided to recommit themselves to their relationship. 34% of these men planned a monogamous relationship with their wives; 46% were definitely going to act on their same-sex feelings without the wives' knowledge; and 20% would engage in extramarital activity with the wife's knowledge and consent.

Other research also indicates that coming out is not a single event, but an ongoing series of disclosures and explorations for both partners (Paul, 1996). Indeed, the disclosure process may actually be a series of "discrete divulgences" such as "acknowledging same-sex erotic attractions, expressing the desire to act on those attractions, disclosing past same-sex experiences, disclosing ongoing same-sex experiences, redefining one's sexual orientation, and talking explicitly about same-sex relationships" (Paul, 1996: 451). How each divulgence is transacted will have a considerable impact on the relationship. Other important considerations include the values held by the couple, the level of concern and emotional commitment expressed by the bisexual partner for his partner, and the availability and extent of social supports. A partner's satisfaction with the relationship, communication skills between the two of them, the presence of other ongoing issues and stresses, prior history of the relationship, the homophobia or biphobia of each partner, the quality of the couple's sex life, and the degree to which the bisexual partner had acknowledged or concealed his bisexual attractions from the partner, will also be part of determining the outcomes.

In relation to postdisclosure/discovery, Atwood (1998) found some wives ended up thinking that a bad marriage is better than being alone, or found many wonderful qualities and gains from the marriage such as economic stability and family stability for children. Hence, they stayed married, at times with psychological and physical abuse from their husbands. As we shall see in chapter 12, many spouses may then become complicit in the secrecy, undertaking strategies of passing such as withdrawing, compartmentalizing, cloaking and fictionalizing (Richardson, 1985). They will keep the disclosure and their partners' gay-related activities secret from friends and families because their partners ask them not to tell or they fear that their partners may lose position or status in their jobs, faith community, or family of origin. However, acting as "accomplices to the very deceptive behavior that hurt them causes moral confusion. Many begin to feel governed by the secret" (Buxton, 2006a: 115).

Several researchers have identified stages through which women partners journey, often not unlike those associated with mourning a death. The five stages of mourning are denial and isolation; anger; depression; and acceptance (Kubler-Ross & Kessler, 2005). Ross (1983) presents three phases: withdrawal-avoidance, disclosure-acceptance, and adjustment-coping. Klaar (2012) presents four stages, as identified by Dr. William Wedin, Director of Bisexual Psychological Services in New York City: humiliation, honeymoon, rage, and resolution. However, as Buxton acknowledges, the very notion of coping in stages "is misleading, since spouses do not proceed in lockstep fashion. Rather, they deal with one or more issues simultaneously and those concerns change in intensity or arise in diverse forms" (2006c:116). This "complicated grief" (Kubler-Ross & Kessler, 2005) is intensified if the individual has prior emotional wounds that were insufficiently grieved. It can be very debilitating because it recurs at unexpected times and can remain a nagging problem for years after the events that triggered it. This cycle is complicated further by what Hernandez & Wilson (2007) refer to as "ambiguous loss," referring to chronic loss for which resolution or closure are inappropriate goals. Nevertheless, there is a generally forward movement. The first stage, "Initial Shock, Denial, and Relief," involves "Facing, Acknowledging, and Accepting Reality":

Slowly they note and acknowledge changes in their partners' behavior, wardrobes, activities, and appearance; their own physical, mental, emotional, and spiritual health; their daily schedule and workplace performance; their attitudes toward life; the relationship and lovemaking; parenting behaviors; the partners' schedule at home and away; and family activities (Buxton, 2006c: 117).

Stage Two is "Letting Go of the Past and Focusing on the Present": accepting what is unchangeable, preserving memories of what was real in their relationship and family life, and "evaluating who and where they are" (Buxton, 2006c: 117). Third comes "Healing," seeking help from varied sources and discovering their core needs, wants, goals and values for the future. The fourth stage is "Reconfiguring and Transforming" their "self-image, moral compass, and belief system" which provides an internal source of meaning and purpose, thereby transforming their lives, whether within or outside of the marriage (Buxton, 2006c: 117). The length of time to reach this transformation stage, Buxton states, is often prolonged by various factors, including:

> the degree of devastation to the spouses' self concept and confidence; their emotional distress and shattering of belief system; the couple's financial situation; the presence of children at home; unexpected events such as family illness or accidents; divorce/custody issues if the couple divorces; and underlying psychological problems (2006c: 119).

Buxton (2006c) also identifies five major emotions which complicate the progress through these four stages: intense pain, unfairness, fear, anger and grief. The power of these feelings helps most spouses move forward, although some become stuck in one place because of the overwhelming force of one or more of these emotions and experience consequent mental health issues.

Gochros identifies the existence of "the precipitating factor or last straw" after disclosure/discovery (1989: 76). Often people cope well with the first hazardous postdisclosure/discovery event and may even handle a series of such events with relative equanimity. However, some final event, either major or trivial "overloads that system, raises stress to an untenable degree, and sends the person into a state of acute disequilibrium, popularly termed 'falling apart'" (1989: 77). Crisis reactions to this excessive stress include aimless activity, immobilization or agoraphobia, dramatic and frequent mood changes, sleep and appetite disturbances, and a range of physical symptoms. They may become extremely dangerous to themselves or others, such as driving recklessly, lashing out at their children, attempting suicide or killing someone. Gochros (1989) also labelled the "I can't stand blood . . . Get me out of here" syndrome where many husbands were truly distressed at the pain they felt they had created and were so excessively guilt-ridden that they exited the relationship (1989: 125). As Lesley describes:

Fine, you've known you're bisexual for quite a few years, now you've told your wife. Expect her to rant and rave. Expect her to be upset, and give her time to come to terms with it before you walk out the door and say, "Right, you can't handle this and I'm gone." (Lesley)

The following eight themes became very apparent in our research as the women recollected their experiences of disclosure/discovery:

1. *The disclosure or discovery was totally unexpected, leaving the woman questioning and re-examining the past and the future for "evidence" of any changes in the course of the relationship*: Some women were completely shocked by the disclosure and were in a state of reexamining the journey so far, "looking for clues," while also experiencing much wariness and insecurity about trusting anyone in the future.
2. *There was either no definitive disclosure or discovery, or it came after years of a gradual growing awareness:* Some women found it difficult to pinpoint the actual time when the course of the relationship shifted. It appeared to be a gradual sailing in a different direction, which some women often struggled to accept or rationalized against. Thus, becoming aware was sometimes met with refusing to know.
3. *The disclosure followed discovery:* Some women discussed how they discovered their partner's bisexuality through coming across objects, notes, websites and other documentation and then had to decide what to do with this "data."
4. *The disclosure or discovery was experiential rather than spoken:* Some women explained how they charted the shifting course of their relationship through sexual and other bodily shifts and changes, and a series of events that caused them to question their partner's sexuality.
5. *The disclosure was initiated by the woman because of her own experiences and/or confessions of same-sex attraction, or wanting the partner's bisexuality to be addressed:* Some women found their own sexual desires and experiences had been shifting and wanted to share this with their partners, often leading to a reciprocal disclosure from them. Other women were aggrieved and exhausted with the obviousness of the bisexuality and its ramifications on the relationship while their partners insisted on maintaining an ongoing silence as if the course of the relationship had not shifted at all.
6. *The shifting sexuality of the partner was part of or brought on by several or many shifts in the course and circumstances of the relationship over time:* Factors which had precipitated or facilitated the sexual midstream shifts were health issues for either or both of them, changes in their sexual intimacy, having and raising children, experiencing financial difficulties,

career and workplace changes, travel opportunities, and circumstances that required them to have time lived apart. Indeed, many women found that until these other issues surfaced and required renavigation, their partners had sometimes not even been aware of their bisexuality.
7. *The deception and betrayal of trust was the major issue in the disclosure/discovery:* For some women, the disclosure or discovery of the partner's bisexuality was less an issue than coming to terms with the amounts and types of deception and betrayal their partners had undertaken. Thus, the course had to be renavigated according to what to do with this knowledge of his ability to deceive rather than the knowledge of his bisexuality.
8. *The disclosure/discovery was followed by negotiations and re-navigations in order to stay together:* Although the travelling and course of the journey required re-navigation, and even though there may have been an immediate and/or prolonged period of angst and ambiguity, some women spoke about staying together and maintaining the same destination as a couple that they had previously set out on.

"I NEVER, EVER REALIZED"

Well, I never, ever realized, and it wasn't until about a month before we separated that he actually told me that he thought he was [bisexual]. The only thing he ever said to me was he wanted time to himself to sort himself out, and find out which direction his life was taking. (Beth)

For some women such as Beth, the disclosure or discovery of their partner's bisexuality was doubly confrontational and shocking as it had been totally unexpected. After ten years together, Beth recalls her husband having given other more 'normative' or 'standard' reasons for wanting to separate. This is similar to Coleman's (1982) study in which most wives were unsuspecting at the time of disclosure. Their responses ranged from calm concern, to extreme upset, to revulsion and disgust.

The lack of prior realization or suspicion of the partner's same-sex attractions leaves the female partner questioning her own behaviors as possibly being at fault. It constructs an ambiguity and helplessness in trying to determine why the relationship has deteriorated and, if the causation is unclear, then how can she determine what to do about it:

I thought "What have I done wrong, and why can't I do something to get back what I had?"... I would have liked the explanation of how this happened. How someone could have been in a heterosexual relationship and tells me that he was in love with me and very, very happy with me, all that time, until right the very end. (Beth)

What is also confusing for many women in the total unexpectedness of the disclosure is their partners often saying their same-sex attractions were also unexpected and recently discovered. There is also the lingering doubt that perhaps the partner is not "telling the truth" anyway about the "not knowing": "he says that he never ever realized before . . . And I've asked if something happened to trigger that, and he says no" (Beth). Thus, both partners are left floundering in the suddenness of the situation and having to quickly accept that the future will need to be completely reconfigured: "He was very upset and devastated about it and now wants to be really close friends. . . . I'd like to be, but it's just difficult" (Beth).

Part of this reconfiguration of the future is the woman's fear that if this can happen to her once, what would prevent this from happening again with another partner? Thus, the total unexpectedness of the disclosure/discovery can have long-lasting posttraumatic repercussions as women feel they can no longer trust their own insights and abilities to determine the sexuality of any future partner, let alone trust that the partner's sexuality may not "suddenly" change:

> Definitely the fear that if that's the sort of man I'm attracted to, is that going to happen to me again? The odd person I've spoken to about it, they see my partner and they say, "Oh, yes, I can tell he's gay." Well, how? Why didn't I know if they know? (Beth)

Kaye (2002) refers to "Gayanoia," whereby women begin to think that "just about every man you meet is gay," and that they are "gay magnets." With time this passes, particularly when women realize they are protected because they "have a pre-conceived mental list of what to watch out for." As will be discussed further in chapter 9, this formula is itself problematic in its implication of what defines 'normal' heterosexual masculinity:

> If a man is nurturing, attractive, stylish, well groomed, well dressed, and/or compassionate, he's an immediate candidate for homosexuality.
>
> If you are meeting a man in his 30's or 40's who hasn't been married before, find out why. This is a red light (Kaye, 2002).

Many women whose partners suddenly come out reflect on the beginning of the relationship and begin to consider how naivety, being young, and making assumptions of heterosexuality had prevented these issues from being recognized and addressed much earlier. What is also intriguing for women is having friends who are gay and yet their own partner's same-sex attractions go unrecognized or undiscussed:

> He was the first serious relationship I'd been in. It was heterosexual and I assumed he was, simply because we were sexually attracted to each other and it didn't dawn on me, even though I had gay friends. (Erin)

Thus, what might at first appear to have been unexpected begins to have threads that extend back, once the woman is aware in hindsight of what she could have paid attention to. However, this still sits in total contrast to what she has known and felt about her partner, and experienced from and with him, throughout the years they were together:

> I thought back over time. I didn't want to make things fit, but I started thinking, well, maybe such and such was a sign that I didn't pick up.... We had a very, very intense and close relationship to the point where I just thought it was completely impervious to anything ever happening, and I think when the shock came at the end, that was what really stunned me so much, ... I wasn't suspicious. He was devoted to me, and I was devoted to him. (Erin)

> It makes sense now in the puzzle ... He used to go out during the week for a drive, but sadly enough it was to the beat.... Our sex life had ceased anyway. It just wasn't working. I kept asking him to see a doctor.... Thinking back now, I think he always knew. I think he was enjoying two worlds. (Pat)

As in Pat's situation, what may be totally unexpected by the woman is something that the male partner has gradually been coming to terms with. Thus, the disclosure is the culmination of what has been either known and pushed away until it can no longer be denied, or eventually it was expected that the same-sex desires would surface and have to be disclosed:

> He said he'd tormented himself, because he came to realize his feelings were actually getting stronger.... And he said he just kept pushing it away and pushing it away. But he was in turmoil and I didn't know. For the last six months of our marriage he was having counselling and I didn't know.... I said to him, "When did you realize?" and he said, "Oh, when I was seven." And he'd kept that inside for all of those years ... I thought that we could talk about everything. He was the first man that I had ever seen cry.... One of the most hurtful things at the end of it all was that he couldn't tell me. (Erin)

A strong indication of how what is unexpected by the woman may have been prepared for or expected over time by the male partner is when he begins another relationship or makes other life changes soon after the disclosure/ discovery. For example, two weeks after separating from Erin, her partner was in a relationship with a man who he had been in a three-month relationship with as a young adult, before meeting Erin. Meanwhile, Erin is in a state of total breakdown:

For the first few days, I was like a zombie. I didn't sleep for nights or days. I didn't eat. I smoked and I drank cups of tea. I was so afraid that I would do something to harm myself that I didn't drink wine and I love my wine. I was in such a deep state of shock that I just felt numb. It was like a state of nothingness. My whole world as I knew it just disappeared. I was pumping myself with sleeping tablets. . . . And he was in a new relationship, and I just couldn't believe that, because he seemed quite devastated by the end of our relationship, just as I was, but of course, he was at a different level. Because he was the one that disclosed his sexuality to me, he was the one that had been psyching himself up for the end of the relationship. He was already six months on from me. He left me the day he disclosed . . . And I was just left on the floor in a heap. (Erin)

Indeed, many women described the physical, emotional and mental health reactions experienced due to the shock and trauma of sudden, unexpected and unprecedented disclosure:

He came out the closet to my best friend. Before he told me. . . . I went downhill quick smart, I couldn't eat, I couldn't drink. . . . It was like a living nightmare. It was hard for me to speak. . . . There were periods of drought where I wanted to cry and I couldn't. I lost a lot of weight dramatically, too quick that made me sick. (Pat)

He was working in a macho type job, it was maintenance of aircraft, and he decided that because he was artistic and doing painting and drawings, he wanted to get into other work. So, he took on working in a display department of a large department store, and it was from that point onwards, when he actually got around people that were like-minded . . . and then I found James was totally drinking like badly, too, writing himself off. . . . and I had no idea, until one day I finally wouldn't leave the bedroom until he told me what was going on, and he said he was bisexual. Oh, it was like my world collapsed. I pretended for six months that that didn't occur. . . . Threw it away, like pretending was a protection thing. . . . yet James didn't want to break up. He was not going to explore who he was. And I was incredibly naïve and didn't want to go there, like, "Don't change my world." . . . [After 6 months] I was incredibly depressed, and I just wrote myself off with alcohol, because I didn't know how to face what was happening. (Mary)

Finally, there were women whose partners disclosed their same-sex attractions after their HIV-positive status was disclosed:

One of the reasons I didn't up and leave initially [after he disclosed both his HIV-status and sexuality] was that my husband said he would commit suicide, and I really believe he would have, and I thought "Do I want to have to cope with that?" . . . I really got terribly upset and depressed and went to see my GP, and I really was almost suicidal at that stage, because I thought we had a really good marriage. (Jane)

"IT WAS A GRADUAL AWAKENING I SUPPOSE"

Sixteen years ago, I noticed that he was having this very playful relationship with the students at the university . . . there was no doubt in my mind that he was exploring, not physically, but emotionally, relationships with some of the students. We didn't have a particularly fantastic sex life at all. . . It was a gradual awakening, I suppose. I thought well, maybe he's exploring, and who knows what's happening, but I've got three children, I just need to keep trucking along here. . . In retrospect, of course I can see a fair bit. (Felicity)

For Felicity, a combination of a growing dissatisfaction with their sex life, and an awareness of her partner's increasing relationships with his university students, led to a "gradual awakening" of an absence in their relationship. Thus, unlike in the first section where women faced a pivotal turning point of unexpected disclosure or discovery, many women talked about a progressive shift in the course of the relationship as they became increasingly aware of "something wrong" before learning of their partner's same-sex attractions. Klaar discusses one of the "fascinating things" in previous research is "the level of Denial" on the part of women even "after having been told that he had contracted HIV, or that he was involved in sex with other men, they doubted the reality of the evidence" (2012: 113). Haag refers to what the critic D.A. Miller called the "open secret": "the secret is always known—and in some obscure sense, known to be known," so that the "social function of secrecy is not to conceal knowledge" or behavior, so much as to conceal the knowing of it (2011: 164). Yarhouse & Pawlowski (2003) believe that disclosure can be partial with the partner sending out a "trial balloon" (2003: 464). They may be trying to read their spouse's reaction to see if it is safe, and if a more complete disclosure will be tolerated.

Buxton (2006a) describes "new factors" that are part of the "gradual awareness," whereby their partners often change so much physically and emotionally that some spouses call them "Pod People inhabited by aliens" (2006a: 57):

I look back at it now and think, "How could I have been so dumb, so thick?" because he was going out a lot and our relationship really went downhill and we didn't really talk to each other much and I found letters that I wrote to him that I didn't show him saying, "What the hell is going on, we need help, it's no good" etc etc . . . The kids were younger then and life just gets in the way basically. (Marissa)

> In bed one night he began caressing me and he was trying to stick his fingers up my backside. I pushed him away five times, and finally in his sleep he mumbled, "I want to suck your cock." Well that just finished it with me, because where he said he never thought about guys, that told me differently. (Jean)

Women also have difficulty accepting how, in hindsight, they had so much "evidence" but, because they did not want to acknowledge it for what it was, a final event led to full awareness:

> I was doing a big clean up in our bedroom and found blood test results that he was doing on a 3 monthly basis, e-coli and HIV etc, etc, and it was in the middle of a Saturday afternoon and kids were all around and I just said, "Oh, what are these?," and he just said, "I had a big check up," and at the time I thought, "Doesn't sound quite right" but because the kids were there I just said, "Yeah ok" and didn't pursue that but then about a month later, he left his phone at home and went off to work and for some bizarre reason I decided to look at it. There were messages there to and from a guy that left nothing to the imagination basically. (Marissa)

Kaitlin described the see-saw feelings toward her partner that she experienced as she grappled with an "awareness" that is based on "gut feeling" but not "knowing." For example, she was aware of certain mannerisms and gestures that made her feel uncomfortable but not knowing why. Likewise, the same security she felt in knowing that her partner would never cheat on her with a woman and yet had many women friends was situated alongside a "gut feeling" that there was something else about this that did not feel secure. Other contradictions also became evident such as the growing awareness that their sexual relationship and pleasure in each other's bodies fluctuated between great intensity to "nothing," but not knowing why; and knowing that he was an excellent father who had experienced a deep depression when he found she was pregnant, but not knowing why. What also became apparent was how she did not challenge this dissonance between what she was aware of and what she knew. She colludes by not directly raising issues, "squashing" her fears in her own need to be a "respectable middle-aged married woman," or attributing "rational" reasons to why certain things are occurring, until she can no longer rationalize certain shifts in long-held signifiers of their intimacy:

> And then he reached the stage where he didn't want to be touched, and he went to bed in a track suit. And, oh, I mean, it was so demoralizing. It was so terrible because when we first got married, he talked me into going to bed naked, which I hadn't done before. (Kaitlin)

For Kristina, gradually becoming aware of the situation between her partner and his boyfriend coincided with an awareness of what she had refused to see or was unable to see. Indeed, she had actually asked him very early on about his sexuality but had accepted what seemed like a very "feasible" and reasonable response. Indeed, Kristina often found herself rationalizing and substantiating certain behaviors or "rumors":

> We met at a nightclub, and yeah, I'd heard rumors about him, but I just asked him straight, and as it turns out, he has an identical twin brother who is openly gay, so he would always say, "Oh, people always mistake me for Nicholas." . . . In those eight months we were together and planning to marry, it turns out he was having a relationship with his flat mate, so the fact I was there six nights a week, like, looking back I think how could I not know? But, yeah, there were a couple of times when I'd just walk in and they'd just be really close, talking, heads close together. And some other things like if he bought me something, he just couldn't do that without buying Justin something and he'd want Justin to come out with us sometimes, and we couldn't go away without Justin coming. But, you see, Justin had come out of gaol, he was sort of like a troubled kid. He was nineteen, and Mark had this whole thing about taking him under his wing and looking after him. . . . and especially because I've always liked the nurturing, helping type, so to me that was something admirable. . . . We'd just bought a new house together and I was thinking, "Hurray, we can get into our own house," but Mark started saying, "Oh, we can fix the upstairs room for Justin" and I'm going, "No we can't, that's not going to happen," and he had this big dummy spit. But it was also bizarre because I used to go to the primary school [where he taught] and help out in the classroom and there were a couple of the other teachers who told me that he'd actually had Justin come down to the school as well, and that there were rumors. Some of the mothers picked up things. (Kristina)

Even as Kristina tried to deflect the emotional reactions by searching for what sounded "feasible" in Mark's justifications, the stress she experienced during those few but very difficult months was evident to others:

> My girlfriend told me that from the time I met him I went from this bright, bubbly, full of self-esteem. She said "You were just down and out," and I didn't perceive it at the time. . . . but you're there, you're pregnant, you want to believe him and you go, "Oh, yeah, that sounds feasible." (Kristina)

The discovery finally occurs due to Justin's accidental drowning. Yet even at this stage, when the coroner is given evidence by other family members of their relationship, Kristina decides to stay in the relationship until further evidence is uncovered when investigating her partner's accidental overdose:

> It was actually the coroner that told me that Mark and Justin had bought plane tickets to London for themselves and an infant, open-ended. Like, Mark's mother knew, Justin's mother knew . . . It was a nasty shock at the time. I left

him for a short while, but I was pregnant and I was obviously not psychologically stable, when I look back on it, and he convinced me that he had never had sex with Justin, it was more of a father/son relationship and everybody's just misconstrued it, and he wanted to be there for me and the baby. So I actually moved back in, and I didn't leave until when she was four months' old, I think, and he got some mysterious illness, which I later found out was an overdose. The doctor said, "Can you go through his bag and see if you can find any medication that he might have taken?" So with his mother sitting there in the corner, I've opened the bag and there's like this gay sex kit thing in his school bag. And so that was it. I just walked out from there. (Kristina)

Lizette met her partner at a nightclub when she was nineteen and a single mother of a four-year-old boy, and was won over by his attention and persistence:

I wasn't interested, and he chased me and wouldn't stop ringing. He would buy me flowers, nearly every day, and it was just such a whirl-wind. . . . and he ended up proposing like three months after we were going out together. I just felt a lot of things were rushed. And we were married about eighteen months later. And we just had the most wonderful relationship. He was wonderful with my son. He was just so so loving and protecting of me, and would do anything for me. (Lizette)

However, a series of events began to indicate growing "cracks" in the relationship that Lizette believed were due solely to his declining health. Indeed, for many women in these situations of gradual awareness, it is difficult to determine whether health and other problems and circumstances precipitated the same-sex attractions or actions, or whether the attractions and actions were always there and shifting circumstances allowed these to manifest or intensify. Again, what also keeps the women rationalizing away any fears or even any idea of bisexuality is the positive qualities still apparent in their partners:

He had a lot of medical problems. Like, he lost his job because he kept sort of blacking out and bleeding from the bowel and they did an investigation and they couldn't find anything. I thought he was very stressed and he was losing a lot of weight. And, anyway, they eventually got that under control with medication. But not long after we bought the house he was diagnosed with diabetes. So, then again we sort of go through the whole rigmarole. From his sickness, I look back now I see little things. Apparently, and I only found this out a few years back, he had suicidal thoughts, but everything was always wonderful. It was the happy little family and we bought a house with the picket fence. . . . But, about eighteen months before he left, he just started to sort of change, gradually. He really took things out physically and mentally on my son. This split personality was evolving. And then he hurt his back at work. And, so, he's at home with a bad back for six months and he's on the Internet and he would contact these guys on the chat line. It became like an obsession, but I'd just jokingly laugh to people and say, "Oh, I'm the computer widow now." (Lizette)

Even as men begin to appear in her partner's life, Lizette turns this in to a positive that she hopes will improve her partner's health and outlook on life:

He started going to a gym and became sort of more obsessive with his appearance. And he said that he met this friend, Craig. And I thought it's good, because he didn't really have a lot of male friends and he always did everything with me. You know, we'd go shopping together and we'd do the theatre. And there were times when I wished he'd go down to the pub, go out with mates. . . . one day Craig rang and Ron sort of snatched the phone out of my hand, and he always raced off to see him, and I thought, "God, he's becoming obsessive with him." And then all of a sudden it just died down. And then he sort of became quite obsessive with this Jonathon on the computer, a young boy from Queensland, and I'd get on there and participate sometimes to have a chat too, and we'd muck about. . . . Then he started dyeing his hair, just the grey hairs he's got, and then his clothes were all changed. They went really young. And then he went into the really young music and I ended up saying to him, "You know, you're going through your second childhood." He said, "I haven't got out of my first yet." (Lizette)

Three months later, his emotions spiraled downward and inconsistencies came forward:

I said, "What's the matter?" "No, no, nothing. I'm just stressed with the kids." But it just continually got worse, and then one night he started to get upset and said, "I've got to go and see somebody about my panic attacks." And I said, "That's okay, we'll get you a counselor and we'll work on this together." He was actually going to GAMMA [Gay and Married Men's Association] every fortnight and was starting to really withdraw from me. He would sleep on the edge of the bed. He would not stand me touching him. . . . And then I found out he was supposed to be finishing work at say half-past two in the afternoon and he wasn't picking our daughter up from day care until half-past six at night. . . . And he decided to take this friend of ours who was married with two children to GAMMA . . . . and the friend was not quite the same after that. And he said, "I'm never going back down there again." And I just had a feeling something had happened. This is what my girlfriend often laughs about now. She said, "I could have just, you know, shaken you, you were so trusting, and so loyal." . . . And in the end, I'll never forget it. It was the 30th of January and he was vomiting. I just didn't know what else to do. He's sitting on the edge of the bed. I said, "Do you think you need a few days away or something?" Well, with that, he had his bags packed, and he was sort of out the door as quick as lightning. Well, I was just absolutely devastated. (Lizette)

Even after it became obvious that Ron had left permanently, Lizette tried to maintain a relationship but found she was still not being told or was aware of what really occurred:

He's staying at this friend's place and I'd have him up for meals. . . . And he said, "Oh, the psychiatrist doesn't know whether I'll ever be able to come home. I'm just too stressed and he doesn't think it's going to help the situation." And I would beg him and it was just pathetic when I look back when I'd say, "Why, why can't you?" He said, "I can't tell you yet." So, this just sort of like went on for I think seven or eight weeks. Anyway, it was affecting my work. I walked out in the middle of a shift twice because I was nearly having a breakdown. I had to have time off work, and I was left with a mortgage and the personal loan to pay, and he just didn't seem to have a care in the world for us. (Lizette)

Finally, after so much time of inconsistencies and ambiguities, Lizette's partner told her and she went into shock:

I honestly do not know what he was trying to tell me. It just seemed to go on forever and ever, and then he came over to give me a hug, and I couldn't stand it. I said, "Get away. Take your wedding ring off." I took mine off and that was just horrible. And he was crying and I was crying. I was shaking and I didn't know what was going on around me. Everything was such a blur. I was rocking myself back and forth. I couldn't sleep, and then when I closed my eyes all I could see was him and another man doing things. (Lizette)

However, even at this stage of disclosure, Ron would not discuss and clarify what had been happening for years:

The next day, he rang and said, "Are there any questions you'd like to ask me?" And I said, "I want to know, have you slept with somebody?" and he said, "I'm not prepared to answer that." And I would ask him personal questions and "I'm not prepared to answer that" and in the end I hung up on him. . . . I remember one time after he left, I was having one of these panic attacks which I had started getting. I was at work and I called him, "Is there anything you're not telling me?" And he said, "No, just what I've told you." And, well, it wasn't. I was just sort of left with the pieces. Ron very quickly got on with his life. He went straight into a relationship. I never got any explanations. (Lizette)

Thus, what Lizette experienced was years of a gradual awareness leading to a traumatic disclosure and finally knowing. However, this final knowing has led to many questions and ambiguity about actions and events from the beginning of their relationship that have never been answered. It is also difficult knowing that people along the way did surmise but very few told her. Another difficulty is dealing now with a man who has gone from years of concealment due to what people would think to someone who carelessly displays behaviors that are not the man she knew and loved:

> I'll never forget the day we got married, and when I walked up the aisle and stood next to him, he was sort of rocking back and forth and I kept thinking, "He's going to walk out at any time" he was that nervous, but now I wonder whether he was sort of having second thoughts and then that family friend that went to GAMMA with him, I have since found out that both of them were caught in a room at high school. . . . And then when it all came out, he says, 'Well, I don't care what people think. This is me and tough luck." . . . I'm not getting any financial support. I'm not getting any support whatsoever from him. . . . He's very sarcastic. Especially when he gets found out about a lie. I just don't cope very well with that, because that's not the person I know. And he does raise his voice sometimes and I'm not used to that. That's not the person I used to know either. He likes that authority. He's very much a controller. . . . People tell you, "Oh, yes, well, we knew," but nobody comes forth at the time, you know. And I really think I would have been able to move on a lot quicker and it wouldn't have floored me as much. (Lizette)

Sally recalls the first thirteen years of their marriage being "really happy . . . really based on loyalty, friendship, support, love and kindness, really doing lots of stuff for each other that made each other's lives easier, I suppose, and I think sometimes in marriage you forget to do those sorts of things." Then followed three years of gradual withdrawal and depression:

> Not wanting to get involved in life at all, so you'd ask him, "What would you want to do on the weekend?," and it was like, "Oh, nothing." And it was like having a chain around him. . . . but it's such a gradual thing, I couldn't actually tell you, look, on this particular day that happened, and I was busy working and studying and looking after kids. . . . it's only afterwards I figure, "Oh, yes, he was depressed." So as he withdrew from life, basically I had to take control of everything, [he was] pretty well much suppressing everything about himself. (Sally)

The three years of gradual decline from happiness to depression culminated in Sally's partner coming out:

> I came back from a trip interstate, and I walked in the door and instead of having a hug and "How are you?" he was very cold, so I said "Something seems to be wrong here. I think you should take some time out for yourself," so he did. He had a day where he just went off and he came back and said, 'I think I'm gay' and it was certainly the last thing I thought. (Sally)

"I JUST HAPPENED TO LOOK IN HIS WALLET AND FOUND CONDOMS"

I have never been able to talk to him about it or confront him. I actually just left the marriage. . . . I found some gay magazines and I found some videos that were both straight and bi, and I just thought, "Well, he's curious," and this might relate to my naivety at the time about having grown up on a farm and being a very trusting person. "Maybe he's printed these magazines [at work at the printery], and he's just brought them home to read them." There was always something that I could say, "Well, this is the reason why" . . . And I remember a time when we were going out that he actually put one of my nurse's uniforms on. And, again, I didn't think anything more of it. It's just something he did, and he wanted me to take a picture of him. . . . I just happened to look in his wallet and found condoms, I thought, "Oh, there's another woman in his life." So on another morning, I just thought, "Oh, I'll have a look in his wallet again" and found a letter. And I had to go to work, and I actually took the letter, sat on the toilet, read the letter and was shaking. All he said was something like, "Dear Fred, I'm married." He didn't tell his real name. He didn't tell where he was from. He said he was black and from the West Indies and that he is turned on by men and wanted to you know what . . . I don't know how I got through that day. I think part of me felt that I'd been set up. I think part of me felt just disbelief. . . . I couldn't confront him and say xyz because I was not supposed to know. And I'm scared because of the violence. To tell you the truth, I'm sure he knows I know. And I'm sure that he planted them [DVDs, magazines, condoms and the letter] for me to find so that it was his way out. (Lisa)

In some situations, as with Lisa, discoveries of a partner's bisexuality occurred a few times but were at first dismissed or able to be rationalized away. However, at some stage, a discovery happened that was unable to be excused. It was so shocking or created such fear of violence from the partner, the woman would choose not to discuss it further: "Those who discovered clues that their partners deny as proof, wonder if they can live with an elephant in the living room" (Buxton, 2006a: 73). Some partners would deny their bisexuality even when confronted with their discovery, such as being found in bed with a man. Thus, some women discussed how they discovered their partner's bisexuality through coming across objects, notes and other documentation, and then had to decide what to do with this "data." The discovery was either sudden and unintentional, or was a deliberate "snooping" due to a growing suspicion and awareness over time, as has been discussed in the previous section. The dangers of "snooping" and "data collection" are dramatized in *The Dying Gaul* (2005), where the screenwriter Elaine is married to a Hollywood producer Geoffrey. She creates the screen name

"Arc Angel 1996" and engages her husband's employee, Robert, in personal conversation in a gay chat-room because she is charmed and intrigued by him. In the chat-room, Robert says he is actually starting a new relationship with his new boss and describes this man enough to make her certain that it is her husband. Robert and Geoffrey do begin a sexual affair while Elaine launches into an elaborate deception of her own, paying someone to hack into Robert's computer and raid the files of his ex-psychiatrist. From that point, the plot descends increasingly into tragedies, as deceptions are believed or created which mask additional truths that may have saved the loves and lives of these characters.

The issue of being able to find or identify "proof" of their partner's same-sex attractions and behaviors has been either endorsed or criticized. For example, Kaye (2001) has a section on her website, www.Gayhusbands.com, called *"Catch Him."* It gives women directions such as checking their computer's temporary Internet files to see if there are any "gay sites" their partners are visiting; and investing in spyware which downloads a program that provides a written report of all their partners' computer activity including passwords, e-mail, instant messaging, and Internet activity and history. Kaye (2001) then lists and dismisses the kinds of "perfectly logical explanations" partners will often give when they are found out, such as accessing these sites for someone else, or out of curiosity.

> Leave a gay magazine lying around. Get on the Internet and have a site there where it's accessible that there happens to be two men together. Their reaction will tell you. (Lesley)

King refers to a powerful weapon women have against DL men, their intuition: "when a woman gets that little feeling inside, when that little voice tells her something ain't right, she has to listen . . . she has to start playing detective to know for sure" (2004: 130). He then proceeds to tell women to "get nosy," to "watch for a few signs" such as if he is overly homophobic, and also advises that "a woman should also keep up with her man's comings and goings" (2004: 131). He relates his own experience:

> When I was living a double life lying to my woman, . . . I knew her schedule. When I was married I was always home for dinner, I never cancelled important events that my wife and I were scheduled to attend. I was home every night in bed with her. We made passionate love often, I told her I loved her, . . . Throughout the relationship I would give her everything she could want or expect from me. When she became comfortable with the relationship and I had passed the test, I would get even bolder with my outside sexual activity (2004: 132; see also Browder, 2005).

Another African-American writer, Boykin, criticizes King for alarming black women with little or no basis and evidence. As a result he has helped to create a culture in which "women are learning to be down low detectives. They are trading tips on how to spot men on the down low, and posting messages [and photos of DL men] on websites to find the tricks of the trade" (2005: 141). He is concerned with women being given advice such as slipping a finger or two up their man's anus: "If he accepts two fingers up his butt, then he surely is DL" (2005: 142). Another piece of advice is asking a gay friend to make a pass at her husband to see if he responds. As Boykin concludes, "King's signs are so broadly constructed that just about anything a man does might raise a red flag" (2005: 143), and the "best way to know the truth is not to spy on your partner, but to create an environment where sexuality can be discussed openly" (2005: 144).

In our research, some women became detectives in trying to piece together information about what had been occurring:

> I was on my way to bed one time and I saw a mobile phone bill and for no rhyme or reason, I suddenly thought, "Oh, I'll just see how many times he rings up this, that and the other." I suddenly realized that this was a phone bill for a phone that I didn't know he had. . . . I saw Anthony's bag, so I dug in it and I found his phone. I took down the numbers that he'd made calls to, then put it all back as it was, but in the middle of all this, he came upstairs, and so I just put the phone away and we just chatted away, and he was digging through his bag. Well, he could hardly say to me, "Have you seen my secret phone?" . . . Michelle [my daughter] had a silent number that couldn't be traced, so she rang these repeated numbers that he had rung. One of them was a gym. One of them was a sauna place, and another one was a bloke, and this bloke he'd rung 44 times in a 30 day period, and I didn't understand that at all. I mean, I should really have understood it. If a woman had answered we would have been suspicious. . . . Anyway, that night when he came home, I just stood there with the phone bill and I said, "Oh, by the way, what can you tell me about this phone bill? I don't understand it." Well, you should have seen the speed that that phone bill left my hands, and he said, "I haven't been unfaithful to you." And I said, "That's funny, I only asked you could you explain this phone bill." Anyway, he said, "Oh, that's so and so's number," and I knew he'd lied because I knew that one of them was the gym and one of them was a sauna. Anyway, the next day he went to work and I rang the bloke that he'd rung 44 times, and I just said to him, "I'm wondering why my husband has rung you 44 times in the month" and he said, "Your husband?" And I still didn't click. Why should I? There was nothing to make me suspicious, and I mean, even if it's dished out to you, it would still be the furthest thing on your mind. . . . my husband wasn't impressed that I'd rung the number. He said, "Look, if you must know, we've been having phone sex and computer sex." I

don't even know whether I cried. I think I was just too stunned. He swore blind it was nothing more than talking because the sex life had gone because I was sick ... Next day I got into all his computer stuff and my God, what I found. All the histories, because he didn't think I'd get there.... [my son-in-law] got into the computer and we both just stood there and cried, and he said, "I don't believe this." So I then had a witness. He'd have wiped it all, which is of course exactly what he did. (Jean)

Loredana's partner said he never had any attractions to men:

The kids found male porno videos and pictures on the computer. Natasha was nine. Christian was thirteen. But it wasn't just once that they found these. We kept moving a lot and so he would find new places to hide them, obviously, and then I would confront him with them, and he'd say, "Well, I'm just interested in looking at male bodies. I'm looking as you look at a beautiful woman, I look at men and see what I could look like." And, I think now, how clever. I'd never have thought of it. It's amazing how I didn't ... But I didn't know what there is to know, what to look out for. (Loredana)

For Loredana, the discovery that was the turning point was a phone call from a mother:

An irate woman rang and accused Christian [my son] of preying on her son, "My son's on the Internet. And do you know that my son's only seventeen?" That was the worst thing because Christian said, "It's not me, it's my father." The computer was right there in the lounge, and I would just walk past him, and I didn't see it. He was actually making me feel guilty for not trusting him. And I used to buy it. And, again, he didn't actually deny that he was emailing the guy. He said, "I thought he was twenty-six." Christian actually got the transcript of what they'd written to each other, and he couldn't look at it at first. But, everything that I'd ever thought should be said to me, hoped would be said to me, it was like that.... They got my GP to come here because I was so distraught when it happened.... our GP said, "What's the matter with him, that he's so naïve to give out his details online." (Loredana)

Other women found out very suddenly without any preemptive words, actions or suspicions. Indeed, women like Sharae suspected other people of having "set up" the discovery in order to "break them up," and thus had to "set up" their own discoveries:

A friend used to use his computer on a regular basis to grab pictures or movies. He came to me this day and said, "Sharae, you need to have a look at the computer, you need to have a look at this stuff NOW," and I said, "No, no, no, it's all right, he's writing files for a friend." And he came back to me about two or three months later and he said, "No, you really need to have a look at this stuff." So I ended up going into the computer and I found heaps of it, files and files. Male to male pornography. There were jpegs, movies, stories, there were many folders of it, there was singles, couples, groups, the whole bit. And I was quite shocked. There wasn't a boob or a pussy in any of it . . . Initially I thought that my friend was trying to break Michael and I up, and putting all this porn on Mike's computer, and so I sort of did a bit of mini snooping on the computer and I set it up so that I knew exactly what was already on it. I took this guy out for coffee and when I came back there was more stuff there and I thought, "Hang on a minute, he couldn't be putting it there." (Sharae)

Even after the discovery, some women like Sharae decide to stay with the information, wait to see what unfolds, or try to find an appropriate time to disclose their discovery:

Michael was watching a show on TV, and I said, "Turn that bloody TV off. We've got to talk." I explained to him that I knew. He initially said, "You've got the wrong idea, this is a file for this fellow." I could feel it in my heart that he wasn't telling me the truth. So I left it for approximately twelve months, but that was how he didn't actually come out to me. I dropped some pretty clear hints over the twelve months. He said I was nasty but I really tried not to be. . . . My brother came out [as gay] in the Easter of that following year, and when Michael was ironing his clothes for work I said, "It's really good that my father accepts my brother's homosexuality because it will be so much easier for you to come out when the time comes" and he just kept ironing his shirt. He didn't skip a beat, he didn't say a word. And I just went off and made a coffee and I thought, "Anybody else, any straight guy, would have slammed his fist down and said, "Will you get this out of your head." So I knew. I was just letting him know that this is okay, so it was quite funny, yeah. (Sharae)

Finally, despite the discovery and subsequent attempts to encourage her partner to disclose, Sharae decided she needed to force the issue out. This resulted in "verbal diarrhea to the max" and the opportunity to reconfigure their future together:

I'd been away for a horse riding trip. I came back and I had been watching all these couples smooching and cuddling, which I was missing in our relationship and I said, "Okay, that's it. You have needs. I have needs too. We're going to have an open relationship" and he just crashed on me. He just emotionally overloaded and dumped everything on me. He took me into the computer room, showed me all his sites, introduced me to all the people he was talking to. He had verbal diarrhea to the max. (Sharae)

"THE BODY DOESN'T LIE"

I started to feel an incredible sense of absence in our love making, and my intuition was screaming at me what was going on. But I didn't listen. I almost got myself into a semi-abusive situation in that I almost allowed myself to be sexually manipulated, because his sexual urges, homoerotic, they always come through no matter how much he might have wanted to suppress them. The body never lies. You can trick it and you can trick other bodies, but in the end, especially through intimacy, the body tells you all the truth, so I started to figure out that he was bisexual through what was going on in bed . . . So that got really sad for me about him because he had secrets, and I found the secrets in my body. (Deanna)

For many women like Deanna, the disclosure or discovery was felt, seen or experienced rather than spoken. They explained how they charted the shifting course of their relationship through sexual and other bodily changes, as well as events that caused them to question their partner's sexuality:

He'd actually taken his wedding ring off at some point, and he said it was too tight and didn't put it on again after that. That was way before I found out. . . . Another interesting thing now looking back, he would never donate blood, like I was always on at him . . . Now I know he couldn't tick off the boxes that he hadn't had male to male sex in however long and also there was this thing about me wanting him to have a vasectomy after our daughter was born, and he wouldn't do it and now he tells me, and it makes sense, if he had a vasectomy he would have no reason to still use condoms when having sex with me which he wanted to do to protect me. (Marissa)

From the beginning of their relationship, Sylvia observed many events and situations that formed a pattern:

We'd go to cafés and I didn't feel he was with me. He was always ranging, you know, roving eye, but not for women. I am horribly observant. I thought, this is shocking, this is awful stuff. I could tell when he walked into a restaurant where he was going to sit. One time I actually said, "Well, I'll sit here and you can enjoy the view." Oh I held my breath having said that. . . . he must have felt it because he sat in a different place. . . . I caught him looking at reflections of blokes in mirrors. . . . I could pick out the sorts of guys he would like very quickly . . . It used to make me feel physically sick, and once in a restaurant, he was looking at a guy. Now, he looked rather mean, very thin, earrings, tats, short hair, dyed blond. Larry was just staring at him and he was sometimes staring back, and I felt like standing up. I wanted to bully him like a jealous girl, "Keep your eyes off my man, fuck off you" . . . I began to write these situations down, there were a couple of A4 pages. . . . Even on television, he would say, "Oh, it's got that young policeman. We have to watch that." Always comments about men. . . . he got these sarongs he used to wear when it got hot, and one time we were going to go out with this architect friend. I was getting changed, but Larry was sitting out on the verandah with his sarong, and when he heard this guy's car pull up, I said, "Look, you better get changed," and he said, "I will" in a really "piss off" sort of attitude, and I saw him tweak up his sarong. He had long legs and no underwear on and I go, "Fuck." And he had no top on. I thought, "He wants to feel nakedness with this bloke." . . . It was secret stuff which I happened to see, because my eyes were on stalks. (Sylvia)

When asked if she ever raised any of these issues and observations with him, Sylvia replied:

I didn't dare, but I knew one day I'd have to. I wasn't scared of him being violent. I was protecting probably myself. If people say, "Oh, I didn't want to hurt him," bullshit, you don't want to hurt yourself. (Sylvia)

After a break-up, Sylvia decided to get back together with Larry, but began asking questions about his behavior:

We seemed to be back on track. I thought well, I'm going to sort the relationship out now, and I knew I had to broach the subject because I was getting weary of the insecurity. One time I said something like, "Why are you always looking at boys?" And he said, "Well, you can always admire the form. It doesn't mean you have to touch." . . . And another time he said, "What do you think I am, a fucking poofter?" and I had to stop myself saying, "Well, not a poofter but bisexual?" . . . Another time, he absolutely hit the roof. "Who the fuck do you think you are. You know you're questioning my real core? You're no good for my fucking psyche," and I said, "Well, I am actually, but you don't want to know." We couldn't go anywhere with it. He hasn't had a girlfriend since. He rang me up after about six weeks and said he missed me, sorry he hurt me. I said, "Well, there are other issues I feel I know about but I could see no resolve with you." He went on about marrying me. . . . . it upsets me, because he is living this horrendous secret, and we could have had a lovely thing. (Sylvia)

The following are excerpts from a letter Sylvia provided after her interview. In it, she listed many of the occasions when she perceived her partner's behavior to be telling her of his attraction to men. At times she challenged him but received no definitive reply:

I was going over some of his old photos; he quickly skipped over those of Paul, dark, quiet looking man, young, outside a café they used to hang out. I said "When's that?" "That's past, that was it" . . . There was a particular male model he would look through my magazines to find and make a cup of tea or do something when he found the page advert he was in so the magazine ostensibly remained open validly at that page. . . . He tried a pair of my knickers on for fun once, said to me, "Don't throw that dress out, beautiful sea blue silk, I'll wear it." . . . These things on their own do not mean anything. I know plenty of guys who've dressed in drag for parties and many European men have manicures and pedicures, but for me it was part of a picture. . . . I also believe he had a crush on my handsome son who was doing his last year of school. He has a lovely body, and I often caught Larry looking at him. Once Benjamin was studying at his bedroom window and Larry was in the garden sitting on a low log. Of course he could see a shirtless Benji from the garden. I felt ill. (Sylvia)

Thus, the issue for Sylvia was not the same-sex attractions manifested in various behaviors and bodily stances, but instead Larry's refusal to acknowledge and discuss them with her.

"I TOLD HIM I WAS BISEXUAL"

We were in the bath one night and I went through and listed the people that I was most attracted to, and said, "Well, I'm most attracted to bisexual people. Then, homosexual, then heterosexual," . . . and that's when it came out. Greg said, "Oh, well, actually I'm bisexual." I think when he was a teenager, sort of mutual masturbation. . . . It made me a lot more comfortable because with me being bisexual and thinking that he was heterosexual, I had been having a problem with Greg in my relationship, that it was just stagnating. (Annette)

As with Annette, some women initiated a partner's disclosure because of their own experiences and/or confessions of same-sex attraction. Some women found their own sexual desires and experiences had been shifting along the way and wanted to share this with their partners as an assumed heteronormative relationship was no longer what they wanted. This often led to a reciprocal disclosure from their male partners. Other women were aggrieved and exhausted with the obviousness of the bisexuality and its ramifications on the relationship while their partners insisted on maintaining an ongoing silence as if the course of the relationship had not shifted at all.

Maura had been attracted to girls from the time she was a teenager, "but being brought up in that Catholic environment, that was a difficult thing to come to terms with." She met James when she was 15 and he was 14 and they became friends. She found she was attracted to him because of qualities that she thought meant he might be gay: "He was a lot more approachable, I guess he had sort of effeminate qualities about him and I did not feel threatened by him." By the time they were 20, they were sharing a flat together as friends and then began a relationship. Later, Maura realized this was not what she wanted due to her own bisexuality, as well as feeling increasingly frustrated that he was not coming out to her:

> After the birth of my daughter I guess I realized that this wasn't something that I could do forever. . . . So from that point on I made moves to get out of the relationship but he didn't want to. He used a lot of emotional blackmail . . . I was too scared to leave. Throughout that time there was plenty of opportunity for him to talk about his own sexual orientation. He didn't. I guess when he finally did come out I felt just ripped off. I had sort of shared things about myself with him and just expected that that person would be honest about who and what they were. (Maura)

What is also significant, however, is Maura's acknowledgment that if he had come out as bisexual, she would have ended the relationship given her existing frustrations with it, which is what he feared: "It [a heterosexual relationship] was a security blanket." Thus, despite her making it open for her partner to come out, her response to it would still have changed the course of their lives together.

"LIFE HAD CHANGED IN MANY WAYS"

> There was a time when he had quite a major career direction change, and he went from working during the day, nine to five, office work, to working in a carer's role, which meant he was working shift work and weekends, and it changed our relationship because our physical lives had changed. Life had changed in many ways. Perhaps we weren't spending as much time with each other because we worked opposite hours. (Erin)

Many women, including Erin, discussed how the shifting sexuality and depth of intimacy of the partner was part of or precipitated by shifts in the course and circumstances of the relationship over time. Cram writes of "triggers" such as "along comes the male menopause or whatever you care to call it" (2008: 20). The trigger could be a period of high stress, such as the threat of redundancy at work, difficulties with the marriage, financial loss, the birth of a child or the loss of a loved one (see also Buxton, 2004a, b; Higgins, 2002; Pearcey & Olson, 2009). Isay discussed how middle age brings an increased awareness of the "finitude of life," and a wish to repair discontinuities between one's needs, wishes, ambitions and longstanding social demands and expectations before "it's too late" (1998: 426). Other factors which precipitated or facilitated the sexual midstream shifts included health issues for either or both the partners, changes in their sexual intimacy, raising children, travel opportunities, aging and retirement, and circumstances that required them to have time living apart. For Lisa, pregnancy and long separations seemed to create a context within which her partner's repressed sexuality came to the fore:

> I have memories of being pregnant and him being away in Ghana for six out of the nine months and we would always be apart here or overseas and I was getting the bends. I didn't really enjoy the pregnancy because I had three jobs at the time. And he became very abusive. (Lisa)

Indeed, many women found that points of major transition and/or crisis became pivotal to the discovery or disclosure of their partner's bisexuality. Hannah had fallen in love with her husband because he was a "softer man, a more considerate man" compared to others of that time. He had an "openness to difference for both of us," and they enjoyed "an active sexual life right through, even towards the end." Indeed, they considered themselves to be "radical," enjoyed travelling and attended protests such as the anti-Vietnam War protests. They had a child, bought a house and continued to live what Hannah reflects upon as "the most joyful time" of "young marrieds," although given their earlier radicalism and love of freedom and travel, their relationship evolved into fitting in to what married couples "should do." Life became "very, very busy" upon having a second child and by the time they were thirty, she recalls "things started to change a bit." This included both of them becoming less satisfied with their sexual lives and having secret relationships with outside partners:

> Dean did come home and say he had been picked up by the police at a beat.... it wasn't as if it was a shock... I'd actually been having sex with other men which I think would have been more of a shock to him... so we thought initially we would live together and have an open marriage. It didn't work for us.... So he moved out and lived with a guy. And I was much more open about my sexuality at that stage. (Hannah)

Thus, both Hannah and her partner experienced shifts in their sexual needs and desires that they had not anticipated and had not been prepared for: "someone of my era, who, you know, things were always hidden" (Hannah).

Jeannette got pregnant so she and her musician partner got married: this was "the only thing you did in those days." A few years later, as his career as a television director bloomed, she learned of the first of many affairs he would have over the years:

> He had an affair with his boss's mistress.... I was hurt, but I thought seeing we've got a child, we've got to make the most of it. We'd start afresh and come to Australia. (Jeannette)

180   *Chapter 6*

In Australia in their late twenties, he managed an orchestra and she had another baby. When he went to hospital to have his tonsils out:

> I opened his bag and brought these letters out. He was having an affair with one of the ballet girls and an affair with the manager of the ballet who was male. (Jeannette)

Jeannette considered her responsibilities and circumstances and decided to stay in the marriage. She found that, despite another affair with another woman, life seemed to smooth out again:

> We had no money, and we were paying off a mortgage. We had counselling, but we didn't discuss the sexual side of it. Well, he sort of settled down and soldiered on and had various jobs, and finally I started my degree and he was fine. He was proud. And also we had a nice house . . . and the kids were doing well at school, and he looked after the kids when I went on my study weekends away. (Jeannette)

However, another work transfer for her partner to Sydney resulted in further economic shifts. It was also when Jeannette began her own business and they celebrated their 25th wedding anniversary. Throughout, she was aware that he was having affairs but not aware to what extent and what his plans were for the future:

> Whatever he was doing, it wasn't involving me and he said he was so wound up with work and things, he wasn't interested in sex. On one side, I think he was just an old tart. . . . I knew there was something really wrong with the relationship. I mean, he was never home, and there were often strange phone calls where men put the phone down. They would never give me messages. . . . I bought a plant nursery I wanted and aparently he thought if he got me into a plant nursery I'd be happy and he could leave me then, but I wouldn't move. . . . I had this incredible 25th wedding anniversary party, he made this beautiful speech and said how wonderful I was and how clever I was, and everything was in something silver and my girlfriend afterwards said he was running around telling everybody he had another place, and it was his farewell speech and he was leaving me, which I thought was a terrible betrayal. (Jeannette)

When the nursery was destroyed through fire, there were further intertwined economic and emotional issues to deal with, as well as sudden health issues that may also have been part of these stressful shifts:

> I had to re-borrow the money to start again, and then the following year he kept saying, "I'm going to have six weeks' break. I've got to be on my own." But it was a permanent break. He had a really good job and a really good salary and

> a car and left me about three weeks later, penniless, working my guts out at the nursery. . . . So he gave me $50 a week for food, left me in the house, and my son was living here and he was paying rent, and I got a boarder, and I had my first heart attack, and I had another one, my depression increased, so then they put me on a sickness benefit and I kept going to the nursery and working. And he was just Mr. Successful. But he lost his successful job and he had to come back home . . . In four months, he said he was back for good and we'd sell the house and pay off the debts. I'd found a unit and we shifted in to live happily ever after. . . . What was I going to do? I was fifty-five. I'd been through a lot of good things with him . . . We had a good cultural life. We had a lot of fun. He played the piano for three or four hours a day, which was fabulous. He was nice to be seen with. I could dress him, which I loved doing. (Jeannette)

However, the reconciliation as an attempt to repair their economic and emotional circumstances was short-lived when Jeannette noticed certain behaviors around her, and was told what her husband was saying:

> My son had a talk to him and he said he just couldn't stand me. He couldn't even sit at a table with me when I ate. It's dreadful and terrible for my self-esteem. . . . [He married me] because I was pregnant and he felt responsible for the child. (Jeannette)

For Steph, from the time they began to have children, a series of events contributed to increasing shifts in the relationship, and are blamed for the lack of sexual intimacy:

> Dean developed pneumonia very badly, and from that moment, I was blaming pneumonia. He was not the same person. Then he had a serious accident a year later. The doctor said that he had slight brain damage but nothing that was tragic, and one of the symptoms is lack of interest in sex, frequent impotence, so I thought there was a health explanation. . . So you just make excuses all the time, so there just wasn't a window where I would have said it's something else. Then, of course, when you have children you put on weight and you think it's you anyway. You're tired and you know it's normal not to have sex as regularly and there was never any indication other than lack of interest in sex. (Steph)

Another important factor that led to further shifts and realizations was Steph's partner being transferred to Vietnam for work while she waited for her last child to complete high school before joining him. This meant freedom from family and Steph, and being surrounded by Asian gay men and an expatriate community of gay men:

> All of a sudden it was sort of like a bolt from heaven, that this is what has been eluding him all his life, and he realized he was attracted to gay men and

had a one night fling in Singapore, and then consequently thought, "Oh, this could alter my life considerably." Of course, he wasn't with me, which meant that probably I was the controlling factor unbeknownst to me. Also, he had a colleague who was gay, and Tom introduced him to the gay community in Vietnam. . . . He used to have the most incredible high blood pressure, and since he's become active with men and he's come out to me, his blood pressure is below mine, damn it. (Laughing). (Steph)

Nine months later, at Christmas, Dean comes out to Steph, although she had already been following "the trail":

He was beside himself because he didn't know how he was going to tell me. He'd actually laid this neat little trail for me. In fact, the trail actually started before he went to Vietnam because he insisted we watch a gay movie. I sort of dutifully watched it, and even then I was thinking, "He's very insistent in watching this movie." No discussion. . . . July we went over to visit and he met us at Singapore airport, and I felt that I'd met someone I didn't know, he was very, very distant. I felt that I was not welcome at all, and the kids felt it too. And then we flew to Vietnam and we stayed in the apartment and I was taken around and I was a bit culture shocked anyway. I had to come to terms with the culture, I was uprooting the family and myself and going, and I had this bloke who was keeping me more than ignorant and removed while he was right out there . . . so I went home to Australia from that thinking, "Well, I'm not sure I want to go if he's going to be like that over there." He started having lovely parties at the house and he was having all these blokes around for lunch. That's okay, that's fine. That's what you do in a very social life. . . . And then I went over and there was gay literature on the shelf, and "Oh, Tom's lent it to me." "Oh, that's fine," I said thinking that Dean wanted to get a bit of background, had to get on with his gay colleague. I mean, you research. And then he had another one of these lunches, and I said, "Oh, who's coming?" He said, "Michael" and the voice was different and in my head I said, "Shit, he's gay." (Laughing). Like that, a bolt out of the blue again. And hung up. . . . And when he came home I sat him down at the kitchen table and I said, "I think there's something really difficult but very important you have to tell me." And he said, "Yes, but I can't tell you yet." And I let it go, because he was quite emotional and I thought, "Well, God, do I really want to go to Vietnam with this man?" (Steph)

What is also significant is that after such a journey of shifting circumstances and ambiguities, Dean's final coming out was initially a relief for Steph, like the end of a difficult journey:

We went down the beach and we walked and then we sat and actually, I didn't pre-empt, I didn't say anything. I just waited. I think it had to come entirely from him. . . . and because I was expecting it, the feeling was euphoria. It was absolute lightness and freedom and relief and I just floated. I skipped down the road and I'm thinking, "This is ridiculous. Why do I feel like this?" But it was just this load off the shoulders for a start and the knowledge that actually I had worked it out and I was right. The knowledge that it wasn't my fault, that the marriage wasn't working, that now I had choices. And it didn't hit me to the next day, when I sort of kept hyperventilating. (Steph)

After the initial lightness and floating, Steph realized the journey hadn't ended as decisions needed to be made about the move to Vietnam and how to deal with Dean's coming out with their children and family:

We weren't sleeping. We were talking all night and I wasn't eating. I lost about three kilos first time over Christmas I've ever lost weight (Laughing). In a sense it was, "But am I going to go with this man into the unknown in an unknown relationship?" I was going to have to cope with the Vietnamese culture and the gay culture. And really it was stubbornness I think that made me decide, "Well, damn it. I love going to new places. He is not going to do me out of going to Vietnam." (Steph)

Steph also noticed another unexpected pleasant shift in the quality and frequency of their sex life. Indeed, some women in our research said that after their partners disclosed, there was often a renewed intimacy because of the relief, euphoria and bonding that came with the new trust and openness, what is often called the "honeymoon phase" (Corley & Kort, 2006; Kort, 2014a):

We probably had the best sex we've ever had in our married life that week after he told me. It was every day, and it's never, ever been every day. I mean, were we clinging to each other because we were terrified? I don't know. And then it regressed. Because when I first got to Vietnam, I thought, yeah, this is going to work. He's treating me really well, because he hasn't always been, often with lack of words or lack of intimacy, lack of warmth. So I thought, "This is heaven. Gosh, if he's going to be gay, so be it. This relationship is the best it's ever been, I can live with this," but then it didn't last. He actually had developed quite a relationship with a bloke in Vietnam. He was starting to behave like an adolescent too.... "I can't juggle work, I can't juggle hiding my sexuality. I can't juggle Steph any more" because it was a juggle. I mean, I was a wonderful expat spouse playing tennis and drinking gin and doing all those sorts of things, thinking, "Well, you don't know half of my life. He's off with men and I'm just the lady of leisure." ... life there was so different, so maybe that's how I did actually cope with it, because not only had life changed in one way, it had changed in another way. I loved Vietnam. I actually have a lot of regrets that I wasn't emotionally strong enough to take myself off to places, to really get to know the culture. (Steph)

Finally, Steph realized she had another decision to make:

> It took me probably a while to decide to actually make the break. . . . I said, "Well, look, I've made the decision, I want to go home . . . and you live here and I'll live there and we'll see each other occasionally . . . You're having a lovely time and I'm not. You're going out and here's me sitting at home doing nothing." And he actually was in denial for quite some time. (Steph)

Sue's partner came out as bisexual after three years together but, despite feeling it was something he would not discuss further, she felt they had the foundation for a workable relationship. As with many women, shifting life stages in regards to having children, negotiating each other's goals and work stress, selling a home and moving in to a new one, begins to coincide, precipitate, or intertwine with cracks appearing in the relationship:

> He'd been away for business for a week, which was not unusual. Came home, and I knew something was wrong straight away. And he told me that night that he had hired a male escort. And that had been his first sexual experience outside the relationship. And that was sort of the beginning of the end. I was totally devastated. . . . we'd been married eleven years, it was all pretty hard to understand why it had happened at that stage when we were building the next stage of life, and we were actually going through the process of building a new home . . . the only way that he could describe it was that he'd had these desires that he'd been trying to suppress and apparently he'd spent quite a bit of time on the net, talking to people in chat rooms. . . . Having two children I think was the precipitating event, absolutely. I think he probably was thinking about responsibility and just freaking out. He couldn't do exactly as he wanted to and in hindsight, I can see that pretty much our life was molded around his needs in terms of his work. I mean, we had a great life. We did a lot of traveling and wonderful things. . . . Our daughter was pretty challenging in terms of not being a good sleeper, and I used to think how lucky I was that I had such a fantastic partner, and all the other women would be bitching about their husbands, and so I had another child. (Sue)

The relationship ended six months later when their second child was eight months old. Soon after, he was in love with a man he'd met on the Internet. Sue found herself trying to understand why and how it had all happened:

> He's a high achiever and has always had very high goals. And I just wonder whether he perceived us as holding him back. . . . I couldn't say that I love him anymore because it seems like he's swept all those years away far too easily, and particularly when I'm left holding the babies. It's been pretty tough, and I feel resentful, because I felt like I'd just given him all this rope, and hoping that he would come to the right decision, that we were more important, but sadly he didn't. (Sue)

For Monica, it was having "three babies in nappies" that she believes was the "trigger" for her partner to come out about something she had always suspected and even known a little about:

> At the time, I think he was expressing dissatisfaction with me and a monogamous relationship which I already knew about. . . . The kids started coming and he sort of realized that maybe he was stuck there. . . . He told me when the twins were six weeks old, which was really fucked up. So he was feeling depressed but look we were both really miserable. He would come home from work, and I had a two-year-old, and I was pregnant with twins and it was a hot summer and he'd say, "How are you?" and I'd say, "Kill me, now, please, kill me." And then the twins were born and I was averaging about three hours sleep at night and he was averaging about four or five hours sleep at night. We had three kids in nappies, oh, it was just a nightmare. (Monica)

For Loredana, her Multiple Sclerosis made her dependent on her partner in ways that changed their relationship, and she believed it occurred at a time of his mid-life crisis as well:

> I have so many physical needs that I can't meet myself, and I needed him. He's a great cook and he's very good around the house. He can make lounge covers, he can make curtains and he's six foot and he's very strong. . . . his way of answering [when she asked about his lack of intimacy for her] was, "Well, we change as we grow older." And, I said, "Yes, we change. We might change in a color that we like but this is about intimacy." (Loredana)

"HE DECEIVED ME FOR SO LONG, AND THAT'S THE MAIN ISSUE"

> The thing that in the end that I really couldn't cope with was the fact that I had been perfectly honest with him about everything in my life and to know that he'd been secretly doing all these things, lying to me, made me feel like a complete idiot. . . . and I know that if I tried to continue the relationship, I would always distrust him and probably become quite bitter myself. He deceived me for so long, and that's the main issue. . . . I mean, we're still friends. I own my home, he pays me rent, we're comfortable together, but we don't have a sexual relationship any more. (Gerry)

After twelve years together, Gerry discovered her partner had "actually been for the last seven years of our relationship visiting gay venues and having casual sex with other men." For women like Gerry, the disclosure or discovery of the partner's bisexuality was less an issue than coming to terms with the amounts and types of deception and betrayal their partners had undertaken. Atwood (1998) also found that the pathology for many women existed not in the sexual practice but in the dishonesty, the deception and the manipulation of others: "The worst thing is not knowing, just having this nebulous thing hanging around. Then I start doubting myself" (Loredana). They feel betrayed by the very persons with whom they thought they had the most intimate of relationships and who should have trusted them with this core information about themselves:

> For many, the disclosure opens a Pandora's Box of previous secrets, lies, half-truths, or omissions. Some spouses wonder what role they may have played unconsciously in the deception and/or denial. Feeling led on and, for some, "used," most lose confidence in their own judgment of whom to trust, including themselves (Buxton, 2006c: 115).

Thus, the course of the relationship had to be re-navigated according to what to do with this knowledge of her partner's ability to deceive rather than what to do about his bisexuality (see also Browder, 2005).

After her initial discoveries, Jeannette found herself being told about the extent of her partner's same-sex activities piece by piece, which only added to the feelings of mistrust:

> He said that he loved me and that he was sorry and I said, "Look, you've lied to me. If you had only been upfront with me and talked to me about this we can go forward, but while you lie about what you've done and what your feelings are we can't move forward . . . you told me you hadn't been with him, it was just phone sex and computer sex. I've had unprotected sex with you. I've got chronic fatigue. If you've got AIDS, you could fight it for twenty years. I'd be dead in twelve months because I've got no immune system" . . . and again, he made it all sound as if it wasn't really his fault and it was only oral sex. Anyway, again I tried to believe him and tried to put it behind us and then a few days later, he told me that he'd had full-blown sex with men in a car park and sex in a park on a Saturday afternoon. . . . If I had the gas connected, I'd have put my head in the oven! We were a mess, both of us, there's no two ways to describe it. (Jeannette)

"WE'RE A LOT CLOSER NOW ACTUALLY"

> I wouldn't accept it at any cost if he was very inconsiderate and we didn't get on. I wouldn't stay in a marriage in which I was unhappy, but it was mostly positive and we're a lot closer now actually. (Maria)

In some relationships, the disclosure/discovery was followed by negotiation and renavigation in order to stay together. Maria's partner began to go to gay nightclubs when she went overseas with the children, and continued to do so when she returned. From this point, Maria confronted him, he came out, and many discussions and clarifications ensued:

> About a year ago I kept complaining about the amount of times he was going out at night or overnight. . . . He wasn't spending any time with me or the children. And that's when he told me that he was exploring a side of himself that he previously didn't know about, but he realized it all made sense to him . . . and at that point I didn't really know what was going to happen, because it sort of felt like we were living a lie, and I wasn't prepared to continue with our marriage as it was. And then I found out that he was so determined not to live a lie himself that he was prepared to walk away from our marriage if that's what it took to stay true to himself. The fact that he was prepared to do that meant it put all the pressure on me. I said to him, "This is really unfair because it's left to me to make all the decisions here." I suppose I was given an ultimatum. I knew he wasn't going to change and would walk away and that would affect me and also our children. (Maria)

Maria decided to stay in the marriage based on certain conditions and concluded that it was the best decision.

There was sometimes a time of ambiguity and indecisiveness as the women came to understand the enormity of what had happened and what it would mean for the future. They experienced a temporary paralyzing limbo-state where they found themselves unable to decide which direction to take from this point. Buxton (2006a, d) sets out the stages through which MOREs typically progress if they initially endeavor to work on the relationship after disclosure/discovery. First is what she refers to as the "Honeymoon Period" when many couples feel closer and more intimate, often sexually. Second is an "Awareness of Differences and Conflicts" as bisexual partners explore their same-gender attractions while their heterosexual spouses express pain, fear, anger or grief about these pursuits. The third stage is "Increase (or Decrease) of Couple Communication, and Mutual Adjustments" wherein couples learn how to renegotiate boundaries and face the nonnegotiable items in their needs, wants, feelings, values or priorities (see also Kort, 2014a). Fourth is the "Reinstatement (or Not) of Trust" wherein heterosexual spouses work to restore belief in the partner's word, ascertain the quality of the relationship and whether or not they believe it is worth preserving. Fifth is an "Increase (or Decrease) of Tolerance" wherein couples make mutually agreed upon changes so that each feels satisfied in the relationship. The next stage is "Integration of the Changes" wherein couples learn to live with the changes as ongoing givens in their relationship. The final stage is "Commitment to Work Jointly to Continue the Marriage" which entails developing "a healthy interdependence . . . affirmed by demonstrated love and marital lovemaking" (2006d: 121). As one of Buxton's participants states:

It was terrifying and exhilarating! There was a sense of breathing free, of shattering old patterns, of opening up to limitless possibilities with no more boundaries to our lives (Buxton, 1991: 19).

In the film *Kinsey* (2004), Alfred Kinsey's marriage is the film's central relationship. Mack is aware of her husband's bisexuality and her emotions range from acceptance to betrayal and jealousy when she becomes aware of his interest in Clyde. Mack and Clyde talk about this sharing of Kinsey. "Most women would have had me murdered", Clyde says. "Oh I considered it," she says but then admits "there have been benefits. It's certainly sparked things up sexually." Here again we see that a bisexual male's relationship with a woman can be enhanced by his simultaneous relationship with a man and vice versa. The outcome of this is that Clyde, acting on a natural attraction, initiates an affair with Mack as well. After their dual involvements with Clyde,

> the film ends with a return to marriage as the basic building block of a successful life [for Kinsey and Mack] . . . To be fair this is often what happens in individual bisexual lives since the pressures of maintaining an unstructured life, of braving social discrimination and abuse, often cause people to choose in favor of something more traditional (Vicari, 2011: 102–103).

For many women in our research, the past relationship, particularly if it had been a very positive one, was not easy to leave behind. Yet, there was the knowledge that the present could not just be a continuation of this past due to the disruption caused by disclosure/discovery, even if the partner believed that it could be so:

> He told me it was such a relief for him and it was like, "Oh, great, I've told Sally, and now I can just get on with life, we can just merrily go on" and I'm thinking, "Hell no, this is a big thing." (Sally)

Yet, a future without her partner, or any kind of different future ahead with no sense of a definite destination, was also unfathomable for some women: "given all that, I'm still not leaving him and I think, 'Am I so stupid or is he that clever?' I don't know" (Loredana).

Although the course of the journey was going to be renavigated, some women spoke about deciding to stay together and maintain the same destination as a couple that they had set out on before. For some couples, a strong religious faith in regard to making lifelong marriage vows which included "in sickness or in health," as well as a strong commitment to each other and the children, were the foundation for staying together:

I thought I just can't live like this. I'll leave. And then I thought you don't leave a marriage when well, number one, you've vowed before God that you won't, and number two, I really love the guy and you don't walk out on someone who was depressed and sick . . . and I know one of my feelings would be I would be a total failure if this marriage fails. He's confessed in recent years that he tried everything to make me leave, and then he wouldn't have had to make the decision to leave. . . . . I've committed to Bill, I've committed to these children. (Fay)

For other women and their partners, it was about recalling the reasons they had married, allowing each other separations to see what it would be like to not be together, and coming back together because of their love for each other, but on a stronger basis of honesty and communication:

We separated for a year and part of that was "Okay, you've got to sort this out" . . . Our separation gave him the space to explore his attraction to men in his own way and time. . . . and we agreed on a policy of microscopic truth from then on. I asked lots of questions, and he shared the information I needed even if he felt guilty or knew it would hurt me. He remained supportive through my bouts of despair and anger. I finally got that this was not about me—that I was not a deficient wife in some way. That I did not cause it and I could not have prevented it. (Krystle)

Given thirteen years of a happy marriage preceded the withdrawal and depression prior to his coming out, Sally and her partner decided to stay together. Sally, however, needed to acknowledge the huge shifts in the relationship which required a new course to be set:

I gave him a big hug and said that we would work it out together. I did what I normally did, I went and got lots of information for both of us, but was still in shock I think. I found support for him through a support group. Then I started looking around for different marriage models. . . . That first year proved to be really hard. I remember going through the most awful stress and being very unsure of everything whereas before I was very comfortable with where things were. . . . It's still there [the relationship] but it's changed. That's the way, not losing your family, because as I said we had a great marriage and we've got great kids and he's a great dad. (Sally)

Soulla also noticed that after a few years of happy marriage and two daughters, her partner became depressed for months:

He then finally admitted that although he loved me, he could no longer hide from me or from himself the fact that he loved men as well. He had fallen in love with a man he wanted to see regularly but he would be devastated if I left him or took the children away from him. He said he felt so trapped and guilty having caused so much pain to the woman he loved, that it was more than he could bear. Anyway, we worked out that he could see the man he loved as long as he still loved me, and with time, we actually found the pain began to ease. There was too much love between us and we enjoyed parenting our daughters, and then there was all the shared hard work to get above our working-class backgrounds, my migrant background, only to lose everything, money, family, each other if we got divorced. That would just add so much more psychological, emotional and economic traumas and in the end we'd all lose. (Soulla)

Thus, renegotiations were made, and the costs and rewards of either staying together or divorcing were considered very seriously before deciding to stay together. What seems to have been very important for Soulla was that her partner still loved her and she understood his need and ability to love a man as well.

Vicky attributes the openness of the regional area around them, renowned for "alternative lifestyles," for allowing them to renegotiate their relationship. Likewise, seeing how another couple had organized a life where the bisexual partner had another partner of the same sex provided a model for a viable future together:

Mike: I think a lot of the turning forty syndrome affected me. Here was little me with the desires and I was scared that I was all of a sudden going to be an old man and never experience some of the things that I would like to have tried, so now I have, it's wonderful. . . . And then of course the wonders of the Internet. A lot of mistakes were made there too I must admit. I met some creepy men, but as it turned out I met—

Vicky: Met a lovely fellow. Who I also get along really well with.

Mike: The whole situation is just perfect. Everyone gets on well and it's a good life. . . . I see him once a month and not always something sexually either. I mean, we went to the Motor Show and were like boys in a lolly shop, looking at cars and because he's got his own business too and we'll meet up for lunch, it's just as simple as that. He comes to our place and we have a little bit of a party and a few drinks and a laugh. (Vicky)

Mike and Vicky believed that if the relationship is solid and loving and there is a strong level of open communication and negotiation, it could be renavigated and stay the course:

Vicky: We were real talkers. We'd sit for hours and discuss things. . . .

Mike: These guys sitting at home with their wives, the wife might have an inkling, and could say, "Would you be interested in another guy?" and there's a door for the poor bugger to say, "Maybe" and that's pretty much how we did it and one thing leads to another and you end up just discussing everything. And most women that are married really don't have a huge problem with their husband if it's done correctly. . . . You don't over complicate things is probably the big thing. (Vicky)

CONCLUSION

In conclusion, our research has shown that many women feel anger and resentment at the dominant assumptions and presumptions that construct the triad of marriage, monogamy and heterosexuality as "unquestioned and unquestionable" (Schutz, 1944). This has rendered them ignorant, vulnerable, powerless and unable to make informed choices and decisions about their lives, health and relationships. Whether their partners disclosed or were discovered, and whether they had reached the end of their relationship's journey or renavigated a future direction together, they found themselves on the borders, devastatingly dragged into or agentically leaping into challenging the "thinking-as-usual" (Schutz, 1944). They often have no discursive framework at the beginning of their relationships for mestizaje possibilities and problematics that may be ahead, both enriching directions and devastating dangers.

Chapter 7

"We've Arrived Where We Started and Know the Place for the First Time"

Women Reflecting on 'Staying the Course' or 'Splitting Up'

If I look at it from here looking back, if I knew what I know now and Bill knew, and we lived in this era, we probably would never have married. I think there's a lot my age in my situation. And I think there'll be less as time goes on. (Fay)

What was it that T.S. Eliot said? Something like "We've arrived where we started and know the place for the first time." Well, we now know why we fell in love and have stayed in love despite the silly world that kept hounding us. The pre-feminism feminist lawyer and the beyond-sexual-labels husband. Because we had a unique love to share and life lessons we could teach others, if they only wanted to know. We are getting old now, with careers and kids and employment behind us, and hopefully relaxation and more joy ahead as the world catches up, and sometimes I wish we had been young now and just starting out in this somewhat less repressive society. But what a journey it's been. (Alice)

Having explored the experiences of women at the beginning of their relationship with a bisexual man in chapter 5, and the experiences of women who discover their partner's bisexuality during the course of the relationship in chapter 6, this chapter will present the feelings of both these groups of women in hindsight, when they look back at the relationship and their decisions. Two groups of women in long-term relationships become apparent:

1. Women who 'stayed the course' in the relationship; and
2. Women who 'split up' with their partners, either initiated by themselves or by their partners.

Ahmed's (2010) reflections on what constitutes happiness are applicable to the women as they reflect on the past. She writes that "happiness scripts could be thought of as straightening devices, ways of aligning bodies with what is already lined up" in accordance to heteronormative and gendernormative constructions of how love and relationship should be lived (2010: 92). To deviate from the line is to be threatened with unhappiness, and yet, as the women who stayed in their relationships find when they look back, in deviating from the apparent happiness of heteronormative conventionality and conformity, they left this happiness "for life" (2010: 77). Ahmed also considers the notion of "bearable and unbearable lives" based on Butler's (2004) concept of livable and unlivable lives. A bearable life is "where what must be endured does not threaten that life, in either the bare facts of its existence or in the sense of its aim, direction, or purpose . . . [and] in being endured can keep its bearings" as was the situation for many women who stayed in the relationship (2010: 97). This is contrasted with an unbearable life which epitomizes the decisions of women who left the relationship: "The unbearable life is a life which cannot be tolerated or endured, held up, held onto. The unbearable life 'breaks' or 'shatters' under the 'too much' of what is being borne" (2010: 97).

For those women who stayed in the relationship, the following themes emerge:

a. *Family and friends became supportive and admiring of the couple* even if they initially may have been doubtful or negative about the women's decision to stay with their partners.
b. The women are *sought out by other women in similar circumstances to become advisers and supporters.*
c. The bisexuality became relatively insignificant due to *ageing which brought new concerns and circumstances.*
d. The women were very *aware of the rewards that came with staying in the relationship*, no matter how difficult it was at times.
e. There was a strong feeling of *personal growth* that came with having survived and thrived in the relationship.
f. There was much *rethinking of normative and traditional relationship structures* and a satisfaction in constructing their own relationship configuration.

For those women who ended the relationship or had it ended by their partners, the following themes become apparent:

a. If they had known about their partner's bisexuality or what would eventuate, *they would never have married their partners.*
b. If they had known what difficulties and dilemmas the relationship would continue to bring, *they would have left the relationship much earlier.*
c. Having left the relationship and the known, there were *fears and uncertainty about their futures.*

d. The women expressed *feelings of freedom, relief and a strong sense of personal growth*, including an interest in establishing new goals and new relationships.
e. The divorce had been a positive experience with *much goodwill in salvaging a friendship and restructuring a future form of family.*
f. *Grief, loss and sadness were ongoing* and required management.
g. Although the relationship had ended, the women *did not regret it because of the positive outcomes* such as the children they had together.

"WE JUST THINK OF IT AS THE NORMAL WAY TO BE"

I know he loves me to death and nothing will change that and we're very secure. . . . we just think of it as the normal way to be. (Vicky)

There is a need for research with "resilient" MOREs who are satisfied with their relationship despite facing significant constraints. What are the "dynamics" and "coping resources" they utilize to keep their love and understanding alive for each other? (Yarhouse & Pawlowski, 2003: 468). Coleman's (1982) clinical experience suggested that for long-term "successful adjustment," both people must love each other, have a high degree of communication, and want to make the relationship work. Likewise, both people have resolved feelings of guilt, blame and resentment; physical contact and intimacy is present; and the woman partner has a sense of worth outside the marriage. Finally, they have worked out monogamous or non-monogamous negotiations; the woman partner is willing to work on understanding and accepting her partner's same-sex feelings; and he accepts his same-sex feelings (see also Grever, 2012).

Buxton found that those who cling to the "marriage-as-it-was" find it harder to keep their marriage alive than do those who redefine their marriages (Buxton, 2004a: 98). Schwartz (2012) believes that acceptance is about knowing that the original marriage/long-term relationship is over and growing beyond the betrayal experience. If the couple is going to remain together, trust and reconnection need to be rebuilt. The decision may be fraught with complexity and based on many factors, including the length of the marriage, the age of the partners, the presence of children, and negotiating a sexual relationship. Nevertheless, the couple must be able to recognize and celebrate the positives aspect of bisexuality and MORE relationships. For example, the participants in Rostosky's (2010) study described eleven specific positive qualities of bisexual identity. At the interpersonal level, there was the freedom from socially constructed labels and gender roles, and the feeling of authenticity and honesty; a unique perspective on individuals and society and love; and "a level of insight and self-awareness that they would not otherwise have attained"

(2010: 134). What might be considered paradoxical, "fluidity and flexibility" were experienced as solid foundations for establishing a sense of self, and to live with self-confidence and security, authenticity and honesty (2010: 135).

The experience of "staying the course" can also be found in a few biographies and novels:

> I realized that bisexuality is a part of what makes him and I, and he is what I needed. I love everything about him and if I could change anything, I would change nothing. . . . We now enjoy a love that only a few people have the privilege of knowing (Scott-Blanton, 2005: 249).

In Brant's novel, one of the wives, Sally, says to her husband:

> This is something I don't understand. All I know is you're my husband. I don't want another man. There's no one else I'd rather spend the rest of my life with. . . Seems to me this is Mother Nature's work. . . . I love you. It's no more complicated than that (2006: 238).

In her autobiographical account, Coon (2012) describes the euphoria of realizing how special her relationship is after the tumultuous journey she has traversed:

> Today I have reached the other side. No matter how dark and consuming my journey became or how heavily my numbed feet dragged along the cold Earth, I inched my way steadily toward the light. The other side for me is a relationship that radiates love and illumination, like nothing I have ever experienced before, with a capacity to evolve even further . . . The best part is that I didn't have to leave my husband to achieve it. . . . Fortunately, by falling more deeply in love with my husband I actually grew to love myself more . . . This book is not about *surviving* a relationship like mine, it is about embracing a relationship like mine (2012: 1–3).

"We think you're wonderful"

Some women found family and friends who were initially doubtful, disapproving of or disgusted by their decision to stay with their partners gradually became supportive and admiring of the couple. They often viewed them as heroic and pioneering, particularly if their own more normative relationships had ended or experienced disillusioning problems. Sometimes this admiration came from one's own adult children:

> The thing that gets me is that people now say, "Oh, I think you're marvellous." And like my daughter's friends now say, "Oh, we've heard all about you. We think you're wonderful." . . . And that's [also] coming from our children, so

now they've got a respect for me in a different way, whereas I think before they thought, "Mum doesn't know what she's doing." (Brenda)

"Some women ring me up and they say to me, "Well, what do you do?"

Some women found themselves sought out by other women in similar circumstances to become advisers and supporters, especially if they were known to counsellors and support groups: "Some women ring me up and they say to me, "Well, what do you do?" (Brenda). However, at times, this seeking of advice from women in heterosexual relationships came from a deficit model framework of thinking that the women with bisexual partners had been through so much more than they were going through. Often, women like Brenda had to correct this position and make the women understand that although the structure and machinations of the relationship may have seemed "worse" from an external perspective, it was often much more loving than the normative relationships women were seeking advice about:

> They say, "I don't know how you cope." When my friend was having hassles with her relationship with her husband she said, 'And I think of all these things [I'm going through] and then I think of you and what you're coping with." I said, "But I'm not in the same situation as you." . . . She's worse off, I mean, I've got a loving relationship. (Brenda)

"We're both old now anyway"

Some women who got to old age with their partners after decades together found that with age, many of the issues they had faced such as negotiating external sexual relationships, had gradually become insignificant or nonexistent. They were glad they were still together to face the new challenges of ageing such as chronic illness and grieving deaths of family and friends. The reasons to stay married were often far more compelling than the reasons to separate. For example, some older bisexual men become less enthused about the gay "scene" and "keeping up with the latest trends" (Edser & Shea, 2002: 26). Brenda's partner (now deceased) was facing the onset of dementia and was beginning to forget many of his past relationships and experiences with other men: "he can't remember all that now, not to the fine detail. But that's another worry that's coming in" (Brenda).

Thus, overall, these couples were respectful of the importance of growth and change, and preferred to experiment with new ways without wiping out the value of what they had built together over a thirty- or forty-year period. Tornstam's (2005) theory of gerotranscendence appears to be very applicable to these older MOREs. Gerotranscendence refers to a state of development where individuals "transcend rigid socio-cultural perspectives about the self, others . . . [and] results in a meta-perspective that is reflective, cosmic, transcendent, and typically, more personally satisfying" (Fleckenstein & Cox II, 2015: 97). It provides a theoretical framework for predicting "adults' openness to the possibility of sexual non-exclusivity and greater satisfaction from sexuality, even as they age" (Fleckenstein & Cox II, 2015: 97). Tornstam discusses how gereotranscendent individuals experience less interest in "superfluous social interaction" (2005: 45). This is very pertinent to some of the older MOREs in our research who gained an insight that certain social interactions are "merely role-playing; where the role does not necessarily fit the actor very well" (2005: 66). They now had the means to refuse to undertake "haciendo caras" (Anzaldua, 1987a). Tornstam refers to "emancipated innocence" as the "delight in doing things that one did not earlier dare to do. . . a new kind of innocence and spontaneity is added to adult judgment and rationality" (2005: 66). Ageing can also bring "self-confrontation" or the discovery of hidden aspects of the self, both negative and positive. This may be coupled with "ego-integrity" whereby "pieces of life's jigsaw puzzle form a wholeness" (2005: 74):

> we probably now are the happiest we've ever been . . . We do respect each other now, and well, I find him to be my main friendship. . . . I guess I've learnt over the years that for my mental health, if I dwell on things I get depressed, and I don't want to live like that. And so what I can't fix I just put aside and hang on to positive things. (Fay)

Examples of where gerotranscendence, "emancipated innocence" and "ego-integrity" had not occurred at all or completely in MOREs who stayed together, were those women who stayed in their marriages because of the decades of "investment" in the relationship. Even though they acknowledged the "love has gone," they considered staying together a better option that facing an old age alone:

> We're both old now anyway. I'm prepared to stay in the marriage as long as he treats me fair. We still have sex periodically but it's nothing like it was before. I don't love him, and I doubt if I ever will, but we're working on it. He says he loves me. . . . we've invested a lot, and thirty-five years is an awful lot to think about, throwing it down the drain, and I know at my age, the chances of finding a decent bloke is pretty remote because all the good ones, the women are going to hold on to them. (Jean)

Other older women found their husbands were grieving a past they never had, particularly as they became vulnerable to ill health:

> Bill nearly died. He went in for a simple hernia operation about seven years ago, and he developed a deep vein thrombosis and within forty-eight hours, the clots had ended up in his lungs. . . . And from that near death experience, he said to me, "I've nearly died and I've never lived the truth. I've never lived who I am." (Fay)

And in relation to this grieving, the women themselves had shifted in their comfort over their partners having another partner:

> a couple of nights ago, I said to Bill, "If you do find somebody, bring them over for tea" because I've come that far in my thinking that it's not the desperate need to hold him so tight that I didn't think I would be able to survive if we weren't a family, but we'll survive, because even if he met another partner, the friendship will always be there. (Fay)

"Many blessings have come from it"

Women often spoke about the rewards of the relationship and staying in it, but were also able to acknowledge there were times of great difficulty to be worked through:

> For us, it is a journey. We don't know the destination, or necessarily whom our travel companions will be, but we are just enjoying the view and the company we have today. It seemed an unforeseen U-turn that was all wrong, but many blessings have come from it. (Krystle)

Many of the rewards came from witnessing and experiencing the ongoingness of the relationship, which they believed they might have forfeited if they had left the relationship and faced the possibility of not finding a new relationship as fulfilling and rewarding as the current one. Thus, the costs and rewards of the relationship often went hand in hand:

> It's a real yo-yo ride, and we felt like we were breaking new ground and he was out there putting it about and I was around suffering or putting it about myself. But, I mean, it all came out in the wash. I'm glad that we went through it, and I'm glad that I let him free because in the end it did work out. I feel as though I did win. . . . We've got that common ground and we'll sit there and we'll laugh and he'll make all sorts of camp comments and for me it's quite normal. (Sherry)
>
> *Greg:* We want to both be individually happy and happy together. We've got a past, we've got a present, and we want a future. But we want it to be an authentic future . . .
>
> *Krystle:* Greg is a beautiful person who is a lovely partner to me and who I love, so why shouldn't we be together. . . . We believe that we will be able to

cope with the challenges, but accept that as in all marriages, there is no guarantee. . . . I certainly couldn't envision that we would be as happy as we are three or four years ago.

For Soulla (deceased), it was reflecting back on their shared joy and pain when she was experiencing terminal cancer, and feeling blessed that after her death, her daughters' lives would be secure:

Would I have married him? If I hadn't I would've missed so much. Compared to the many married men I know and hear about, there is no way I would give him up without losing so much. He is a wonderful husband and father and my best friend. (Soulla)

"I have learnt an awful lot"

Many women expressed a strong feeling of personal growth that comes with having survived challenges and thrived in the relationship:

I think it's been overwhelmingly positive . . . There's certainly been hard times, gut wrenching fears, you know, but overwhelmingly, it's been so important in me, in the way I see the world and . . . it has challenged so many dominant things and that's only healthy. . . It's quite exciting to think gee, I have learnt an awful lot. (Katie)

Ava considered her growth in dealing with the relationship as being similar to dealing with any change, including her migration to Australia from the United States:

Like anybody I have my depressed moments. My moments of questioning and thinking what have I gotten into. The reasons that I went into it haven't gone away just because sometimes it's hard. Sometimes living in Australia is hard. When it's Thanksgiving, you know all your family is getting together and they're having a big party with the turkey and everything. But, you sort of get away from the minutiae of it and you realize this is not the best of all possible worlds and not everything can be perfect. (Ava)

For some women, there was also the personal growth that came with establishing a flourishing relationship after a history of heteronormative relationships that did not work out:

I had three bad marriages before Luke. This one is less needy. It's honest, it's simple, if I want something I say it . . . So very much the study and the reading that we do is about living in the now, be in this moment and operate from that. (Simone)

"There's him and there's me and how we live together"

Women who stayed with their partners often spoke about having to re-think normative relationship structures. They gained satisfaction and strength in having constructed their own relationship configuration, negotiating their investment and identity in the relationship, and honoring all the experiences they had gone through together: "There's him and there's me and how we live together, it's up to us" (Monica).

> Being in this relationship has made me evaluate myself a lot and my sort of pre-formed opinions of the way relationships can be. It sort of makes you think about how much society has influenced the way we think and so I guess in a lot of ways it can be a good experience, but at the same time you have to really work through it and be ready for it. (Lauren)
>
> I want people to know it's not a doom, gloom situation. In fact, I feel happier than I ever have. And I have no crystal ball and I can't say that we are going to last, but I couldn't say that even if I was in a heterosexual situation . . . In fact, I kind of believe that we've got more of a chance than most because we are very honest. (Rosemary)

For some women, the relationship had begun with a strong sense of commitment and love, and continued to be so. Thus, for Monica, there was a feeling that having renavigated the relationship in the face of so many challenges, dealing with her partner's bisexuality was considered "a small thing" that just required more of the same relationship adjustments:

> He's adorable. I love him and I know everything about him, all the yucky stuff as well and I still love him and he says, "I really love you back. Not pretending to." . . . and it certainly wasn't okay to begin with. It was a big shock so I wouldn't want other women to think that you get told and then you just happily move on so quickly. There were a lot of tears and a lot of trauma and a split up . . . but if I don't want to be with him any more then we'll break up but it won't be because of that issue, it will be because I don't want to be with him anymore, whatever reason that is. . . . You know, from when I was 22 to 30 I had uterine cancer. I had three miscarriages, I had three children. I've married. I've set up one business that failed. I set up another business. . . . if he was going to leave me he would have left me when I was sick, when we had no kids, we had no ties. . . . And he was diagnosed with depression and he'll be depressed on and off for the rest of his life. When he is at his absolute worst, am I prepared to put up with that for the rest of my life and I am because the times I am happy make up for all the bad times. . . . His sexuality seems like such a small thing compared to all the other stuff that we've been through together. (Monica)

Other women had become very pragmatic about relationships in general, stripping them of the romanticized media images of what being in love is and focusing on what foundations are required to keep it together. They also arrived at a point of comparison with other more normative relationships and realized there were common issues of dysfunctionality in any relationship structure. Overall, they were glad for what they had:

> It's a bit about the devil you know. You've seen all the horrid parts. You've seen all the good parts. You know the extremes and you can live with it all, and they can live with you, because you've done the same thing. And all three of us manage to live together. I think it's just being realistic. (Nicole)

For Rachel, it was the comparison between her previous husband in a more conventional relationship who was cheating and her current husband honestly seeing other men:

> I'm happy with him and if this relationship does continue I'd be happy. If not, I actually don't think I'll ever have a relationship with a man again. . . . It could be a lot worse with someone else, or no one. So, why give all that up? I mean, I was in another relationship with someone who told lies. He saw prostitutes and that really freaked me out. Sometimes he didn't use condoms. I was just devastated when I found that out. We'll just take it as it comes. (Rachel)

"WE HAD TO LEAVE IT BEHIND"

> If I'd known from the beginning I'd have walked away a lot sooner. . . I sort of look back on my twenty-five years of marriage and think, "What was it?" It was sort of null and void, really, so we had to leave it behind. (Steph)

There were many women in our research who arrived at a point where they were relieved and grateful that they and/or their partners had ended their relationships. This involved women looking back to when they started to know about their partner's bisexuality, accepting the negative and/or irreconcilable dilemmas since then, and letting go of the past. As well as the unworkable pragmatics of the MORE, partners also rid themselves of unrealistic images, assumptions and expectations about themselves, their partners and their marriage. It is a time when "Needs are examined and prioritized, strengths were unearthed or discovered, and weaknesses admitted, and strengthened" (Buxton, 2006a: 57). Grever's (2012) interviews with women who had left their MOREs identified common practices that helped them recover: it was important to live in the present, recognize the importance of closure, see themselves as complete, decide not to be a victim, and reject hurtful actions without hating the perpetrator. Indeed, in the spirit of gereotranscendence, many women discover unexpected joy in a revitalized life after they adjust to their new reality, including a new relationship, reveling in their newfound freedom and satisfying single life.

In House's (2006) play, Clive and Bennett, both around 65, recall their love when they were 19, before Bennett married Maybelline. Clive has cancer and has come home to die. The play is full of gentle recollections of the two men as they take their daily strolls on the jetty, watched from a distance by Bennett's wife who describes them as "Two old birds. . . and me here watching, like a curious little girl" (2006: 29–30). As she describes her life with Bennett, and despite the wonderful love, we hear snippets of a heteropatriarchal life that as a woman, wife and mother, she has accepted for decades, and thus her ageing is also a significant factor in looking back and looking forward. For decades, she has been aware of a love poem to her husband from someone unknown, which he thinks he keeps hidden and frequently reads. She suggests a meal together and creates a comfortable bonding between her and Clive. After the lunch, she asks Bennett to tell her about him: "I want to be included in something that for a lifetime you kept for yourself; and that nearly destroyed me. . . . I deserve more." She reassures him that she will understand:

> I have done all of my coming to terms with this. . . . I found the bloody poem 30 years ago . . . We will get this out the way and I won't say another thing, and we will just carry on as usual. . . . Please my darling. I will understand anything you say to me. We've got forty years behind us! I've been happy!. . . I love you; and the kids, and what we've had (2006: 41, 44).

With her persistent questioning, Bennett shifts from "once or twice" having sex with men to a "few times" to "maybe ten times, in forty years, that's all probably! . . . just, nothing Maybelline; nothing" (2006: 44), to which she erupts, screams hysterically and starts hitting him as she had asked him a few times over the years "if there had ever been anyone else, ever!" Bennett explains: "You asked me if there had ever been another woman Maybelline. . . . And I answered you, no" (2006: 47). He tries to explain:

> I wasn't playing a game; it wasn't avoiding who I really was; it wasn't because of how people thought then . . . it was never that simple for me, homosexual or not, I married you Maybelline because, you were you (2006: 58).

But there has been a massive shift for Maybelline and she decides she has to leave in order to gain a long-lost sense of independence and freedom: "I've never had the car for just me, in all these years; it's always been a big deal. I'm driving on the Great Ocean Road for a while, maybe a month or two, or three; who knows; living in a tent. . . . like I always wanted to do" (2006: 60). When Bennett says she never told him she wanted to do that, she replies, "Oh, I did, Bennett, many times over forty years. You just didn't hear me" (2006: 60):

> Life's running out Bennett, quickly, and I want a bit just for me. . . . And anyway, there's someone else who needs you now. You be here for Clive; this next month or two with the cancer, with the dying, it's going to be very hard for him . . . You've been my everything since I was 20 years old Bennett; I have loved you with every single little bit of love and care I have inside me; I thought you were the greatest man on earth; even greater because I'd read that poem and knew that there was a little bit of you that you had turned away from, controlled, given up or whatever, bcause of your love for me. But here and now, you need to let me go; I need to go, get away from you and all that's been (2006: 61).

"I'd say don't, don't enter into the marriage"

This subheading is a simple statement from Helena, illustrating how many women said they would never have married or entered into the relationship had they known about their partner's bisexuality from the beginning, or what the sexuality would mean in the relationship:

> If I was 21 now, and the same situation arose, I think the questions may have arose and I might have read something or I might have questioned him, or I might have questioned myself . . . I think perhaps women do have an advantage these days, that it's not going to be a problem that we're going to see in perhaps fifty years. (Steph)

"I wish I'd never taken him back the first time"

Some women, like Jeannette's statement in the subheading, expressed regrets that they had not ended the relationship earlier: "I almost can't conceptualize how I stayed in there for so long and put up with it and cried day in, day out" (Kristina). They considered their earlier reasons for staying as saying more, in hindsight, about their own insecurities and problems, which they were now overcoming:

> I should have probably taken the kids and gone and with a bit of luck may have found someone else. . . . the thought of being alone a lot of the time was not an attractive proposition at all, but now I'm starting to think, no, it wouldn't have been such a bad thing. I mean, I have a lot of friends, and there are lots of interests that I would've liked to take up. (Jane)

Likewise, if they had known what difficulties the relationship would continue to bring, they now believe they should have left rather than keep trying to make it work. This was emphasized when, in the long term, their partners left them and they found themselves adjusting anyway, with more strength than they thought they had:

> I never wanted to be a woman who said after her husband left that it was the best thing he ever did for me but I learned to try and move on in my life, and now I have this opportunity to learn how to grow. So I like who I am now, and I like what I've learnt about myself. I would never have chosen this for myself. . . and it happened anyway, and hope that it helped me to develop into a better person and that's always the opportunity that crisis gives people. (Scarlett)

For some women, the sexuality wasn't why they needed to leave but rather the way they were treated by their misogynist emotionally abusive husbands, although their responsibilities as mothers kept them there:

> If I hadn't fallen pregnant seven months into the marriage, I know it wouldn't have worked because of the way he treated me, and if he hadn't been away seven months out of that first year we were married, I'd have left. Because I think I deserved better and he's treated me like shit and you can't change that, not even taking the sexuality into account, . . . but once you've got children, things change, because they come first. You can live in a hovel on your own, but you can't do that with children. (Jean)

"I've learnt to not think too far into the future"

Having left the relationship and the known, many women expressed fears and uncertainty about the 'unknown' future:

> I feel angry that the future that I was looking forward to is going to be very different to what I had anticipated, and I think, "How dare you do that to me." I was looking forward to retiring from work and doing all sorts of things together, and now what am I looking at? (Jane)

For a few women, this fear of the future was further complicated by an ex-partner's HIV status, the possible ongoing obligations to support him and the complexities that would create: "I'm looking at perhaps him being sick, and I think oh, maybe it's taught me that I have to live for every day, . . . and I've learnt not think too far into the future" (Jane). Or it could be around their own health and financial situations: "Look, my main worry now is financial. I need people to cook for me, I need people to wash and iron and whatever. I can't do those things. I can still teach, and that is great" (Loredana).

For other women, the uncertainty and fear was around establishing a new relationship: "It's like you're scared and you've got a shield in front of you"

(Pat). The uncertainty and fear could also be around whether the old relationship could be resurrected in some way:

> If I had a clear direction of where he is, then maybe things may be different but you can't work with something when you don't know what it is so that's why I think we're better off to be separate while he works through his issues and then whatever comes out of that, comes out of that... you're completely different people from when you started [the relationship] to when you finish. (Sally)

Uncertainty and fear could also be all of these issues in a convoluted form creating many uncertainties, such as for Heather who wonders if the relationship is actually over given they are still living together and demonstrating much affection to each other. She wants both her partner and herself to find new partners while simultaneously worrying about how she will react to her partner having a new relationship:

> I suppose what I'm scared about in the future is that the timing's not going to be right, and if Ian finds a partner and decides to leave, it will feel as if pow, the carpet's out from under my feet again. (Heather)

Another fear many women shared about the future was the sense of "shattered" self-confidence: "Because I've been so wrong for so long, I think well, what else have I been wrong about in judging people and judging all sorts of situations" (Jane).

"My life which I have now is absolutely as I've created it."

Many women expressed feelings of freedom, relief and a strong sense of personal growth after the end of the relationship, including establishing new goals, new relationships and constructing a stronger sense of self:

> My life which I have now is absolutely as I've created it. . . . I did courses on self-improvement and if nothing else, that's put me back into a sense of reality. . . Life is fabulous. My son's twenty-nine. My partner's gorgeous. We go away for weekends. We've going over to the UK. It's just like he's everything I ever wanted, and I'm happy now. . . . as far as I'm concerned it will be the relationship that I will have for the rest of my life. (Mary)

> I'm thinking of selling up and getting something different for me. The way I want to put things together, the colors I want to paint things, not what he wanted. . . . I have learnt my independence being on my own, my freedom, standing on my own two feet. Got my divorce, got my name changed back to my maiden name. . . . I have come to a point in life where if he came back to me and wanted to start again I couldn't do it. (Pat)

For Jeannette, the impetus in creating a new life came from her ex-partner's mother:

> See, when this was all over, his mother rang me and said, "Right, I've got the villa. It's just outside Venice. You come and stay for a month." And there were three of us women and we hired a car and we just had the most magical time. Going down from there was a farm, and it had an olive grove and white flowers coming up through the grass. You could see the whole of the Venetian plain and way over there were the lights of Venice. And I sat there one day and I thought, "Well, they can all go to hell as far as I'm concerned, all the men that wanted him and I'm standing here." . . . I am now saving for a trip down the Nile. (Jeannette)

For other women, it was just an overall sense of being real, living with strength and wellbeing as if their previous lives had been unreal:

> My emotional, physical, everything, is better. I've come through it. Sometimes it's just like you were living a movie, you know, and people wouldn't believe the things that have happened. It's just like an out of body experience, there was no control, it was horrible. (Lizette)

> I saw a long corridor with all the doors closing and as I looked deeper I saw a doorway open to the sky and nature, trees and water. I looked down on so much beauty, how could I want my life to be any different. (Nirupa)

Others found that personal growth meant going back to who they were before they began the relationship with their ex-partners: "that core person has come out again and taken hold, if you like, . . . It was just wonderful to bring back that little girl that I left behind" (Loredana).

"Out of it has come a special and loving relationship"

Many women believed the divorce had been a positive experience with much goodwill in salvaging a friendship and restructuring a future family. Jess and her ex-partner had established a new family:

> Neil and Anton are our family and we love it. . . . Anton is a special person and as a married couple we both loved and respected each other. Through thick and thin we still upheld those values and out of it has come a special and loving relationship. (Jess)

For Pat, the relationship had evolved into a friendship where they could go "window-shopping" together. Thus, rather than other men being the problem that split them, there is now a sharing of their mutual desire for them:

> The funny thing is like, nowadays, if we walk together or if we go to the beach just to get fish and chips, we check men out with each other. . . . (Laughing.) So we're there window shopping, having a laugh about it. (Pat)

What was important in reaching this point of friendship for many women was a shared feeling that the years together had not been wasted, or being able to work through the losses of what might have been:

> Ross and I would both say there's no sense of those years wasted whatsoever. It was a good marriage and we did well in that and we are very different people because of each other. I mean, it took a bit of time to come to the richness of saying that. (Kaitlin)

"The brick wall is still there for me"

Some women spoke about how grief, loss and sadness were ongoing feelings after the trauma of the relationship and its breakdown. They did not accept standard clichés such as 'letting go,' 'moving on,' 'forgiving' but spoke in terms of "managing," "accommodating" and "learning" from these experiences:

> It's been a huge grief in my life and it's always going to be a part of the landscape of your life and like so many things, we actually have to find a way of accommodating them, because often you will hear people talk about letting go or moving on and all these sort of clichés and it's really, really hard when you've suffered something that has devastated you personally, no matter what it is, for people to tell you that you'll get over it or learn to accept it . . . that brick wall will always be there and you have to chip away at it but both of you have to have a hammer in each hand, chipping away at it. My husband decided that he could no longer commit to that, and so he walked away from the brick wall, but the brick wall is still there for me . . . I can manage that now and it will always sadden me. I don't try and forget it, I don't try and pretend it didn't happen, and that's what we do with griefs. It's like losing someone dying. You never forget them, but you have to learn to actually accommodate that void that they leave. (Scarlett)

For some women, the ongoing pain was tied to the regrets and sadness that despite how wonderful the relationship had been, it had ended:

> I can't deny that there were many years of happiness, and a wonderful, trusting relationship. So that's why it's such a great loss because there was negotiation, and we were very open throughout the whole thing, but it doesn't make it any less painful. . . . the end result is creating a broken family, which is the last thing I ever wanted to do because I had a pretty unhappy childhood myself. (Sue)

Also for Sue, the fact her life was so linked to her ex-husband kept the sense of loss fresh in her heart:

> I'm still living in the family home. He's still supporting us completely.... I suppose the thing that I found hardest to deal with was the profession of his love for me, right up until the day he left. You think, "Well, then why are you doing this?" I just have to cut off, because if I leave anything open, it's just open for hurt, so it's better to just say, "You're gone" and I have almost nothing to do with him other than we have a very quick nightly conversation if he rings up to speak to the children, and it's just the logistics about, "How did they sleep?" and "Do you have his blue jumper?" That's a real loss. (Sue)

"Something really fantastic came out of all this"

Although the relationship had ended, many women did not regret it because of the positive outcomes and opportunities that came from the relationship:

> I can look back now and see that I've got five wonderful grandchildren and two wonderful kids. You know, there was something really fantastic came out of all this. The results now far outweigh probably all the anger I feel. I mean, I wouldn't have had them and if I hadn't stayed with him for so long we would never have come to Sydney to work and they wouldn't have met the people that they met. I'm enjoying my grandchildren, every now and then a trip. I'm loving my job. I mean, how at sixty can you get a job like that? (Jeannette)

CONCLUSION

As we have seen in this research, many women expressed anger and resentment at their partner's closeted bisexuality and/or anger and resentment at a society that made him feel deception was necessary to construct a 'liveable' life (see Butler, 2004). Choosing to or being coerced to inhabit this "third space" (Bhabha, 1990) or "unscripted space" (Swan & Benack, 2012) meant many women positioned themselves on the border of "stranger/homecomer" (Schutz, 1944). They entered the MORE relationship as strangers to either or both the external societal "thinking as usual" and the metissage of their MOREs. They were also homecomers, coming home to themselves in either exhilarating ways via exploring their strengths and desires, or in devastating ways by facing their disillusionment and rewriting their futures, whether they were 'staying put' or 'splitting up.'

Part III

MAPPING THE LANDSCAPE

Chapter 8

"New Rules, No Rules, Old Rules or Our Rules"

Women Designing MOREs with their Partners

> If you're not being hurt and if you're not being coerced, then it is actually possible to design a relationship with a bisexual man. (Monica)

> Oh, it tears me apart. I just adore him and I don't know the rules any more.... That's what I would love [some rules], because I often liken myself to just floating in space looking for a planet to attach myself to. And if we had some rules, I'd feel a lot more secure. (Heather)

This chapter will provide an overview of the shifting subjectivities, agency and resistance of those women and their male partners who undertook processes of "designing" their long-term MOREs and the "ground rules" and "boundaries" this would entail. As Rust writes, "Ground rules serve to protect the primary relationship from the potential threat of outside relationships, to ease feelings of jealousy, and to promote honesty within the primary relationship" (1996a: 488). Trahan (2013) refers to "relationship literacy" to articulate how and why we do relationships the way we do, and how these factors are affected by existing normative and oppressive external power structures. Some theorists such as Barker (2013) utilize a continuum rather than an either/or model to assist in constructing rules for a relationship (see also Peterson, 2001; Rambukkana, 2010). Barker delineates between emotional and sexual monogamies and discusses the continuum of emotional closeness or love from "monoamory," which is one close intimate relationship and no close relationships outside this; to polyamory, which is multiple close relationships. Her second continuum is of sex and physical contact: from monosex, no sexual or physical contact outside the relationship; to polysex, multiple sexual encounters. Barker's third continuum of relationship literacy is of freedom: from togetherness in making decisions which will entail a range of compromises to one's choices and freedoms; to being free to make one's own decisions and leaving the other partner also free to make theirs. These continua call to mind Heckert's theory of "nomadic exclusivities" wherein relationship partners "create space to discuss, define and refine their boundaries, which are always open to change" (2005: 196). "Nomadic autonomy" is very empowering as it entails self-organization and self-realization "through co-operation and self-management (i.e., power-to) rather than domination and representation (i.e., power-over)" (Heckert, 2005: 243):

> *Vicky:* Mike and I discuss absolutely everything . . .until we can get to a final thing in which everybody is happy with what's happening.
>
> *Mike:* If something starts to interfere with the primary relationship, it has to be nipped in the bud. . . . and that is probably our main golden rule, nothing can affect our marriage.

There appear to be three overall groups of 'rules' within which specific 'designs' for MOREs are created:

1. *"Old Rules"*: Monogamy is considered the only workable or desirable rule, and a partner's inability to adhere to monogamy would mean the end of the relationship.
2. *"New Rules"*: A range of negotiations and design-specifications establish nonmonogamous boundaries and operational strategies.
3. *"Our Rules or His and Her Rules":* Decisions are made regarding to what extent will the rules be equitable to both, or are there separate regulations for each partner.
4. *Ongoing rule revisiting, redesigning and renovation*: Rules are not necessarily permanently fixed but require re-visiting, re-designing and renovation based on individual, temporal, spatial and other contextual shifts.

Negotiations, regulations and machinations were put in place or wanted by women in order to develop or maintain a healthy MORE, or facilitate the ending of the relationship if the rules could not be agreed upon:

> You can make agreements and arrangements about your relationship with your husband or how you work out the sex thing, whether you both have partners or whatever. I mean, people come to all sorts of agreements, but what you need to do is accept that if you don't or can't negotiate to keep the marriage together and that your marriage ends, then it's not your fault. There's no blame attributed anywhere, it's just the way it is. (Erin)

There were also women who believed that the less rules the better, thereby allowing their relationship and those with others to take whatever course it needed to:

> We're very uncomplicated. Whatever there is to talk about, we talk about and relationships don't last with other people that aren't willing to do that as well. . . . everyone knows where everyone is at. . . it's like we would check with each other before we organized a dinner party. We'd check with each other before we book our holidays. We'd check with each other before we sleep with someone. . . I'm his primary partner and if that should change, well, we'll discuss it and we'll arrange something that works for both of us. (Jacinta)

"I'M JUST NOT PREPARED TO SHARE"

For some women, monogamy was the relationship design of choice. This contradicts mononormative and heteronormative cultural discourses about "commitment-phobic" bisexuals, and that bisexuals are "incapable of monogamy" and "deep feeling" (George, 1993: 83; see also McLean, 2004). Mark et al. recently found that bisexual individuals, particularly bisexual men, did view monogamy as "less enhancing" and "more of a sacrifice" than gay, lesbian, and straight individuals. Nevertheless, many did report that their own relationships were "monogamous and traditional" (2014: 263). What is significant here is that monogamy was not an externally ascribed presumption and automatically performed. Women were clear that they had "the opportunity" to think agentically, or what Wosick-Correa (2010) calls "agentic fidelity," about what they wanted from a relationship: "it is very much for me a one-on-one thing and I couldn't consider anything else. I'm just not prepared to share" (Sue). Scarlett's comments below point to the fourth theme, permission to shift and reconsider previously set rules regarding nonmonogamy:

> Allow yourself the right to say, "Look, I tried that [open relationship], it's not working, I don't want that. I thought I could but I can't." So that's okay to change things. (Scarlett)

Many women who chose monogamy also discussed how they believed they would become open to the idea of nonmonogamy as the relationship developed over the long term. Katie provided examples of the types of discussions she and her partner had when they revisited the monogamy status of the relationship:

> We check in with each other probably once every six months, you know, "Are you still comfortable with staying monogamous? Is there anyone you've met in

the past six months that you'd like to explore a further relationship with?" We have kind of scripted a conversation we'd have if we did meet someone. (Katie)

Other women also explained how they had negotiated a monogamous relationship for the present but remained open to the possibility of this changing in the future:

We have talked about bringing other people into it, but it's not something that we're totally comfortable with yet. . . . I think as I get more comfortable with it and with him, as I begin to trust him, I think I'll be happy with bringing someone else into it. (Lauren)

Indeed, for some women, the external ascriptive definition of monogamy was also open to deconstruction and re construction into specificities, such as 'gendered monogamy' whereby a bisexual partner could only have sex with other men:

Vicky: I don't see it [her partner having male partners] as an invasion of our marriage. It's an extension of what we have.

Mike: If I was seeing another girl it would be different, totally.

Vicky: Yes. I mean, it's still a monogamous relationship in my view.

Another variation was 'shared-partner monogamy' where women stated their relationship was monogamous if they were sexual together with another male, or had agreed on certain forms of nonmonogamous pleasure for both herself and her partner that they defined as "faithful":

My partner is faithful to me and I am faithful to him . . . and if he wants to watch me with another man, he will sit in the same room and watch, but I will never cheat on him. (Tamara)

Interestingly, sometimes women who constructed a monogamous relationship felt they were being judged by what they perceived to be an increasing societal perspective to do otherwise. Indeed, many women like Scarlett found themselves feeling as if this was a very "old-fashioned," "archaic" position to take and that they "should" have been able to negotiate some form of open relationship. This is very ironic given that, as we shall see later, women who did negotiate a nonmonogamous relationship felt as if they were perceived to be "deviant" or "foolish" or "abnormal" from a more mainstream societal perspective. Thus, the level and forms of panopticonic scrutiny, misrecognition and coercion most women faced, regardless of their decisions, became apparent: "If you want monogamy, say that you want monogamy. There's a variety of ways of living and you're allowed to pick" (Scarlett).

"KNOW THE GUIDELINES AND WHERE TO SET THE GOAL-POSTS"

> We didn't really start doing anything for a long while with other people simply because we wanted to get ourselves to a stage where we were able to sort of say, "Okay now the time is right"... We just kept bringing up the worst possible scenarios just to be able to talk it through and know the guidelines and where to set the goal posts. (Christine)

Most women in consensual nonmonogamous relationships had negotiated a wide range of boundaries and rules, usually involving lengthy and detailed discussions and scripting of possible scenarios (see Anapol, 1997; Easton & Liszt, 1997; McLean, 2004, 2011; Sheff, 2006). Other women did not delineate detailed boundaries but constructed a framing code of communication that would be used to address circumstances as they arose:

> I didn't really have expectations necessarily of monogamy, and as long as there was also room for me to have a relationship with him. But no, there were no boundaries.... because no matter what happens, if there's a trust and a truth that does come out in the very beginning, then you have some strength to deal with whatever comes up. (Nicole)

From their empirical research and analysis of other existing research, Conley et al. (2013) conclude that currently there is no evidence sexual exclusivity invariably leads to greater intimacy and relationship satisfaction than consensual nonmonogamy (CNM). Despite the common belief that monogamy is a way to prevent feelings of jealousy, Conley et al. (2013) conclude research has shown that levels of jealousy were actually *lower* for those in CNM relationships than in a monogamous sample. Moreover, research by Ritchie & Barker (2006) found that polyamorous communities have developed new words to describe both the positive and negative aspects of potential (or actual) jealousy. For instance, those in polyamorous relationships sometimes derive pleasure from a partner having other partners, known as 'compersion.' Feelings of discomfort or uncertainty about a partner's sexual activity with others is referred to as being "wobbly" or "shaky," akin to what others may describe as jealousy but milder and less traumatic. Indeed, some preliminary empirical evidence suggests that those in CNM relationships actually exhibit *secure* rather than insecure attachment (Moors et al. 2012). Moreover, both qualitative and quantitative research have shown that participants in CNM relationships report high degrees of honesty, closeness, happiness, communication and relationship satisfaction within their relationships (Barker, 2005; Klesse, 2007). Conley et al. suggest three dimensions that "might yield differences between CNM and monogamous groups—extraversion, agreeableness, and openness to experience.... Those who are successfully maintaining multiple romantic or emotional relationships may be higher in such relationship-stabilizing attributes" (2013: 11).

The following are the kinds of 'rules' negotiated in MOREs:

The Genders of External Partners

This was a very common issue, with the most common consensus the 'same-sex rule': only being allowed external partners of the same gender: "He decides what to do with the men and I decide what to do with the women" (Temptress). In some situations, the 'same-sex rule' could extend to the kind of pornography and other sexual imagery permitted in the home:

> My partner does have male pornography in the house and some people say that in watching male porn, it's a threat to me, but I'm not going to be threatened by a box of pornography. (Sara)

Other women talked about the differences between sex with a woman and sex with a man, thereby perceiving the "same-sex rule" as removing any threat or competition:

> I said to him: "If you ever have sex with another woman our marriage will be over straight away"... It's like I can't compete with a man, like I don't have what he's got, whereas another woman you do feel like there is a bit more competition. (Marissa)

Thus, there appeared to be, on one hand, a socially recognized and endorsed acceptance and adherence to a gendernormative binary construction of male and female sexualities. On the other hand, this binary was strategically deployed to assert their primacy as the sole female partner in the relationship:

> He's told me how he's felt after having sex with a man, completely different to being with a woman. Men are very aggressive, hard and fast and women are much softer. There's just really no competition. However, if he showed an interest in a woman, I would get very upset. An invasion of my territory sexually. (Rachel)

> They're getting different things [from a man]... getting filthy... I could put on a strap-on and pretend to be the guy but it wouldn't be the same as being a real life penis. (Leanne)

Women who were very happy with their sexual relationships tended to encourage their partners to have male partners. For example, Monica believed that if her partner could experience satisfying and open relationships with men, his increased happiness would only further augment their relationship:

> His previous homosexual encounters before he and I got together were furtive and nasty and secretive and deeply unpleasant and . . . our sexual relationship has been the exact opposite, you know, it's been loving and supportive and fun. So I have spent the last two years saying, "Access some porn, if you want to get a male prostitute, let's get one together." . . . and I suppose I'm keen to explore whatever makes him happy. (Monica)

There were some women who allowed their partners to have other women as sexual partners, particularly if this was as a shared partner:

> It was a strange thing at first [another woman] . . . but now I'm fine. . . . I thought, do I really want this lifestyle and this freedom of the lifestyle, and I did. (Simone)

Other women allowed this after much discussion regarding what his needs were and whether he was looking for a "replacement" of her. Thus, some women worked to find a middle ground between a values system that advocated sexual freedom for both of them and a concern that in having sex with others of the opposite sex, their primary relationship could be threatened:

> I didn't want to feel that I was tying him down, that freedom thing was very strong. . . . I look at the sorts of women that he really gets attracted to, whether he has sex with them or not, and they're all perfect replacements for me. So there's a foundation for me to feel insecure. So I talked to him about that and said that we need some rules, and only a few rules are needed . . . I haven't been attracted to any other men, and it's possible it might come up. But we would deal with it the same way. (Raven)

An effective strategy some women used was to get to know the other women partners in order to allay any fears:

> I find, bizarrely, getting to know the other person is so much better. Keeping them at an arm's distance, you make up all these things about who they are, and why they're going to threaten you. (Rose)

Sexual Health Negotiations

Every woman listed STIs/HIV as a primary concern requiring clear rules and honest communication: "Always has to be safe, and he doesn't have anal sex. . . . even using a condom, if they go anal sex, they can still break and there's that risk factor." (Lesley)

Some women discussed safer sex negotiations about "fluid-bonding" (Barker & Langdridge, 2010), whereby vaginal and anal penetration between the primary couple do not have to include condoms and other STI precautions while sex with anyone else will be restricted to safer sex practices: "If we do get to bed together with another guy, the two of us will not use condoms with each other, but anyone having sex with us will" (Naomi).

Emotion Management

The degree of emotional attachment or 'emotion management' with outside partners was also a strong point of negotiation. While some women preferred their partners to settle in to a "closed loop" of partners (Barb) or have a polyfidelitous relationship with one other partner as this would minimize the health risks of random sexual encounters and establish emotional stability and continuity, other women wanted their partners to experience sexual connections with many partners, but not establish intimate loving relationships, which they saw as exclusively for the two of them. Thus, many women and their partners differentiated between "sexual monogamy" and what Anderson (2012) refers to as "emotional monogamy." For some, cheating occurred "if one member of the couple began to privilege someone else in their emotional attachment, or in providing another person with care and nurture at the expense of the partner" (2012: 81).

For those women whose partners were just embarking on exploring their bisexuality, it was agreed that this question of "love or sex" would remain unresolved but open to honest communication along the way:

> We started to have rules about how he was going to go out and play. Did he need a male to love, did he need a male just for sex? He was only just coming to terms with the fact that "Hey, I'm bisexual, I like guys" . . . and he didn't know whether he was going to really want to go any further or just look at some pictures. . . . So we had to develop rules. (Sharae)

A few women wanted to avoid any possible form of emotional investment as well as any sexual health risks by allowing their partners to only see a male sex worker:

> We have been talking for a while now about my partner using the services of a male sex worker and then we will see what effect it has on us and the relationship beyond that. . . . It feels like a contained and manageable thing. (Jude)

Energy Management

Another area of discussion was the pragmatics of the everyday: 'energy management' such as time management, parenting, home duties, work/career demands, economic/financial resourcing; as well as the sexual energy and rosters required to be intimate with more than one partner. Many women were very clear that any energy given to sexual or other activities with outside partners was not to sap away energy required in the primary relationship:

> Mike and I decided not to stay overnight at a lover's place. It was important for both of us to be there, for the kids, in the mornings. Our opinion was the house and family dealings should be disrupted as little as possible. (Sharae)

Another code was to not engage in any outside activities with other partners if they were experiencing problems within the primary relationship (see Spears & Lowen, 2010):

> We make sure we are emotionally up to handling outside relationships. At times of stress we simply take time out from our same sex relationships to focus on each other and whatever the problem is. (Shelley)

Some women designed systems of time compartmentalization whereby their partners had their temporal, sexual and emotional "gay time" and the rest of the time was for the female partner, children and home. Other women wanted geographical compartmentalization such as no outside sexual relationships in the town where they lived. This was particularly pertinent for women who lived in rural or remote townships:

> He travels out of town a lot, which provides opportunities, because it's a small town. While we're here, we're a unit, we're a couple. He treats me respectfully. He supports me. That's what I want, and what he does when he's away, as long as it's safe, I don't care. I don't see it at all as a threat to our relationship. . . .[but] I'm not having my home and my child and my job interfered with. . . . I'd rather keep the two in separate boxes. (Jolene)

There were a few women who did not place "time restrictions" on their partners but wanted their partners to enjoy a sense of freedom to manage their own time:

> Our relationship in terms of the time we spend with each other is very free. . . . If I'm worried about where he is, like is he in a car accident, then I'll ring his mobile . . . but it's not a "Where is he? I should know where he is!" that ownership thing. (Raven)

From DADT to TMI

Many couples spoke of constructing agreements regarding how much detail about outside relationships would be discussed, or simply be known without discussion. As outlined in chapter 6, Haag refers to the importance of "the knowledge of the knowledge" or "the open secret" (2011: 165). She refers to Judge Ben Lindsey who in the 1920s coined the phrase "adultery agreements" which could involve "no candid agreement, but simply a tacit ignoring of the facts" (2011: 226). Similar to Petronio's (2002) theory of Communication Privacy Management, Finkenauer & Hazam call for a more nuanced understanding that under certain circumstances, "secrecy has a neutral, if not positive, impact on relationships" (2000: 247), depending on the reasons why the secrets were kept such as to protect family members from stress or pain. Barker (2013) talks about the continuum of privacy and disclosure from complete disclosure to complete privacy. In our research, while a few women preferred the DADT (Don't Ask, Don't Tell) rule, most women wanted to know something about their partner's other relationships and sexual activities without overstepping a comfortable boundary into TMI (Too Much Information):

> We've done enough group sex, I know roughly what things Gennaro likes, so that's no great mystery to me, which I like . . . I don't suppose we talk about every tiny little detail but we do talk about how it feels generally, the really good points, the really bad points but maybe not the exact minutiae of it cos that could be a little harsh on the other person. (Lizz)

Sometimes, women needed to know sufficient detail in order to feel secure and reassured about their own relationship: "I don't want to know details really but I do want to know our relationship's on track" (Barb). Other women wanted to know and have a say in what sexual practices their partners were engaging in outside the relationship:

> Once I realised that he hadn't partaken in anal sex, something clicked . . . I said, "Well, I'd like that boundary to remain." I had to feel that there's a little bit of him that is still mine—not that I use that particular part—but it was representative. (Krystle)

For other women, being informed before a partner had a sexual relationship with someone else allowed for "emotional preparation" (Joanne) and any discussions that needed to be had.

Some of the older women stated that, because their partners' sexual activities had decreased with age, they were therefore happy to listen to whatever activities might occur:

There's no secrets, I want to hear all about it.... But he doesn't go out that much now, or he'll go into town and then he'll drive home.... I said, "Well, who did you meet?" and then he'll tell me, "Oh, I met this nice man, so we had tea together." (Brenda)

Other women would shift in how much detail they wanted, and expected their partners to be responsive to the level of detail they required at various times:

You don't give more detail than the other person wants to hear. And, even in a relationship as open as ours, there are times I don't feel like the details. I'm not in a self-confident enough state that I want to know how gorgeous this other person was. And he respects that. And there are other times when I'm in a fun mood and I'm like, "Oh, yes, so, what was he like? What happened? And then what?" It might even titillate me. (Jolene)

The "Sacred Bed" Rule

Many couples set agreements on where sex with outside partners could occur. Many women did not allow their partners to have sex in their shared bed, being very clear about keeping their bed as "sacred space" with only their "sex energy" in it, "but we have another room ... with all of our crap in it, but it also has a bed in there so that if we do have another lover we go into that" (Joanne). For some women, the sacred bed extended to the whole home:

This is the family home, okay. I have children. You want to fuck somebody, go to their place or go to the park, or wherever it is. But, you're not doing it here. It's our sanctuary. (Suzette)

Informing the Other Man's Partner

Some women specified that their partners could not become involved in a relationship which involved the other men cheating on their own partners, particularly if they were placed in positions where they became complicit or accomplices in the cheating:

I don't want to be cheated on, and I wouldn't do it to another one. That's one of my ground rules. That's it, end of story, and he's happy with that, because we did do it once with a cheating married guy and it was a shambles.... I would hate to be the other woman, so I won't do it to anybody else. (Lesley)

Mike didn't want to be the other man. So we set a rule that if the other person was married, they must have disclosed to their partner as well. It has to be total disclosure. (Sharae)

Separate or Shared Partners

Some women negotiated a relationship wherein any outside partners would be shared rather than either or both of them having separate partners:

> It's always with me, in a small group situation or usually just a threesome, with certain parameters with that person: they have to be a bit bright and actually have a conversation and be a little bit interesting as well. There has to be some connection. (Simone)

Others wanted the encounters to be between the men and not include them, while a third group was happy to negotiate either way depending on the levels of attraction, circumstances and contexts:

> We've set our own guidelines and as far as we're concerned, if my husband wants me around when he's with one of his guys, that's fine, or if he wants to be alone with the guy, that's fine as well. . . . and for me to be alone with a woman, that's fine too, and if I was with another woman and he's playing with the both of us, that's okay, because I'm there and I know that it's a fun and games thing. (Christine)

> Some of the guys have been straight who fancy me, or other times it's been someone who's gay and fancies Nathan. And then we say, "That's my partner, how do you feel about that?" and then it goes into either a threesome or the two guys together, it doesn't bother me, . . . there's no kind of competition or power. So long as I feel everyone is alright. (Naomi)

Women often described the processes involved in seeking and finding couples who were compatible for a wide range of activities and levels of relationships:

> If he wants to be with somebody or if I want to be with somebody or we find a potential partner to share, nothing is to happen until all parties involved have met or already know each other. A phone call would be sufficient. (Kirsten)

Rules for Socializing Together

Couples would negotiate behaviors and protocols for when they were out socializing together. For many, it was important to set the parameters beforehand. These rules for socializing are part of what Davidson calls "adhering to a 'no surprises' policy' where 'thinking ahead and communicating thoroughly' are required in order to prevent the emotional upheavals of 'out of the blue' developments" (2002: 2): "If we were going some place together, we would sometimes negotiate well, okay, we're here together, we're going home together, or maybe not, that sort of stuff." (Evelyn)

> It's just this respect thing that we are here at this place together and if this person really wants to see you they can contact you tomorrow and organize it. (Naomi)

How to Handle Mistakes and "Cheating"

Some women stated that the possibility of rule violation required acknowledgment, which then required designing strategies to address this. Indeed, the rules for breaking the rules in polyamory and other forms of non-monogamy seem "less regulatory and more participatory, encouraging an overall commitment to oneself, current partners and potential partners rather than restricting certain sexual and/or nonsexual interactions" (Wosick-Correa, 2010: 55).

> My feeling is that if someone gets in certain situations, they just happen, and I'd rather not have to feel, "Oh, my God, you've ruined our relationship by having sex with this person and I will never see you again." (Evelyn)

Some women, however, were adamant that there was no allowance for rule violation as the whole point of designing workable boundaries for non-monogamy was to avoid this scenario:

> I've told him, ever catch him going behind my back and he can say goodbye to his balls, they'll be hanging from the rear view mirror. [laughing] . . . I probably wouldn't go to that extent, but his bags would be packed before he got home. Especially when we're open about it, there's no need for him to go behind my back. (Lesley)

The Female Partner having "Veto" Power

Some women spoke about having "veto power", the final say in whatever occurred in their nonmonogamous relationships. Simone said her partner wanted this as while he was comfortable with his sexuality and relationship style, having lived with it since he was sixteen, he was aware that this was all new for her. Hence, he wanted Simone to be in control of the developments both within and outside their relationship: "he has left it that anytime that I'm not comfortable with anything between us then I'll just say. With a look or a word, anything can stop or start" (Simone). Thus, in some relationships, it was the male partner who insisted on running potential new partners past his female partner:

> He has met guys on the Internet. So he might send me a photo saying, "This is who I am really interested in, what do you think?" He sometimes sends me the guys' emails they've sent him. In the end he'll go, "Does this guy sound genuine, does he sound alright?" Then we will all arrange to have a coffee or dinner

and have a chat with the guy. I actually prefer that he has sex and meets the guy first, and sees how he feels about it. I mean honestly, I am not that fussed. (Naomi)

In some relationships it was agreed that the woman would meet all potential partners before any relationship was established, and had "veto power" if they believed the other man 'wasn't right':

Vicky: If I have met a guy that Mike had been looking at and I said, "I don't like him, I don't think he's got it all together" or "he's hiding from his wife," it wouldn't be on.

Mike: I've got to get approval.

Vicky: Not that I've got him under the thumb or anything but it's just an equal relationship.

Mike: I know what's right and wrong and if Vicky has been so wonderful she gives me the freedom to go away and have a little bit of fun, I respect that so I've got to abide by the rules and I'm quite happy to do so . . . They must meet my family, they must meet my wife, and they're pretty basic things.

Other women insisted on "veto power" in relation to where sex occurred and to what extent they were prepared to participate:

I don't do that [have sex on the beach together with his other partners]. It's not legal, and the sandflies. [Laughing] . . . he wants to include me and share it with me, and I'll say, "Up to a point I will play games with you, but not where it steps over that line where I don't feel comfortable so, shut up, go away, have fun, and come back when you're ready. I'll read my book." (Jolene)

In some relationships, the "veto power" was extended to external partners, although the priority was given to the female partner's veto:

First of all everybody needs to know veto rules and that any other people in the relationship, we have to obey their rules as well, or a new set of rules needs to be negotiated. . . . but he needs to get my okay before he could approach them. (Kirsten)

For Jenna, "veto power" began from the time of initiating swinging and other socialsexual encounters:

We used to arrange swingers' meet n greets—one had attendance of over 120 people. I am the one who registers on websites, controls profiles, and vets potential sexual partners. I am very fussy. After initial contact we swap a few emails.

After swinging now for three to four years, I can quickly assess what type of people I am speaking to. Very few make it to the next stage which is the swapping of face pics. Even fewer make it to the next stage which is a meet face to face over a coffee or drink, we always meet in public for safety. After discussing our personal boundaries, safe sex etc if we both agree and "click" with the other person, we are happy to play on first meet . . . We have found that in situations with couples, that the women control the whole scenario, profiles, rules, choices, sexual partners etc. (Jenna)

Resisting Relationship Myths

Many women, particularly those in polyamorous relationships, believed in the need to completely rewrite the 'rule book' about relationships and intimacy, and debunk many of the social myths that prevailed in the mainstream, rather than just reconfigure them for specific issues (Anapol, 2012; Davidson, 2002; Barker & Langdridge, 2010). This kind of rule rewriting occurred within ongoing processes of conversations/recognitions and actions/reconstructions:

You're doing a project together and the project is constructing this life that is going to work for both of you in all its aspects and have both fulfilling your potential. . . . I didn't even know this level of communication was possible. . . . and there's nothing to control, there's only something to create. Like, we're constantly bringing something into existence that didn't exist and we can only do that together. (Jacinta)

For some women, it was important to not only rewrite the rules for their partners but for themselves as well, leaving behind heteropatriarchal and monogamist systems and rules in order to completely redesign and redefine what relationship and home could mean:

I feel very lucky as I've had the opportunity to live two parallel lives for the last five years with two men, one my heterosexual husband of fourteen years and the other my bisexual husband of nine years. Negotiation, co-operation and trust that I love them both make the relationships work. The benefits the men gain is freedom from the traditional rules full-time wives might impose on men. Both are very independent men who have strong feminist principles. My straight partner chooses to be monogamous with me and my bisexual partner has male partners, but it's up to them in the end. My homes are with my partners where they live, where my clothes, toothbrushes, books reside. Home is also my suitcase in which I permanently keep things like hair-dryer, a bag of underwear . . . . It's like I'm a modern turtle carrying my home with me . . . . But in becoming polyamorous and poly-home like this, I've had to leave behind home as a place of social approval, or else I would've had to leave behind my bisexual partner in order to stay in that traditional thing of one home, one husband. (Naomi)

Butler refers to these new potentialities of embodied interaction as a "materializing of possibilities" (Butler, 1990: 272). She adds that our understanding and experience of what Hidalgo et al. (2008) call the "dyadic imaginary" is deeply wedded to a fantasy notion of "one true love." Yet, those in dyads are in reality faced with their lover's past, simultaneous and potential relationships, feelings and desires that are not entirely related to the current dyad. One set of concepts that some people find useful when discussing polyamory are the notions of "primary," "secondary" and "tertiary" partners. Anapol (2012) defines "primary" relationships as long-term, committed, marriage-type relationships, where lovers share finances, parenting and decision making; a "secondary" relationship may also be long-term, committed sexualoving relationships but lovers usually live separately, have separate finances and see themselves as close friends rather than immediate family; and a "tertiary" relationship describes lovers who spend intimate time together only once in a while or for a brief time and who are not part of each other's daily life. Thus, for some women in our research, rewriting the rules for a polyamorous relationship required much work on the self and an understanding of how "natural" polyamory felt. It also required being flexible in negotiating the right rules and levels for each relationship due to individual needs and differences within that partnership:

> All the relationships I've had have been open relationships. Some of them have had different levels of openness, different levels of negotiation. . . . And it means in every one of those relationships, there tends to be a discussion about what's the primary partnership and what's outside of primary partnership, and there are different levels of emotional commitment. I think there are some people who are naturally polyamorous, and some who aren't. (Rose)

> Even though, you know, it sounds very nice in theory, but in practice, sometimes you do get the jealousy. So, you just start going through the whole mental process, it's like everything else, you balance it. I mean, I don't think I'd be happy in a monogamous relationship either. (Ava)

"THERE ISN'T A POWER IMBALANCE"

> We decided on similar rules about how he would play, how I would play. (Sharae)

These discussions have already shown the prevalence of issues such as equity, balance, power and agency in women's negotiations with bisexual male partners, and the awareness that there would be ramifications of imbalance and inequity (Sheff, 2005). Apart from sexual equity, 'activity equity' was also negotiated; one partner could not be having fun while the other was not:

> It's a great pleasure to feel that our relationship is equal in that way, that there isn't a power imbalance. . . . I am happy for Gennaro to go out with a guy and have a good evening, come home or stay the night, or whatever. But I have to kind of have some plans as well cos I don't want it to feel like I'm sitting at home doing nothing and I would like it to be in the reverse situation as well for example when I'm seeing someone I don't want Gennaro to feel I am randomly going out and ignoring him. (Lizz)

It was also important for many women that the male partner strive for equity between NRE (New Relationship Energy) and LTRE (Long-Term Relationship Energy) in the amount of attention and affection shown to new partners and long-term women partners:

> It's really, really important to maintain balance. . . . I think the woman needs to have her needs fulfilled first, before he goes outside . . . I've noticed that he becomes gushy over the other new person. I must admit it's that adolescent, that new feeling . . . and if I'm getting what I need within our relationship I won't begrudge that at all. (Sharae)

Sharae's comments regarding the rush of early lust and infatuation in a new sexual encounter/relationship is often referred to as the "honeymoon period" by polyamorists and others in nonmonogamous relationships, which has to be emotionally prepared for and understood (Iantaffi, 2010).

Women discussed two issues of what could seem inequitable from the outside but which they understood as 'fair' within the context of the relationship. First, there was the issue where the male partner did not want her having outside relationships for fear that she would become too attached. For example, while Maria's partner was able to have outside male partners "just for sex," he was worried that she would not be able to do the same:

> I think he would be [worried and unhappy] because he knows that if I did find someone else, it wouldn't just be a casual thing for me, it would be a more emotional thing, which would be a real threat. So I think he would think it wasn't fair. (Maria)

Second, some women were satisfied knowing that equity was theoretically in place, even though they were not interested in being nonmonogamous:

> He professed that it was a two-way street, that whatever applied to him applied to me. He actually encouraged it. So as much as I entertain ideas in my head, which is completely different to actually doing them, that was enough for me . . .I think he pushed for it because he thought that it was selfish in a way for him to do things with people and me not. (Maz)

"IT JUST CHANGES AND SHIFTS AND FLOATS AROUND"

> I guess I've always been the kind of person who, if it's two o'clock in the morning and there's no visible traffic, I will go through the red light. So, there's rules for a reason and you work out what the reason is, and then the rule is flexible. . . . you just do what everyone's comfortable with and then it just changes and shifts and floats around. (Jacinta)

Many women discussed the need for recognition that negotiations would shift according to individual, relational, external and other contexts and circumstances, thereby requiring rule remapping and reevaluations (Rust, 1996a). As Wosick-Correa (2010) writes, renegotiations serve the purpose of recognizing that individual needs and desires within relationships are "not static." This entails a commitment to flexible borders over rigid walls coupled with an understanding that "just because one can go anywhere, one does not have to go everywhere" (Heckert, 2010: 260). Women's experiences of remappings also concur with Davidson (2002) who presents how agreements often proceed through stages of self-assessment, communication, negotiation and experimentation, with subsequent ongoing application or reconfiguration:

> Talking and establishing ground rules just sounds so military but then again, I am flexible in so far as I think if he changes or if I change that we can discuss and not let it become a problem. . . . I mean, it's not like I'm holding the upper hand or anything, because we came into this together on equal ground. (Suzette)

Some of the older-aged couples who had been together for decades explained that flexibility and responding to shifting needs gets easier over the years as individuals strive to fulfill any unfulfilled desires "before it's too late" (Alice). They had also arrived at a place and time in their relationships where they no longer felt the need to set any rigid rules, nor undertake any surveillance, and that they had such faith and deep love for each other, they would be able to resolve and adjust to whatever the future held (Tornstam, 2005):

> *Paul:* Even though I'm old, I've suddenly found the man I want to live with.
>
> *Alice:* In fact, I encouraged Paul to try living with him. "You deserve to try it, Paul, after all these years. Don't die without taking that opportunity. I'll still be here. Plus you know I can take care of myself."

Some women who had been together with their partners since they were adolescents spoke of how this allowed them to design their relationship as they went along:

We had ideas about how this sort of thing [relationships] works, but not from direct experience, and that's evidenced now by the fact that I'm the full-time worker and he's the full-time carer of the children, . . .we're always realistic and . . . take it day to day. . . . I've always just assumed that one of us may have sex with someone else. You can't be together since you're so young and getting to our old age and that won't happen [Laughing]. (Monica)

Having the relationship withstand the tests of time also meant previously sacred rules, such as 'the sacred bed' rule, could be wavered:

I came to realize later it's only a bed for heaven's sake, the sheets can be taken off and washed. And the same with the house. These things I had to come to my own conclusions because society doesn't teach us this . . . . You've got to have all those guidelines because society puts you in a box. You then put your own relationship in another box. (Sharae)

Thus, even what could be considered the most radical relationships such as polyamorous ones showed deep levels of traditional lifelong commitment. Indeed, the "12 pillars of polyamory" include both traditional and nonnormative foundations: "authenticity, choice, transparency, trust, gender equality, honesty, open communication, being non-possessive, consensual, accepting of self-determination, being sex positive and understanding, and embracing compersion" (Haslam, 2008 cited in Antalffy 2011: 1):

The thing with me and Pete is that it feels like there is a natural depth and just a history of deep friendship and on top of that, several years of deep nutting out our relationship, through which we've both grown in each other and together. But, it is a theoretical possibility that he will come across, or I will come across somebody with whom we have a naturally deeper relationship. I'd be surprised, but it's possible. And I just think why would you want to restrict that? Why would you want to damage that? If that's there, go for it. . . . I want him to follow what he needs to follow when he needs to follow it . . . .the only times I myself have ever experienced jealousy, it has been clear to me that it has been my problem. I have been feeling insecure for whatever reason and feeling, you know, needy and left out and like I want Pete to look after me and all that sort of stuff. . . . and Pete experiences jealousy very easily and we've had to fight and fight and fight over this one. (Anne)

Some women, like Anne above, were very upfront in stating that the ongoing "sorting out" would sometimes result in arguments and could be quite confronting:

We're still sorting it out. We have moments where I say, "No" and we have a knock down, drag out, screaming match at each other and then it's done.... Most of our drop down arguments are when we're on the Internet and if he says something to somebody that I don't like... Well, from my standpoint, don't sit back and say, "Yes, yes, yes" and just go along. Think about it. If you've got an objection, say it, give your explanation. (Lesley)

We evolve as human beings, very few decisions are cast in stone.... sometimes a lot of heart breaking discussion because it almost feels like one's continuously re-examining the most important thing in life, and that can occasionally be a bit daunting, it can be quite confronting, but then again on the other hand I think if we didn't try and re-examine it we probably wouldn't have any peace and quiet. (Lizz)

At times, making shifts in the relationship involved periods of separation to reflect, have other experiences, and reconnect based on new realizations and negotiations:

Separating was kind of the only way, in my head. A big, big part of it for me was, "I can't do any more here. The only way now is to go, and you have to take responsibility for yourself." I then talked about if there's any inkling we want to be together, these are my [new] boundaries, and basically said what I didn't feel comfortable with. (Krystle)

CONCLUSION

We are very happy.... and we enjoy our life together. We are both very open about his attraction to men and I enjoy many jibes at his expense! (Krystle)

These findings on how women with bisexual partners design relationship rules and boundaries support the findings of existing research that partners who design successful MOREs share a number of characteristics:

Mutual sexual pleasure... open communication, primary commitment to the marriage,... rewriting marriage "rules," love, honesty, the wife's autonomy and acceptance, the husband's compromise, and personal capacities of empathy and flexibility (Buxton, 2001:157, 163).

When Krystle returned her transcript, she had attached a letter detailing their careful and considerate negotiations. The following examples may not suit every relationship, but it illustrates an outcome of processes of negotiating 'the rules' for this specific couple:

We manage his same-sex attraction by:

*keeping perspective on our relationship—that this is just one part of who 'we' are

*accepting that sometimes it will overwhelm each of us for a time, and supporting that person unconditionally when it does . . .
*negotiating that from time to time, when the need builds up in him, he has a sexual experience with another man, with my full knowledge and blessing, on the grounds that:
*this person must respect our relationship
*it must be safe sex
*it has physical limits
*he enjoys it!
*we continue to have counselling from time to time, and seek support when we need it
*if he ever has sex with another woman—we are dead!
*if he ever lies to me—we are dead!

The rules and commitments in Krystle's letter also illustrate how internal recognition and "day-to-day interactions through which to modify parameters of their marriage" (Buxton, 2001: 183; see also Carlsson, 2007) were also significant traits that counteracted external community and societal misrecognition. As Whitney writes: "they are the reluctant pioneers of a different family form" (1990: 114); and "in making their choices these couples have agreed to live with an on-going reformation" of their relationships (1990: 136). In these ways, MOREs are influencing the broader reformation of social ascriptions, understandings and recognitions of various relationship forms and options.

These border spaces where women with bisexual male partners dwell exist as entities in themselves with all the dilemmas of weaving new patterns and constructing new discursive boundaries of identity, truth, and reality as they negotiate and resist the dichotomous patterns and discursive boundaries that exclude or distort them. As Zerubavel writes,

> We very often experience boundaries as if they were a part of nature . . . . It is we ourselves who create them, and the entities they delineate are, therefore, figments of our own mind. Nonetheless, our entire social order rests on the fact that we regard these fine lines as if they were real (1991: 3).

Bisexuality and MOREs reveal the tenuousness of those "fine lines." Certainly, as discussed in chapter 2, agentic practices and discursive knowledge always exist within determinate historical and spatial bounds. However, if agents were unable to originate new forms of activity then "it would be impossible to account for the extraordinary variation in social conduct that has been exhibited in the course of human history" (Cohen, 1987: 291). For example, new labels can be constructed to define new forms of relationships, such as "queer-kinship" and "polyamory," the latter invented in the early

1970s by Morning Glory Zell (Sulak, 2013; Zell, 1992). It is fitting that I conclude this chapter with the words of a research participant in Buxton's pioneering research:

> Our relationship has internal validity regardless of outside standards . . . It took a while for us to write this script for ourselves (1991: 231–234).

Chapter 9

"The Problem Is That He's A Man, Not That He's Bisexual"

Women Discussing Masculinity, Misogyny, Privilege, and Power

> If a woman is having a shit time with her bi partner, the problem is that he's a man, not that he's bisexual. The problem is that he's an old-fashioned sexist bastard who thinks he can do whatever he wants whenever he wants, and then come home to be Mr. Powerful Hubby, and she's there to be Mrs. Meek Little Housewife and Mummy. Being bi hasn't taught him anything. (Naomi)

In this chapter, women discuss how constructions of masculinity, gender-normativity and patriarchal inequities impact on their partners, themselves and their relationships. From the most misogynist conformist masculinity displayed by abusive bisexual male partners to the most profeminist antimasculinist behaviours and attitudes displayed by other bisexual male partners, women's perspectives range from never wanting to be in another relationship with a bisexual male to never wanting to be in another relationship with a heterosexual male. Sometimes the very qualities that initially attracted women to their partners were later revealed to be the qualities they came to understand as being nonheterosexual. For most women, it is ultimately the way the men perform their masculinity, rather than their bisexuality, that becomes a determining factor as to whether the women are satisfied with their relationships and decide to stay or not. Indeed, many women referred to and indeed refuted the stereotype that women in relationships with bisexual men are passive, meek and naive, and have no power in the relationship. While some women definitely recount experiences of abuse and disempowerment, other women strongly explained and demonstrated that women in relationships with bisexual men, and who indeed choose bisexual men as partners, are very independent, very feminist, very strong.

Steinman states that although there is a rich multidisciplinary scholarship on masculinity, there is "great need for research integrating critical gender studies and bisexuality studies, and especially a need for empirically oriented research to learn how the relationship between masculinity and bisexuality is played out in various communities and social contexts" (2011: 405; see also Pallotta-Chiarolli, 2015b). Beemyn & Steinman believe questions which require further research are: "Is there something distinctive about bisexual men's engagement with masculinity? ... How do bisexual men perceive their masculinities, and how are their masculinities perceived by non-bisexuals around them?" (2001a: 10). This research requires engaging with simplistic views such as those of Jeffreys who frames all forms of nonmonogamy and BDSM as examples of how "a bisexual politics privileges men and patriarchy" (1999: 284). It also requires exploring how for some men "a bisexual politics" involves divesting oneself as much as possible of patriarchal privilege. Likewise, are bisexual inclinations and behaviour foundationally at odds with claims to heterohegemonic, hypersexed and hypermasculinity? (see Buchbinder & Waddell, 1992; Burleson, 2005).

These issues regarding bisexual masculinities are explored in some films. In *The Trio* (1998), the character Zobel represents male bisexuality as patriarchal hypersexed masculinist privilege. In *The Matador* (2005), the hard drinking, charismatic, hypersexual world class assassin Julian Noble, who is also bisexual and clumsy, is played by Pierce Brosnan, who has usually played heterosexual, hypersexed and hypermasculine spies including James Bond. "Time and again the awkward Julian calls attention to himself, stumbling drunkenly like a bisexual bull in a heterosexual china shop helplessly making an incriminating display of his bisexual needs" (Vicari, 2011: 103). When Julian visits Danny and his wife Bean in the middle of the night needing a place to hide from the vengeful Mr Stick, this scene seems to be edging rapidly toward a sexual threesome, again subverting the heteronormative action hero and his possible threesomes with more than one woman. This film supports Eisner's (2013) contention that being a bisexual male in mainstream culture automatically means "failing at performing the proper standard of masculinity." Yet this failure, Eisner explains, "is the key to the subversive possibilities that male bisexuality can offer in relation to masculinity and patriarchy" (2013: 231).

Sheff's (2006) research on polyhegemonic heterosexual masculinities, or the hegemonic masculinities performed by some polyamorous heterosexual men, is very applicable to bihegemonic masculinities, as well as her application of Connell's (2005) terms of complicit, marginalized, subordinate and resistant masculinities. For example, Sheff refers to "complicit masculinity," meaning bisexual men who occupy conventionally privileged positions in hierarchies based on race, class and gender, while others fit additional norms such as hypermasculinity, hypersexuality, and/or competitiveness (2005: 79; see also Pease, 2010). Thus, although bihegemonic men may not have the socio-cultural capital of heterosexual hegemonic men, they may compensate for their marginalized sexualities by adopting or hyping traditional masculinist traits. Thus, bihegemonic men may use their misogynist treatment of women or performance of certain abusive or aggressive masculinities to display a superior masculinity, thereby retaining traditional gender roles within nonnormatively gendered MOREs (Sheff, 2006).

Sheff also distinguishes between "poly subordinate and resistant masculinities from dominant hegemonic masculinity" with the former espousing and practicing "more egalitarian, sexpositive, and gender-neutral relational styles than are characteristic of dominant hegemony" (2006: 632). These subordinate and resistant men attempt to subvert hegemonic power distribution and relationship structures by engaging in emotion work (Hochschild, 1983): acknowledging their own emotional needs and cultivating emotional connections with other men and women. Indeed, Sheff found that "their resistance was the primary feature of their masculinities" (2006: 639), as men who wished to engage in long-term MOREs cannot operate on emotional 'auto pilot' as can some traditional men in heteronormative relationships who relegate the responsibility for emotional maintenance to women.

More recently, McCormack et al. examined bisexual men's experiences of coming out across three age cohorts. They found a correlation between older men having more negative experiences of being bisexual with "elevated heterosexism" and misogyny. This "highlights the importance of growing up in homohysteric cultures . . . where misogyny raised their masculine capital" (2014: 8). This "masculine overcompensation" was far less evident in the younger bisexual men who had grown up in less homohysteric cultures. These men appeared "more confident, socially competent and at ease discussing their sexuality," correlating with exhibiting "softer masculinities . . . less heteronormative views and [they] did not use the misogynistic language like the older bisexual men" (2014:11). Decreasing homohysteric cultures also meant bisexual men were more likely to come out early in their relationship and seek relationships with either men or women, rather than the older cohort's more common system of having a relationship with a woman in order to have children and live a heteroassimilationist life, and only have casual sex with male partners (Anderson et al. 2015).

Four major themes became apparent in our research as women discussed how constructions of masculinity, gendernormativity and patriarchal privilege and inequities impacted on their partners, themselves and their relationships:

1. *Bisexuality did not necessarily mitigate against an abusive misogynist masculinity:* Many women spoke about the use of gendered power and privilege by their partners, whereby the men displayed "bi-patriarchy" and "bi-misogyny." Significantly, some women could also identify bi-patriarchy as a compensatory response or result of their partner's frustrations within a heteronormative system.
2. *Bisexuality was significant in the resistance to gendernormative and partriarchal performances and privileges of masculinity:* Many women praised their partners for behaviors, outlooks and performances of "resistant bi-masculinity" that critiqued and surpassed limited heteropatriarchal constructions of masculinity. This was particularly evident in their sexual relationships and, as named in chapter 8, "energy management" in relation to childrearing and work/home negotiations.
3. *Bisexual masculinities were compared to heterosexual masculinities in predominantly positive ways:* Some women compared their bisexual partners to their previous heterosexual partners in their heightened level of self-reflexive constructions and performances of more gender equitable masculinities. However, the varying behaviors of heterosexual men and bisexual men were not seen as being in opposition but often on a continuum from misogyny to profeminism, and framed within a dominant heteropatriarchal sociocultural framework within which all men were externally positioned or self-positioned.
4. *Bisexual masculinities were relevant to women challenging or being constrained by prescriptive and limiting constructions of femininity:* in analyzing their partners, many women discussed their own femininity in relation to their masculinity, and how either bimisogyny constrained their own gender and sexual expressions, or bimasculinity encouraged and enhanced their own resistances to normative submissive femininity and passive sexuality.

What will also become evident within this chapter is how women often resorted to essentialist homogenizing dichotomous language and constructions of masculinity and femininity even as they endeavored to identify, scrutinize and problematize these very constructs and address the socio-cultural frameworks within which these 'gender rules' and scripts were being adhered to and performed. There were other women, however, who were aware of these gender regimes:

> [Masculinity and femininity] is an amusing, antiquated language. It's just so dissatisfying . . . because I think it's perpetuating this whole dualistic nature of everything to even talk about having feminine and masculine aspects to yourself because you don't, you have human aspects of yourself. (Ava)

"THEY SAY THEY'RE BI BUT THEN START ACTING ALL SEXIST"

> Women are a bit sick of men who say they're bi but then start acting all sexist because they believe that with women, you can just get away with anything and we are there to serve you. (Susanna)

Many women related experiences of their partners displaying "bipatriarchy" and "bimisogyny," with a sense of entitlement to patriarchal privilege with which they had been raised within a heteropatriarchal culture:

> I think men are not socialized to hear the word "no" so I think it's very difficult for bisexual men to imagine that they have to deny themselves anything, and there's also that stuff about "we don't control our sexual urges, they're driven from the brain." You know, "have penis, will seek orifice." (Scarlett)

However, as we shall see in this section, many women also identified bi-patriarchy as a response to or result of their partner's sexual and gender frustrations within a heteronormative system of stigmatization, subordination and the limitations of sexual dichotomies (Connell, 2005; Pease, 2010). Some of the manifestations of bimisogyny and bipatriarchy included the following:

- going out whenever and for as long as it suited them without discussion and agreement with female partners;
- female partners not having the same rights to independent socialising and/or outside sexual partners;
- holding certain expectations regarding their female partner's prime role as undertaking domestic chores, parenting, and providing for and attending to his needs;
- women partners having minimal say in their expenditures and financial decisions;
- inattentiveness or indifference to a female partner's sexual, emotional and mental health;
- indifference, harassment or neglect in response to their women partners' sexual needs and desires;
- domestic violence, sexual assault, aggression manifested in various forms toward female partners and/or children.

It was also evident that the exploitation and disempowering of women were more likely to occur if the male partners:

a. had not disclosed or 'come out' as bisexual;
b. were not secure or comfortable with their own bisexuality;

c. were experiencing internal conflicts and mental ill health due to biphobia and homophobia, and their desire to be 'a real man'
d. held traditional expectations of women and were invested in maintaining a heteronormatively defined 'successful' lifestyle replete with being able to claim heteropatriarchal privilege
e. either perceived or coerced their female partners into being 'weak', 'less confident', 'naïve' and adhering to traditional femininity

These findings illustrate what Gochros (1989) refers to as two interwoven syndromes: "male chauvinism and liberation ethics." In other words, bisexual partners claim as their right, as a man or as an oppressed minority, to "discover and fulfil his desires, meet his needs," and that it is the woman partner's duty as feminine and "symbolic oppressor," to help him "cheerfully" (1989: 110, 126; see also Atwood, 1998):

> If the guy's got to be in control, which is sort of the typical patriarchal thing, and he's in a heterosexual relationship, and then if he's going to go out and be bisexual as well, then he's just going to be a bigger arsehole isn't he? . . . he's still being the control freak and keeping her really intimately controlled. (Raven)

With time, these subjugated women feel so inadequate and begin to play what Kaye (2004) calls "the 'if only' game": "if only I could be a better wife, if only I was more attractive, if only I was better as a lover, if only I was a better housekeeper, . . . then maybe he could love me enough not to think of men" (2004: 44). This is interlinked with the "twister game" or "the blame game," where men twist the situation around so that women will blame themselves:

> I was a caretaker and over-functioner in our relationship and very much saw if our relationship wasn't working then somehow or other it was my fault, and that was the way that women were raised to believe, . . . he had taken on a job where he was working interstate in the political area, and so I was home a lot with three small kids and trying to paint walls and work and study and also then feeling quite demoralized when he would continue to express feelings of unhappiness in the relationship, and he wasn't very good at taking any steps to work through that . . . . every anniversary virtually from our first anniversary, in every card I had apologized for the fact that we hadn't had a great year, for somehow or other making our relationship not work as happy as he thought it should be and in his cards it was always quite the reverse. (Scarlett)

Some women would refuse to abide by gendered rules and were aware that some of those masculinist expectations and entitlements had been imprinted into their partners from childhood when their mothers, and indeed society, were seen to cater for their every need, construct a sense of privilege, with little communicative effort required from them:

> He'd go out at the weekend and he wouldn't come home for lunch until the middle of the afternoon and then get cross if his lunch wasn't there. So I said, "Well, if you're not going to come home, I'm not going to hang around. I'll get your lunch ready and if it's dried up it's fine, or if I'm going out, you get it yourself or go without." Because he was very spoilt by his mother. I mean, she used to put his clothes out, everything. (Brenda)

> You can be bisexual and you can be very different from all these macho things, but you still fall into saying things about women, never in a million years would he say that about a man. . . . but what we're up against is men who have been brought up to actually do that. (Sara)

Some women who had initially been attracted to their partners for their transgression of "blokey" norms found it extremely difficult adjusting to the fact that these nongendernormative men could also display a form of bipatriarchy and bimisogyny. Indeed, certain masculinist assumptions and behaviors were given an extra dimension due to bisexuality:

> He can be really emotional and feminine. There was a time when that wouldn't bother him at all, but then that changed about 2 years before we broke up. . . . He became really blokey. He started to get tougher, and yeah, mean and selfish. . . . We had big talks about it now and then but a wall came up for him. He really couldn't handle the fact that I really liked him because he was like that [emotional and feminine], and then he started to get really nasty. Like, he started to punish me for it . . . I felt like a second class citizen. (Susanna)

Some women concurred with Kaye (2008) who attributes the fault-finding some of these men display to frustrations around their sexualities:

> When you live with someone who's going through that suppression of not coming out properly, they become very particular and perfectionist. Michael is very picky about anything that happens within the house. So it's almost like they can't control that [bisexual] side, so they'll control something else. So it was around the housework and I remember I would dust and he'd come past and go like this [indicating wiping a finger along a ledge] . . . you would do something and he would just look at you and you'd go, "Oh, God, that wasn't right, okay, I'll go and fix it up." (Sally)

Many women discussed feeling resentful and disempowered that they either complied with or were coerced into complying with gendernormative roles in the household, with childrearing, and in maintaining good family, friend and community networks:

I'm responsible for making sure that the family stays together and the children are all right, and that nobody knows about this [his bisexuality] and the church, they shouldn't know about it. It was very totally disempowering. (Felicity)

It had all been about what his needs were . . . You think, "Wait a minute, what's going on here? I am totally turning into somebody I never wanted to be" . . . and here I was with a new born baby, breast feeding in the middle of the night and he was going out clubbing. And then being really tired and wanting to sleep the next day, and I'd be feeling like, "You're tired? What about me?" . . . he went out and bought a two-seater Mercedes just after our second child was born, where we really should have been looking at a less expensive family car. (Sue)

Some women acknowledged their complicity with or upholding of dominant constructions of gendernormativity, gendered roles and what constitutes success, status and privilege for women within a heteropatriarchal socio-economic framework. This complicity gradually came to work against them:

He kept sort of apologizing [for his bisexuality] and saying everything would be different and he really wanted to be married and I said, "Oh, well, he's a nice guy and a sort of pillar of society," so you just pretend. . . . nice house, nice friends, drove the right car. All the trappings. (Jeannette)

He's very flashy. He likes to be displaying antiques and that sort of thing, but it's the power that he needs. Oh, and the grandiose, and he used to say to me like when we were fighting and after I found out [about his bisexuality], "I should have known better than to pick a woman from the suburbs" because I was from like the rough end of town, and he used to talk about how his ancestry went back to the King of Scotland or something. Anybody that came in the house he had to go and show them all his stuff and his blue blood and to throw it at me. (Kristina)

In the following, Helena described very clearly the seductiveness of being married to a wealthy, powerful and sophisticated husband, as well as the costs and expectations placed upon her in return:

I felt that I became just another prop. You know, the beautiful wife doing all the right things, cooking the exquisite dinners, producing the beautiful children. So, I became this sort of accessory and didn't know how to manage it . . . I said to him, "You know I'm not the hired help" . . . Oh, he'd give me gifts. I mean, a pair of pearls and other stones. (Helena)

Sylvia got divorced after twelve years of marriage when she could no longer perform the role of dutiful wife, despite the material and social capital she had access to in exchange for agreeing not to "rock the boat":

> I couldn't express myself then, because you married as a nice girl, you know, get the twin set of pearls, bit of money, husband had been at boarding school all his life, you travelled all over the world, pretty wealthy. So he didn't want me to rock the boat, so I didn't. You know, protect him, and you followed him. (Sylvia)

In Atwood's (1998) research, all the husbands were described as having always been or having become stereotypic male chauvinists. They often displayed sociopathic tendencies, combining "aggressiveness, impulsiveness, irresponsibility, lack of remorse and charm . . . they have a keen capacity for rationalising (*sic*)" (1998: 164). Helena relates the time she collapsed at home and the subsequent hospital stay as another example of her husband's abuse and indifference:

> I rang my husband when I was lying on the ground and getting a bit panicky because I knew I couldn't move. And he said, "Look, just calm down. I'm going to a meeting" . . . So I got an ambulance. . . . And the next day, I said "Could you bring me some slippers and a dressing gown and toothbrush?," and when he arrived he said, "Oh, I was so exhausted. I just had to go and eat something." He hadn't got my few things. And, I mean, I was in hospital and I said to him, "Excuse me, do you just keep me on the backburner? It's not a lot to ask." (Helena)

The issue of women accepting men's abusive and patriarchal behaviors and still being able to evaluate them as 'perfect' became very obvious in some interviews. The women would relate very distressing experiences and still be able to discuss their love and satisfaction with their partners:

> He never ever really would say that I looked beautiful or anything like that. He was never probably overly affectionate, but then, we very rarely had arguments, and he was just so understanding of every situation I was in, and I could talk to him about anything. (Beth)

Heather, after discussing bouts of depression, isolation, emotional and even physical abuse, was able to say after separating but living within the same house:

> It's sort of like nothing's changed other than Ian sleeps downstairs. I mean, we still watch TV together at night and I still cook for Ian and do everything I always have. He's a fantastic father. He's a great friend to me. Yeah, I just adore him. And yeah, I suppose he's self-absorbed in a lot of things, and he's extremely lazy and sleeps a lot. Besides that, I mean, he's just a perfect person in my life. (Heather)

This also points to the power of gender-scripting, as is evident in Gerry's comments whereby a woman living without a man is considered more difficult and frightening than living with a domineering man:

> Simon can behave in quite a chauvinistic way. . . . He has a sharp but brief temper, and avoids any discussion that may become emotional. He obviously has attracted me though, he is physically very attractive, we share a sense of humor and he is most charming and fun-loving . . . But, no, I would never look for a bisexual man because I thought he had particular positive qualities. . . . A lot of it is just not being on your own all the time. It's having someone that you know that you can live with on a daily basis. (Gerry)

Some women suggested the physical abuse and violence they had been subjected to, as well as their partners' denigration and disempowerment of them, arose from the frustration, internal conflict and stress over their hidden bisexual selves:

> Initially I saw him as an incredibly aggressive, controlling man. . . . I found it more masculine than anyone I've ever met. Which is really odd. But, it was I think, from just wanting to control everything in his life. (Nicole)

For Kristina, this became manifested in very abusive and violent behavior which she found difficult to extricate herself from and over which she continued to experience anxiety:

> Obviously they're projecting the blame and that's certainly my experience. And it becomes the old DV [domestic violence] triangle. . . . I thought I saw him in the supermarket one day and I actually hyperventilated, I'd just gone white as a ghost and it wasn't him at all. I've been working on it with myself, rehearsing what's going to happen the next time I see him because I need to show no fear because he knows he's got it over me. (Kristina)

Several other women also related experiences of domestic violence and aggression, whether they believed it was linked to their partner's internal conflicts over their bisexuality or was a symptom of aggressive patriarchal masculinity:

> He was abusive, both violence and aggression. . . . he treated me like shit. . . . I mean, the domestic violence issues were the last straw. . . . But, if he'd told me he was bisexual and there wasn't the DV issues, then maybe we could have worked it out and maybe we could have had an open marriage. . . . I don't know what he's capable of, that's why I steer clear of him. (Lisa)

> Ian came in very, very late after a party, and after he'd been asleep for an hour, he got up and he opened one of my drawers, and he pissed in it. And I needed the

light on to clean it up, and every time I turned the light on, he'd go ballistic, and in the end, he punched me. And from that point on I just thought, "Who is this man?" I was literally black and blue all over my chest, and I just felt like all the inside of my breasts had just changed their shape. . . . he really was punching with so much hate, and I thought is it hate or frustration? He later said that he's very, very sorry. And that he would never mean to hurt me. (Heather)

Maz's description shows the complex connections between her partner's issues of self-hatred and frustration with himself and his hatred of and frustration with the behavior of others:

He really had a lot of baggage [about] the bisexuality . . . one time he punched a hole in the wall. The first time he grabbed my arms so hard I got bruises and the other three times he grabbed me around the neck . . . in my view he hated himself. He just seemed so messed up . . . quite disgruntled with humanity, he got really irritable with people being fake and insincere. (Maz)

Of course, as I address these realities of bisexual men's violence, it is also important to remember that these realities may become the only media representation of bisexual men, sometimes in dangerous biphobic ways, as will be further discussed in chapter 11. For example, the compelling eight-episode Canadian documentary *The Staircase* (2004) follows a murder trial and court proceedings, showing how an innocent man may have been convicted of murder because he was outed as a bisexual (Szymanski, 2012). Mike Peterson is convicted of killing his wife, after it looked like she fell down the stairs in their home and fatally hit her head. Some gay porn and e-mails are found on his computer, while his liaisons with a male sex-worker and that he is out as bisexual are revealed. The jury could not believe that Peterson's wife knew about his bisexuality and knew that he was going out to meet the sex-worker, nor that she may have condoned it. The prosecutor could not even say the word "bisexual" without choking, a fact that the team of documentarians point out in the extra interviews. Although his parents and brother knew about Peterson's bisexuality since he was a child, the prosecutor said, "We found every aspect of Mike Peterson's life was a lie" (Szymanski, 2012: 443).

Schnarrs et al. found that many bisexual men were often attracted to women depending on how well they performed the "traditional feminine role." They were more likely to describe the women they were attracted to as nurturing, more open emotionally, caring and attentive, and attractive, as these traits were "a representation of their own masculinity" and high status (2012: 259). However, not all traditional stereotypes of women's roles were found to be attractive. In many instances, participants valued women with a "specific kind of 'feminine' intelligence" (2012: 259).

[In his view] women should be having an education and they really have a hard time in life and men really don't understand the good qualities that they have and then in the next breath, "I hate women. I can't stand women." . . . Women just absolutely love him. He's quite entertaining, good sense of humor, good wit and does have this way of making women feel important. But, then if it really comes to the crunch, like with friends of mine, as soon as they become mothers, "Oh, hopeless. They're just demeaning themselves being mothers." (Nicole)

Some women provided the 'stable' heteronormative home within which their partners could perform the normative dominant husband while they also lived queer, nonnormative lives away from home:

I was becoming very responsible and I wanted to pay the mortgage off and start getting somewhere, and also I had to support him through his ups and downs of employment. . . . he was going out to parties all the time and started doing lots of drugs, and meeting lots of gay men, and pretty much living the high life—and he then would come home to me . . . . Being pregnant and about to have the child, it was really hard. . . . he often just wouldn't come home. When he did, after I hadn't seen him for a couple of days, he'd be wearing someone else's clothes and he would have lost clothes I'd bought him and he'd have no excuse. (Rachel)

Sometimes, such misogynist and patriarchal entitlements did not surface until the men wanted to become fathers: "he did say to me he had wanted children, and he spotted me and thought, 'Well, she looks like a good breeder'" (Barb):

Things were fantastic, and then when we had the twins he wouldn't get up at night to pass the babies to me or help me and I was feeding every twenty minutes around the clock. And the pressure was so great, I don't know if I had some sort of breakdown then or not, but I really felt very isolated at that time . . . There's just the sheer neglect. (Heather)

Thus, as life brought more responsibilities and challenges, including raising children, the men increasingly regressed to bihegemonic modes of masculinity. They asserted control over their female partners if they felt their masculine dominance was being threatened by age, dependence on a female partner, unemployment and other financial factors: "he cut up the keycard for the bank account denying me access to money . . . One time he set fire to the kitchen curtains" (Josie).

He was also going through a mid-life thing and got himself into quite a lot of financial difficulty. . . . I think age is a big factor in those sorts of things, too, because men feel age more than it seems to me than women . . . but maybe it's that work thing [for men]. Like, when I was the bread winner and he was studying, it was extremely, extremely difficult for him to accept that. (Nicole)

I kept saying to him, "Why haven't you paid these bills? You've got the bank account with all your wages in it," and he said, "Because there's no money in it. I spent it on the flying lessons." . . . It was his money as far as he was concerned. He was still living the life of a single man, you see. He always had money for alcohol. . . . Every time he used to get us into debt and flittered the money away, I always put the children into day care and I had a job within the week and I honestly think that was the worst thing I could have done because I never made him face up to his responsibilities, but at the same time I did love him. Yes, and you keep on thinking they'll learn, they'll change, but of course they don't . . . he chose these [curtains] without any consultation with me, like he chose everything. He used to say, "This is what I'm going to buy. This is the furniture we're going to have." . . . I'm telling you these things so you can understand I was married to a domineering man who thought his word was God, and to try and show that even though I was a strong-willed female, you lose the battle. (Jean)

Interestingly, it wasn't until Jean discovered her husband's secret relationships with men that she began to feel as if she could assert herself. It is difficult to discern whether this was because she now perceived him to be less of a man or whether the fact that he wasn't above reproach had now been destroyed:

Because I had something over him, I became stronger. And where he used to say, "You will do this," I then said, "Sod off, do it yourself" whereas before I would have just said, "Yes, Anthony" and done it, but this changed me . . . it gave me an inner strength to rebel a bit. (Jean)

Many women also discussed how, when men begin to weave their bisexuality into the relationship, their behaviors becomes less domineering and sexist. Thus, when allowed to express their transgressive sexuality and masculinity openly rather than maintaining the charade of heterosexuality, they also drop the performance of stereotypical masculinity commonly associated with heteropatriarchy:

I think that from the beginning he was probably sort of like trying to come across as "Hey, I'm a man and these are the things that I'm supposed to do and these are the things I'm not supposed to do," but because we were able to explore our sexuality and we were able to sort of communicate a lot more, we've come to realize now that we're equals. (Christine)

Sexual relationships were another area where men often asserted their masculinist privileges and power. They showed indifference, harassment or neglect toward their women partners and demonstrated gendernormative assumptions about women's passive sexual needs:

I've met some really offensive bisexual men who think that bisexuality equals free love and "I get to come on to whoever I want and if they don't agree with me and have sex with me, then they're just frigid" and it can be used as another way to oppress women. (Joanne)

The erosion to women's self-esteem was very evident in Josie's experience where sexual put-downs, coupled with threats of suicide and her double workload, led to a major crisis and eventual turning point. One of the first changes Josie made was to go out and have sex, yet her partner's patriarchal double standard rose again:

> He continuously told me the reasons why he wasn't attracted to me was that I was fat, that I wasn't a good lover etc. . . . So I started going out to have some fun. He changed once I was seeing someone, becoming possessive . . . he started throwing him [her new partner] out the house. He became progressively more angry about the situation, usually when things were not going well with his lovers. (Josie)

"BISEXUAL MEN MAKE BETTER LOVERS"

> I think in some ways bisexual men make better lovers because they've got a greater repertoire to their sexuality because it involves men as well as women. Often they can be more thoughtful about a woman instead of just being the same old, you know, I stick my penis in, and then I come, and then sex is finished. . . . I think that there may be a tendency for bisexual men to look more into that kind of stuff because sexuality is an issue for them. They are more likely to research it and think about it. (Joanne)

> It's a sort of a wider range of interests than a blokey bloke. Not just the beer and the football, whereas it's the beer and the wine and the football and the art gallery and it's the sailing and it's painting and whatever. (Jane)

In this section, we will explore women's experiences and perspectives regarding how bisexuality in their partners resisted gendernormative and patriarchal performances and privileges of masculinity. Many women, including Joanne and Jane, praised their partners for behaviors, outlooks and performances of 'bimasculinity' and sexuality that critiqued, resisted and went way beyond limited heteropatriarchal constructions of masculinity. Whitney's study also found that 54% of the women stated having a special attraction to gay or bisexual men because they believed that they possessed certain positive qualities: "sensitivity, humour, warmth and compassion, creativity, interest in women as being more than sex objects, willingness to express emotion, spiritual and intellectual depth, and liberated behaviour" (1990: 43). More recent studies on this topic have also shown that heterosexual women express a desire for androgynous men or men who display both so-called masculine and feminine characteristics (Hill, 2006): "one of the real beauties of relationships with bi men: the ability to reinvent gender roles with another" (Julz, 2005: 217; see also Ward, 2015).

An interesting historical example of women's desire for androgynous men is the relationship between Oscar Wilde's former partner, Lord Alfred Douglas, and the woman he married, Olive Custance, who was at the centre of an important group of writers "negotiating and re-imagining fin-de-siècle and early twentieth-century constructions of gender and sexuality" (Parker, 2011: 226). When she met Douglas in 1901, Custance discovered a man who perfectly fit her fantasy construction of androgyny:

> His golden, effeminate beauty and connections with Wilde enticed her with homoerotic connotations, yet he was also willing to have a relationship with her. Most crucially, he was disposed to play along with the idea of being objectified, and enjoyed occupying the feminine role of beloved (Parker, 2011: 221–222).

In her early letters to Douglas, Custance describes herself as both a "page" and a "princess," which appears to be a way of arousing Douglas', and her own, bisexual desires by playing with shifting gender dynamics. She also sent Douglas a photograph of herself "briefed out as a pretty boy" (in Parker, 2011: 229).

In his autobiography, Douglas (1931) cites Custance's active role in their courtship as one of the principle reasons for his attraction to her. He also emphasizes his lifelong preference for occupying the feminine role, the pursued rather than the pursuer. Theirs was a union, he explains, in which the boy was "just as beautiful as the girl" (Douglas, 1931: 209 cited in Parker, 2011: 230). What is also of interest is that problems occurred when their flexible gender roles became fixed after their marriage in 1902. In this socially sanctioned relationship, Parker (2011) believes Douglas felt pressure to perform the "manly" role of patriarch. By Douglas' own admission, the decay of his and Custance's marriage was in part due to his increasingly masculine behavior: his reaction to the pressures of married heterosexuality was to "suppress or keep under . . . the 'feminine' aspects of his personality in order to conform to Victorian ideas of masculinity: "The more manly I became the less attractive I was to Olive" (Douglas 1931: 215 cited in Parker, 2011: 235). Indeed, Douglas' efforts to perform the archetypal masculinist role appear to have had a stultifying effect on her creativity. Her life from 1911 onwards is a narrative of conflict, depression and ill health. Many women in our research would have agreed with Custance about having male bisexual partners as their "queer muse": "I think on an unconscious level I really related to gay men's approach to the aesthetics of life. I identified so strongly that I felt like a gay man" (Nirupa).

Several women believed being bisexual had placed their partners in situations of heightened social and self-scrutiny about their own marginalization and 'difference', which gave them a heightened awareness of gendered power and privilege:

> They have often been on the outside, of not being able to fit in to society which gave him more of a depth of connection and understanding and therefore he was more creative with emotional intimacy. (Nirupa)

> I think his sexuality has made him very honest with himself and with challenging what people view as right and wrong. Luke became very much of a loner because he has sat on the outside with most people with this secret. (Simone)

For some women, a positive bimasculinity was seen in their partner's equitable participation in domestic work and childrearing:

> Both of us enjoy cooking and we share a lot of the workload. . . . I've got such a young child who still wakes us up through the night and he hears our son more than I do, but that again is because he's more in tune to the women's work as well as the guy's work. (Christine)

At times, however, other people's drawing attention to these qualities could be quite annoying:

> He actually took his annual leave to stay home and look after the children while I went overseas and I really got quite fed up with hearing how wonderful it was to do such a thing and I thought, "Who do you think looks after them the rest of the year?" (Scarlett)

For other women, a positive bimasculinity was particularly evident in their sexual relationships, as has been discussed in chapter 4. Women's sexual desires, fantasies and needs were more attended to and encouraged, and their partners' sexual practices were more varied and exciting, such as desiring penetration from a woman; engaging in BDSM; affirming non-monogamy and same-sex desires in their women partners; checking out men together and/or sharing a male partner:

> We worked out over the years a number of different variations where you control as a woman so we can both get our satisfaction. Like, we've done all kinds of variations on it, [penetrating each other and BDSM] . . . he approached relationships like a woman does and that's how come he's always interested in this and that kind of sexual act. Yeah, I think the sensitive new age guy that everybody says they want is a bi guy. (Jacinta)

> They've usually had some guy try to take advantage of them, kiss them, get drunk and be stupid with them, and they're usually much more understanding of how that feels from the other end, and therefore they don't tend to do it so much, don't end up sort of with their tongue half-way down to your stomach, you know. (Rose)
>
> I really like the power play that you can get with queer men ... like they can play that objectification role a woman can play in heterosexual relationships.... [a straight boyfriend said] "Oh, God, baby, why are you having sex with gay men? Where's that going to get you?" And it's like, "It's going to get me a good root." (Sascha)

Other women talked about partners' levels of demonstrativeness, affection and communication, particularly if their partners could be open about their bisexuality and/or have male partners:

> He's much more relaxed. He was sensitive before but he's more attuned [since he came out].... and picks up on what I'm feeling. He doesn't hold things in. He'll just walk up and give me a nice cuddle ... Patient, a lot more patient with absolutely everything, which is just astounding, because he was very short fused, usually. (Vicky)
>
> I think I've never been with a guy that's cried as much as Robert does.... we went to the movies and I'm like, "Oh, yeah, that was good" and I turn around and he's just blubbering like a baby and I'm like, "Oh, let me get you a tissue." (Yvonne)

Peterson attributes this increase in emotional openness to the fact that coming out meant experiencing feelings was a new phenomenon. Having previously denied their sexuality, "they also lost the ability to 'feel' ... After coming out, they suddenly find that they can express their feelings, and for the first time, some of them cry and love easily" (2001: 206).

Another quality women often commented on was their partner's attention to their appearance which they found very attractive even if others around them, as well as themselves, may have defined it as "looking gay":

> People said, "Oh, he looks gay," but he dresses very well and was always really well groomed,... I think that quality is what attracted me to him. Well spoken, confident, always sort of aware of his appearance, not that it was obsessive, and the cleanliness. (Beth)

Naomi was aware of how identifying as bisexual after endeavoring to pass as gay became freeing for her partner in terms of how he refashioned his masculinity:

> His hair got longer, he stopped smoking so much, put on some weight, and stopped trying to fit in to a certain gay look . . . stopped worrying about his clothes all the time although he would still cycle in his tight pink shorts, other times he looks like a dag, . . . he has found his midpoint. (Naomi)

"NOW I DON'T LIKE STRAIGHT GUYS"

> Now I don't like straight guys. Because they're usually quite chauvinistic. . . . I tried to conform with conventional straight guys but oh, look, I can't be bothered bullshitting. (Susanna)

In this section, we will explore how many women made comparisons between bisexual masculinities and heterosexual masculinities in both positive and problematizing ways, particularly in their constructions and performances of masculinity. They linked their desire for equitable, flexible and satisfying relationships with their actively looking for bisexual or gay men as partners and never being able to go back or try to be in relationships with heterosexual men. They believed bi men had interrogated hegemonic constructs of heterosexual masculinity and the interlinked traditional gendered expectations and assumptions of women.

> I like a guy who's not afraid to wear eyeliner or jewelry or pastel colors or a tight shirt or long hair or seem a bit effeminate or wear a skirt or dress up as a woman . . . Bi guys are not turned off by a woman with a strong personality. Many straight guys are uncomfortable with women with strong personalities because they feel, as a man, they should be the more dominant one (Lambert, 2010).

> Having met all these bi guys and if anything ever happened to Corey I think I would only want to have a relationship with a bisexual guy because in my perception they are better communicators, they are more empathetic, they are more equal, egalitarian, they are more creative lovers. They are interested in your clothes and your hair, they notice, they make comment. (Jacinta)

This was particularly poignant for Mary, whose partner had died of AIDS and whom she still loved and upheld as the perfect partner:

> He had patience, he was compassionate, he was loving. He would not want to do anything that would hurt me . . . , I still have that love for him. . . . so from seventeen until I was forty-three, he was my confidante. (Mary)

Many women had been in previous relationships with heterosexual men and made blunt comparisons: "[straight men] think they're king dicks"

(Yvonne); "I lived with a pig for eleven years" (Suzette). For many women, the issue was that heterosexual men, due to heterosexual privilege and dominance, did not have to interrogate their masculinity and sexuality, thereby preventing them from having a depth and insight into themselves and women:

> They're insecure bloody unselfaware men, because they've never had to examine themselves because they are part of the dominant culture. Whenever anything comes up, there is a glib dominant culture answer to it, and they have managed to live on that all their lives. You get women to support you all your life and you never have to think about it. ...[My previous husband] had difficulty talking about anything deep . . . our process of dealing with things would be something would come up and he'd freeze and he'd get really uncomfortable and then he'd spend three weeks throwing himself up rivers and down rocks and doing outdoor stuff, and then it would all percolate and then he would come back and be able to talk about it . . . I had been doing all his emotional work for him, like all the women in his family did, but I then got to a point where I was unable to do his work, and I needed help with mine. (Anne)

Krystle discussed how, during the process of deciding whether she would remain in her marriage with a bisexual man, she began a relationship with a heterosexual man:

> I had three sons. I had to get into cars and football. . . . I did have a connection with a 'macho man', and what I learnt in that time was, yes, I could discuss football and cars and whatever, but this guy had no fucking idea of his emotional state. He lacked a huge amount of emotional intelligence and therefore integrity. That relationship really helped me to work out that everybody is a package and straight men will have bits I don't like in their package. Sure this gay part is part of a package with Greg, but I get someone I can have deep discussions with, is intelligent and creative and who is emotionally aware. To me, having that real honesty and a soul mate was important. But if I hadn't had that other experience, I wouldn't have learnt and been sure of that. (Krystle)

Some women believed that the performances of masculinist strength and supremacy in previous heterosexual partners were actually attempts at disguising insecurities. Their current relationship was 'more equal' because their bisexual partners, in displaying an emotionality and so-called effeminacy that heteronormative society would define as weakness and inferiority, were actually being stronger and more secure in their gender and partnering roles than heterosexual men, and expecting the same from their women partners:

> I always had weak kind of [heterosexual] men. They wanted someone to make decisions, do everything, another mum. . . This [current relationship] is, I would say, the most equal relationship I've ever had, and every single day I

look at my actions and make sure that I'm being fair and make sure that I'm not railroading . . . I remember my nanna actually saying to me before anyone realized there was any real relationship going on, "Gee, I bet you wish that he was straight" and I said to her, "Well, actually I don't because he wouldn't be the person that he is" . . . I guess there's always the assumption that gay men are sort of sissies, weak. And I've said time and time again to people he's actually the strongest man I've ever dealt with. (Rosemary)

Other strong points of comparison for many women were the appreciation of and attention to women's bodies and sexual desires, and being responsible and proactive in relation to sexual health, all qualities they did not perceive in or experience with heterosexual men:

Straight men don't want to have a look inside [the vulva and vagina] . . . . There's something incredibly powerful about the image of a cunt, and raw powerful female sexuality [that bi men are into]. (Sascha)

I don't imagine myself getting seriously involved with a heterosexual man because I guess I would be horrified if I was seen as a bit of a play toy like "Guess what, I've got a bisexual girlfriend, so aren't you all jealous." Or being seen as a means of fulfilling a man's fantasies . . . I think a bisexual man is a bit more likely to understand that because they're there too. (Joanne)

Joanne's insights above into presumed FMF threesomes by some heterosexual men connects to Sheff's (2014) reference to the "unicorn hunter syndrome," wherein a male-female couple try to establish a triad with another woman who has no other partners herself: "Such a myopic view of a woman willing to fold herself into someone else's existing plans as if she were a mere ingredient can only exist if that fantasized woman is (at best) two dimensional, certainly not a multidimensional human with plans and lovers of her own" (2014: 83). What would also be of interest is whether and why aren't male bisexuals coming into a threesome not defined as a unicorn?

Some women did express contradictory comparisons between their bisexual partners and previous heterosexual partners. For example, while enjoying the fact that their current bisexual partner did not perform the patriarchal dominance of previous heterosexual partners, they also expected and expressed a desire for a performance of 'manliness' particularly in order for them to perform their femininity as a counterpoint to this. Temptress expressed her mixed needs with her current partner who lacked certain expressions of a gendernormative man that she would like as a counterpoint to her constructions of gendernormative femininity, even though her descriptions of what that entails in her could be perceived to be quite traditionally masculinist:

> I want to be fucked by a man, and I love the whole masculine thing. I love being in the kitchen. I love cooking. I love taking care of a man. When it comes to decision-making, I also like him to take charge, you know. I'm the little girl with the big man. . . . What's good about our relationship is that we can share feelings and hug and cry and all that, but at the same time, it's a disaster, because no one's strong, no one's the man. . . . I don't want mummy's boys. . . . the one I have now, he's half-half. So, he's the woman I need for understanding me and letting me scream and push and shove, and he's also now learning with me to be a man, . . . he always went with his mum shopping. He even did her hair. So, he's learnt to be a woman, even the way he walks. I taught him how to walk again. He used to lift up his feet, to have that elegant thing like a woman. He practiced at home. Walk in a straight line. (Temptress)

On the other hand, there were facets of his masculinity which were still problematically similar to her previous heterosexual partners, such as an obsessive interest in pornography and an overt dominance over women in social situations:

> I don't understand, he can't go a day without looking at porn, like, what the fuck is that? Get a life! Go read a newspaper, a magazine, get creative, get intelligent. . . . Every time he's with a woman, he does the wrong things, speaks too much, touches too much, gets in there. My God. He meets a woman, "She's nice. She liked me. I want to fuck her. I want to do this with her, I want to do that" Vroom, vroom, vroom. (Temptress)

"I'M NOT A DOORMAT"

> I'm not a doormat. I'm very strong and independent. I always had my own professional life, great confidence in myself. I was a feminist even before feminism became a household word. I demanded his honesty, his love, his equal parenting and domestic sharing, and a good sexual, affectionate relationship but sexual ownership was something I worried about only for a few months after he began his first relationship with a man, and then I realized I was worrying because society said I should. (Alice)

A final theme that was very evident in women's discussions about their partner's challenging of prescriptive and limiting constructions of masculinity was how they were also able to challenge prescriptive and limiting constructions of femininity. Bimasculinity encouraged and enhanced their own resistances to normative submissive femininity and passive sexuality:

> I think to be in a relationship with a bisexual man, to have that meaning that you're abused, it's so inaccurate from my experience. . . . It also makes me

feel quite angry, because my role in this relationship is one of equal power and equal decision-making capacity, economically as well, which is important for women. How happy I am in this relationship depends very little on his sexual identification.... It all intermingles, incorporating my own feminist politics and his queer politics. (Katie)

I think with a guy who's bi, you actually need to be fairly strong, and you need to be able to cope in unexpected situations and difficult situations. I think that you have to be fairly emotionally mature, too, because the woman is going to be dealing with really complex questions from outside sources, the people who are butting their nose in, and then trying to comfort and support their partner. (Luna)

If the women were weak, they would probably go for the straight, macho guys, because they're the ones that come across as, "I know what I'm doing and I put my foot down and you're going to have to toe the line and follow whatever I say."... [my bi partner] realized that I've got a lot of male traits in me. I can just look at the street directory and holding it upright I know which way it is that we should turn. I can back into any parking spot without a problem. I'm very focused on work and business and stuff like that.... I don't come across like a dumb blond... I guess that's why we have this balance and he lets me take over a lot of the stuff like our finances. (Christine)

Other women spoke about how their partners and their relationship forced them to become more equitable, resilient and independent even if, at times, performing dependence and neediness may have been desired by the women. In Jacinta's case, this independence was interwoven with a togetherness and one-ness that she found challenging and yet deeply secure:

We'll be driving home from somewhere and he starts up a conversation and I'll go off being all disempowered and helpless and pathetic and we'll get home and he'll just turn the engine off and he'll stay in the car like for half an hour until either I get the thing resolved for myself or I admit that I'm unwilling to resolve it right now and I'm ready to leave it... I was in Melbourne, delayed overnight, I've come straight here from the airport. He's got the kids up, he's got them breakfast, he's getting them dressed, he's getting all their gear together to go swimming. But that won't mean I owe him one... we don't keep score. It's just one life. (Jacinta)

Sally felt her work and the dependence of her partner robbed her of elements of her femininity which she eagerly regained after the relationship ended:

My attitude in work is very focused and very driven, so I actually lost a lot of femininity.... I had to make all the decisions at work and then the decisions at home and really mother Michael completely. I definitely had three kids, because he just wasn't capable of really doing anything or in control of anything . . . [Since breaking up] just a bit more girly I suppose. I used to wear a lot of trouser suits, I didn't really think about it, yeah, but just taking a bit more pride in your appearance. (Sally)

There were also women who discussed how bipatriarchy did constrain their or other women's gender and sexual expressions, and indeed, disempowered women by making them financially dependent and insecure. This was more evident if the women already held traditional notions of heterofemininity within a framework of heteropatriarchy, such as needing a man as a provider and protector:

There's a huge fear out there of being on your own, and these women have been made dependent [by their bisexual male partner]. . . . If he's the breadwinner, how are you going to do it [leave him]? Unless you are absolutely able to, you go into a lot of poverty. . . . also if you're not that madly into sex, what's the big issue if I'm looked after, and the kids are looked after? You'd be prepared to compromise. (Hannah)

Other women believed this type of exploitation and disempowering of women was more likely to occur if the partners were not out or comfortable with their own bisexuality, coupled with their holding traditional expectations of women as partners. It was also more likely to occur if the women were already "weak" or "less confident" and "a bisexual man who doesn't want the responsibility of communication would choose a woman who would put up with his shit." (Joanne)

It's very easy for me to think of a situation where there's a couple out in the country and one day she finds out that he's been having sex with other guys, and she has nowhere to go, and no one to turn to. And she probably has no money or a job or any career prospects of her own. So in that case it can be an exploitative thing where, you know, "Well, I don't care if you don't like it. This is just what I want to do and you don't have a say about it." (Ava)

In Loredana's situation, there were multiple levels of dependency on each other, based on her adhering to the gendernormative female nurturing role while he was also required to be the carer due to her disability:

When Peter got the job in Kuala Lumpur last year, I wasn't going with him, but he said, "Look, I think we can make a go of it." . . . People don't faze me, whatever level they are in society, whereas he is. So he actually established himself through me. So, although I may be disabled, as a personality I certainly am not and he has needed that, and also my emotional support he's needed . . . we found our apartment, and I took care of everything, you know, whatever needed to be done, in setting up. . . . The only time that he had to do anything for me was when we went out, socially, to push me in the wheel chair. But I felt that he began to feel really uncomfortable with him pushing me. Just wasn't careful. I actually fell right out of it one time because he hit a step and I know he's impatient, but I just felt unwanted. (Loredana)

Some bisexual polyamorous women were also aware of differing gender dynamics between their relationships with female partners and with male partners. Indeed, women like Georgina experienced frustration when they witnessed their male partners behaving patriarchally with other female partners who responded submissively rather than challenging him the way she did:

The other woman that we're in a relationship with, he's still manipulating her through self-esteem, you know, "You're stupid, you don't know what you're talking about," blah, blah, blah, . . . And once, she was crying on my shoulder and saying, "I've always been supportive. I've always let him go out and do his thing. I've never passed judgment and it would be nice if it was reciprocated." . . . Now, it's very difficult to pull back when [women] don't want to do anything about it. (Georgina)

CONCLUSION

In this chapter, we have seen how women differentiate between bimisogyny and bimasculinity in their partners, and how these gendered performances are based on the need to navigate social ascription, community acknowledgement and self-ascription in regard to how to be a man, how to be a man in a relationship with a woman, and how to be a bisexual man, and in a MORE. Self-surveillance is a result of panopticonic regulatory forces (Foucault, 1977). The consequences of social and community scrutiny are the projection of external inferiorization and social powerlessness as a man onto exercising superiority and power over a woman in one's domestic domain. However, some men refuse to undertake such compensatory actions and instead choose to live on the borders with their partners, together reconfiguring what is externally deemed to be demeaning to masculinity into what is personally and relationally positive and enhancing.

Chapter 10

"What Do We Tell The Kids?"
Women Talk about Bisexual Fathers

> So many times when situations arise around his bisexuality, we've looked at each other and asked, "What do we tell the kids?" So what we've done always is be honest, and it's been very painful, often. And yet we've got three people who we love, and who seem to be well and truly adjusted wonderful people. (Hannah)

Many women had children or were considering having children with their partners, as they believed their partners' bisexuality did not affect their ability to be good fathers. Indeed, some women were adamant that a partner's bisexuality augmented his capacity to be a good father: "we would have had a gorgeous child ... if I was to have a child it would definitely have been his" (Nirupa). Sometimes, the women knew this even if their partners had internalized heterosocial norms that only straight men could be good fathers:

> I knew that he would be an excellent father.... But the reality of being a bisexual father, he just didn't want it. He didn't want a child to have a bisexual father. (Susanna)

Other women expressed concerns about having children with their bisexual partners: "Well, I wouldn't get that far into a relationship where I would consider having children to a bisexual man" (Louisa).

There were also situations where having children had actually precipitated the father's disclosure. They had revealed behaviors that indicated they seemed to be wanting freedom from the responsibilities of parenting:

> I challenged him every day. "It's not acceptable to go out and not come home until 7 o'clock in the morning and leave me at home with the baby" and then he would go into this tantrum thing, "Why are you doing this to me? Why do you

make me so unhappy?" You know, completely turn it around so he's the victim and I'm the perpetrator. (Kristina)

He'd always done the right thing and he was finally breaking free, instead of getting all of that stuff out of his system in his late teens, where everybody else does, he decided to do it in his mid-thirties when he's a father, when really it should be like, "Hello, I'm a Dad now and let's be happy with that life." That's why I felt very much that the children were pivotal in the change. (Sue)

There were also fathers who did not disclose their bisexuality until their children had grown: "Well honey, the kids are grown and now it's time for me to pursue my own life" (Kaye, 2001).

However, for all women, whether they had children or were contemplating having children, the issue of when and what to tell their children about their partner's sexuality, as well as considerations about the rewards and ramifications of this, were major issues in our research. Indeed, in all interviews with mothers, there was an awareness of their children being within and between two worlds: that of home and that of the world outside the home, such as at school. Thus, this chapter presents the double-edged sword familiar to all queer family configurations. On the one hand, MORE families suffer from a lack of social presence which disadvantages them in terms of legal, economic, and institutional rights and acceptance. On the other hand, fears of misunderstanding, demonization and othering by the media, health, education and service providers make MORE families, including polyfamilies, reluctant to disclose their families to the wider societal matrix in which they exist and operate (Pallotta-Chiarolli, 2010a, b; Pallotta-Chiarolli et al. 2013).

This fear of disclosure of MORE families and bisexual fathers is linked to a major absence in popular culture of positive representations of bisexual fathers. In *The Naked Face* (1984), Rod Steiger's police officer summed up Hollywood's view of bisexual fathers quite succinctly with the line, "A bisexual is a fag with a family" (Bryant, 2005b: 310). In the black comedies, *Something For Everyone* (1970) and *"Dry Cleaning"* (1997), enterprising young men enter the heteropatriarchal family unit as outsiders and attempt to reorganize it around their bisexual desires, including seducing the paternal head of the household into sex with them. This plot is similar to Pier Paolo Pasolini's *Teorema* (1968) in which a handsome young man seduces male and female members of a wealthy Italian family, as will be discussed further in chapter 11.

In *A Home at The End of the World* (2004), childhood male friends Bobby and Jonathan become lovers, are both eventually involved with the same woman with whom they have a child, and move to the country to raise their daughter as very loving fathers. However, at the end of the film and novel (Cunningham, 1990), Claire takes the baby and leaves. It appears that becoming a mother redefines Claire as someone intolerant of unconventional sexuality. One of Claire's first real moments of unease around Bobby and Jonathan is in watching them tenderly playing with her newborn daughter. Not only does she feel left out of their cofathering, she seems to unexpectedly experience the sight of male intimacy as wrong in itself. In the film's final shot, as Claire drives away with the baby, Jonathan goes into the house first while Bobby lingers outside for a minute, staring at the landscape before finally joining Jonathan. According to Vicari, this "is meant to suggest Bobby's bisexual nature, divided in this case between the part of him that wants to remain with Jonathan and the part of him that is still very much tied to Claire and their daughter" (2011: 136). Vicari contrasts this "pessimistic choice for Claire" by the author Cunningham and the film director Mayer with how Techine ends *The Witnesses* (2007) "with a melange of straight, gay and bisexual characters coming together to raise the new baby—the next generation" (2011: 140). Another positive representation of a father understanding his bisexuality is in *The Lost Language of Cranes* (1991). When Owen's son declares his homosexuality, Owen begins to question his own long-hidden bisexual behavior and indeed tells his son that he believes "everyone is bisexual." He eventually comes out to his wife and begins to bond with his son in a way that they have never been able to before. What is disappointingly stereotypical is the representation of the wife/mother as cold and hard. As an editor of romance novels, she is depicted as immersed in the romantic erotic language of the novels while her own love life is empty. What isn't explored is what came first: her dispassionate manner or her awareness of her husband's sexual secrets. At the end of the film, Owen does say she is the love of his life, has never loved anyone like her, and never will.

In *Brokeback Mountain* (2005), both men are portrayed as capable fathers who wish to maintain loving relationships with their children as well as their position as fathers. In particular, Jack's authority as a father is challenged by his father-in-law, who appears to suspect that Jack is not "a real man." We see Jack asserting his position as head of the household, much to the delight and approval of his wife. We see Ennis losing much contact and access to his daughters after the divorce and his ex-wife's remarriage. However, the film ends with his adult daughter coming to find him in the caravan, where he lives alone, to invite him to her wedding.

In *Priscilla, Queen of the Desert* (1994), the drag queen character, Tick, has a wife and son in Alice Springs. Indeed, it is his wife's nightclub he travels to by bus through the Central Australian desert with two fellow drag performers in order to financially support her with a drag show. And it is his son with whom he reestablishes a relationship and takes back to Sydney to live with him. Tick was actually based on well-known Sydney drag queen Cindy Pastel (aka Ritchie Fingers), whose son grew up in Sydney with him, and whose mother eventually joined them there. In the film, his son actually soothes his father's anxieties about coming out to him as his mother has told him all about Tick and his lifestyle in Sydney, and "it's not a problem."

Another film, the dark British comedy *Death at a Funeral* (2007), presents a father whose bisexuality is not revealed until his blackmailing gay partner turns up at his funeral. We see the adult offspring struggle to connect the image they have of their father as a dedicated "decent" man who adored their mother, with the new images of their father in typical gay dance-party attire in the arms of his male partner. Indeed, the dead man's wife is earlier depicted wondering how she will live without her very considerate and loving husband. The slapstick humor involved in the events that ensue, such as trying to conceal this new information about their father's other life in order not to discredit him in front of his family and friends, and trying to conceal the accidental death of the male partner by placing him in the coffin with the father, give way to a sobering eulogy delivered by one of the sons. In this eulogy, the father is described as inspirational to his children in teaching them to aim for their desires in life and whether they succeed or fail, the importance is in the endeavor. Words like "decent" and "loving," which had been applied to the father before his bisexuality was dramatically and comically exposed, are reclaimed and reaffirmed in the eulogy. Indeed, new descriptions such as "exceptional," "understanding" and "good" are added, as well as the man's family and friends being asked to gain wisdom and reestablish commonality in accepting the complexities, chaos and confusion of life, love and being human.

A Spanish film, *Dark Blue, Almost Black* (2006) explores through humor the impact a father's bisexual lifestyle has on his son Sean, who takes blackmail photos of a masseur when he is performing sexual favors on his male clients. One afternoon, Sean sees his own father naked on the masseur's table, and this revelation of his father's bisexuality is difficult for Sean, although not treated as a crisis but as a source of offbeat humor. For example, he immediately begins to anonymously blackmail his father for money which he uses to buy the van his father is selling. Frustrated with the lack of honesty in his household and with his own growing sexual insecurities, Sean confronts his father who denies that he is either gay or bi: "I won't explain myself to you." Then, when Sean angrily exposes his father's secret to his mother, she is mad with Sean because she knew all along her husband was bisexual. "This sucks" Sean says, defeated. The mother says, "No, it sucked before when your dad was always bitter and made my life hell. He's learnt to live with it and so have I." As if "to underscore the fact that his parents' marriage worked successfully, Sean later overhears them having loud passionate sex" (Vicari, 2011: 133). In a final twist, he visits the same masseur and gradually finds himself being turned on by the hand-job and wanting it more regularly.

Indeed, he and his father work out alternative days to visit the masseur. Thus, he begins to understand his father more as well as realizing he is not gay himself. They are now connected through a shared unlabeled sexuality. As the director Arevalo says, "in the contrasts you encounter the richness of nuances." Thus, these two films, *Death at A Funeral* and *Dark Blue, Almost Black* substantiate Hart's (2005) theory: through humor, shock, "grossness," and mockery, which effectively engage a mainstream voyeuristic audience, can come opportunities for moral lessons and cultural interrogations.

Bisexual fathers have been absent in research literature. A literature search conducted by Ross et al. (2012) found only seven studies reported any findings specific to the bisexual participants included in their sample. In most research, bisexual parents are simply clustered together with lesbian and/or gay parents. Likewise, Garner (2003) believes that bisexual parents who are married to someone of the opposite sex are often overlooked because they are mistaken for heterosexual couples. Thus, "exclusion by inclusion" (Martin & Pallotta-Chiarolli, 2009; Pallotta-Chiarolli & Martin, 2009) is very evident in most studies of bisexual parents.

In their review of existing data, Ross & Dobinson (2013) found that many bisexual people have or want to have children and indeed bisexual men and women may be more likely than gay men or lesbians to have children (see also Edser & Shea, 2002). Coleman (1982) found that maintaining a loving relationship with their children was one of the main reasons why many men continued to have a close relationship with their spouse or former spouse. 77% of his sample had children, all men had truly wished to be fathers and expressed a deep sense of love and admiration for their children (see also Peterson, 2001). Ross & Dobinson (2013) could identify no research exploring experiences of bisexual parents disclosing or wishing to disclose their identity to younger children. Further, while excellent age appropriate resources are available to assist in discussions about lesbian and gay families, such as children's picture books, they were aware of no such resources discussing biparented families. They also could not identify any research that has specifically examined experiences of bisexual people coming out to their children's teachers.

Ross et al. (2012) examined the experiences of bisexual people in the adoption system: "few bisexual participants chose to disclose their orientation to their adoption workers, perceiving that identifying themselves as either heterosexual or gay/lesbian . . . would prevent exposure to workers' potential biases about their 'fitness' to parent as bisexuals" (2012: 151). With respect to legal and child custody matters, negative stereotypes about bisexual people in Family Courts and welfare systems are sometimes used to justify denying child custody or limiting visitation (Mallon, 2011). In particular, the assumption that bisexual people are not capable of committed, monogamous relationships and therefore cannot create a stable home for a child was both experienced and anticipated by bisexual parents as they negotiated the child welfare system (Mallon, 2011). These stereotypes are upheld in the French film *To the Extreme* (2000) wherein Thomas is a hedonistic young bisexual male in a long term relationship with Caroline, an older widow with a thirteen-year-old son named Greg. When Caroline is killed in an accident, he finds himself wanting to take care of Greg. Thomas never conceals his bisexuality from Greg, and indeed Greg would like to live with Thomas but the court system will not grant Thomas custody. Greg is placed in an orphanage pending adoption but he runs away to see Thomas, who descends more and more into promiscuous sex and male prostitution. In a pivotal turning point in the film, he invites Greg to a late-night sex party where he stares at all the sex acts "with wide eyed horror." He finally sees Thomas in makeup being anally penetrated and "a look of cold disappointed disgust comes over Greg's face" (Vicari, 2011: 113). What is problematic about this filmic depiction is the assumption that a bisexual man cannot be both a competent father and enjoy an active sex-positive life. The film ends with Thomas dying in a street accident when saving Greg who police are chasing to return him to the orphanage. Vicari comments upon how this ending symbolizes the heteropatriarchal order "would rather return Greg to no father at all than to a surrogate father who has subverted the masculine role through androgyny and bisexuality" (2011: 115).

The experiences of children being raised by bisexual parents also lack substantial research (Garner, 2004; Buxton, 2006a; Pallotta-Chiarolli, 2006a; Karlson, 2007; Block, 2008; Tye, 2003). It is likely that these children share many of the same anxieties as children of lesbian and gay parents, such as the potential discovery of their parent's sexual orientation, subsequent assumptions about their own sexual orientation, and bullying or harassment at school. However, as indicated by the emerging literature on the strengths of children raised by lesbian and gay parents, there may be advantages to being raised by bisexual parents that are worthy of study. In my previous research, Rita, 17, and Mateusz, 18, were bisexual young people who had grown up with a bisexual father:

> When I first came out bi he was so excited, and so was my mom, and they congratulated me like I'd won some major school prize, and then they took me shopping for cool queer clothes. I wore them the first chance I got to some school function and I'm sure my eyes said, "Fuck you" to any cloney Barbie and Kens from dysfunctional fake Brady Bunch set ups who dared to stare at me as if I had the problem (Rita in Pallotta-Chiarolli, 2010a: 153).

> My dad and I went on a holiday as part of a father-son bonding session, just the two of us. . . . we'd talked about doing our own thing that night. So I thought

I'd take the chance to explore the "gay" side of the town... Well, there I am stripping down in the change-room, and there's my dad getting dressed on his way out! Talk about mega-awkwardness. The strange thing is that we carried on as normal afterwards for the rest of the holiday and didn't talk about it at all. It's like we pretended it never happened . . . It didn't affect our close relationship . . . but it left me confused about who's really in the closet here. About six months later, and totally out of the blue, Mum sat me down for a deep and meaningful to tell me that Dad was bisexual and that she'd known this when she married him and that it was nothing to worry about and I wasn't to let Dad know she'd told me. Well, what do you do? I told her her son is one of those too. Anyway, we're still a real close family and Mum and Dad have accepted me, and we joke that it's "in the genes" or "you men's pants" as Mum says. . . . My father is happily bisexual and married, and one day I hope to be too, with a guy or girl or both! (Mateusz in Pallotta-Chiarolli, 2010a: 154).

This issue of nonmonogamous or polyamorous bisexual parents has begun to gain some research (Barker & Langdridge 2010; Pallotta-Chiarolli, 2010a; Pallotta-Chiarolli et al. 2013; Riggs, 2010). Goldfeder & Sheff's (2013) research highlights the benefits and pitfalls of polyparenting as experienced by her participants, including the extra emotional and practical resources of having multiple parents and role-models who emphasize open communication. Drawbacks included the problems of attachment following break-up, in common with many monogamous parents, and stigma due to being polyamorous.

Buxton's work (2006c) has been the most significant in addressing the impact of the bisexual partner's disclosed orientation on their children. A major concern of the heterosexual parent is to support their children and protect them from getting hurt from teasing or stigmatization by other children, neighbors and the wider community. They may also experience "conflict between their own hurt from disclosure and their desire as a co-parent to preserve the children's bond with their parent who has come out" (2006c: 113). Most parents usually tell the children when they themselves feel "comfortable enough" with the information and before the children hear the news from outsiders who may not be accepting or have appropriate knowledge. Indeed, the heterosexual parent models how the children process the disclosure and relate to the disclosing parent. Parents advise not telling the children about divorce and the partners' sexual orientation at the same time as the children blame the disclosing parent for the divorce. In some cases, the disclosing bisexual parent may neglect the children for a period of time or engage in ineffective parenting behaviors either if they stay married or post divorce. This can upset the children and trouble the heterosexual parent (see also Buxton, 1991, 1999). Lubowitz (1997) reminds us that the children will need to be reassured they are loved by both of their parents. In fact, research shows that children respond well to their parents' openness, and that early awareness can foster the social skills needed to problem-solve around disclosure to peers (Paul, 1996).

In our research, the following themes arose in relation to disclosing to children:

1. Telling the children was *essential and wanted* in order to foster family health and closeness, foster the child's understanding of sexual diversity, and develop confidence in espousing human rights in the wider world.
2. Telling the children was an *unwanted, problematic but necessary consequence* of the fissures in the family, with the added concerns of the ramifications of this information on the child's wellbeing.
3. Telling the children *required negotiating the child's level of outness with others* such as peers, schools, family members and the wider society.
4. Telling the children was *determined by a range of factors* such as the child's age, gender, health status, and closeness of the relationship with the father.
5. Telling the children was *not an option*.

"FOR THEM IT'S JUST NATURAL"

> If it comes up in conversation, we answer the questions completely and honestly. . . . one morning, one of my twins trotted in and went, "It's like I have two daddies. It's like mummy married two men" and we all just went "Yeah." For them it's just natural. (Jacinta)

Many parents believed their children knowing about their father's bisexuality, and/or the family's mixed sexualities and nonmonogamies, was essential in order to foster family health and closeness, the child's understanding of sexual diversity, and develop confidence in espousing human rights in the wider world:

> I certainly think my partner's children [who have a lesbian Mum] will grow up with quite diverse understandings because of the way their families are shaping up. And I think it's just showing children that there are all sorts of ways of living and expressing themselves in intimate relationships. (Jude)

> He sees mummy and daddy snuggling up to all sorts of people. He's more concerned about their vibe. He'll pick up whether you're a nice person or not, and it doesn't matter what sexuality you are, if you've got the wrong vibe, he don't want to talk to you. And I actually use him as like a little radar type of thing. (Kirsten)

In some families, this openness about parents' sexual diversity was just another component in a life of experiences, both positive and problematic, in understanding the diversity of human lives and values, and the role of parents in facilitating this:

> My daughter's a little bit sensitive, because like any adolescent, she doesn't like to think of her parents having sex. The fact that Charlie is bisexual has been mentioned. No big deal. His son is very understanding. He has a friend who he works with who's gay and it didn't shock him. His daughter has a relationship with another woman who just had a baby by another man. (Jolene)

Some parents spoke in hindsight, realizing what a difference it had made to their adult children: "I think we raised them to understand the special love their father and I always had for each other and they trusted us to never do anything that would hurt them or each other" (Alice).

Mothers of children "in nappies" spoke of telling their children soon as part of developing an openness and closeness within the family that many felt they themselves had either experienced or missed in their own childhoods. Another motivation was to tell children as soon as possible before they learned negative and discriminatory attitudes from the wider society:

> One day they'll find out, and I'd rather they find out from us . . . They soon won't be in nappies any more. . . . I was fortunate in a lot of ways in that I had this sort of hot house with my parent and got to know her really well as a person, and was forced to appreciate her as a person at a very young age. After my father died, my mother had a nervous breakdown and was in and out of psychiatric care. . . . Grace was so delighted to tell everybody at the doctor's surgery that daddy had depression, which I thought was hilarious. She's at the age where they just say whatever they think. I'd love to tell her before she knows what it [bisexuality] means and then when she does know what it means, she'll have that life knowing her father for years and loving him for who he is. I knew gay people when I was a kid before I knew what gay meant. It never occurred to me that it was weird. I was like thirteen before I realized that gay was not considered normal as far as everybody else was concerned. By that stage, I'd already had thirteen years of love from these family friends, who were all gay. (Monica)

Other parents believed they were modeling effective communication strategies, particularly in relation to sexual and relationship diversity:

> They ask questions and repeat what we have said to indicate that they have grasped the concept. They couldn't believe that some people wanted to hurt our feelings. (Shelley)

My kids joke about, "Don't ask mum a question, she'll get the bloody books out and she'll show you pictures." When they were younger they used to listen patiently and now they just go, "Can I have the short version, please?" (Scarlett)

Indeed, some children were very angry if they realized that their parents hadn't told them immediately. Then, as in Kaitlin's example, the issue became incorporated into the everyday dynamics, bantering and humor of the family:

> She [daughter] was enraged that we hadn't told her as soon as Ross had told me.... I just said I wasn't ready to do it. "I could have helped you", she said.... the humor in the family changed, and it was a bit hard for Ross, because some of it sounded homophobic, but I think it was really, really healthy. I remember Nicholas in year 12 came out in these tight little shorts because he got them in Year 9. I said, "Nicholas you can't wear those, you'll be raped and pillaged if you go out in those" and he had this twinkle in his eye and he said, "Oh, I better watch out for Dad then, hadn't I?" (Kaitlin)

Sometimes, the children assisted their mother in understanding and accepting what their father was going through, and even showed strong insights into why their father might be displaying mixed or negative emotions and behaviors: "They say, 'Oh, he's confused, mummy, he's just upset and is not functioning very well'" (Felicity).

> I said to my husband, "You've got to tell the kids. I can't bear this anymore, me being this emotional nut case." ... there just was always this underlying thing of mum unhappy, and Dad distant and my daughter said she remembers terrible loneliness in her childhood ... Anyway, he told her and he also told her that I'd had an affair with this Indonesian guy and had an abortion.... and she wasn't shocked at all.... She said, "Mum, it's not a problem. I've learnt so much from Mum and Dad." And she's not being a martyr. I mean, she calls a spade a spade. If she's had enough, she'll let me know, as will my older son ... my daughter said to me a couple of weeks ago, "Mum, I know your unhappiness in the marriage has been but Dad has really struggled and suffered with that as well, you know, not being able to be who he is." (Helena)

At other times, parents expressed their concerns at the possible outcomes and reactions to the coming out, which proved to be unfounded. Indeed, the children had other concerns which were more generic such as imagining a parent being sexual, and in relation to the family's wellbeing and togetherness:

> We sat down with the girls and after dinner was finished, we were biting our nails and really had butterflies in the stomach. We said, "Okay kids, this is the way it is." We asked if there were any questions. They said, "Are you going to split up?" "No!! Not because of this. I love daddy because of who he is. That

will never change. If we break up it would be no different than if we broke up and we were a heterosexual couple." "Okay. Can we watch Chicken Run now?" That was it. . . . We said, "Do you know what a bisexual is? Well, daddy likes to have sex with men." And Stephanie sort of cringed when the penny dropped [about the sex]. Unfortunately we made them think about it. (Laughing) (Sharae)

Other parents spoke of how their children would sometimes drop hints or initiate conversations regarding what they already knew or surmised. In Helena's case, one son began to talk about dreams and memories of an incident with his father when they were away on a father/son holiday; the other son had always sensed a loneliness in his mother within a troubled marriage; and the daughter was able to have blunt honest conversations with her father about his sexuality and piece together what she had always felt about him:

> When he was eight, we went to the beach, his Dad had gone to the toilet and I was a bit concerned that he's gone so long. So, we walked over and fucking hell, wouldn't you know it, there were these two pairs of sneakers facing one another in the cubicle. . . . [So recently] he's going, "God, if only dad had told me. It would have made so much difference to understanding" . . . to Magnus [other son] I said, "When I'm around Dad I often feel very alone" and he just looked at me and said, "He's an alone kind of guy." End of story. . . . she [daughter] told me the last time she'd been to see him she had a conversation with him about "pussy" versus "dick" and he'd said, "Well, actually, I'm not really that interested in either of them. I just have never been very sort of sexual." My daughter said to me, "You know, when I looked at your pre-marriage photographs, he just looked so asexual." (Helena)

In Maura's situation, her daughter asked the question and Maura felt able to respond honestly, knowing how beneficial this knowledge would be to her daughter's growth. She was also aware, as were many parents, that belonging to a sexually diverse community and having access to sexual diversity discussions in the media and popular culture not only led to the question but also allowed for a framework of knowledge and understanding within the children:

> She is well aware about discrimination or that some people think it's a terrible thing . . . she sees that we are all just like normal people. We have got gay friends and we've got loads of straight friends. So she sees a whole lot of relationships and that some of them work and some of them don't. It's not about the sexuality, it's about the people. (Maura)

Sometimes, children wanted more information than they had been given:

> About a month ago he [son] was in bed and he called out to me, "I just want to ask you a question, well, I can't ask you unless I have the doona over my head,"

and the question he comes up with is, "Did Dad cheat on you with men?" and I said "He did, and that's pretty much why we've separated," and he said, "Well no one ever told that to us." (Marissa)

Several women talked about the significance of childhood experiences, and openness and understandings of sexualities, relationships and queer culture because of seeing their parents being part of a queer community:

> She's got a big thing about marriage at the moment and she wanted me and Mark to get re-married because she wasn't there for the wedding. . . And the other day she said to me, "Before you and Dad got married, he was married to a man, wasn't he?" And I actually don't mind that she knows that because we have just within our street different kinds of families and she knows lots of our gay friends and their boyfriends. (Sara)

Other children felt grateful that their parents had opened their lives up to the broader realities of the world beyond the narrow parameters of their schooling. Sixteen-year-old Terry, the son of Vicky and Mike, refused to apply sexual labels to himself. He felt disillusioned with schooling because supportive and nurturing MORE families had never been discussed. Indeed, he was angry that his parents' livelihood could be severely jeopardized if he spoke about them at school within the small rural community. Thus, he passed his family as monogamous and heterosexual while he also believed that his "real education" was occurring outside the school gates:

> *Terry:* Since Mum and Dad opened this world up to me I've found there's so much more out there. There's a lot more bisexual people out there, and I'm more happy to know that instead of it hidden away from me. . . . [At school] all you hear about is the basic mother, father, and child. There's not all varieties, and that's not the way it works. . . . I feel lucky to tell you the truth, that I've got such an open family and I look around and see all these people who are living with this very small mind, and I can look around with this wide open view and see the real world . . .
>
> *Mike:* Even watching something on TV and there will be a nice looking guy come on there, you'll ask me what I think of him.
>
> *Vicky:* Mike'll say, "He's got a cute bum, that one, hasn't he?" and they'll [the sons] all go "Yeah."

Being out about a father's bisexuality and being open to new configurations of family were discussed by Jess. Her main objective was to maintain a relationship between her son and his father after she remarried a heterosexual man and had another child and her ex-husband established a relationship with a gay man. They have developed into a supportive family, a queer kinship:

I think first and foremost, for both me and Anton it was keeping Harley's life as happy and unaffected as possible. . . . And, as Harley gets older and more aware of his own sexuality, I think it's going to be more important that his whole life is just totally balanced and that he feels comfortable where he goes as well. . . . Another fantastic thing is the support the kids have. Between the four of us there is always someone to take them to school, pick them up and it makes our lives easier and the children's lives richer. . . . We all share a lot of the same interests so we are keen for us all to go out and do lots together—holidays, family activities, dinners and always try to share Xmas Day together. Mother's Day I am so spoilt and Father's Day is a big occasion too. (Jess)

"ONCE PANDORA'S BOX HAD BEEN OPENED, IT WOULDN'T CLOSE AGAIN"

I think we both realized that once Pandora's box had been opened, it wouldn't close again . . . and one of my reasons for kind of bringing a stop to it all [difficult marriage] was because he [son] was so young, . . . his dad not being in the same house as me would just be a normal environment. (Jess)

Many women expressed their concerns and indecisiveness about coming out to children. At times, women such as Jess would accelerate the process of splitting up in order to establish a new normativity of family structure. Telling children was often considered an unwanted, problematic and yet necessary consequence of the father's sexuality and/or the fissures in the family, with the added concerns of the ramifications of this information on the child's wellbeing. Some of the problems stem from the need to separate one's personal anger and value system from the well-being and mental health of the children. As Buxton writes, "No matter how grievous the children's embarrassment, anger, or confusion, their love for the disclosing parent does not diminish" (2004a: 100).

You have to be honest and give them the integrity of handling their own emotions. If they're upset, they're crying, they won't die because you have told them. (Sylvia)

Some heterosexual parents become concerned about the children's exposure to same-gender hugging and kissing or sleeping arrangements (Buxton, 2005). In a homophobic manner, Kaye (2001) discusses how women may rightly try to keep their children away from their fathers in order to prevent them from being "exposed" to same-sex intimacy. Lizette's daughter experienced great discomfort in seeing her father and his partner together. However, to what extent was this because of a lack of discussion with her mother, a reflection of her mother's unnamed anxieties and homophobia, as well as the acquiescent homophobia of health service providers around her?

> She came home telling me that she'd seen her father and the boyfriend in the shower together. They were always very explicit about their affection in front of her, and Kate was just very uncomfortable about it. And, anyway, she just didn't want to go see them. Well, then he was blaming me for things like that when it was actually her . . . You know, he did not give anybody any time to adjust. . . . She's got a disability and she had to have a major operation. I've walked into the ward to go and visit Kate and my ex-husband and the boyfriend were there waiting. And this is so in your face. I think it's the time of mum and dad to be there with the daughter. He [boyfriend] just sort of took over everything. . . . it was very difficult because he would sit very close, almost on his knee, and being sort of a little bit affectionate. You know, there's a time and a place. My daughter's just been operated on. I don't need this. Social workers, the staff were all aware of the situation. They were all supportive to the point where the social worker said, "Do you think it might be an idea just to ask if only your dad come and visit for a while" because wherever dad goes the boyfriend goes. (Lizette)

Fears of negative scenarios and consequences on their children often led to parents stalling the 'telling' until their children had given them indications that they were ready to receive the news, or knew it already. Even when the children indicated they were ready to know the truth and understand it, some parents were unable to come out in ways that would have modeled a positive confidence in oneself:

> I didn't tell my kids for years, because their father was in the closet. . . . We told them in two blocks. The oldest boy, when he turned sixteen, started asking me a lot of questions about the split so I said, "I've told you as much as I can. You will have to ask your father the rest." And I felt at that point he was very ready to get the truth, because he was really digging for it. So I called his father straight away and he came around that afternoon and took Al out for a drive and told him and Al said, "First I thought of all the stereotypes and then I thought he's still my Dad" . . . When Chris was sixteen three years later, I felt very strongly in my bones that Chris had made a few little comments and was starting to work it out for himself. And, Matthew was eleven and I thought I'm not having Matthew being the only person in his family who is not being told the truth, so it was important to tell them both together. And it was when my ex was about to move to this new house near us and I thought someone's going to see him walking down the street with the boyfriend . . . So I pulled him up and said, "It's time to tell the kids" and he really didn't want to. And in the end I had to say to him, "Look, I'm telling them six o'clock, Monday evening. Be there or I'll do it on my own" and oh, he argued and argued. But he came around and I let him do the telling, which later I regretted. He burst into tears

and I felt really sad and then he said, "Please don't tell anyone or I'll lose my job." I thought he shoved the kids into the closet with him, and it was such an opportunity for him to say, "Well, yeah, this is what happened, and I'm really sorry about the upset it's caused the family but I am who I am, and I'm not going to apologize for who I am," and then the kids would have been shocked, but it would have been the beginning to be really proud of their Dad for having integrity.... but how can they when he's so ashamed of it himself and it was just a missed opportunity. (Paula)

Some women had less concerns about a father's bisexuality and more concerns about raising children in a nonmonogamous family:

I wouldn't mind having kids with him, and I don't think it would be a problem for them to know about his bisexuality but I don't know if I would feel comfortable with them seeing other people in our relationship. (Lauren)

We don't even do it [have other partners] in our own home.... the kids are growing up, they're more inquisitive, they don't go to bed at an early hour, and you also get these guys that get real possessive and if it doesn't work out, you don't want them coming around and harassing, knowing where you live.... It's just a precaution. One gentleman that we met, he wanted to meet for dinner one night, and we said, "Look, we can't do that, we've got the six kids." And he said, "Well, that's fine, they can come" and that was a shock. But we went out to dinner and it was a nice evening. (Lesley)

Some mothers felt that with divorce or estrangement had come a detachment or disengagement between the fathers and their children. Thus, informing their children of their father's new "social" life as a bisexual man would only increase the hurt of losing the closeness of the previous father-child relationship: "his priority for his social life before family time ... he wouldn't see them for a long time" (Josie).

Where's the father figure? Forget about us and the relationship, but no responsibility to your children, and when I discussed this with him, he didn't want a bar of it because he always said that I was over-protective anyway and now I'm saying, "Just as well, at least maybe they've got somebody that they can rely on" ... My son can't stand his father. He won't call him "Dad," he just calls him "Peter." I think part of the problem is "Who is this person? Somebody that I thought was this and this." (Loredana)

At other times, mothers found themselves being blamed by their children for not having prevented the situation, or dealing with their children's emotional fallout. Simultaneously, they were trying to protect their partners as well as the relationship between their partners and their children:

My daughter took it all out on me, as if I'd caused it. So abusive. "How stupid you are, mother! Couldn't you have stopped it? I'm sure this is going to break up the family. You're the mother. You're supposed to solve all problems, and you haven't solved this one. What are you going to do about it?" (Steph)

She's a pretty complicated little girl. She's a very bright little girl, but she will certainly every now and again just break down, "I remember the night that Daddy left, when you were sitting on the bed. I'm the only one that doesn't have a daddy. Why did he leave?" I don't get it so much now, but I was always the one that was hearing that and of course she's never said anything to him. And I've tried really hard not to bad mouth him at all, just, "Oh, Daddy's changed. Daddy wanted different things. He didn't love mummy any more" but it's really hard to say. (Sue)

However, what often began as a range of difficult decisions and choices with potentially damaging consequences proved to be rewarding and positive to both the children and the parents in the re-configuration of a new family form or queer kinship: "In the long term, none of the children's difficulties seem to have detrimental effects" (Buxton, 2004a: 100):

Anton's a really, really involved Dad, and Harley's really clear that Anton's his Dad and I'm his mum, and Dave's my partner and Neil's Anton's partner. . . . Some of the challenges are ensuring that Harley's discipline and boundaries are constant across two homes. . . . At the end of the day we are all reasonable, all love Harley, we just try to ensure Harley's life is consistent and we are all happy . . . . We have a unique, cool and loving family unit for our kids. When Dave and I had Emma we asked Neil to be her Godfather and he was very chuffed. The day she was born, her first dirty nappy in hospital, and Dave, Harley and Anton and Neil were all there celebrating. I asked Dave to change it and he started to do it, then when he looked confused, Anton gave him a hand. But even the 2 of them got a bit stuck and so Neil stepped in and took over, changed her nappy, just like he's done it 100 times before! (Jess)

I was very devastated and upset and our children were extremely upset. They all say now that they can't imagine us together anymore and they think it's the best thing since sliced bread. They would say, "We understand other parents [breaking up], because we see how they hate each other and you guys love each other and what in the hell are you doing separating?," so it was a very, very bad time. . . . we worked very hard. We continued for about six months with Friday night fish and chips family night and no one was meant to go anywhere . . . we still continue to do things as a family unit for the kids' birthdays. . . . then both of us took second relationships, he with a man and me with a man. . . . I found it very difficult the first time he rolled up. And then Jason did become part of our extended family and Emma turned him into her older brother that she never had, and he's a bit of a big kid and a big cuddly bear. (Scarlett)

For other women, the splitting of the relationship and reestablishing of new family configurations for the child had not resolved a range of fears and concerns. What needs to be highlighted here, though, is how the dilemmas over the father's sexuality become interwoven or conflated with more mainstream dilemmas such as custody issues, children possibly wanting to spend more time with the father than the mother, child support issues, the child's behaviour after they have been with the father, and having to support a father-child relationship even though the father was an abusive partner:

> One day I'm going to have to tell Milly. I guess my fear is when she gets older, she'll want to spend time with him and he's already said completely irresponsible things like, "I can't wait until she's fourteen and I want to buy her a house and she can move out of home" and all this sort of stuff . . . I used to take her to see him, I just did everything I could because I really thought it's her father, but now she's got Ashley [stepfather] and we're our own little family. Even with everything there was, I was quite happy to let him be a part of her life, but you can't do that when he's overseas because he doesn't want to pay child support. (Kristina)

> I feel like I'm protecting my ex. I feel in some respects my son thinks the sun shines out of him . . . He doesn't see his father very often, and I find that's incredibly difficult as I've got to get him to have a relationship with his father who is abusive to me. . . . I have some African friends who are mutual friends and I hear things about how he raves about his son but he doesn't put the work in and whenever my son sees him, he comes back and he's just revolting. (Lisa)

"EVERYONE'S GOING TO THINK I'M A PEDOPHILE"

> He is a great dad and there is no question about that, and we actually have 50:50 care of the kids which is great,... Mick was worried that once the kids knew and their friends knew, that their parents would stop them from staying at his house like sleepovers and he said, "Everyone's going to think I'm a pedophile," and I said, "Look Mick, if they do think that, then they're idiots and they won't be our friends so don't worry about it." (Marissa)

One of the issues that arose in coming out to children, whether it was considered a positive or problematic step, was the ramifications of children knowing in relation to their own peers, schools, extended family members and the wider society. In other words, would the children be able to tell others, and if so, who and when? As with children from same-sex families, it is most likely children with bi parents will experience ongoing tension between their selves within their families, "which feels 'normal' and safe and nurturing," and their experience outside their families, "in which they often feel invisible or vilified" (Wright, 2001: 288). In our research, many parents tried to prepare their children for the consequences of their public disclosure, and provided them with verbal, mental and emotional strategies to counteract or deflect negativity so that they would be active agents rather than passive victims in educational and health institutions. Parents were concerned that having access to other knowledge and ways of being, and joining in the questioning of 'heteronormal' constructions of family, might place their children permanently on the borders of society, and they would most likely experience some degree of marginalization and harassment. It also led to self-questioning dilemmas for parents borderdwelling between a philosophy of raising their children with a broader understanding of sexuality, family and relationships, and a protective concern that their children could be ostracized because of this philosophy (Pallotta-Chiarolli, 2010a; Pallotta-Chiarolli et al. 2013). This is a prime example of the deleterious effects of the panopticonic interconnection between lack of visibility and fear of disclosure: minimal social visibility means it is harder to disclose, and yet with increased disclosure, and its possible difficulties, would come increased social visibility, which would herald in gradually easier disclosures for future children from MORE families.

Wright explains how feeling that the outside world has no way to understand or talk about their kind of family can create a sense of unreality, fear and lack of acceptance for children, "as if one is seeing something that others cannot see" (2001: 288). To protect children from this cognitive and emotional dissonance, and to protect themselves as members of local communities and recipients of legal, health and educational services, many MORE parents will pass as heterosexual and monogamous to their own children. The alternative imposes a difficult either/or decision for parents: either allow children to "go public," with attendant risks to the children; or risk damaging the children by expecting them to keep a secret:

> I don't want anything to come out until they've got the strength in themselves to deal with any jibes, which is still a huge concern to me, given that my daughter will dissolve into tears about somebody saying there's something wrong with her hairstyle. . . . She's the type of child who will be going out there and saying, "My Daddy lives with a man, they sleep in the same bed, and they love each other" which is absolutely fine and I need to be fine enough with it to make her feel good about it so that she's not picking up that she has to feel ashamed about it. That's why I wanted him to wait so that I am emotionally strong enough so that she's emotionally strong enough to deal with any sort of backlash. Because, yeah, it's a nice middle-class to upper-class area and you think, yeah, people are all really nice, but you know the bottom line is, you only have to go to a party and hear a few blokes talk and that's where it will all come out. (Sue)

Thorson's (2009) work using Petronio's (2002) communication privacy management (CPM) addresses how parents and children negotiate "information ownership," privacy rules and enact "protection and access rules" (2009: 34). Bi-parenting may involve working with one's children to redefine, reconstruct, compartmentalize, cloak, and/or fictionalize the family for the outside world (Arden, 1996; Richardson, 1985; Sheff, 2010). For some MORE families, these strategies provide protection and the ability to live out family realities with little external surveillance or interference (Kentlyn, 2008; Kroeger, 2003). Paula talked about the detrimental effects on her sons' education as stemming not from having a bisexual father and the family's arrangements, but from her sons' inability to connect their "multiple lifeworlds" of home and school (Cope & Kalantzis, 1995). It appears that attending school imposed a silence on her sons that was removed as soon as they left school. Indeed, one son dealt with the home/school dissonance by removing school from his life:

> The youngest is still at school and manages by not talking about it at all, while the older boys talk about it a little now. But when they were at school they were terrified of anybody knowing, but then both told their friends, one soon after leaving school and one in his last year. Actually, the one who said nothing, left school halfway through his second-to-last year. He was doing so well, the teachers were whispering that he was a likely school captain the year after, and soon after he finds out his Dad's bisexual, he suddenly decides he wants to leave school. His Dad's boyfriend lived quite close to us, and his neighbors had kids at the same school. . . . He couldn't bear the stress of thinking word would soon get around school, so he's lost a solid education and the school lost a great student leader. All because having a bi Dad in love with a man as well as your mum is not talked about. (Paula)

Although these findings fit in with the broader literature on LGBT parenting/families (see Garner, 2004; Goldberg & Allen, 2013), what nonmonogamous MOREs are going through may be more difficult due to the even greater levels of invisibility and/or stigmatization. Wright believes the children of queer families, such as those from "queerly-mixed" or MORE families, may not understand this form of "situational ethics" (see Fletcher and Wassmer, 1970) and may feel "particularly torn by this strategy's similarity to lying . . . . 'I don't tell, but I don't lie cos they don't ask'" (Wright 2001: 283). They may devise strategies such as waiting till other people get to know their families and like them before they tell these people about their families. Thus, as Sheff found, the reality or potential of external stigmatization in any interaction outside the MORE home may require children to manage the stigma of their parents' relationships, for which parents "express remorse about the pain their relationships have caused the children" (2010: 178). A strategy used to alleviate this was "stigma management" (Goffman, 1963) whereby parents strived to make the family and poly/bi/community a space/place of intimacy, positive role models, and peer support in order to diminish the impact and significance of external stigmatization:

> We do worry how our children's friends will treat them as they grow older and we also worry that they won't handle the hassles they might get. We hope they will join some online peer support groups so they can talk to other kids in the same situation from around the world. We also plan to start taking them to Pride events in the city next year. We have to prepare them mentally so they can deal with homophobic attitudes from their peers here in the country. (Shelley)

Stepmum Raven worried about how their child would handle regularly moving from a very affirming and normalizing queer/bi community to the heteronormative world of the child's biological mother. Indeed, Raven expressed her concern not only for their child but also for her partner whose joy in fathering and his relationship with the child could be damaged:

> The first time it came up he named the bi group he's in, and she said, "What's that?" She thought it was a bicycle group, or Harley Davidson and I just said, "Don't explain this yet, I want to have a conversation about it before you talk to her because the world that her mother lives in, is not necessarily as accepting of this stuff" and the mother is very plugged into the school and the other parents . . . they should go out and get a life rather than sit around and think up ways to be destructive. . . . So if he wants her to understand bisexuality then maybe let's go over there [to her Mum's house] and talk about that . . . at the moment they could undermine his capacity as the role of the father. Like, he could start turning up at school and everyone could shun him, right, not give him information about when his daughter is performing at school or something like that. So when she's getting, say, near the end of secondary schooling, they won't have so much power to hurt him like that. (Raven)

As with Raven, the school was the main public site that needed to be discussed and prepared for in relation to bi parents coming out to their children, and then their children's outness with others (Pallotta-Chiarolli, 2015a). Thus, parents' efforts to raise children in nonhomophobic environments may be undermined by the school's actions:

> *Sharae:* When the class was asked, "What are you going to be when you grow up?," she [daughter] said, "I'm going to be a lesbian." Anyway, I got called up to the school over this, because the principal asked "What are you teaching your children at home?" . . .

Michael: It's like, well, we teach our children that they could be purple with green spots and we don't care.

Sharae: I was so furious . . . I remember saying something along the lines of "We've brought our children up with tolerance. Did you bother to discuss it with Stephanie to find out what her understanding of 'lesbian' was?" And they hadn't. I said, "Well how about we call her up now?" So she was called up and I said, "Stephanie, you had an incident in class. What do you understand a lesbian being?," and she described it as a woman who sleeps with another woman and "I've slept with you and I've slept with Shannon, haven't I mummy? And I've kissed you, mummy, I've kissed Shannon" and it was like she didn't understand the sexual part of it. After she left I said, "You've taken a very innocent comment from a child. You haven't even bothered to question the child further."

Michael: And they set up a horrible thing in Stephanie's head now that it's not the right thing to be a lesbian.

Sharae: Yeah, so the school has done more damage than we've ever done.

Sharae's last comment is significant in that sites like schools would consider growing up with a bisexual father as 'damaging' the child, whereas the "damage" comes from adult educators in moral panic mode making a child feel that something is wrong at home.

Elia states that the "plight of the alphabet soup approach to inclusion" in schools means that "for all intents and purposes, it is an empty B" (2010: 457). Yet, school-based sexuality education across the curriculum and in school culture could potentially play a significant role "in mitigating, if not eliminating altogether, the erasure and ensuing violence from which bisexual people and their allies have suffered" (Elia, 2010: 459):

> She goes to a Catholic school. And they had to write stories about their families. Well, she wrote, "I live with my mum and my brother. My dad left me to live with another man." And they were sort of trying to cover it up. I just don't think they want to deal with it. They're not equipped to deal with it. (Lizette)

Paula attributes her sons' differing decisions on whether to talk about their Dad at school to the particular kind of school they had chosen to attend before their father came out. External constructions of religiosity and hegemonic heteromasculinity act as particularly potent silencing and policing frameworks:

> My son who left school early was in a Catholic boys' school which I had always felt had a very homophobic atmosphere. But he said he was happy there, felt really settled there and then leaves halfway through a year. . . . It was a real rugby-, football-playing school and bad luck if you don't fit in. There wasn't

even a school counselor there. They had a priest who was supposed to help the boys, but there's no way they'd approach him. . . . They did cadets, military stuff, and they pushed that instead of health and personal development courses. You were a wimp if you didn't join. Even the headmaster would say that the state personal development curriculum was airy-fairy wimpy rubbish. . . . my son wanted to be like his friends, you're not the real man if you don't join cadets. But it got too much for him. . . . My youngest son wanted to go to a Catholic school too, coeducational, and he says nothing about his Dad, but says he likes the school. At least they talk about sexuality with the students there. They have health and personal development there. . . . My other son went to the local high school, . . . had a gay teacher who was just wonderful, and I think really inspired him, and I was really pleased that he had that at the time that he found out about his Dad. But, again, he still didn't tell anybody until his final year. A group of them went on a skiing holiday and he told me, "When we were skiing I got drunk and told them all and they were okay," and I thought that was a real sort of turning point for him, particularly as his very, very best friend comes from a fairly fundamentalist Christian family. He was clearly in an environment where he could be himself . . . You could just tell the way he blossomed in that place, and the sort of friends he had. A lot of the boys from the private schools would come around our house and there'd be a lot of homophobic talk, but I didn't notice that with my son's friends from the new local government school. (Paula)

Thus, it appears that the more traditionally masculinist the school, particularly if it is a single-sex religious boys' school, the less likely it was for her sons to feel comfortable and supported enough to come out about their father.

Another very important border that families inhabit is the temporal one, the preschool and after-starting-school border (Buxton, 2006a, b; 2007). Preschool children may come from a happy family where MOREs are accepted and 'normal'. However, after starting school and becoming more aware of the larger world's dominant discourses of family, they question the previously defined 'normality' of their family:

We both have good family support and they're very lucky little boys . . . We sort of had this [attitude], "It will be easy. We will just sort of bring them up in a gay community and we'll let them know from day one and everything will be just fine." And we feel differently now, we now worry about school's treatment of them. . . . We will never send our children to a school of any religious philosophies. We feel that would probably be one of the worst environments for them to go to in terms of the church's stand on a lot of these things. . . . Bullying these days involves cyberspace and really serious stuff. There's some really troubled kids out there. I just don't want my children paying the price for somebody else's screwedupness. (Rosemary)

Kirsten kept a "parenting later file" where they were preparing for their children's school days. The aim was to find a supportive school and also create a loving and supportive environment for their children so that by the time they went to school, any narrowness they encountered there would be easy to dismiss given their home foundations: "Some people have come up with some very good ideas which I sort of like bookmarked or downloaded and saved and put in the 'parenting later' file" (Kirsten).

Some MOREs and their children see themselves as polluting outside worlds by coming out and presenting their relationships as legitimate and worthy of official affirmation. Thus, they not only claim public space but compel institutions to adapt to new and expanding definitions of family. Proactive MORE parents speak of a plurality of resistances (Foucault, 1978) including subversive strategies such as gaining positions of parent power and decision-making in schools and local communities, or establishing solid working relationships and friendships within neighborhoods, church and social groupings. These strategies consolidate their security and give access to policy making, community thinking and action, as well as making it possible to forge strong trusting bonds with other "deviant" minority persons in the community (Pallotta-Chiarolli, 2006; 2010a, b). And yet, being out in schools creates what Garner calls "the spotlight effect" for the children (2004:6):

> [The] sense of being in a fishbowl has as much to do with how these children "turn out" as does the sexual orientation of their parents. Issues surrounding a parent's sexuality [/relationships] become confused with issues that could well be unrelated (Garner, 2004: 6, 23).

Children of MORE families may feel the need to pollute/pass as perfect in order to signify the success and functionality of the family (Pallotta-Chiarolli, 2010a; Sheff, 2010), a process that Garner describes as "straightening up for the public" (2004: 179). It could also be termed "monosexing for the public" in relation to MOREs. As Garner notes, "Our families currently lack the 'luxury' to be as openly complicated, confusing, or dysfunctional as straight families" (2004: 6). Thus, the children may develop what Garner calls the "poster-child mentality" (2004: 29) to deflect attention from their supposed family deficit:

> We fear normal won't be good enough. So instead, we strive for perfect. . . . I was one of those children who pushed myself to become an overachiever, striving to build an airtight case for my family's success (Garner, 2004: 2–3).

Panopticonic self-monitoring by MORE-family children in order to pass as perfect may also mean some children will pass their schools as perfect to their families to avoid distressing their loved ones (Garner, 2004).

Several women made practical suggestions regarding how schools could incorporate bisexuality and MOREs into their official curriculum and culture, but not confined to health education: "the longer we leave it in the health context, the longer it stays linked to freakishness and unwellness. It's the freak show at the circus still" (Raven).

> I think the first thing they need to do is change the language, talk about partners as opposed to Mums and Dads, . . . School libraries could stock a lot of interesting books. Curricula materials and then with pastoral care, I think that school counselors should have a role. . . . invite people in to talk about their family to encourage children to talk about their family and to celebrate them. (Paula)

Many women support Bryant's wish to see everyday characters in the media who happen to live in MORE families, and make these available in schools:

> [On TV and film] I would like to see bisexual parents who are honest and open with each other and their children. I would like to see monogamous bisexuals and polyamorous bisexuals. I would like to see bisexual people of color . . . bisexual health service providers, teachers, cab-drivers, fire-fighters, athletes, activists and software developers. I'd like to see what I see in my everyday life (Bryant in Alexander, 2007: 123).

As Epstein (2012) writes, nearly all the queer parents portrayed in children's books are gay or lesbian: "as long as they are monosexuals and as long as they are not too queer" (2012: 292; see also Pallotta-Chiarolli, 2015a). My own novel for young adults, *Love You Two*, is an attempt to address this absence of bisexual men with its multicultural, multisexual and multipartnered characters. Based on people in my research over fifteen years, the characters disrupt, subvert and agentically construct their own sexual identities and families according to their own needs (Pallotta-Chiarolli, 2008). For example, Zi Don is sixteen-year-old Pina's bisexual Italian-Australian uncle with a Vietnamese-Australian partner, Wei Lee. After being outed to Pina by an ex-boyfriend who wonders if Don "still likes girls," Zi Don explains to Pina:

> "You can't fit the straight box? Okay, there's the gay box over here that comes with a whole lot more dents, shredded wrapping and graffiti from having to survive bashings from the straight box. Then along comes this intelligent, beautiful, passionate strong woman"—he gestures to Wei Lee—"and my box begins to split at the seams. But I can't jump out of the gay box and knock on the straight box and say, 'Let me in, I belong in there,' because that's not true either. And Wei Lee wouldn't live with my illusion" (2008: 164).

Some children also expressed their wish to be able to seek support from schools, as they experienced isolation and sadness in dealing with what was happening at home:

> He said to me, "Mum, the number of times that I'd have loved to have just gone up and talked to one of the teachers about it." And I never thought he'd want to . . . He used to go to school and I'd drive away. And then I'd come back and he'd be sitting in front of the tree so the teachers couldn't see him crying. (Brenda)

Some children were adamant their parents were not to come out until after they had finished school, and were part of a more diverse community such as a university:

> [My son] said, "Once I finish school, you can start telling people." Now whether that's going to be the case or "Once I finish university you can start telling people" . . . Penny [daughter] thinks it's all a lot of hot air. She wouldn't care who knew. She's been at uni and I think she's found diversity at university. (Steph)

Even if the school teachers were supportive, some parents worried about the impact of other parents in the school. Indeed, several women believed the parent community of a school was responsible for the school not addressing sexual diversity. In previous research, a gay young man referred to this as the "Three Parent Syndrome" (Martino and Pallotta-Chiarolli, 2003; see also Pallotta-Chiarolli, 2005a). In other words, a vocal complaining minority of parents could prevent any sexual diversity program from going ahead. Whether parents would actually complain or not is often not the issue. It is the panopticonic fear or anticipation of parental surveillance and policing that prevents certain programs from even being initiated (Foucault, 1977):

> I'm a bit hesitant about it getting kind of out in the school community just because kids being kids and other parents being people and schools are pretty back-biting, gossipy kind of places. All those bored women in the school go every afternoon for half an hour, they have to do the gossip. But I'm fairly philosophical about it. Kids are going to get picked on for something. I'd rather my kids were picked on for their parents' sexuality than for being smart or their body shape or something like that. I was picked on for having glasses. . . . I figure it's their life and they'll deal with it and they enjoy spending the time with Martin and Alice [outside partners] and they get all the benefits of an extended family and they know we're happy. (Jacinta)

At times, children became proactive in coming out at school, indeed undertaking some peer education amongst their peers:

> Isabel asked when we first told them, "Can we tell our friends?" and that was her main concern, and we said "Yeah you can, it's no longer a secret but you don't have to go show it for Show and Tell . . . you don't need to go and make a big general announcement" . . . and the 8 year old said, "Oh, I'll just tell them that my Daddy is visexual." She said it with a "v" and I said, "It's bisexual, with a 'b'" and she said, "Oh, that's right just like the girl at the end of the Dodgeball movie" . . . and then Isabel came home from school and said, "I told Kelly about Daddy today, I just said that Daddy's bisexual." She didn't know what it meant. Well, I tried explaining it to her and I just said, "It's like he's gay but he also likes girls." (Marissa)

This confident outness to their peers could mean that the parents became role models to their children's friends who were coming out: "one of Shannon's friends came to us and she really talked to us a lot. . . . she identifies as being bisexual" (Sharae). In some situations, both the parents and the children were open to the whole school community about their MORE families. Jess discussed how wonderful it was to participate in a school with openness about family diversity. She worried, however, whether this would continue as the children got older:

> He's at the stage now him and his friends are starting to talk about things like that. So, I think he understands it in word terms. I don't know if he understands everything attached to it. He talks about Neil as his Dad's partner. . . . But I've got to say, the parents of his friends at school, seem to have accepted it really, really well. I've certainly never felt any situation where parents have been uncomfortable with it like they don't want Harley playing with their kids. . . . all four of us go to school events. And a couple of the parents actually came up to us afterwards and commented on what a loving environment Harley was in and how proud he was showing us around, and that was really nice. I mean, I'm sure there were just as many people who saw it and said, "Oh, God, how terrible, that poor child." . . . See, what's going to be hard for him [as an adolescent in high school] is his basis of what's normal is going to be so different from everybody else's and he's going to have all these teenage boys with testosterone running through their veins saying how wrong the situation is. (Jess)

"WE WERE SO STRATEGIC ABOUT THE WHOLE THING"

> We were so strategic about the whole thing. Ross decided he wanted to write them letters, just to say that his care for us was the same, even stronger, but that he had to be honest. . . . He handed them the letter, and asked about any questions. Anna was absolutely grief stricken, and Nicholas you'd have thought had no impact. So Anna for about three weeks just cried and cried every night . . . . And then she got very passionate about gay and lesbian issues, justice, and she

was a firebrand, and she needed to share with people but found it really difficult to quite know when and how. (Kaitlin)

For many parents, telling the children required strategic planning and consideration of a range of factors that differentiated their children as individuals with unique responses. Indeed, as in Kaitlin's example, even with the most careful planning based on what they thought they knew about their children, the responses could be quite unpredictable and/or shifting between siblings. It consistently appears that the age/maturity level of the child is a significant factor that parents endeavor to take into account when making decisions about disclosure/exposure of their MORE partnerships (Davidson, 2002; Pallotta-Chiarolli, 2010a). Generally, it appears that preschool youngsters can handle disclosure in a more matter-of-fact way. They may sense tension, anger and pain in the postdisclosure household and do not understand sexual orientation, but they know about a parent's love and same gender friendships. School-age children, who have had exposure to normative constructions of families through schools, a wider range of peers and mainstream media discourses, tend to experience varying degrees of embarrassment and discomfort, and may feel conflicted when hearing outsiders' discriminatory remarks about their parents. Adolescents are likely to experience the strongest anxieties and confusions as they are facing puberty issues in regards to their own sexualities, relationships and identities. They are also the most likely age group to keep their MORE families secret, given that they are also more aware of wider dominant moral, political and social discourses which construct cultural understandings of what constitutes a healthy family (Buxton, 2004b; Weitzman, 2006, 2007).

Older children looking back say it is best to tell sooner than later so that they do not feel they were not trusted. If the disclosing parent is out, they want the children to know before hearing from outsiders who may have homophobic attitudes or inaccurate ideas about bisexuality and MOREs. No matter when they are told, children gradually become more open, especially if they can meet others in similar families. Most develop pride in their parents over time, simultaneously acknowledging any struggles their straight parents may have experienced (Buxton, 1999):

> Well, we'll start with the middle son. He's fine. He's twenty. And he's got a really good relationship with a girl. And he just goes, "Obviously if people can't make it together you have to separate." My daughter however, who is 22, she got very confused and still may be a little confused about her own identity, but at the moment she's got a boyfriend. I just pointed her in the direction of someone and said, "Look, just go and get some help because you're moving around in a fog." But she was devastated about us separating, and I think she doesn't understand about her father. And the youngest, well, he's deep and I

said [to his father], "Look, I don't know what's going on with Nick, but it's better for him to know than not because he's sixteen and he's struggling with his own [sexuality], either you tell him or I will." So he told him fifteen minutes later. (Felicity)

Jessica, the middle daughter, actually asked the question in the car on her own with me. . . . Now, she's the observer of human behavior and the most inclined to want to actually talk and I said, "Well, I think you need to speak with him, and then when you're finished, if you want to come back and talk with me, that's fine." So she was all of eleven, yeah, [laughing] and so she talked to her father and he told her what I imagined he would tell her, give her a bit of a non-answer. . . . and so I told her to ask him if it was okay to talk to me and he said yes, so she did. She came in and sat on the bed and said, "Well, can you help me understand a little bit more about this?" . . . I remember the girls and I were out at our favorite little Chinese restaurant that we used to go to as a family. And they had fortune cookies and Jessica ended up with, "You will meet a tall, dark, handsome man" and Jessica said, "Gee, isn't it amazing how it knew that I was a girl," and I said, "No, that could equally have applied to your Dad" and it was so funny because Jessica laughed and Emma, my eldest, said, "Mum, do you mind, I'm in denial." And the youngest one said, "Do you have to talk about this now?" Harry had not wanted to tell them. He said that it was none of their business. I think when I told him that he needed to talk with Jessica, he got very angry with me and I said, "They're not stupid. They need to understand what you're going through. They need help and guidance. They need you to actually help them put things in place so that they can feel that you at last know what you're doing and they can feel secure in working around that." (Scarlett)

Thus, coming out to children was determined by factors such as the child's age, gender, sexuality, health status, personality traits, other life events occurring simultaneously, and the closeness of the relationship with the father.

In regards to age, those parents who waited for their children to become adults often found their offspring more conservative, which sometimes led to a decision not to disclose:

He's a wonderful grandfather [to their children]. I just wish we could tell our children but I don't think they're as open-minded as us. They haven't had enough experience. One day, when life takes them over cliffs and they have to learn to fly, they might be better equipped to understand. (Antonietta)

Brenda found that her adult children would ask questions based on normative societal constructions of relationships; for example, asking why their mother did not leave their father given they thought this was the 'normal' thing to do. At other times, adult children could provide emotional support for their parents, but this was not always positive for the children:

> Edward used Michael [son] for his emotional upsets when I was in England because his partnership with the young married man with the two children didn't work, and Michael was getting all Edward's emotional hang-ups and he was going through a very emotional time of his own and he needed support and Edward wasn't listening. (Brenda)

Indeed, older children like Michael who had been told much earlier could also react in belated anger when they looked back, and indeed blamed their own mental health issues on the coming out:

> He wrote this very bitter letter in his late twenties. . . . it was really devastating when we got it, saying how we'd wrecked his life. . . . Oh, now, yes, yes [that has changed]. But it's taken a long time. I mean, he's seeing a counsellor. When he went overseas he very nearly committed suicide but he thought of us and what it would do. (Brenda)

The film *The Pillow Book* (1996) is an examination of male bisexuality from the viewpoint of a disturbed and vengeful heterosexual adult daughter, the Japanese woman Nagiko. She is "directly on a course of war" against bisexuality since it "brings back painful memories of her much adored and much eroticized father" (Vicari, 2011: 123) who she had witnessed as a child having sex with another man, his publisher. Rather than accept her father's homoerotic desires, she rationalizes the gay sex must have happened against her father's will: He was not a good enough writer to be published without acquiescing to sexual blackmail. She seduces the bisexual Gerome who becomes "a passive instrument for Nagiko to use" (Vicari, 2011: 125), offering to go to the publisher as a living manuscript with her words written all over his body. She does not tell Gerome that the publisher was also her father's lover. Nagiko follows them in a van, watching Gerome and the publisher carry on as a happy couple. She calls Gerome over and berates him, "you're enjoying it too much," as it evokes memories of her father and how he "must be cast as an unwilling victim of gay desire, not an enthusiastic participant in it" (2011: 126). Heart broken, Gerome swallows an overdose of pills and dies naked in Nagiko's bed with her pillow book covering his genitals.

A poignant memoir by an adult daughter of a bisexual father is by Honor Moore (2008) about her father, Paul Moore, who served for two decades as the Episcopal Bishop of New York. He had affairs with both men and women, and was married twice to women who he loved deeply. They were both aware of his bisexuality but never discussed it with him. The memoir also explores her own relationships with both men and women, and her questioning whether bisexuality was something she inherited from him. She begins the book two weeks after her father died: "If my father's privacy was his privilege, what of his life was I, his daughter, entitled to know?" (2008: 15). Moore then recalls the day her father told her: "It's come out that I've had gay affairs" when he was accused of having sex with a younger priest (2008: 286):

> My father's contradictions came crashing in blurring any clarity I'd had about my family past. . . . How impossibly sad and painful to live a whole life torn in two, to move forward as husband and father while kept from another kind of desire, and as a priest. ... My father the priest a liar? (2008: 286).

The memoir chronicles her mixed feelings of pain for both her mother and father, her endeavoring to piece together his past, his "other life." These include words he had spoken which in hindsight were now hints about his sexuality, and how he endeavored to reconcile his sexual desires, his life as a husband and father, his role as a Bishop, and his fervent religious feelings which he said came from the same place as his sexual desire. She also addresses the anger and sadness she feels when she rereads his own memoir, *Take A Bishop Like Me*. She realizes so much remained unsaid or distorted, particularly in relation to her mother who he painted as "a depressive lunatic," as she knows now it was "to keep his complicated secret" (2008: 302). A significant part of the uncovering, discovering and recovering is meeting his father's "close friend" of over 30 years, Andrew Verver, who makes contact wanting to visit her father's grave: "At the end he was becoming more gay and I . . . was going in the other direction," and he tells her about the woman he is engaged to marry (2008: 324).

Toward the end of his life, Honor manages to get her father into a therapy session where he gradually begins to open up about the past and his feelings:

> He said bitterly in one of the therapy sessions, looking away, "I can't help how I was made." I could hardly bear the sadness. What was wrong with how he was made? . . . Hadn't he taught me all creation was perfect? (2008: 328–329).

She also comes to understand how so much of what her father did and chose to conceal was due to the times he lived in, and that his "situated agency" (Foucault, 1988) would have been very different in today's era. This understanding comes largely through speaking to a gay priest whose partner had died of AIDS:

> "In my understanding" he tells me, "your father had to make a choice. It seems to me that he understood that he could accomplish his work only with that concealment." . . . But what of the suffering? It was my father's sacrifice and his gift (2008: 345).

In our research, another major factor in when and how to disclose was the gender of the child. Many daughters seemed to deal with the knowledge more smoothly than sons and indeed, fathers seemed more reluctant to tell their sons than their daughters:

> I said to Edward, "Look, I think now's the time. We've got to tell Janet everything that's happening because she's going away to school." So we told Janet, and she wrote a very interesting essay on it in Year 11. So I said to Edward, "Well, I think you should tell Michael" and he said, "Oh, no, you tell him, I don't think I can." We went for a walk down to the creek and I told him. And he was devastated. He never got over the fact that I told him and Edward didn't. (Brenda)

Having children who were or could be gay, lesbian or bisexual was another factor to be considered:

> I don't think it's necessary for them to know, but I'm aware that they may need to know if it affects their sexuality—if they seem to be heading that same way then I would discuss it, use it as an example maybe. (Maria)

After their son came out as gay, Fay struggled with telling their son about his father. Fortunately, Andrew's concerns were generally temporary or about minor issues such as seeing his father in shared gay spaces:

> If I knew what I knew now I would have said something to him at fourteen so he didn't struggle. And I think he was about seventeen when he came out, and it was no surprise to us, and we just said, "Look Andrew, you're our son, and we just love you so much and we're here for you. It makes no difference." . . . So he came out to Andrew and Andrew was angry. He just thought Dad was wanting to copy what he was and for quite a few months, there wasn't a lot of communication at all and Bill was heartbroken and I said, "You've got to give Andrew time, he's just finding out and even though he's gay he still needs time to adjust." So then Andrew just slowly came around and said, "Well, what the heck." I think he thought Dad might want to start going to places that he went to. [Laughter]. (Fay)

Another interesting example of how age, gender and sexuality are significant in the coming out to children was discussed by Krystle and Greg in relation to their adult eldest son, his having gay friends, being part of gay arts communities, and yet there was still something difficult in having a father come out as bisexual:

> *Greg:* . . . we haven't shared it with two of our three sons yet. We wouldn't have told Josh probably except that he found the book [about married gay men]. . . . I mean, kids generally don't want to know how their parents get their rocks off.

Krystle: I think that it's different too with different ages. I think it's hard at the ages that the boys are now. . . . And I also think that, particularly with three boys, there's the whole sodomy thing with men being gay, which is different to lesbians.

Greg: Women going together is a turn on for straight men. . . .

Krystle: Later on when they're married and they've got their own partners and support systems, then that's a bit different. Their identity won't be so tied up in this. At school our kids used to get, "Oh, your Dad's gay." It makes you extra careful, more careful. . . . [When Josh found the book] he rang me and said he's coming around and needed to talk to me. Josh didn't want to talk to Greg at that point, but we worked out that Greg would come down the next day and I'd pack a picnic. The three of us would go down to the beach. Greg said, "You can ask me any questions."

Greg: It was good because he kind of shared a little bit of experience that he had.

Krystle: That's right, he said, "Oh, yes, I kissed a guy in year 10. I just had to find out. But I wasn't, so that's all right." He's now 23, about to get married. She's an ex student and she knows us really, really well. And she's been okay. .. And we said right from the beginning, "You talk to the people that you need to talk to to feel okay about this." Josh was in acting school and his friends knew us quite well. Josh has got lots of gay friends, but Luke hasn't, the middle one, and I don't think the youngest has at this stage . . . it's different when it's your Dad. That's what he [Josh] identified. I don't think he's homophobic at all. He wrote a play for the queer festival last year, working with young gay guys who were coming out, and he shared a house with a lesbian friend.

Sons could find themselves questioning their own sexualities as well as doubting their father's ability to be a good model for them:

> Nicholas crashed in a heap . . . He said, "Dad's no longer a role model for me. How do I know what it means to be heterosexual? Do you think I'm heterosexual?" And I said, "I've no idea, Nicholas. I think you are." So I needed to give him reassurance, needed to give him freedom. . . . I said, "Well, certainly Dad is not a model for you of heterosexual behavior, but he'll always be a wonderful model of a man of great integrity and compassion. You haven't lost that model." (Kaitlin)

Some boys like Terry, however, acknowledged how significant it was having a bisexual father in terms of thinking about their own relationships with women in the future:

> I hope when I find a partner, which will most likely be female, I'm going to be more attention wise on what she wants because I know the way Dad's been, he

wanted to do something and just couldn't quite do it, and if I ask questions and give her opportunities, then maybe she'll go, "Okay, do you want any opportunities," and it will come. (Terry, Vicky's son)

"THEY DON'T NEED TO KNOW"

They don't need to know, I think that would be really hard for them. I think as long as they see that we've got a good relationship. And as long as they learn the basic fundamentals to a relationship, which I just think is honesty and strength and all that sort of thing. . . . I wouldn't feel comfortable with telling them because unfortunately we are brought up in a heterosexual world . . . A little bit [shifting] but it's not bringing a lot of the bisexual stuff, . . . you're either heterosexual or you're gay. There's no inbetween and I just think it would be too confusing. (Yvonne)

For some parents or potential parents, telling their children about a father's bisexuality was not an option, either for always or for a particular amount of time. Buxton (2006b) found that if the relationship is monogamous, parents may choose not to tell as it is a private matter and will not impact the children (see also Leavitt, 2006). Even when children initiated a discussion or had come across evidence', some mothers believed it was not necessary to tell the whole story:

I haven't told my son. He's ten, and actually came home one night and told me, "I found this magazine under Dad's bed." It was a sex magazine. I said, "Oh, what, boys and girls?" "No, boys and boys." And I just said, "Oh, okay. Well sometimes Dads are curious and like to look at things like that." (Lisa)

Some parents said they did not disclose because their children did not want them to, even if they had overheard conversations or surmised a situation:

I think probably the oldest one, she has been home from parties at 3 in the morning to hear enough of the conversations that go on. I don't think they want to know, it'd probably gross them out. . . . we've just told them that people's sexuality is entirely up to them and it's not relevant unless you want to sleep with them. (Leanne)

I don't know if he knows. I think he does. He was always brought up to accept that homosexuality was never a problem. My partner always went out with friends and my son to the football, and they were all referred to as "the girls" and my son couldn't understand why and thought it was a bit strange, but at the same time, too, it was quite acceptable. He's 32 now. And we have a friend in common. She stayed here, and so she knew what was going on, and I have no doubt that she would have said things to him, but there's never, ever, been any conversation about it. (Nicole)

Klaar argues secrets can be toxic when they are held in a family: "those who are not privy to the secret are often aware that information is being withheld from them." This can lead to distrust and anxiety (2012: 112). In our research, a major reason for nondisclosure was not to disrupt the positive image the children had of their father, nor distress them with news of such things as the father's HIV-positive status:

> My initial reaction when Richard said "I've got HIV" was "Don't tell the kids." And I still don't want them to know. My daughter, who is the elder, has had a series of fairly unhappy relationships with blokes. She's looking for a nice guy, and they all seem to let her down, and I just think this would really destroy her attitude to men. I think why do they need to know. I mean, he has been a very good father to them. I think it would destroy the relationship with him.... I think our son would probably be all right. He's in his late twenties, he's engaged with a girl who's a terrific person. And I think that they would weather that together quite well. But obviously I can't tell one child without telling the other. And the reason I haven't told any friends is because I feel I can't tell friends if I haven't even told my kids, and when I do tell my kids—and I suppose eventually I'll have to, or he will have to - they're going to say, "Who else knows?" and if I say, "Well, I've told this friend and that friend," they'll say, "Why didn't you tell me?" (Jane)

Other parents believed it would be placing a huge burden on the children and thus disclosure could be constructed as quite a selfish act:

> *Krystle:* ... as the eldest one said after he found out, he wished he didn't know. Part of me too feels, I now have to deal with this every single day for the rest of my life. Do I want that for them?
>
> *Greg:* See, it's the dilemma of a fine line between being honest and sharing something to get it off your chest. So then you're freed up and you can move on but you've dumped it on somebody else.

CONCLUSION

In summary, some bisexual people may choose not to marry or have children, may raise children to whom they are not biologically related, or may raise children in the context of monogamous and nonmonogamous family forms, such as polyamorous families. Examination of the ways in which bisexual identity informs beliefs and decisions about family and parenting is an important area of study yet to be thoroughly undertaken.

Borderdwelling in MORE families means the child is a stranger/foreigner "questioning the unquestioned and unquestionable" (Schutz, 1944; Bauman, 1990) of the Center. It requires the child to make decisions about how they will define and construct their sexual and intimate relationships with peers within the heteronormative social space of a school, as well as deal with the realization that they will most likely experience some degree of marginalization and harassment. It may also lead to self-interrogation and problematization for parents who are borderdwellers between a parental philosophy of raising their children with a broader understanding of sexuality, family, and relationships; and parental protection. Bigner (1996) provides some guidelines for an appropriate, planned disclosure of homosexuality to children, which is applicable to bisexuality: Parents need to come to terms with their own sexual orientation first; children are never too young to be told; it is important for parents to discuss their sexuality with children before the children come to know or suspect; disclosure should be planned, and should occur in a quiet setting where interruptions are unlikely to occur; disclosure should be "informational," not "confessional"; it is important to reassure the children that relationships with them will not change as a result of disclosure; and children can be assisted to learn how to control boundaries (e.g., via selective or nondisclosure of their parent's sexual orientation).

It appears fitting to end with the words of Coon (2012) who did the ultimate "outing" to and with her children by writing about their father and family. When she first tells her children that she is going to write a book, her son is happy with the idea whereas the following eventuates with her daughter:

> She was nearly a teenager at the time and thought that anything to do with sex was disgusting. I can remember her coming into my bedroom at the end of that day. She lied down next to me on the bed, put my arm around her shoulders and asked me solemnly if I really believed my story could make a difference to someone else's life. I told her that from the bottom of my heart to the bottom of hers I truly believed that it could. She replied simply that I had to write the book then. . . . I used to think being a parent meant teaching my children about life and love. I had no idea how much I was to learn from them, their strength and natural tolerance of people's differences. (2012: 193–194)

Chapter 11

"Spreading Disease With the Greatest of Ease"

Negotiating Sexual Health Issues

It's like everyone thinks bisexual men are "spreading disease with the greatest of ease" like that jingle in the old Mortein flyspray ad about flies. And some are, and lots aren't. But no one thinks of the circumstances, of why. I mean, why do some guys have secret unsafe sex with other guys and not tell their female partners? As soon as you start wanting to be sexual with a guy, ask him who else he has sex with, guys or girls or both, and does he do safe sex and does he get tested. (Naomi)

In this chapter, we will be exploring how sexual health, STI/HIV issues, are negotiated or not, and the health impacts on women and their relationships. It is a difficult and sensitive issue, as Naomi points out, because it is discussing a strong stereotype of bisexual men as STI/HIV vectors between the homosexual and heterosexual worlds. Nevertheless, we need to think about what Naomi raises as "the circumstances," or biphobic contexts within which some bisexual men do have "secret unsafe sex."

As stated in the first chapter, a dominant misrepresentation in the media and mainstream society is "bisexual men as AIDS carriers" (Worth, 2003). Dodge et al. (2012) also argue that a consequence of the narrow focus on disease in research is that much of the contemporary knowledge related to the intimate and sexual behaviors of bisexual men has been constructed solely in the context of "risk" and disease transmission (see also Malebranche, 2008; Sandfort & Dodge, 2008). They consider this ironic as it "may have resulted in work that provides us with a very limited understanding of the behaviors and interactions that much of this work seeks to change" (2012: 28). All the bisexual young men in my previous Australian research were aware of this stereotype in the media (Pallotta-Chiarolli, 2005b, 2006b, 2010a, b). In young women's magazines, readers are advised that all bisexually active young men are secretly engaging in sexual relations with other young men; having a bisexual boyfriend is "dangerous" and "risky," as all women in relationships with bisexually active men are unaware of or have no say in their partner's sexual practices, and therefore are at high risk of contracting STIs. They are also informed bisexual men are predatory and will have sex with "anything that moves."

Two films which depict HIV-positive bisexual men are *Savage Nights* (1992) and *The Twenty-fourth Day* (2004). In *Savage Nights*, a film based on Collard's (1989) autobiography, the bisexual protagonist goes to many beats around Paris, is HIV-positive and has unprotected sex with various partners including his 18-year-old heterosexual girlfriend, Laura, and his bisexual boyfriend Sammy. His character upholds the stereotype of the bisexual man as HIV vector because although he can say, "I loved Laura, loved Sammy," he also says he "loved the vices of my savage nights" (1989: 59). In *The Twenty-fourth Day,* this stereotype is challenged. Tom cannot forgive himself for, as he believes, indirectly causing the death of his wife through contracting HIV and also causing her the painful realization of his secret affairs with men. This devastating guilt is projected onto the imprisoning and torture of a promiscuous gay man, Dan, who he has had sex with in the past. Tom forcibly takes his blood for an HIV test, accusing Dan of unsafe sex practices and endangering the lives of his sexual partners: "If that test comes back positive, I'm going to kill you." During the tense hours of waiting for the results, the two men's conversations and reprimands are about sexualities, relationships, social expectations and discriminations. Interestingly, in the piecing together of Tom's flashbacks, the conversations also include the possibility that Tom contracted HIV from his wife. At the end of the film, we are still left with ambiguity and complexity about who infected who. Ultimately, the film seems to be saying it doesn't matter. What does matter is the deception and betrayal, and the social contexts which frame these, and within which unsafe sex occurs. A third film, *The Velocity of Gary (Not His Real Name)* (1998) goes beyond deceptions, divisions and devastation to provide an affirming example of possibilities amidst tragedy when Valentino, an ex-Adult film star, who is very much in love with his girlfriend Mary Carmen and boyfriend Gary, is rushed to hospital after collapsing and is diagnosed with HIV/AIDS. His two partners are forced to push aside their jealousy and differences to take care of the man they both love while he is dying. Ultimately, they find comfort, understanding, and strength in the other.

Many of the studies into bisexual men in the 1980s and 1990s focused on HIV/AIDS, with the men being "vociferously blamed for the spread of HIV (even though the virus is spread by unprotected sex, not a bisexual identity)" (SF Human Rights Commission, 2011: 11). However, the data from San Francisco collected in 1994 found bisexually identified men weren't a common vector or bridge for spreading HIV from male partners to female partners "due to high rates of using barrier protection and extremely low rates of risky behavior" (SF Human Rights Commission, 2011: 11). Overall, however, studies of bisexual men internationally indicated a large proportion engaged in high risk sexual behaviors; did not have a good understanding of safe sex practices especially in male-to-male sex; did not necessarily practice safe sex with either their male or female partners; generally resisted informing their women partners of the nature and extent of their sexual contacts with men; and were prepared to allow their women partners to remain ignorant of the risk of HIV infection to which they may have been exposed (Kosky, 1989). The resistance of many men to identify themselves as homosexual or bisexual and the associated denial of the reality of their same-sex contact may have explained some of this behavior. Bisexual men who did not identify with the homosexual community may not have had access to sufficiently explicit information on safe male to male sex, whether at school or as adults, and therefore may have been putting themselves and their sexual partners at risk unwittingly (Goodenow et al. 2002). Socially marginal, they may experience isolation, loneliness, and stress, leading to increased levels of "acting out" and risk behavior (Jeffries & Dodge, 2007). In one Australian survey, only 15% of bisexual men who perceived their sexual behavior as making them highly at risk of HIV infection told their female partners about their behavior, while no men reported using condoms with their regular female partner (Palmer, 1991).

Some studies of the 1980s–1990s found a "differential perception" of risk of HIV infection with male and female partners (Boulton et al. 1992: 165). For example, Boulton et al. (1992) found that only a minority of behaviorally bisexual men engaged in unprotected anal sex with their male partners while two thirds had unprotected vaginal sex with their female partners (see also Fitzpatrick et al. 1989). Interestingly, amongst men living in a predominantly bisexual social context, safer sex appeared to be the normative practice in all sexual encounters. This may reflect the influence of the bisexual community both in facilitating men's openness to women about their homosexual activities and in making them aware of the importance of safer sex with both homosexual and heterosexual partners. Those who lived in a predominantly heterosexual context tended to have unprotected sex with women and no unprotected sex with male partners. This may be simply because men who lived in a heterosexual context were less likely to have a 'regular' male partner, which is the context in which most unprotected penetrative sex occurs. Alternatively, it may have been because men in a heterosexual context were particularly careful in their relationships with other men as a way of keeping their homosexual activities 'private' or 'secret' from their female partners. In other words, restricting themselves to safer sex with male partners allowed unrestricted sexual activities with regular female partners, amongst whom condom use was not expected and might require 'explanation'. Also, the men did not feel they were at risk of infection from their female partners. An Australian study with men having sex with men found 23% reported unsafe sex with men while married. Due to the ongoing secretive nature of some of this external sexual behavior, these men faced little accountability within their marriages (Higgins, 2006). Another factor to consider was that when participants perceived a woman wanted to become pregnant, using condoms became more difficult (Schnarrs et al. 2012).

By the beginning of the twenty-first century, there was some evidence that men who had penetrative sex with men and women were changing their behaviors. In her review of the available studies, Worth concluded:

> It would appear that the threat of the bisexual infector is more inferred than it is real. . . . With this conclusion comes the obligation to avoid demonizing or making scapegoats of men who have sex with men and women (2003: 84).

Indeed, by the mid-1990s, researchers such as Paul (1996) were concluding that bisexual men, although possibly concealing their bisexuality from some partners, were not unmindful of the need to protect their female partners and were less likely than heterosexual men to engage in high-risk sexual activities. Jeffries & Dodge (2007) found that condom use by bisexually active men with their most recent female partners was statistically higher than those of heterosexually and homosexually active men. This finding contradicted earlier studies from the 1990s which suggested bisexually active men used condoms at lower rates than other men (Doll et al. 1992; McKirnan et al. 1995). Other researchers have found that bisexually active men engage in high rates of insertive and receptive oral sex with men (McKirnan et al. 1995; Stokes et al. 1993). Thus, it is very likely these men reported lower rates of condom use with other men. Although the risks for STIs other than HIV are considerable, unprotected oral sex carries substantially less HIV risk than unprotected anal sex (Reece & Dodge, 2003). This trend regarding oral sex continues to be found in more recent studies. Schrimshaw et al. (2013a) found that many nondisclosing bisexual men limit their sexual behavior to only oral activities at sex-on-premises venues out of fear of discovery, thereby leading to fewer sexual risk behaviors.

On the other hand, there continued to be a number of psychosocial, cultural and economic factors that increased the likelihood of risky sex and infection with HIV. One of these is ethnicity, while in other studies, men who have sex with both men and women were more likely to use injecting drugs and were more likely to have drinking problems (Wold et al. 1998). As Worth (2003) writes, when thinking about the risks to women associated with having sex with a man who has male partners, the epidemiology of HIV results from a relationship between the people having sex, the environment and the virus itself. For example, participants in Cerdeno's (2012) study of Latino men argued that they could gauge sexual risk by the appearance, gender and type of partner, and they admitted not using condoms with male or female partners they felt they could trust. This was the case especially for women back in Mexico and/or women who had recently arrived from Mexico, as they were often perceived as more sexually conservative and therefore trustworthy. In contrast, casual male partners and commercial female sexual partners were perceived as more risky. Thus, their risk appraisal was generally based on morality, familiarity, stereotypes and trust, rather than objective inquiries about sexual histories or verified HIV/STI tests.

In 2011, the San Francisco Human Rights Commission challenged "the misleading hysteria about men on the 'down low' infecting unsuspecting female partners, particularly in the African-American Community" (San Francisco Human Rights Commission, 2011: 18). In an earlier study, McKirnan et al. (1995) found that compared to White respondents, Black respondents were more likely to self-identify as bisexual, reported more female partners, and were less likely to have disclosed their bisexual activity to others. 31% reported unprotected anal intercourse with a man in the past six months. Black respondents reported more unprotected sex with women, more casual male partners, and were more likely to exchange sex for money. Goparaju & Warren-Jeanpiere report "men who identify with the term 'down low' do not primarily identify as heterosexual, do not engage in greater sexual risk behavior with their female or male partners and are less likely to be HIV-positive than non-down low identifying men who have sex with men" (2012: 880).

The U.S. Department of Health and Human Services, Centers for Disease Control and Prevention (Mosher et al. 2005) stated that the rate of heterosexual HIV infection for newly diagnosed women was 80% and the preponderance of these women were African-American and Latina. Only two studies placed women in the center of analysis relative to their experiences and attitudes regarding outwardly heterosexual, nondisclosing African American men who have sex with men and women. First, Voetsch et al's (2010) survey of black female college students found that 11% reported having had sex with a bisexual man in the last 12 months and engaged in more risk behaviors, including not using a condom in vaginal or anal intercourse. In addition, 23% of the women who reported having sex with a bisexual man somewhat agreed or completely agreed that, "The biggest cause for the spread of HIV is the black men who are living on the down-low on campus." Second, Whyte et al. (2008) conducted in-depth interviews with 11 African-American HIV-positive women aged 47–69 years who reported being infected by their long-term male partners. They believed their male partners acquired HIV as a result of engaging in extrarelational sexual encounters with men. Although having awareness of DL African-American men, some women reported not always engaging in direct communication with male partners about HIV status, sexual behavior practices and condom use history, thus demonstrating that awareness does not necessarily lead to safer sexual behaviors. The women in Goparaju & Warren-Jeanpiere's (2012) research reported how racialized images of black hypermasculinity negatively influence their perceptions of male homosexuality and willingness to speak with their male partners about same-sex behaviors, partially for fear of losing financial support from their male partners. The women reported being aware of DL men and being concerned about the potential of becoming infected with HIV, being reinfected with a different strain of HIV or another STI.

Overall, past research has found that in comparison to exclusively homosexual men, bisexual men report significantly lower intentions to use condoms; higher numbers of sexual partners; hold weaker peer norms favoring risk avoidance and safer sex; ascribe more to culturally specific gender roles and norms; and have lower safer sex self-efficacy scores (Goodenow et al. 2002; Jeffries & Dodge, 2007). For example, Dew et al's (2006) study showed that 25% of bisexual and gay men who reported high numbers of sexual partners via the Internet were having regular (1–3 times per week) sexual intercourse with their wives. Yet, less than 30% of participants had disclosed to their wives any information about their sexual activities or their health risks, indicating that most respondents were engaging in these behaviors in secret. Schnarrs et al. (2012) found that one of the most common reasons for not using a condom was not having one readily available, especially in cases of unplanned sex with men and in conjunction with substance use influencing decisions and leading to decreased inhibitions (see also Dodge & Sandfort, 2007). The lack of planned sex with men may be an outcome of larger social processes ascribing sex with other men as taboo, thus possibly making it harder to plan for sex with men and therefore prepare by having condoms available. However, overall, 68% reported using condoms with men. Also, participants often cited lack of feeling, comfort and sensation as barriers to condom use with women. However, others explained it was easier to use condoms during vaginal sexual activity compared to insertive anal sexual activity with men, because women were more "naturally" lubricated so sensation was not as drastically decreased. The researchers concluded that better understanding of how behaviorally bisexual men "physically experience men and women's genitals, including the anus, as well as how they are perceived, may give better insight into decisions regarding condom use" (2012: 275).

In the first decades of the twenty-first century, the research literature indicates bisexual men may engage in less reciprocal anal sex and have less sex with male partners than do homosexual men. Hence, the risk of sexual transmission from a bisexual male partner may be less than previously thought (Carlsson, 2007; Iantaffi et al, 2015). Another factor is that even if female partners are unaware of their partners' bisexual behaviors, they may indeed know of these men's confounding risks through sex work, using drugs during sex, and having multiple partners. As a result, they may perceive their male partners as being of greater risk and mandate that they use condoms during sexual episodes (Scrimshaw et al. 2013a).

Hence, given the above overview, the research findings since the 1980s could be categorized into three specific groups regarding perceptions of HIV risk in bisexual men and their partners. First, some do not see HIV as a risk because they always use condoms; second others view HIV as the most severe sexually related health issue; and third, some perceive HIV as a risk, but this is not specific to whom they have sex with, but rather an issue of unprotected sex. In most cases, they realize HIV and STIs are potential risks, but often describe STIs as treatable and less severe, and express a lower perception of STI/HIV risk with women. Thus, sexual health service providers need to address these varying groups and factors. The 2008 San Francisco Department of Public Health HIV/AIDS Epidemiology Annual Report, where the only time the word "bisexual" appears is as an infection source for heterosexual women, states, "When a man says he is married or partnered, there are often no subsequent questions asked about other sexual partners. Health care providers need to become aware of how to serve this often-overlooked community and its unique concerns, looking at a patient's sexual behavior rather than simply a patient's sexual identity" (2011: 20).

Throughout the decades, some studies have exclusively relied on samples of HIV-infected men. By doing so, they have assumed a level of sexual risk for the general population of bisexually active men that has not been empirically tested. There have also been studies finding bisexually behaving men were less likely to have ever been tested for HIV/AIDS, and when they did test, they did so less often than homosexual men (Jeffries, 2010; see also Wright et al. 2011; Iantaffi et al, 2015). Again, a range of factors need to be considered in relation to HIV-testing similar to considering them in relation to unsafe sex practices (Worth, 2003). For example, Filipe et al. (2005) studied 250 HIV-positive, heterosexually identified and bisexually identified men in Brazil and found the majority of bisexual HIV-positive men did not use condoms, and did not perceive themselves as being at risk for HIV before learning they were HIV-positive. However, the earlier San Francisco Men's Health Study found while 2% reported having had unprotected vaginal intercourse, no unprotected anal sex with women was reported in 1988–1989 (Ekstrand et al. 1994). The researchers speculated that the decreased rates of unprotected vaginal sex (from 16% to 2%) among HIV-positive men suggested that in the San Francisco social, economic and political contexts, "at least some of the HIV-positive men may have modified their sexual behaviors with women after their HIV antibody testing" (Ekstrand et al. 1994: 918).

Given such a wealth of research and discussion with and about bisexual men and STIs/HIV, there has been an accompanying dearth of STI/HIV research with women in relationships with bisexual men even though the likelihood of transmission from a male to female is much higher than the reverse. Any realistic assessment of the extent to which the partners of bisexual men are at risk of contracting the virus has always depended on the lack of awareness of and/or denial by women of the homosexual behavior of their male partners. Reviewing the past research with women with HIV/AIDS, Satcher et al. (2007) found that a small proportion of cases were attributed to sex with a bisexual man (see also Miller et al. 2007). In her Australian study, Kosky (1989) cited the difficulty of making women aware of the need to practice safe sex when they were largely unaware that they were personally at risk. She suggested that there are really only two alternatives: to target the women partners of bisexual men or to target bisexual men, giving them the onus of responsibility for safe-sex practices with their partners, female or otherwise. In the 1980s, priority was given to the latter. Indeed, for many women, the risk of HIV infection was a considerably lower priority than the need for emotional support, information about bisexuality and its implications for the relationship: "These women gave the impression that if they were to insist on safe sex they would be confirming the often unpalatable fact that their partner was having sex with men" (Kosky, 1989: 35). Several women in Kosky's (1989) research believed themselves powerless to negotiate safe sex as their insistence may have precipitated further violence from already violent partners. Some of the other women were very concerned about the risk of HIV infection and wanted information about safe sex practices, while others were more concerned about meeting the needs of children, partners and parents over and above concerns for their own wellbeing. As Klaar states, "women can only request that their partners use a condom but cannot force them to do" (Klaar, 2012: 104). Attempts to educate women about the need to protect themselves have been less than effective because these initiatives have not taken into account gender roles and patriarchal power issues.

About 10% of the women in Kosky's (1989) research had engaged in anal sex with their bisexual partners and all but one did so unprotected. Only the woman who had protected anal sex had tested for HIV. Fitzpatrick et al. (1989) also found evidence that anal sexual intercourse may be an important factor in male to female transmission of HIV. About three-quarters of the women who continued to have sex with their partner after finding out about his same sex experiences did so unprotected. Slightly more than half of these women had not determined their HIV status (see also Doll et al. 1992; McKirnan et al. 1995; Reid et al. 1997; Stokes et al. 1996). The Australian study by Richters et al. (2002) with sexually diverse women reported that while overall rates are low, sex with a man remained the main risk for HIV transmission. In total, 27% said they had ever had sex with a gay or bisexual man. This included 2% of the lesbian, 8% of the heterosexual and 25% of the bisexual women participants. 25 women had recently had unprotected vaginal or anal intercourse with a male gay/bi partner, while 16 women said their regular male partner was bisexual. Eight women had an agreement he must always use condoms for anal sex with men and three women had an agreement that he have no anal sex with men. Thus, these women seemed to be relying, without explicit negotiation, on the men's safe-sex practices with other men for their own protection. Richters et al's (2002) conclusions in regard to the sexual health of women in relationships with gay and bisexual men resonate with the broader concerns of our research in relation to cor-relations and contradictions between sexual identities, sexual behaviors and sexual cultures, and how MOREs become erased within heteronormative and homonormative categorizations:

> If a lesbian were to contract HIV from a gay male sexual partner, the diagnosis would be recorded in the category 'heterosexual contact', a phrase that is misread by many as meaning 'sexual contact between heterosexuals'. . . . It may be more useful to conceive of women and men as being part of particular 'cultures of health'—associated with bars and dance parties, with large community events, with other mixed social venues, or with clinics. This might then move attention away from individuals and their identities to social practices in context (2002: 201).

In our research, four themes were evident:

1. *Trust as a major approach and stance* by women in relation to their partners' safe sexual practices. This would often be manifested in two major trends: first, pre-disclosure where women trusted men without prior discussion of their sexualities and negotiation of their sexual practices; and second, postdisclosure where women trusted men after discussions and negotiations of their sexual practices, and often examples of their safe practices were already in place. The former often resulted in STIs.
2. *The negotiation of safe sex practices and rules for either or both the couple*, usually only in relationships which were open about the partner's bisexuality.
3. *The coming to terms with HIV and STIs* that had been contracted in themselves and/or in their partners as a result of unsafe sexual practices in their partners.
4. The *mental and emotional health issues* that women experienced in relation to unsafe sexual health practices and STIs.

"I MEAN, IT COMES DOWN TO TRUST"

> Obviously, it [HIV] has certainly been discussed. I mean, it comes down to trust. I trust that he would tell me if there was any other relationship and I know from his past relationships that they have all been safe, that he's very fastidious. He's very well educated. (Rosemary)

For many women, trust was considered to be a major approach in relation to their partners' safe sexual practices as well as their own if not monogamous: "he tells me that it is safe. So it can only be based on trust. I mean, I'm not there to see him" (Jolene). Ryan (2000) found that in love relationships, condoms are abandoned partly as an attempt to differentiate sex in this context from impersonal sex. Thus, there is a reluctance on the part of women to use condoms with the men they love or are committed to, as it signals a lack of mutual trust, and infidelity rather than monogamy or consensual nonmonogamy:

> I'm lucky. I've got all this honesty. I absolutely trust my partner. If I had caught him out once or if I had seen any sort of behavior that would indicate to me that he was seeing someone he hadn't told me about, then I would instantly back off. (Rose)

In some situations, women trusted men without prior discussion of their sexualities and negotiation of sexual practice. Indeed, they maintained this trust until there was some kind of discovery or disclosure, sometimes through having acquired an STI themselves. In other situations such as Rosemary and Rose above, women talked about trusting men after discussions and negotiations of their sexual practices had occurred, and often had examples and track records of their safe sexual practices already being in place. Nevertheless, women were also aware that while trust existed between them, the male partners of their partners might not be trustworthy, thereby adding another dimension: "he said he does rely a lot on the guys that they talk and tell him. So you're relying on trust that they're telling your partner how safe is the sex that they've been having" (Barb). It is poignant to consider the trust narrative in relation to research that shows married men who have sex with other men would rather undertake suicide than risk admitting it and losing their families (Jenn, 2007).

Substance abuse at gay sex venues was considered problematic by the women in our research as it created a situation where despite trust, their partners were not in the state of mind to practice safe sex effectively:

> They'd [her partner and his partner] go to a sauna party and other gay parties around and they'd take two or three Ecstasy tablets each. Injecting came much later. One day he flipped out. That's when I started saying that he needed to decide - I'd had enough. It was emotionally draining for us all . . . They both

lost a lot of weight and got really unhealthy looking. I talked with the boyfriend that I really wasn't happy about that part [drugs] and the more he gave my husband because he knew it was a way of getting at me. (Rachel)

Many women in sexually negotiated relationships explained trust was based on openness, discussions and negotiations rather than assumptions of heterosexuality and monogamy:

I have trusted him completely. And he has been completely open. . . . [The first time] talked about what precautions he'd used and condoms had been used and I said, "Well, hey, nothing is foolproof." So, yeah, sent him off to be tested. . . I suppose maybe for me, being in the hospital setting, you say, "Well, I'm sorry but low risk still means there's a risk which means goodbye." I have that scientific mind and I'm probably being black and white but unsafe sex meant the relationship was doomed. (Sue)

Some of the women provided a temporal boundary in how they felt about trust as a sexual health strategy, dividing it into the pre-AIDS and post-AIDS eras: "The only time I started worrying was when the AIDS crisis arrived in Australia. But we talked some more and worked that out" (Alice).

I remember when HIV became more part of the scenery, as it unfolded, they kept changing the timelines on it. You know, if you'd had relationships in the last two years, you better go and get checked. And then they said actually, if you've had relationships in the last five years you better go and get checked, and I remember everybody was sitting there doing a mental count of how long they had been monogamous and how many relationships they had before . . . And so that was worrying and also a little bit of anxiety about the fact that Harry had had male sexual partners before we married, so thinking about that, I was giving blood on a regular basis and I knew that they were actually regularly checking the blood and so I figured that even though that would be a horrible way of ever finding out, if there was anything untoward, I'd probably be rung up. So I just trusted in that. (Scarlett)

HIV hit really quite big in Australia when he was in that three-year relationship, just before I turned up, so him being in that monogamous relationship actually most probably saved his life and being sick [with cancer] meant that when he went to Europe, he didn't sleep with anyone. And so I think that cancer in some ways has saved his life. . . My partner got testicular cancer so it meant that he couldn't have children, which meant that I could go off the pill. So we have never practiced safe sex in our relationship. (Sara)

Hannah reflected on a past when safe sex meant being on the pill and despite awareness of her partner's sexual activities outside the relationship, safe-sex discussions did not appear to be important:

Hannah: I think I was probably at risk at that time. And I've never actually talked to him about the kind of sex he had. . .

Maria: Did he ever worry about sexual health, STIs?

Hannah: No, and I must say that I didn't either. I now know, God almighty, I went through the era where the pill changed everything. You had sex without any thinking, and after I had children, I got my tubes tied so pregnancy wasn't an issue. I never thought about STDs. I can't believe that. I mean, I know a lot of people who actually during that time did get genital warts and all that.

Some women expressed absolute trust and confidence in their partner's having been and continuing to be monogamous:

> I've always been confident of Joe's monogamy and my monogamy. We've always used condoms, and that's more a measure taken against unwanted pregnancy. I mean, maybe perhaps earlier on, when I was coming to grips with it I sort of did think, "Shit, what if he goes out, does this, comes home, it could happen." But I think that can only be dealt with with honest communication. And neither of us has ever had a kind of history of irresponsibility. . . . [When we broke up for a while] there was one guy who he had one encounter with. . . . He said they were safe. I suppose I could have said, "I need you to go and have a blood test," but I didn't, and so yes, if Joe hadn't been such an honest person, it could have been really dangerous and devastating. I'm lucky I suppose. (Katie)

Other women expressed doubts about the safe-sex practices of their partners even after establishing rules that supposedly allowed them to be trustworthy. For example, after establishing a trusting relationship based on negotiated safe-sex rules, Hannah was still "insisting" her partner be tested for HIV due to ongoing suspicions: "he hasn't been tested as yet, . . . I don't think that he has been having safe sex and I think that's not very courteous to me" (Hannah). Other women secretly continued to have regular tests themselves:

> He says he does [practice safe sex] and in that I have to believe him, but I guess I also have to be careful to myself and even if I go for a pap smear I get one of those [STI/HIV] tests as well. (Sherry)

Another interesting issue that surfaced involved women who believed they could trust their partners absolutely but were engaging in unsafe sexual practices themselves:

> He's absolutely fanatical about safe sex, so I don't have to worry about policing him. I once had unsafe sex with a guy, I knew I had condoms in my bag in the car and it was just like at that point I didn't care. He goes, "I don't want to stop."

But Corey was really annoyed about that. He just said that was irresponsible, and I agreed it was irresponsible and not to do it again and went and got a morning after pill. And I got tested. (Jacinta)

Lilith talked about how men seem to trust her without knowing her STI/HIV status, and how another reason why she trusted her partner Adam was because of how scrupulous he was with safe-sex behaviors:

> They [guys] assume that I am safe and they don't care. They will do anything, they just assume that you know it all. Whereas Adam is really like, "I'm sorry I would be one of those guys who would not go down there with another woman. I don't know what's going on inside the woman." . . . I feel funny about that. I'm thinking, "Well I don't expect a guy to use a dental dam on me cause I know that I am safe, I've never had thrush and I have never had any of those things. Yet I am assuming that Adam won't do it with another woman." So where do you go with that? It's one of those intricacies. (Lilith)

Callis (2013) found that for heterosexual females, the most often cited reasons for not dating bisexuals had to do with health concerns. They felt bisexual men would be more likely to have STIs, or that their need to "express both sides of their sexuality" would result in an increased probability of health problems. Goparaju & Warren-Jeanpiere (2012) state that it is essential women ask questions regarding their male partners' sexual history early in a relationship in order to establish a baseline of information regarding partner risk. They suggest the following questions: What is your HIV status? Have you had any STIs in the past six months? How many male and female partners have you had since your last HIV test? Do you always use condoms with your sexual partners? Ultimately, trust connected with communication and safe sex practices; personal contact with HIV-positive people as an ongoing alert to the realities of potential infection; and belonging to sexual cultures where safe sex practices are automatic, provided a safe and secure context in many relationships, as Lizz explained:

> I've seen him in practice with me and other new people in my presence and from that behavior I think I've got enough of a knowledge to know what he considers pretty automatic. He does just roll on a rubber when he thinks he's going to poke his penis into someone. I can see that's an established pattern, I don't need to fear . . . . he can see through my practice that safe sex was an issue for me, so again he knows that he can trust me, my protective kind of instincts . . . My most personal contacts with people who essentially got sick and died with AIDS were not necessarily people in the gay community but a lot of what I would class as young bi men who were also IV drug users. . . . Previously I had sex with HIV-positive people but because I had to practice safe sex anyway it wasn't something that struck me as particularly scary. (Lizz)

However, even in sexual subcultures such as swinging, where safe sex is a number one rule, some women felt they had to police their partners' sexual behaviors:

> We must both be present in the same room while play is occurring. I imposed this when my husband put both of our health at risk when we were separated in a "seek n concur" scenario with another couple and he had given and received oral sex with no protection. This rule was imposed so I could monitor situations and ensure that we are not put at risk. Men seem to take more risks than women. (Jenna)

"GETTING TO THAT NITTY-GRITTY STUFF"

> He said that he doesn't have anal sex, only oral, but without condoms because who has oral sex with condoms on? . . . so that's getting to that nitty-gritty stuff, and he goes to a clinic and has a gay doctor and has all these STD tests regularly and has been doing that right from the start. . . . And then we also talked about that he hadn't gone to beats because you couldn't be really checking them out [for STIs] in the dark . . . And I thought, well, as long as his tests are going to be clear, there's not much point me, independently, going off and being tested. (Barb)

Barb's explanations provide one example of "getting to the nitty-gritty stuff" when negotiating safe sex practices for either or both of them. For example, partners would discuss a possible restriction of sexual activities to mutual masturbation and oral sex between the male partner and his male partners. Many women provided examples about their knowledge of the protected sexual activities of their partners:

> We'd go out in the car and I'd say, "For goodness sake, pick up your rubbish [condoms]." You know if he'd gone to a sex venue the night before, these little packets, they'd be in the glove box. I'd say, "Oh, that looks really great." [laughing] (Brenda)

> He does occasionally have anal sex with men, him receiving usually, but mostly just oral and mutual masturbation. He assures me that he always uses a condom for penetration whether it be with males or females. . . . and because I'm a nurse, we talk quite frankly and intimately about the risk of hepatitis, the risk of whatever, and so I'm very fortunate. (Jolene)

These frank conversations were of course only possible in relationships which were open about the partner's bisexuality or both partners' nonmonogamous relationships, as contrasted to couples where the male partner was engaging in secret sex with other men and thus there was no discussion until an issue led to disclosure or discovery:

> The first time [I had sex with him] I was a little bit worried because I had a lot of technical knowledge about safe sex, but not had a situation where I felt that it was really, really, really absolutely, vitally important. . . . We both got tested. . . . and we did talk about it afterwards. (Evelyn)

> It was such an unknown for me. I had to do a lot of reading and I remember saying to Dean, "Of course you haven't been promiscuous," and he said, "Well, actually I have." That out of anything really rocked me, that he could disregard my health and safety. . . . He said he had [been safe], mostly. And not always anal sex, and he made it sound like it [HIV] was sort of very unlikely. But it's everything, it's all the other sexually transmitted things. Anyway, we got off without having anything terrible. I made him get tested every six months. (Steph)

Many couples would get tested together, or the woman accompanied her partner to the clinic and was able to ask questions:

> He is very pedantic about all that and paranoid. He would go every 3 to 6 months to the clinic for the full check up thing. . . . I actually went along with him to the clinic and just had a chat to one of the doctors there and it was interesting about the oral sex and is that safe sex, this and that and the other. (Marissa)

Other women became the prime educators of sexual health to their male partners:

> I just made sure he always had condoms available. . . . I went along to the AIDS Line meetings and made sure I accessed what literature I could, and forced that in his face and made him understand what safe sex actually was, because he wasn't particularly well informed for his age group. . . . I thought, well, it's our problem so I'll have to educate him. (Rachel)

Research with polyamorous MOREs has shown a high level of negotiation and "nitty-gritty" discussions (Weitzman, 2007). For Annette, decisions within her poly/bi relationships were based on whether sex was occurring within a "closed circle" or if there were other external partners:

> I don't have safe sex with Jen. She's not active with anyone else, so it's a closed circle but hey that could change. With Greg, myself and our female friend, Greg wears a condom with her, although she has at times asked him not to and I've put my foot down and said no, not because of her but because of her male partner and I don't know what he's doing. And I asked him [the male partner] one

day about safe sex and his comment was, "I just don't think about it" or something really weird like that. . . . I've spoken to Greg about the condom with her and he said, "Well, it's not an option not to [because of her partner]." (Annette)

Thus, specific sexual relationships and configurations within the larger bi-polyamorous group require particular negotiations:

All parties are tested before we do anything. You never know, you might have something you don't know about. Although, once we were in a committed and full-time relationship, things might change because it would be polyfidelitous . . . I've had far too many boyfriends cheat on me in the past. It's like, "Excuse me, I don't care if you sleep with somebody else, but at least use a condom. She might have chlamydia. I don't want it, thank you very much. You wouldn't know, she wouldn't know. You could be bringing something home that you don't want to know about." (Kirsten)

There was a four-way happening, and I said, "Right, we're going to have to have safe sex. We've got three guys and me in this thing. The condom bit's easy because you just use a new one every time, but how are we going to do the gloves? With a three-way it's easy. You've got two hands, so you've got one hand per person and you don't have to worry. You know, just don't swap them. With four people it's a bit harder. So, let's label each glove with the person's orifice. You want to touch that bit, you use that glove." I think it's an important thing to say that group sex can still be safe sex. I can do it with a glove and still make it work and still make it fun. (Lilith)

Louisa had been a sex worker and was now a social worker with male sex workers. Her experiences as well as her participation in a gay culture and the information male sex workers gave her about some of their married and/or bisexual clients, kept her very aware of the presence of HIV and its potential impact on both the men and any female partners they might have:

I got a lot of the boys just come in and sit down and talk. They were worried because there was a few clients that would drug them and have sex with them when they were drugged. They'd be raped. And, so, they had issues about condoms being used. . . . And even with the condom, I'm still frightened of HIV, because as a sex worker I was sort of exposed to that swapping partner thing, and been around these men when they talk and laugh about oh, yeah, this one was with this one last night, and this one was with this one tonight. (Louisa)

One common point that arose with many women in their negotiations with their partners was their desire that safe sex be practiced outside their relationship in order that they could have unprotected sex together. This usually entailed a very gendered discussion of a set of safe-sex rules for issues that their male partners may or may not have been aware of. For Lizz, the issue of contraception was of significance and required negotiations she and her partner had not previously undertaken:

> Gennaro and I don't practice safe sex with each other . . . when we first met we sort of used condoms and I used gloves but then we sort of thought well it looks like we're going to be together for a while and we discussed all these issues about non-monogamy and being bisexual and we did the "Talk Test Test Trust" routine thing . . . Also I had to deal with the issue of contraception which I have to admit I hadn't really ever dealt with in a focused way before because most men that I had sex with were gay men who insisted on safe sex, or were other bi men who I didn't have as permanent relationships, so it was always safe sex so that was my method of contraception. . . and I have to admit I wasn't really content with the decisions that I came to which was to take the pill because while it works very effectively as a contraceptive it seemed to have more side effects than I ever considered worth it. Gennaro who has spent a lot more time in the heterosexual community didn't really seem to consider it an issue which struck me as a very strange thing. I think he'd not encountered any women who were not just automatically on the pill. . . .men don't have to talk about it, whereas I actually needed some discussion because it was a brand new idea for me as well [Laughing]. (Lizz)

> He felt very responsible, "I can't give her anything, she's married, she's a mother, it's not just her, it's her children, her other partner." I didn't want to use condoms in our relationship but he wouldn't stop until he had been through the tests . . . There are times when he has gone overseas and he has come back and said, "I have done something unsafe and I need to get tested so back on the condoms," and it could be like, "I think I got some pre-cum in my mouth when I was doing oral sex" and I'm the one that's gone, "Don't worry about it," but he does. In a way I really appreciate that . . . It has never been the anal stuff. He's really really careful with that. (Naomi)

"HE GAVE ME AN STD"

> We have unprotected sex and that has started to bother me a little because he gave me an STD which he didn't know he had. The doctor told me that I shouldn't be trusting him, that if he went out one night and had unprotected sex, I can't trust him not to do that again. (Lauren)

In this section, we will be exploring how some women did face the reality that they and/or their partners had contracted an STI or HIV as a result of unsafe sexual practices on the part of the male partner. HIV prevention education for women partners of bisexual men requires two approaches: First, all sexually active women must be made aware that sexual relationships between women and men who also have sex with men are relatively common; and second, women who do know or suspect that their partner is bisexual are able to quickly find support and advice in negotiating safe sex and dealing with the multiple emotions, such as feeling their privacy has been invaded when they go for HIV testing (Buxton, 2004a). There is also a dearth of research related to the effect on the male/female relationship when one is diagnosed with HIV and the other partner is monogamous, and neither are intravenous drug users. After all, when one partner is diagnosed, the other may have already been put at risk. Klaar (2012) studied the lived experience of wives who were heterosexual, monogamous, non-drug-using and exposed to HIV through sex with a husband who has sex with men without the wives' knowledge. The themes that revealed themselves were anger, betrayal, disillusionment, isolation, denial and self-blame. Interestingly, the participants were willing to accept either the fact of the HIV-positive diagnosis, or the fact of the husband's sexual orientation, but not both. They were willing to tolerate the first disclosure, whichever it was, but drew the line at the second: "It was only when the second blow was delivered that they could no longer delude themselves" (2012: 115). Jane explained how finding out about her partner's same-sex relationships came after he found out he was HIV-positive:

> He got very sick and we thought it was flu. So I moved into the other bedroom and played the dutiful wife-cum-nurse maid and was waiting on him hand and foot and the doctor said he thought it was probably a very bad dose of flu, but he'd get him tested for a few other strange viral diseases that were around like Ross River Fever. And after about two weeks of being really very sick, he said would I come and sit next to him on the bed, and he said, "I have to tell you I know what I've got. I've got HIV," and I was totally stunned. And, of course, my next question was "How did you get it?" So then it came out, but it came out in short bursts. I mean, he led me to believe at that stage that this had only been going on since he lost his job. You know, "I did this because I was feeling so low and so desperate and you're so successful. You have it all, and you're held in high esteem by your peers and you've got lots of friends, and I don't have any of this" . . . So it was all rationalization. (Jane)

This double whammy left deep psychological scars, which were then further deepened when Jane had to have an AIDS test. Jane felt she had entered another world, an AIDS subculture, and was unable to continue a sex life with her partner despite wanting to stay with him:

> I really felt demoralized and demeaned, and he took me along to see his doctor. It also made me terribly, terribly angry because I'd realized that we'd

never had safe sex. So for years he'd been putting my life at risk, and so for all the "I really love you's", "You're the only person I care for," I think, "Yeah, but you care for yourself more, because you weren't prepared to be totally responsible all the time." And he answers that with, "Well, everybody behaves irrational at times." . . . And just going into the clinic and having to be tested for AIDS by doctors who, I must say, were always very lovely, but I'd never seen them before. The clientele at the clinic were different. Some of them obviously had not just HIV but had AIDS. So I was exposed to a whole different scene there too. So that doubly confounded and confused me I think. . . . I say to my husband, "You've ruined my sex life in a sense." I mean, I actually haven't had full intercourse with him since. I'm still scared but my counsellor says to me, "Oh, you'll be fine as long as you use condoms," but I guess it's a psychological barrier that I have to overcome somehow. I mean, initially I just didn't want him to even touch me, and I still actually cannot kiss him on the mouth. . . . I was talking to him only recently and I said, "Well, if I said I was going to leave you, then you'd be free to have sex all day, every day, if that's what you wanted," and interestingly he said, "I think if you left me, I'd end up with another woman." And I said, "Well, you'd have to find one who was a very accepting person, who would accept the HIV, who would accept all the other things that come with it." He says to me, "I won't lie to you again. I've told you the truth." (Jane)

Reisen et al. (2010) found of the participants who had ongoing relationships with heterosexually identified men who have sex with men, only 5% knew that their partners were HIV-positive, and only 38% knew that their partners were HIV-negative. In an earlier study by Ekstrand et al. (1994), nearly one quarter of bisexual men who died of an AIDS-related illness were married at the time. In the following interview, Gerry was at first very unsure of how to talk to me about her partner's HIV-positive status. Leading up to the following excerpt, her body language and subdued voice indicated her shame and sadness. Once I asked for clarification about his status, she relaxed and gratefully spoke about it in much detail.

Gerry: It took me a month to suddenly realize that I had been exposed to a lot of risk health-wise. And I said, "Look, for heaven's sake, go and have an AIDS test, please." And he came back and this is the bit I'm not supposed to tell you, but we were both tested and I am not HIV-positive.

Maria: But he is?

Gerry: That seems to be it, yeah. So, that was also a very nasty moment in our relationship and because we were concerned for each other more than anything. . . It's a huge, huge shock. . . .he'd actually had an HIV test two years before this. And he was okay then, and this time he went to somebody who specializes in the sexual health of gay guys, basically, and I went to the same guy, and he was great . . .he doesn't know [how he contracted it]. I mean, he thought that he was practicing safe sex all the time, except that his fetish is, in the gay world he's the bottom and the other guy's at the top, and as far as I can tell they could be doing anything to him and he wouldn't know. . . . I'm glad it didn't take me any longer to get tested because the longer I'd continued to have a sexual relationship with him, the more likely I would have contracted it myself. . . .what my biggest fear now of course is that he'll become ill while we're together and I'll end up devoting a large chunk of what remains of my life to caring for him. And, on the other hand, there are occasions when I think, "Well, if he needs caring for, I'll care for him." So, who knows? Yeah, we haven't worked that through yet. (Gerry)

In other situations, contracting an STI or HIV, or experiencing the fear of having contracted it, came after the disclosure of a partner's secret same-sex sexual relationships and often led to further traumatic discoveries:

He gets herpes, and I'm like, "What's that about?" [He says] "It was you. I got it from you." . . .but it's like, "I wasn't asking you where you got it from, I'm just asking you what it's about? You know, maybe you were diagnosed five years ago and you're having a relapse. You know, people have had herpes. It's no big deal, but protect me from it." . . . one of the reasons why we broke up is because I asked him to go and have tests, and he refused. Once the herpes thing came up and I wasn't getting any clear answers, I went, "Okay, we go to the sex clinic together. We find out where it came from, we find out where it finishes, and then we get on." No, he didn't go through with it, and that's where I wasn't okay with everything, because when you love somebody you do what you can. (Deanna)

The very first time I really questioned it [his sexuality] was when I discovered I had crabs. Well, it was just disgusting. I mean, I was showering and I actually picked one off and it was in my hand, and when I saw this thing moving, my God, I'd never seen anything like it in my life . . . . and then I called to Ian, and he came rushing in and then it was me that had to go to the chemist, and I said to this chemist, "How on earth do you catch them?" And he basically said, "Well, I'd be looking at who your husband's sleeping with, love." And I went home and Ian said, "Don't be so stupid, I work with clients with intellectual disabilities and it must have been that I caught it off a toilet seat or something." I actually felt stupid. My instincts were saying, "That's bullshit" and then I would question Ian again later and he would say, "Look, don't be stupid. We catch things off our clients" . . . [Since then] he uses condoms when he's giving anal sex. He doesn't receive anal sex. Oral sex, he doesn't use condoms, and he's actually had gonorrhea, and he showed me the secretion. . . . the very first thing I did, I made an appointment at the doctors. I had a physical examination, and I went to pathology that same day, and I found that just terrifying. But everything was clear. (Heather)

I had these two tickets to go to the opera and we were driving along in the car and we were all dressed up, and I started scratching between my legs, and I said, "I don't know how I'm going to sit through this. I think I seem to have some dreadful infection" and he said, "Well, I better tell you, I've been having an affair for a few months with somebody, and I got infected with lice. And I got rid of mine, but, you keep re-infecting me." And I sat through the opera thinking, "How low can you get?" and this man who has got a really good position in society, it's all sort of a front. I felt we were nice, clean people. I didn't tell anybody. . . .I realize I was so naïve. I mean, I was lucky it was only the lice and another time the genital wart virus. . . .Why should I be exposed because of his sexual games? . . . The doctor also explained to me that I had been constantly exposed to the AIDS virus as Maurice didn't use a condom and he had discussed with her that he was sleeping with men. I was also tested for the hepatitis strains as he had the antibodies and had been exposed to that too. (Jeannette)

He told me that from the time I was pregnant to the time Milly was four months' old, that he'd slept with well over thirty people, men and women, and he also used needles intravenously, shared them, the whole works, yes. . . . I actually vomited, I thought "Oh, my God." Milly had to have four AIDS tests at six month intervals for the first two years of her life, so that was quite scary. (Kristina)

There were also women in our research who contracted an STI after their partners had unsafe sex with another woman, while maintaining safe-sex practices with other men:

Always condoms with men, but not with the women. And he stuffed up with one of the women. . . . And I went straight to the doctor and I said, "I'm getting thrush and it's fucking killing me. I was a careful, careful girl, is me." And I had tests, I had scans, scrapes, and he said, "We can't find anything on you. Let's check your partner." And apparently he's got some fungi he caught from her, so we both had to take this special pill. But it was like, "There's a lesson for you to learn babe." (Temptress)

Some women in our research knew women who happily lived with HIV-positive bisexual husbands, particularly because, as with Lilith's friend, the men were already HIV positive when the relationship began:

My Italian-American friend says she's a lesbian but is married to an African-American bisexual HIV-positive husband! She's a doctor and she loves cooking him plates of wholesome pasta as part of his therapy. Her home-therapy also includes Southern Italian women's peasant witchcraft including the removal of the mal'occhio ["evil eye"], which she does by pointing her forefinger and little finger of her right hand at everyone while chanting Catholic prayers to Mary, mother of Christ, and the Rosary to ward off anyone else's evil thoughts about him. (Lilith)

Luna talked about her HIV-positive status and not being sure from which of her two bisexual partners she contracted it. There was an interesting pragmatism and acceptance in Luna's perspective and she gave reasons for why she had no resentment or anger toward her bisexual partners. Her only sadness is her daughter's reactions of fear to her mother possibly dying:

When we first got together with my first partner, I remember talking about it [HIV] one night. He had friends over for a heroin session, and I remember thinking that if anyone was going to catch it would be us, you know, just the way we behaved. . . . I guess we really just didn't do that [use condoms], even though I knew that [I should]. I guess at that age he was like almost my hero so I'd said my bit and explained it as well as I could and then left the decision to him [about condoms]. But I don't know when he contracted it exactly, but a lot longer before I did I think. I've only been positive for just over eighteen months now. And there wasn't a lot of anger about it because we lived the life that we did. I think both of us are a bit more careful now of other people's rights than we ever were of our own. . . . My second partner for a few years, he got HIV. He never told me he had it but I found out from friends . . . So, it's really unsettling. But I don't regret it at all. I just wish it had have been easier for them. . . I guess I was blinded by love. [My first partner] got into drugs, and I don't know whether that was from the emotional trauma growing up or whether it was just part of the scene that he was into. We always smoked and then he tried speed fairly early and then he got into crack and eventually ecstasy, and then eventually he got into heroin and now I think he's still sort of struggling with that. So sometimes I see him three or four or five times a week for like eight months and then it could be six months or a year until I see him again. He says, "I just can't cope at the moment, gotta do my own thing." I mean, I'll still take him back, for sure. I guess it's like that honesty thing. I've never been able to tell anybody everything I think, and I guess that as a teenager I didn't feel very attractive, and he gave me a boost, and the fact that there haven't been big fights or any sort of dramas. . . . I didn't think that my other experience [relationship with a straight man] I had is very real. I think that was very plastic. But, with Ian, it was the level of honesty and intimacy, everything was planned together. He respected me. . . . and he was honest about himself, too. After he did something bad, he never said, "Oh, I won't do it again," he'd just say, "This is what happened and this is how I felt and this is the result." . . . he never made false claims and promises. . . . . . . [My daughter]'s got this real fear of death, but I think that's because of the way that it was initially explained to her, that her mum's going to die, so it's just going to be a thing that year by year she sees that I'm still here. (Luna)

This journey of the full gamut of emotions experienced for an HIV-positive partner and how the virus actually brings them closer again is related by Mary as she recounts her relationship with her partner:

> I had a life that's different and that is my past and I honor that. . . . I'd string some of the beads for him [for his costume] and we'd sit down and get ready for him to go to Mardi Gras. I was all excited and I'd be watching it even before the parade was famous when there was nobody on the streets watching it. And I remember he was going to the party one of the early years and he said, "There's a disease that's out there and they don't really know what it is, but there's a blood test that you can have for it. It comes out in a rash. I don't know the name." So he went and had the test and then he had to tell me he had it . . . And it was almost like an innocence around it, because we didn't know the impact or the repercussions and then when it became a deadly virus was when you go, "What about me and my life?" It was a shock. . . . I took an AIDS test and when you're waiting for the tests to come back it's not much fun. It's really disbelief that, "How could this occur to me?" . . . "Why did he do this to me? That's not my life, I want to have a normal life. Husband, wife, children, home, family, like, hello, this is not happening. Sorry, picked up the wrong book here, you know" . . . . So, that took me a good few years to even want to peek out from under that blanket. It was like totally terrifying back then thinking, "What does this mean that I'm now in this life with a mortgage and a six-year-old son? What am I going to tell him? What am I going to tell my parents? What's everyone going to think of me?" . . . So, I went back into my life and I did go to a lot of counseling because I didn't know how to shift who I was. I've lived hell, like, day in and day out, was walking around with bricks on my feet. . . . he had a mark on the leg, and he took me for a walk along the beach and said, "There's the first example of it and that can get worse." He'd be talking about treatments and he would investigate and suss it all out. Just gradually, gradually got worse and because we were so close, we spent a lot of time together in the last couple of months. He was incapacitated. I'd document everything, because he had it under control, how he was going to die. He was getting vague and, "Once I get dementia, you're my line, you are totally it." So I was like an extension of him. The only thing that didn't occur to me was the death. He had other support people come in. We did the caring courses together about three years before he died to get a feel for what it was going to be like, and I became a volunteer with people living with AIDS, took on a client and the client died. So sad. It was for me to go through a death in a way that wasn't going to be so nice, so that I could get a feel for it. . . . Apparently dying men find me a comfort, so it worked really, really well, and there was a demand on me to do more of this volunteer stuff and it was great to get the experience, but it's not something I want to live through daily. . . . And my partner died and I'd been looking after him for a good year and towards the end I took some leave and we just stayed with him. My son, his girlfriend and their baby and James's friends stayed with

him until he died. . . . Like, it was disgusting, how the body has to get through something. I went through every step of that with him, and it was as if I was like walking a path with him, but when he died, it was an absolute shock for me because I thought, "What do I do now?" (Mary)

"I KNOW IT'S TAKEN ITS TOLL"

I know it's taken its toll and I really feel that this stress has perhaps been a contributing factor to the breast cancer. . . . when I first got this news about my husband [having sex with men and being HIV positive], I simply wasn't coping with things. . . . So, it's a battle but yeah, I can still hold down a job. I can still entertain friends. I can still go out to dinner with people and have perfectly reasonable conversations and I actually can have time when I don't even think about it, and I never thought that would happen. . . But, mind you, it took its toll because I couldn't eat. I still don't sleep very well. But I'm determined I'm not going to let it grind me down now. I've got my fighting spirit back again, which I lost for a while. And, then, when I was diagnosed with cancer, I thought, "Well, do I just throw it all in and give up?" but I didn't. (Jane)

Like Jane, many women reported experiencing a range of mental and emotional repercussions and health issues due to the disclosure of their partner's secret sex lives and the consequent STI/HIV that either/or both they and their partners experienced. Often, these factors came on top of other life and health issues already "taking their toll." Physical symptoms often include excessive activity, and emotional highs may also alternate with depressive states. Sleeplessness or extreme sleeping, headaches, digestive disorders, chronic coughs, hypertension, ulcers, fatigue, poor appetite or overeating, and anxiety attacks are commonly reported by women, as well as sexual suppression and depression. Emotional and cognitive signs of depression include moodiness, disinterest in life, inability to experience pleasure, excessive guilt, hopelessness, low self-esteem and poor concentration. They think about suicide and may attempt it (Grever, 2012).

CONCLUSION

This chapter has shown how bisexual men lie at the heart of social and public health writings about sexual health risk for women, and the varying reports on to what extent this link is real. It is important to undertake public media and other health promotion campaigns to raise awareness of STI/HIV issues as well as simultaneously destigmatize and not demonize the men and their partners. As will be discussed further in chapter 16, professional development and training of medical and health service providers is needed. "Contact points" are required where women can obtain Internet information and access centers for printed information about safe sex and its negotiation with a bisexual partner, information on bisexuality and its implications for women partners, and further referrals to appropriate services. A women's officer being employed in STI/HIV services, particularly in AIDS Councils and Gay Men's Health Services, would make these services more approachable to women. Finally, safe-sex knowledge and sexuality education for girls in schools should incorporate information about the future likelihood of having sex with a man who also has sex with men.

Part IV

BORDER DWELLING AS OUTSIDERS BELONGING

Chapter 12

"Minute by Minute Maneuvering"
Navigating the Heteroworld

> Adam and I live our truths, finding shelter in the silences and darknesses of gaps and undergrounds. We venture out into the sunshine to enjoy straightworld happy times among straight allies, or when we feel strong enough to brave the chills and the storms from straightworld. And all this minute by minute maneuvering will link us to those that come after us who will change straightworld. (Lilith)

> The unhappy queer is unhappy with the world that reads queers as unhappy (Ahmed, 2010: 105).

> I'm not concerned with bisexual people. I'm concerned with how the world treats bisexual people. My issue is that Dave is a victim and I became a secondary victim because of him. And my issue is that it's not the man's fault that he's not telling you the truth, it's society's fault that he's not being given an opportunity to express himself truly as who he is. That shit is what broke us up. . . I can't stand mono hetero culture. It makes me sick. (Deanna)

A major theme in the women's discussions was who, when, and how to tell, and how to live within a predominantly heteronormative, heteromonogamist, and heteromonosexual world. Issues of social isolation and stigmatization, as well as panopticonic feelings of the need for self-surveillance, or as Lilith described, "minute by minute maneuvering," were strongly voiced:

> The hardest part of our marriage was the secrecy with work colleagues and family, and the agonies and hurts we caused and had to face when some loved ones found out along the way. But as we got older we got tougher and braver. That's a good thing about aging. You stop worrying about being judged. And along the way, we've watched other so-called "normal" marriages crumble or just dry up, especially the relationships of some of our knockers. (Alice)

As Zivony & Lobel (2014) write, given that bisexual men have little public visibility, it is unlikely that heterosexuals can gather much knowledge from media representations or direct contact with bisexual individuals. Therefore, heterosexuals draw their knowledge from indirect sources and they might not consider their behaviors and beliefs as prejudicial at all. Even sympathetic individuals might behave inadvertently prejudicial towards bisexual men and their partners, thereby leading to closeting:

> I've now learned how to live in the closet, parts of me invisible, camouflaged, masked, to meet the gaze, the scripts, of others, slicing my life into digestible pieces for others while I live its intricate patterns on the inside. . . .the world is not ready for people like me and my partners . . . everything on TV and the bloody soapies is about bisexual men doing the bloody cheating and killing. It's like, "OK I know that happens, like straight men do it too. But there is way more, you know." (Naomi)

Thus, being in the closet is where the multiple-within can be lived with minimal scrutiny and ascription: "While we lied to others, we never lied to each other" (Buxton, 1991: 24). The concept of the closet as a sociopolitical strategy is discussed by many mestizaje borderdwellers:

> Even as I am suspended between borders, between definitions, . . .I survive by remembering that going in and out of closets is a strategy for working to remove the conditions that make my closets necessary in the first place (Aruna, 1994: 374).

Evidence of greater disenfranchisement of bisexual men than gay men was provided by the Pew Research Centre (2013) survey. It found gay men (66%) say society is a lot more accepting of the LGBT population than bisexuals (41%) do. More specifically, 70% of gay men have come out to their mother compared with 40% of bisexuals. Similarly, 53% of gay men have told their father compared with only 24% of bisexuals. Gay men are also more likely than bisexuals to have shared this information with a sister (75% versus 50%) or brother (74% versus 42%). This recent survey upholds the findings of a 1999 national survey in the United States (Herek, 2002), which found ratings for bisexual men and women were lower than for all other groups assessed—including religious, racial, ethnic, and political groups—except injecting drug users. Heterosexual women rated bisexuals significantly less favorably than they rated homosexuals, regardless of gender, whereas heterosexual men rated male nonheterosexuals less favorably than female nonheterosexuals, regardless of whether the person was bisexual or homosexual. An earlier study by Eliason (1997) had also found that bisexual people were less acceptable to heterosexual people than either lesbians or gay men. Further, bisexual men were less acceptable than bisexual women, particularly for heterosexual men.

"Binegativity" works through "a broad set of oppressive practices, which include forms of violence (interpersonal, legal, institutional), discrimination (social, cultural, legal), as well as epistemic erasure and denigration through negative representations" (Klesse, 2011: 234). These heteronormative practices impose on bisexuals the burden to engage in "fierce 'kin work,'" if they want to receive validation of their relationship(s) or achieve integration into closed social circles" (2011: 238; see also Ochs,1996; Mulick & Wright, 2002). As Kentlyn (2008) explains, queer family lives are lived within "queer" homes as a "safe space" and simultaneously a "scrutinized space" from the outside. Thus, the queer home of MOREs provides a safe space where people can cast off the constraints of heteronormativity and "do" gender, sexuality and family permutations not sanctioned in external contexts. Thus, the queer home becomes a subversive space as well as a place of belonging, intimacy, security, relationship and selfhood. As Haag describes: "These pioneers have Oreo marriages—traditional on the outside, untraditional on the inside" (2011: xv). The scrutiny of MORE homes can be expressed as sympathetic support, simple curiosity, identity policing and forms of hostility including snide remarks, physical violence and damage to property (Kentlyn, 2008). Living on the queer borders requires stigma management (Goffman, 1963), a form of agency. Stigmatized people's lives are characterized by a constant focus on intertwined processes of concealing, passing and information control. "Disidentifiers" such as props, actions or verbal expressions are used to distract and fool those who would scrutinize and ostracize. Leading a "double life," maintaining different lifestyles with two or more distinct groups of people that have significant meaning and connection for an individual—for example, one group that knows about their 'deviance' and one that does not—is another form of agency (Evans, 2003).

As discussed in previous chapters, Stiles & Clark (2011) find that much of the literature on concealing secrets espouses the benefits of revealing them, including improved mental and physical health, and the harm of concealment in close relationships. Other literature provides warnings regarding the consequences of revealing secrets, or suggests concealment might be warranted if one has good reasons, such as the need for protection. Thus, to tell or not to tell is not a simple decision, but shaped by a variety of factors. Stile & Clark's (2011) study with individuals in the BDSM subculture resulted in the emergence of six levels of concealment, all applicable to MOREs. After "absolute concealment" is "thorough concealment" which encompasses those who tell only close friends, while "scrupulous concealers" are those who have disclosed only to family members. The "partial concealment" category encompasses those who tell some friends and some family while the "fractional concealment" category encompasses those who only conceal to one or two individuals. The "open" category encompasses those who do not conceal to anyone. Finally, there are individuals who have been exposed against their wishes, experiencing accidental or intentional outing.

In previous chapters, passing in the heteroworld has been discussed as potentially agentic, as people may "pass in order to bypass being excluded unjustly in their attempts to achieve ordinary, honorable aims and ambitions" and in order "to be more truly themselves" (Kroeger, 2003: 2; see also Richardson, 1985). If a border person such as a bisexual man and/or his partner are not "passing by default" but instead "passing deliberately," passing can become a subversive defiant act, a performance on the very stage of social scrutiny and surveillance (Samuels, 2003: 243). Revealing one's bisexuality and/or MORE to an institution such as a school, hospital or church, can result in stigmatization and stereotyping, again leading to closeting. Disclosure may leave a woman vulnerable to the simplistic ascriptions applied to her and her partner and relationship, and with which she will be permanently labelled and classified in her extended family, communities and wider society. Also, as discussed in chapter 10 in relation to the link between increased visibility and increased vulnerability for children, the negative consequences of disclosure will often encourage women to 'closet' any future information about their lives in order to avoid further humiliation, and yet it also avoids further engagement by her communities and society with the intricacies of her life outside their boundaries. Fuss refers to this paradox as an "interior exclusion" where to come out can further "jettison" one from becoming an insider (1991: 4). This is a theme in Brant's novel:

> Shasha snorted contempt. "Yes, I made the stupid mistake of telling her [mother] . . . . James has always been her wonder-boy. Mother's trying to figure out how it's my fault. . . She asked me this morning if I've been attentive to his needs" (2006: 265).

Shippee (2011) discusses how not confronting the stigma, but instead minimizing its disruptiveness, is an agentic strategy. Drawing upon Goffman's (1963) work, he discusses strategies of "covering" and "deflection," in which actors redirect attention from the stigma by accentuating positive attributes such as being a good husband and father, and "creating different arenas of life," depending on which situations are risky for disclosure and how much energy is required to pass in various circumstances (2011: 117). In addition to avoiding harm, passing removes the imperative to account for their differentness: they "are not expected to advocate, apologize, or otherwise comment on a personal attribute" (2011: 117). Shippee categorizes passing into two strategies: "camouflaging"—deliberately presenting a self that does not have the stigma; and "avoidance"—refraining from interaction, thereby creating ambiguity about the stigma's existence. These include the following potential strategies, which are very important to women in this research and their MOREs: "Appropriateness": what are considered proper topics of conversation, and what personal information is frequently out-of-bounds in everyday interaction; "Just Let Them Believe What They Want": unless told or indicated otherwise, audiences usually assume that one is heterosexual; "You're Not Willing to Say it: Not Asking": audiences were customarily expected to not ask about relationships or other "personal" details; "Not Telling": choosing to not disclose information, thereby preserving the ambiguity that customarily surrounds one's personal life; and "True Without Actually Saying: Sloughing": constructing creative answers to questions about their personal lives (Shippee, 2011: 134). Poulos also argues that there may be "occasions-perhaps even daily, in many people's lives—where it is best to withhold, edit, or avoid revealing so-called secret knowledge, thoughts or fantasies" (2009: 32). Poulos refers to this as a "strategy of silence" whereby withholding information prevents disclosures that may lead to grief (2009: 38).

These strategies of passing and deflection problematize the simplistic assumption that MOREs completely benefit from heterosexual privilege by disguising their relationship as heterosexual (Carlsson, 2007). Heterosexual privilege consists of the spoken and unspoken rules, rights and privileges given to the dominant heterosexual community (Pease, 2010). As introduced in chapter 1, bisexual partners in MOREs need to negotiate and border a major paradox: the contradiction between the heterosexual public identity, which places them comfortably in the mainstream of society with an affirmed marriage, family, and social identity; and their stigmatized and forbidden homosexual desires and behavior, which would position them outside this privileged zone (Buxton, 2007; Joseph, 1997; Pallotta-Chiarolli & Lubowitz, 2003; Weinberg et al. 1994). Brownfain's (1985) study found that partners living in MOREs drew boundaries between the various worlds in which they lived out their sexualities and relationships. Usually, the outer world was far more powerful and influential and thus limited disclosure was often necessary to avoid losing a great deal. Nevertheless, some women also expressed their joys and relief when those in the heteroworld understood and accepted their relationships, celebrated their positives, and empathized with any difficulties. Indeed, polluting the world around them with their open deviance was seen by some women as stripping the external world of its power via bi-furiosity (Baker, 2015): "the more it's out there in society and just talked about as though it's normal then the less power people have over you" (Raven).

Thus, MOREs often implemented protection rules: two internal (maintenance and cultural); and one external (protecting the family from outside scrutiny) (Thorson, 2009). As discussed in previous chapters, Communication Privacy Management (CPM) suggests that withholding information from others can serve as a positive function (Petronio, 1991, 2002; Petronio & Caughlin, 2005; Vangelisti, 1994). Access rules are guidelines that individuals or groups use to determine when it is appropriate for information to be discussed with others. They can be driven by motivation, such as intimate exchange, exposure, urgency, acceptance, conversational appropriateness, relational security, important reason, permission, or context (Vangelisti et al. 2001), or by the need to communicate to a new family member they are accepted. Access rules may also be determined by one's perceived risk-benefit ratio (Petronio, 1994, 2002). Privacy rule management involves three related processes: (a) "privacy rule foundations" which focus on privacy rule development, privacy rule attributes, and privacy rule change; (b) "privacy boundary rule coordination" which focuses on the ways people manage their personal privacy boundaries and collective privacy boundaries; and (c) "privacy turbulence" which erupts due to the complexity of managing privacy boundaries on multiple levels and in coordination with others (Petronio, 2002).

As discussed in chapter 2, Foucault (1977) uses the panopticon model as symbolic of the power of regulation and surveillance of the wider social order (see also Kazmi, 1993). Women with bisexual male partners are particularly aware of how their multiple realities are subjected to the panopticonic gaze. This leads to their scripting performances of normativity: scissoring, simplifying and homogenizing their selves and lives. Nevertheless, within this system, panopticonic conformity to social norms can be gratifying, profitable and pragmatic in order to avoid discrimination and harassment. Mason calls this wider societal code the "discourse of silence" that renders MOREs "both unseeable and unknowable" (1995: 87). Within this code, MOREs question whether they are really unhappy with their partners or are told by a wider society that they should be unhappy, and if they aren't, is there something "deviant" about them as women? (see Ahmed, 2010). Gochros refers to this either/or conflict as "cognitive dissonance" without alternatives and outlets that would assist women in navigating these limited polar presumptions (1985: 110).

Binegativity can come from the heteroworld in the form of microaggressions. These are "brief and commonplace daily verbal, behavioral, or environmental indignities, whether intentional or unintentional, that communicate hostile, derogatory, or negative slights and insults toward members of oppressed groups" (Nadal, 2008, p. 23). There are three posited forms of microaggressions: "Microassaults" are the usage of explicit and intended derogations either verbally or nonverbally; "microinsults" are often unconscious verbal or nonverbal communications that convey rudeness and insensitivity and demean a person's identity; and "microinvalidations" are also often unconscious and include communications that exclude, negate or nullify the realities of individuals within oppressed groups. There is a link between microaggressions and structural violence, the latter being legitimized through the use of religious, scientific, linguistic and artistic symbols and practices (Nadal et al. 2011).

This chapter will explore the components of the heteronormative world that women not only felt influenced their MOREs but also needed attention:

1. extended families
2. friendship networks
3. workplaces
4. local communities/neighborhoods/small towns
5. the wider society and its media and popular culture

For each component, the women delineated between their networks and their partners' networks as responses often differed. For example, while her family members might be supportive, his family members might not be or vice-versa. A further point of delineation often occurred between her desires regarding who and when to tell and the partner's desires. Many female partners were disturbed by covering for their partners. Krystle explained how she wanted to be out, pollute, about Greg's bisexuality as it was a nonissue for her, but found he did not want her to tell:

> *Krystle:* It's not my secret but it's still an enormous part of my life and it's a major thing in our marriage, but it's his secret. It's that thing of the guy comes out of the closet and the woman goes in. . . .
>
> *Greg:* I mean, Krystle is a very open, verbal person. Has always been like it, she just communicates and it's a no holds bar communication. . .
>
> *Krystle:* It feels like an internal battle about how much to come out.

Another point of differentiation was the responses within family, friendships or other social categories. For example, while some friends or siblings could be supportive, others would not be. Hence the women felt that their everyday lives, and those of their partners, required this detailed panopticonic "minute by minute" attention because of the variable responses from within each of the groups, real or surmised.

"IT'S MORE TABOO FOR THEM"

> I'm concerned about telling my mother because she'll go, "What will the neighbors think?" and I think all our parents for some reason they would be far more upset about the idea that Corey is bi than that I am. It's more taboo for them. . . And maybe I'm wrong, who knows, because I've never had the

conversations. Maybe they'd all be fabulous. . . . .I've put on a good show of it on the surface, and I'm still doing that for our families, definitely, but over the last year or so I know that it's going to come around. It becomes more and more public knowledge and eventually someone will say something and the information will get back to our parents . . . there's nothing I'd really like more than to have my parents cheering at the Mardi Gras parade. . . .[and] to have birthday dinners and stuff like that where the whole family is sitting around and have Martin and Alice [our other partners] as part of that. (Jacinta)

Jacinta's words illustrate the meandering between wanting to tell and simultaneously being aware of the concerns it would raise in their families if they did so. She highlights the "show" or performances of heteronormativity that many women and their partners displayed to their families while simultaneously trying to live their real queer lives, which then led to the awareness that at some point these would clash and require coming out. What is also significant and unanimous among all women, including Jacinta, was the desire for family togetherness: the "ideal" of sharing quite conventional experiences of family, such as birthday parties, while simultaneously wanting that traditional family to engage in queer spaces and queer experiences (see Bertone & Pallotta-Chiarolli, 2014).

In her research, Gochros (1989) found some wives lost the support of their parents and in-laws and in one case an entire extended family. Some families were supportive, some were punitive, and some were simply not told. Most wives expressed conflict between wanting parental or familial support, yet not being sure how much they wanted, how much was fair to ask for, and how capable a family was of coping with nonheterosexualities. Nevertheless, Gochros advised MOREs: "If you are so closeted that you don't permit yourself such help, you may prevent some hurts, but you'll also add to the already excessive intensity in your marriage and prevent the relief that comes from both support and finding many of your feelings and problems shared by others, no matter what the sexual ballpark in which they play" (1989: 179).

As stated earlier, there was sometimes a discrepancy between what the woman and her partner wanted to say and to whom:

I told my family, but Dean didn't tell his family. He just said that we were splitting up. They were shocked. We were the perfect couple. Had the kids. Had the house, had the renovations done. All the things you do. I used to still go and visit the family, do things with them. I was there when his father died. So we've kept connected but there was always that lie. It was a kind of a pretend. And it's interesting that you do that to protect people from life. (Hannah)

Mick was absolutely petrified, he refused to tell his family and I said, "Well I can't function like that because I need to have people I can talk to, I need to tell my family." I'm very close with my parents and my sister and brother, so I did tell all of them. They were all completely shocked because Mick is a real Aussie bloke, into the footy and under the car and any given moment playing with grease and oil but they were also extremely supportive of whatever I decided to do and I know it was really difficult for them to see me with him, they didn't want me to be with him, but they never actually voiced that. (Marissa)

Complexities could arise where a woman told family members but requested they not tell her partner that they knew:

This is just between you, me and the bedpost, I told my mum about him before we got married. So she's known for ages and Mum said, "Well, that's okay. You love him, he loves you. You know what you're doing" and she's been very supportive of him. And so they get on really well. Better than I do with my mother half the time. In that respect it's frustrating. He doesn't know that she knows and I think he would die if he did. (Sherry)

The situation was exacerbated when family members would have differing reactions, meaning the decision who and when to tell was difficult for both the woman and her partner:

Actually, when I just met him he had come out to my family. So, yeah, everybody knows. And I guess when it comes to our relationship, I'm sure everybody thinks it's as strange as strange can be, but now that it's really been put in their face that, "Hey, we're married and there's now another baby and you've sort of got to take it a bit seriously". . . And of course when he told them [his family] we were getting married, they said, "Oh, you told us you were gay" . . . The only problem I have had is with my father. I'm still unsure as to who he was trying to protect, me, him or Jack, because he was always giving a different story. Like he'd be on the phone to me and he would be, "Gee you're not being fair to Jack, no one can live a lie," and then the next thing that would come out of his mouth is, "Maybe the children should call him Uncle Jack because it's going to be painful for them later, when he does get a boyfriend." . . . but at the end of the day, I think what it really came down to with him was that everybody knew Jack as gay and then all of a sudden it was quite embarrassing for him to have to now say to all these people, "Well, yeah, now my daughter's actually marrying that gay guy." (Rosemary)

What is of ironic interest in Rosemary's situation is her father introduced her to a world of sexual and gender realities, which influenced her ability to understand and negotiate her relationship with Jack:

He's always been very brutally honest and his lifestyle is certainly not your average father's sort of lifestyle. At one stage when I was 12 or 13, and I think he thought he was giving me a life lesson and he would do really bizarre things like say, "Right, we're going out to a cabaret show tonight," and I would sit there and watch the whole cabaret show thinking, "Gee, they're all good looking women" and then at the end of the show of course they'd all strip and show that they were truly men, and my father would be rolling around in the aisle thinking that was the funniest thing in the world. You know, the girls that I would befriend during the day, I would find out at a later date that they were also [male] hookers at night. I learnt a lot of really hard life lessons that a lot of other people have no insight to. I mean, I was never in danger personally or anything like that. I think he really believed he was just sort of showing me the world as it really is. And my mother would have had a seizure. . . . but when it came to who I would choose as a partner, I was sort of always looking for a much safer option, somebody that was a complete opposite to him that wasn't playing mind games all the time. (Rosemary)

Some women gave examples of the biphobia expressed by family members that either prevented them from coming out, or occurred after they had disclosed:

My parents have both been aware of my bisexuality since my teenage years and they have dealt with it very poorly. Well originally they kicked me out of the house. . . They said on several occasions that it meant that I could never be a functioning part of society and that I could never have long term relationships . . . they both think Gennaro is a bit of an odd fish but they don't dislike him [laughing] which is good. I suppose they kind of respect the fact that he does work hard in his professional life, and that's the only thing that they can really judge him on and his appearance which they think his hairstyle is a bit strange and they think his clothes are a bit strange, but they don't really know what to make of him so they leave it at that. (Lizz)

At times familial support was bittersweet, such as the family celebrating the break-up of the marriage despite the break-up itself not something the woman had wanted:

My silly parents upset me over the whole thing. When I told them that I was leaving my husband my father cracked open the champagne. They've never liked him, and I still defend him to my parents. I don't want my parents to feel that they can tear him apart to me. (Helena)

Thus, dealing with a partner and a family often led to torn or divided allegiances, particularly if it involved biphobic judgements of the male partners or not understanding why a woman would want to consider an ex-husband still part of her family:

I was justifying to them [family] why I was handling things like I was. I mean, they all think I'm a saint because I've kept Anton in our lives in such a big way. I got to the stage with my family that I said, "Look, if you want to help me, just accept Anton as part of our lives, because sure, this has happened, but this is how I've chosen to deal with it, and if you can't deal with it, then you're only making it hard for me." And they've all been fantastic now, they really have. (Jess)

At other times, family members seemed to make suggestive comments, as if providing avenues and openings for the disclosure of what they possibly already knew: "his mother kept suggesting that there were all these men interested in him" (Jeannette). The suggestive comments and apparent humor were at times experienced as harassment and "ganging up," as Jeannette experienced when her gay brother decided to announce he had slept with all her male partners, including her husband. This also illustrates how a gay man is more acceptable to family because of his simple binary delineation as homomonosexual and thereby aligning with heteromonosexuality (see Eliason, 1997; Herek, 2002; Pew Research Centre, 2013):

> We were having a dinner party one night and they [friends and family] all got drunk and my brother Bruce explained to me and the other people there that he'd slept with all my boyfriends. My mouth was open. How does one react? I rang Maurice and he said, "Oh, what a joke" . . . and Maurice was going to Spain with Bruce [later in the year]. I said, "Now Bruce'll write to me and say he's now slept with my husband." . . .Well, I was hysterical. I felt as though they're insulting me. . . For years Bruce had been writing to me about wonderful gay friends he had in Spain and now he was taking Maurice. . . . [Later I found out] all my fears about them sleeping together were true. I cut off all correspondence from him altogether. (Jeannette)

Other women had disclosed to their families and continued to address the questions, concerns and confusions as they arose. There was also much understanding and acceptance from these women that their families, particularly the older members, would have difficulties because they were from another generation or sociocultural context:

> Mum's aged 91 and I couldn't tell her I was leaving him. I mean, she has trouble accepting homosexual people. She finds it all very strange, you know, "It didn't happen in my day dear." And then she says, "Well, maybe it did, but" but she really doesn't want to know about it. . . .she keeps saying to me, "Oh gosh, you've got the most wonderful husband. He just adores you." (Jane)

> My parents would be absolutely horrified, they would be the sort of parents that would forbid me—not that I'd listen—to see him ever again. I don't think they'd know the difference between pedophilia and homosexuality. Totally wrong generation. (Steph)

In other situations, some women found it easier to tell at least one parent as they got older or neared death as their attitudes changed:

> I did tell my mother and she was supportive. I think with growing older, people question their beliefs, they mellow a bit. . . . When I initially told her that he was seeing a man, she just was like, "Oh my goodness." She didn't say, "Oh that's disgusting." She just felt like, "He is sicker than we ever thought," you know, "you poor thing." . . . It was funny because when my mother was dying she was in the hospice . . . she asked James to come to her bedside and she made some peace with him. (Maura)

Coming out to families required an understanding that family members would now also have to deal with questions of who to come out to in their own networks as well as having their own traditional aspirations for their children challenged (Bertone & Pallotta-Chiarolli, 2014). Because of the complex interconnections of lives in a family, critical events create "counter-transitions" wherein events that occur in the life of one member also affect others in the family (Boxer et al. 1991: 64). Indeed, familial disapproval of the partner's sexuality was often intricately interwoven with a range of negative reactions to the multiple ways the couple were not adhering to middle class, gendernormative and heteronormative ways of living:

> Joe came out to his parents, and it was quite traumatic . . . I'm not interested in being married. Joe's not interested in being married, and in a way they've [his parents] kind of responded to his coming out by bugging us even more about getting married. . . . I love his parents, and I don't want them to feel upset or confused. I know that their dreams of Joe and Katie building a house in the suburbs and making babies is just not going to happen, and I feel sad for them. (Katie)

> I know that when we first got married, my mum, I think along with lots of other people, just thought, "Oh my God, this is going to be a disaster," but actually we've been together longer than my mum was with my dad and actually longer than every other relationship that they know of. . . . Mark's mum was a single mum because her husband had died and when Mark was 18 before he had sex with any men, he said to her, "I'm bisexual" and she completely and utterly collapsed and said, "Oh, my God, what have I done wrong?" . . . She's very kind of normal heterosexual white woman from the fifties and even when Mark got married to me and now has a child, he still doesn't do what she wants him to do which is to be really normal, live in a house in the suburbs. (Sara)

At times, it required a resignation to the fact that familial support and understanding would be limited and that a full expression of one's needs would not be responded to effectively:

> He's out to his brother and sister, and one of his cousins, but they're not really supportive. . . . he couldn't go, "Oh, I'm going through this real trouble, can you help me." I'm out to my mum and my sister and my surviving grandmother, and

they're supportive. I probably wouldn't be able to say, "I'm having these real problems." . . . I wouldn't get much sympathy necessarily from them. (Joanne)

Thus, for some women, it appeared easier not to say anything at all so that these issues for their families would not have to be addressed, given their limited capacities to understand the situation within their own sociotemporal constructions:

I don't think they would have a problem with him being bi, but I think they might have issues with me in a relationship with him. I'm not sure because I haven't really talked to them about it. (Lauren)

I couldn't tell my father because I got the lecture about marrying someone of a different race early on, but he found out from a relative of mine and his reactions were, "That poor girl. I hope she's had an AIDS test." And has never spoken to me about it. (Lisa)

Some pointed out to their families they had been "taught to be tolerant" and thus now expected their parents to live up to and/or continue to display this openness in relation to their relationship:

For their generation, they're relatively open-minded, but my mother's not been happy about my relationships with bisexual men. . . I say to them, "You taught me to be tolerant. How can you do this [be unhappy]?" But, in the end, my mother's 75. I don't think I'm going to have a lot of influence on the way that she reacts to these things, and she's accepted it insofar as it's more that she worries about me. She knows enough about AIDS and Hepatitis and all that sort of thing to know that these are the high-risk groups, and not enough to know just what level of protection that you can organize if you do the right things. (Evelyn)

Many women appreciated being able to tell family members and receiving full support, whether this was instantaneous or had to be processed: "My parents, sisters, brother, and nephews all love him. They think he is wonderful and are thankful that we found each other" (Tamara).

Tovi's mother's amazing. And sends him clippings of guys she thinks would be cute. I mean, she was one of those, you know, "Hey mum, I'm bi." "Yeah, I know. I've been waiting for you to tell me." My mother did have a moment a couple of years ago where she kind of said, "Oh, my God, your sister's coming out, what have you done to her?" and it's like, "I didn't do anything, mum. What's wrong? I thought we were all fine with this?" "Oh, I thought you'd grow out of it." "Okay, let's get over that myth," and once we got over that, it was fine. (Rose)

Other women sought advice from family members who they believed had been in difficult situations to assist them in making decisions:

> I thought I have to speak to my mum who lives overseas because when she was my age my dad left her. He decided that he wanted to move to Australia with or without her, and I thought there were big parallels with what was happening to me. So I spoke to her—I was very upset and tearful—and said, "If you were in that position again, would you do the same thing and let Dad leave, or would you stay with him?" and she said she would stay with him and would have come to Australia too, because of all the upset that it caused to everyone, and that they could have tried to work things out. Then she asked me why I was asking and I told her, and she's been very helpful. I realized then that it was all up to me to work things out. I thought, you make your own life, your happiness is up to you, attitude is everything. (Maria)

Sometimes a family member took it upon themselves to ease the coming out and make sure the woman and her partner were feeling supported and loved. This person, which in Sharae's case was her mother, drew upon their own life experiences and networks to understand their daughter's situation:

> I went to mum and of course she's got a gay son and she'd worked in the gay community, she turned around and she said, "Do you love Michael for his sexuality or for who he is?" and it was like the penny dropped and it just all made sense. Had he done anything wrong to me? No. Had he beaten me, abused me? No. Did he love me and look after me well? Yes. How could I just throw my hands in the air and walk away from that? . . . I think everybody in the family knows. I was chatting on the phone to my sister and I said, "Yeah, relationships can be funny" and she said, "Yeah, look at yours and Michael, he's bisexual, isn't he?" And it was okay. So my mum has obviously told various members, which is fine. We had a birthday at the house and my mother brought over a cup cake with a candle in it and she said, "Here, Michael blow this" and then she put her hand across it and said, "No, no, no, you've got better things to blow." [Laughing] The jaws all hit the kitchen table and we just stared at her. We all just cracked up. Mum has been very sick for the last twenty or so years. She was diagnosed first with polymyalgia and then with arthritis, everything seems to be seizing up. I don't think her and dad have had sex for a lot of years. I suspect, but I don't know for sure, that the relationship is very open between the two of them as well, because my dad has needs that she's not able to supply for him. (Sharae)

This was very different to the reactions of her husband's mother, despite her own life experiences with older children in her family:

> Michael's mum is so totally against talking about it. She didn't think we'd last longer than six months. I should also mention here she had bounced Mike's

elder brother all over the kitchen when he was fourteen when he said he was gay. His mother doesn't accept this at all. Mike's other brother identifies as bisexual and he came out recently to his mother and he has been harassed a lot by the younger brothers and Mike's sister. And of course Michael didn't actually come out and say "I'm bisexual." . . .It was just discussed around the family and she found out he went to clubs that she knew were gay clubs. I was quite cheeky in the family, if ever we had a family get-together, it would always come around to sex somewhere in the conversation. (Sharae)

Overall, the women whose families had gay members and a range of experiences of relationship diversity found it much easier to accept bisexuality than those whose family members had limited experiences with diversity:

I have a lot of family who are gay, cousins mainly. . . . Growing up my mum had a lot of weird friends too. Like she might have been a strict Catholic but amongst her really good friends she had a woman who was the first wife of a harem. He had at least four. I knew that and I understood that from a very young age of about twelve I think and it wasn't an issue, because mum never saw it as an issue. (Sherry)

Other women forged a bond with their partner's mother who had also lived with a bisexual husband or established nonnormative nonmonogamous relationships: "I can feel the bond there, like a silk cord, because she loved a bi man, his father, until he died . . . . And when I am back in my closet, I know she is there for me" (Lilith).

At times a partner's family would blame the wife for their son "turning gay": "His family don't speak to me—apparently it must be my fault!" (Josie). At other times, it was the woman's family that blamed a marriage break-up on their daughter and wanted her to stay, while her husband's family were wanting her to "kick him out." Either way, many women would have preferred less judgment and blame allocation, and more support and empathy for both her and her partner:

I went over to see them [my parents] and tell them. Oh, that was shocking. They blamed me for the marriage breaking up. They told me I should have stayed with my husband. . . . And then there's the big silent treatment like, you know, act as if nothing's happened whatsoever. In fact, my whole family just left me to it. . . . Ross's mum was just feisty. And so she'd say, "I'd kick him out, Kait, I'd kick him out." I said, "Well, I'm not" and she just thought I was wonderful, but I had to reign her in. (Kaitlin)

At other times, the woman partner was gladly accepted by the male's parents as a sign of the increasing 'normality' of their son, whether it be that she was a woman or that he was now in a committed more conventional relationship:

> He came out to his parents when he was going out with his previous male partner. I think they're rather happy that he's now married to me . . . .it wasn't like, "Oh, a woman." It was more of a case of his being in a committed and caring relationship, because the last relationship was quite destructive. (Kirsten)

"IT'S AS IF WE'VE GOT TWO SETS OF FRIENDS"

> It's as if we've got two sets of friends. We've got the straight friends, the family friends, you know, the ones that we have Christmas parties with and then we have the other group, which is friends who know us as a bi couple, friends who are bi themselves and yeah, it seems kind of strange because you're sort of like having to lead two separate lives. (Christine)

> We have very accepting close friends, while others politely tolerate us, and still others wait for disaster so they can pounce. It's like our closet has swinging doors on it, like those saloon doors in cowboy movies. Some people will probably never be told, others will be eased into it gradually, and still others know and don't want to know and so they pretend they don't know because they don't know what to do if they admit they do know. [laughing] Others have become these armchair anthropologists researching this peculiar social phenomenon that we apparently are. (Lilith)

Heterosexual friendship networks, which friends to tell and when, and how to deal with the outcomes of telling was another major theme for the women in this research. As Lilith and Christine explained, it often became a situation of having two or multiple sets of friends based on who knows and who doesn't. Issues of disclosure would have ramifications for the future depth and level of the friendship, as well as requiring coordination when planning social events and deciding on who gets to share various life events. Furthermore, many women were not just concerned with their own status and support within friendship networks, but also very aware that coming out to friends would have implications for their partners as well:

> I think it was just hard for him. If he slipped up, if he brought into the conversation anything that might put him, you know, as a poofta, he'd experience a lot of rejection. We had our group of friends from when we were teenagers, and they just accepted that as Neil's business. But anyone else that sort of came along was pretty hard for him. . . it meant that if we went out or if we did anything, Neil always was trying to show that he was a man's man, his body language would be really stiff I guess, and very calculated. Yeah, there wasn't as much

> eye contact as there could be. He'd try to talk about subjects that he had no interest in, football, all that. . . . and the questions about me always came after they saw that the acceptance on my side for him was total and real, "Well, why? How could you let him do that?" And they never consider that if I didn't want to be a part of it that I could leave. And very few people would be the same after they'd sort of known about us. (Luna)
>
> He had his 50th birthday and he really wanted his party, and I said to him, "Is everybody coming to the party going to know about you?" And he said, "Well mostly yes" . . . and he only invited people he didn't mind knowing about it, so he didn't invite anyone from the footy club or the car club. (Marissa)
>
> Amongst the friends who don't know are actually life-long friends that Jack has had from kindergarten, and now they're also having children and getting married and they sort of reacquainted themselves. . . I always say to him I don't understand how people couldn't know, but he doesn't understand what I'm talking about. "Of course they don't know. People don't know unless you tell them." He doesn't realize how truly obvious he is. But I heavily suspect with these people that they're just relieved that, "Oh, he's married, so we were obviously wrong." And we're not scared of telling them or anything like that, but there's just really no need to tell them, you know. . . .One thing I really hate is whenever we run into past acquaintances of Jack or even past people that he's been with, it's sort of a shock, and I hate them looking at me like, "Oh, the poor girl." And I say to him, "You make sure you tell them that I know because I don't want them thinking that I'm an idiot." (Rosemary)

Barb explained how her partner came out to his friends after one friend asked him. What followed was a sharing of secrets whereby the friend revealed he was having an affair with a woman:

> He'd been on a bike ride weekend with a friend of ours and apparently they'd sat down for dinner and the guy had said, "Are you bisexual?" and Andrew was taken aback and said, "Well, actually I am." And this guy said "Oh, we've all always known," and then this guy went on to tell Andrew that he was having an affair with a woman, and so they both said, "Well, obviously what we've said is confidential" and when Andrew told me that, he said, "Oh, this guy won't say anything because now I've got something over him." So a few months after, this guy's wife came around and was heart broken because he'd just told her that he was leaving, he was having this affair. . . . she just was a wreck and I told her where we were at. Now she actually knew, because her partner had told her anyway, and she said to me, "I don't know how you are holding it all together." (Barb)

The above example among male friends correlates with Ripley et al's (2011) findings that heterosexual males, particularly younger ones, dismiss the "one-time rule of homosexuality" and are increasingly accepting of non-heterosexualities (Anderson, 2008b; Anderson et al, 2015; McCormack et al, 2015). Nevertheless, and problematically, being openly bisexual and cheating on a partner were considered on par by these friends:

> Some people say, "Oh, well, that's no different to a man having an affair is it?" I mean, well, yeah, it is actually. So they just don't get it. It was really important to me that nobody judged Greg negatively, but I wanted some resonance of my experience. I felt like I was an alien, and a warped one at that! You would find people who would run or others who could listen, but not people who could walk next to you through your journey. (Krystle)

Some women were aware that the gender of the friend was significant, particularly in relation to their bisexual partners telling their heterosexual male friends. This appeared to be much harder than a bisexual woman telling her heterosexual female friends: "I think it's because their crew, their social group, it's just not cool for them. Men have intimacy issues that are different to ours. It's really sad" (Deanna).

Some women also expressed how their partners' reticence toward them talking to their friends about their relationship limited the support they gained and thus, in turn, their ability to support their partners:

> I kept the secret for a year and then it got to the stage where I just felt like I was cracking up really completely and needed support. . . You'd go to picnics or friends and they'd say, "How are you going?" and you're thinking, "I can't tell you that I'm falling apart on the inside." So keeping up the pretense was the hardest thing for me, keeping up the smiling face and, you know, nothing's wrong, but everything is wrong. . . . Now I've started telling friends, and I tell Michael that I told them. (Sally)

Indeed, Loredana found herself leaving a country where she and her husband had lived as expatriates for many years because she could no longer keep lying for him:

> I'd made lots of friends there. It was lovely. I didn't want to go, I really didn't. But I couldn't cope with the pretense. . . . I had to lie for him. I mean, I'm sick of it, had been lying for a long time. It's like, well, who am I lying for? It's nothing I've done. He was quite jubilant in a way, "Everybody knows you're going back for your health," and I said, "Yes, everybody may think that, but you know different, don't you?" and of course he didn't like that. (Loredana)

Many women experienced confusion and ambivalence over who and how many friends to tell in heteroworld, and felt that expecting understanding and acceptance from these friends could lead to further denigration and dismissal:

Andrew has said all along it's up to you who you feel comfortable to tell, but obviously I've been going through this hugest thing in my life. I mean, so has Andrew, but he's got support of our gay friends . . . but I don't feel enough people know in my life and yet I don't want them to in a way. So I'm sort of all a bit mixed up myself about that . . . . it's not the sort of thing you just want to ring up and tell someone on the phone. . . .it all seems so much more complex, . . . I feel we mix with a reasonably well educated, well informed group of people, but even when I talk about just mainstream sort of sex ed things I have talked about with our kids, they will say, "Oh, have you? We haven't told our children any of that yet." And I just think, "Oh, are we back in the dark ages?" So I do feel quite overwhelmed. I think, "Where do I begin?" (Barb)

I was needing just to get all this stuff off my chest, just somebody to listen, so I went to each friend, and each one in succession basically did the same thing, just throw away a seven year marriage, "He's a pervert," "He wants to have his cake and eat it too." Because they only see the stereotypical. . . . It's like "Excuse me, he's the same person, it's just his sexuality," but they don't see that. And I just couldn't cope with that. (Sharae)

Indeed, sometimes women had invested so much time and energy in presenting a heteronormative façade to conceal the queerness of their lives that when they did tell their friends, there was quite a shock at how different their relationships were in reality to what they had perceived:

It was quite funny when we first started talking about all this [bisexual and polyamorous] stuff, the number of people who said to me, "I didn't think you two even had sex. In fact, I wouldn't have thought you'd even like sex." You know, because I had the armory up. I was just this suburban matron, mother of three, who looked really, really conservative. (Jacinta)

Many women would talk to friends who they believed had been through similar or other challenging life experiences, were comfortable with diversity, and would be able to empathize:

Most of my friends work in sexual and reproductive health so they understand. . . another friend said, "Oh, I've known for a long time." She had a friend whose father was bisexual, and she could see all the signs and apparently my ex was eyeing off her friend's father at our wedding and of course, I didn't realize. And I said to her, "Well, why didn't you tell me?" and then she said that I wouldn't have believed her anyway, which is probably true given my background and upbringing. (Lisa)

Her husband had been killed in a helicopter accident and when he died, there was all sorts of things they discovered, including that he'd been having gay relationships, and so I know for my friend it was really important to hear it from somebody else because I don't know whether she'd discussed it. (Helena)

Other women would deliberately talk to friends about their partners and their relationships in order to educate and create openness or to disrupt heteronormative and gendernormative ways of thinking:

> If I talk with three or four people about my particular situation, my beliefs and values, how they've changed, and what's been confronted, I really think that reverberates quite far. (Katie)

> I've had a lot of trouble [with straight friends]. I remember the last time I did open my mouth it was at a straight party. They were hip, in their late twenties, thirties, and they talked about these women who had a lot of money, good jobs, working overseas and they would have affairs when they were overseas and would never tell their husbands. I talked to them at length because I'm into, "Haven't we moved beyond all this secretive stuff?" and I absolutely got nowhere with them. . . .So those straight people were into the whole package they'd been given by their parents which was you have adulterous affairs and it used to be the guys and now it's the women, and you lie and you keep secrets and you avoid the jealousy and they thought that was all okay. So guys got their just desserts because women can do it now. But I said, "I thought we were saying there was something wrong with that, not we should be able to do it too." They absolutely refused to contemplate that. Now that's a very powerful scenario to be trying to break through with things like diverse sexuality and polyamory in my relationship. (Raven)

Some women found that even those friends who purported to be nonhomophobic expressed concerns and prejudices against bisexuality and the mixed-orientation nature of the relationship: "I think actually my friends are all very accepting [of homosexuality]. But not my relationship" (Jane). Other women found that friends displayed an intrigue in their MORE due to its "difference," thus maintaining interest in them in a form of exoticization: "It was just like a curiosity thing, you know, is it really true, is he really bi, do they really do this? So you become like this exhibit A" (Luna). Other women were very selective and screened their friends carefully before telling a few trusted friends. Thus, they set up distinct groups or boundaries between friends: the inner circle who know and those in the outer circle who don't, and expected them to respect the boundaries:

> Very early on after Shane's disclosure, a guy that I'd been friends with for many, many years, who after I told him got on the phone with about ten or twelve of our friends without my consent. (Erin)

Another duality was between "her friends" and "his friends," and what would happen to the usual combined nature of these friendships after the revelation: "the difficulty lies in that a lot of my friends I suspect would take sides and they would probably try and pressure me to leave" (Jane).

> I think some friendships that Anton and I had when we were a couple have changed... Like, they just didn't want to back one of us or the other and so they kind of just stood back. (Jess)

Thus, there are different layers and depths of friendships requiring navigation, remembering what was said and to who, and preempting possible consequences as circumstances shift:

> In the end it just gets too much and the friendships suffer. But then there's other friends that have supported me, stuck with me and I've made a very good woman friend who has been through a similar experience with a still close ex-boyfriend who has become gay. I've lost some friends and gained others and I've had to make decisions and choices.... I think my biggest regret is losing friends over it. (Rachel)

In the case of Marissa, her partner outed both of their sexualities, exposing the flaws, limitations and prejudices of existing friendships to the point where they could not continue:

> In order to soften his own experience of coming out he outed me to people. That was a really humiliating experience because I wasn't telling anyone.... It was that sort of scandal side of it people enjoyed, like, "Look what's going on behind their doors."... I just felt completely vulnerable and I felt like I had been cut open and laying in the noon day sun.... those people that I had known for all those years who knew us as something else really had to go so that I could move on and become the person that I fundamentally was and it was difficult to take that path. (Marissa)

Many women spoke about the significance and joy of having friends with whom they could share the crisis of discovering a partner's bisexuality:

> I had people taking time off work, they took sick leave for me so that I wouldn't be alone. They brought me soup, they made me tea. They made sure that I had water. They made sure that I had a shower every day. These were things that I didn't even think about doing, I didn't care about. . . . they would listen to me and they would talk to me, without passing judgment, knowing that what you said was confidential. (Erin)

> I immediately rang my best friend that I've been friends with since I was five, and she's been fantastic. She doesn't put any pressure on. She says, "Your own journey is your own journey and when you need to do things, you'll do them." And she says, "I know I couldn't live with a partner like that. I'd need to develop my own space. But if you can live with him, that's just fantastic." (Fiona)

Making new friends also required decisions about what to tell and when. This needed to be part of the process of establishing rapport or, as Jess described, a kind of "shock value" to see if the friendship was compatible with one's values and lifestyle:

> When I make new friends, I feel like I'm deceiving them if they don't know about this part of our relationship. Here's such a major thing in my life and a part of me is dealing with it every day, whether I'm up or down. (Krystle)

Establishing new friendships also provided opportunities to become involved in groups and activities where it was more likely that accepting and open-minded friendships could be formed, as Kirsten and her partner set out to do by joining a university choir: "in the choirs you get a lot of people who are alternative in various different ways. . . . And a number of people we know have open relationships of various kinds" (Kirsten).

> A lot of our friends are from the role playing community . . . We've even developed a phrase, "Partner once removed" because at the moment there is a guy who is going out with my girlfriend who is going out with me, who is going out with Tovi who is going out with another woman, who is going out with another guy. (Rose)

"THE WORST PLACE IS THE WORKPLACE"

> I think the worst place is the workplace. I think the workplace is so straight and conservative and full of fear and I understand why. I understand that anything that upsets the manager and the hierarchy is a potential problem for people's jobs. . . There's not enough air flowing through those spaces and so full of neurotic activity. (Raven)

Many women talked about the workplace as another major heteroworld in which they and their partners had to navigate and negotiate when, who and what to tell about their sexualities and relationships: "He's had an extremely high profile, very sensitive government job. Just don't shit on your own doorstep" (Jolene).

> We are painfully aware that being bisexual, which doesn't exist according to his workmates, will lose him any promotions and his current position in the company. Chances are his workmates would refuse to work with him or respect his position of authority. . . . Staff in his department are still repeating homophobic sayings that were around 30 years ago such as "What does AIDS stand for? Arse Injected Death Sentence." Another is "What does AIDS backwards stand for?: Stick Dick in Arse." (Shelley)

In her summary of research on bisexuality in the workplace, Köllen (2013) believes biphobia creates a negative working climate. Bisexual employees face various stereotypes and, together with the tendencies to be silenced within organizations and the internalizing of biphobic attitudes, their general vocational scope is narrowed. Mechanisms of exclusion can range from mere unfriendliness to different types of aggression (Barker et al., 2012; Eliason, 1997). Thus, bisexual employees have to decide how to deal with their bisexuality in the workplace on a day-to-day basis. More open bisexuals tend to have a higher level of "organizational citizenship behavior" (Köllen, 2013: 127), while pretending to be heterosexual can negatively affect the individual's vocational self-consciousness, mental capacities and workplace performance. Furthermore, biphobia can cause self-alienation, isolation and intensifies cognitive dissonance. Köllen's summary also finds bisexual employees who work in a more encouraging and affirmative climate tend to be more open about their bisexuality, and "organizations may also profit in economic terms, because of the aforementioned positive consequences (on the individual and organizational level) that being more open about one's sexual orientation brings" (Köllen, 2013: 133).

Indeed, Köllen's (2013) review found bisexuality is rarely addressed by organizations. Even employers who have implemented diversity actions on sexual orientation often fail to explicitly address bisexual issues (Towle, 2011). Marketing activities often focus on gays and lesbians; when images are employed, they are mostly same-sex couples. Likewise, LGBT workplace networks are usually almost exclusively composed of gay male and lesbian employees (Köllen, 2007; 2012). As Köllen writes, "By making bisexuality a topic of an article on the business's intranet or in a staff magazine, employers can show that they do not measure all sexualities (with the exception of heterosexuality) with the same yardstick and indicate that bisexual employees are recognized and appreciated as they are: bisexual" (2013: 127). The Pew Research Center (2013) found that among employed gay men, 60% say their workplace is very accepting of gay men while 44% of bisexuals say their workplace is very accepting of bisexual employees. About half of gay men (48%) say all or most of the people they work with closely know they are gay, while only 11% of bisexuals say the same about their bisexuality.

In our research, workplace biphobia was particularly apparent in working environments with strict religious frameworks:

Greg: I work at a Christian school . . .only a couple of my workmates know, but no details or extended discussions. But I mean, in reality, a lot of people must wonder. I've always had kids at school make the assumption that I'm gay.

Krystle: And the parents.

Greg: And then be totally surprised I've got a wife and children.

I'm working for Mormons now. I'm an office manager, it's a very Mormon environment . . . they are very homophobic, exceptionally. I just make a mental note to not throw out any obviously camp lines and we'll just let it go at that. (Sherry)

Some women believed their workplaces were gay friendly but biphobic or had stronger stereotypes or misunderstandings of MOREs than same-sex monogamous relationships:

There was a guy there who was gay and the partner used to come over to the office lunch time and so sit around with us and have a chat. And I found that most people were pretty accepting of the fact. But I don't think the situation would be the same if someone had said, "Look, I'm not gay, I'm bisexual." (Christine)

Yes, he has big work issues in the army. I mean, he's supposed to be getting ready for a top secret clearance at his work . . . and he's just worried that they're going to find out about us. . . .the simple fact that there are a lot of lesbians in the army I find really interesting. It's sort of like, well, if they can be so open about it and it doesn't stop them progressing then why on earth should it stop him? . . . I think he's seen one of his bosses at the local beat close to work one night and kept that to himself, for future knowledge. (Sherry)

Some women reported situations of harassment at work or unfair work practices which were difficult to pinpoint as harassment:

He's on stress leave, because somebody off the Internet, because we said no [to having sex with him], e-mailed his employer saying that he was gay and sells his services on the Internet. And, of course, because of political correctness and discrimination, work's not going to say that, yes, that's why they're giving him harassment, but through colleagues from his work, we found out that's what it's come from. . . He is a fully qualified paramedic. He has been one for eleven years. And he went from being a station officer himself in relieving little towns around here, to getting crap jobs, put on a bus picking up the invalids, taking them to the hospital or the doctors for their appointments and then home. . . .. It was actually the superiors that got the e-mail and let it leak to the other officers. And I know for sure that they did get it because we had them here. One night he had an attack and I had to call an ambulance, and it was staffed by his superior officer. I was really angry, and I said, "Most of what's going on is your fault because of the harassment Jeff's getting. I've been informed by other officers as to what it is." And he turned around and said, "Oh, that's a load of rubbish, we never got an e-mail like that" and I never mentioned the Internet, okay, to this station officer, and he said, "But he does have a site on the Internet, doesn't he?" So he knew. And I turned around and I said, "I never even mentioned the Internet." I'm quick. I've got six kids. You can't miss a trick, you know. [Laughing]. (Lesley)

It appeared that, for many, coming out was based on what kind of workplace it was, but even the most 'relaxed' workplace could present some concerns, panopticonic responses and stigmatization. These were not necessarily in relation to sexuality but more so to polyamory and open relationships, as well as the employer worrying about their status in the wider society and among their client base. Interestingly, this could occur in both heteronormative and homonormative spaces: "when I worked in straight places, I didn't really talk about his bisexuality. When I worked in gay places, I never talked about mine or his, so I was in the closet in a gay workplace [laughing]" (Sara).

> There's quite a few bi people at work and gay people and it's just so completely an accepting environment.... Even the boss, I was talking to him one day and I said I was organizing this dance party. He was fascinated to find out that we were bi and poly and so mostly I find where I work it's great. Really into personal development and everybody's really positive and there's not a lot of negative gossip but at my previous place, they actually took me aside and said, "People are going to react negatively, don't spit it out publicly while you're in a leadership position here because they don't want the word on the street, 'Oh, yeah, that place is really into this weird blah, blah, blah.'" (Jacinta)

Others found the workplace culture, particularly the ages and lifestyles of colleagues, allowed for open discussions so the workplace became a friendly and supportive setting: "We're so lucky . . . both of us working in the arts, so it feels like a really open community" (Monica).

> It's a university so there's a great deal of acceptance of variety there to begin with. A lot of them found polyamory completely alien, and they were happy to say so, but that wasn't necessarily in a negative sense, they were just going, "I really don't get it and it's weird but cool," kind of thing.... One woman was a lot older and considered Christianity an important part of her life. I have to admit that she wasn't in the least judgmental, but while she was happy to hear about our success and failures as a couple, she didn't necessarily want to hear that we had sex with some of our friends . . . And a lot of the younger people there were talking about who they went home with from the pub or from the nightclub or what flat mate they bonked was all fine conversation. (Lizz)

The question of telling became more urgent if the woman or her partner were experiencing illness and emotional trauma over any crisis in the relationship and this was affecting their productivity and/or required sick leave:

> I had two weeks sick leave. Having to explain why you needed that much time off for not being sick was just unbelievable. . . . I felt so ashamed. I thought that people would think that I was dirty. (Erin)

> I look back and I used to say I didn't know why they didn't sack me, I was like a living zombie. We'd have meetings and all of a sudden I'd just go. When they did find out, it's like you get people saying, "He should die". . . It's hard to sit there and make conversation with them at work, cause they will never understand what it was like. (Pat)

The silences and fears in the workplace also meant that women were unable to access friendships with other women in similar situations, thereby unable to make the workplace a site for support and wellbeing:

> Isabelle and I always clicked as far as working together. We always had something in common, which was quite strange . . . . And one night Edward went out and he didn't come home before I went to work, and he never did that, and anyway I went to work and I was really quite upset. I was just about to tell Isabelle about Edward and she said she had to dash home. And she was having the same sort of problem at that time, too, because she only just found out about her [gay] son. And it wasn't for another two years before Isabelle rang me and said, "What are you both doing next week? Would you like to come out for dinner?" I thought that's strange, you know, we've been good friends, but we've never sort of [socialized outside work hours]. . . And she said, "Oh, I'll tell you what it's about. I've got two gay men." I thought oh, I didn't hear that right . . . and [when I saw her at work] she said, "Oh, have you got over the shock?" and I said, "Well, sort of, but did you say one or two?" We just gave each other a big hug in the corridor. It was just amazing. So we went out for dinner the next day. (Brenda)

In line with Barker's (2015) notion of "bi-furiosity", other women spoke of being "explicitly" out in the workplace in order to help shift social attitudes and, indeed, support other queer colleagues:

> I get bizarre reactions from straight work colleagues occasionally, but I had one year where eight different guys came out to me as gay or bi, because they see coming out to a bi woman who's in a relationship with a bi man as an easy person to come out to. Straight colleagues will often have those discussions with me where they sort of go, "Oh, I couldn't do that. I don't understand how you can do that." . . .And we talk about it. It's all fine. I know that Tovi is very explicit at work, he's in an industry where you've got a lot of people playing computer games after work and people making sort of silly homophobic comments, and someone will say, "Oh, suck my dick," and Tovi will say, "I'd love to." And he sees that as a bit of a crusade to be explicitly out, yes, you can be a long haired guy who dresses the way he does, who is a little bit feminine, but is just one of the guys, and who is bi. (Rose)

As Ava found, however, work colleagues could be "cool" and full of "admiration" but discrimination could manifest itself in other ways, including sexism:

> My partner's open at his work place. He's a suit. He works for a software company, and a really big one, and they don't tend to be the most liberal and open-minded people, but they seem to have taken to it quite well. And actually he had people ribbing him the other week about, "So, at the Christmas party are you going to bring one of your sweeties or both of your sweeties?" He's like, "Mm, I don't know, if I bring any one it's going to be neither of them, it'll be someone else altogether". . . . I think there's probably less stigmatism and more a relaxing admiration. Like, even if people think he's wrong for doing it, there's still a sort of, "Yeah, that cool guy, he can keep up with two women. Wow, that's pretty good." . . . You know, his virility in being able to keep two women happy. Whereas if he were female, then maybe it would be like, "Oh, what a slut." (Ava)

"IT'S A RED NECK TOWN AND YOU WOULD BE CENSURED"

> There's a lack of trust and there's a lack of discussion about it because it's a red neck town and you would be censured. There's no venues. There's lots of toilets, but it's very, very covert. There are people here in this town thirty years old who are born and bred here and have never been to a city. Like, how much do they know about the world? (Jolene)

Many women discussed the specific challenges to their partners and relationships that came with living in small towns or rural and remote areas: "you talk to the people from the country and it's like, "No, that doesn't happen in our country town." (Louisa).

> Living in rural Australia means that he has to be careful. If you are gay/bi and smart you hide who you are. . . . living with the fear of what might happen if the wrong kind of people found out. We lack "out" people to spend social time with. . . . A person's sexuality is still fuel for scandalous gossip at that. (Shelley)

> We live in a semirural area. We are very discreet. We have different circles, rarely do they cross. . . . It can certainly impact the availability of people with similar mindsets. (Jenna)

Nevertheless, a few women did discuss how they were challenging these small-town views by taking small steps and connecting with old friends:

> *Vicky:* We're a very touchy family, and I get frustrated when Mike says goodbye to his partner and he might be in the town in view, that they can't do that.

They've got to like pat each other on the back. I'm sure a lot of the community have an inkling because when Mike goes to work he's dressed completely different to when we go out and he'll wear bangles and necklaces. . . . If they want to ask us straight out, you know, is he bi, is he gay or whatever, we'd answer but we're not forwarding the information . . . we don't walk up to someone and say, "Are you heterosexual?" . . . Being where we come from, in the community we are, there are boundaries miles high.

Mike: But on the contrary, there are a lot of people that are very, very accepting too. Now, this mate of mine I've known for twenty years and I mean he's a 100% straight guy, and he has actually met my boyfriend and he reckons he's a great guy and said, "You're the same guy that I had a beer with last week and we went motor bike riding the week before or camping, you're no different, in fact probably a better mate that you've taken my trust."

At times, women would delineate between various areas in a city or various Australian cities according to the level of diversity, size and acceptance: "They're slowly coming to terms with the gay and lesbian population in Perth. But I think hey, there is another group of people out there too" (Christine).

I suppose the living out in the western [lower socioeconomic] suburbs, suburbia, the biggest problem could be my neighbors, . . . I don't know my neighbors well enough to talk. (Evelyn)

However, most city-dwellers agreed that the level of anonymity worked in favor of their relationships: "I never see my neighbors anyway. I can go months and never see them" (Jane). Or they were able to be open and not perform a persona in public:

He came from a very religious rural background, and it just was not on [being bi]. But coming to the city from this very isolated country area, he's been able to. . . .there's not this division between what I am and what I tell people I am. (Nicole)

City-dwelling also meant people were more aware of sexual diversity and there were more opportunities for male partners to find men. This was something that some of the women were not comfortable with, given what they observed in some men and knew about their own husbands:

Greg: Sometimes we go to Melbourne and we think maybe we could just kind of be more ourselves and just fit in with a group over there . . .

Krystle: But sometimes I find Melbourne a little bit confronting in that way, like I'll just be crossing a road and some guy will just smile and say hello to Greg and it will just be that 'gaydar' recognition thing, you know.

Greg: Krystle always brings it up before I do.

Krystle: He wouldn't know he was being come onto until his pants were around his ankles. [both laughing]

We live in the inner city and there are people up and down our street who are nice, heterosexual, white married couples who I have great interest in their husbands and what activities their husbands may or may not do [laughing]. (Sara)

"HOW DO WE WIN IN OUR CULTURE AND OUR SOCIETY?"

We don't have to tell everybody every aspect about ourselves, but how do we win in our culture and our society? . . . the basic fear for people is that they're going to be rejected. And "you're a weirdo, you're a freak, you're deficient, bugger off." All you now are is a bisexual man or the wife of a bisexual man. . . . it needs very much that process of normalizing [bisexuality] and I think there's too much pathologizing. (Scarlett)

In this chapter, we have explored the various locations and sites within heteroworld that women and their partners have to navigate and maneuver. Framing these specific worlds is a larger dominant society, media and popular culture of heteronormativity, an infrastructure and institutionalized world of unquestioned heteroprivilege:

I become more invisible being straight than I do when I was a lesbian. . . . it's such a weird privilege being heterosexual. Like, it's so weird going to family lunches and being able to talk to my grandma about my boyfriend . . . Now I'm just like everyone else . . . getting close to thirty and normal and fucking boring . . . And I sometimes feel like I'm suffocating. And it's so weird holding hands when you're walking down a street and women talk about, "Don't you just hate the way guys leave the caps off the toothpaste?" in the bathroom and like, "Ahhh, a heterosexual conversation" and I feel like I'm going to shrivel up and die. It's a burden being heterosexual, it is. It's fucking scary. (Sascha)

I remember after Greg had told me, the next day wanting to get a card saying, "To my gay husband, I love you," but of course there just wasn't one. I stood at the cards with tears running down my cheeks and the lady said, "Can I help you?" and I said, "I don't think you've got a card for what I want." . . . So you have these times when it really hits you and you feel very acutely how different you are. (Krystle)

Indeed, part of the women's need to shift and challenge heteronormativity was becoming aware of the panopticonic fear and self-regulation that many adopted in order to shield from the harshness of societal discrimination, and to not allow this system of social judgments to prevent living a liveable life:

> We pass for a nice straight young couple. We get smiled at by shopkeepers, stopped by tourists wanting to use us as a frontpiece to an Australian backdrop. I remember the day an old woman reading a newspaper at the bus-stop watched us share a breakfast apple, kiss and hug, before going separate ways for work. She then said to me, 'It's so nice to see a decent young couple like yourself these days. He looks like such a lovely young man. There's so much evil in this world. I've just been reading this." She showed me the article on bisexual men doing the beats, going to orgies, while their poor wives knew nothing until the day a doctor told them they had a STD or HIV. "There's just no self-control anymore," she said, really disgusted. "Not like in my day. We weren't even allowed to talk about such things." I really wanted to tell her. Tell her about the other realities that existed, had always existed, all around her like right there with me and Adam. But I didn't, and I hated myself for it. This old woman seemed so relieved, so excited that there were wholesome young couples around, and what would it mean to have this image destroyed? And anyway, weren't we 'wholesome'? I just couldn't bear the thought of those aging disillusioned and furious eyes drilling into my back for the fifty-minute bus ride. . . . Yeah, I think people are afraid of people like Adam and me. We represent too many possibilities, so we need to be kept out. The straight world allows us to hold hands and kiss in cinemas, on public streets, shop together and receive lots of smiles. But if we talk about our shared interest in men, we're soon shown the exit out of that world. (Lilith)

For other women, there was sadness in knowing how their partners would perform affection for their wives in public in order to 'pass as straight', a performance which ended as soon as they were in the privacy of their own home: "Often we'd be out, and he would put his arm around me. He would be quite affectionate actually, so we'd get home and I'd think oh? But nothing. So it was a show for people" (Loredana).

Hence, for many MOREs, a major determinant of how silently or openly their relationship is conducted is determined by the discourses surrounding them in their communities and the wider society. Many women spoke about their frustration with the 'myths' that were perpetuated in society as a system of control by the dominant group. They talked about the damage those myths do to people, both those in MOREs and people who pathologize them, as they miss out on so much engaging, learning and connection with others, as well as avoiding acknowledging aspects of themselves:

> The most difficult time was establishing the relationship. No role models. We hurt each other, we hurt other people we loved. But somehow we made it. The most difficult issues are the amount of editing and lying that occurs, and the lack

of sociocultural and legal recognition of my relationship with Andrew. Frustrations include knowing that some people, especially other men, would think my straight husband was weak for so-called "allowing" me to have a bisexual male partner rather than recognizing how strong he is and how much I love him. It's also a problem for some feminists who think relating to one man is bad enough, what woman would want two? It's also been interesting discovering what I call the armchair feminists who say women should be allowed to do anything and live anyway they want but then disapprove of me being polyamorous... Sometimes, I feel as if whatever I do, I'm being watched, especially when I'm with him. Sometimes I feel the letter A is tattooed in neon lights on my forehead as well as sequined on my chest like in that book about the adulterous woman in Puritan America, *The Scarlet Letter*.... I feel like we're illegal foreigners, who would be completely thrown out if people knew. So we stay on the periphery, moving in and out. As if there's an amoebic space within which I hover and circulate around. I feel it a lot when I actually manage to have both my partners together. I want to say, "See, we are like you," as we sit and chat, or just roam around the streets or go to the supermarket or to dinner or the movies, as well as, "We are different." (Naomi)

Although not readily available in the media, greater knowledge about MORE history is gradually providing alternative models and frameworks and is a powerful way of inserting these issues into a mainstream interested in celebrities and other public figures. For example, Foster et al. (1997) researched and compiled a collection of biographies of threesomes from ancient times to contemporary times, many of which include women in relationships with bisexual men (see also Roiphe, 2007). Actors such as Charles Laughton and Sir Lawrence Olivier, and film director Tony Richardson, were three bisexual film celebrities married to women. Another memorable bisexual man in theatre was the composer Leonard Bernstein who wrote the musical score for *West Side Story* in 1961. He was married for more than twenty-five years, had three children, and had relationships with a number of men (Bryant, 1997). Bernstein was always quite open about his bisexual lifestyle. In 1967 he embarked on a trial separation from his wife, thinking that now the children had grown, he would feel easier in a less ambiguously gay environment. He was back with his wife the following year (Jones, 2000). Another famous bisexual man from the music world is Clive Davis. In his autobiography, *The Soundtrack of My Life,* Davis (2013) details a five-decade career in the music business with three successful music companies, Grammy Awards, a place in the Rock and Roll Hall of Fame, and the many renowned international musical artists he has managed. In the 551-page book, he discusses his bisexuality in only four pages, toward the end. After the break-up of his second marriage, he explores his desire for men, and refutes the many assumptions about men in his position:

> I didn't feel as if I had found, or was even searching for, my true self. I had not been at all repressed or confused during either of my marriages. I hadn't fantasized about men. I had never experimented during my adolescence or between my first and second marriages. I was not at all interested in anonymous sex (Davis, 2013: 545).

He also explains why he "stayed outside the public glare": "I tried to custom-craft a life that felt good... I didn't want to be typecast... admitting you're bisexual is to invite derision from all sides with no one ultimately benefiting" (2013: 546–547).

Vita Sackville-West, a writer, and Harold Nicolson, a politician, both bisexual in early-twentieth-century England, have had their multisexual polyamorous relationship discussed in biographies, one of them written by one of their sons, Nigel Nicolson (Nicolson, 1973; see also Glendinning, 1983). Nicolson summarizes his parents' relationship as

> the story of two people who married for love and whose love deepened with every passing year, although each was constantly and by mutual consent unfaithful to the other... Each came to give the other full liberty without enquiry or reproach. (1973: 3–5)

It is also thought-provoking to analyze the way Vita and Harold attempted to articulate their relationship in the absence of queer discursive frameworks that would provide, in decades to come, labels and other positive terms of reference:

> *Harold to Vita:* I know that your love for me is central, as is my love for you, and it's quite unaffected by what happens at the outer edge... I know that for each of us the other is the magnetic north, and that though the needle may flicker and even get stuck at the other points, it will come back to the pole sooner or later (Nicolson, 1973: 189).

> *Vita:* I know of no truthful record of such a connection- one that is written, I mean, with no desire to appeal to a vicious taste in any possible readers; and... I hold the conviction that such connections will to a very large extent cease to be regarded as merely unnatural,... [and] it will be recognized that many more people of my type do exist than under the present-day system of hypocrisy is commonly admitted (Nicolson, 1973: 101).

The Nicolsons' relationship resonated with many women in our research who tried to explain and resist the connection between external regulation or the fear of it, and internal regulation and panopticonic performances that damaged the self and relationships. Georgina discussed how her bisexual monogamous partner questioned his masculinity, not over his own sexuality but over his female partner's bisexual polyamory:

> It was the "What would people say? I'm not a real man. Real men don't let their women go and have a relationship with another woman" . . .And the stupid way our society insists that there's one person for ever and ever and you're the one. . . . I know it's hard, but try not to look at your relationship through society's eyes. I think that's where a lot of us come undone, but rather than say, "Hey, how do I feel about it, how do I see it?" we sort of say, "Oh, how does society see it, how does society see me?" (Georgina)

Women imagined people's responses based on dominant societal constructions, preventing them from even initiating conversations that might have broken the damaging silence and led to much more support:

> I lived in a world which was grey, because people would ask me, "Are you involved with someone?" and if I said yes then I would have to open up and divulge my life story which I didn't want to do and if I said no then they would say, "Well why aren't you?" so it was a very difficult time. (Nirupa)

Some women spoke of navigating a midcourse between telling and not telling by wearing "signifiers" or performing certain actions that only "insiders" would be able to read in public, thereby being both visible and invisible at the same time:

> for both of us it's not something you go around shouting. I mean, you've seen the [rainbow] hat I'm wearing, I've got [bi and poly] tags on the bag. I've got the subtle hints there for those who know. But, I'm not going to go around saying, "Woo, hoo, look at me!" because what's the point? That asks for trouble that you wouldn't otherwise get and that you don't really want to invite. (Kirsten)

> Tovi's got long hair. He can look feminine from the outside. He's slim. He's not tall, and we've been called 'leso' many times from cars, from people who assume that we're women. And we were standing in the city and Tovi had had a very bad experience, and he was crying on my shoulder and I was stroking his hair, and I had a hat on and five guys walked by, and one of them grabbed my hat and I said, "Come on, give me my hat back. This is ridiculous," and they started saying, "Lesos," and Tovi then looked up and they went, "Oh" you know, there was this kind of moment of recognition, of, "Hang on, this is a guy." And they then went through this weird thing where they could tell there is something about us that is inherently queer. And they said, "Oh, what's this? Do you have the strap-on?" And I was so tempted to say, "Gee, how could you tell?" That was a situation where if I'd said that, the violence and danger that we were in. And Tovi's masculinity kind of kicked in and he wanted to start hitting

them, and I'm sort of holding him back going, "Now, come on, come on, don't do this," and so they're going, "Oh, see, you're so gutless, your woman's who's strong, isn't she." And in the end I got my hat back and the guys left us alone and nobody got punched. But that was really an intimidating situation. (Rose)

As is discussed throughout this book, the media and popular culture were seen as very responsible for perpetuating heteornormative imagery and thus making same-sex or bisexual public signs of affection very difficult:

> Like, they're [films with bisexual men] so few and far between, especially something of quality, not something trashy. Because it's [the media] selling products in the market and I've been thinking instead of calling it popular culture, really it's marketing culture. Deeply disappointing. (Raven)

Where bisexual men with women partners have been presented in popular heteroculture such as film, the representations are similar to the earlier representations of gay men and lesbians as discussed by Russo (1987): demonization, derision, pathologization, criminalization, and as objects of entertainment and humor:

> I can no longer watch many films and soapies, nor listen to music, without another commentary, a jarring buzzing at the same time inside my head as the torn-between-two-lovers, the evil adulterers, the emotional torture of being unfaithful, are screened in full technicolor gory and salacious detail on the screen, on the radio, on advertising that also titillates with the possibilities of extra-marital desires. I'm always looking for signs for something else that looks like us. There is nothing that makes me real. And of course, anyone who is watching me and catches a second or two of my reality thinks they know the whole plot of my relationship because they watch it on the screen or hear it on the radio day in, day out.... When I do find something that gives me glimpses of my situations I cry because other people watching these glimpses would never understand, accept my reality. "It's OK on the big screen," I can hear them say, "That's where anything is possible. But not in real life. It just wouldn't be allowed, it wouldn't work. What would happen to society?" Yet they're the ones who could give it permission, they're the ones who could make the space for it to work. They are the society, its prisoners and its guardians. (Naomi)

Three theories which endeavor to analyze and understand the relationship between media texts and media consumers are pertinent to this discussion. First, Cultivation Theory (Gerbner et al. 2002) states that exposure over a prolonged period of time to portrayals of reality as defined by the media will lead to perceptions of reality that are consistent with these portrayals, a process called mainstreaming. Thus, the negative representations of bisexual men and MOREs will lead to media consumers believing these misrepresentations. "Resonance" is a sub-section of cultivation theory. It exists when viewers' real-life environment, such as women in abusive relationships and experiences with bisexual men, is like the world of media. This provides a double dose of messages which resonate, entrench and amplify cultivation, as the media provides no alternative views with which the consumer can reflect and consider their own situation as just one of various ways of being, albeit a negative one. Second, Social Cognitive Theory (Bandura, 2002) states that individuals observe media portrayals for insight into how they themselves could behave, especially if they are performed by individuals perceived as attractive, powerful and popular and if the outcomes are viewed as appealing. So if being in functional and fulfilling MOREs results in a desired outcome of health and happiness in the film, television program or festival event, individuals will engage in similar behavior believing that in doing so they will gain the same benefits. Third, Cinema as Therapy Theory (Izod & Dovalis, 2015) posits the movie theatre as a "sacred space" where spectators are "freed from their usual inhibitions, which allows them to connect to their emotional lives." In identifying with certain characters or situations, they are able to "project disowned parts of the self on to the screen" (2015: 1). Thus, film and cinemas provide viewers with a "transformative intellectual and psychic experience in which self-discovery can occur" (2015: 2). Vicari presents the above theories in more direct language in his study of bisexuality in film:

> In the taxonomy of visual representations we recognise elements of the living world better once they have been catalogued by movies. Nothing exists as full as it does until it exists within a film. . . . Movies and life are perhaps best thought of as parallel realities, . . . The two can be made to bleed over into each other and they can be made now and then to intersect like train tracks that sometimes switch with each other. They can be testing grounds for each other but one thing remains: to be shut out of the movies or always depicted unflattering in them is to experience a special kind of pain which only the members of the heavily saturated media culture can know. It stands to reason that if the intricate mimesis of film can reflect lives which people already live, then they can also inspire lives which people might possibly live (2011: 10).

The relationships between media and consumer in relation to bisexual men and MORES have been discussed by many queer-media theorists:

> bi representation in the media is usually sensationalized, brief, uneven, and unexamined. . . . We're only a curiosity at best, and then when relating to AIDS or some form of sexual "impropriety," not as real breathing girl/boy next door people whom you might know and love or work with and understand. This is mass denial (Hutchins in Alexander, 2007: 116).

Capulet explores how despite some famous male entertainers coming out as bisexual, their sexual status never becomes a subject of media frenzy: "these disclosures never amount to more than a blip on the pop-culture radar" unlike how women bisexuals dominate celebrity news (2010: 8). Interestingly, the actor Alan Cumming has always been matter-of-fact about his bisexuality to the point where his recent family memoir weaves in information and reflections about his past and present male and female partners with no sensationalism or specific attention: It is all part and parcel of his life (Cumming, 2014).

Bryant refers to bisexuality as "the love that dare not speak its identity" in visual media (in Alexander, 2007: 117; see also Amy in Alexander, 2007). Bisexuality may be constructed as a temporary 'phase' or experimental, as in the films *Threesome* (1994) and *Just One Time* (1999), with a return to the more 'mature' and 'authentic' (straight or gay) monosexuality and/or marriage by the end of the film. Bisexuality may also be connected to violence and crime, as if the former precipitates the latter. Araki's violent movie *The Doom Generation* (1995), is a road movie about Amy and Jordan, young "druggies" who get involved with a bisexual named Xavier who, in common metaphoric representations of bisexual people, is presented as a drifter: rootless and going nowhere. He has also just shot a Korean convenience-store owner, and from there, the three unwittingly commit a series of murders. Thus, we have what could be surmised as the typical bisexual criminal introducing a somewhat fragile, somewhat naïve heterosexual couple to "the dark side" of crime and murder. And yet, simultaneously, Xavier challenges the couple's ideas about the gay/straight duality (Hart, 2005). Indeed, the film explores the attraction between the two young men and their relationships with Amy. The film ends with the brutal killing of Xavier and Jordan, with Jordan's penis being severed and placed in Xavier's mouth, by neo-Nazi gay-bashers. This occurs just as the two young men are about to consummate their sexual relationship without Amy present. Hart argues that despite the "unexpected, remarkably brutal bloodbath" at the end of the film, "it effectively represents Araki's way of making an incredibly powerful statement about the repressive nature of hegemonic ideology in the United States in relation to bisexual men and other nonheterosexual individuals" (2005: 54–55). Indeed, Araki has given his three characters the surnames of Red, White, and Blue.

Bryant (2005a) documents how bisexual youth growing up in the 1960s to the early 1990s, who later became adult men trying to live their bisexualities, saw an array of negative bisexual stereotypes at their local cinemas. Among them were bisexuals who spread AIDS and a number of bloodsucking bisexual vampires. One common theme was the number of bisexuals who end up dead in films of this era, including being murdered in love complications and treacheries. Clinton Green is murdered in *The Last of Sheila* (1973); bisexual burglar Jean is murdered by his boyfriend in *L'Homme*

Blesse (1983); rock singer Karon is strangled in the men's room in *Hot Child in the City* (1987); and Sasha and Grace, both bisexual gangsters, are blown up by Sasha's wife in *Inside Monkey Zetterlandland* (1993). In *Second Skin* (1999), the very insecure and frightened bisexual husband is torn between his wife and male lover, is cruel to both of them, cheats on both, and finally dies in a motorbike accident. In contrast, his gay partner is a doctor, noble, kind and generous. His wife is a good patient mother. *Romance* (1988) is a Brazilian film in which the bisexual politician is killed at the outset and the premise of the film is to discover which of his many enemies was responsible. In *Deathtrap* (1982), Michael Caine's character dies a violent death at the hands of his male lover after they kill Caine's wife. In *Burglar* (1987), Whoopi Goldberg discovers that the murdered bisexual, Christopher, was killed by his own lover, the lawyer. Araki's film *The Living End* (1991) shows a masochistic, young bisexual man who is stabbed to death after picking up one of the film's leading men for sex. Bisexual fencer Michiel is killed in a match with his lover in *Touché* (1991). There have also been films in which the bisexual character was a suicide victim, including *Advise and Consent* (1962) and 1928's *Geschlecht in Fesseln* (*Sex in Bondage*), where a young man and his wife kill themselves when extorted by the man's former lover.

In *The Rocky Horror Picture Show* (1975), it is the bisexual Dr. Frank N. Furter, a self-proclaimed "sweet transvestite" from the planet of Transsexual in the galaxy of Transylvania, who is killed at the end of the movie by his own servants. He seduces both Brad and Janet, a newly engaged middle-American heterosexual young couple, who arrive at his castle symbolically lost on a stormy night. It should be pointed out that, despite the "evil" and deception in both the bisexual doctor and the overall plot, the young couple's dormant and ignorant sexualities are awakened and they leave the castle far wiser (see Hart, 2005). Indeed, the theme of the bisexual man disrupting a mainstream heterosexual couple who will never be the same again is a common trope, ending in the murder of the bisexual. In *Dry Cleaning* (1997), a couple goes for a night out to a "seedy" club to get some erotic spark back into their hard-working lives. They meet the young drag queen performer Loic, who falls in love with them and engages in sex with them after he becomes their employee. The husband accidentally kills Loic when Loic is penetrating him anally. In *Leaving Metropolis* (2002), a gay artist becomes a waiter for a dysfunctional married couple, leading to the disintegration of everyone's life. The wife is depicted as bossy and maternal, with dolls and doll-houses representing the perfect normative happy life she aspired to. However, she is also capable of having very passionate sex. In *Teorema* (1968), a bisexual "stranger" enters a bourgeois family, and, as stated in the film's blurb, is both "God and the Devil." The interactions are both divine and diabolical because after the seductions when he is about to leave, they all have to reevaluate their belief systems and goals. This involves both pain and gratitude to the "stranger" for the wisdom they have gained.

Thus, as we have seen, many films are bleak or grim, with characters who compete or are ruthless with each other (Bryant, 2005b). As previously presented, in *Cabaret* (1972) Brian is in a relationship with Sally, and together they have a friendship with Baron Maximillian. When the Baron leaves the country without warning, Brian seems relieved to see him go. "Screw him," he says. "I do," reveals Sally. Brian stops her cold by responding, "So do I." Married men and younger male hustlers is also a common theme. *Forty Deuce* (1982) is a bleak film about troubled and exploited teens, where all the hustlers seem to be gay. Orson Bean plays the married man whose interest in underage males makes him an easy target for the hustlers, who attempt extortion by blaming him for a boy's fatal drug overdose. In *My Addiction* (1993), Glenn is a married man who has fallen hopelessly in love with a bisexual hustler named Dick. The problem is that Dick is not interested in a relationship with Glenn, but Glenn refuses to leave until Dick physically throws him out. Indeed, the bisexual married man is usually portrayed as a closeted homosexual and/or a man who has sex with other men behind his wife's back. In the Spanish film, *El Diputado* (1979), known in English as *Confessions of a Congressman,* the Fascist party learns everything they need to destroy the career of Congressman Roberto Orbea by setting him up with a young male lover, Juanito, the "gay-for-pay" adolescent. The right-wing extremists murder Juanito and force Orbea to be discovered with the dead boy's body. Before this grim ending, Orbea's wife has come to accept Juanito, and he plays the role of "trophy boy for Mr and Mrs Orbea" (Prout, 2005: 161). In *Straight for the Heart* (1988), a photojournalist who travels war zones returns home to a personal war he has been indifferent about and refused to attend to. He finds both his male and female partners gone, after a ten-year polyamorous triad. She is pregnant and again, heterocoupledom and nuclear family arrangements are endorsed.

Bisexual men as thieves is another mainstream representation. Patrick Dempsey plays a bisexual bank robber in the film *Bank Robber* (1993). In Bertrand Blier's French comedy *Going Places* (1974), Gerard Depardieu plays the more despicable of the two thieves, the bisexual one. In 1986, the actor and director teamed up once again on the film *Ménage,* in which Depardieu plays another bisexual thief who seduces a poor straight couple sexually and into a life of burglary, then later sex-work dressed in drag. In *L'Homme Blessé* (1983), a bisexual vice squad detective employs the younger bisexual, Jean, to pick up men at the train station and then rob them after sex. The film presents many older gay/bi men paying for younger men to "service them," although Jean is also seen regularly visiting the woman who loves him.

Dog Day Afternoon (1975) is based on a real incident when a down-and-out bisexual man named Sonny robbed a bank to get money for his boyfriend's sex-change operation. In 1975, John Stanley Wojtowicz, on whom Al Pacino's character was based, wrote a letter from prison to *The New York Times* to challenge the inaccuracies of the movie portrayal:

> A third scene shows me speaking to my female wife, Carmen, on the telephone. (The actress who portrays her in the movie is an ugly and greasy looking women [sic] with a big mouth, when in real life my wife is beautiful and very loving wife.) . . . I did not like the horrible way they tried to make her the blame or the scapegoat for everything that happened, especially because of the Gay aspects involved. . . . [it] inferred that I left her and winded up in the arms of a Gay man because of her. This is completely untrue, and I feel sorry for the actress for having to play such a horrible role. . . . I did not think it [the movie] was funny because it was about me and my loved ones. I felt the movie was in essence a piece of garbage. It did not show the whole truth, and the little it did show was constantly twisted and distorted. So it left you, the viewer with so many unanswered questions. . . . But Hollywood wants to make money, and if sacrificing the truth or exploiting the lives of real people is the way to make money, then that's what they do. I feel deeply hurt by the movie.

Abuse of women by bisexual men is also a common theme for many filmmakers. To imply that all married men who enjoy sex with other men must hate their wives, or are using their wives for concealment, simply perpetuates an entrenched biphobic stereotype and misogyny. Married bisexual men are portrayed as wife beaters in *The Leather Boys* (1964), *Petulia* (1968), *American Gigolo* (1980), *Blue Velvet* (1986), and *Total Eclipse* (1995). Michael Caine kills his wife in *Deathtrap* (1982), as does Peter Weller in *Naked Lunch* (1992). The bisexual husband in *Michael's Death* (1984) bites his wife's genitals so hard that she must be hospitalized. In the Italian film *Investigation of a Citizen Above Suspicion* (1970), a bisexual police homicide inspector goes so far as to murder his mistress so that he will be a hero for 'solving' the case.

According to Vicari (2011), negative plotlines still figure even when some of the bisexual characters are "good bisexuals." The good bisexual/bad bisexual trope figures in films such as *The Mysteries of Pittsburgh* (2008) where the "bad bisexual" boyfriend suicides. In Ozon's *Waterdrops on Burning Rocks (*2000), middle-aged business man Leopold has brought the teenage Franz back to his apartment. Franz is the good bisexual—sincere, loving and sensitive—while Leopold is the bad bisexual—misogynist, manipulative, predatory, patriarchal and self-centered. His ex-partner Vera had a sex-change to try and maintain his interest; and the young woman Anna, who wanted to marry the "good bisexual" Franz and have children, gets seduced by Leopold into abandoning her dreams. It is as if everyone becomes Leopold's creatures and creations, losing their idealism and innocence. Indeed, suicide is the good bisexual Franz's only way out and the final certification of the fact that he's more human than the other characters. *Criminal Lovers* (1999), also by Ozon, involves bisexual Luke and his girlfriend Alice murdering an Arab student. Only in the last moments of the film is a sense of bisexual love finally rested free from "a thicket of depravity and perversion and even so, this love is . . . blood stained and doomed" (Vicari, 2011: 94). Again, the film cannot present a happy ending for the bisexual protagonist:

> Luke's cruelest fate is to be used by the larger agency of repressive society to punish both his female and male lovers. Throughout the film Luke has been searching for his masculinity . . . But he does not actually find his masculine self until the very end in the helpless pain of losing both partners . . . Indeed the revelation of his bisexuality is finally the failure of even bisexual inclusiveness to protect a man from loneliness, punishment and death (Vicari, 2011: 99).

As already presented, *Brokeback Mountain* received tremendous international publicity in 2005. There was an outpour of public sympathy for the men whose lives were complicated by living lies throughout their marriages because of the social taboos of the time. Many queer theorists believe the two male leads in *Brokeback Mountain* are arguably bisexual, not gay (e.g., Bryant, 2011). Others were highly critical of the bias of the film:

> After watching *Brokeback Mountain* at a movie theatre I felt sick to my stomach. Everyone was talking about the poor guys who had to hide their sexuality. What about the loving wives who are left behind to pick up the pieces of the family and try to make sense of it all. What about the loneliness and isolation of the women who are devastated by the unexpected loss of their trust and the lives they thought they had. . . . It seems like the media until very recently has been skipping over the plight of straight wives because it is not sensational or alluring or sexy. We are often ignored, yet must overcome great adversity and despair. . . .I am one of the women who the media left behind (Cram, 2008:11)

More balanced or ordinary love stories in positive filmic representations have appeared recently (Lambert, 2011), as will be discussed further in Chapter 17. What is of significance is how many of these films are not US-or UK-made. *Habana Muda* (2012) is a documentary about Chino, a deaf man struggling to raise two children with his wife in Cuba. All of the couple's financial troubles could soon disappear because Chino has a well-off boyfriend, Jose, in Mexico. Jose, who works for a Deaf organization, visits Chino and teaches him Mexican sign language. When the documentary begins, the plan has already been hatched and everyone is on board, but soon enough, the viewer is led to wonder if this unique arrangement can ever really work out. A film called *3* (2010) has a high-profile couple gradually forming a relationship with a stranger, culminating in a pregnancy and positive reconfiguration of family. A portrayal of powerful possibilities and win/win situations where bisexuality in marriage is acknowledged and affirmed is very evident in two of Ferzan Ozpetek's films, *Steam* (1997) and *The Ignorant Fairies* (2001). What is absent from Ozpetek's films and so many other representations of married bisexual men with both male and female partners is seeing these bi-poly relationships as flourishing, with the absence of death and crisis as tropes.

TV talk shows have discovered that bisexuality is "a sexy topic" (Rust, 1996b: 129). Far from educating the public however, these shows mainly reinforce stereotypes:

> Actually, I shrieked in horror a couple of weeks ago. I was watching that stupid "Beauty and the Beast" on TV. Someone wrote in about their bisexual boyfriend. And they absolutely slaughtered them. "Oh, you silly, they're disease spreading pigs, bisexuals are the most selfish people in the world." . . . in five minutes, the ignorant masses that watch this bloody show and who get all of their opinions, it's such a load of bloody crap. (Rosemary)

> Shows like "Neighbors" and "Home and Away," any of the serials that are watched by a large audience of families and young people. They've got the opportunity to show open communication, because if it's on the television it can be so easily then brought up in a home at the same time, by parents or by kids. . . . I mean, they're there for entertainment and not education, but they provide a fantastic avenue. Yeah, I think it's just getting it on commercial stations (Luna).

We finally saw a positive representation of a bisexual man, Captain Jack Harkness, on a television series avidly watched by young people, *Torchwood* (2006–2011). Time-travelling Jack, played by John Barrowman, first appears in *Doctor Who* as a con man and matures into a hero. In the final episode, he kisses both the Doctor and his assistant Rose when he leaves. Indeed, in his first appearance in the episode, *The Empty Child* (2005), the Doctor suggests that Jack's sexual orientation is more common in the fifty-first century, when humanity will deal with multiple alien species and become more sexually flexible. The labels "pansexual" and "omnisexual" are also frequently applied to him. In *Torchwood*, Captain Jack is romantically interested in his team's policewoman, Gwen, as well as having a long-term loving and sexual relationship with his employee Ianto Jones. One episode also recalls his marriage in a different era. Thus, his sexuality is a given, "matter-of-fact," not to be problematized or interrogated. Indeed, Captain Jack refers to the sexual orientation classifications of the twentieth and twenty-first centuries as "quaint" (Jensen, 2007; Channel4.com's LGB Teens Health Site, 2007). What makes *Torchwood* important is that it fits with what Hills described as the "non-agenda agenda" of showrunner Russell T. Davies, whereby queer identities are made unremarkable and textually incidental rather than an "issue."

However, there have been criticisms of bisexual representations in *Torchwood*. Amy-Chinn, for example, acknowledges it is "a breakthrough show" but there are important ways in which

> it compromises its radical credentials: from the outset, bisexuality is cast as 'alien,' and as the program moves from the narrowcast channel BBC Three to mainstream BBC One, the scope for characters to explore their bi potential is restricted, and normativity progressively reasserts its privileged position. In the end, the show bows to forces that mitigate against true visibility for non-normative sexualities (2012: 640).

Amy-Chinn (2012) points out that Jack's relationships with men tend to take place outside the normal time-space continuum while Jack's past relationships with women seem to take place within the framework of linear time. Equally significant is that Jack's relationships with men are presented as being short lived and/or casual, whereas his relationships with women have a much more emotional inflection and appear to be more permanent and committed, much more in keeping with the type of relationship that gains cultural approval. The episode, *Children of Earth,* not only reflects back on another of Jack's past relationships, but one through which he fathered a child, Alice. This reveals him to be a father and a grandfather, hurt by his estrangement from his mortal family:

> this secures him firmly into the heteronormative matrix and makes the sacrifice of his grandson to save the children of Earth all the more devastating and poignant, while reminding queer viewers of the impossibility of a securing a queer future through reproduction (2012: 73).

In terms of bisexuality in novels, Epstein writes, "I believe that there are two major types of reading that people do: we might read books to see ourselves reflected (i.e., mirror books) and we might also read books to see other selves (i.e., window books)" (2012: 287). In Lambert's anthology of bisexual short stories, she tries to avoid stereotypically manipulative and deceptive characters and plotlines: "I steered clear of stories that relied too heavily on infidelity or the surprise reveal of a same-sex attraction for their only sources of drama" (2014: 9). Recently, some writers are deliberately endeavoring to portray more positive representations of bisexual men:

My own new adult romance series, *Magic University*, features a bisexual hero as he makes his way through four years of college... Within the framework of romance and building on the pre-existing tropes of fantasy and the paranormal that lend themselves to sexual exploration outside the gender binary, ... Kyle's bi nature is crucial to the plot and to saving the human race... Elizabeth Schechter's steampunk romance *House of Sable Locks* was multiply nominated for many awards and features the rare bisexual hero paired with a female heroine.... Romance has a reputation as a hide-bound, restrictive genre, while science fiction's reputation is the opposite; rule-breaking and upsetting the status quo are supposedly in the genre's DNA. But perhaps like bisexuality itself, a kind of hybrid vigor results of a mix of the two. I plan to keep my eye on paranormal and futuristic queer romances in the hopes that a new hotbed of bisexual representation is about to flourish (Tan, 2015: unnumbered).

Many critics, like the women in our research, believe bisexual men in honest, open relationships are still rarely portrayed in print media (Antalfy, 2011):

> I've read some really terrible articles in women's magazines that perpetuate myths ... all this really strange language, the deviance kind of language.... I stopped reading them when I was about nineteen thank goodness. I needed to purge, you know. (Katie)

Kaitlin spoke about the dilemma some women faced when their partners wanted to be in the media talking about the issues:

> I felt very vulnerable and very diminished, sounds a silly word, because when Ross came out, I went in, because he was so upfront striving for justice for gay and lesbian and bisexual people in the church, and some of that went into the newspaper.... his name was in print and he was on television one night, and I was so upset for his family, because I thought here he is, doing all of this and they're going to find out in the most inappropriate ways, and he just didn't care.... He needed to be public, I needed to be intensely private, and so we had arguments from time to time. (Kaitlin)

The vast majority of mainstream articles that mention polyamory, for example, are actually focused on infidelity/cheating and consider polyamory an extension of the idea of "getting some on the side" (Antalfy, 2011: 2–3). Titillating articles tend to portray polyamory as something more salacious, forbidden or desirable than it actually is in order to present the reader with voyeurism. Antalfy (2011) concludes that as the polyamory movement continues to develop, so too will its media representation.

> It's just so frustrating that of all the people that he probably interviewed for that article [on MOREs], that he couldn't have found some people who were

happy and well-adjusted and didn't seem sort of tawdry and pathetic and shallow . . . I think books and websites are a great thing. Because it's such a private thing reading them. I mean, you can take them and read it in the loo. . . . and to be able to learn, to have other people's lives available in texts when you can't access them in your life. (Ava)

A *Good Weekend* magazine article, inserted into *The Age* (2008), had the usual depiction of married gay and bisexual men, as well as gendernormative depictions of the type of women in these relationships. The headline reads: "Fairytale marriage" (2008: 39), followed by the topic sentence: "The perfect couple, beautiful kids, the picket fence, it's the dreamy existence until the wife finds out that it's all based on a lie" (2008: 39). When this article was published, letters from readers were published, including some from women who had experienced this scenario. Interestingly, however, the letters that Sara and I wrote about our research findings, Sara's work with the Women with Bisexual Partners Network, and from some of the women in our research who had negotiated strong and ongoing relationships with bisexual husbands, were not published. We were all left asking why positive examples were still being ignored in mainstream reports.

A similar situation arose in 2004 when Glenn Vassallo and other men from the Australian Bisexual Network were asked by a journalist to assist in the preparation of an article for a women's magazine. Again, as Glenn wrote at the time to many of us working in this area:

> The issue did not include any of my quotes, and instead spun the article into a doom and gloom story. . . In true journalistic style she [the journalist] ignores the local statistics and studies I provided her . . . I'm getting pretty damn pissed off with the double standard that being a bi man is bad, while [the same women's magazine and another one] had a pretty positive article about bi women not so long ago.

Several bisexual men responded to Glenn's e-mail such as the following:

> I now wish that this person had interviewed my wife and myself to see how a happily married man with three aware kids and a boyfriend manages with bisexuality. We are not bad people.

> There are well-known Australian women who are in that situation right now and they're not going to speak out because of the amount of crap that they're going to get (Sara).

Sara's point is very significant given the occasional news item about well-known Australian men who are openly bisexual, or who are outed as bisexual by the media. Of renowned dance choreographer and dance company director, Graeme Murphy, and his long-term relationship with dancer Janet Vernon, journalist Jones wrote:

> It really is a terrific love story, albeit an unconventional one that has been punctuated by other relationships. . . . In a 1998 interview Murphy was quoted as saying, "I know people like to speculate about my sexuality but that doesn't really worry me. You wouldn't exactly have to be Sigmund Freud to work out my history. It's all there in the past 20 years of my choreography" (2000:17).

Benzie (2002) wrote about Jackie Weaver and her relationship with the writer Richard Wherrett who later died of HIV/AIDS. On Wherrett's list of eight great loves, Weaver was the only woman. She says:

> I knew he had affairs with men as well and I just fell in love with him. . . . He didn't have boyfriends while we were together or anything. I mean, whether if we had stayed together longer that would have been the case, who knows. . . . I lived with him for the last month of his life (in Benzie, 2002: unnumbered).

Olympic gold medalist jockey from New Zealand, Mark Todd, found his bisexuality publicized in the media when he was caught having sex with another man and allegations of drug use were made against him (Burney 2000). Todd is quoted in the newspapers as saying he's not gay, he just likes sex with men, and likes being married to his children's mother. What is significant is Burney's disparaging commentary about Todd's statements, calling him "irresponsible," "careless," "untrustworthy," abusing heterosexual privilege for his public gain as well as abusing the gay scene for his personal gratification.

South Australian politician Mark Brindal, 57, was outed by *The Advertiser* (see Bevin, 2005; Bildstein, 2005a; 2005b; Larkin, 2005) after having sex with a 24-year-old man in his office, who then proceeded to seek financial compensation when the relationship ended. He discussed how his wife of 9 years, Pam Bennett, and his four adult stepchildren knew about his bisexuality and rather than it being the cause of any potential divorce, his wife stated, "Compensation? That's bloody outrageous. What, are you expected to compensate a person because you are no longer having an affair with him. . . If you ever pay that man one cent then you have lost your marriage." A committed Christian, Mr. Brindal said,

> I don't need to be ashamed, I don't need to hide. . . you make wrong choices because your choices are limited, or, in fact you allow yourself because you are

vulnerable to be able to be blackmailed or any other sleazebag effort that comes along, and that's not right (Bildstein, 2005a).

Larkin (2005) reported that Mr. Brindal used his announcement to launch a fierce attack on homophobic elements in his Liberal party and threatened to expose other state MPs' secrets:

> if my personal life has been fair game I really don't see why anybody else's shouldn't be. That includes serial womanizing, drinking, gambling debts, many, many things. If I get one hint of hypocrisy from anyone in that place . . . I might just tell the truth about other things (see also Bevin, 2005).

As he proceeded to tell Bildstein (2005a), and what resounds so strongly with the women in this research:

> I'm not contemplating that I can go off and do anything I like and she [Pam, his wife] sits home while I do. But we need to determine what is appropriate for me and what is fair to Pam. . . . It will be about making sacrifices, compromises and choices.

MP David Campbell was filmed leaving a gay sex sauna in Sydney using a concealed camera. What is significant in this situation, unlike Brindal's 5 years earlier, is how the media began a fiery debate not about his sexuality but about the mix of hypocrisy and homophobia accompanied by a new low in so-called journalistic standards:

> The Channel Seven newsroom has split this morning over the ethics of . . . [the] icky scoop exposing transport minister David Campbell's "double life" as a bisexual man. . . . The minister's private life had been an open secret in state government and media circles for years (Crook, 2010: page unnumbered; see also Jones, Kamper and Haynes, 2010).

Hosie writes:

> We're also assuming his wife didn't know, when maybe she did. They wouldn't be the first couple in politics or out of it to have a particular arrangement around this stuff- but that's hardly the kind of arrangement you can explain to the general public (2010: 11).

Mr. Campbell married his wife of 33 years when he was just 19 and only last week he had been telling colleagues of his relief that her cancer was in remission. The gay sex sauna that Mr. Campbell was filmed leaving refused to comment to the media. Sources said its patrons are usually older men from suburbs across Sydney. Llama asked:

Why did he lead a double life? . . . Because fuckwits like Peter Meakin continue to treat sexuality as 'scandal', instead of allowing their stories to be useful and help change public perception that might allow people to come out, they go for the ratings and the sensationalism pretending it's in the public interest (2010: page unnumbered).

Wheatley's (2000) article about the politician Neal Blewett and the artist Robert Brain, both in their 60s, reflects on their relationship from their meeting in 1952 at university in Hobart, having an affair, doing military service together, and then splitting when Brain decided to travel overseas. Blewett went on to become the Minister for Health in Australia, as well as marrying Jill. As Brain explains:

> He was in Adelaide, married with children, monogamous and stable with a serious career. I was living a promiscuous and lascivious life in an old monastery in Tuscany and running an opera festival.. . . Neither of us understood the other's life, I think.

It was only after Jill's death that Brian made contact again:

> Ten years ago I'd lost both my Italian partner and my best woman friend and was looking I suppose for a new life. I was staying in Bondi when I heard on the radio that Jill Blewett had died. I wrote to Neal a letter of commiseration and then after about six months he came to see me. Neal's children were grown up and he was extremely lonely. I was the sort of person he needed, nestbuilding, domestic, this womanly thing I've got. He could provide what I wanted, loyalty and stability.

A former South Australian Premier, Don Dunstan, was bisexual and this is finally discussed in the biography by Hodge:

> Dunstan's life surpassed the sexual identity politics that dominated thinking in the twentieth century. . . [he wanted to] love freely, negotiate honestly, and embrace passion's boundless opportunities. He was wily in resisting categorization but, had Dunstan been receptive to the suggestion of any label, it would be more accurate to say that he was a willing polyamorist (2014: 304).

What is significant, as it is for many in our research, is how these sexualities and relationships were lived without having access to or wanting to attach labels and discourses such as "polyamory":

> Dunstan's social democratic and libertarian philosophy in his public life, augmented with the bisexual polyamory of his personal life, never sat comfortably with Gay Liberation but anticipated Queer by several decades (Hodge, 2014: 312).

I was honored to be asked to launch the book in June 2014. I emphasized how much even the cover of the book reflected Hodge's efforts to interweave and yet allow for the multiplicity/intricacy and beyondness of Dunstan, and uphold his lived self/selves that could not be contained, constrained, fixed and manageably classified. Media reviews began to also consider Dunstan's multiplicity rather than singularizing him: "In the context of the times Dunstan's private life was a mystery for a married man with three children who left the family home, married a much younger Asian woman, Adele Koh, and spent his last decade in a gay relationship with Cheng, an Asian science graduate" (Debelle, 2013: 8). Steven Cheng said Dunstan had not tried to hide his bisexuality. He was comfortable with who he was but refrained from talking about it publically as it would be a distraction from what he said (Shepherd, 2013). Ruth Starke, who is also writing a personal biography about Dunstan, explains:

> Dunstan's trajectory is not a straightforward story of a gay man repressed by the times, who finally comes out. . . . In fact Dunstan's heterosexual affairs in the 1970s were more passionate than his homosexual affairs . . . I think it was a complex sexuality that really flowered after his separation from Gretel (Debelle, 2013: 8).

A letter that Dunstan wrote in 1990 to one of his lovers, "Tony," who asked him what he thought of wanting to marry a woman, reveals Dunstan's positions on MOREs:

> Of course you may make a marriage agreement which rules out any homosexual behavior on your part for the future . . . .But the pressures which you will inevitably suffer sticking to such an agreement will put very heavy strains on you and create an emotional situation within the marriage partnership which will strain it severely. Now that all that is said, I know of two cases of men from the Australian Ballet who from adolescence led active lives as homosexuals . . . .Sometime afterwards, both of these men . . . married women dancers who were also leaving the stage. The past was fully known to all. They have formed very stable and happy marriages . . . .So it is possible to do as you propose. All will depend on your natures, tolerance, and understanding (Dunstan, 1991a, b).

An article about the famous Australian artist, Margaret Olley, in the *Good Weekend* (Hawley, 2005) documents her love affairs with both bisexual and heterosexual men, and her one lesbian experience. Particularly in relation to bisexual theatre director, interior designer and ice skater Sam Hughes, she says, "Sam was bisexual, but that didn't worry me. I take things as they are" (Hawley, 2005: 25). Olley would reach her fifties before Hughes, her longest lover and 15 years her senior, finally moved in with her. They lived together in Paddington for a decade until he died from cancer. "Sam was the only one I let move in with me and it was marvelous because he would go off for a month at a time to Europe and do his own thing and then I'd join him" (Hawley, 2005: 25).

CONCLUSION

This chapter has shown the importance of broadening limited sociocultural heteronormative discursive frameworks within which MORES are either rendered invisible or misrepresented, and/or within which they find themselves lacking agency and control. Foucault (1977) uses the panopticon model as symbolic of the power of social ascription. Women with bisexual male partners are particularly aware of how their multiple realities are subjected to the panopticonic gaze. Hierarchical, continuous, and functional surveillance, as felt by all participants and their partners in this research, is organized as multiple, automatic, and anonymous power. "It is the fact of being constantly seen, of being able always to be seen, that maintains the disciplined individual in his subjection" (Rabinow, 1984: 199). As was evident in this chapter, this leads to their scripting performances of normativity, finding the "ready-made code and having to accommodate oneself to it" (Trinh, 1991: 136; see also Richardson, 1985). Nevertheless, we also saw that in the face of "oppressive and unfair" systems, passing may at times be more effective than protesting because the former may enable the passer to "meet his[/her] personal aspiration in the here and now" (Kroeger, 2003: 132).

In his later work, Foucault (1988) elaborated a notion of situated agency. As many of the women, their partners and families in our research show, situated agency means the self must "grasp the points where change is possible and desirable, and to determine the precise form this change should take" (Foucault, 1984: 46). Foucault's notion of situated agency acknowledges that even critical skills and practices of resistance are themselves socially produced and constrained by cultural discourses (see also Pallotta-Chiarolli & Pease, 2014). As introduced at the beginning of this chapter, this dilemma is discussed by Ahmed as how to find queer happiness within the unhappiness of a heteroworld:

> A queer lover might not be able to cause happiness for her beloved if her beloved cannot bear being rejected by the straight world. . . . To be happily queer might mean being happy to be the cause of unhappiness . . . as well as to be happy with where we get to if we go beyond the straight lines of happiness scripts (2010: 100).

As Brant's character realizes: "It dawned on him then. He felt complete. At odds with the world maybe, but complete" (2006: 61).

Ultimately, some women look back and wish that they had spoken out earlier and broken through the panopticonic forces imposing silence and pathologization in heteroworld: "I feel I've been duped, keeping up appearances. I just wanted the world to know" (Jeannette). Other women acknowledge the difficulties of the present sociocultural contexts but contextualize contemporary discriminations by either looking back to more accepting historical times, or forward to a time when bisexuality will be fully supported:

> We went out and had coffee and we were sitting there and I was holding Corey's hand and Martin's hand and we were just all talking and the people at the table next to us sort of did this huge double take and stood up to go and Martin was in hysterics, . . . I think we're benefiting from the fact that we've had the women's liberation and the sexual liberation movement, and bisexuality is kind of lagging behind but it's the next wave. . . but then in ancient Rome and Greece and places like that it was just expected, it was like nothing weird about it. (Jacinta)

Other women decide to be completely open, to pollute, as a form of overcoming their experiences with their partners, and feeling like what has happened to them is not something to be ashamed of, or as Rosemary explains, not something to romanticize but rather see as ordinary:

> The homophobic comments I hear everywhere around me. About Jack, about others, on the street. I fight it on every level, because I think to myself, even if they just walk away and before they say something so derogatory or something so homophobic to the next person, they might think, "Well, shit, I might get shot down in flames like I just was." . . .I have also had a lot of positive feedback. I don't know why they're saying, "Good on you" as if it's a heroic or brave or romantic kind of thing. Obviously I get a trillion and one comparisons to whatever movie is out at the time. "It's just like your life, isn't it?" I think people sort of get a few romantic ideas about it, a bit of a trail blazer. . . . And you get the usual, "Oh, your relationship is so creative" and it's sort of like, "Well, no, some of us are as boring as piss." (Rosemary)

Despite potential stigmatization and discrimination, insights and understandings do come from refusing to pass or passively self-police in response to panopticonic policing in heteroworld. The research participants in this study positioned themselves on the borders of heteroworld and as we shall see in the next chapter, homoworld. From these sites they could see the instability of social categories, their temporal and spatial shifts and fluctuations, where contradictory either/or discourses overlap, or where discrepant kinds of meaning-making converge in both/and manner.

> Walking bare-footed on multiply de/re-territorialized land . . . where she confronts and leaves off at the same time a world of named nooks and corners, of street signs and traffic regulations, of beaten paths and multiple masks, of constant intermeshing with other bodies—that are also her own—needs, assumptions, prejudices and limits (Trinh, 1991: 334–335).

Chapter 13

"Ewww, Girl Germs"
Women's Experiences and Perceptions of Homonormativity

It's like gays go "ewww, girl germs." (Leanne)

In the previous chapter, we discussed women's experiences with the heteronormative world. In this chapter, we will focus on what women said about gay and lesbian communities. As has already been discussed, many women, whether they were heterosexual, lesbian, or bisexual, spoke about how their relationships placed them and their bisexual male partners on the borders of the homosexual world/"gay community" and its criteria for belonging. Homonormativity is complicit in "compulsory monosexuality," the ideological institutional privileging of either heterosexuality or homosexuality; and in compulsory monogamy as "providing the engine toward and enforcement of mono-sexuality" (Phellas & Coxon in Phellas, 2012: 21). While the common assumption is that bisexual men exploit their ability to claim heterosexual privilege, Solot & Miller (2001) found that bisexual people in MOREs were more likely to have an awareness of their "heterosexual privilege" than many heterosexual-identified people, and sometimes chose not to get married because of this. Some said that they might rethink their decision to marry if same-sex marriage were legalized. Others did get married and maintained their bisexual visibility as a means of breaking down heteronormative norms. However, the researchers also found that too many married bisexuals fade from the gay community, no longer feeling the need to fight biphobia and homophobia, and "even check the 'heterosexual' box on forms ('I'm monogamous,' they say, 'so my sexual orientation doesn't really matter to anyone')" (2001: 85). Solot & Miller (2001) do not discuss, however, the extent to which exclusion or marginalization from gay and lesbian communities lead to the person in an opposite-sex relationship crossing over and assimilating to "the other side."

375

The film *Together Alone* (1991) consisted of dialogue, sometimes heated, between two men who have just had sex, one of whom blatantly states he is a bisexual man with a wife and children: "It's not a black and white world. You have to allow for greys. . . not everyone who has sex with a man is gay." The gay man replies, "You're making me into an object if you say you're bisexual, a blow-up doll." In his discussion of the film's reviews, Potoczniak (2007) notes that no commentary within the gay media used the word "bisexual," despite the obvious bisexual material. He sees this as indicative of the gay male community continuing to "hold tenaciously to the dichotomous, monosexual, and essentialist nature of sexual orientation" (2007: 125; see also Brown, 2002). As Bashford wrote: "When homophobia ceases to exist among our enemies, queers will perfect it for decades to come" (1993: 67). Already discussed is *Brokeback Mountain* (2005), a film in which the characters have been defined as "closeted gay men," or gay cowboys, and is about the tragedy and pain experienced by these men due to homophobia (Roughton, 2014: 83). Could they not be closeted bisexual men who, together with their wives, experience the tragedy and pain of biphobia? In *Cock* (Bartlett, 2013), the bisexual John is challenged to claim a straight or gay identity by both his long-term male lover and the woman he is falling in love with. His male partner says:

> Most people seem to come together pretty well, their atoms hold. . . but you, you don't seem to have grown coherently. You're a collection of things that don't amount. You're a sprawl (2013: 30).

John tries to explain how coming out at university as gay was a kind of seduction as it meant he "was part of a scene":

> everyone said the real me was emerging, that I'd been repressed, and so I thought I must've done the right thing then, but it didn't feel like that to me. I had to make more of an effort than before (2013: 96).

This "homosexualization" (Dowsett, 1997) is linked to the desire to retain "the immutability defense" which bisexuals apparently threaten, even though bisexuality and immutability are not necessarily inconsistent: there could "be four immutable categories—immutable heterosexuality, immutable homosexuality, immutable bisexuality, and immutable asexuality" (Yoshino, 2000: 405). Goffman (1963) uses the phrase "concern with in-group purification" to describe the efforts of stigmatized persons to "normify" their own conduct and also clean up the conduct of borderdwellers in the group. For example, as discussed in chapter 1, bisexuality and MOREs problematize mainstream gay and lesbian strategic use of two arguments: first, the assimilationist argument to 'seduce' or 'tame' the dominant heteroworld with the 'we are just like you' or 'we will be just like you, not a threat to you' position, as seen in the same-sex marriage debates; and second, the argument of distinction and boundary maintenance that states that gays and lesbians are so distinct from heterosexuals there is no danger of 'messing' or 'blurring' the segregationist boundary between them. Thus, there will apparently be no infiltration and pollution of the heterosexual side by deceptive and untrustworthy bisexuals, and no reaping of heterosexual privilege by bisexuals who still wish to claim marginality alongside gays and lesbians.

> We would go out partying and all of a sudden they [gay guys] would have that desire [for me as a woman]. I know that Gennaro particularly when he had that cute image of a young gay boy a lot of women who identified as lesbian and were actually really quite negative about bisexuals propositioned him and his famous response very publicly yelling loudly in a bar was "Until you identify as bisexual I'm not pulling my dick out" [laughing]. (Lizz)

Bennett et al. (1989) found that fewer than one-quarter of the bisexual men in their research identified with or participated actively in aspects of organized gay culture. Many pursued a rather clandestine or secretive bisexual identity where the quick and anonymous opportunities for homosexual contact at public toilets and other beats denied them the development of intimate ongoing relationships with gay men. In the 1990s, Ochs (1996) noted that some gay men may be uncomfortable with bisexuality because of the fear that they are themselves bisexual, which would create the possibility of having to go through the pain of a second "coming out" process (see also McLean, 2008). More recently, Goetstouwers (2006) found bisexual men appear to be seen by gay men as a challenge to their sense of security and fixity, of boundary and delineation, in regard to their own sexual identification and culture. The Pew Research Centre (2013) survey found gay men (72%) had higher community engagement than bisexuals (33%) in a variety of LGBT-specific activities, such as attending Gay Pride events, rallies, marches or being a member of an LGBT organization. And more recently still, a UK study fund the highest levels of biphobia were experienced within the LGBT community and health services (Rankin et al, 2015).

In the late 1990s, I came across some very concerning and disconcerting reactions from members of the gay and lesbian communities in Australia in relation to bisexuality (see Pallotta-Chiarolli, 2011). With shock, sadness and disillusionment, I witnessed and had to navigate my way through a situation of "hegemonic gayness" (Dowsett, 1997) when bisexuals and transgendered persons, who also 'mess up' sex-gender dualities, were rejected as members of the Sydney Gay and Lesbian Mardi Gras. Applicants who indicated they were bisexual on their Mardi Gras application forms had to "state succinctly what special factors might persuade the board that [they] should be admitted." Reynolds stated that this act of discrimination indicated how

> bisexuals remain second class sexual citizens in one of the world's most important celebrations of sexual diversity. Yes a bisexual could always just tick the gay and lesbian membership box if they want to, as one proponent of the proposal suggested. But think about it, gays and lesbians have struggled for decades to win visibility and acceptance for our desires and identities. Are we really prepared to ask bisexuals to forego theirs? (2000: 12).

While the debates and discriminations were occurring, my mestizaje border zone became a site of conflicting identifications, allegiances and memberships. In my personal and professional life, I was researching, teaching and actively campaigning against homophobia and endorsing the importance of cultural events such as the Mardi Gras. Simultaneously, I was personally and professionally linked with bisexual communities around Australia and was declaring my work to be about sexual diversity and inclusivity rather than the construction of new sexual hierarchies. And yet, here I was working and associating with otherwise outstanding gay and lesbian leaders who were ousting bisexual members from the leading national queer cultural organization. Thus, for a few years, I experienced and negotiated the tensions and contestations around me, ensuring that I maintained my border status by critiquing and supporting the various groups I was affiliated with, and enduring their mixtures of criticism and support of me and my work. This entailed working and associating closely with some of the major critics of such a regulatory biphobic/transphobic admission system. As Reynolds stated, it was important to repeatedly "debunk the bisexual peril" myth (2000: 12). As was satirized and sensationalized in the following gossip column in a gay community newspaper in Australia:

> GOSSIP this week is first with the latest news of the ongoing outbreak of Het C (Heterosexual Coupling) in our community... A current and a former Board member of Mardi Gras, of *opposite gender,* are the most high profile coupling so far spotted, but they are just the tip of an unfortunate iceberg (GOSSIP, 1996: 12).

A few years later, due to the effective campaigning of bisexual, transgender and other organizations, bisexual and transgender applicants were "admitted" again. Indeed, by the thirtieth anniversary of the Mardi Gras in 2008, celebrating its evolution from a protest march resulting in police aggression and many arrests, to a major cultural, political and international tourist event replete with police marching bands, the bisexual Korean-American comedian, Margaret Cho, led the parade with the honor of "Chief of Parade." In the same year, Sydney bisexual drag queen Cindy Pastel (aka Ritchie Fingers) on whom the Australian film *Priscilla, Queen of the Desert* (1994) was based (see chapter 4), retired from performing (Watson, 2008). Pastel explained in an Australian gay newspaper interview:

> The Priscilla thing didn't really work in my favor . . . after it came out to the world that I was bisexual. . . It's time now to pull away from the scene because I just don't feel like I fit in (Lamont, 2008: 5).

Hence, in this specific intersection of art and life, it appears that art presented the border possibilities for the character Tick that were not available to Cindy Pastel in real life. Instead, the filmic portrayal and publicity of this reconciliation of multiple worlds of a bisexual father/drag queen at the queer border problematized his border reality as a bisexual father/drag queen in the real "homoworld" of inner Sydney.

In this chapter, the following themes presented by the women in our research will be discussed:

1. *Negativity, biphobia and misogyny from gay men and gay communities* towards women in relationships with otherwise 'really' gay men; and towards their male partners due to their being in a relationship with a woman.
2. *Negativity, biphobia and misandry from lesbians and lesbian communities* towards women in relationships with bisexual men and towards their male partners.
3. *The positive relationships with gay and lesbian communities and the creation of queer rather than gay and lesbian spaces* wherein sexual diversity rather than sexual dichotomy were acknowledged and affirmed.

"THE POOR LITTLE WOMAN WHO HAS NO IDEA"

> I hate the way my bisexual partner is put down by some gay men, and the way some gay men think I don't know about his bisexuality, and so they paint this picture of the poor little woman who has no idea. . . When we got together, I went from being a nice girl to being the slut and the fag hag, "Oh is this why you got involved with the gay community? To convert a gay guy?" All that kind of crap. We went through some pretty tough times. (Naomi)

Many women related experiences and perceptions of negativity, biphobia and misogyny from gay men and communities who believed their partners would be gay if not for the women's interference; and towards their male partners due to their being in a relationship with a woman. This supports the findings of previous research by Buxton (2007) who identified that gay friends disparaged marriage to women as an external negative force that affected otherwise 'really' gay men. As Julz writes:

> my own lover has dated some gay men who have treated me, and my relationship with him, with scorn and derision. Fortunately, these guys get voted off the island quickly now. . . . Some gay men can be mean about considering women partners a "phase" they are eager to help our fellas get over. . . . Some guys seem happier interacting with closeted cheaters with unknowing wives at home . . . I have a lot of complicated feelings about my lover's difficulty finding boyfriends. . . . that I'm the barrier to his ability to meet other boys. . . And ironically, gay men often say that they feel *they* will never be able to compete with a woman for a bi man's affections (2005: 219).

This issue of competition felt by gay men needs to be considered as it highlights homonormative reactions to heteronormative power, wherein gay male partners and friends are reluctant to be 'second best' or 'inferior' to the prime heterorelationship pedestalled by heteroprivilege:

> My partner lost half his gay friends when he came out as bi after falling in love with me. . . . He would like a more long term relationship with a man, but when he tries to set that up, as soon as he mentions that I'm in the picture, it gets problematic for gay men. (Naomi)

> You're seen as fence sitters. You're seen as you've got all of the rights and privileges of being het because you look like it—especially people like me and my partner, because we have a child, we're married, we've got all of the white Anglo Saxon heterosexual privileges, supposedly. (Kirsten)

The question of what comes first, either negativity and inferiorization towards bisexual men and their female partners from gay men and their community, or negativity and inferiorization from bisexual men and their female partners towards gay men and their community, seems to have proponents on either side of this debate. For example, Simpson (2006) denounces gay men for their negativity toward bisexual men:

> when they're not eagerly cruising bisexual men in laybys, saunas and chatrooms, are too often keen to denounce the "dishonesty" and "double lives" and "repression" of bisexual men—because they have the temerity to not be just like them, and instead lead "normal" lives that happen to include a discreet, "deviant" sideline, rather than order their lives and their wardrobe around their deviation. . . . Another, perhaps more elitist gay response to male bisexuality

is to insist that men are not "really" bisexual unless they take it up the arse; this seems to me to be a peculiar requirement. . . . Many homosexual men are exclusively active; are they not "really" homo?

Bradford (2004) found that members of the gay community may think a bisexual person cannot be trusted to commit to a relationship. They might wish for their partners to claim lesbian or gay identity to signify commitment. Common erroneous assumptions are that all bisexual people need both male and female partners to be satisfied or that, given the choice, they would prefer the privileged status of other-sex relationships, and can neatly avoid the difficulties associated with same-sex attractions by "going straight" (Cashore & Tuason, 2009; Rust, 1995; Udis-Kessler, 1996).

Many women in our research discussed the queries and assumptions gay men made towards their partners about their relationships with women:

Alice: He got stronger in standing up to these gay activist types who couldn't figure out why he didn't leave me and lead what they called a "normal" gay life.

Paul: Come to think of it, that word "normal" gets used by everyone to knock someone else.

Some women also discussed when they had felt disrespected, and shown a lack of concern or compassion by gay men if they had experienced emotional and sexual trauma with bisexual partners: "what he has done to our lives is unforgivable and the gays he's with don't care"(Lizette).

Michael: I was a monitor in a gay chat-room and it took me a good eight months to get the guys to stop bi-bashing. . .

Sharae: Initially when Michael put me around to all his chat rooms, I had a lot of guys message me and say, "Well, you've lost your husband already. Why are you pursuing this?" and I was battering back saying, "No, my relationship is very solid, thank you very much." They'd say, "There's no such thing as bisexual. He's gay, he's suppressing it," and I said, "No, he enjoys sex with me, thank you very much and he can get a hard on with me, that's not a problem."

We [Rachel, her partner and his boyfriend] all went to Mardi Gras together. We had dressed similarly to a theme and were obviously three people together. His friends saw that and no doubt told him in no uncertain terms that it was a crazy situation to be in. After that, for a while, my husband was turned off the scene. He'd been hurt. . . . I'd always supported the gay scene however I was very hurt and I did become almost anti-gay for a while. I felt quite betrayed because every time my husband got into a friendship with any gay man, they would try to drive a wedge between me and him. . . . we were on holiday once in a small town, drinking in a bar, and a gay guy just came straight over and starting chatting to my husband, wanting him to leave with him, completely ignoring me. Give me a break! They don't respect any relationship boundaries at all and that really started to piss me off, because I've always been so accepting of them, and instead got a major slap in the face for it. (Rachel)

Jack said quite recently they [gay friends at the gay organization he volunteers at] all wanted to know what the deal was, and they said, "Oh, does she know?" and he goes, "Well, yeah. I am allowed to have a boyfriend if that's what I would like" and they give him that sort of condescending look, "Oh, yeah, you wait and see if you try it, that's just what she says." That attitude really annoys me, because no one knows my mind like I do and I don't like people assuming that they do. (Rosemary)

On the other side of the debate, research has found that some bisexual men are negative and discriminatory toward the gay community or "lifestyle," thereby seeming to support the assumption that bisexual men only use gay men and the gay community for sex but are not committed or loyal to it. For example, Whitney (1990) found that 26% of the men admitted they might prefer to be with a man but they could not tolerate what was perceived to be the "gay lifestyle" (see also Leavitt, 2006). Dodge et al. (2012) found that several men expressed feeling uneasy around men they describe as "stereotypically gay" or men who acted feminine (see also Dodge et al. 2008). Steeped in her usual gay/straight homophobic thinking, Kaye also believes that the

> gay world wasn't something they could identify with—it was a bunch of freaks who blatantly bragged to the outside world that they were proud of this fluke of nature. It lacked sincerity, commitment and depth. Everything was focused on one thing—sex. . . . The straight lifestyle offered him a security blanket. A loving wife, adorable children, respectability, stability (2000: 150).

As discussed in chapter 3, there were some women in our research who commented on how their husbands altered their styles to ways considered "gay" or signified belonging to gay culture: "it's all competitive out there in the gay scene. . . . your money has to go towards that scene. Drugs are involved. That's why he let go of me cause he couldn't live two lives" (Pat).

Many women in our research talked about experiencing discrimination when undertaking simple activities such as going out to a gay venue or volunteering in gay community services and activism. For some women, these regular occurrences created animosity towards the gay community:

> To get into a nightclub, [me and my male partner] get, "Do you know that this is a gay and lesbian night?" and oh, it's like the cat claws were coming out. It's like, "Fuck man, you guys criticize us for not accepting you. What the fuck are you doing to us?" And I walked out. And they go, "Fuck you, too." . . . So,

I'm in a mixed world at the moment, very outside in my community . . . we went to another gay night club and like, oh, God, we couldn't touch each other. We were frustrated. Everyone was staring at us. . . . I thought come on, this is ridiculous. . . . they're hypocrites in a way, fuckin' gays. (Temptress)

I sensed from them, you know, what's a straight woman doing here. And I can understand that the spaces that I was entering into with Joe were queer spaces, and I didn't identify as queer, yet I was in a relationship that is quite queer, you know. . . . [For example], because of my background in dance performance, I decided to volunteer and perform in one of those [gay events]. I felt like I wanted to somehow support, encourage, get enthusiastic, embrace, all of those things, by performing in this dance performance, and a lot of the women in that group had very binary understandings of sexuality, gay/straight. I was thinking at the time, as a straight woman I don't experience homophobia. But, I did feel that I was in a relationship that was affected by all the homophobia. (Katie)

We are just too queer for the queer . . .I mean there's Adam, thinking he'd found a comfortable, respected, and quite popular place in the gay community paradise, when I came along, turned him upside down, shook him up, and when he was on his feet again, he was rearranged, like patchwork, seeing and feeling the realities of his suppressed desires for the first time. . . .It makes me sick cos I know the other truths in the gay community. Like the well-known community activist, classified gay, who's in a secret relationship with a well-known community writer, classified lesbian. Away from the gay parliament, they have been meeting for years to write politics, to plan community events, and to fuck. They're like Romeo and Juliet from the houses of Gay and Lesbian, dynasties which will cautiously and politely do business together to ensure their province is under control and thriving. But there is to be no sexual liaison, no romantic love that will tarnish and disrupt these very corporate structures. And I know a well-known writer who tells me he's really bisexual but his books wouldn't sell so he's a "public gay man, closeted bisexual." He told me how one of the big boys in gayristocracy heard I was attending an event and screeched out, "Well, if she's coming, we'd better leave our boyfriends home!" (Lilith)

I worked in the gay media early in my career and more of my friends were gay than straight and it's [heterosexuality] never been an issue. How come I got to be part of this community when I'm straight and now I'm not allowed to be part of this community when the man I'm with is bi? (Monica)

Other women were aware of 'othering' in gay spaces, not through marginalization but exoticization: "I've been to gay clubs and they flock around you, because you're this sort of odd person. . . .you're this wife" (Steph).
What often made situations worse was if their partners also became complicit in ignoring or disrespecting them within gay spaces and with gay men:

we were having a cup of coffee at a coffee shop. And one of Ben's gay lovers was there. He was like a semi-regular bonk [laughing], fuck buddy, and he treated me really badly, and I got really upset about this and I got really upset with Ben. It was like, well, to use an old-fashioned phrase, he's dishonored me, and Ben didn't really see how I could be as offended as I was. Ben still wanted to continue his relationship with this guy, with no problems. We had screaming rows about it . . . so Ben doesn't see him anymore. (Joanne)

Suresha (2013) conducted research with national US queer organizations that "demand equality for everyone" to find out if they are themselves paying attention to the particular needs of "bisexual folks, not merely as lip service, not just as an afterthought, but in any sort of tangible way." The communications contacts for these organizations were given a month to reply by phone or e-mail to questions on "Eight Metrics of Bisexual Representation and Leadership." He noted that none of the 10 national organizations he surveyed include the word "bisexual" or even the letter "B" in its name, and that "there is nobody devoted specifically to bisexual issues or bisexual advocacy in these groups." Suresha's (2013) findings resonate with many women who experienced awkwardness, indifference or lack of understanding and resources from gay organizations:

> From the gay community it's like, "Oh, he's confused" and how hard it was for him and because it's not to be seen as gay bashing or anything like that, I had no permission to say, "Well, he's just a bastard." If I was in that situation again I would not access anything to do with the gay community. (Kristina)

It was also significant how, by not adopting the label of lesbian, the bisexual women in our research shared their partner's experience of ostracism and marginalization from the gay organizations:

> The flag wavers, you're going to do your cause more damage than good because don't start pigeon-holing us again. . . I was looking at role models and saying that's not me [lesbian], I don't want to be like that, and hey they're throwing the baby out with the bath water [because] I am not lesbian, hey, where do I fit? Oh, I don't. (Annette)

> I have to admit I am starting to resent that [hatred from the gay community] a little bit. At first I just tolerated it because I thought OK here's a community that suffers a lot and they have a right to vent a bit of spleen and then I thought bugger it I suffer a bit too and I really don't want to have someone else venting their spleen at me when I consider them to be part of my community. . . . it's this kind of hierarchy of picking on people. (Lizz)

> I explicitly stood up at the Gay and Lesbian Rights Lobby, during a discussion and said, "Okay, so I'm walking down the street with my boyfriend and his boyfriend

and we're bashed up by a gay person because we're bi, would you protect us?" and they said, "No." (Rose)

Luna found that being HIV positive had made it easier for her partner to find his place in the gay world: "I think he feels more protected and accepted now in gay type of communities, through his HIV status, and that's good. . . . he's sort of found friends" (Luna).

A few women also felt that bisexual people should respect gay boundaries: "they get enough shit in straightworld and don't want images of it in their faces in their spaces" (Lilith).

> To come out as gay you have to completely leap the fence and it would be profoundly irritating having taken that risk, particularly the older ones who have really suffered through persecution, and then to have these people who look to them like they're trying to have it both ways or get what they can. . . . Why would bisexual people get heated up about joining? We all form our own group. (Jacinta)

Kristina described the reasons why her partner was disliked in the gay community and how this was less to do with his bisexuality but more about his exploitation of younger men:

> He went to South America and found a boyfriend who was a refugee who had just turned eighteen. He sponsored him to come back and it was him going out with this strange, exotic thing on his arm. Six months' later he's bored shitless and he just ups, goes overseas and leaves this poor kid who he's completely isolated. . . . This kid was made totally dependent. So the gay community actually looked after him, like, took him in and supported him. (Kristina)

Hudson (2013) found that there is limited research on gay long-term lovers of bisexual men. Personal narratives do surface on occasion (M. Jones, 2007; Schleicher, 2006). Two novels which have looked at the perspective of a gay man being in a relationship with a bisexual man are *Insignificant Others* by McAuley (2010) and *We Think the World of You* by Ackerley (1960), the latter being made into a film of the same name. In McAuley's novel, the gay partner has a "high opinion of Benjamin's wife, Giselle, and their two kids. The lot of them had become familiar and dear to me, like characters in a play who are frequently mentioned but never appear onstage" (2010: 6). Indeed, Benjamin's good looks and attention to his appearance are attributed to his being married even if it also caused other health concerns:

> He laid the blame for all of his vanity, the curly locks, the longish hair, the pubic trimming-on his wife. Married men always did. All in all, he showed fewer

signs of aging than I thought he should by right, considering the messy tangles and contradictions he lived with. True, he suffered from ulcers, occasional panic attacks, and a nervous tic in his right eye that some times got so bad I had to cup my hand over it until it quieted down. But what decent person in his situation wouldn't show a variety of neurotic symptoms? Despite the multiple deceptions, Benjamin was an exceptionally decent person (2010: 7).

Indeed, the narrator explains why he prefers married men:

Having been well trained by their wives, they're almost always clean and polite. The vast majority are sexually submissive and hugely appreciative of getting on the side what they can't get at home... On the whole, they're obedient, they get regular checkups, and they never call after business hours (2010: 10–11).

He also states that having been together for three years, he has come to think of Benjamin as his husband, although he is aware of the straight-husband world Benjamin does live in as very separate from his:

He was, after all, *a* husband, and in some way that was heartfelt but also, I realize, entirely ridiculous, I saw it as my responsibility to protect his marriage from a barrage of outside threats and bad influences. It was the only way I could justify sleeping with him, and it wasn't an easy job. . . .There was the whole cushy, boring infrastructure of Benjamin's suburban life to preserve—the pointlessly large house, the cars, the dog, his wife's horse, the after-school activities, and the Christmas decorations. In my most deluded moments, I thought of myself as a distant, benevolent relative to whom his family had never been introduced (2010: 9–10).

By the end of the novel, however, Benajmin does leave his wife and they connect, although we are not told if he then "turns gay."

The issue of protection of a married bisexual lover, Johnny, and his beloved dog is also a strong theme in Ackerley's (1960) novel. This protection does not willingly extend to Johnny's wife however, who he marries while he is in a relationship with the gay protagonist, Frank. She is seen as a threat and a manipulator who is aware of Johnny's male partner and indeed exploits his desire to financially and otherwise support the man he loves. For example, when Johnny goes to prison after a drunken fight, he asks Frank to take care of his family:

"Johnny! You're *not* going to ask me to help that disgusting woman of yours! . . . She means trouble for me and always has . . ."

"She's jealous, that's where it is," said Johnny, blowing his nose. "She can't 'elp it. . . . She's expectin'." . . .

"What, again!" This would be the fourth. "I thought you weren't going to have any more?"

"We wasn't. *But* you know 'ow these things 'appen." Then he burst into tears. . . ." We owes some back rent. Who knows what'll 'appen."

". . . I'll see you don't lose your home. And I'll go and talk to your mother, . . . I expect we can fix things up between us" . . .I kissed him. ". . .But whatever I do, Johnny," I said as I got up to go, "I do for you. I wouldn't cross the road to help that tart of yours." . . .

"Megan's sorry for what she done, Frank," he [Johnny] said, fixing upon me his beautiful luminous gaze. "She says she won't never open your letters no more or stop me coming to see you. And I've told 'er I'm going away with you for your 'olidays when this lot's over. . . She thinks the world of you now." (1960: 5–11, 17).

The holiday never eventuates and as Frank says to Millie, Johnny's Mum, "He ought to take away from her and give to me. . . It's all give and no get" (1960: 50–51).

Earlier in the novel, the reader finds out that Johnny's parents know of the relationship and indeed also show strong affection for Frank, as well as financially exploit him:

"Why on earth did he marry her?" I continued bitterly [to Johnny's mother]. "I warned him not to and he always said he wasn't such a mug. Everything was perfectly all right when he was just living with her and the twins in Chatham, and coming up to stay with me or you as he pleased. He belonged to us all then. But as soon as Dickie was on the way she got working on him, and he was too weak to stand up to her," (1960: 12).

To which Tom, Johnny's Mum's partner replies: "Well, she's 'is wife for better nor worse. . . and you can't come between man and wife" (1960: 31).

The bisexual man's gay partner has also appeared in film expressing betrayal, anger or jealousy. In *The Dying Gaul* (2005), Robert complains about his relationship with Geoffrey, "I think he's just using me for sensation because his marriage has gotten stale," an inaccurate assumption. In *Leaving Metropolis* (2002), after his closest friend dies of AIDS, David recognizes the instability of his own position as a gay man in love with a man who will sacrifice him at any time in order to maintain his own straight image. At a gay bath house, David has visions of dead gay men arising, and he begins to feel that "sleeping with a straight man is a betrayal of homosexuality itself" (Vicari, 2011: 152).

A powerful Peruvian film, *Undertow* (2009), has a gay lover of a bisexual married man as both a literal and metaphoric undertow of secret same-sex attraction. Miguel is portrayed as a good husband and father, and integral to the social and religious life of his small fishing community. After Santiago drowns, he appears to Miguel as a ghost, symbolic of his secret invisible love. Indeed, Miguel tries to prevent the drowned body from being found so that he can have the life with Santiago he would have wanted with both his strong and beautiful wife and his gay partner. For example, there are scenes of the two men walking hand-in-hand along the main street of the village, and the three of them sitting at home on one sofa watching television. Eventually, the body is discovered and heralds the disclosure/discovery of Miguel's past relationship with him. Miguel decides he must be strong and give Santiago the public and traditional religious burial at sea that he deserves, at the cost of possibly losing his wife, his child and the respect of the village. At the burial rituals, we do see some people, including some young men, come forward to participate and offer support, indicating there will be future acceptance of same-sex relationships in the village as Santiago had always wanted.

"I USED TO THINK IT WAS A LOAD OF RUBBISH THAT LESBIANS WERE MEN HATERS"

I used to think it was a load of rubbish that lesbians were men haters, and they are. "Why do you want a man? All it is is trouble, when you can use things like vibrators." It's just real derogatory things that they say against men. (Lesley)

Several women, particularly bisexual women, talked about the negativity, biphobia and misandry from lesbians and lesbian communities towards them and their male partners: "there certainly is a lot of prejudice in the lesbian community against women who sleep with the enemy and just can't make it all the way into true women loving" (Ava). The following is an example of a lesbian separatist coercive stance on bisexuality: "Our disbelief in bisexuality works to women's advantage ... [because it] ensures their inclusion in the lesbian subculture" (Murphy, 1990: 88). Stein (1997) coined the term "coming out, again" to describe the practice of lesbians relinquishing this identity and subsequently having to "come out" with a bisexual identity. While fleeting sexual encounters with men were tolerated, ongoing sexual involvements and emotional attachments were considered especially problematic. McLean's (2008) lesbian participants who had any attractions to or sexual encounters with men felt that this threatened their sense of identity and place in the lesbian community. They often felt like "traitors" and were concerned about being seen as untrustworthy. Using words like "100 per cent," "complete" and "total" to describe a lesbian, they clearly articulated a language that essentialized lesbian identity as fixed and unchanging (2008: 309). As a result, they changed their identities from lesbian to bisexual, lesbian to heterosexual or from lesbian to 'fluid' in order to find new spaces of belonging where they could express their desires [for men] without guilt or shame (2008: 311).

While Martin argues that rigid categorization in lesbian communities is a response to the need for stability and operates as a "defense against the continued marginalization, denial and prohibition of women's love and desire for other women" (1996: 103), it is clear that within this imagined lesbian community described by many women, these boundaries had significant impacts on bisexual women's sense of belonging:

> I've had really bad lesbian community responses... there was a call that went out for inclusion in a lesbian art thing. And I wanted to be involved, and everyone went around the circle and introduced themselves, and I said, "I'm a bi woman" and they ended up having to vote as to whether I was allowed to participate, and they ended up voting no because I would infect their art with bisexual images. They didn't understand that I was not there to make images about men. (Rose)

These issues were particularly pertinent for women who did identify as lesbian or for whom this was their first relationship with a man, and they wanted to maintain their belonging in the lesbian community:

> I've basically been socializing in the lesbian community, so it's quite a big thing for me to start this relationship with a man. . . . I was part of the Lesbian Reading Group and I resigned from it when I had a conversation with the woman who oversees it. I found that she was asking questions that didn't really see my partner as kind of a whole person. . . . things that kind of depersonalized him... some of the more lesbian separatist feminists, and some of the essentialist feminist notions of somehow women being better than men, I don't buy into any of that at all. (Jude)

> I'm not wanting to go to them [lesbian community] and say, "Oh, by the way, now I've got a bi male partner." . . . I'm aware of the potential damage, and that's interesting because when I lived in the women's community, all feminist lesbians, like Dykesville, and it didn't bother me at all then [when they made comments against men, and women sleeping with men]. . . . You know it's like a pack thing they get into. . . . if I left my partner, I would never have to take this shit so just because I want to be with him, I've got this whole shitty world, and I resent that enormously. . . .but it's not just the sexuality. That's just about women being mean. I'm so disappointed women are so lacking. (Raven)

> I know that opportunities were made for me to be a lesbian spokesperson at times, because, you know, young, funky dyke—yep, she'd be a great

person for this, let's get her to do it. . . . I guess they get disappointed, not in you, but disappointed for the community. They feel like it's a bit of a genocide. . . . worried about losing members, yeah. . . . I feel really, really comfortable in a dyke scene and really normal but I also feel like, it's so weird, when I sit down with lesbians now, and then I start talking about my boyfriend, I always feel like sometimes I've got to explain the subtext, because I don't want them to assume that I'm straight, automatically, which they do. (Sascha)

"I'VE DEVELOPED WIDER CIRCLES OF FRIENDS, A LOT OF THEM QUEER IDENTIFYING"

I've developed wider circles of friends, a lot of them queer identifying and it's a lot more comfortable place to be. There's an alternative queer scene which is not based on what you look like, and how much money you have, and your sexual label. So I'm much more interested in being part of that community than some sort of wealthy white conforming community. (Katie)

Some women described positive and supportive relationships with gays and lesbians. Even those women with difficult experiences within the wider gay and lesbian communities could identify and acknowledge supportive subgroups of gay and lesbian friends:

I have a couple of lesbian friends who I have remained in very close contact with. . . . in the evening, might spend three or four hours just dissecting the world and/or my relationship, if there's a problem, if I'm lonely. (Jolene)

We have friends over and there are gay men and there are bi and there are straight, . . . We all sit out there and clown around and carry on, and I'm usually the brunt of all their jokes, trying to send all the gay guys bi for the bi guys. You know, it's just a real big play around. (Lesley)

Mulick & Wright (2002) found that homosexual individuals may be more sensitive to the issues involved in discrimination due to the prejudices they face themselves: "We have found birds of a feather flock together" (Jenna). Their research also shows that many women partners of gay and bisexual men become politically active, particularly in the gay rights movement or the women's movement. As Lambert's (2010) *12 reasons why I love dating bi men* includes: "I don't have to leave the queer community to date him. Because he is already part of it."

Some women specifically talked about how getting reassurance and support from gay men was particularly consoling:

> They [gay friends] did say to me, "Look, it's not your issue, it's his issue, and this isn't your fault," and I guess I felt some support from that . . . knowing that they were gay, and they said it was quite normal, that [married men having sex with men] does happen. (Beth)

This support and reassurance was, for some women, based on a relationship of reciprocity with her partner's friends and lovers:

> If Edward got into trouble or any problems we had, I would go to our gay friends first before I'd go to family or straight friends. Because they're more understanding I think, and they're more genuine in their feelings. Edward will always introduce me to his friends if he really likes them. He'll bring them home. But often they won't come because they can't believe we get on so well. A lot of the young boys used to come home, Edward wouldn't be there, and they'd visit me to sit and talk because they couldn't talk to their parents. (Brenda)

There is a growing bisexual community, which participants in Rostosky et. al.'s research saw as "in contrast to the gay/lesbian and heterosexual communities. . . welcoming to people of all sexual orientations" (2010: 139). Some women in our research found the creation of queer community spaces, some of which they created themselves in their own homes, to be more affirming and celebratory of sexual diversity rather than sexual dichotomy. Glenn Vassallo (2002), at the Seventh International Bisexuality Conference in Sydney, spoke about how bisexual social spaces are a strong and inclusive border zone between repressed and exclusive polarities of "Homo and Hetero spaces." He provided Table 13.1:

Table 13.1 Glenn Vassallo's Table of the Inclusivity of Bisexual Spaces

In Hetero Spaces	In Bi Spaces	In Homo Spaces
Must explain and justify	No explanation, no justification	Must explain and justify
Exclusive	Inclusive	Exclusive
Invisible	Visible	Invisible
Behavior policed	Anything goes	Behavior policed
Monogamous with opposite-sex partners, or single	Mono, poly, single, with partners of any gender	Mono, poly with same-sex partners, single
Not belonging	It is ours and for all who love and support us	Not belonging

Of concern, however, are the number of bisexual people who believe there is a lack of such local bisexual specific community spaces and events (Rankin et al, 2015). Dodge et al. (2012) discuss how building a sense of community among a population that participants described as "invisible" or "unspoken" presents many challenges:

> Defining what a 'bisexual community' would look like, as well as conceptualizing building and evaluating community capacity, is particularly problematic... Because behaviorally bisexual men exist outside of a contained geographic region and are representative of a variety of social and personal characteristics, previous conceptualizations of community need to be explored to better address how to establish a bisexual community (2012: 1105).

And yet, couldn't this be the case for gay and lesbian communities: the diversity within?

> *Mike:* This is a really nice place that we go to once a month. It's a gay, bi, lesbian friendly place and they have a little bit of an amateur dance show. I got roped into doing a performance on stage. My little drag show. I went out to the toilet to get all the make up and everything off and this quite big guy came in and he was chatting with me. A big solid bloke, but he was also very feminine and he was straight, straight as. He said, "This is just the most wonderful place to come to, great atmosphere, lovely people," and he was there with his girlfriend....

> *Vicky:* Actually, I've had the most positive feedback from everybody at this place. We always have kisses and cuddles...

For behaviorally bisexual men, Dodge et al. (2012) found anonymous and confidential spaces could subdue fears of disclosure, violence and stigma while providing a space for these individuals to connect with similar others, as well as provide opportunities for delivering appropriate and relevant health-related services. For many married bisexual men, being on-line assists them to "develop a sense of community through receiving support from dozens of other men like themselves and no longer feel that their situation is unique" (Peterson, 2001: 195). They often create queer cyberspaces—"cyber-families," "cyberfriendships" and "virtual communities"—with other men (2001: 199).

CONCLUSION

As we have seen in this chapter, Probyn's term "outside belonging" (1996: 9) is applicable to the women in our research and their bisexual male partners who see themselves as 'outside' the dominant constructs of gay identity and gay community in Australia with its common marginalizing of MOREs, while simultaneously 'belonging' due to their partner's and sometimes their own same-sex attractions and relationships. "Border reinforcers" such as gay men who refuse to be in a relationship with a bisexual man are "interfacing with the borderland in their very refusal to interact with it... Individuals of all sexualities react to the sexual borderlands, by crossing them, inhabiting them, fortifying against them, or denying them" (Callis, 2014: 77). The "multiple within" realities of women in MOREs seeking a community for networking and support call for the following questions to be addressed: How do we use the word "community" without meaning homogeneity; and where and how are the boundaries of exclusion and inclusion of a community drawn (Martin & Pallotta-Chiarolli, 2009; Pallotta-Chiarolli & Martin, 2009)? How do we work with gay communities/services in order to construct spaces for women in MOREs to negotiate their multiple-within realities and decisions? How do we engage with the "bisexuality reaps heterosexual privilege" contention, and can such privilege be put to good use? As Angelides asks: "is it not conceivable that such privilege provides it with potentially subversive possibilities for the infiltration of the economy of (hetero)sexuality?" (1994: 42; see also Angelides, 2001). In our research, this subversive potential is very pertinent to many openly nonmonogamous bisexual men who construct publicly proclaimed families with opposite-sex partners, thereby infiltrating the "economy" of heterosexual families.

An area that did not appear in our research but requires further investigation and community engagement is what Dobinson et al. (2005) found: that rejection based on bisexuality can come from other bisexual people as well. Internalized biphobia may create additional challenges for bisexual people, as internalization of common negative attitudes about bisexuality may produce barriers to developing a positive bisexual self-identity, which in turn may influence confidence in and experiences of relationships, friendships and community (see also Israel & Mohr, 2004). Likewise, hierarchies within bisexual communities are constructed in response to external gay marginalization. For example, quantitative research conducted by Weinberg et al. (1994) revealed how attendance and allegiance to a bisexual community and being politically active led to the establishment of a new hierarchy within bisexual groups. Some bisexual activists position bisexuality as hierarchically superior to the "monosexualities" of gay and straight. For example, Weinberg et. al.'s (1994) respondents revealed a set of five basic understandings about the "true" nature of bisexuality: Everyone is basically bisexual; bisexuals have more options and avenues for sex; being bisexual means sexual freedom and flexibility; bisexual people are more open to personal growth; and sexual relations with both sexes means wholeness and completeness.

STSP paper w/ Mmm JU
↓
how does occult intersect w/ religion to shape h. outcomes btw black and GL adults?

Chapter 14

"The Priest Told Him to Marry Me and He'd Go Straight"

Bordering Religion and Spirituality in MOREs

I don't think he'd actually had sex [before our marriage] because the eyes of God were on him. . . . Oh, fucking Catholics, he hates Catholicism apparently, but it gets to you if you're a choir boy and your mother's had six kids and dad's a born and bred poofter basher. And I wonder what the fucking priests did to him. You can't confess it. Who could he tell? . . .basically before he got married, he went to a priest and the priest told him to marry me and he'd go straight. (Sylvia)

In this chapter, the impact of religious values and spirituality, and belonging to religious communities, will be explored. While some religious and spiritual belief systems are relatively neutral about diverse sexual orientations (e.g., Buddhism and Hinduism), others historically have been more condemnatory (e.g., Christianity, Judaism and Islam), with same-sex relationships seen to conflict with dogma regarding extramarital or nonmonogamous relationships. Even within religious traditions which have been historically disapproving of nonheterosexual orientations, there has been an emerging and growing theological paradigm in the past 30 years that accepts and supports diverse sexual orientations (American Psychological Association, 2011). However, to what extent these are accepting of MOREs is difficult to ascertain and has not been thoroughly explored. Toft (2012) discusses the ramifications of Christianity, specifically Anglicanism, perceiving bisexuals to be promiscuous. He quotes from the House of Bishops (2003):

If bisexual sexual activity involves simultaneous sexual relations with people of both sexes, then this would be the implied promiscuity or infidelity or both. Furthermore, bisexuals are seen as having a choice about their sexuality. . . If God's overall intention for human activity is that it should take place in the context of marriage with someone of the opposite sex, then clearly the church needs to encourage bisexual people who are capable of entering into such a relationship to do so (in Toft, 2012: 42).

These views of bisexuality construed by religious authorities were known by Christian bisexual research participants in Toft's research. They stated that homosexuality was "justified as God-given as is heterosexuality, leaving bisexuality as being seen to actively deny the choice to be heterosexual." This led them to separating their sexual and spiritual lives and "act" heterosexually within religious spheres, even though these strategies were "not ideal and created great inner conflict" (Toft, 2009: 84–85).

In their review, Rodriguez et al. (2013) found that scholars researching the religious and spiritual experiences of sexual minorities have focused nearly exclusively on the study of lesbian and gay individuals. Of the little research about bisexuals, the focus has primarily been on personal experiences and autobiographies such as in the poignant book *Blessed Bi Spirit* (Kolodny, 2006). In the biography of the bisexual Archbishop of New York, Paul Moore, his daughter recalls her mother's anger with the Church. She knew about his relationships with men, including some Church clergy, while she performed their heteromonogamist roles as a minister and his wife: "now, nearly spitting in anger at my father she [mother] had shouted, 'The church is just second rate', pounding the dining room table" (Moore, 2008: 287). Moore also recalls a time at the cathedral with her father "gesturing to include his body when he told me that he believed that sexuality and religious feeling came from the same place in the psyche. . . "There is no conflict . . ." my father had said that day" (Moore, 2008: 287–289). In her recollections, Moore comes to understand some of her father's actions before he left the office "as if the ritual of succession became tangled in the turbulence of his private life, as if forces long held in check had abruptly surged to life" (2008: 291). For example, he elected the first lesbian woman to the Episcopal Church and had an old teacher who had been removed for homosexuality reinstated as a priest. When he was outed, Moore recalls: "Although my father looked terrible and sad, he had no intention of leaving the priesthood. He would ride it out. . . . He had not exaggerated when he imagined the worst consequences of revealing the entirety of who he was" (2008: 297). She discusses her anger and, much later, her understanding why he had not talked about his sexuality in his autobiography, *Take a Bishop Like Me*:

> At the time I was disappointed in his lack of courage but after our conversation in Hartford I realized that perhaps I'd been asking too much of him. I could write what I wanted to, but I was from a different generation. I had no spouse or children and most important I did not have a public life as a religious leader.

But when I read the actual text in bound galleys . . . I was furious. Without disclosure of his own sexual secret, his description of my mother made her seem selfish and irrational. He did not admit to having been unfaithful, therefore it was inexplicable that she had banished him from their marriage bed. . . . How could he lay bare our mother's vulnerability without taking any responsibility for his part in the collapse of their marriage? . . . For years she had known of his sexual relationships with men but in pain herself and sensing his suffering had never confronted him (2008: 300).

The suffering which ensued due to the conflict between his intuitive understanding and Church doctrine allows Moore to engage with the multiplicity of her father's lifeworlds:

As my father lived his sexuality with men it certainly was something else, something that moved beneath the surface of the life he lived with his wives, with his children, with parishioners and colleagues. . . . forming his theology and his compassion. If my father had disclosed that existence to his wives and children he would have had to give up one life or the other, which is what eventually happened (2008: 326–327).

Indeed, after his death, she is contacted by Andrew Verver who had been his lover for over two decades and with whom he shared holidays and official ministerial trips. As part of deep discussions with which she is able to fill in some ambiguities in her father's life, he informs her he is now marrying a woman.

Toft (2009) discusses the either/or dilemmas bisexuals have to think about. Do they question traditional interpretations of the Bible, focus on the life-enhancing values of the church or the dogmatic rules? Do they dismiss the Church as the authority on the word of God who is seen to have created all sexualities as good, and deny the relevance of the Church to one's life? Do they selectively embrace only positive values from their religion, or erase religious frameworks from one's life as much as possible? The available research finds that bisexual individuals may experience privileges based on certain aspects of their identities and encounter oppression due to other characteristics and this complex relationship requires further exploration (Rodriguez et al. 2013). For example, a bisexual Christian in an other-sex relationship may experience more privilege than a bisexual Christian in a same-sex relationship, while both of these individuals may experience Christian privilege because they belong to the dominant religion in the Western world. Bisexual individuals may also differ in terms of the role that religion and spirituality play across the lifespan. Some of the specific findings in Rodriguez et al.'s (2013) research were: those who viewed bisexuality as a choice scored higher levels of religiosity/spirituality, and those who were older when they decided that they were bisexual were more likely to view religion as oppression. Those bisexual participants who were more open about their sexual orientation were less likely to attend church regularly, and those with a more liberal political view showed higher levels of spirituality, and were also more likely to have alternate religious beliefs.

Peterson (2001) found that spirituality, organized religion, and personal religious beliefs and experiences were the subject of frequent posts by bisexual men on Internet lists. Among the concerns commonly addressed are feelings of guilt and shame over their sexuality, the ramifications of coming out at church, and the process of finding a church, denomination, or denominational group (for example, Dignity for Roman Catholics, Integrity for Episcopalians, or More Light congregations for Presbyterians) that is supportive of bisexuality. Several pastors on these Internet lists shared sermons, hymns, poetry and other commentaries to assist subscribers in understanding themselves within a spiritual framework. Men also recommended and sometimes offered detailed reviews of religious and spiritual books to each other. In Whitney's (1990) research, 22% of the men listed moral values and religious beliefs as being the primary concern of their relationships. Included in this group were couples affiliated with religious institutions that considered homosexuality immoral and couples affiliated with religious institutions that considered sexual relations outside of marriage immoral. For the most part, those whose behaviors or desires were inconsistent with their belief systems were tremendously unhappy and at least two cases reported being suicidal. This conflict will be evident in some of the men in our research, including religious ministers.

The issue of religion has been prominent in discussions about DL African-American men. As Boykin writes,

> If you want one explanation as to why men are on the down low, look no further than our local churches. The church is the arbiter of moral decency in the black community ... In fact many of our churches have invented special ministries and campaigns simply to convert the homosexual men in their midst. ... We create them [DL men] with our condemnation of homosexuality. We create them with our insulting stereotypes and we certainly create them with the offensive words we use in our families, our communities, and our churches (2005: 154).

In relation to religious women in MOREs, Gochros (1989) found they face severe dilemmas around moral integrity. They took their marriage vows of forsaking all others, in sickness and in health, and till death do us part, very literally, although this did not necessarily prevent them from accepting their husband's extramarital activity, while making it difficult for them to consider extramarital sex an option for themselves. Less fundamentalist and nonreligious women were caught in similar moral dilemmas but framed these as questions of ethics rather than religion, where questions of right and wrong were based on personal decisions or the spirit rather than the letter of church doctrine. "For example, was there a moral, ethical difference between homosexual and heterosexual acts in defining infidelity?" (1989: 115). Atwood also found that women with strong religious backgrounds were the most likely to stay in marriages where husbands are bisexual: "They do not think in terms of choices, they think in terms of endurance. . . . Frequently these women turn to God for support and learn spiritual survival skills" (1998: 154). Buxton's (2006a) research also concurs with these findings. Some wives will condemn the sin but continue to love the sinner, some reconcile what their religion says with their own positive experience of being married to such an "evil person," while others discard dogmatic beliefs and work out their own moral position. They will then "stay quietly in their church or temple, choose another denomination or lose their faith entirely" (2006a: 56). For some women, having a bisexual husband was seen as punishment for not following Biblical teachings: "I married a man who lied to me and died from AIDS because I wasn't obedient to the word" (Lajoyce Brook Shire in the Foreword to Browder, 2005:11). Hernandez & Wilson (2007) also found that those who believe that only good things will happen to good people find it most difficult to cope, as is evident in the deeply religious African-American wife of a DL man in the film *Cover* (2008). She feels a deep anguish in having been betrayed by God as well as her husband, given she has been a good woman and wife and kept her faith. Such women describe a lifelong belief that God would prevent heartache if they live righteously, and they report praying earnestly before choosing to marry their husbands: "the women were confused about what they had previously interpreted as answers to their prayers or signs from God that they should get married. All of the women in this sample prayed that God would preserve their marriage and enable their husbands to love them and be happy as men" (Hernandez & Wilson, 2007: 192).

Discussing religion with women in our research revealed four major themes:

1. *the negative impact religion had on either/both the woman and her male partner*, particularly in relation to ignoring either or both of their sexualities, and the subsequent detrimental effect this had on their partner and relationship.
2. *the positive use of religion in supporting the couple* in working through their concerns.
3. *the differentiation made between problematic religion as dogma and rules, and spirituality as life-enhancing and liberating.*

4. *the absence or erasure of any religious or spiritual beliefs and values* as these were considered anathema to a healthy relationship, or as a response to past negative influences on the woman and/or her partner.

"IT WAS BAD, IT WAS A SIN, IT WAS WRONG"

> He came from a religious family and if there was any sort of conversation or television or any publicity centered around gay issues, he said the message he got quite clearly from his family was that it was bad, it was a sin, it was wrong. (Erin)

Many women directly attributed their partner's repressions about his sexuality to his religious upbringing and ongoing religious beliefs where same-sex attraction was condemned or silenced. This has been found in much previous research. For example, Higgins (2006) found that coming from a background of religious fundamentalism, particularly as proscribed by parents, may explain the high level of internalized homophobia at the time of marriage in previously married gay men, or in the case of our research, bisexual men, and may be a factor that contributed to the choice to marry a woman. Rodriguez (2009) and other researchers have identified several causes of conflict and anxiety between gay and religious identities which are applicable to bisexual identities. These causes are *"extrinsic,"* coming from outside of the individual and more dependent on acceptance by others, and *"intrinsic,"* coming from within the individual and generally held as internalized moral ideals. Some of the extrinsic causes are: strict adherence to established Christian tenets, usually those promoted by the conservative Christian religious right; acceptance of anti-gay Christian doctrine; acceptance of other gays' and lesbians' negative outlooks and experiences; and contradiction with the religious beliefs of family members and friends. Intrinsic causes include a fear of divine retribution and strong beliefs that their sexuality and spirituality are incompatible:

> A very strong Irish Catholic background, he went to a Catholic school, and it was very strict and everything was a sin, really, and then his parents believed the same, and they just really reinforced it, yes. . . . He had an uncle and a first cousin who were Brothers in the Catholic Church, and so the church was paramount in the family. (Loredana)

> He had that God stuff when he was a kid. The God stuff is still there. I think he's a bit embarrassed about it if anything, you know, that here is this logical, analytical guy, lawyer, scientist, writer, and it really bothers him that the big man in the sky is still such an issue for him in his emotional and sexual life. (Monica)

Antalfy (2011) analyzed many publications coming from a religious conservative angle, which describe polyamory and its connected sexualities as unacceptable on the grounds of morality, potential harm to traditional marriages and children, and in total opposition to what "true human nature" is supposed to represent. Anne discussed how belonging to an evangelical religion led to much repression of her own bisexual desires, as well as awareness of the hypocrisies when she was sexually abused by the clergy. This subsequently led to a sexually miserable marriage before finally finding her own way forward to her bisexuality and polyamorous relationship with Peter:

> I never actually fitted with that sense of evangelists, you know, go and convert the world and we're right and they're wrong. . . . I was a very committed Christian. Went to church every week, prayed, read the Bible. It was a major focus of my life up until I had a fairly drastic falling out with the church over being abused by a priest who was found to be abusing a number of other women. . . . Oh, it was absolutely the standard, straight down the line sex is only within marriage, and in fact I did not engage in actual physical intercourse—this is penis in vagina stuff—until I got married at the age of twenty-eight. Now, I think this is one of the stupidest things I ever did in my life, and I have grown a lot since then, and I was so pissed off that the sex in my marriage was so bad, because I thought I'd saved myself for this for so long. I masturbated, but I felt hideously guilty about it. . . . And, it [bisexuality] intrigued me because it totally went against everything I'd been taught. . . . it [bisexuality] was just something that got condemned, utterly condemned. . . . I also managed to repress my awareness of it [love for Peter] for long enough to get married to someone else. . . . We tried not seeing each other. We tried staying friends. We tried everything, everything, and it didn't work, and this [love between them] was so much more important and so much deeper than anything else. And the church had no idea how to deal with it. Its advice was to stop seeing each other. . . . I was already moving out of the church, anyway, dealing with the abuse. . . . and to say that God or the universe or some supreme all powerful person wanted that superficial, boring, uncommunicative, unhelpful, damaging marriage instead of this other, deep, loving, open, honest, intimate, caring relationship, it was just ridiculous. It didn't fit with my experience of God and the universe. The church taught me not to trust myself and that I was not trustworthy. Once I started trusting myself, I knew I never wanted to be in that situation again where somebody could hold over my head some arbitrary set of rules that had no relevance to my experience. (Anne)

As Anne's example reveals, women from religious backgrounds, whether they are wanting to understand their own and/or their partners' bisexuality

> have been taught by the church that "God is love," but love has not been demonstrated toward them. They have believed the church's teachings, but have been

damned by its leaders and members. Resentment over such prejudicial treatment usually drives the entire family out of the judgmental church (Grever, 2012: 77).

Particularly for straight partners who discover their partner's bisexuality after marrying them within fundamentalist frameworks, she is "the innocent bystander in the situation. She is again collateral damage" (Grever, 2012: 77). Hernandez & Wilson found that the women in their research often experienced disorientation: "The sense of order and predictability was now gone, as was their assumption of how God intervenes in people's lives" (2007: 191). Some women found they were given comfort if they presented themselves as victims "of a horrible and sinful hoax," but this comfort was removed if they endeavored to remain in friendships or relationships with their partners and accept this bisexuality. Women would often experience a sense of spiritual abandonment: "God, Where Are You?" (2007: 192). Indeed, watching their husbands also suffer spiritually had a profound impact on the spiritual lives of the wives.

For those women experiencing a difficult and abusive marriage with their bisexual partners, religious beliefs that created naivety in women and defined marriage as lifelong made it extremely problematic to leave:

> Growing up as being pretty naïve, not knowing what the real world was all about. . . .I married for better or worse and I think that's possibly why I stayed with him as long as I did. The abuse started basically as soon as I had my child. I did leave about two years into it, but I came back because my religious beliefs were that marriage was for keeps. (Lisa)

Felicity's husband was actually a church minister, and she believed the wedding was a performance of the heteromonogamist ideals the church expected of him:

> He's a priest in the Church of England . . . And somebody said to me after our wedding that it was "Ron's Production," and I didn't know what they meant, and of course our wedding was a huge sort of affair and I just thought yes, it's something about stating ideals. . . . I think it's the fact that possibly he went into the Church to hide. . . .it's [being a minister] a persona I suppose, and it keeps everything kinda controlled too. (Felicity)

Fay's partner was also a minister and she recounts how they used their roles as a minister and his wife, serving their congregation and maintaining a stable lifelong marriage, to avoid the hard questions about themselves:

> After our marriage, we were pastoring in a church that was probably one of the hardest, and having a heart for people who are hurting, I think we both just

shelved our own hurts and I put my energies into other people and at that stage I believed my commitment to the marriage was it's for richer or poorer, you just don't walk out. We took on this type of thinking that you do find in the church, that you sacrifice for other people and forget about how you feel yourself anyway so we never really faced up to what was happening in our marriage. Our house was always full of young people in trouble. And there was no way I could walk out on it, and I thought I just have to make the best of this . . . . I just wonder if Bill and I had been honest and been able to separate our life from the church, it would have given Bill a chance and me a chance. And we say this to one another now, "It's too late for us" . . . but when you're young and you do these things, you're idealistic. I've talked young Christian people out of trying to copy what we did. (Fay)

Other women acknowledged that both their partners and themselves were prohibited from exploring their sexualities by the religious frameworks within which they followed the heteronormative script of no premarital sex and then only 'vanilla' heterosex after marriage:

To me religion is very hypocritical. . . When we were together, the label I would have on us was probably very Catholic. You don't really do it [have sex] and we had a lot of hang-ups about it in those days. We were not imaginative in being who we were sexually. (Mary)

It's very hard to break away from the traditions that you were brought up with and I actually tried to conform and fit in with the religious family ways and it wasn't until I was much older that I actually started questioning things. In fact, it wasn't until after my divorce. . . . It was the Salvation Army and they're tolerant of homosexuality, but not practicing. I had a relationship, yeah, with another [female] soldier. . . . I actually decided that I would step down out of the uniform before I had that relationship, because I was starting to question my sexuality and . . .for my own peace of mind. I have been back to the corp a couple of times with this particular person, who was still in uniform and still practicing. And I know that she had a relationship with an officer. So it's certainly happening in the Salvation Army. (Nina)

Indeed, many women who previously felt comfortable within their religion and religious families and communities, now struggled when they found their bisexual partners were deemed unacceptable or unnatural:

I was breaking new ground [with my bisexual partner] and that's why I left the Catholic Church. I mean, I got so pissed off with it. All it came down to was a threatening bunch of white, middle-class ancient old men, celibate men at that, or supposedly celibate men, who don't know what it's like to be a young woman with kids in this sort of a situation, just to get a role model to connect with or empathize . . . I really wanted a blessing of the church upon my marriage and, quite frankly, the marriage I have now is not okay with the Catholic church. And I think I would have felt better or had a more peaceful transition if I'd realized that it was okay, that every relationship is different and it's not such a big deal after all. (Sherry)

Indeed, Fay struggled with her religious faith in realizing that both her partner and her son were ostracized from church due to their sexualities and subsequent mental health issues:

I've learnt to be angry with God. I sort of say to God, if you're God, why did he [son, Andrew] have to number one, inherit the gene of manic depression, and being gay? . . . I think the church can't practice what they preach. They say that they're all inclusive and that they will accept all people, but they don't, and I have it in two scenarios in my home with mental illness. We had to put a wall around Andrew and protect him from the church because his psychosis is reality to him but not to anyone else, and they were coming saying we want to pray with Andrew and cast out the demons. They would want to do the same with the gay issue. . . . It just broke my heart in the Mardi Gras last year to have these people with their banners saying that God condemned you to death and my understanding of God and the God of love and fairness who creates us all, has created gay, and it's a beautiful sensitive people of the world who are suffering, the bipolar and the gay. And, if you skim those people out of the world, you're left with a huge hole. . . . When Bill had his first mental breakdown, the pastor said to Bill, it's time that he shook himself and got out of his depression and loved his wife and got on with life. And with Andrew, thirty years down the track, I was having the same friends ringing me and saying how could Andrew be depressed when he's had such loving parents and such a home life as he's been brought up in. And so the church to me, thirty years down the track, hasn't caught up. (Fay)

"MY RELIGIOUS FAITH HAS SUSTAINED ME"

He agreed to chaperoned outings, a quick wedding conducted Greek style, and allowing our two daughters to be raised in the Greek Orthodox Church. . . . My religious faith has sustained me in knowing there is a reason for everything. I am now very ill and cannot leave my bed after battling cancer for two years and I know why God sent him to me. The love, devotion, and care he has given me is the answer. Knowing that when I die, the girls are in good hands. (Soulla)

There were some women in the research who drew upon their religious beliefs as sources of strength and support, such as Soulla (now deceased) who considered her happy marriage to Keith to be destined by God in order to care for her during her terminal illness and be a good father to her daughters. The work of Shallenberger (1996) in relation to gay and lesbian Christians highlighted three key issues also relevant to bisexuals on their continuing spiritual journeys: questioning their religious beliefs as they relate to their experiences as bisexuals or women in MOREs; reintegrating their religious identity with their bisexual or MORE identity by reading relevant literature, talking with loved ones, and identifying and approaching others grappling with the same issues; and reclaiming by seeking out safe spaces where they can reconnect and interweave their bisexual, MORE and religious identity in a community of supportive, like-minded individuals. Participants in Jefferies et al.'s research (2008) tended to use their religion or faith to manage the stress of negotiating intersecting identities, such as the psychological benefits that affirming religious or spiritual experiences may have for Black bisexual men, while others discussed the protection they received from God. Jeffries et al. conclude that, although further research is needed to examine the relationships between spirituality, coping and sexual orientation, spiritual coping is "perhaps a vital mediator of bisexual stigma and the internalization of it" (2008: 475). Toft found that bisexual Christians believe that Christianity "is about the promotion of good moral values and following the teachings of Jesus and the Gospels, rather than the Bible in general. . . [and] was a matter of personal reflection and meditation" (2009: 79). Indeed, Christianity was about "being in tune with oneself rather than being God-fearing or rigid about one's faith" and bisexuals were far stauncher in their rejection of authoritative structures such as attending weekly Mass than gay Christians (2009: 80).

As Yarhouse et al. (2003) state, only a few studies have explicitly looked into the role of faith and religion as a positive resource for women and their partners in MOREs. The research that does exist shows this often means weaving a tapestry that includes elements of organized religion with personal spiritual beliefs and rituals. For women in MOREs, religion is seen as "a transcendent power's intention in bringing them together" in both commitment to the marriage and sense of a higher power's "divine will in the couples' life together" (Yarhouse et al. 2003: 391). In their research, Hernandez & Wilson (2007) found many women read voraciously in order to support their observation that their husband's orientation was not a choice. Others joined another religious denomination that was more inclusive, while others tried to educate their congregations through writing and speaking. Thus, women must examine "church beliefs, rules, roles, and experimenting with new ways to interact with church members" in order to "experience spiritual and emotional growth" (2007: 192). Yarhouse et al. (2003) and Yarhouse & Seymore (2006) found many couples cited one of their many reasons for maintaining their marriage was to "obey God" in their commitment, or maintain their "covenant," and their religious faith was a significant source of support.

Religious activities, such as prayer, communal worship and social support from church members were also helpful coping resources.

In looking at the role of the black church for the African-American community, Boykin points out how the church has developed "a paradox or reputation as the most homophobic institution in the black community and also the most homo-tolerant" (2005: 264). He urges the church to continue the historical tradition and use of religion by African-Americans "for good in our community to fight against slavery and segregation . . . and to comfort those in need. . . . We know that religion should be used as a tool for love, not as a weapon of hate" (2005: 268). In their research with black bisexual men, Jeffries et al. (2008) found participants spoke of their religion in terms of "public expressions of faith (e.g. church attendance), and their experiences within a broader religious (primarily Christian) community that included family and community members as well as non-denominational religious groups (e.g. Christian clubs at school)" (2008: 467). Some regularly attended religious services while others were actively involved with their churches' music ministries. Jeffries et al.'s findings raise issues regarding the quality of life implications that religion has for bisexual men, and the need for these to be researched further:

(1) do bisexual men reap long-term health benefits through religious participation? (2) does religious participation buffer racial and socioeconomic marginalization for bisexual Black men?, and (3) how might bisexuality mediate social and psychological effects of religion upon well-being? (2008: 474).

For some women in our research, the church was the place where they met their partners and with whom they shared common religious interests:

I met Dean at the Presbyterian Fellowship . . . Oh, he's such a danger. And he's got the frock and the rings you know. . . he should be off to Rome [laughing]. . . . I think we were kind of kindred spirits. We got very involved with the church as far as, like, we ran the young dances every month. . . And we used to have coffee lounges where people brought various stuff and he used to sing and he also organized a theatre production in the church, which was quite innovative in those days, and the Sunday evening we went around the churches and did this kind of play. It was some kind of a controversial thing and we had projectors and lights and we just kind of came down the aisle, it was all very demanding and all very exciting at that time. (Hannah)

Some women also reported how they found solace in their religious beliefs, practices and communities when the relationship ended. Kaitlin, herself a minister, related the responses of fellow ministers and congregation members and how rituals were used to mark the change in her relationship with Ross:

part of what saved me in a way was every Sunday I had to leave to worship and preach, and every Saturday night and Sunday morning I thought, "I don't know how I can do this" and I told a team ministry member, "I'm not going to use you as the counsellor because it's very important for us, for boundaries, not to do that with each other, but I want you to keep an eye on me and tell me to take time out if you see I start to make bad decisions because I'm stressed," but that person who always had been pretty supportive of gay and lesbian justice issues, when it was up that close, couldn't cope. He didn't speak to me another time about it or how I was going for eighteen months. And, in the meantime, he was leading up a team that assessed somebody who was a candidate and who was lesbian, and he voted against her. . . . we had marriages all the time in that parish because of young families and doing weddings I found it so dreadful, but I did good weddings, and I never knew how. But some days I'd come there and I'd be around real strugglers, and I'd look at them, and I'd think, "Yeah, there's real therapy being with them, they're in the shit, and I'm in the shit, we're all in the shit together and we're trying to make sense of it as best we can.". . . Anyway, after we were divorced, we very much wanted to have a service and we ended up calling it "restoration at the end of a marriage." And it was just lovely. We had a lament and I wanted to use my tears from the box [I had collected]. So, I sprinkled the tears around the church, and I said, "I don't need them. It's tears now. I'm letting them go as water" because your tears are also refreshing. And then we had a big afternoon tea and it was just lovely. Some people brought gifts. So it was lament and reading and wonderful singing. We made promises to each other, . . . And the way it healed me doing marriages was, we have "As long as we both shall live" or "Till death us do part" was the old language and for me that was where I suddenly saw, no, we were not living in that relationship, and we were beginning to really die. And so that was a permission to separate and to be in a new kind of relationship. . . . The kids were there, yeah, they wanted to play music for us, Anne would play the trumpet and Nicholas played the French Horn and it was just great. A couple of real fundamentalists said, "Look, we don't believe in this, but we know you and we know Ross, so we'll have to think again." . . .When I went to my new parish, they had a morning tea for me the first Sunday and I had Ross and Anna and Nicholas up on the stage, and I just introduced them, you know, this was my husband, this is my great friend, Ross. So, we don't call each other ex's. We can't stand it. (Kaitlin)

Another research participant, Fay, whose husband was a minister, heard about Kaitlin and contacted her. She related how affirming it was hearing about Kaitlin's "service of separation":

They had a service of separation. A blessing service where they both had their friends and the folk from the parish went to it. . . . they cried in the service and they talked about the positives of the marriage and their love and respect for each other and of their new lives. They had like a divorce ceremony I suppose you'd call it and asking God to bless them. (Fay)

Kaitlin's experiences connect to Hernandez & Wilson's finding that it may be difficult to know how to explain their spouse's orientation to children in the context of religious beliefs about sexual expression, particularly if they have heard church leaders or peers disparage gay people: "Children can experience spiritual and emotional crises of their own, especially if they believe their parent will suffer eternal consequences" (2007: 190; see also Kaye, 2001). Also, with increasing openness and outspokenness in their religious communities can come problems for MOREs and their children. As Kaitlin and Ross became increasingly involved in publicly supporting gay rights and MOREs, fostered by their religious faith, negative repercussions were felt from within the Church:

> Oh, it was absolutely disgusting, some of what we tolerated when Ross was in the paper and on television news and when there was the Daring [Uniting Church GLBT] Conference, he was of course one of the organizers of it, very much upfront with that. And people then turned against the Uniting Church, were vitriolic, and we had phone call after phone call, crank, revolting calls and Ross never got any of them. I got them as a Uniting Church Minister and wife for not speaking out against gays. And, then, I had threats on the phone. It was just terrible. . . . I also had death threats against the kids, and, in fact, one guy was arrested. He came in the night and tried to knock through the window. I had Anna's friends sleeping in the lounge, and we had to have them crawling up the passage. "Keep down, flat." So I called the police but the guy across the road already had, because he could hear what was happening, this guy was threatening to shoot the kids. Oh, it was just shocking and it went on until I left the old parish. Mostly it had died down by the time I left, but still suddenly at two o'clock in the morning or in the middle of the night you'd suddenly get a call. Nicholas was great. He would just say, "Mum, put the phone down." He would just take it out of my hand and put the phone down. (Kaitlin)

Kaitlin also accessed the Metropolitan Gay and Lesbian Church but found her needs as a heterosexual woman were not always met:

> The Metropolitan Church were lovely, caring people. It's just that I thought, "They don't understand about my issues having to go through the question what's wrong with me that I fall in love with a man like him?" You know, all of this stereotype stuff that I had to work through before it could go. (Kaitlin)

This calls to mind Barker et al. (2012)'s statement that although there are community organizations for LGBT Muslims, Christians and Jewish people, there are few bisexual-specific groups and there may be low levels of bisexual awareness within such LGBT groups.

Other women such as Raven selectively rescued what was supportive and useful from their religions and discarded the rest:

The last question I had to resolve is was there a God or not, because if there was, there was something to the religion I'd been brought up with, and so I had to reconcile that with all the problems that came with that. . . . you can't tell people what to do. And it's interesting, that belief came very strongly from the religion that I was brought up in, The Christian Brethren. . . So you didn't have like a priest telling people what to do or having more power, and you'd all sit in a circle in the church for your Sunday worship and there wasn't supposed to be a leader. So I got the theory of the democratic approach, although the elders were all men and all that power play, gender roles. . . . I grew up with the oppression in that religious world, the total control they had over me, and yet at the same time the theory I learnt about freedom that didn't mix with that. So since then, I have tried really hard to create the world in my own image . . . They [religion] taught me participative democracy, equality, freedom. They didn't live it. (Raven)

For some women like Deanna, religious faith was strongly linked to culture rather than a set of rules and regulations:

Because I'm a Roman Catholic Italian down to the core, because if you're taught these things when you're a child, it formulates how you think as an adult, and so it's just not going to happen [discarding her religious background completely]. Like, it would be like asking a black person to become white. . . . So that was a big time for me when I was with a Jewish person. That really kind of made me realize that I'm very Catholic. . . . I'm against pretty much everything that the Catholic church proclaims to be, but I look at it more from a cultural point of view, like Italy is not Italy without the church. The church is not the church without the Italian community that sits around it. It's similar to Judaism in the sense, in the way that a lot of Jews identify themselves culturally as Jews, but not religiously as Jews. . . . It's huge to be brought up in an environment where the only thing you see is Christian iconography. Like, it's intense, and I am devoutly a religious person, but I don't follow that Catholic God. He's not real to me. (Deanna)

Some women reported how family members were relieved that, despite 'alternative' sexualities and lifestyles, they had maintained their religious faiths: "My mother's met my girlfriend. She thinks it's great that I'm seeing a Jewish girl, finally" (Rose). Fay related her and her partner's journey to maintain what mattered to them in their religious beliefs, to explore various religious communities and other beliefs, and establish a personal spiritual relationship with God:

My faith in God has not wavered. I've built up a relationship with God where I can be pretty angry with him and I remain pretty angry over some things. But, it's a living proper relationship with God I have, but I don't have any trust in the church. I've been hurt so much. I go to worship now to a church where I find total acceptance, but I wonder sometimes if I go because of my respect and love for Bill, for the want of a better word, and for my son, who's also gay, knowing that they're not accepted in the church. It does fulfill all my needs because the female minister follows a total feminist theology, and she's a broad leader in feminist theology. So most of the people at that church are either gay, lesbian, bisexual, or have mental illness, and it's beautiful fellowship of people, and there are heterosexual couples, who have been hurt by the church and who also worship and found their way there. . . . So Bill and I are still grappling with this whole issue of church, because if you take out your whole belief system in what you have for years believed in, you're left with a void. And probably ten years ago we lost everything, house, everything through the church and through shady dealings that the church dealt us. And so we've been fractured and torn apart if you like. . . . .for quite a few years we went nowhere near the church. . . . Bill's ministry fell in a heap. For him, that was a huge loss, and then he did his nurse training and he was the first male midwife in our state. And so the nuns at the hospital had a big influence on his life at that stage, which sort of had a big influence on my life, because we went back into ministry, in a Charismatic ministry, and that lasted probably two or three years, where our life was sort of turned around again, and we were back on this roller coaster, where I was in a position where I needed to believe in talking in tongues and if you believe, then this will happen and that will happen, and yet I couldn't see anything happening in my family situation. . . . Yet, now I go into somewhere like this church where it's all inclusive and you feel this wonderful warmth of acceptance. (Fay)

There were also women who had grown up without any religious faith but now found support in very structured religious settings. For example, Helena and her husband converted to Islam:

It was something just extraordinary, a sense of there being something in Islam, and to this day, along with my husband, I felt it was something to do with the structure in Islam. You know, that it was having come out of this sort of no discipline, no guidelines, no road maps, sixties childhood, there was something that gave me some guidelines. . . .I haven't got a problem [with homophobic stereotypes of Islam]. . . if you can't defend yourself politically, why would you bother. And I can see why there's a million things wrong with Islam. . . . but there's a connection there for me. (Helena)

Suzette found strength in Buddhist philosophies:

I read a lot of books on Buddhism and Eastern philosophy and I loved the philosophy very much. I was thinking, "That's exactly the way I think, and this is how I would like to live my life" and tried to adapt myself accordingly. That helped me, to not get upset about what other people think and say. (Suzette)

"MY SPIRITUALITY WAS MUCH BETTER EXPRESSED OUTSIDE OF THE CHURCH"

I found that my spirituality was much better expressed outside of the church. (Anne)

Several women clearly differentiated between religion as problematic heteropatriarchal institutions, dogma and rules, which they discarded or refused to consider, and spirituality as life-enhancing and liberating from heteropatriarchal monogamist dogma and rules:

> I would say some form of spiritual practice, a form of honoring, is completely essential. Honoring the mind and the body and the spirit I would say is very important; to incorporate your own chosen spiritual practice. So we might incorporate some tantric practices. People can create their own honoring, whether it's you light candles or you bring flowers into the center, have certain colors or fabrics that become a part of you. We have special things just for us that we don't incorporate with other people [we are in sexual relationships with].... I was in a leadership role in one of the biggest churches in Australia. So yeah, absolutely enormous change. I've come half a century through this life and I have a right to make my own choices and I'm probably more spiritual and more aware of God than I have ever been. I've come top, come dux in theology classes but now I would say I have permission to be who I am. (Simone)

These findings correlate to those of researchers such as Jeffries et al. (2008) who found that because many African-American nonheterosexuals including bisexuals have encountered condemnation from churches, they often esteem personal faith in God or a personal non-mainstream spirituality higher than the Bible or their religious institutions. Indeed, they believe spirituality may have considerable prominence given the psychosocial struggles bisexuals have due to rejection from heterosexuals and homosexuals. They often "evoked a naturalistic view of sexuality, one that presumed that sexual orientation was instilled by God at birth and, therefore, beyond their control" (2008: 470–471). Yip showed they also reinterpreted church teachings in light of their own sexualities:

> Spirituality denotes a self-based internal journey of experience with the divine. It is about the relationship between the individual and her/his faith, not necessarily mediated through the church. It is personal and experiential (2003: 139).

> Spiritually, I like paganism, it's a non-restrictive religion. It's something that I can choose and it's flexible.... I don't have to deal with doctrine. And you know the basic tenet of paganism is do whatever you want. Just don't hurt anyone, and I think that that's a wonderful thing to live your life by and try and

minimize the harm you do to other people, because so often, religious doctrine has been about how many people have died over crusades, and I like the fact that women have an equal if not greater focus in the religion, and I like the balance as well that there's a goddess and a god. Yeah, that fits in very well with my feminism and with my bisexuality, and I see a lot of links between bisexuality and paganism that it's not about restricting one part of yourself, it's about going with the flow and celebrating all parts of yourself. (Joanne)

Indeed for women such as Temptress, maintaining a spiritual faith despite the dilemmas that religion had created for her was seen as essential to her sense of self and culture:

I don't go to confession or church because I believe if God's everywhere, well, then I can talk to him. He knows exactly what's going on here, so don't bullshit me I have to tell someone about it. I don't believe in the Pope, but I believe there is a power beyond us or a belief in our heads, or in our bodies. If I lose this faith, I lose a part of me, a culture, a background, everything. I can't lose that, because that's who I am. And I don't want to. (Temptress)

Along with her more structured religion, Islam, Helena talked about the significance of spiritual practices in her life:

Spirituality, it's very much part of my life and it's sort of kept me as sane as I am I think and as anchored as I am, and sometimes when I think my life's a mess, I think well, it [spirituality] hasn't done much, but you don't know what it's done, relatively, and I embraced a spiritual meditation community, they don't proselytize. It's about getting to know yourself basically, but it's like what I call an active meditation. And it doesn't separate you from the world. It's very open. It's multi-denominational. It's multi everything. . . .it's an active meditation because you sing, you dance, you cry, you scream, you go to sleep. You know, whatever's happening is what you do. (Helena)

Like Helena, Kaitlin combined both religion and spirituality. Although a Minister in the mainstream Uniting Church, her spiritual metaphors supported her after her partner came out:

I found that I changed incredibly in the spirituality, because I'd been quite an academic. I swapped that where metaphor became really important for me... I really became alive to symbols in a way that I never had before. . . . An example of that, it was a really ordinary one. On the front verandah—because it was a dumpy old house - was a cracked concrete verandah, and one day, when I was really low, I came out to the verandah and there was just this little plant coming up through the concrete. And I watched it, and it was right back under the eaves, so it didn't get very much water and I thought, "Right, I'm having to battle here with a feeling of very little nurture and no watering and if I'm going to get through this, you have to too." So, I would speak to the plant, and it grew and it grew, and it was a violet. Even the color was just so symbolic. . . . Yes, that was a long haul, and it finally flowered and then it died right away. That was interesting, because it flowered around about the time of twelve months from when Ross had told me. I thought, "I've done really well." I felt really strong and I felt maybe I didn't feel as bad as I thought I would . . . and so the flower died off and it all went crispy, crunchy, but then again the following year it flowered too, and I looked at it and thought, "Yeah, I feel crispy, crunchy like that and just dried out and desiccated. There may be life or there may not." Ross came one day and he looked at the violet and he said, "You've got water under your verandah" and I said, "That's nothing to do with water under the verandah, that's the spirit of God there. Just leave that alone" and he looked at me as if I was crazy. I said, "That's nothing to do with science" so that was really my spirituality there. I could have roamed around without seeing that particularly before. . . [another day] I stopped off at a gallery, and they had this pottery box of Australian sand dunes in stone color and it was just gorgeous. And I thought, "I'll buy that for Ross," because he's a great lover of outdoors and nature and it was just so beautiful. Anyway, when I got home, I realized it wasn't for him, it was for me, and it became too painful to see all these sand dunes, and I thought that's how it feels plodding up the sand dunes. You get to the top and there's another bloody sand dune. And I put it away in the box, in the brown paper bag at the bottom of my wardrobe, and I left it there for about eighteen months, but every morning—because I had my clothes and shoes in there—even though it was in a brown paper bag and inside a box, I could still see right through it to see it, and I thought, "Rotten thing." I wanted to throw it out, and I wanted to smash it and I couldn't. And then one morning I thought—and I was getting better by then—I will just take this out and look at it and see if it's how I remember it. And it was exactly how I remembered it, except that I hadn't remembered how beautiful it was. And I thought, "Yes, this pain has had that beauty in it too. I really deeply know myself. Ross deeply knows himself. We're very marked by pain but I'm sure neither of us would want to go back to who we were then." (Kaitlin)

"BAN RELIGION. BAN RELIGION!"

Ban religion. Ban religion! . . .spirituality and organized religion that accepts diversity doesn't exist, and it should do. . . . Yeah, basically I see religion as being probably the biggest sticking point, because once you no longer have those religious biases, then you can change people's attitudes really easily. (Kirsten)

There were women in the research who erased any religious or spiritual beliefs and values in their lives as these were an anathema to a healthy relationship or sexual expression, or had negatively influenced them and /or their partners:

> I did go to a Catholic girls' school. However, that was mostly negative, and probably distanced me from the Catholic Church, which is probably a good thing. I don't think I suffer from any kind of Catholic guilt or any of those popular things. (Katie)
>
> Maybe it's because I'm irreligious, but I don't equate sexuality with morality at all. I believe that if you're not hurting anybody, and everybody knows where they stand, then sexuality is something that should be embraced. (Mary)

CONCLUSION

As this chapter has shown, religious frameworks and communities are strong forms of external ascription and community (dis)approval for many women and their partners in MOREs as they navigate their insider/outsider/no-sider belonging. In response, strategies of passing (normalization), bordering (negotiation) and polluting (noncompliance) are undertaken, dependent on the level of stigmatization and/or affirmation within these contexts. There is no denying that lesbian and gay people within religious communities are experiencing increasing social visibility, political clout and theological affirmation. However, a "rigorous and robust theological destigmatization of bisexuality has yet to be developed" (Yip, 2010: 38). Yip believes this is partly because bisexuality, as far as dominant theological and popular discourses go, is even more subversive, particularly in terms of "dyadic relationship form and monogamous management." This may generate much pressure on bisexuals to "opt for normality, namely being in a relationship with a different sex person" (2010: 38). It would be interesting to see how queer affirming theologians incorporate the range of bisexual lives and identities, such as dyadic and triadic relationship formations, and kinship forms that problematize religiously sanctioned monogamy, commitment and dependency. For now, being bisexual and Christian can lead to a "privatization of faith" with "de-traditionalization and less reliance on over-arching structures (such as organized religion)" while still relying on religious teaching (Toft, 2009: 85).

Chapter 15

"It's A Matter of Family Honor and Shame"

Negotiating Ethnic and Racial Identities and Community Codes

> One of the sad things is that I can't talk openly to my parents about this because of their old thing about their face in the community, you know, it's a matter of family honor and shame, "what will people say." It's like that's way more important than your own kids' individual happiness. (Naomi)

In this chapter, women explore the impact of ethnic, Black and Indigenous family, community values and belongings in their lives with bisexual men. For so many women, including Naomi, their individual lives and relationships were framed by a far more important collectivist construction of their "face in the community." "Haciendo caras" (Anzaldua, 1987a) or making a face to maintain family honor, prevent embarrassment and shame, were paramount and greatly impacted upon the relationship. The previous chapter explored religious community lifeworlds, though it is important to state that culture and religion are often interwoven panopticonic frameworks. Indeed, it is often difficult and yet necessary to distinguish between religious/spiritual codes, and cultural man-made dogmatic interpretations of those codes, and constructions of cultural rules justified by using religion. As Jaspal writes,

> One observable commonality between British Asians of all three religious traditions [Hindu, Sikh, Islam] concerns their cultural prioritization of the notion of *izzat* (honor) and their trepidation about experiencing *sharam* (shame) (2014: 428).

In *The Two Krishnas* (Dhalla, 2011), the married Hindu, Rahul, and the young Muslim, Atif, fall in love in the Indian diaspora of Los Angeles. One of the ongoing themes is how to reconcile their sexualities with their cultures and religions, both now and in the past. After reading the Koran,

Atif concludes: "So it was prohibited on Earth, but Muslims could look forward to homosexuality in Paradise... Legendary mystics like Jelaluddin Rumi and Farid ud-Din Atta had written evocatively about the love between men... The tales of Shiva and Agni, of Shiva and Vishnu, Krishna and Arjuna...He resented how believers ignored those stories" (2011: 43). Even Rahul's wife, Pooja, in trying to fathom her husband's differing love for her and for Atif, and her position as an Indian wife and mother in her migrant community, has to confront the fact that her Hindu deities "to whom she had prayed for the preservation of her marriage were themselves unfaithful... who had disregarded their vows and turned forbidden passion into a criterion for nothing less than perfect love" (2011: 213). She turns to the Internet and discovers studies in India on same-sex marriages and queer sexualities in the ancient texts, as well as modern-day queer Hindu movements in India.

As stated in chapter 1, the cultural diversity within bisexual groups and subcultures is not adequately acknowledged or explored in research (Dobinson, 2005; Hutchins & Ka'ahumanu, 1991; Pallotta-Chiarolli, 1995, 1999, 2005a, c, 2006b; Noel, 2006; Sheff & Hammers, 2011; Volpp, 2010). Beemyn & Steinman (2001b) state there is a need for issues of race and class to be incorporated into all critical analyses of male bisexuality. Examples of the available research include Paul et al. (2002), who found that the highest prevalence of suicide attempts among nonheterosexual males was among Native American bisexual or nonidentified respondents. Likewise, Goodenow et al. (2002) found that bisexually active males were more likely than others to be members of ethnic minorities (see also Reisen et al. 2010). Thus, race, ethnicity and class may be complexly interwoven in the ways bisexuals envision their communities and understand their masculinities and sexualities within them. For instance, themes of agency and subversion are often articulated in bisexual activist writing. These reflect notions and experiences of independence and individualism that are largely specific to white, middle-class individuals. How do these themes fit with the collectivist sociocultural and possibly lower socioeconomic locations of ethnic/men of color bisexual males and their partners? Likewise, rarely are the sexual practices of white men "racialized; or attributed to particular ethnoracial sexual norms within white culture" (Ward, 2015: 24).

Whilst some bisexual men may see their membership in multiple groups as a source of strength and pride, others may experience these multiple group identifications as a source of conflict and pain, due to coercion from one or more groups to make their primary allegiance to identification with that group (Goetstouwers, 2006). King (2011) discusses the lack of an integrated model which addresses the experience of individuals holding multiracial bisexual identities. Research specifically related to individuals identifying as multiracial/biracial and bisexual is usually based on observations (Stanley, 2004); exploratory discussions (Collins, 2000, 2004); or first-person accounts (Israel, 2004; Thompson, 2000) rather than empirical evidence. Existing literature suggests that multiracial bisexual individuals have a unique experience with regard to identity development (Dworkin, 2002) and that multiple marginalizations may lead to either acceptance or rejection of the messages and attitudes of the mainstream (Rust, 1996b). Fukuyama & Ferguson (2000) acknowledged that previous biracial identity models, such as Poston's (1990), could be relevant for individuals who identify as bisexual. Likewise, Reynolds and Pope developed the Multidimensional Identity Model (MIM) to reflect the multiple dimensions of identity, human diversity and within-group differences. They highlighted the fluid nature of identity choices, "based on personal needs, reference group[s], or [their] environment," suggesting that individuals could move about throughout their life course without needing a stable identity choice (1991: 179). The intersectionality of each of these dimensions represented the reality that no single dimension could be understood on its own, and that multiple identities could be engaged in at one time (Jones & McEwen, 2000).

Kich (1996) explored biracial and bisexual identities contiguously in an effort to illuminate the similar marginal experiences of both populations. Likewise, Collins (2000) provided the biracial-bisexual identity model as a four-phase structure which consists of Phase I—Questioning/Confusion, Phase II—Refusal/Suppression, Phase III—Infusion/Exploration, and Phase IV—Resolution/Acceptance. Collins (2000) also identified the influences of family, peers and the environment, as well as external forces which place the individual into different roles based on life course stage, sex, gender, class, sexuality and race. Thus, situational identification was believed to occur, where biracial-bisexual individuals changed themselves to blend into specific contexts. However, Collins (2000) made an assertion about this phase that was not clearly supported by King's (2011) later study: that "participants 'over-identified' with their minority side" (2000: 245). For example, if the participant was Japanese and White, he or she would identify as Japanese. This experience might hold true if the participant held White /non-White identities, but one half of the participants in King's study held non-White multiracial identities. King (2011) also critiques as idealistic and unattainable Collins' Phase IV—Resolution/Acceptance where biracial bisexuals develop a multiple identity that is "intermeshed [and] cannot be separated" (2000: 246):

> She suggested that to reach this stage the individual has shed stereotypes, confusion and self-devaluation. She also presented it as an end stage without room for growth or movement . . . [the participants in this study] all expressed that

they would continue to evolve and grow as they learned more about their racial heritage and/or gained comfort with their sexual identity (King, 2011: 111).

In the light of these findings and critiques, King (2011) developed her own model, with the four elements involved in the identity development process being (1) confusion/awareness, (2) parallel exploration relevant to context, (3) transitioning to safety, and (4) acceptance of dynamic identities. The "parallel exploration" phase was the degree to which participants were able to ask questions, research or physically explore. This was tied to context and the openness of that environment, including community, family, friends, religion and the school setting. In this phase, participants were not yet able to explore both identities fully because often, one identity was supported over the other. If communities were not racially diverse, for example, then participants may not explore their multiracial identity. If communities were not supportive of nonheterosexual identities, then participants focused only on their racial identity, which was the identity they could acknowledge and investigate. The "transitioning to safety" phase occurred where individuals could find "like-minded others, like-appearing others, or student organizations, resources and supportive others that provided validation of explorations, feelings and identity labels" (2011: 114). King's fourth phase, "acceptance of dynamic identities," was one of acceptance of the chosen identities and recognition that as humans, growth and evolution were inevitable. Although uncertainty may still exist, participants were content with that notion and excited about the possibilities of change and redefinition in the future.

Another model that endeavors to encapsulate bisexual-multiracial identities is Yuk & Singh's (2010) Bisexual Youth of Color (BYOC) intersecting identities development model. It includes aspects of four identity models (racial/ethnic, LGBTQ, bisexual and gender identities) but differs by directly addressing intersections of these identities within the sociopolitical context. It posits that if individuals learn to adapt and overcome different types of discrimination, they emerge strengthened by adversity and better prepared for the next set of challenges. This resilience subsequently affects the intersections of identities. The model includes two large concentric circles that encompass a cluster of seven smaller circles. The largest concentric circle represents the sociopolitical context (macrosystem) in which the bisexual youth of color live. The cluster of seven smaller overlapping circles signifies distinct, but overlapping, identity development processes (racial/ethnic, LGBTQ adolescent, bisexual, gender identity development, ability, socio-economic and religious/spiritual). The BYOC identity microsystem may increase or decrease in size depending on the individual's sociopolitical context (macrosystem) and personal resilience (found within the microsystem). For example, many youth of color are raised within families that share the youth's racial and ethnic identity. If family support is strong enough to offset discrimination encountered at the sociopolitical level, then healthy racial and ethnic identities are more likely. However, families of color may or may not have experience with or knowledge of concepts of sexual and gender fluidity, which may lead to limited support for the sexual and gender minority identity development of youth. In the worst cases, outright rejection of sexual identities can significantly impair bisexual identity development. Larger areas of overlap between racial and ethnic identity development and bisexual identity development might occur in situations where BYOC are raised in cultural traditions that are more accepting of sexual fluidity such as the two-spirit tradition in some Native cultures. Increased intersection of identities may also occur where BYOC discover LGBTQ communities which are inclusive and affirmative of bisexual individuals. For example, Thompson's (2012) research with bisexual and mixed race women showed they all expressed discontent with the "established" gay and lesbian community for being monolithically White in racial composition and also biphobic. This supports Rust who argued that for biracial or multiracial individuals, "painful decisions are often associated with the (perceived) necessity of choosing between an ethnic/racial community and the (White) queer community" (1996b: 419). Bisexuals of color reported feelings of marginalization in both communities because they felt compelled to divide themselves along identity lines and leave part of themselves "at the door" (1996b: 420). Although they view their multiple identities as connected, the majority of the interviewees in Thompson's (2012) study were involved in several organizations, fragmented across demarcated lines of sexuality and race, which could lead to the internalization of this division. Several participants discussed feeling more affinity and connection to racial/ethnic based communities or organizations, due to the "visibility" of their race/ethnicity. In other words, they felt more included within racial/ethnic organizations in which they "look like everybody else" than in gay and lesbian organizations, where they share a more covert identity yet stand out physically.

Specifically in relation to bisexual men of color, Munoz-Laboy (2004) uses the term "configuration" instead of identity in describing the lives of bisexually active Latino men. Nondisclosure may be a healthier option given the possible negative personal consequences of disclosure in the racial, ethnic or cultural community contexts in which they live. Bisexual men of color can be influenced by and adhere to strong male-dominated norms, values and cultures in which there is little or no validation other than for heterosexual attractions, behavior and relationships. The bisexual person of color in any European country lives in both a more traditional cultural environment and in the dominant culture, and is affected by both the more conservative values regarding sexual expression and by the more liberal values of the dominant culture. For European bisexual men whose religious and cultural background is Islamic, for example, there is a strong influence of heteropatriarchal thinking on the one hand and a parallel development of an Islamic-based European feminist movement. These countervailing trends raise issues of multiple identity and loyalty issues.

In their review of literature about DL black men, Pettaway et al. (2014) found there were inconsistent definitions of the DL identity and incorrect understanding of behaviors linked to the DL, particularly as they related to the issues of bisexuality and HIV/AIDS. They also found that the "failure to mention bisexuality" throughout much of the reviewed literature and the collapsing of bisexuality and homosexuality into a single category "is striking and difficult to explain, especially given the fact that the term 'down low' was most consistently defined in the same articles as a Black man who has sex with men and women" (2014: 214). Boykin's book dispelled what he calls "deadly lies" about DL men (2005: 164) and scrutinized their construction and application:

> For some whites it confirmed their pathologizing hypersexualized perception of black people, and for some blacks it confirmed their hypersexualized perception of gay men... For those of us who had been victimized by black men, it gave us a way to express our grief and our rage (2005: 151).

Boykin believes talking about the DL is a way of avoiding talking about racism, homophobia and AIDS and "our collective responsibility to find solutions for these problems" (2005: 5). Two films which explore the interface between African-American DL married men, framed by their cultures and church, and the white society, are *"Wes"* which is part of *The Down Low Chronicles* (2007), and the already discussed *Cover* (2008). Issues explored via personal stories include being bisexual or gay as "the white man's disease"; and how parental expectations of black men to succeed in a white world encompasses not only being financially and professionally successful, but being married with children, and being heterosexual. In *Wes* (2007), DL men are described as being between "a definition and a designation," living in a grey liminal or borderzone. Likewise, the documentary by Angela Childs, *On the Downlow* (2007), presents a range of gay and bisexual men talking about their families, sexualities and community/societal responses. Boykin relates meeting King (2004) and after the conversation, he remained deeply suspicious about the whole transaction with him and King's motivations for writing his book:

> after all JL King was providing the perfect iconic image for white America to understand. It was a stereotypical image of black men as pathological liars,

surreptitiously satisfying their primitive sexual cravings by cheating on their wives. That would have been an easier image for white news anchors to swallow than the image of black men who accept their sexuality and are comfortable with it. To promote positive images of black gay and bisexual men might actually help some black men to deal with their sexual orientation, and soon there would be no scandal to cover. . . The worst part of the down low story is that it is being promoted by a black man who is using America's fear of black men to advance his own agenda. Few black figures are more compelling to white America than the black man who is willing to criticize his own people (2005: 116, 130).

Other studies into ethnic bisexualities have found men's heterosexuality is determined by penetration, not the sex of whom one penetrates. For example, the emphasis on penetration as active and manly has led to a belief by some Latinos that "homosexuals" are those men who take a receptive role in anal intercourse, whereas "men" (i.e., heterosexuals) are those who take an insertive role, regardless of the gender of the partner (Munoz-Laboy & Dodge 2007). In Reisen et al. (2010), more than two thirds of the survey respondents reported they had sex at some time with a man who identified as heterosexual, and three-fifths reported the straight man was their main sexual partner during the time of the ongoing relationship. Nearly three quarters of the partners with whom participants reported having had an ongoing relationship or specific sexual encounters were also Latino. "Thus, for the most part, these sexual encounters and relationships occurred within a Latino cultural context" (Reisen et al. 2010: 1014). In addition to general social isolation, Latino men may fear being disconnected from family support and resources if they indicate they engage in sexual behaviors with both men and women. "Familism, a cultural value associated with strong identification with family (including extended family and friends) has been shown to be critical among Latino men, including those who are bisexual" (Martinez et al. 2012b: 1074; see also Munoz-Laboy 2008; Munoz-Laboy et al. 2009). Cerdeno et al. (2012) found that the ambition of heading a family, and being provider and protector, figured high among the goals of Latino bisexual men and their accepted social values of masculinity. Similarly, Ross & Dobinson (2013) found that in a study of Brazilian men with HIV, there was no difference between the bisexual and heterosexual men with respect to their desire to father children. Indeed, a number of bisexual Latino male participants in Martinez's (2012a, b) study reported not using a condom with female partners because of their desire to have children, or did not see pregnancies as a negative sexual health concern.

Cultural factors shape attitudes about sexuality and identity in ways that have implications for HIV risk, as discussed in chapter 11. Most studies undertaken with ethnic bisexual men have been largely in relation to HIV/

AIDS risk and transmission, and the debate has centered around whether these men are of higher or lower risk than white middle-class men. For example, Jeffries & Dodge (2007) found that racial/ethnic minority status predicted increased likelihood of condom use, even after adjusting for factors known to differ between minority and White men, namely marital status, socioeconomic status, sexual risk behaviors and drug use. This is comparable with others' findings that racial/ethnic minority men use condoms at higher rates than White men (Mosher et al. 2005). It is possible that minority men, like bisexually active men, know the sexual risks purported to exist within their racial/ethnic groups and thus use condoms at higher rates (Laumann et al. 1994).

However, some studies have found otherwise. For example, Martinez (2012a) reported that Latinos represent 14% of the US population but accounted for 18% of new reported HIV/AIDS infections. There may be event-specific and culturally-specific factors that shape sexual behaviors and HIVrisks of Latino men, such as the sexual partners' gender identity, who is engaging in the insertive or receptive role in sexual practices, levels of acculturation, and whether they engage in sexual activities under the influence of alcohol and drugs. Although female partners of Black and Latino bisexual men may be aware of their partners' behaviors, gender differences in relational power (Millett et al. 2005) or the perceived lack of partners within their racial/ethnic group (Malebranche et al. 2004), may result in these women knowingly engaging in unprotected sex (Jeffries & Dodge 2007). Shared experiences of racial discrimination may also contribute to women's empathetic attitudes regarding these men, even though some women reported the belief that homosexuality is a sin. Goparaju & Warren-Jeanpiere (2012) state that healthcare and social-service providers should be aware of women's cultural values regarding same-sex behaviors in order to assist them to become more comfortable speaking with male partners about bisexual behaviors.

Martinez also reported that migration seems to play an important role in some of the participants' sexual behaviors: "for instance, a small number reported having sex with male and female partners when visiting their native countries... Programs should be careful to take account of the fluidity of sexual activity as it relates to the migration experience" (2012a: 301). As well as sexual practices in the homelands being possibly more fluid, migration into the new land also allows for more sexual exploration. Some migrant men participate in the homoerotic scene because "there is something in them that is inhibited in their places of origin that becomes uninhibited when they arrive in the USA" (Parrini et al. 2011: 421). Two factors can lead to this disinhibition: the sociopolitical factor of living in a new cultural context, and the sociocultural factor involving the use of alcohol.

The issue of sexually fluid practices in home countries, particularly in relation to precolonial and/or pre-Christian practices, is discussed by several writers (see Low & Pallotta-Chiarolli, 2015). Reynolds (2002) reported that "sex between Afghan men [in Afghanistan] is an open secret, one most observant visitors quickly surmise" (in Burleson, 2008: 260). According to Reynolds, men commonly adorn themselves with eyeliner and henna and proudly walk arm in arm with other men. Most relationships are between older men and twelve- to sixteen-year-old boys, referred to as *halekon*. Reynolds reported that Dr. Mohammed Nasem Zafar, a Professor at Kandahar Medical College, estimates that about 50% of the city's male residents have sex with men or boys at some point in their lives. "A typical life for many Afghan men: get married, have children, and keep a *halekon* on the side" (in Burleson, 2008: 261). Lewis' research into Arabic poetry found that the "requirement to decide on a preference was perhaps rhetorical, as suggested in this verse by ʻAlī ibn Maʻsūm of Mecca (d.c. 1708): "I feel longing in a heart still divided between love of the turbaned and the veiled" (2009: 705). The love for boys, or at least the poetic expression of it, continued to be normative at least through the time of Rifāʻa al-Tahtāwī's visit to Paris (1826–1831), for al-Tahtāwī seems taken aback at how roundly the French condemn pederastic love. He informs us that one cannot say in French, "I loved a boy" (ghulām). When translating from Arabic, he notes that Europeans deliberately change the gender of the Arabic locution to feminize it (Lewis, 2009).

Despite such examples of earlier Muslim cultural references to same-sex love, contemporary narratives such as *Kafavis' Syndrome* by Bouzid (2010) focus on the plight of bisexuals living in the Muslim world today, and the lack of knowledge about Islamic queer history (Beckett et al. 2013):

> I was alone and scared, left to my devices. It was not a problem which one could discuss, and find a solution to. . . . My problem was eternal. I started to blame my father when he had penetrated my mother thirty five years ago. . . Sometimes sexual intercourses, short of a *besmala*, resulted in bringing to the world people like me with a blurred sexual identity. I read this in a religious book. I felt like a bastard. . . . I had been given a secret I could not handle. It was too confusing, and it popped up every time I saw a nice man on the street . . . Once, in a moment of despair, at the outset of my fourth depression, I had confessed my sexuality to him [my brother]. His ideas were completely backward. He thought I was impotent, and that was why I sought pleasure through other means. . . . He thought my marriage would erase the bad gene in me, that I would see the light. He was wrong. It was not a mathematic equation (Bouzid, 2010: 36–41).

Nevertheless, even among such difficulty, the protagonist appreciates his bisexuality: "What if I had had just one orientation in my life? Sure if I had been just old me, from my new point of view, life would have seemed tasteless . . . sometimes I think it was an advantage to stand on both sides" (Bouzid, 2010: 81–83).

In *The Witnesses* (2007), Mehdi is a Muslim Arab man in France, an aggressive vice squad cop with a reputation for closing down gay bars and arresting prostitutes. Early in the film, the viewer understands that Sarah and Mehdi have negotiated an open marriage, with opposite-sex casual affairs occurring occasionally. The teenager Manu awakens strong and surprising feelings in Mehdi, who later experiences confusion and guilt over their affair. Mehdi attempts to rationalize the relationship as nothing more than a physical sexual release but when his young lover contracts AIDs, Mehdi is emotionally devastated. Vicari describes the borderline Mehdi must reside upon, using metaphors of surface respectable assimilation and unacceptable private noncompliance, not only sexually but as a cultural and religious minority:

> When Mehdi and Manu are conducting their sexual affair, they use flying lessons as part of their cover. We are told that the affair is good for them because it teaches them to fly under the radar. This is the kind of complicated knowledge used for life enhancing ... which all minorities—gays certainly but also refugees, immigrants and transplants must learn at some point. As a bisexual, Mehdi occupies a strange position—he's both under the radar and above it, or more precisely to the extent that he is an accepted member of society and a vice squad cop—he technically is the radar (Vicari, 2011: 49).

It has been noted by some ethnic researchers that media coverage of minority male bisexuals is often pathologized, while white male bisexuals are characterized in a much more sympathetic manner. For example, *Brokeback Mountain* (2005) has been critiqued as one of many examples of racist representations of bisexual characters as a black bisexual husband/father has never been presented in such an empathic manner. Using content analysis of more than 170 newspaper and magazine articles written between 2001 and 2006, Pitt found black bisexual men would be called "dishonest and delusional" as well as "deceptive and dangerous" by public health officials because of "bringing diseases home to their partners." On the other hand, stories about white bisexual men included comments from family therapists, social workers, support groups and married couples "who pity men trapped in mixed orientation marriages" (2006: 255–256). Ward writes: "as white supremacy and privilege 'smooth over' any imagined inconsistencies in the sexual behavior of whites, especially white men, the sexual fluidity of men of color falls subject to heightened surveillance and misrepresentation" (2015: 21). Overall, Pitt concludes that stories about black bisexuals "tend to aim their criticism at the men themselves while stories about white bisexuals focus their criticisms at homophobic cultures that force these men into closeted lifestyles" (2006: 257). As Brown writes in his autobiographical essay, negative stereotypes of black bisexual men combine racist stereotypes of African-American men and biphobic stereotypes of bisexual men: "now we have a dumb, lazy, over-sexualized, indecisive, hyper-masculine individual" (2014: 12).

A strong example of the above inequities and stereotypical representations can be found in the trilogy by E. Lynn Harris: *Invisible Life* (1994), *Just As I Am* (1994) and *And This Too Shall Pass* (1996). In these books, bisexual black men are portrayed as "duplicitous and possibly dangerous" with stereotypes of "the predatory, married, closeted, bisexual black man" (Frieden, 2002: 86). Kelvin may have killed Candace by infecting her with HIV; Basil is a married straight-identifying homophobe who occasionally "deals in trade"; and Quinn, like Basil, lives a life of secret sexual duplicity. These characterizations are unfortunate given that Harris' work was the first time black male bisexuality was the central theme of an American novel. For many African Americans, the protagonist Raymond Winston Tyler Junior became the embodiment of black bisexuality and Harris "had introduced the nation to . . . black bisexual men who liked sports, held professional jobs, dated women and looked just like other black men" (Boykin, 2005: 36). In the first novel of the trilogy, *Invisible Life,* bisexuality is represented as transitional, "merely an intermediary step" in "psychological growth toward sexual self-identification as a gay black man" (Frieden, 2002: 88). The subsequent two novels celebrate monogamous relationships and "reduce black male bisexuality to a single character who is associated with secrecy and lies" while an openly gay male is represented in far more positive ways (Frieden, 2002: 88).

A less stereotypical representation of a bisexual African-American is the memoir of Samuel Delany (1988), a black gay science-fiction writer living in poverty in New York, who was married to Marilyn Hacker, a New York poet from a wealthy Jewish background. They were dating as teenagers and she was pregnant when they got married:

> "But look," I said, 'you know I am queer, that's not going to change', I explained.
> "I'd be very silly if I expected it to," she said. . . .
> "You really wouldn't mind that I'm going to be sleeping with men, probably a lot?"
> "I haven't minded it up to now," she said (1988: 103).

The memoir chronicles an interracial MORE of nineteen years, replete with the tensions, negotiations and joys of nonmonogamy and shared partners, including the development of a long-term relationship with a white bisexual married man. The memoir also chronicles the controversies their interracial marriage caused in the 1960s. For example, they could only get married in two states and so had to move. In talking about his writing, Delany also provides metaphoric insights into the duality of his life and love, and the importance of blending "the spaces between the columns" and writing "in both directions over the gap" (1988: 69).

Indigenous concepts of sexuality recognize that sexuality is not immutable and that it can evolve with age, location and political involvement while preserving an element of consistency. The colonization of sexuality has had a profound effect on Indigenous forms of sexuality around the world. In his account of the global influences on sexuality, Altman (2001) provides numerous examples of how Indigenous sexual cultures look to Western concepts of 'gay' and 'lesbian' to both positively and problematically inform the way in which they view themselves. However, Indigenous peoples are now moving some way towards defining their sexuality according to their own traditional values and beliefs (Low & Pallotta-Chiarolli, 2015). Maori society, discussed in chapter 1, has evidence that multiple partners and same-sex relationships were not uncommon (Aspin & Hutchings, 2007; Te Awekotuku, 1996; 2003). Walters et al. explain how the First Peoples in North America developed the term "two-spirit" to embrace tribal histories as it "transcends the Eurocentric binary categorizations of homosexual versus heterosexual or male versus female; to signal the fluidity and non-linearity of identity processes" (2006: 127). Robinson acknowledges that the two-spirited identity risks replicating "the dichotomous constructions of sexuality that obscure bisexuality" (2014: 19) particularly when "colonial value transmission" frame or co-opt two-spiritedness into meaning gay and lesbian (2014: 28). To avoid this risk, Robinson calls for the need to frame and define binary thinking as colonial and create spaces in which traditional two-spiritedness claims its legitimacy by "distancing us from White sexuality models" (2014: 29). Likewise, she states the identity of "Aboriginal" itself "is a fiction, conflating distinct nations, cultures, and histories." Therefore, there is no "single model of Aboriginal sexuality. . . Rather than telling others who we are, two-spirited identity invites others to ask whom we love, how we live, and what we have to offer our communities" (2014: 29–30).

In our research, the following themes became apparent:

1. having an ethnic or non-white background and belonging to an ethnic or non-white family and community require *silence and denial of one's MORE* to avoid bringing shame upon family honour.
2. bisexual men *deny or repress their sexualities in order to maintain their place within an ethnic or non-white family and community.*
3. some women and their partners are *able to comfortably navigate and negotiate their belonging and identities within their ethnic or non-white community* and indeed, claim their ethnicity, Blackness and Indigeneity as pivotal to who they are.

"THEY WILL DIE NOT KNOWING"

> My parents just wouldn't understand, absolutely not. I think it's just coming from an Italian background and their sort of traditional mold about what relationships are all about... To them, it's just black and white, there's no shades of grey.... there's no way, not in a million years I would tell them. They will die not knowing. (Yvonne)

For most women in our research, having an ethnic background and belonging to an ethnic family and community required silence and denial of one's MORE. Sometimes, as in Yvonne's case, it is not a malicious stigmatization of the relationship they envisage from their family, but a genuine lack of comprehension of the possibility of bisexuality and a viable MORE: "a lot of Muslim people just kind of say, 'There's no homosexuality, we don't have them', and it's just like it's just so foreign to them" (Hannah).

> Coming from an Asian background, it's something that you don't really talk about. So, no, they don't know.... I guess if I had been a gay person it would have been different. Because then I would have said, "Look, this is how I am and take it or leave it," but because I identify as being a bisexual, they know that I've always been with guys and I'm now married to a guy.... It's sort of like, "Even if you are, don't talk to me about it, because I still want to know you as the mum, the wife of this guy, so whatever you do in the bedroom, just don't even bring it up."... I find that a lot of the Asian people cannot take my way of thinking. It scares them. I don't conform within their guidelines. (Christine)

Loredana discussed her naivety in growing up in a sheltered environment where many issues and assumptions around sex and relationships were not discussed or interrogated:

> my background, being Italian, has had a fair bit to do with my needs for family and that whole family thing yes.... and I can see now how naïve I was, how trusting. I just assumed that it [her own relationship and family with her partner] would all be okay. I did grow up in very much that. I was in two worlds actually, and I liked the world that I was going into at university. In fact intellectually, yes, I believed in sexually liberated relationships, but at an emotional level I couldn't do it.... there's things from my background like guilt and shame and la figura [public shame]. (Loredana)

However, alongside this naivety, Loredana spoke at length about the dysfunctionalities in her Italian family background that remained unspoken and unresolved. For both Loredana and Lauren, their experiences of heteropatriarchal Italian masculinity were pivotal in their choice of husbands, as they were "different" to those masculinities. And yet, they were also ignorant of possible reasons in regard to why they were different:

> the thing that attracted me was always that he wasn't like other guys. Well, for a start, the Italian men I met would have wanted me to leave school, certainly not go to uni, to have children and to be at home, and I was not interested in that. I didn't fit the typical migrant girl background. He was very different to the other men I'd ever been with, given that I was not allowed to go out with boys anyway. So, yes, I liked the fact that he was gentle, he was softer. . . . and I liked not feeling bad because I didn't want to have sex. . . . You know the Italian men, gosh, you have to push them away. And that was what I liked about Peter, that I didn't have to push him away, that I could be respected, and so I just didn't ever conceive of anything else. . . . . . and my father was a very cold, distant man. So, I think very early on, I was actually satisfied with very little if that makes sense . . . I just didn't see. . . . I didn't expect the sexual orientation. (Loredana)

> He's totally different. I used to date a lot of more traditional, Italian boys. . . . I think because he knew from a really young age that he was bisexual and that's given him an emotional maturity. Both of his parents have died and he's just done a lot with his life and it just really made me think about where I'm going and what I want to be doing. . . . he is very supportive of my ambitions…which is different to before, when I was dating the Italian men, it was like, if I wanted to do something that didn't suit them they didn't want me to do it. (Lauren)

Deanna also spoke about Italian masculinities and why she couldn't tell her family about her bisexual partner, not even after they had split up:

> My brother would fuckin' kill him. . . . Italian men, I know that my brother would beat him up for being a poof and deceiving his sister's virtue. All good reason why blessed David is a scared bisexual boy. . . . my brother always says to me, "There's something about him. I don't know." . . . it's male culture. It's fucked, it's violent, it's bad. You know, we feel the ache and the pain of violence in our community, and as women, we're great. We help each other out, but there are so many poor, blessed, sweet-hearted boys out there who feel the same way about violence as we do. . . . Dave was attracted to my tradition because he comes from a traditional background too. I think that they [his traditional family] think it's [being part of her traditional family] going to fix him for them. Women are band aids, aren't they. (Deanna)

Another issue involved the hard work and suffering, as well as closeness and support, migrant families give their children, with the expectation that their sacrifices will be rewarded through their children's economic success, heteromonogamous marriage and the provision of grandchildren. Subsequently, this creates guilt and a feeling of being unable to hurt their families who have strived so hard for them:

I went through some years of great anger and frustration where each of us at different points tried to commit suicide. But being part of a strict Greek community prevented me from ending the marriage because of the shame it would bring to my family. (Soulla)

My grandmother married a man who was something like twenty years older than her, and I think she did it because it was a ticket out of post war Poland, and I don't think there was any love in that relationship, and when she moved to Australia I don't think she was very happy. They basically just worked all the time, and that, combined with my grandmother had schizophrenia, I think that it left my dad being very controlling of things and self-reliant, and the European quite conservative background. He wanted me to be just like him, and when I turned out not to be just like him, he couldn't handle it, and when he finally found out that I was bisexual, that was the straw that broke the camel's back and he disowned me. (Joanne)

This is a sad thing, I think my parents know. But they do the good old Italian thing, just do not talk about it . . . That is one thing that I really admire about my partner's Anglo background, because he is so upfront with his mum. Everybody just talks about it even if they don't like it, it's said and then it may not get said again but it's known. But then he says, "The closeness that you have with your family I don't have with my mum," and I'm thinking , "Oh god, your mum has bared her soul, you have known that she has had two partners for almost three decades, you have all lived together. She knows that you are bi." I have gone over to England to meet her and she accepts me, a married polyamorous woman. I say, "That is so much closer" but he says, 'No, there is something there that you guys have that we don't have," and he likes being around my extended family and doing things as a friend even though they don't acknowledge him as my partner, maybe don't even know he's my partner. I don't know, what is closeness? (Naomi)

Some women found that their ethnic communities in Australia were far more entrenched in homophobic attitudes than their communities back home:

I find some of the Pacific Islanders in Australia are plain bloody hypocritical. It's [homosexuality and bisexuality] so much more open in the Pacific and they talk about it here as if it doesn't occur. They say it's a Western thing. I get really angry about that, because I've lived in the Pacific and I know, come on. . . . and the great shame if grandchildren are at risk [of being not straight]. (Kaitlin)

This relates to the earlier discussion of an increasing reclaiming of pre-colonial and pre-Christian constructs of sexuality and gender, such as the Fa'afafine in Samoa and the Fakaleiti of Tonga, occurring in "home countries" (Murray, 2002; Low & Pallotta-Chiarolli, 2015).

As an Anglo-Australian businesswoman in a predominantly Italian community, Anne was very aware of the collectivism, conformity and cohesion in migrant communities, with its underlying problems for anyone who was not seen to conform, including herself:

> I work in a big Sicilian community and you tell anybody anything there and it goes right around the entire community. I didn't tell them about Peter until about two years ago. I just told them that I was divorced and single and kept him out of the way as much as I could, and there are still some people who are still just finding out now, five years after I started working there, that I have a partner. There is a very rigid approach. One of my clients who is my age, even before they moved in together, she and her boyfriend wanted to go away for a weekend together on their own to the family holiday house and her parents spent an hour or two berating her for being such a slut as to make it obvious that she was sleeping with him. That kind of attitude. . . . you know, you get a lot out of that community. You never have to be alone, but the cost to yourself is horrendous. (Anne)

Another issue that arose was when women's ex-partners or other family members were from homophobic ethnic families and communities and created problems with the new bisexual partners and access to children: "I have grandsons from a daughter married to a European man who has very strict barriers with all these morals, I just couldn't tell her" (Simone).

> I know that my children's father is probably another reason we haven't told them [the children] too much [about their bisexual stepfather], their father is quite homophobic and he's from a strict Catholic Spanish background. (Leanne)

Where their family liked their partner and felt joy and relief that their daughter had found a stable and loving man, it became especially difficult for the women to tell them something they may not see as positive or be unable to understand: "They like my partner, they get on great. He loves my mum and she's very maternal to him" (Yvonne).

> My Greek family couldn't understand it. They loved him very much. He was the best son-in-law. It [splitting up] rocked their boat. And then he did speak to my parents, told them why he's let go of the marriage, that he didn't want to lead two lives, and so that I could have my life. (Pat)

Sometimes women experience a quandary where there are signs that parents may know anyway, such as the use of humor and hints. However, taking the risk of talking about their relationship is considered too difficult and permanent:

My dad loves him because he is the only person out of all our friends who likes my dad's homemade wine... and he says things to Andrew like, "Thank you for taking care of my daughter," and Andrew goes a bit shy... and then my parents say things like, "Well whatever you want, so long as you two [Naomi and her husband] are OK it doesn't matter." They have these kinds of statements. But I don't know [if they really do know], and I am not really going to just come out with it. (Naomi)

"HE HAD TO BE A MAN"

There was a Portuguese community so he had to be a man, you know. "Woman at home. I go out, I go party, I've got to do everything with the boys," you know.... Family orientated, follow the tradition. Your father is named after your grandfather, he was named after his father... and sex, sex, sex, sex, sex, sex, sex. That's a biggy for them, macho men who are always on about sex.... His family have smothered the kids so much, and his mother has tried to look so much for love and not found any and tried to grab on to the sons and not let them go. And wherever they go, the parents go as well. Because of their culture and them coming here from Argentina. (Temptress)

Like Temptress, many women talked about how bisexual men deny or repress their sexualities due to familial and cultural expectations of heteromasculinity and familial duty. Indeed, these men may perform hyperheterosexual misogynist behaviors (see Chapter 9) in order to maintain their place within an ethnic family and community, which in itself reinforces the dependence and closeness in their sons and men that women spoke about in the previous section. Indeed, as Lisa and Pat suggest, the family and community may be complicit in letting the man have a wife as an acceptable "cover" for what may be known as his bisexuality, and should the relationship fail, the wife is to blame. As discussed in chapter 9, these heteropatriarchal constructions and expectations of women's roles in marriage cause much pain and conflict for women, whether they are from those communities or marrying into them:

I haven't told people about his bisexuality who were directly associated with his community, because I know that it's a very small community and it's that whole black man thing, you know, the sexual prowess and all that sort of stuff... And everyone used to just comment that we had this perfect relationship, and out of all the mixed race couples around, ours was this great relationship. Well, we did for a while. And then it fell down in a heap. But we both put up a great front.... A Ghanian man about six months after I left, I went to one of their functions, and he came up to me and said, "What did you do?" So the role of women in that society is different to the role of women in our society. But there's a contradiction there because there are some people in that community who know exactly what my ex-husband was like, that he's a Jekyll and Hyde. . . . I felt well and truly used. I mean, I think he cared for me, and friends have said, "Look, I think he did love you but you're not the person for him." But I felt a lot like I was set up to be his cover, for him to be out screwing men. . . . But apparently there have been some rumors in his community and it has caused quite a bit of a problem around that whole issue of him denying his sexuality, and I guess making me out to be a bit of a liar. . . . But he was also very homophobic to the point of saying there were no gay men in Africa [laughing]. (Lisa)

I met my husband here in Sydney. It was arranged. We liked each other. We met a few times and we agreed to marry. . . . Those days you weren't allowed to go out. It was strict. . . . But later it was telling his family he was bisexual, shock horror. They went into denial for three weeks and when they came out I copped it all. . . . Failed as wife, couldn't have children. His parents were living with me, in the granny flat. They lasted here approximately a year after he moved out. . . . then eventually his parents left. I just couldn't cope with them anymore. But you do get pressured in a lot of ways by family cause it's just not acceptable in a Greek family. . . . it's a taboo and they usually say someone pushed you and made you. It's like a little magical trick, that you turn like that. So it was harder for me in the Greek background because first thing when a couple separates it's who's to blame, whose family. With us because we always happy couple, we were a good couple together, the only thing missing was a baby. So of course the first things were, he left her cause she wouldn't have baby, and the other things were why did he wait so long to leave her if they couldn't have a baby. . . . Eventually when we did tell why, just everyone was horrified. It was just unacceptable to them and it was like they could strangle him for what he did. They kept on saying he should move back home [with me] and he can have his secret life. It came to the point where I sat down and explained it in pornographic view, words, named it, that he wanted a man in bed and I didn't want that. And then I was with him when he did sit down and tell them, but they're old. They will always be in denial. His family keep him to a distance. When they need him. Otherwise they don't want that much to do with him. If he goes to see them he can't talk about anything to do with his life, they don't even ask. (Pat)

Beneath the heteropatriarchal surface of ethnic communities and families, women reported the underbelly of men meeting for secret sex, such as "doing the beats":

Yvonne: It would be hard for an ethnic man to come forward and admit to beat sex.

Robert: I see it all the time. . . . There's lots of nationalities [at the beats]. . . . There was a guy, he's from the Carabinieri [Italian police force] and he came here thirty years ago, he told me. You start chatting.

Yvonne: How old is he?

Robert: Oh, 60's.

Yvonne: 60's and he can still get it up. Oh, good luck to him.

Robert: But that's the thing, he wants a hug as well. A lot of the Italian men, they like having hugs.

I take the kids down the park. Through the day, you've got the Lebanese and Turkish weddings, and come six o'clock you've got the beat. I just find it amazing how it comes to a certain time and the park just completely changes. And these Lebanese and Turkish guys doing the beat, before they go home to the wife and kids. And she may or may not be aware that he's doing the beat . . . Yeah, and she's ostracized by everyone if she was to be the cause of the family breakdown. (Louisa)

Of course, some of this closeted behavior is also due to internalized biphobia. Ava believes biphobia is still present in her partner, despite him being openly bisexual and polyamorous away from his ethnic family and community:

I think it has to do a lot with his cultural conflict, because he is very Greek and from a very conservative Greek family and also just having been brought up that way he never really accepted that in himself. (Ava)

"I LOVE BEING BISEXUAL, I LOVE BEING ITALIAN-AUSTRALIAN. THEY CAN COEXIST"

Sam and I are bisexual, we occasionally have other lovers in ongoing relationships, we are very happily married, and we love being Italian and hope our children cherish their cultural heritage the way we do. But all these contradictions are not meant to exist. . . . From when Sam and I were teenagers, we knew we were different. Not only different but supposedly nonexistent. It's as if we were the only kids on the whole planet who were not gay and not straight, who wanted to have the good old-fashioned Italian wedding and raise an Italian family but not accept what would've been traps for us like monogamous and heterosexual. Well, we still feel like we're the only Italian-Australians that have ever been through this and it's so isolating sometimes. There's no one else to talk to, no one else to tell you your lives and identities are realities, your sort of marriage exists. But every now and again, we wonder which other wogs are living similar realities but also in absolute silence? We're real. We're flesh and blood. He's there cooking the barbie and playing with the kids and I'm here scoffing my face with tiramisu and our parents are there seeing what they want to see and not needing to know the rest. These days it's all about multicultural identity and gay identity and every now and again there's stuff about a multicultural gay identity, but neither the multiculturalists nor the gay activists are prepared to publicly discuss our realities. But more of us will come out of the woodwork. I love being married, I love being bisexual, I love being Italian-Australian. They can coexist and they do right here in this suburban backyard. (Gloria)

As Gloria exemplifies, some women and their partners were able to navigate difficult journeys and negotiate their multiple group belongings and multiple identities to ultimately claim their ethnicity as pivotal:

Antonietta: Bill married me, a second-generation Italian woman, hoping that his feelings for men would subside. They didn't. Ten years and two children later, he came out to me. We separated but somehow we couldn't bring ourselves to divorce. There was always something that drew us together, especially my Italian family, the rellies and the community. Although they knew about him, my parents and most other members of my community still wanted him to be present at festivals, weddings and other parties. They loved him for who he was, and the way he was a good father to our children. That surprised me. I thought they'd be so homophobic. You know, ignorant Italian peasants are supposed to be according to all the stories. So we've remained married. Our kids are young adults now and I've fallen in love with an Italian man but I still love Bill as well.

Bill: Her new partner is just sexually so interested in her which is good for her I think. And I'll be there for her whatever happens with him. He's a bit homophobic and jealous of me. He's confused about us but he's a good man in other ways.

Antonietta: A couple of rellies have said Bill shouldn't have said anything, but do what he had to do with men and not disrupt the family.

Bill: It's funny but this community is so strong, so much fun and so supportive, I don't want to leave it and I don't want to leave Toni, and if I got divorced or tried to live as a gay man, I'd have to stop my sexual and loving relationship with Toni and I'd lose all this.

Other women identified facets of themselves, such as their strength, ways of communicating, perspectives on men and the type of relationship they desire, as being culturally derived. Also, creating some independent space away from an insular migrant community allowed more positive and supportive aspects of their culture to come through:

I'm old school Italian. I might have had this amazing education, and I might have a really open mind, but I'm kids and pasta for dinner. You know, like monogamy, fuckin' oath I am. Like, I'm not necessarily managing to do it under this particular canopy, but in my heart when it comes to having children and love, I grew up in a really, really, good home with really good values, and I have to stay very proud of that because otherwise I'll just lose it because I feel compromised constantly, because I've been given a new country and I've been given an amazing education. I've been given opportunities by the millions and I've taken every single one of them. . . . So, in light of being with a bisexual boy, then I feel like in a sense my Italianess and my gender views are very, very tightly knotted together. (Deanna)

Now that I'm disabled, and I can't get out as much, I stay with my different aunts and uncles and cousins and they all want me to stay with them of course. And what I needed was to feel totally loved, which I certainly did there [in that community]. So that gave me strength to start thinking, feeling, I deserve better [than my husband]. I could cope with it [his sexuality and her leaving him]. They were making me feel much stronger. (Loredana)

There were also women, such as Lizz from a Czech background with an Italian partner, who believed being bisexual was like straddling different cultures and allowed for a greater understanding of cultural diversity:

I kind of tend to think bi people in some ways could have an advantage in the sense that we have an understanding of what different cultures are like because there is not always a full inclusion in heterosexual community or the gay community. Much like non-English-speaking people have an understanding of what it's like walking into a mono culture where English is the complete language. (Lizz)

CONCLUSION

This chapter has highlighted the significance of exploring MOREs within a culturally diverse perspective and crosscultural histories, particularly in precolonial and postcolonial settings. As Burleson speculates, "What if Pashtun culture dominated the world in the same way Northern European culture does now? Would married men walking hand-in-hand with their young male lovers wearing eyeliner say of us, 'Western men don't keep *halekons*? How strange: how primitive.'" (2008: 263). As with religious communities in chapter 14, the issue of ethnic and racial group allegiance and identification create situations where women and their partners in MOREs need to normalize, negotiate or noncomply with the in-group codes and regulations as they endeavor to live in multiple lifeworlds with multiple marginalities, as well as striving to make these communities places of multiple strengths. Increasingly, multicultural/racialized queers are finding ways of acknowledging the potential of interconnectedness and the problematics of multiple discriminations.

Chapter 16

"When Your Relationship Isn't Recognized by Relationship Services"

Misrepresentations and Erasures in Health Services

It's really stupid expecting women to go out there and get support for your relationship when your relationship isn't recognized by relationship services. You go to the doctor, they have no idea where to send you and have a hard time even talking about it. You go to a women's health service, "just leave him, that's it, he's gay." You go to a gay health service, "just leave him, that's it, he's gay." You go to a counselor, they think there's something wrong with you to find yourself in this relationship. Can someone just listen, and maybe I just need to chat and it's mostly not a problem anyway? (Naomi)

In this chapter, we will be exploring the experiences women and their partners had in accessing health services to support them and/or connect with others in similar situations and relationships. Overwhelmingly, as Naomi describes, women's experiences were negative due to invisibility, misrepresentations, erasures, pathologization and problematization, and the lack of resources.

Certainly, as evident throughout this book, the years of experiencing emotional abuse from their partners was somehow linked to the women's existing or developing ill-health:

I began to get sick and I said to the doctor, "Please will you do a blood test for glandular fever" because my glands were all up. I was also tired. I was sleeping umpteen hours a day. By this stage, I couldn't go to work. And he said, "There's nothing wrong with you. You're just the sort of woman that needs anti-depressants for the rest of your life." Yes, I kid you not. That's what he told me. And that was the best thing he did to me because as I came out of that office I thought, "No, I'm not that sort of woman. I've basically raised three kids on my own. It's not in my mind. I know I am sick" and with that I went elsewhere . . . and this other doctor said to me, "Now, tell me all your problems."

> Well, I never had a doctor say that to me so I told him all my problems, and he said to me, "I think you've got chronic fatigue." And I just sat there and cried, because I didn't know what it was, but I knew I'd got something with a name. (Jean)

> I've slowly deteriorated. I can't drive a car anymore, so I'm much more dependent on other people. . . . Oh, absolutely my emotional state over him has contributed to my MS. The mind does affect the body, the emotions. I can actually tell if I'm feeling wonderful, happy emotionally, and then suddenly something happens and I feel emotionally upset, immediately the MS starts to seize up. I don't think about that too much because if I do, where is that going to take me? But I do feel that's another resentment. I was going pretty well and I thought I'd be okay for at least ten years, and so did the doctors [until finding out about her husband] and the emotional stresses, all the financial, sexual, combined, and in the last two years I've deteriorated a lot more. (Loretta)

In some cases, women also spoke about experiencing anxiety and other mental health issues over their husband's lives, but were grateful to be able to talk to their husbands about it:

> I would all of a sudden get a sort of attack. I would start hyperventilating and I didn't know what to do with myself and I could phone him up and talk to him. I'm so lucky. . . . he knew he was putting me through a lot. (Maria)

While describing their own mental and emotional health issues, some women also pointed out they were aware that their partners would also be experiencing their own:

> I've noticed a lot of bisexual men in marriages have a lot of health problems. . . . Greg had been seeing a psychiatrist for about two years [before their relationship] . . . they're depressed or they feel guilty for what they're doing and it's terrible. You just feel like going up to them and saying, "Hey, look it's okay. You know, it's really not that big an issue. And it sure beats trying to play it straight anyway." (Annette)

In their review of "scholarly attention previously given to mental health among bisexual individuals when compared to homosexual and heterosexual individuals," Dodge & Sandfort found the number of articles that present "relevant information specific to bisexuals in terms of mental health is a miniscule proportion of the published literature on sexual orientation and mental health" (2007: 41; see also Persson & Pfaus, 2015; Volpp, 2010). As already discussed in this book, a particular method of invisibilization is "exclusion by inclusion" (Martin & Pallotta-Chiarolli, 2009; Pallotta-Chiarolli & Martin, 2009). This is evident in the way health organizations focusing on same-sex attraction gain funding for projects that appear to be inclusive of bisexual people by including bisexuality as a category in their project outlines and submissions. However, they do not follow through with bisexual-specific recommendations, outcomes and services (Malinsky, 1997; Russell & Seif, 2002; Ryan & Rivers, 2003). There are many of these examples of bisexual "exclusion by inclusion" in international health research (Cabaj, 2005; Garofalo et al, 1998; Hatzenbuehler et al. 2008; Hughes & Eliason 2002). Likewise, in some research, bisexuality may be problematized even if there is no evidence of its links to health and well-being concerns (Miller et al. 2007).

In Australia, the importance of bisexual-specific health research became evident when Jorm et al. (2002) publicized their alarming findings into Australian bisexual youth health: Bisexual people have more current adverse life events, greater childhood adversity, less positive support from family, more negative support from friends and a higher frequency of financial problems. International research also showed similar findings. For example, research conducted in Canada found bisexual people have worse mental health and greater substance use outcomes than their homosexual or heterosexual counterparts (Ross et al. 2014; see also Dobinson, 2005). In the UK, King & McKeown (2003) found bisexual men experienced higher psychological distress, such as worry, depression, sleep problems, fatigue, concentration difficulties and irritability, and were more likely to have used recreational drugs compared to gay men. Gay and lesbian participants were more likely to be open about their sexuality to doctors and mental health professionals than bisexual men and women. Brennan et al. (2010) found bisexual men were slightly more likely to report fair or poor physical health than either gay or heterosexual men. Gay men were 4.1 times more likely and bisexual men 6.3 times more likely than heterosexual men to report lifetime suicidality. Also, those who do not self-identify as gay or bisexual but engage in same-sex activity are likely to be at highest risk for poor health outcomes. Warner et al. (2004) found bisexual men reported more frequent and severe low mood, depression, non-health-related worry, general anxiety, phobic anxiety, panic attacks, impulsive behaviors and obsessions. More recently, Schrimshaw et al. (2013b) found the lower levels of mental health among bisexual men relative to gay men may be attributable to the greater likelihood of bisexual men concealing their sexual orientation. This is due to the hypervigilance associated with concealment, particularly among men who lived with women, identified as heterosexual or had a lower frequency of sex with men.

> Bill had breakdowns. . . . and when Bill would be in a high, the spending would be big, and then he'd sink into a low and we'd be in debt. And trying to juggle everything, you become very clever at hiding your own feelings, and so you just suppress it all and so that's what I've done for years. You take on almost this

martyr complex, just so long as we get through today and everything's okay, and we've paid the bills ... And then we had the baby and a husband who didn't talk to me for five months. He'd say, "Good morning" and "Good night" and he was so depressed in between.... I'd get frustrated, I'd cry, I'd carry on. I can remember taking Leanne for a walk when she was about two, in the pram, and crying all around the streets. (Fay)

Interestingly, there have been some films about health workers/counselors who are bisexual themselves. In the comedy *Beyond Therapy* (1986), every major character is either a psychiatrist or a client, yet the psychiatrists are the ones most in need of help. The bisexual protagonist Bruce meets a woman through a personal ad who is having sex with her therapist. He also discovers she has always been afraid of gay and bisexual men. Nevertheless, she likes him, but her therapist is outraged that she could believe a bisexual man to be a better lover than he is. His diagnosis of her "problem" is that she is a "fag hag" while dismissing his own premature ejaculation problem (Bryant, 1997).

Paul Goodman was an openly bisexual therapist, becoming one of the founders of the Gestalt therapy movement in the 1950s. The documentary *Paul Goodman Changed My Life* (2011) features interviews with his second wife, Sally, his daughters, Susan and Daisy, and Goodman's poems to his children and his lovers. Goodman was

a dedicated family man and prided himself on "always being home for dinner." Nonetheless, he was an inveterate cruiser as well. ... "He was no fun to cruise with. He made passes at everyone," according to one observer. (Bryant, 2012: 541).

In 1969, Goodman wrote an essay called *The Politics of Being Queer* for and about Stonewall-era homosexual and bisexual men. He reflected that

on balance, I don't know whether my choice, or compulsion, of a bisexual life has made me especially unhappy or only averagely unhappy. It is obvious that every way of life has its hang-ups ... I have persistently felt that the world was not made for me, but I have had good moments (cited in Goodman, 1977: 491; and in Bryant, 2012: 541).

Before exploring women's experiences with health services, it needs to be stated that some women in our research did not rely on external services at all. For example, Heather preferred to undertake natural healing:

if they just try to get back to nature a bit. Yeah, you know, walk on the beach or in the bush. Miles and miles of it. Well, it's not so much the space, it's the pounding, it's the heartbeat. Perhaps it's a bit euphoric, a bit of an escape. . . . and even if your mind's confused, your body is still functioning, and underneath I'm thinking all the time, "Get a strong body, get a strong mind." (Heather)

While Heather did eventually tell her doctor about the mental health ramifications of her partner's bisexuality, she was thankful she hadn't relied upon her from the beginning and had sorted through many issues on her own:

My poor little doctor I think was blown away. Her little head was spinning and she didn't really know what to say, but she did make it clear that she was there any time I needed to talk to her. (Heather)

Other women, including Nicole and Gerry, also discussed how they learned to cope on their own. However, this was linked to the feeling that services were nonexistent or unable to understand their situation. Indeed, in Nicole's case, even the lecturers training future counselors were not considered able to engage with her situation:

I didn't take any medication. I didn't seek any support because I didn't think anyone would really understand. I'd actually taken up a Post-Graduate Diploma in Psychology, and at the time I was sort of sussing out the people concerned and whether I felt that they would understand those sorts of situations, the lecturers and people who were in professions in that area, but still didn't feel that they would actually understand. (Nicole)

One of the reasons I was happy to deal with it myself because I'd never found anybody who was in this situation. I mean, the sort of people who are counselors are well meaning but I'm the only one who can finally make decisions, and I don't expect anybody else to do it for me or be able to explain what's happening for me, so really it gets very tricky. . . . And never to take medication if you can help it. I took one Valium once and I sat and waited for the effect to wear off for six hours. It was just horrific, and I threw them in the bin, and I would never touch another one of them. I'm sure that a lot of medications cause more problems than they solve. People are constantly looking for crutches, but honestly, I really think that in the long run the crutches are more trouble than they're worth. Learning that you can cope makes you stronger. (Gerry)

What supported Gerry in her decision to deal with it herself was that her partner was seeing a very supportive doctor and she felt able to let him deal with matters without requiring her involvement. Thus, she did advocate for doctors to be informed and supportive of bisexual men as that would also support their women partners to remain independent and minimize their health issues: "I think I was very lucky that my partner had gone to the doctor that he went to, because he was just great" (Gerry).

In most of the previous research, bisexual participants were likely to report health-service providers "invalidated and pathologized" the sexual orientation of the client by either assuming the client's bisexuality "was connected to clinical issues when the client didn't agree, or assumed that bisexual attractions and behavior would disappear when the client regained psychological health" (Page, 2004: 139; see also Dobinson, 2003; Page, 2007). The San Francisco Human Rights Commission (2011) stated that it is imperative for health care providers to create a safe, affirming atmosphere for bisexual-identifying and behaving clients in order to facilitate dialogue on well-being and improve the delivery of health care (see also Barker et al. 2012; Rankin et al. 2015).

Given these discussions and previous research findings, the following questions arise in relation to our research: To what extent do bisexual men and their partners and families feel invalidated and pathologized by health services; and how do they develop healthy self-esteem and engage in healthy relationships despite such invalidation and pathologization? These questions will be discussed in this chapter in regards to the women's access to the following health service sites:

1. *Doctors and General Practitioners (GPs),* usually as women's first port of call seeking referrals to more specific services
2. *Counseling services* for themselves, their partners and/or as a couple
3. Attending *women with bisexual partners groups* and/or their partners attending *groups for married gay and bisexual men*
4. Seeking *bi-specific social and support groups*
5. Seeking out *other health services* that address their issues
6. Accessing *resources* such as books, films, Internet lists and sites

"I TOLD ONE OF THE DOCTORS . . . AND HE SORT OF THREW HIS ARMS UP IN THE AIR"

I told one of the doctors that I was going to and he sort of threw his arms up in the air. . . . and then after that he was just a bit brusk, so I don't go to him anymore . . . That's the first thing they say, "Why don't you leave him?" I say, "But I love him." "But how can you love him?" (Brenda)

For many women, telling their doctor was usually the first step to the view of seeking referrals to more specialized services and networks. Unfortunately, many GPs had little knowledge or sensitivity toward their situations. Kaestle & Ivory (2012) found that in medical literature read by doctors, fewer than 20% of the articles discussing bisexuality actually analyzed data for bisexuals as a separate group. Thus, the medical literature used for the training of doctors and their ongoing professional development does not outline a clear agenda specific to bisexual health. Kaestle & Ivory (2012) also found the medical literature on bisexuality did not address intersectionality and diversity among participants, and did not provide adequate information about basic demographics and socioeconomic status. When bisexuality is examined explicitly in the medical literature it is largely problematized, with STIs and sexual risk behaviors being by far the most common outcomes examined, followed by illicit drug use, mental health, tobacco and alcohol use. More than 20% of the articles framed the bisexual individual as an infection bridge or vector, which Kaestle & Ivory (2012) considered very problematic:

> Vectors in epidemiology are usually a completely different species, such as mosquitoes.... Framing bisexuality as a sexual bridge ... is of particular concern in the medical literature because access and treatment are influenced by subtle and unconscious provider biases (2012: 44).

Articles considered positive in the medical literature were quite rare. By 2007, only slightly more than 18% of the articles which specifically examined bisexuality framed it as valid and as a distinct sexual identity. Kaestle & Ivory speculate that the emphasis on the negative consequences of bisexuality may result from

> a natural bias within the medical literature to frame issues as health problems to justify further research in the area; and indeed there are clear health inequities facing this population. However, the emphasis in the literature on risks rather than resiliency or resources may also reinforce stereotypes of bisexuality (2012: 44).

They recommend future research on protective factors, resiliency, resources and positive outcomes related to bisexuality which could provide important insights and balance to the medical discourse on this topic. Finally, because the vast majority of articles were atheoretical and thus provided a lack of guidance for achieving a full understanding of the influences on bisexual health, Kaestle & Ivory (2012) recommend more recent theoretical developments, which treat sexual orientation as multidimensional rather than dichotomous, be presented and discussed in medical literature.

Women in our research complained that medical practitioners tended to try to identify some pathology in them rather than recognizing that the problem was really that of their partner. The reception some women received when first engaging with health professionals reinforced their concern that there would be no support for them, and they would have to justify and defend their position:

I went to the doctor, and I explained what had happened, and she just pulled a prescription pad out and said, "You want some uppers? Do you want something to help ease the anxiety? Do you want something to help you sleep? You tell me what you want." And I just looked at her and I said, "I don't want anything. I want to know where I can go for help." And she just looked at me and there was silence. I was just in tears the whole time I was in there, and she just didn't know what to say to me, and this was my regular doctor. And all she wanted to do was give me drugs, and I was so afraid of taking any drugs, only because I knew the way I was. . . . and even when I was in that state, I just thought, this isn't going to take away the pain I have. And she said in the end, "I don't know what to do for you." I just felt so lost and she didn't even offer to sort of, "Oh, look, I'll see if I can find out." . . . In the end, she pulled some pills out of a drawer and said, "Look, I've got a sample pack here of sleeping tablets. Do you want these?" And I said, "I'll take them." And because I hadn't slept for that long, I was too afraid to close my eyes, and when I did, I was crying continually, I must admit I did go home and I took a couple of sleeping tablets and half an hour later I was asleep. . . . So, it was the first night that I slept after four nights. And Shane came to see me and he held my hand as I fell asleep. . . The next day, she [the doctor] rang me and she seemed really flustered. It's very odd for a doctor to ring someone's home. And she said, "I'm just ringing to see if you're okay" and I just fell silent. And she said, "I was afraid you might harm yourself." And I thought, well, she's had time to think about it obviously, and I said, "No, I won't harm myself. I'm with friends. I've got people looking after me" and just left it at that. . . . In anyone's job you get asked questions you don't know the answer to, and no one expects you to know everything. It's okay not to know, but, "Look, I'll find out" and then you can make a few phone calls or bloody get on the Internet, Google it. But there was just nothing and even her phone call, she said, "Oh, you're with friends. Oh, that's okay" and let then it go and obviously she still had no idea, it was very disconcerting, and she didn't say, "Look, you need counseling" or, "Why don't you go to this place?" (Erin)

I really thought I'd found a doctor that I could perhaps talk to about these issues. She said, "Oh, you just need to take time out for yourself. If you weren't married to someone who was gay, they could have alcohol problems or something like that. And so, what you need to do to survive in the situation is take yourself off on a picnic and read a book." And I thought to myself, "Well, okay, Betty, you're a terrific doctor, and I'm happy to go to you for medical things, but it's immediately closed the book on going to you about this." . . I wanted to hear Betty say to me, "Fay, it must be tough. You must be lonely at times. Come and talk to me if it gets really hard." . . . . you want a hearing board, where you can talk and get referrals and somebody who won't come up with necessarily solutions, but will listen and understand what you're saying. (Fay)

Thus, women suggested "shopping around" to make sure they found a GP that would be informed and nonjudgmental. They also advocated doctors be made to understand these issues and have information available as part of their work:

> The problem is the doctor or medical professional is stereotypically only educated in monogamous, straight relationships, and probably these days they probably get a fair amount of gay or lesbian relationship situations. And you're put into your little pigeon hole, and if you don't fit, you've got problems. But, yes, they should be educated in accepting a relationship on its own merits. I'd suss my GP out. I'd be very careful of watching what the immediate reaction was. And if it was not going to be supportive and positive, I'd just say, "Thank you very much. I'll go and see another doctor." Well, any GP will have prejudices and their prejudices will influence the quality of health care you get. You do actually have to interview them. And most women don't. (Kirsten)

Some women did receive supportive responses from their doctors which provided reassurance that they could discuss anything and be listened to. However, as Temptress and Josie found, even within the same GP clinic, responses could be very individual and diverse:

> My doctor's amazing. I got Fernando also to go to my doctor. You know, he's straightforward, I love it. He was away once and we had a doctor next door... He [the other GP] started talking to us about AIDS and stuff and getting stuck into Fernando and like, no, it was the wrong approach. First investigate, see what's going on.... They should be there to help and inform and guide, but not to point the finger. (Temptress)

> My doctor was helpful. It was scary the first visit telling him about the situation because he was the first person I told, however he was supportive. He also ran a range of blood tests on me to check I wasn't at risk of anything. This was very frightening but reassuring at the same time. I asked him to refer me to a counselor. The one he sent me to was horrible, so I would suggest that they know well the skills of the specialists they refer their clients to. (Josie)

Some women stated that GPs should find ways of opening up spaces and possibilities for conversations and questions around sexuality, sexual health and relationships so that the onus is not on the woman to have to initiate any discussion: "the GP opening up possibilities in conversation where questions might be asked . . . build trusting relationships" (Jude). One facet of support Scarlett experienced involved the family GP revealing he had gone through a similar situation. However, he presented his experience in a way that made Scarlett think he was encouraging her partner to leave her, as he had done with his wife:

I was quite okay with this guy's decision to do that [leave his wife]. What I found difficult was that he was equally encouraging Harry to do the same, and I felt quite betrayed by this man, who we had confided in. (Scarlett)

Indeed, some women reported negative concerns with gay doctors who believed their partners were gay and the relationships should end:

He saw a gay doctor for a while. I went to see the same doctor and realized that his agenda was to split my husband and I up so I didn't bother going to the shrink he recommended. The doctor told me I needed to get help for my problem which was not being able to release my gay husband. The boyfriend [of my husband] who also shared the same doctor also said that to me, and accused me of being tolerant towards my husband's sexuality because that was the only way to try to keep him in my life. (Rachel)

"SHARAE BURNED OUT THREE PSYCHOLOGISTS"

Michael: Sharae burned out three psychologists because they couldn't understand that she could stay with a man who was bisexual. . . .

Sharae: [laughing] The first counselor, it probably would have been a big shock and out of her league so she sort of ran away screaming, but she put me on to this other person, but he didn't last very long, and then I went to this other bloke, and he kept saying that I was coping so well and should just keep at it. Now I spilled my guts, basically, to all the counselors, and there was nothing. There were so few resources, there was nowhere that they could point me. I was looking for anything that I could read. Documentaries that I might be able to get a hold of off the Internet, anything. So they listened to me babble on endlessly about what I was thinking and emotions and what was going on in our relationship, but they really had no answers

Sharae and Michael's experiences unfortunately reflect common experiences women have when seeking counselors. This section discusses the experiences women have with three types of counseling: seeing a counselor by themselves; their partners seeing counselors by themselves; and doing couples counseling. In presenting these experiences, I will also be presenting what women are seeking in counseling.

Counseling for Themselves

Heterosexual spouses seek counseling for an array of expressed concerns and require deep empathic responses from counselors, unlike the ignorant, blaming and trivializing responses that Coon describes in the following:

Sadly, I have to say that the so-called professional counselor I saw sent me plummeting back even further . . . She was not surprised that my husband had cheated on me and with a man as well, when I was as obesely overweight as I was. According to her that was reason enough to send any man across to the other side. She had also ascertained from what I had told her in our short time together that I was lazy, demanding, and a bit of a cry-baby as well. Maybe if I was to . . . pretty myself up with some good-quality clothing, put on some makeup and get a suitable hairdo things would be very different. If I could keep the house nice and tidy and clean, have dinner on the table for when my husband walked through the door after his long stressful day at work, I would be much more appealing to him. . . . And one last piece of advice for me, if I could give him what he wanted in the bedroom or perhaps out in the living room every now and then or in the laundry sitting on the washing machine while it was washing—the vibrations are fabulous, that would work a treat. . . . The only things I took from that session was a belly full of shame and the belief that this really was my fault (2012: 30–31).

Buxton explains how each "presenting problem is the tip of a complex composite of the issues, coping behaviors, and emotions." If therapists know there is this "underlying and unspoken chaos," they can be of immense support (2006d: 124). She lists the following as the most common concerns that heterosexual spouses present with: weight loss or weight gain; smoking, increased alcohol or other substance abuse and overdoses; being unable to sleep, work, or take care of the house or children; sexuality concerns, such as "alleged frigidity, loss of sexual desire, feeling that they are sexually starved or inadequate, or desire to enhance marital sex"; worries about STIs/HIV; hypertension and heart attacks; breakdowns, depression, suicidal thoughts and self-harming (2006d: 124). Some want to improve communication with their partners, avoid outbursts of anger or to resolve arguments. Still others want to know how to set boundaries, negotiate and manage monogamy or non-monogamy, or "how to distance themselves on the path to divorce" (2006d: 128). Psychological issues include the heterosexual spouses' disbelief that their partners are bisexual, self-blame, shame or embarrassment; low self-esteem, lack of confidence, and/or feelings of worthlessness. These self-perceptions are often heightened by their partners' blaming. Many spouses also present with cognitive conflicts, feeling unable to comprehend their partner's attraction to both men and women or the partner's deception. Others are troubled by the conflict between their love of their partner and their religious beliefs that condemn homosexuality and condone only heterosexual marriage. In response to these multiple and interwoven needs, Treyger et al. (2008) recommend "Solution-Focused Brief Therapy" (SFBT) so that the client is able to create her own solutions, rather than feeling judged or pushed in one way or another towards a specific path, and become oriented toward the future. SFBT focuses on what they are already doing well in order to increase the use of strengths, as opposed to focusing on weaknesses and behaviors they want to decrease (see also De Shazer, 1994).

Apart from a lack of awareness and resources, some women were shocked at the downright negativity, insensitivity and stereotyping expressed by counselors when what they wanted was an opportunity to consider all possibilities and potential ramifications:

> That was his comment, "Oh, well, you know, it's [the relationship's] going to die" and shit I was wild. I was so bloody angry, because I'm thinking, "Hey, you're supposed to be supporting your patient, and hey, I know how you're going to couch it, you're going to say, "Oh, well, I don't want to give you unrealistic expectations." . . . I felt like saying, "Well, okay, what's happening with the straight marriages with the affairs [coming to see you]? They're not doing much better." (Annette)

> I was seeing a counselor, who I've just found out was gay himself. . . . [when] I said to him, "I'm going to have an AIDS test," he said, 'Well, maybe he just had thoughts and feelings about men, not everything else. Maybe you don't have to rush into this straight away." I said, "I don't care. I'm going to have it. I want to sleep at night." . . . when I went back he said, "Have you had that test?" and I said, "Yes, I did. I don't care what you say, I went ahead and did it." He said, "Well, I'm pleased because I've had a talk with his doctor and he said Rod's been fucking around on you for a good while. There's a lot more that he disclosed but I can't disclose it. Yes, I'm pleased you got it." That really floored me. (Lizette)

Gochros (1989) found that most therapists, whether they themselves identified as heterosexual or homosexual, examined MOREs from within hegemonic constructions of sexuality and gender. While straight therapists were most likely to focus on the "battered wife syndromes," gay therapists were "apt to focus on hysteria and vindictiveness of wives following disclosure" with wives' behaviors ascribed to "neurosis and homophobia" (1989: 138–139). The women in her study also found the following problematic in mental health professionals: pretending they knew all about MOREs when they didn't; admitting lack of knowledge and leaving wives to "flounder around by themselves"; hiding behind confidentiality as an excuse for either inability or unwillingness to provide information and guidance in coping with the husband's sexuality; playing "trivial behavior modification games while ignoring basic issues"; terminating treatment prematurely and inadvertently creating anxiety and guilt about the need for future help; and automatically discouraging efforts to save a marriage (1989: 151–153). More recent empirical work still demonstrates that even therapists who believe they are free from sexual orientation bias are more likely to view bisexual-identified clients, as compared to gay- or heterosexual-identified clients, as confused and conflicted, even in the absence of clinical evidence to support such a view (Brooks & Inman, 2013; Rostosky et al. 2010).

Brooks & Inman (2013) found it is important to explore the potential influence of clinicians' cultural and religious beliefs on one's comfort with discussing bisexual-related issues. Carlsson also believes "it is imperative that the therapist's counter transference is kept in check" (2007: 123). Therapists need to be aware of their own internal dialogue as their clients talk about their bisexual feelings and experiences: "If you find that you are exceptionally uncomfortable assisting an individual with bisexual concerns it is best to refer to another qualified therapist" (2007: 123–124).

> I saw one counselor in the early days and she said to me, "That's normal, all men have affairs, but you know, men with other men, that's not normal." I just retreated from the room and said, "Thank you." ... She was very much putting her own personal slant on it all. She had a very cultural bias and she said that herself, she just absolutely couldn't relate to it at all. ... And she was also saying, which was so wrong, "He'll get over it all. Maybe he just needs to work this out of his system and then he might realize what he's got and just come back," and I thought for a tiny second, "Oh, yes, maybe that's how it would be" and then I thought, "Oh, don't give false hope to people. That's a terrible thing to do." That's what I remember thinking that day, "Gee, if I'd been a real mess and I'd gone to see her, I don't know how I'd have come out." (Barb)

After traumatic experiences with her counselor led to her hospitalization, Helena found the counseling she received from a cardiologist, with his very simple messages, to be the most useful:

> It [the collapse] happened after a session where I really got in touch with my pain, and she didn't back me up, and I went home and I had this collapse. I ended up in an ambulance in casualty. ... I saw a cardiologist just before I left [hospital] as a sort of final check up, having done a stress test. He said, "Look, I see lots of women like you, go away and get validated." And I read his letter that I picked up from my GP after that and he had said, "This woman has compromised most of her life." He was amazing, and I know from this experience that I've had in my new job in this school, kids adore me and I adore them. And the staff think I'm great. So, I'm actually getting some validation that I've never had before. I don't have a whole lot of faith in counseling services. ... I think they've got to be careful that they don't just sort of compound the shit. (Helena)

The women who did have positive and useful sessions with counselors remarked on their openness, lack of judgment, and having resources to suggest (Brooks et al. 2010):

Jane: I don't think I would have got through last year without contact with my counselor. I just think that I would have curled up and stayed in bed for like a sort of nervous breakdown. I used to think, oh, well, if I can just get through today, it's only two more days until I see Jeff, [the counselor] and I used to weep and wail and be very distressed and he was terrific. He was only a young bloke, in his twenties. And he was amazing. He used to say to me, "I think you're getting a bit stronger. I can see strength there and you're going to be fine.". . . I still talk to my counselor but not every week any more. It's usually about once a month, so it's getting less and less time I spend with him. And just every so often I feel I need to pour it all out. . . . I go to a counselor for the HIV and the bisexuality issue and I go to a counselor for the breast cancer issue, so I have to try and think, "Hell, which counselor am I getting today.". . .

Sara: So had you ever been to counselors before?

Jane: Never, no. I mean, I thought I was very much together. I mean, I'd never really been depressed in my life. But this just went on and on and on and on. My life is very full just with going to counselors and support groups. So it certainly has changed. But, out of it all, I do think I'm getting stronger.

I went down into a slump, I'd drink myself to oblivion. It was the only way I could sleep. . . . counseling was fabulous and it was then helping me push through the limits I'd put on myself. . . . Mainly the thing I'd want to say is for women that maybe take it or have taken it as hard as I took it, actually own up that you need support. You don't see reality. For me it's like getting into a barrel for a good seven years, and it was totally black. I didn't contemplate suicide, but if I'd thought about it at the time, I could have done if someone had offered it, you know. Just really take on that there are people out there that are skilled in assisting you and having you get out of the situation. And you become stronger in life. (Mary)

The biggest issue is cost as well with counseling although you can get GP referrals and my friend put me on to this woman in a low cost counseling center, . . . she was totally supportive of whatever I was doing and when we were trying to stay together it was all ways of trying to improve the relationship, and then when it was time to separate it was all about me feeling ok about myself, you know, she shifted the focus. So not making decisions for them and not pushing them in any particular direction, letting them go their own direction. The girl that I see sort of describes my path as a 3-year grieving process and she said it was like the first year was shock, the second year was sort of anger and denial, and the third year was getting ready to go. She actually described it to me like someone turning up on your doorstep with an elephant and saying "Here, hide this, don't let anybody see, keep it away from the kids" and I've spent the last 3-years rushing this elephant from room to room trying to hide it from everybody and suddenly I could let everybody see the elephant and it was such a relief. (Marissa)

It was also interesting to have research participants who were counselors or studying human sciences, as they were able to provide both personal and professional insights and how they interweave:

> I've formed a bit of a niche for myself so that people would refer those types. And then because I've had some experiences in my own life, my professional supervisor has often tried to encourage me to work in that area. . . . and so when people ask me in counseling, "What do you think?" I say, "All bets are off, whatever works. Do what you need to do and it will eventually work itself out." . . . .I know a couple of therapists who don't go anywhere near it. There are some counselors who actually feel quite confronted by this and so they routinely don't ask the question or if they do, they might say, "So sex life okay? Good. Thanks." So in one way or another they actually silence the couple on that. Now, I'm not saying that I'm not often confronted with some experiences that people describe that really are outside my realm of comfort but that's why hopefully we do professional development and we learn to actually sit with their experience and it's about them, not us. . . . you don't end up being a third person in the relationship and you don't want to become voyeuristic in the counseling process, and you certainly never want to be abused in the counseling process. You have to make people feel okay about their sexuality and their expression of sexuality and even if it's outside your realm of understanding, be okay with that. So I can say, "I don't know anything about fisting. Tell me how it works." . . . I suppose helping people to find a voice is really important in all of this, particularly the women where they're living with a bisexual man, really helping them to actually understand how they can control this themselves and not feel like victims. (Scarlett)

> I try to teach them the differences between secrecy and privacy and remind them that they have every right to be private and they don't need to tell anybody if they don't want to. I use a basket of toy eggs. You've got this much energy. How much energy are you going to put into looking after or guarding yourself, or taking care of those who don't cope? . . . They need to know their symptoms are—if you call them symptoms—absolutely normal, and they also need very much the freedom to find their way of going. I won't talk to them about my story unless they ask, and so I think they mostly need to be treated as people who hold in themselves their own answers that are very good, but usually they don't know that they've got an answer. It's just exactly like a death in the grieving and so they need to know I'm there for them. I always say this number is okay to ring any time of the day or night, because the feelings don't strike at predictable hours. That's where services are a problem, because they're open nine until five or whatever hour. You know, the minute that they're ready, have the courage to talk and get support, they need to be able to. So, again, if a counseling service has a six week waiting time, that's too much for someone. . . . They really need containment in those early days. They spin out in behavior sexually, in ways that I know nearly all of them are going to have really big issues dealing with later. They're real risky behaviors, so, you know, real loss of care for themselves, and

to say, "Look, let's not do things that are going to hurt you." So how to help them to look at their own values that they always prized, discard ones that are no longer valuable for them, . . . part of helping them is to say, "I've got four bedrooms there—come and stay there as a time out. See if you can get somebody to look after your children if you've got children. Have not a day or two, but a week, you know, and come back for another week," so that they've got time just to breathe again and find some things that are life giving. What helps them to stay feeling sane. . . . I can say to them, "Look, we can experiment with not taking something [prescription drugs], because it doesn't matter two hoots if you don't sleep tonight. You're on holiday anyway," so sometimes medications can be tough to break away from, but a lot of them will want to. (Kaitlin)

Louisa saw her role as a sex-worker as being a counselor to many men who were unable to discuss these issues with their women partners:

They can't talk to a wife or a girlfriend that they do love. They're not open to receiving that type of information about their husband or their partner. . . And it's a shame because they are spending such a lot of money on male prostitutes. . . . a lot of women don't know that they can access sex workers who can help them access health services for themselves and their partners. But there needs to be a lot more training for sex workers around these issues. And a lot more advertising. (Louisa)

Counseling for their Partners

Rust (2007) emphasizes the importance of validating bisexual identity and viewing bisexuality as one among several healthy sexual orientation identities (see also Persson & Pfaus, 2015). Clinicians need to apply the basic tools used in all good clinical practice including respect, empathy, positive inquisitiveness and a bias in favor of the client's uniquely unfolding development (Moore & Norris, 2005; Rankin et al. 2015). They need to remain alert to ways that bisexual clients may have internalized cultural bias deeply into their sense of self and wellbeing. It is also important to offer information and resources to clients. In order to do this, counselors need to take the time to become accurately informed about local community resources.

> The therapist can offer a place in which dominant societal scripts such as the orientation script and the monogamy script are not assumed, so the client can be free to examine the ways in which he does not fit them. Thus, the therapeutic session can provide a place where unscriptedness, confusion, and contradiction can occur, temporarily free of the demand to make sense or make decisions that the queer spouse no doubt feels acutely in the rest of his life. In this way, the therapist can offer a small island of moratorium in the midst of an adult life of responsibility (Swan & Benack, 2012: 62).

Thus, therapists need to be willing to "step outside their own scripts and enter unscripted territory along with the queer spouse" (Swan & Benack, 2012: 62; see also Kort, 2007).

As discussed in the previous chapter, bisexual clients from diverse racial, ethnic and class backgrounds require counseling be familiar with and sensitive to the particular issues that arise from clients attempting to integrate multiple marginalized identities (Pallotta-Chiarolli, 2010a). Rust (1996b) set forth a number of competencies for working with ethnic-minority bisexual clients (see also Brooks et al. 2010). It requires recognition not only of the unique problems such clients confront, but also the unique resources that are available to them. For example, "The counselor who is unfamiliar with a client's culture might perceive only the greater familial control, failing to realize that the same strong family ties virtually guarantee family support within the face of disapproval" (Rust, 1996a: 71–72). The counselor might also misinterpret messages a client receives from his family, resulting in attempts to explore misunderstood or nonexistent issues while failing to recognize the real issues. For example, a counselor might interpret a family's "unwillingness" to discuss the client's sexuality as "a rejection of the client as a family member," not recognizing that "the family's demands that the client marry are in part a demand that the client express ethnic loyalty" (Rust, 1996a: 72). Connecting the client with bisexual people of their ethnic background and/or literature from their culture's history that is supportive of diverse sexuality may be beneficial in broadening the definitions of ethnic loyalty and heritage pride (Beckett et al. 2014; Low & Pallotta-Chiarolli, 2015). In developing competence with Asian-American bisexual clients, Collins (2000, 2004) recommended awareness of the barriers to treatment for this population, such as the notion that counseling is antithetical to a collectivistic worldview and perhaps shaming to one's family. In addition, Collins (2000, 2004) highlighted the struggle of Asian-American bisexual individuals having to choose between their ethnic community's support and the LGBTIQ community's support. Thus, exploring ways to bridge ethnic and sexual identities is an important part of therapeutic work. Furthermore, integrating positive coping strategies developed through the client's spiritual beliefs may be beneficial.

Some women in our research discussed how their partners did not want to go to counselors despite being encouraged to or needing to:

> I tried a range of options to get Dean to attend counseling especially when suicidal and it was very difficult and he wouldn't justify the cost of going to counseling for the benefits he perceived there to be little so he thought he had to struggle through on his own. (Josie)

> It was his first experience of seeing someone about this issue, and that person also met with me once and we talked about how it was going to be very difficult

working with him because he was extremely intelligent and extremely capable at deflection. Now as a psychologist and a counselor, I know very much what he means and that some people can't let you into their inner world, . . . But Harry did continue doing counseling for some time, and it seemed to help him a little. (Scarlett)

Several women had major concerns with counseling services for bisexual men. For example, Heather found that her partner had actually met his counselor over the Internet and was sexually intimate with him:

I rang him [the counselor] a couple of times and I said that I didn't want to interfere with his privacy, but it was really important to me [to know what was going on between them]. And he just said, "I think you need to speak to Ian about that." And he said it was hardly a relationship [between them], it was casual sex. (Heather)

Other women considered counselors to be quite biased toward making their husbands identify themselves as gay and leave the marriage:

Anyone who has ever tried to give him therapy who's gay they've actually been fairly conservative as well. They haven't been able to get their heads around what we are to each other. And that's actually really infuriating, me being his primary partner. (Rachel)

There were women who expressed relief when their partners began to see a counselor even if everything that was suggested was not followed through:

It just got harder and harder for him to hold it all together and he got more and more aloof and then it really did start to unravel at the seams and I was beside myself. And then he went to a counselor who said, "You've got to tell. This is just killing you, let alone what it's doing to anyone else." And the counselor suggested did he have a support person in case when he told me, I threw him out of the house or whatever. So he went and told his mum. And then he came home . . . He said to the counselor, "Something I've always loved about Barb that she is such an independent, secure woman, and here she is becoming all teary and insecure," and the counselor said "It's so natural that she's feeling insecure, like it would be so abnormal for someone in a situation like this not to be wanting some reassurance, whether it was a hug, a kiss, a verbal everything is okay or whatever." And Andrew said at the time yes, he could see all of that. But he hasn't really adopted any of those reassuring policies . . . . I think he's so preoccupied for what's going on for him and he said, "Empathy, I don't know what it is." He just said he's not someone who can even begin to put himself in anyone else's shoes. . . . the counselor said to him, "Look, it is your life together," and Andrew was the one who said, "Well, I want to try to stay together." (Barb)

Couples Counseling

Many women described the problems they experienced with couples counseling. These included a lack of awareness, openness and understanding, as well as quite homophobic, sexist or other stereotypical assumptions (Bradford, 2012). In previous research, the most frequently stated criticism concerning counselors working with MOREs is that counselors lose sight of the issues for which services are being sought:

> We went for quite a few sessions and this marriage counselor was bringing us to the point of divorce and separation, and it absolutely floored me. Bill said, "No more counseling, all I want to do is cuddle Fay and give her a kiss and go home and start again." ... I was told in one marriage counseling situation, "You're so passive, why don't you stand up and be assertive?" I said, "Well, I don't want to be assertive because all I was mixing with at work were assertive women who were quite angry with the world and I had to learn how to be assertive but not lose my sensitivity." (Fay)

As Buxton explains, in couples counseling the couples "bring two sets of issues in the same areas of sexuality, marriage, children, identity, integrity, and belief system in addition to relationship concerns" (2006b: 128). Goals include those for each partner, interaction between the partners, and actions for partners to take jointly. Many couples want help evaluating the relationship to see if it is worth preserving. As Buxton contends, the "most realistic and promising counseling objective is not to save or to end the marriage" but rather to help the spouses work out "ways to redefine their relationship so that it meets both sets of needs, wants, and values" (2006: 131–132). In couples counseling, heterosexual spouses want equal treatment and "neutrality toward both spouses ... to let each spouse speak without fear of repercussion" (Buxton, 2007: 406).

Davidson (2002) explores how therapists can work with people who are exploring polyamory, and being aware of how culturally-based assumptions that only monogamy is acceptable impacts and informs therapeutic practice. However, what Davidson calls "The Shadow Side of Polyamory" must also be attended to (2002: 3). This may include coerced consent, manipulation, dishonesty, or other dysfunctional patterns that are no more representative of healthy polyamory than healthy monogamy. It is also important to distinguish troubled relationship dynamics from troublesome passages in predominantly healthy polyamorous relationships. For example, the exuberance attached to some aspects of polyamory will be counterweighed by corresponding surges of pain or grief over other aspects. Weitzman (2004) also found that relatively few counselors have heard of polyamory and fewer still have worked with polyamorous clients. Thus, the "poly-affirming" counselor has the opportunity to be "a leader among her peers" even if the latter express prejudice against the counselor who affirms the validity of the polyamorous lifestyle (2004: 160). Weitzman (2007) recommends basic practical changes to show that the counselor is poly-friendly, such as changing the language on intake forms to the name of partner/s, not name of spouse, and noting in counseling centre brochures and websites that polyamory is understood and accepted.

In our research, some women found their experiences with couples' counselors to be problematic in many ways:

> I think the counselor we had never dealt with the situation before, and how she dealt with it is that I would go in sobbing my eyes out, and we would explain what had happened, and she would turn to Shane and start asking him what he was going to do about his sexuality and how he was going to cope beyond the marriage, about his other relationships, and I would sit there and just think, "Well, what about me? What about now? How am I getting over what's happening?" I said to her after the first session, "I thought we've come together because we want counseling together." And she sort of honed in on him and all his issues and I just felt completely cut out of all that... So I went to a session on my own with her, and she still referred back to Shane and his issues. And we had only one other session after that together. (Erin)

> We went to couples' counseling and I could have smashed the woman, I swear to God. You know, "We're not here to blame anybody, we all play a part" and I'm like, "Excuse me, like I know what you're saying, I can see the framework you're delivering in but common sense here. Unless there's some responsibility taken, then how is this couple ever going to get to a point where they're not going to kill each other."... I think what I really needed was just an arena to be able to just really off load. If someone had just been able to say, 'So that must make you really angry.' I just didn't get that opportunity to be able to go "Yeah, that did make me angry." (Kris)

Couples counseling was also rendered ineffective if the partner's bisexuality was not raised:

> *Kaitlin:* Ross didn't present what he, by then, knew was the real reason [for marriage problems], so yeah, it was just too superficial. The counselor got nowhere with that at all.... The counselor taught things on communication that were really very basic, that we were already pretty good at...
>
> *Maria:* And never at any point raised the issue of sexuality?
>
> *Kaitlin:* No, not at all.... It must be to do with work, and it must be that they can't talk to each other properly.

After some time and continued counseling, the sexuality issues were discussed and, indeed, the counselor suggested family counseling, which proved to be far more effective:

By then, Ross was grieving about things, wanting things to be more back the way they'd been and I'd moved on to a different spot [wanting to move on out of the marriage]. . . . The counselor spotted that the issues that would be big for the children were as much the issues of whether we'd stay together or we separated, and he asked them some questions about us splitting up. (Kaitlin)

Other counselors could be dismissive of both individuals in the couple as Coon and her partner experienced:

The psychiatrist recommended we both go home and take a good hard look at ourselves and grow up! There were people out there dealing with real tragedies in life, much more serious issues than the rubbish we had presented her with. Then she proceeded to tell us, for the duration of our session, that she was still paying off her husband's (or was it her ex-husband's) gambling debts. And if we ever wanted to understand real pain and suffering then try dealing with that (Coon, 2012: 32–33).

Some women felt fortunate enough to have been able to access very supportive and thoughtful counselors:

she was very skilled, and she had the right kind of framework to work from. She wasn't slick and smart like some. . . . We went for six months, and I really realized in the end that he could not put himself in my shoes, and I was trying very hard to put myself in his. So it was just traumatic because every attempt to make a connection just sort of failed. And it was just he wanted to keep the marriage going in name, but the marriage counselor at one point said, "We're talking about a Clayton's marriage, and that's really what it would be," and he got very angry. But that's what it would have been to me, just keeping the marriage going. Like a business arrangement. He said to the counselor, "Well, I do like sleeping in the same bed with Felicity." Oh, God almighty, is that all we want for the next forty years? "And it would be lovely to grow old together." Oh, shit, you know, so totally different kind of ways of looking at the relationship. . . I was just so lucky [with the counselor's] support to decide whether to stay or leave, heaps of emotional support. (Felicity)

I decided that we should get some couples counseling, mainly because I had needed a third party there when I said things, which I thought might be misconstrued or upset him. We did go to someone who was experienced with different sorts of relationships. And she was very good. She was very nonjudgmental. . . . And although she didn't make nasty comments to my husband, she certainly let him know that he'd rewritten the rules around the marriage without letting me know. (Jane)

In relation to religious counseling, Yarhouse et al. (2003) argue that the role of Christian counselors is not to use religious beliefs in order to "change" the beliefs and values of the client, but to allow the client's religious beliefs and values to be congruent with and a value-added part of therapy. Specific training in religious coping activities and the relationship between religious/spiritual activities and various measures of mental health and well-being may be warranted. If the couple's request for therapy touches on several areas that appear to fall outside of the Christian counselor's areas of competency, the ethics code encourages them to make a referral to someone who can provide professional services:

> We went to religious counseling and while he was nice and he was cheap, he wasn't talking about the problem. We were talking about our wedding vows to each other and what they meant. It was more of a Bible lesson. I am a great God person, I really am, and I have Bible study every week so that shows how God really is in me, and at one meeting I said, "You're missing the point here. He's had sex with men. We need to address this." Anyway, he saw that session out and he then said, "I don't think I can help you. I think you need to go somewhere else" and he suggested we speak to somebody about sexual problems. . . . We see an absolutely super dooper girl. . . . now Anthony has learnt through her to listen to me, and not just blame me, to respond to me, and this has made a big difference to the relationship. It's like a building. If you've got a good foundation, you can build a tower, but if your foundations are rocky, that tower will rot and fall down. . . . I would want religious counselors and organizations who don't know how to deal with this to say, "This is out of our jurisdiction, we can't deal with this." Redirect us to the people that can. Don't take our money, don't see us for nine months and we're no further down the track. We go to you with faith, and you can't help us. (Jean)

For Scarlett, couples counseling involved a very thoughtful and skillful counselor with whom they could work through many individual and relationship issues. Ultimately though, the results were not what she had wished for as it was during counseling that Scarlett's partner announced he was leaving her:

> We worked with a male counselor for twelve months, and I thought we'd made some really huge changes in our relationship, and I thought we were going absolutely really well, I was finding my own voice and recognizing that even though I am very talkative and very emotive and had been identified as the dominant partner in this relationship because I was quite able and active, and he was considered to be the dominated partner in the relationship, that in many ways I began to recognize that he, indeed, had been quite controlling with his passive aggressive manner . . . and this guy we were working with the sexuality issue as well, and finding ways of him exploring his sexuality without being actively sexually involved with men. . . . one of my main complaints in the relationship was that there wasn't much passion. The sex was fine, but Harry was always having to monitor himself and so censure himself . . . The counselor was actually helping him get in touch with his internal world. . . . And then almost a year

after we had begun counseling I came home from work one evening. We were going to counseling and I'd had a really good day and I got a bottle of champagne and I thought after the counseling we'd sit down and have a nice evening together, and in that counseling session Harry announced that he was going to leave the marriage.... Which was horrible, and a little cowardly I thought, understandable in a way, but it was horrible to hear it there. It was not what I had thought at all. (Scarlett)

"I WASN'T THE ONLY ONE FEELING LIKE AN ALIEN"

Then I came to the women's group, so I wasn't the only one feeling like an alien. It's good to have women at different stages, that had just sort of learnt about it like me, people in a year, two years, three years down the track, you listen and they tell you what the stages you go through.... The sad thing is that not a lot of groups going that help women. All I can say is it would be good if it was more known or publicized about these groups and I think you'll be horrified, you would see how many women would come forward, that have just kept it to themselves. (Pat)

Maria: You know that there's a bisexual married men's group and things like that here in Adelaide?

Lauren: No, I didn't think so.

Maria: You wouldn't want to approach any of those groups?

Lauren: What for?

There was a program run from the AIDs Council for women partners of bisexual men. I never really felt that was for me, though, because I always saw that as straight wives. And sort of dealing with perhaps relationships breaking down because of it which seemed negative to me. (Joanne)

As the three women above demonstrate, although a few women couldn't see the purpose of support groups for themselves, others spoke about the need for support and social groups, particularly in order to meet other women going through similar experiences:

I got in touch with the AIDS Council over here and said, "Why is there no support group for partners of bisexual men?" and they said, "Oh, well, we'll put it on the agenda" and that was about 3 years ago. The AIDS Council is run by men for men and they couldn't really care less if women need support in those areas or not. I did get in touch with Amity Pierce Buxton and she sent me some info about setting up our own support group but then to do that we would need to go public whereas if something was done through the AIDS Council then it's through an organization and not an individual. (Leanne)

> The Gay and Married Men's Group [GAMMA] gave me the name of one woman who was running a support group, which met once a week during the day, on a day that I worked, so that was of no use to me, and it was also closed. . . . And I was getting the GAMMA viewpoint, which was just, "Well just take your medicine and basically be a doormat, and you just have to do whatever is good for him." (Sue)

> I was just sort of left on my own to deal with it, and I was like chasing my tail. And they'd [gay services] go, "Oh, sorry, we didn't get the funding. The gays and the lesbians get the funding here." I was devastated . . . And I went to a women's health center at one stage . . . but it's like lesbian counseling, lesbian mothers' support group and this and that, and I thought, "Well, hello, we're [straight women] here too." (Lizette)

In this section, we will talk about the various groups women attended, the most popular one being a women's-only support group for women with bisexual male partners. Buxton (2006a) discusses her role as executive director of the Straight Spouse Network. Internet lists, support groups and contacts in every US state and 11 countries means she is connected with women representing a cross-section of location, ethnicity, race, socioeconomic class, education level, age, religion and political party. Auerback & Moser (1987) found that the main role of group leaders was to direct the group members' thinking to their own needs. They advocated for a heterosexual male leader, as his presence as someone "who could accept and respond to the mixed feelings that were expressed about men [by women] was extremely valuable." Another reason was "the extreme ambivalence and distrust the women held towards homosexuals and bisexuals" (1987: 323). However, bisexual men in positive MOREs could also be healing and aspirational for women. Treyger et al. (2008) found that group therapy for wives of bisexual men and for bisexual men and their wives could be very useful. In particular, while bisexual men may have access to a huge support network once they come out, their partners do not have such support and can benefit greatly from such groups. Support groups can be therapeutic, permitting each partner to receive support from and provide support to others in similar situations, thereby reducing isolation, self-doubt and stigma. They allow for insights into various ways of negotiating their relationships and sexualities, provide realistic expectations, and model healthy conflict resolution (Paul, 1984):

> I think going [to the support group] in itself was a bit of an affirmation to myself that I was accepting this thing, and up until then, it was like, "No, this isn't happening. My marriage isn't ending. This is all going to blow over, and any minute now he's going to come back and say, 'I've made a mistake.'" That moment never came. . . . But once I'd accepted that "Well, I'm in the situation and perhaps it's time to meet some others in the same situation," I took myself

along to the support group and that support group led on to another support group, and it was all word of mouth. It was something like, Women Partners of Bi And Gay Men. There were women in the group who were in relationships, with families, and their husband was sexually active with other men, and they wanted to keep the relationship together. It just opened my eyes to the world because I just had no idea that those sorts of marriages existed really. It wasn't ever a static group. There was a core of women that were always there, but then there were always people that drifted in and out . . . Oh, look, just venting, venting, being able to talk to people who understood where you were. Even though they were all very different, I mean, there's common themes, obviously, and common feelings. . . . I knew that because we were strangers to each other and because there were certain rules in place for the meetings, it was just a comfort to know that you could speak openly and that it wouldn't go anywhere, that what you said would be respected . . . . There was laughter at times that I just thought why are we laughing at this, but we were laughing because we all understood. But occasionally there would be people crying and then there would be this comment that would make people laugh, and we'd all sit there and start crying again, hard to explain, but you could only appreciate the humor in it because you were there and you were in the depths of something far deeper and you knew it wasn't flippancy. . . . every month we'd go back and we would tell our stories until it didn't hurt any more . . . I remember the first few meetings I went to, new women coming into the group. It was just like you see yourself all over again, not being able to speak and just crying at every moment. . . . So, I suppose part of healing has definitely been telling the story. Telling the story reinforces the truth of it to you, and reinforcing the truth means you have to accept it. You can't deny it. . . . She [group facilitator] was just a very incredible woman. She's very understanding and nonjudgmental. She was very calm. And sometimes the sessions got quite emotional. There was always a way of gently leading us along, just gently pushing maybe but not enough so you think, oh, no, that's too much. But she kept the group cohesive. Yes, you need a process and we went around the circle, told our story and then we'd discuss and if someone had an issue that they wanted to talk about or something was coming up, then we'd focus on that. So, we all had time for ourselves and each other. It's great to have people together, but it's not just a chit-chat. It needs to have some structure, but not so structured that you feel as though you can't move beyond that. And the great thing about the group was there were probably three of us that got together outside of the group and we became friends. (Erin)

When I used to come home from the support group, was really encouraging knowing that you [Sara] were in a relationship that you sorted out, you know, that wasn't the conventional relationship, and that kind of almost gives you an understanding that you can work it out how you want, it doesn't have to be this way or that. (Jess)

Some women also tried mixed gender support groups for people with bisexual partners but found the gender dynamics created problems:

In theory I suppose I thought it was a good idea, well, surely it doesn't matter what our gender is or what our partners' gender is, the fact is we're all going through a similar thing. . . . I let the group go after a few months, and it was mainly the guy, I must say. I didn't tell the facilitators. There were two women that facilitated the group, and they were very good. I don't normally have a problem with men. . . . he was quite sexist, and look, sexism, I just don't cope with, and I just have to stand up and say, "Don't speak to me that way, I'm not going to put up with that language" and that just puts me on the wrong foot with some people and that's okay. (Erin)

Krystle and Greg were a couple who were keen to establish a mixed group that would be open and supportive to all:

Krystle: We're having this barbecue to hopefully contact other new couples. . . . I'd like it to be open at home, that people can ring and send emails . . . We find it really hard to find couples who have the success—this sounds really awful, but the level of skills and relationship that we have, and so we really do want to support other people. . . . . What I'd probably love is even to have a weekend, a camp or something, where people in our situation from around Australia come. Couples that do want to stay together. That doesn't mean necessarily exclusively, depending on each situation, . . .

Greg: I'd love to meet other couples who are equally committed to having a future together basically. That would be fantastic.

Krystle: Without compromising themselves as individuals. . . . Well, some compromise, but a compromise about choice, not an enforced compromise . . . To talk about how do people negotiate and how does it work in practicalities. How do you cope with feeling like shit and how does he cope with the guilt.

Some women also discussed how their partners joined men-only groups for married gay and bisexual men, but overwhelmingly their perspectives on the efficacy and empathy of these groups were negative. This was particularly evident if the groups advocated for secrecy and complete compartmentalization between the men's lives with their partners and with other men, with female partners having no say or rights in what the men were doing:

Pat: Finally he [her partner] found the Gay Married Men's Group.

Sara: Right. The speaker is making a wanking [masturbating a penis] movement that you can't see on the tape [laughing].

Pat: [laughing] I don't like that group.

Krystle: Greg went to this Gay and Married Men group where he had sex with the coordinating guy and I think that's really poor ethical practice for a support group, and I'm not pleased [Laughing]. . .

Greg: I found it online as a sort of support group. It was kind of a pick-up group.

Maria: Did it meet other needs, apart from sexual? [Laughing]

Krystle: It certainly met those. [Laughing].

Greg: No, because I only went the once.

In their study with bisexual men's groups, Miller et al. (2007) found that the group facilitators did encourage honesty, particularly with sexual partners, with plenty of acknowledgement that it was not an easy process. However, the group's curriculum included a focus around bisexuality, sex and dating with men, and safety and safer sex with men, but it "did not include discussions about women and the women in their lives" (2007: 66; see also Moore & Norris, 2005).

> There's lots of misogynist comments made. And my partner has really pro-feminist ideas . . . I think organizations can't ignore they might have wives that they love dearly, and they don't like having women spoken about badly. (Jude)
>
> Well, we accessed the men's group eventually, which wasn't a very good experience for me, because whilst they were totally supportive of John, they really didn't give me anything . . . the only information I got about the other women from the men was, you know, their really emotional responses and that they were all bitches. . . . Well, he enjoyed going there, so I suppose he felt that he could be more himself, and meet people of like minds. And it made him feel better about what he was doing. Which I don't know was necessarily very good for me. It taught him to be very selfish I think. (Sue)

Another support group that some women and their partners tried was PFLAG (Parents & Friends of Lesbians and Gays):

> We can be ourselves at PFLAG. Until Bill came out, we were there as the parents of a gay child. And then one night, you know how they go around in a circle, Bill said, "I'm the gay husband of thirty years." It was probably the first time in my life I had support where the secret was out and it didn't matter. You felt secure and safe. It was a place where we all, the three of us, could go and talk and we were accepted, . . . We've been away to a conference, we've marched in Mardi Gras with PFLAG so it's friendship as well . . . it's me now that keeps wanting to go to PFLAG. . . . The convenor rang me the other day, and she said she had a young woman who's just married and is crying and was angry and would I talk to her and I said, "Yeah, that's fine." (Fay)
>
> I found PFLAG extremely useful. I'd say that was the best thing I did. I didn't need it for very long, but I certainly needed it for a few months, and I didn't speak that first time. I just couldn't. The whole place was so emotionally charged that I knew that I would not get one word out without bursting into

tears. Well, when I did eventually stand up and speak, I did burst into tears but it didn't matter. And this wonderful guy came rushing over afterwards and gave me this huge hug. He was gay. He'd just left his girlfriend of four years because he'd told her he was gay and he was such a warm, lovely, guy.... PFLAG was a good start, but it certainly wasn't going to be an ongoing support because all their difficulties and problems are so totally different to what us women are going through. (Sally)

"I NEEDED THE BISEXUAL SOCIAL GROUP"

I needed the bisexual social group.... At least have them, bisexual groups, where we can just get together and talk and not feel estranged from society. (Temptress)

Some women wanted to join social groups for bisexual people and/or polyamorous people and their partners of diverse genders and sexualities. Belonging to a visible bisexual community is often a determining factor and major strategy for MOREs' public acknowledgment of their relationships (Weinberg et al. 1994). Swan & Benack (2012) report that two decades ago, there was no organized community of people in MOREs. Social and support communities have now developed, including online groups and organizations. Thus, a public discourse is increasing to create new social scripts for MOREs:

We love attending social and activist gatherings on bisexuality. There's such an exhilaration in being with so many people who are so similar in very different ways in this community that other communities don't want.... I mean, where else in the so-called queer community could a gorgeous Size 20 suburban housewife with manicured nails proclaim herself bisexual and run several businesses, including evening swingers' clubs in her home in good suburban taste, cos couples don't have sex on the first date. "It's like your friendly neighborhood get-together where you talk about the footy, the kids' schools, the latest fudge recipe, while sizing each other up for fuck-potential next time," she explained to the group. "Except we're more honest about it, and get hurt less. And the next time, we have another party and I give them clean towels, assign rooms, and we have a nice breakfast in the morning."... Hovering over everyone is the bi- Goth boy who bites necks and spits out the perfume as if it's the ultimate vampire repellent. He tells the group that Goths assume you're bisexual unless you declare otherwise. Yeah, I love these groups because when you attend you find that no matter what the bigger world thinks of you, in this group we feel very staid and ordinary, Mr. and Mrs. Queer. And that feels so nice! (Lilith)

There's no visible bi night club. I mean, the closest you get sometimes are the Goth night clubs.... and yes, in the last couple of years we've started to have more than one bi float in the parade so you do have the bisexual support networks and then you've got the bi pride networks. (Rose)

Mike: This little club we go to, a really nice, friendly environment . . . that you can walk into with your wife or mate. You can take your kids, you can have a quiet meal. You can have a couple of quiet drinks, listen to music, you can have a dance and everyone is very, very friendly . . .

Vicky: If someone sat on their own for more than two minutes, someone will always walk up and talk to them and make them welcome.

Mike: And one of the other golden rules there is no drugs. Everything is always kept under control, they don't need security guards and all that sort of rot.

"A SERVICE WHERE IT WAS OKAY TO TALK ABOUT THE UNSPOKEN THINGS"

I think women's services could do it [address these issues]. I think if we had a service where it was okay to talk about the unspoken things, because it's about shame, it's about betrayal, it's about I'm a lesser person if he's gone off with a man. . . . where it's one of the health issues so it's written out there so that people see it . . . it becomes part of a health package, so there has to be some kind of advertising where that's part of a parcel. That this is part of women's health. (Hannah)

Many women, including Hannah, believed all health services, but particularly women's centers and services, should openly provide resources, "parcels" and "packages," and resource-persons so that women could comfortably access materials as part of their regular health and wellbeing maintenance:

I was actually dropping a friend off at a Women's Health Service, and they actually had pamphlets on Alternative Sex Life Partners or something like that. And I actually grabbed a couple of those, and we [she and her partner] had a read of them. They weren't too bad, but they put too much of the negative in them I think. As in making these women think, you know, your husband's going to leave you for a man because he prefers to be with one now and then. . . . they get in there [health service] and they preach it at women that it's wrong to have a bisexual husband. He's going to give you STDs. So I don't read any more of their rubbish. I'd rather read something that's informed like a website [with bisexual and MORE resources]. (Lesley)

In their research, Dobinson et al. (2005) found MOREs had problems with health service providers positioning bisexuality as a deficit, with having multiple partners, and experienced inappropriate jokes or comments. Most commonly, their participants felt bisexuals should have bi-specific services as well as being able to utilize broader LGBT services for other health and wellness needs. Ideally, the broader LGBT services should have bisexual specific education and include bisexual providers and staff members. Some of the separate services that people felt would be helpful for bisexual people were counseling, mental health services, coming out groups, support discussion groups and telephone support or information lines. Dobinson et al. (2005) wanted health service providers to have competency or sensitivity training which included an awareness of resources in order to make appropriate referrals to books, websites, support groups and other sources focused on bisexuality (see also Moore & Norris, 2005).

Another issue that often arose was how difficult it was to access services for women with bisexual male partners because such services were not readily publicized:

> Gayline said, "Oh, a wife, oh, no. Look, we can't help you." . . . The Women's Information Switchboard were very good, put me on to the woman who was running a support group. . . . And, of course, none of this is ever advertised. (Erin)

Some women in our research believed these health services could be working in schools to introduce these issues at a much younger age so girls go forward into life with a greater understanding of sexual and relationship possibilities: "go into schools to kind of dispel myths" (Katie):

> Sex education shouldn't be about you can be gay or you can be straight, but it should be about different types of relationships. You can have monogamous relationships, you can have nonmonogamous relationships. . . . I think instead of the 'tick a box', it should be young women should be given options about the diversity of relationships. (Joanne)

Rural health services addressing MOREs were also considered necessary. However, concerns were expressed because of their locations, the framing conservatism, the need for confidentiality as well as the overall lack of services: "I had to travel nearly two hours away to go to a counselor once, and there was just nothing [in my rural area]" (Lizette).

> You would have issues of confidentiality more so in the country than you do in the city. . . . I think a women's health nurse or a GP in a country town probably wouldn't have a handle on it and so maybe they need to be upskilled just to what are the resources that are available for these women to tap into? Are there support groups in the area? Where are the sexual health clinics? . . . but, then again, there are stereotypes about who goes to a sexual health clinic. (Lisa)

Given these concerns, virtual support groups may provide important interpersonal contact in small or rural communities (Rostosky et al. 2010). Service providers need to educate themselves about bisexual community resources that are available in their geographic regions and on the Internet, such as Facebook, chatlists and other forms of social media. Many participants described the importance of their involvement in "giving back" through community engagement as educators, role models and social activists.

It was also interesting listening to women with bisexual male partners who were health workers discuss their efforts to make these issues part of their services:

> Certainly at our center we try and have representations in all sort of ways of the diverse lives of women. . . And, I think, that probably the biggest challenge for us, as workers, is to not bring so many assumptions to our conversations with women so that we open up spaces for women to say, "Well, actually, my partner has sex with men as well" or "I'm not in a monogamous relationship." (Jude)

> I'm a women's health nurse, but like me, they may not be aware of the issues. I have become aware of the issues through experience in it. It was something that was never really dealt with when I did the courses and sexuality is something that we often don't do a lot of discussion about and you basically pick it up as you go along. (Lisa)

Messinger (2012) reflects on how many bisexual individuals and families interface with a range of agencies and organizations that could do with "organizational bisexual inclusivity" training and awareness: employment agencies, immigration, education, child welfare, criminal justice and welfare systems. Providing education and in-service training will help decrease organizational biphobia or monosexism: "staff members who complete such training could be given 'Safe Zone' signs or stickers for their work spaces, or the organization could have one posted near the front door to signify that it is a space free of antibisexual violence" (2012: 369; see also Rostosky et al. 2010).

"BISEXUALITY IS MAINSTREAM. IT'S JUST NOT IN THE MATERIALS"

> A documentary that I could watch, that would be great. Websites. Privacy. In your own home. It's educational. It's fact-based. It's also visual media. . . . bisexuality is mainstream. It's just not in the materials. (Deanna)

Whether women wished to access any health services or not, all women believed there was a need for information, resources and texts such as books, films, and Internet sites, and these needed to be readily available publicly as well as privately. This was particularly important for women who did not wish to talk to GPs, counselors or other health workers but who sought independence and/or anonymity by accessing their own resources via the Internet. In their research, Dobinson et al. (2005) found participants called for a large-scale positive media and public information campaign for bisexuality awareness, education targeting the gay and lesbian community, and the development of bi social spaces, groups and communities. Also important were texts striking a balance between listing potential problems and presenting affirming examples and a diversity of options in regard to MORES:

> I think those sort of anthologies of different people's writings can just be really lovely, because you can find yourself somewhere in there, and I think they sort of show the diversity of bisexuality. (Jude)

> I went along to Hares and Hyenas [queer bookshop]with Ross one night. I had to have a book, and I found this book where the women in that book all became my mates. (Kaitlin)

Mental health professionals can also raise social awareness about polyamory. Barker & Langdridge (2010) report that there is still no consideration of consensual non-monogamy within mainstream psychology or relationship therapy texts, while internationally best-selling relationship self-help books continue to present almost exclusively heterosexual lifelong monogamy as the natural mode of human relating and the "happily ever after": "I have been hunting for years now and I have found lots of books and videos and groups over the Internet, blogs, e-lists on polyamory" (Naomi).

The Internet was discussed by many women as a place that could provide information confidentially and anonymously, again with a balance between negativity and affirmation. Peterson (2001) studied men's online support networks and found men often readily provide support to others in need. Previously private e-mail messages and postings from other lists are likewise shared, in part to stimulate discussion. A number of professional therapists subscribe to the lists and are able to answer the men's questions, such as how to determine if a potential counselor is sympathetic, what are appropriate responses from a counselor, and does the counselor's own sexual orientation make a difference. Silenzio et al. (2009) found that online social support helped prevent bisexuals from experiencing higher rates of suicide ideation. Hou & Lu's (2013) study analyzes the participants' use of bisexual websites in Taiwan for social support in terms of four groupings: screening potential friends; participating in the bisexual virtual community; coming out and releasing stress; and looking for romance. The Internet is "interactive, anonymous, hyperlinked, multiple-mode representative (e.g., pictures, animations, and sound)... accessible, affordable, and approximate" (Hou and Lu, 2013: 1283–1284; see also Robinson & Moskovitz, 2013). However, it is problematic when the researchers conclude that "the Internet provides opportunities for married bisexual men to search for the real self [underlining is mine]" as if the self being lived in the physical world is not real (2013: 1292).

> Currently I'm on Polyfamilies, PolyOz. I was on AusBi, on Wombat. It's "Women of Beauty and Temptation." It's a female bi list in America. Females or female identifying. And they're a great, very, very, very talkative group. (Kirsten)

> I guess the Internet is an incredible place, incredibly supportive. There are bi support groups, bi mailing lists ... and there are polyamory lists and that's where I got support when my ex-boyfriend and my ex-girlfriend went off together, because there were people who knew how to deal with that and understood those sorts of things. (Rose)

However, some women reported that the negativity on some of these websites for women in MOREs was problematic (Coon, 2012):

> I think a lot of it's [a negative Internet site] probably been done by a woman whose husband hasn't told her and he's been doing it for God knows how many years. And she's probably caught something ... and I think I would do too, get on the net and vent it out. (Lesley)

Indeed, Sharae set up her own website in response to a lack of positive and varied information for MOREs:

> *Sharae:* ... although I've mentioned some of those sites on my website so that I'm not biased to say you have to stay in a relationship, because there are some women out there who if they're with really yobboish men, they might be having a really hard time. And I've got a Google search or Google Alerts. It sends me information and I still haven't found too many resources that are positive ... I get emails saying thank you for the site. I have women coming in where their husbands or partners have given them my site address...

> *Michael:* We know of at least 210 men who are on another list that are bisexual and are not telling their wives, screwing around.... Another group that's on there, it's a very secretive group. You can't get in without being invited.

CONCLUSION

Like the health of all people, bisexual men and their women partners' health is influenced by other demographic factors, such as race and ethnicity, gender, age, disability or chronic health conditions and financial resources. It is also influenced by attributes of one's social environment and personal history, such as mental health stigma, HIV stigma, access to transportation, history of imprisonment, history of sexual victimization and many other factors (Ebin, 2012). Understanding more about the health causes and outcomes of people in MOREs can help us improve their health by learning when and how to tailor health education, outreach and messaging; by helping individuals become empowered health consumers and advocates; by assisting health providers in becoming culturally competent; by learning from successful strategies that bisexuals or bisexual communities may be using to support their health or the health of their communities; by understanding how their beliefs about health and health care may affect their health status; and by supporting funding for efforts to enhance MORE health.

It is important to acknowledge that, as with race and ethnicity, it is generally understood that bisexuality and being in MOREs in and of itself do not cause negative health outcomes. The health status is adversely affected by social factors including minority stress, which may be furthered by MOREs being a minority within minority communities, and the related factor of MORE invisibility (Miller et al. 2007). Health services, sites of power and gate-keeping, must not do what Britzman describes as refusing "difficult knowledge" (1998: 118). Likewise, they must avoid what Richards & Barker call the "clinical illusion" whereby all bisexual men and MOREs are instantly problematized as that is all that health service providers see of this group (2013: 11).

> There is a revolution occurring in our consulting rooms, our clients are no longer coming to us because they want to be normal, they are coming to us because they want to be whole. . . . Our job is no longer to help those who seek our assistance to achieve the cultural ideal, the mythical norm of well-adjusted middle class heterosexual adulthood (Firestein, 2007: preface, page unnumbered).

Part V

NOT JUST BELONGING BUT BLOOMING IN THE BORDERLANDS

Chapter 17

"A Door that hasn't been Opened"
Women's Final Words for Future Women

> It's okay if you're in a gay relationship and you have children, but it's bisexual men and women, that just seems to be a door that hasn't been opened, and we're supposed to be an open-minded society. I just think it's a shame, particularly for the women that are stuck in traditional type relationships, that they have nowhere to turn. (Louisa)

In this chapter, we will be presenting 'final words' women wanted to say for and to others who would be getting to know them through this book. All research participants believed that women in relationships with bisexual men was both a social and research issue that had not been addressed as its multiple realities required. This rendered them "unspeakable" and therefore erased from existence:

> Whatever is unnamed, undepicted in images, whatever is misnamed as something else, made difficult to come by, whatever is buried in the memory by the collapse of meaning under an inadequate or line language, this will become not merely unspoken but unspeakable (Adrienne Rich, 1979: 199).

Hence, very pertinent to our roles as researchers is Madison's discussion of research as "co-performative witnessing" (2007: 826). It is *"being there and with* as a political act in the excavation of subjugated knowledges and belongings for the creation of alternative futures" (2007: 829). As presented in chapter 1, the interview/conversation became a space for women to think through issues, to feel empowered, and to ask us for contact details of various groups and individuals they could access, including each other.

As the project developed, it became apparent that the participants were also "queer coyotes" alongside ourselves as researchers (Valadez & Elsbree,

2005). In providing their experiences and insights for future women in MOREs, as well as families, communities and colleagues who will love, live and learn with them, they are serving as 'mediators' in future queer border crossings. Throughout this book, and as again becomes evident in this concluding, yet forward-opening chapter, they fulfilled and continue to fulfill four characteristics of border crossing research as set out by Valadez & Elsbree:

- operating in "secreto": being protective of future women and their MOREs, using the research process and this book to help them move forward and cross borders;
- knowing "los codigos": knowing the codes of both the border zone and Center that future women live within, between and beyond, and thus teaching, explaining and working with the codes of each to the other. This included relaying the needs of future women and MOREs to health services as well as conveying the existences of resources and resource persons to other women;
- having "la facultad": reading the different situations and contexts of future women and their MOREs quickly and accurately; seeing into the deeper realities below the surface such as understanding the wider heteronormative framings, often interwoven with particular cultural and religious framings, within which future women and their male bisexual partners experience oppression and undertake resistance and agency;
- expressing sincere "compromiso": having a commitment toward social transformation, social justice and the politics of recognition (2005: 176–77; see also Pallotta-Chiarolli & Pease, 2014).

Louisa's use of the term "traditional type relationships" appears to have two meanings when we read the final words of these "queer coyote" women in this chapter:

1. "traditional type relationships": *women are oppressed or vulnerable in relationships* with bisexual men who conform to traditional patriarchal constructions of relationships wherein men control their lives before and after disclosure; and women play the traditional subservient gender role of maintaining family and home functioning.
2. "traditional type relationships": *women and their partners are constrained and oppressed not by their own relationship dynamics but by societal forces and expectations of relationships* which make it difficult for them to construct new relationship models that suit them, and which would be conducive to nurturing what the partners in MOREs have between them.

Ultimately, all women asked other women to take control, given the reality of situated agency, and make decisions that suited them in regard to what kind of relationship they wanted with their partners:

> Whatever your individual choice is, the new meanings of fidelity is to be faithful to yourself, to what you believe, to whatever commitments you make and the person you love has consciously decided to make. . . . To leave form behind means that we will have to operate from new levels of responsibility and self-awareness. Being aware enough to choose, being ongoingly conscious enough to evaluate (Kingma,1998: 191, 197).

The above calls to mind Tornstam's (2005) theory of gereotranscendence, as discussed in chapter 7. Can this transcendence of panopticonic surveillance and restriction occur before old age? It would seem that many women posited that it could and hoped that future women would develop a "code of their own":

> This is a time of unrest. The world is losing its boundaries. . . . and the closets are opening. . . [As] displaced persons. . . we live with a code of our own.
> (Happy Ho in De Ishtar & Sitka, 1991: 8).

"WHY SHOULD HE HAVE HIS CAKE AND EAT IT TOO"

> Don't put up with it, have some self-respect and sense of self-worth. It's not your problem, love them, support them, remain friends if you can but not at your expense. You need to enjoy life too—why should he have his cake and eat it too! (Josie)

Many women like Josie wanted women in "traditional type relationships," wherein they were oppressed or vulnerable because of bipatriarchal masculinist domination, to take control and refuse to tolerate it. They could understand the love and togetherness that often kept women adhering to or tolerating abusive relationships, but they wanted women to recognize when their partners were taking advantage of their desire to adhere to their important traditional roles as wives and mothers. Often they were able to "justify" or rationalize to themselves their reasons for staying in the relationship and how, while no one else knew what was happening, its façade could be maintained. Ultimately, however, this was preventing women from living full lives themselves:

> They'll [the readers] probably wonder why I stayed or how I coped. And if they're in the same situation themselves, they can justify why they stay and also, no one knows what's going on . . . it [her experiences and those of other women

in the book] may help other women make a decision that life's pretty good and not be sort of screwed around. (Jeannette)

I've been dealing with a child, and I've only just realized now. Basically follow your feelings, your sixth sense, really believe in it, and don't blame yourself. Don't keep giving him the benefit of the doubt, and really try and find out who you are if you're not sure, because who you are is maybe allowing this person to perform this way. . . . ask them to be honest with you, if nothing else, because then you feel you have control back. Otherwise you're being manipulated, you're not being respected as a person, and that is the most damaging—that not feeling that you are respected. (Loredana)

Women often advised caution, communication and compassion in negotiating and navigating the future of their MORE in order not to create even further devastation:

Your first thought is, "Kill the bastard. Kick his balls. Run the cricket bat up his arse. Burn all his clothes, tell his mother, a page in the newspaper or sky write what a bastard he is and what he's done." Those are all the initial reactions, but take time, sit down, talk about it. It must be harder for them than it is for you, even though they don't admit it . . . . Don't pack their bags, you need each other. You had something once. If you've had children together, try to talk it out. Set up the ground rules between yourselves . . . Even if you separate six months or twelve months down the track, do not do it on the spur of the moment. (June)

I think it's essential that you never try to make a guy choose between yourself and another guy because you're different. There's no choice there. . . . I think it's really important to make sure that you've got yourself anchored somewhere, that you're fulfilled and that he's a bonus. I think also there is a tendency for the woman to want to cope all the time. . . we overcompensate for the difficulties that they [partners] have . . . so you need again to take care of yourself. . . . have some savings for yourself and just make sure that you're okay, and maybe expect a little bit more out of them. They're adults too. They're part of the relationship. . . . Even though 95% of the time you accept it and respect it and life's really happy like that, there are times I think when everybody, no matter what their persuasion, feels insecure, and if you're having a PMS day or a bad hair day or whatever, it's really easy to feel depressed with the pressure from around you. (Luna)

Similarly, Lee advised women to face the facts of their partner's bisexuality and think about what they can handle and what they can't, rather than expecting their partners to "change" their "sexual urge":

If their partner is bisexual, they're bisexual. They're not going to be able to change that. . . . if you honestly, after a period of time, cannot handle it then get out . . . you can't just grin and bear it, because that's not a marriage any more. (Lee)

Interestingly, as Vaid (2012) states below, if the relationship is based on traditional notions of commitment and loving the whole person, then these traditional values can be put to good use in working toward staying together in a more honest, negotiated and nontraditional way:

> There is an uneasy relationship between most social justice movements and notions of tradition be they embodied in traditional culture, traditional family, sacred tradition or inherited teaching that is accepted as the natural order of things.... We argue for new worlds, radical new possibilities even as we pursue accommodation and renovation of the status quo to make ourselves more comfortable (2012:11).

Hence, although as quoted above, Lee was urging women to get out of marriages they could not handle, she simultaneously believed in the traditional notion of love being able to handle everything and adapting this to designing a nontraditional marriage:

> If you love your spouse, you can make it work. That's what it all comes down to in the end. You married one person for the whole person, and if you value your commitment then you will work through anything. (Lee)

Relationships with children featured in Marissa's words for other women considering whether to leave or stay:

> I was thinking, "Oh look, every marriage is different and we can do this, we are both really good for our kids and it'd be really great for our kids if we're together" but I think over those 3 years I came to the discovery that actually, I myself wasn't good for the kids in that situation because I had so little head space for them and I'm feeling like I'm doing it much better now. I have them on my own for a week and I can devote my week to them pretty much apart from when I'm working and then I have a week where I don't have them here all the time and I've got space to think . . . I felt like tons had been lifted off my shoulders when I separated from Mick. I really didn't think it'd feel like that but it did feel really really good. (Marissa)

Other women strongly connected the reluctance to leave their relationships or resist change to the upbringing they may have had, and the cultural mythologies they were greatly influenced by, in relation to what marriage and women's roles were to be:

> There were stories of tragedy and hope. The tragedy lay not only in the marital and personal break-downs but in the fact that some marriages might never have been made and others might never have broken down had it not been for society's sexism and homophobia and that so much of that pain had been needless.

The hope lies not only in the happy endings that eventually came to pass, but also . . . that they learn from and use their own experiences to help others, and that the failures of one generation can hence be turned into the successes of its successors (Gochros, 1989: 255–256).

You know, someone who has been brought up within a religious background, has very clear definitions of what life is. You know, the 2.4 kids and the Volvo. If at the age of 45 you suddenly find out that for 20 years, your husband has been having sex with men and you knew nothing about it, it can be quite devastating. (Jolene)

We've got Hollywood, we've got weddings, we've got honeymoons. They're the fantasy that keep everything going maybe, because we stink as a whole race. If you look at what we do to this planet, realistically, we're parasites, and truly, just to destroy it basically, so maybe we need these fantasies. We've had myths and legends and religion and philosophy, intellectual pursuits, fairy tales when we're kids, all that kind of stuff. Maybe we need that. . . . You see people compromising because they see they're not meeting expectations, whether they're society's expectations or their family's or whatever, and all of a sudden, because I can't meet them, then am I second class citizen? (Nicole)

It was important to hear from women in open and nontraditional relationships wanting to speak to women in traditional relationships:

If he's happy you should feel happy, and if you're jealous that he's got another man, well, don't be. If you think that's not fair, then you should not have chosen a bisexual man. . . . It's "I've chosen this path and it's okay, this is what I want, this is what you can give me, but what do you really feel and who are you really, and when we have that clear, that's it." (Temptress)

If you've got low self-esteem, don't get walked over. If you are not bisexual yourself, and you have a bisexual partner, you're on a steep learning curve and as such, be open, but don't let them get away with stuff, because like any boy, they'll try and get away with things. . . . communication is very, very important, as is honesty. (Kirsten)

Shelley wanted to speak out to bisexual men who were cheating on their partners, letting them know MOREs like hers distanced and differentiated themselves from these kinds of men to the point of not labelling themselves bisexual and married:

Advice to men who are bi: Make sure your relationship is a healthy one. A bit of advice for bisexual men who sneak and cheat on their wives: Just be a man and be honest with your wife. You are the lowest of the low and you give bis a bad name. You think you are so cool and I know the brotherhood thing you have going with your guy pals doing the same thing and I just want to say you are the most selfish and pathetic humans I have ever come across! . . . Advice for other women: if a man wants to go both ways, believe he's with you because he wants to be with you and so let him do it. It's an aspect of him. It's not superceding the woman. It's not that they love you less. Some women feel they have to fulfill every need of a guy but that's energy draining. Women can find it freeing because if he can talk to a woman about it all, then he won't do it behind her back. Be confident and secure. (Shelley)

This advice was also forthcoming from the bisexual male partners of the women in our research:

I'd like to say to guys that are bisexual that they have to be, first of all, honest with themselves to admit that they have those desires and be honest with their female partner. I mean, I spent most of my life hiding things, my desires, in the closet as they say and after Vicky and I discussed all this stuff, we were actually laying in bed one day and I said, "You know what I'm going to do today? Clean out that closet and that's it." So from then on no secrets. (Mike, Vicky's husband)

"WE DON'T HAVE A TRADITIONAL MARRIAGE"

It is hard to say if our relationship is better or worse for hubby's sexuality. This is normal for us and it's all we have known. It is hard to imagine if being of a different sexual orientation would change our love in any way. Hubby being bisexual simply means that we don't have a traditional marriage. We are more than happy with our lives. I think our levels of trust run a lot deeper that it does in a lot of people's relationships. Trust is more important than monogamy to us. (Shelley)

Many women in nontraditional relationships wanted other women to know that they also could construct new relationship models that suit them and their partners. These would be conducive to nurturing what they have between them as partners, rather than trying to constrain themselves into normative relationship structures or feel that, if they couldn't, they would have to exit the MORE. As Shelley reflected, what external society may construct as abnormal was what she and her partner happily called "normal for us." Indeed, theorists have contextualized the social ascription of abnormality to MOREs as being similar to previous eras' notions of abnormal relationships which today are considered normal, as Gochros reflected in the late 1980s:

Just a decade ago interracial marriages were "unthinkable" and usually failed not because of the partners' biological racial differences, but because of the isolation, stigma, and lack of support they received. Today they are more accepted and relatively viable... Similarly, it can be expected that as acceptance, information, and support increases, the problems I have described will decrease... These [MORE] couples were pioneers traveling uncharted trails without the companionship of the wagon train or the leadership of a wagonmaster. Given the handicaps they faced, what seems surprising is not that so many marriages failed or that so many women sooner or later fell apart, but that so many women tried so hard and recovered so well, that so many marriages were still intact with the potential for survival, and that some had not simply survived but were flourishing (1989: 251, 256).

In 2014, Kort echoed Gochros' comparison by referring to "mixed-orientation miscegenation [which] is as taboo today as black-white miscegenation was fifty years ago" (2014a: 148). As Hudson writes, bisexuality "has inherited, by default, the same negativity and condemnation that homosexuality has endured so frequently throughout history. In doing so, it has victimized the wives and demonized the husbands" (2013: 531). Thus, as these researchers and clinicians state, we need to

> revisit the past to build the future... People partake in controversial and vitriolic debate on sexual orientation, frequently popularized via online blogs and journals, often based on inconclusive empirical investigations and publications in scientific journals, psychological expertise, personal testimonies, and other forms of supposed evidence. It is unfortunate that so much time is wasted... The bottom line is that some people will continue to partake in what gives them pleasure, not what gives them an identity (Hudson, 2013: 548).

Indicative of this border between the residual and the emergent, some women did position their relationship within temporal shifts in what constitutes a traditional or non-traditional marriage, what is considered radical or normal, and how these shifting definitions and judgments are determined by the absence or availability of knowledge, which I and all the women hope this book contributes to:

> I think the old thing is knowledge. One generation after another, it's changing. Like my daughter's reaction to it [bisexuality] was completely different to what my reaction would have been at 24 ... It's like my mother saying, "Oh, maybe he's a faggot," and me saying, "He's this wonderful human being," and then my daughter saying, "Well, he doesn't know whether he likes pussy or a dick, maybe he just likes both." (Helena)

The following are excerpts from a poem Jude sent to us about looking back at her relationship from the hindsight of shifting times and understandings, and how if she could have the time again, she would choose to stay with her partner:

If I was with you now
I'd tell you how in love
With you I am
How much joy I know
Because of you.

. . .

If I was with you now
I'd watch you with expectation
Wanting to know more of you
All of you
Waiting to be surprised

What many women also pointed out, however, was the need to see, hear and learn more about nontraditional relationships, or what happens when "putting down the two faulty maps—the essentialist script and the monogamy script—that the culture has given them and exploring the territory of their loves and desires on their own" (Swan & Benack, 2012: 65):

> I think the one thing I did realize is that it's important not to keep thinking, "What would other people do, and is this acceptable behavior in a marriage?" And worrying that I was being a doormat by staying and trying to work things out. . . . Life is short, don't overanalyze things or agonize over them, wonder whether you fit into 'normal' society, or wonder what other people might be thinking. (Maria)

> Set some rules, boundaries, and listen to your heart. Don't ever take each other for granted and get to know your husband's partners. They make great friends. Keep things positive and never use your husband's sexuality as a weapon against him during an argument. . . . Not all marriages are meant to last, it has to be a win-win situation for both of you. The last thing you want is to be in a mentally cruel situation. Know when to let go and move on. (Shelley)

> It's just phenomenal, the difference that it's [creating a poly-bi relationship] made and I want to get that out to the world in as many forms as possible, so that people can sense at least that that's possible for human beings to do it and start looking for it and creating it for themselves in their own relationships. (Jacinta)

Sharae sent us a copy of the e-mail she sent to Bonnie Kaye in remonstration against the ignorance of her website and publications. In her research interview, Sharae had stated:

This woman is perpetrating the lie that bisexuality doesn't exist and that women who stay with their husbands are simply deluding themselves. I couldn't help myself, I had to answer the calling of putting her in her place. I am really sick of these women who devalue the relationships we have with our partners. The fact that some of these so called authors are counselling women as well just scares the pants off me. (Sharae)

Here are some excerpts from her letter, which is an emphatic example of "bi-furiosity" (Barker, 2015):

Dear Bonnie
With your husband treating you with such contempt, I believe you had every reason to leave and to dislike his behavior. However, I do believe that you could word your articles a little differently, so as not to force your own misguided opinions so strongly upon others. In your article, you mention that women who stay with their husbands are not accepting the truth. That is a load of Codswallop. I am not too scared to face the truth. On the contrary. I am a very emotionally strong woman who has chosen to love my husband "Unconditionally" regardless of his sexuality. I have enough self-esteem to know that he is with me because he wants to be, not because he HAS to be. Or because it provides him with some form of normality/stability. . . . I fully recognize that my husband could just as easily leave me for another man. . . as he could another woman. I could sit around and dwell on that paranoid delusion for the rest of my life. But I don't live with that fear. I "choose" NOT to. . . . why should I deny myself the happiness of a relationship that supplies both my children and I with fulfillment, contentment and love, just because a few people don't agree with the relationship mode I have chosen!?. . .

I would also like to say that I believe that counselling women to relabel their husbands [as gay], as you have, for their own empowerment, is somewhat irresponsible and reprehensible. I understand you are bitter about the relationship that you lost, (even though you have a wonderful relationship with your husband now.) But by re-labeling a person you effectively take away a part of themselves that they believe is valid. This in effect lowers that person's self-esteem. . . . A designer is not just a dressmaker. A poet is not just a writer. A bisexual is not just gay! I find it difficult to believe that an educated counsellor would dishonor and damage another person's self-esteem so intentionally. . . . Or perhaps this is a lot about making money off the books? The very concentrated focus on books has not escaped my attention!

What is your opinion about bisexual women? I would sincerely love a response to this question. Because quite frequently it is not regarded as disgusting or abnormal for a woman to be bisexual. Only a male. . . .

Wishing you all the best in your path to enlightenment.
Cheerfully yours   Sharae

In our research, women with bisexual partners speak of wanting equal acknowledgment and affirmation for their relationships alongside other relationship and family structures. They want to hold out their relationships as evidence of what happens when mythical norms about sexuality, gender and relationship are believed and uncontested, such as discovering their partners have been having sex with men while performing according to the myth of heteromonogamous marriage. This begins with an awareness of how they are currently 'in-between' normative and deviant constructions of relationship and family and an acknowledgment of how this 'outsiders within' positioning influences their subjectivity, public identity, and the way they love, parent and negotiate the public and private settings of their relationships and families. As discussed in previous chapters, Ahmed (2010) uses the metaphor of happy and unhappy queers:

> We must stay unhappy with this world.... The happy queer, who has good manners, who is seated at the table in the right way, might be a strategic form of occupying an uncivil world. But strategic occupations can keep things in place.... A revolution of unhappiness might require an unhousing; it would require not legitimating more relationships, more houses, even more tables but delegitimating the world that "houses" some bodies and not others (2010: 105).

What kinds of alternative kinship stories are possible, which are not organized by the desire for reproduction, or the desire to be like other families, or by the promise of happiness as "being like"? (2010: 114). Queers can be made unhappy by the conventional routes of happiness, an unhappiness which might be an effect of how normative happiness makes nonnormatives unhappy: "To be happily queer is to explore the unhappiness of what gets counted as normal" (2010: 117). As Som writes, the "queer kitchen" then becomes its own site of happiness:

> "You can't have your cake and eat it too," they tell me. Well, sure I can, if I learn to bake it myself. Then I can not only eat cake forever, but I can have all different kinds. I can even have bread.... welcome to the queer kitchen! (1991: 146).

Our research supports the pioneering research of Nahas & Turley (1979), Whitney (1990), Gochros (1985; 1989) & Buxton (1991; 2001; 2004a, b; 2006; 2007). They called for inserting knowledge and debates about MOREs into the wider society so that the personal agentic strengths and strategies deployed by many women and their partners is increasingly acknowledged and supported by wider cultural, structural and institutional frameworks:

> No longer are we squatters trying to lay claim to a bit of heterosexual territory and a bit of homosexual territory in order to fashion a makeshift identity... Instead, we have created new territory by defining it in our own terms (Rust, 1992: 301).

In chapters 1 and 2, Derridean deconstruction was used to introduce MOREs as inhabiting "difference," defined as hybrid, fluid and multiple rather than just a point of comparison and contrast between two fixed polarities. As the conclusion of this research, and as questions to take into future research, we can reflect on the four facets of "difference":

- "difference beyond": What differences have we seen women in MOREs experience which challenge or go beyond mainstream understandings and constructions of "different" relationships?
- "difference as excess" or "a point beyond which language and explanation cannot proceed": How have MOREs illustrated limitations and absences in language and discourse? Has this book struggled in discussing and explaining lived experiences within a language and discursive framework that does not allow for them?
- "difference within" that shows how "a thing is also partly what it is not, what it is differentiated from": What mixtures and differences among and between MOREs have we seen exist which problematize any attempt at homogenizing and generalizing discourses?
- "difference against" whereby conventional norms and dominant discourses are questioned and their gaps revealed: how have the lives and loves described in this book disrupted and questioned conventional assumptions and accepted silences in relation to sexualities in relationships? (Burbules, 1997: 106–108).

As presented briefly in chapter 12, we are now seeing some increasing shifts in positive bi/MORE/poly representations in film, interwoven with cultural diversity. Two of Turkish-Italian director Ferzan Ozpetek's films, *Steam* (1997) and *The Ignorant Fairies* (2001), epitomize the truths and possibilities that could be encompassed by MOREs and their worlds. In *Steam*, a successful, married male professional from Italy explores bisexual pleasure while in Istanbul. He is then discovered with a male lover by his previously estranged wife, Marta, who consequently discovers a new eroticism within herself in watching her husband with another man. In *The Ignorant Fairies*, a successful female physician in Rome becomes part of her dead bisexual husband's sexually, culturally and gender diverse community: "she stumbles into the elective family of her husband's lover, made of 'fairies,' immigrants, and queers, who are presented sympathetically through her surprised and bewildered gaze" (Anderlini-D'Onofrio, 2007: 122). Thus, monosexual, monogamous and monocultural identities and communities premised on either/or competitions and constraints are discarded for the emotional sustainability and enrichment offered by a both/and world of intermixture and collaborations "to model an ethic of care, respect, and emotional sustainability" (Anderlini-D'Onofrio, 2007: 124).

In both Ozpetek films, women are presented as experiencing a growth in their self-knowledge regarding their own sensual, sexual and erotic power, possibilities, confidence and desires, including the pleasure derived from watching and/or participating in erotic play and sex with gay and bisexual men. For example, *Steam* introduces Madame, a single, classy, Italian émigré in Istanbul who describes herself as the first Western mistress of a men's bathhouse. She admits to having chosen this occupation because surreptitiously witnessing men's private pleasures intrigues her. It is her death that causes Francesco's trip to Istanbul, where he enters her space and becomes bisexual too. After Francesco is killed by the mob that opposes his plan to restore the steam bath because they want to destroy the old buildings and make a commercial center, Marta decides to stay in Istanbul and becomes the new expatriate Italian *maitresse* of a men's steam bath as well as best friends with his lover and part of his lover's family. It is important to note that Marta had actually followed Francesco to Istanbul to get a divorce and marry Paolo, her male lover of two years. But she falls back in love with him because she likes the way in which bisexuality has transformed him. Thus, while Francesco knows his marriage is in crisis when he leaves Rome for Istanbul, he leaves as a straight man who discovers his bisexuality, not homosexuality, and it is likely that if he had not been killed, a bi-poly relationship would've been established with his wife and his Turkish lover.

The Ignorant Fairies begins with a death, this time a fatal accident. A recent widow and her late husband's male lover are both grieving the sudden death of the bisexual man between them, Massimo. They shared this man, unknowingly, for years. Antonia, the wife, was not aware of Massimo's secret life. Michele, the gay lover, believed Massimo's marriage was a fiction. But the reality is that Massimo loved them both and was unable to speak it. The void left by Massimo's death in the emotional lives of both his partners is vast. The fact they were rivals does not count in the end, as they fall in love. Indeed, Anderlini-D'Onofrio contends that "if all three were alive, they would form a polyamorous triad" (2009: 151). In various scenes, Antonia and Michele are seen grappling with the reality of their shared lover's "other lovelife," Antonia realizing the group sex Massimo engaged in with Michele, and Michele visiting Antonia's beautiful villa: "the two lounge chairs side by side in the garden next to the two swings, then the two armchairs half-way turned to face each other in the living room" (Anderlini-D'Onofrio, 2007: 130). In an ensuing scene, Antonia and Michele finally accept the fact that they are drawn to each other:

> She hugs him and the hug gradually turns into a French kiss. The diegesis interjects the image of Massimo's face in between cuts of the kiss. . . . Massimo, the different memories that Antonia and Michele have of him, and their grief for his loss, is the force that connects Antonia and Michele erotically (Anderlini-D'Onofrio, 2007: 130).

This bisexual kiss is used by Ozpetek to represent the fluidity and multiplicity of erotic desire that humans experience, and is representative of the upshot of the intense bisexual and polyamorous inner dialogues that have transformed Michele and Antonia into people capable of multiple inclusive forms of love.

The movie ends on an ambiguous note. "Ozpetek certainly won't deliver happy heterosexist endings in a Hollywood style" says Anderlini-D'Onofrio (2009: 132). Antonia finds out she may be pregnant from Massimo but keeps this information from Michele and the other members of her newly acquired "queerly mixed" family. When she leaves for an unspecified amount of time, she knows the child won't be an "orphan" but rather a baby with a whole bunch of parental figures, including herself, Michele, their elective family of foreigners, fairies, and queers, and Antonia's mother: "a baby stands a chance to acquire some good parental figures because some adults have matured beyond monogamy and monosexuality" (Anderlini-D'Onofrio, 2009: 150).

Thus, Ozpetek's films explore bi/poly/queer complexities wherein the characters "give up conventional dreams" of happiness (Ahmed, 2010), whether they be heteronormative or homonormative. Certainly, Michele's homonormative gay identity and Antonia's heteronormative identity as a monogamous heterosexual woman are being queered by their falling in love (Anderlini-D'Onofrio, 2009). However, what is absent from Ozpetek's films and in so many representations of married bisexual men with both male and female partners is seeing these bi-poly relationships as flourishing, with the absence of death and crisis.

Two more recent films have travelled beyond desultory plot devices. First, *Angels of Sex* (2014) is a Spanish film that begins with two happy seemingly heterosexual couples wherein the two men, Bruno and Rai, discover their erotic desire for each other, while Bruno's partner Carla also falls for Rai. As Szymanski writes, "The movie doesn't have room for labels. Rai doesn't identify, and Bruno, when asked directly if he's bi, simply says, 'I don't know'. There's a satisfying ending for all bisexuals, and that again, is unique for stories like this" (2014: 302). Indeed, although there is a motorbike accident, the riders do not die. Each character works through normative, challenging barriers and boundaries to meet on the borders in Barcelona, exuberantly dancing in their apartment symbolizing they are both free and committed in their new bi/poly/queer relationship configuration. They are also compared to the unhappy seemingly heteromonogamous chilling marriage of Carla's parents wherein her father is openly having an affair, creating much humiliation for her mother.

The second film that opens the door into a queerer future is Tom Tykwer's *3* (2010). Hanna and Simon are a couple together for 20 years living in modern Berlin. Although their connection is still strong and loving, there is a lessening of sexual passion. First Hanna and then Simon meet Adam, whose middle name is, aptly, Born, and begin independent romantic relationships with him. The three characters "come together at the end to forge a new experiment apart from the mundane and stifling long-term coupledom that is expected of them" (Ruthstrom, 2010: 602). As the story shifts among the three different relationships, the viewer can easily accept the love and affection that is expressed within each configuration. In one of the scenes, Simon makes clear to Adam that he doesn't identify as gay and is unsure of what he should identify as. "Adam's comfort with his own bisexuality and inability to worry about restrictive definitions prompts him to counsel Simon to 'Say goodbye to your deterministic understanding of biology' (Ruthstrom, 2010: 604). Indeed, there are many references to fertility, new life and biogenetics in the film. As Ruthstrom writes, "it's no shock when Hanna discovers she is pregnant. And it is when she dashes to Adam's apartment on a rainy night to tell him of her pregnancy that all of the secrets burst forth" (2010: 604). Ruthstrom concludes:

> *3* is the most satisfying film about bisexuality that I have seen in years.... The last 15 minutes of the film provides an incredibly liberating narrative.... A close-up of the three of them spooning in bed together seems almost too sentimental for Tykwer to end upon, so at the very last second he shrinks the image into a petri dish and removes it with a researcher's hand. Is this just another experiment? (2010: 605).

Or is it a sample of what will grow from an embryonic social experiment in today's times to a future of opening up ways of doing MOREs?

In so many ways, these four films are symbolic of where this book and our research ends, as an opening of a door to new lifeworlds:

> All sides of the issue need to be considered in the media, research, social theory, and religious thought... we need: social realists to affirm society's need for stability by exploring alternative marriage and family arrangements, and sexual realists to point out the diversity of sexual orientations as part of the natural order and but one aspect of the individuals who make up society (Buxton, 1991: 275).

It is also intriguing to reflect that these films are from countries other than the mainstream movie production companies of the United States and

United Kingdom. Thus, these films are from borderlands daring to challenge the more stereotypical and problematic representations of bi/poly/MORE individuals and relationships constructed from within these dominant media locations. These films are from "sites of creative cultural production" that have produced sites of creative representations (Rosaldo, 1989: 208).

> as long as the complexity and difficulty of engaging with the diversely hybrid experiences of heterogeneous contemporary societies are denied and not dealt with, binary thinking continues to mark time while the creative interval is dangerously reduced to non-existence (Trinh, 1991: 229).

In chapter 1, and as symbolically depicted on the cover of this book, I presented two previous historical "creative intervals" which we have seen in this book as having ongoing and future "potential for border breaking" and being "revolutionary" (Callis, 2014: 71): the precolonial Maori Te Arawa love story, which concerns Tutanekai, Hinemoa, and the flute-playing male companion, the takatapui, of Tutanekai called Tiki (Te Awekotuku 1991, 2001; Hutchings & Aspin, 2007); and the English painter from the colonial era of the nineteenth century, Edward Burne-Jones, evoking a similar narrative of Hinemoa, Tutanekai and Tiki in his painting *The Garden of Pan* (1886–1887). Similar to the multiple interpretations made available in *The Garden of Pan* and the Te Arawa story, contemporary MOREs are forging further "creative intervals" to foreground queer mestizje realities that resist and pollute heterocolonialist, monosexist, and heteropatriarchal dichotomous and fixed presumptions of gender and sexuality. The emerging representations and understandings of MOREs are challenging the residual beliefs voiced by D.H. Lawrence's character, Ursula, as quoted in chapter 1, that MORE-loving is "false, impossible." In Birkin's refusal to revert to the residual, we find the possibility of the emergent: "whether we love men or women—or both, or neither—will be as unimportant as whether or not we love cats or dogs—or both, or neither" (Weinrich, 2014: 545).

We hope our research and this book perform their part as cultural productions in the extension of the creative interval into the creative intransience.

References

Abbott, A. 2013, *Fairyland: A Memoir of my Father,* New York: W.W. Norton & Co.

Ackerley, J.R. 1960, *We Think the World of You,* NY: New York Review Books (reprint edition, 2011).

Ahmed, S. 2010, *The Promise of Happiness,* Durham, NC: Duke University Press.

Albury, K. 2015, 'Identity-plus?: bi-curiousity, sexual adventurism and the boundaries of 'straight' sexual practices and identities', *Sexualities,* 18 (5/6): 649–664.

Alexander, J. 2007, 'Bisexuality in the Media: A Digital Roundtable', *Journal of Bisexuality,* 7(1/2): 115–124.

Alexander, J. & Anderlini-D'Onofrio, S. 2010, *Bisexuality and Queer Theory: Intersections, Connections and Challenges,* New York: Routledge.

Altman, D. 2001, *Global Sex,* Chicago: The University of Chicago Press.

Altork, K. 1995, 'Walking the Fire Line: The Erotic Dimension of the Fieldwork Experience', in D. Kulick & M. Willson Eds *Taboo: Sex, Identity and Erotic Subjectivity in Anthropological Fieldwork,* London: Routledge.

American Psychological Association 2011, *Guidelines for Psychological Practice with Lesbian, Gay, & Bisexual Clients,* <http://www.apa.org/pi/lgbt/resources/guidelines.aspx>.

Amy-Chinn, D. 2012, 'GLAAD to Be Torchwood? Bisexuality and the BBC', *Journal of Bisexuality,* 12(1): 63–79.

Anapol, D. 1997, *Polyamory: The New Love Without Limits: Secrets of Sustainable Intimate Relationships,* San Rafael, California: Intinet Resource Center.

Anapol, D.M. 2010, *Polyamory in the 21st Century: Love and Intimacy with Multiple Partners,* New York: Rowman & Littlefield.

Anderlini-D'Onofrio, S. Ed. 2004, *Plural Loves: Designs for Bi and Poly Living,* New York: Harrington Park Press.

Anderlini-D'Onofrio, S. 2007, 'Bisexual games and Emotional Sustainability in Ferzan Ozpetek's Queer Films', *Journal of Bisexuality,* 6(4): 121–134.

Anderlini-D'Onofrio, S. 2009, *Gaia and the New Politics of Love: Notes from a Poly Planet,* Berkeley, CA: North Atlantic Books.

References

Anderson, B. 1983, *Imagined Communities: Reflections on the Origin and Spreads of Nationalism*, London: Verso.

Anderson, E. 2008, ''Being Masculine is Not About Who You Sleep With…:' Heterosexual Athletes Contesting Masculinity and the One-time Rule of Homosexuality', *Sex Roles: A Journal of Research*, 58(1–2): 104–115.

Anderson, E. 2009, *Inclusive Masculinities: The Changing Nature of Masculinities*, New York: Routledge.

Anderson, E. 2012, *The Monogamy Gap: Men, Love, and the Reality of Cheating*, Oxford: Oxford University Press.

Anderson, E., Scoats, R. & McCormack, M. 2015, 'Metropolitan Bisexual Men's Relationships: Evidence of a Cohort Effect', *Journal of Bisexuality*, 15(1): 21–39.

Angelides, S. 1994, 'The Queer Intervention: Sexuality, Identity, and Cultural Politics', *Melbourne Journal of Politics*, 22: 66–88.

Angelides, S. 1995, 'Rethinking The Political: Poststructuralism and the Economy of Heterosexuality', *Critical Inqueeries*, 1(1): 27–46.

Angelides, S. 2001, *A History of Bisexuality*, Chicago: University of Chicago Press.

Angelides, S. 2006, 'Historicizing BiSexuality: A Rejoinder for Gay/Lesbian Studies, Feminism, and Queer Theory', in K.E. Lovaas, J.P. Elia & G.A. Yep Eds *LGBT Studies and Queer Theory: New Conflicts, Collaborations and Contested Terrain*, New York: Harrington Park Press.

Antalffy, N. 2011, 'Polyamory and the Media', *SCAN: Journal of Media Art Culture*, 8(1): 1–10.

Anzaldua, G. 1987a, *Borderlands/La Frontera: The New Mestiza*, San Francisco: Aunt Lute.

Anzaldua, G. 1987b, 'Del Otro Lado', in J. Ramos Ed. *Companeras: Latina Lesbians*, New York: Latina Lesbian History Project.

Anzaldua, G. Ed. 1990, *Making Face/Making Soul/Haciendo Caras*, San Francisco: Aunt Lute.

Anzaldua, G.E. & Keating, A. Eds 2002, *This Bridge We Call Home: Radical Visions for Transformation*, New York: Routledge.

Arden, K. 1996, 'Dwelling in the House of Tomorrow: Children, Young People and Their Bisexual Parents', in S. Rose & C. Stevens Eds *Bisexual Horizons: Politics, Histories, Lives*, London: Lawrence and Wishart.

Aruna, V.K. 1994, 'The Myth of One Closet', in S. Lim-Hing Ed. *The Very Inside: An Anthology of Writing by Asian and Pacific Islander Lesbian and Bisexual Women*, Toronto: SisterVision.

Aspin, C. & Hutchings, J. 2006, 'Maori Sexuality', in M. Mulholland Ed. *State of the Maori Nation: Twenty-First Century Issues in Aotearoa*, Auckland: Reed Publishers.

Aspin, C. & Hutchings, J. 2007, 'Reclaiming the Past to Inform the Future: Contemporary Views of Maori Sexuality', *Culture, Health & Sexuality*, 9(4): 415–427.

Attali, J. 2005, *Monogamy: Here Today, Gone Tomorrow*, <www.foreignpolicy.com/story/cms.php?story_id=317&fpsrc=ealert050906>.

Atwood, A. 1998, *Husbands Who Love Men: Deceit, Disease and Despair*, Providence, Utah: AMI Publishers.

Auerback, S. & Moser, C., 1987, 'Groups for the Wives of Gay and Bisexual Men', *Social Work*, 32(4): 321–325.

Autumn, E. 2013, 'Challenging the Binary: Sexual Identity That Is Not Duality", *Journal of Bisexuality,* 13(3): 329–337.
Baird, B. 2007, 'Gay Marriage, Lesbian Wedding', *Gay and Lesbian Issues and Psychology Review*, 3(3): 61–170.
Bammer, A. 1992, 'Editorial', *New Formations*, 1(7): 7–11.
Bandura, A. 2002, 'Social Cognitive Theory of Mass Communication' In B. Jennings & D. Zillmann Eds *Media Effects: Advances in Theory and Research,* New Jersey: Lawrence Erlbaum Associates.
Barker, M. 2005, 'This is My Partner, & This is My... Partner's Partner: Constructing a Polyamorous Identity in a Monogamous World', *International Journal of Constructivist Psychology*, 18(1): 75–88.
Barker, M.J., 2015, 'Depression and/or Oppression? Bisexuality and Mental Health', *Journal of Bisexuality*, 15(3): 369–384.
Barker, M. 2013, *Rewriting the Rules: An Integrative Guide to Love, Sex and Relationships*, London: Routledge.
Barker, M. & Langdridge, D. 2010, 'Whatever Happened to Non-Monogamies? Critical Reflections on Recent Research and Theory', *Sexualities*, 13(6):748–772.
Barker, M., Richards, C., Jones, R., Bowes-Catton, H., Plowman, T., Yockney, J. & Morgan, M. 2012, *The Bisexuality Report: Bisexual Inclusion in LGBT Equality & Diversity*, London: The Centre for Citzenship, Open University.
Barker, M., Yockney, J., Richards, C., Jones, R., Bowes-Catton, H. & Plowman, T. 2012, 'Guidelines for Researching and Writing About Bisexuality', *Journal of Bisexuality*, 12(3): 376–392.
Barrington, J.S. 1981, *Sexual Alternatives for Men: Facts and Fantasies*, London: The Alternative Publisher.
Bartlett, M. 2013, *Cock,* New York: Dramatists Play Service Inc.
Bashford, K. 1993, 'Fanning The Flames', in K. Bashford, J. Laybutt, A. Munster & K. O'Sullivan Eds *Kink*, Sydney: Wicked Women Publications.
Bauer, C.K. 2013, *Naughty Girls and Gay Male Romance/Porn: Slash Fiction, Boys' Love Manga, and Other Works by Female "Cross-Voyeurs" in the U.S. Academic Discourses,* Hamburg, Germany: Anchor Academic Publishing.
Bauman, Z. 1973, *Culture & Praxis*, London: Routledge & Kegan Paul.
Bauman, Z. 1988, 'Strangers: The Social Construction of Universality and Particularity', *Telos*, 78: 7–42.
Bauman, Z. 1990, 'Modernity and Ambivalence', in M. Featherstone Ed. *Global Culture: Nationalism, Globalisation and Modernity*, London: Sage.
Bauman, Z. 1997, *Postmodernity and Its Discontents*, Cambridge: Polity Press.
Baumeister, R.F., Shapiro, J.P. & Tice, D.M. 1985, 'Two Kinds of Identity Crisis'. *Journal of Personality*, 53(3): 407–424.
Baumeister, R.F. 2004, 'Gender and Erotic Plasticity: Sociocultural Influences on the Sex Drive', *Sexual and Relationship Therapy*, 19(2): 133–139.
Beasley, C. 2010, 'The Elephant in the Room: Heterosexuality in Critical Gender/ Sexuality Studies', *NORA: Nordic Journal of Feminist and Gender Research*, 18(3): 204–209.
Becker, H.S., 1973, *Outsiders: Studies in the Sociology of Deviance*, New York: The Free Press.

Beckett, S., Mohummadally, A., Pallotta-Chiarolli, M. 2014, "Queerying Muslim Identities" in Ata, A. Ed. *Education Integration Challenges: The Case of Australian Muslims,* Melbourne: David Lovell Publishing.

Beemyn, G. 2011, 'Looking Back on Publishing with the Journal of Bisexuality or How a Genderqueer Person Ended Up Editing the First Works on Bisexual Men', *Journal of Bisexuality,* 11(4): 389–393.

Benn, P. 2012, *The Versatile Husband,* Melbourne: Argosy Media.

Bennett, G., Chapman, S. & Bray, F. 1989, 'A Potential Source for the Transmission of the Human Immunodeficiency Virus into the Heterosexual Population: Bisexual Men Who Frequent 'Beats'", *The Medical Journal of Australia,* 151: 314–318.

Bennett, K. 1992, 'Feminist Bisexuality: A Both/And Option for an Either/Or World', in E.R. Weise Ed. *Closer to Home: Bisexuality and Feminism,* Seattle: Seal Press.

Benzie, T. 2002, 'Leaving Me This Way', *Sydney Star Observer,* 28th Febuary: 23.

Bertone, C. & Pallotta-Chiarolli, M. Eds 2014, *Queerying Families of Origin,* London: Routledge.

Bergler, E. 1956, *Homosexuality: Disease or Way of Life?,* New York: Collier Books.

Bersten, R. 2008, 'Marginalia: Living on the Edge', *Gay and Lesbian Issues & Psychology Review,* 4(1): 9–18.

Bevin, E. 2005, Brindal Claims He's Victim of a Witch Hunt, *The Adelaide Advertiser* <www.theadvertiser.news.com.au/common/story_page/0.5936.16261863%255E2682.00.html>.

Beye, C.R. 2012, *My Husband and My Wives: A Gay Man's Odyssey.* New York: Farrar, Strauss and Giroux.

Bhabha, H. 1990, 'The Third Space' in J. Rutherford Ed. *Identity: Community, Culture, Difference,* London: Lawrence & Wishart.

Bhabha, H. 1994, *The Location of Culture,* London: Routledge.

Bigner, J.J. 1996, 'Working with Gay Fathers: Developmental, Postdivorce Parenting and Therapeutic Issues' In J. Laird & R.J. Green Eds *Lesbians and Gays in Couples and Families: A Handbook for Therapists,* San Francisco, CA: Jossey-Bass.

Bildstein, C. 2005a, 'Extortion Claim Over MP's Gay Liaison', *Adelaide Advertiser* 8th August.

Bildstein, C 2005b, 'Brindal Fears Gay Sex Was a Set-up', *Adelaide Advertiser* 11th August.

Blank, H. 2012, *Straight: The Surprisingly Short History of Heterosexuality,* Boston: Beacon Press.

Blee, K.M. 2003, 'Studying the Enemy', in B. Glassner & R. Hertz Eds *Our Studies, Ourselves: Sociologists' Lives and Work,* Oxford: Oxford University Press.

Bleiberg, S. Fertmann, A., Todhunter Friedman, C. & Godino, A. 2005, 'The Layer Cake Model of Bisexual Identity Development: Clarifying Preconceived Notions', *National Association for Campus Activities Programming Magazine,* 37(8): 1–19. <http://www.nyu.edu/residential.education/pdfs/article. bisexual.identity.pdf>

Block, J. 2008, *Open: Love, Sex, and Life in an Open Marriage,* Berkeley, CA: Seal Press.

Boden, D. 1990, 'The World As It Happens: Ethnomethodology and Conversation Analysis', in G. Ritzer Ed. *Frontiers of Social Theory: the New Syntheses,* New York: Columbia University Press.

Bostwick, W. & Hequembourg, A. 2014, 'Just a Little Hint': Bisexual-specific Microaggressions and Their Connection to Epistemic Injustices, *Culture, Health and Sexuality,* 16(5): 488–503.

Boulton, M., Schramm, E.Z., Fitzpatrick, R. & Hart, G. 1989, *Bisexual Men: Identity and Behaviour in Sexual Encounters,* Paper presented at the Twenty-First Annual Conference of the Medical Sociology Group, Manchester, England.

Boulton, M., Hart, G. & Fitzpatrick, R. 1992, 'The Sexual Behaviour of Bisexual Men in Relation to HIV Transmission', *AIDS Care,* 4(2): 165–175.

Boulton, M. & Fitzpatrick, R. 1993, 'The Public and Personal Meanings of Bisexuality in AIDS', *Advances in Medical Sociology,* 3: 77–100.

Bouzid, H. 2010, *Kavafis' Syndrome: An Odyssey of a Bisexual Moslem,* Baltimore: PublishAmerica.

Boykin, K. 2005, *Beyond the Down Low: Sex, Lies and Denial in Black America,* New York: Carroll & Graf Publishers.

Bradford, M. 2004, 'The Bisexual Experience: Living in a Dichotomous Culture', in R.C. Fox Ed. *Current Research on Bisexuality,* New York: Harrington Park Press.

Bradford, M. 2012, 'Couple Therapy with GLB-Straight Relationships', *Journal of GLBT Family Studies,* 8(1): 5–22.

Brant, M. 2006, *Five Married Men,* Self-published.

Brennan, D.J., Ross, L.E., Dobinson, C., Veldhuizen, S., Steele, L.S., 2010, 'Men's Sexual Orientation and Health in Canada', *Canadian Journal Of Public Health,* 101(3): 255–258.

Britzman, D.P., 1998, *Lost Subjects, Contested Objects: Toward a Psychoanalytic Inquiry of Learning,* Albany: State University of New York Press.

Brooks, K.D. & Quina, K. 2009, 'Women's Sexual Identity Patterns: Differences Among Lesbians, Bisexuals, and Unlabelled Women', *Journal of Homosexuality,* 56(8): 1030–1045.

Brooks, L.M., Inman, A.G., Klinger, R.S., Malouf, M.A. & Kaduvettoor, A. 2010, 'In Her Own Words: Ethnic-Minority Bisexual Women's Self-Reported Counselling Needs', *Journal of Bisexuality,* 10(3): 253–267.

Brooks, L.M. & Inman, A.G. 2013, 'Bisexual Counselling Competence: Investigating the Role of Attitudes and Empathy', *Journal of LBT Issues in Counselling,* 13(1): 65–86.

Browder, B.S. 2005, *On the Up and Up: A Survival Guide for Women Living with Men on the Downlow,* New York: Dafina Books.

Brown, R. McGruder 2014, 'Say It Loud, I'm A Black Bisexual Male and I'm Proud' in R. Ochs & S.H. Williams Eds *Rec.og.nize: the Voices of Bisexual Men,* Boston: Bisexual Resource Center.

Brown, T. 2002, 'A Proposed Model of Bisexual Identity Development that Elaborates on Experiential Differences of Women and Men', *Journal of Bisexuality,* 2(4): 67–91.

Brownfain, J.F. 1985, 'A Study of the Married Bisexual Male: Paradox and Resolution', *Journal of Homosexuality,* 111(2): 173–188.

Bryant, W. 1997, *Bisexual Characters in Film: From Anais to Zee,* New York: Haworth Press.

Bryant, W. 2005a, 'The Bisexual Biopic', *Journal of Bisexuality,* 5(1): 114–118.

Bryant, W. 2005b, 'Is That Me Up There?', in R.J. Suresha & P. Chvany Eds *Bi Men: Coming Out Every Which Way*, New York: Harrington Park Press.

Bryant, W.M. 2011, 'Bi Film Retrospective', *Journal of Bisexuality*, 11(4): 582–586.

Bryant, W.M. 2012, 'Paul Goodman Changed My Life', *Journal of Bisexuality*, 12(4): 539–542.

Buchbinder, D. & Waddell, C. 1992, 'Myth-conceptions About Bisexual Men', *Southern Review* 25: 168–184.

Burbules, N.C., 1997, 'A Grammar of Difference: Some Ways of Rethinking Difference and Diversity as Educational Topics', *Australian Educational Researcher*, 24(1): 97–116.

Burleson, W.E. 2005, *Bi America: Myths, Truths and Struggles of an Invisible Community*, New York: Harrington Park Press.

Burleson, W.E. 2008, 'The Kinsey Scale and the Pashtun: The Role of Culture in Measuring Sexual Orientation', *Journal of Bisexuality*, 8(3–4): 259–264.

Burney, J.A. 2000, 'The Myth of Mark Todd', *Express*, 6th July: 8.

Butler, J. 1990, *Gender Trouble: Feminism and the Subversion of Identity*, New York: Routledge.

Butler, J. 1993, *Bodies That Matter: On the Discursive Limits of 'Sex'*, New York: Routledge.

Butler, J. 2004, *Precarious Life: the Powers of Mourning and Violence*, New York: Verso.

Buxton, A.P. 1991, *The Other Side of the Closet: The Coming Out Crisis for Straight Spouses*, Santa Monica, CA: IBS Press.

Buxton, A.P. 1999, 'The Best Interest of Children of Lesbian and Gay Parents', in R.M. Galatzer-Levy & L. Kraus Eds *The Scientific Basis of Child Custody Decisions*, New York: John Wiley & Sons.

Buxton, A.P. 2000, 'From Hostile to Helpful: Parallel Parenting after a Mixed-orientation Couple Divorce', in J. Wells Ed. *Home Fronts: Controversies in Nontraditional Parenting*, Los Angeles: Alyson Publications.

Buxton, A.P. 2001, 'Writing Our Own Script: How Bisexual men and Their Heterosexual Wives Maintain Their Marriages After Disclosure', in B. Beemyn & E. Steinman Eds *Bisexuality in the Lives of Men: Facts and Fiction*, New York: Harrington Park Press.

Buxton, A.P. 2004a, 'Paths and Pitfalls', *Journal of Couple and Relationship Therapy*, 3(2–3): 95–109.

Buxton, A.P. 2004b, 'Works in Progress: How Mixed-Orientation Couples Maintain their Marriages After the Wives Come out', in R. Fox Ed. *Current Research on Bisexuality*, New York: Harrington Park Press.

Buxton, A.P. 2006a, 'A Family Matter: When a Spouse Comes Out as Gay, Lesbian, or Bisexual', in J. Bigner Ed. *An Introduction to GLBT Family Studies*, New York: Haworth Press.

Buxton, A.P. 2006b, 'Healing an Invisible Minority: How the Straight Spouse Network has Become the Prime Source of Support for Those in Mixed-Orientation Marriages', in J. Bigner & A.R. Gottlieb Eds *Interventions with Families of Gay, Lesbian, Bisexual and Transgender People: From the Inside Out*, New York: Harrington Park Press.

Buxton, A.P. 2006c, 'Counselling Heterosexual Spouses of Bisexual Men and Women and Bisexual-Heterosexual Couples: Affirmative Approaches', *Journal of Bisexuality*, 6(1–2): 106–135.

Buxton, A.P. 2006d, 'When a Spouse Comes Out: Impact on the Heterosexual Partner', *Sexual Addiction and Compulsivity*, 13(2–3): 317–332.

Buxton, A.P. 2007, 'Counseling Heterosexual Spouses of Bisexual or Transgender Partners', in B. Firestein Ed. *Becoming Visible: Counseling Bisexuals Across the Lifespan*, New York: Columbia University Press.

Buxton, A.P. 2011, 'Reflections on Bisexuality Through the Prism of Mixed-Orientation Marriages', *Journal of Bisexuality*, 11(4): 525–544.

Cabaj, R.P. 2005, 'Other Populations: Gays, Lesbians and Bisexuals', in J.H. Lowinson, P. Ruiz, R.B. Millman & J.G. Langrod Eds *Substance Abuse: A Comprehensive Textbook*, Philadelphia: Lippincott Williams & Wilkins.

Callis, A.S. 2013, 'The Black Sheep of the Pink Flock: Labels, Stigma, and Bisexual Identity', *Journal of Bisexuality*, 13(1): 82–105.

Callis, A.S. 2014 'Bisexual, Pansexual, Queer: Non-binary Identities and the Sexual Borderlands', *Sexualities,* 17(1–2): 63–80.

Capulet, I. 2010, 'With Reps Like These: Bisexuality and Celebrity Status', *Journal of Bisexuality*, 10(3): 294–308.

Carey, B. 2005, 'Straight, Gay or Lying? Bisexuality Revisited', *New York Times* July 5th <http://www.nytimes.com/2005/07/05/health/05sex.html?_r=0>

Carlsson, G. 2007, 'Counseling the Bisexual Married Man', in B.A. Firestein Ed. *Becoming Visible: Counseling Bisexuals Across the Lifespan*, New York: Columbia University Press.

Carpenter, D. 2005, 'Brokeback Mountain: A Dissenting View", *Indie Gay Forum* <www.indegayforum.org.authors/carpenter/carpenter81.html>.

Cashore, C. & Tuason, M.T.G. 2009, 'Negotiating the Binary: Identity and Social Justice for Bisexual and Transgender Individuals', *Journal of Gay and Lesbian Social Services*, 21(4): 374–401.

Cerdeño, A.F., Martínez-Donate, A.P., Zellner, J.A., Fernando-Sañudo, H.C., Engelberg, M., Sipan, C. & Hovell, M. 2012, 'Marketing HIV Prevention for Heterosexually Identified Latino Men Who Have Sex with Men & Women: The Hombres Sanos Campaign', *Journal of Health Communication,* 17(6): 641–658.

Cerny, J.A. & Jansen, E. 2011, 'Patterns of Sexual Arousal in Homosexual, Bisexual, and Heterosexual Men', *Archives of Sexual Behaviour* 40: 687–697.

Channel 4.com's LGB Teens Health Site 2007, 'Am I gay or bisexual?', <http://www.channel4.com/health/microsites/L/lgb_teens/boys/are-you-gay>.

Chun, K.Y.S. & Singh, A.A. 2010, 'The Bisexual Youth of Color Intersecting Identities Development Model: A Contextual Approach to Understanding Multiple Marginalization Experiences', *Journal of Bisexuality*, 10(4): 429–451.

Cicioni, M. 1998, 'Male Pair Bonds and Female Desire in Fan Slash Writing' in C. Harris & A. Alexander Eds *Theorizing Fandom: Fans, Subculture and Identity*. New Jersey: Cresskil.

Cloven, D.H. & Roloff, M.E. 1993, 'The Chilling Effect of Aggressive Potential on the Expression of Complaints in Intimate Relationships', *Communication Monographs* 60: 199–219.

Cohen, I.J. 1987, 'Structuration Theory and Social Praxis', in A. Giddens & J.H. Turner Eds *Social Theory Today*, Oxford: Polity Press.

Cohen, Bentley M. 2013, *Confessions of a Bisexual Husband*, <www.markbentleycohen.com>.

Cohen, S. & Taylor, L. 1976, *Escape Attempts: The Theory and and Practice of Resistance to Everyday Life*, London: Allen Lane.

Coleman, E. 1982, 'Bisexual and Gay Men in Heterosexual Marriage: Conflicts and Resolutions in Therapy', *Journal of Homosexuality*, 72(3): 93–103.

Collard, C. 1989, *Savage Nights*, New York: Overlook Press.

Collins, F.J. 2000, 'Biracial-Bisexual Individuals: Identity and Coming of Age' *International Journal of Sexuality and Gender Studies,* 5(3): 221–253.

Collins, F.J. 2004, 'The Intersection of Race and Bisexuality: A Critical Overview of the Literature and Past, Present, and Future Directions of the Borderlands', in R. Fox Ed. *Current Research on Bisexuality*, New York: Harrington Park Press.

Comeau, D.L. 2012, 'Label-First Sexual Identity Development: An In-Depth Case Study of Women Who Identify as Bisexual Before Having Sex With More Than One Gender', *Journal of Bisexuality*, 12(3): 321–346.

Confer, J.C. & Cloud M.D. 2011, 'Sex Differences in Response to Imagining a Partner's Heterosexual or Homosexual Affair', *Personality and Individual Differences*, 50: 129–134.

Conley, T.D., Moors, A.C., Ziegler, A. & Constantina K., 2012, 'Unfaithful Individuals are Less Likely to Practice Safer Sex Than Openly Nonmonogamous Individuals', *Journal of Sexual Medicine*, 9: 1559–1565.

Conley, T.D., Ziegler, A., Moors, A.C., Matsick, J.L. & Valentine, B. 2013, 'A Critical Examination of Popular Assumptions About the Benefits and Outcomes of Monogamous Relationships', *Personality and Social Psychology Review*, 17(2): 124–141.

Connell, R. 2002, *Gender*, Cambridge: Polity Press.

Connell, R. 2005, *Masculinities*, Sydney: Allen & Unwin.

Coon, L. 2012, *Sexual Biversity: Loving my Bisexual Husband*, Oakleigh South, Melbourne: Barker Deane Publishing.

Cope, B. & Kalantzis, M. 1995, 'Why Literacy Pedagogy Has to Change', *Education Australia*, 30: 8–11.

Corley, M.D. & Kort, J. 2006, 'The Sex Addicted Mixed-Orientation Marriage: Examining Attachment Styles, Internalized Homophobia and Viability of Marriage After Disclosure', *Sexual Addiction and Compulsivity*, 13(2–3): 167–193.

Cover, R. 2010, 'Objectives of Desire: Romantic Coupledom Versus Promiscuity, Subjectivity and Sexual Identity', *Continuum: Journal of Media and Cultural Studies,* 24(2): 251–263.

Cram, H. 2008, *You're What?! Survival Strategies for Straight Spouses*, Minneapolis: Beacon Hill Publishing.

Crook, A. 2010, 'Channel 7 to Out Star' *DNA Magazine* <http://www.dnamagazine.com.au/articles/news.asp?newsid=12104 >.

Cumming, A. 2014, *Not My Father's Son: A Family Memoir,* Edinburgh: Cannongate.

Cunningham, M. 1990, *A Home at the End of the World* New York: Farrar, Strauss & Giroux.

Davidson, J. 2002, 'Working With Polyamorous Clients in the Clinical Setting', *Electronic Journal of Human Sexuality*, 5 <www.ejhs.org/volume5/polyoutline.html>.

Davies, R. 2005, 'The Slash Fanfiction Connection to Bi Men', in R.J. Suresha & P. Chvany Eds *Bi Men: Coming Out Every Which Way*, New York: Harrington Park Press.

Davis, C. 2013, *The Soundtrack of My Life*, New York: Simon & Schuster.

De Ishtar, Z. & Sitka, C. 1991, 'Connecting Cultures', Paper Presented at *Living as Lesbians*, Sydney Lesbian Conference, July.

De Shazer, S. 1994, *Words Were Originally Magic*, New York: W.W. Norton.

Debelle, P. 2013, 'Don't Cut me Out of Don's History', *The Advertiser* Saturday April 27th p1, 6–9.

Delany, S.R. 1988, *The Motion of Light in Water*, Westminster, Maryland: Arbor House.

Denes, A. Lannutti, P.J. & Bevan, J.L. 2015, 'Same-Sex' Infidelity in Heterosexual Romantic Relationships: Investigating, Emotional, Relational, and Communicative Responses. *Personal Relationships*, 22: 414–430.

Derrida, J. 1981, *Positions*, Chicago: University of Chicago Press.

Dew, B., Brubaker, M. & Hays, D. 2006, 'From the Altar to the Internet: Married Men and their Online Sexual Behaviour', *Sexual Addiction and Compulsivity*, 13(2–3): 195–207.

Dhalla, G.S. 2011. *The Two Krishnas*. New York: Magnus Books.

Diamond, L.M. 2003, 'What Does Sexual Orientation Orient? A Biobehavioral Model Distinguishing Romantic Love and Sexual Desire', *Psychological Review*, 110(1): 173–192.

Diamond, L.M. 2005, "I'm Straight, But I Kissed a Girl": The Trouble with American Media Representations of Female-Female Sexuality', *Feminism and Psychology*, 15(1): 104–110.

Diamond, L.M. 2008, 'Female Bisexuality from Adolescence to Adulthood: Results from a 10-year Longitudinal Study', *Developmental Psychology*, 44(1): 5–14.

Diamond, L. 2009, *Sexual Fluidity: Understanding Women's Love and Desire*. Boston: Harvard University Press.

Diamond, L. & Butterworth, M. 2008, 'Questioning Gender and Sexual Identity: Dynamic Links Over Time', *Sex Roles,* 59: 365–376.

Dobinson, C. 2005, 'Improving the Access and Quality of Public Health Services for Bisexuals', *Journal of Bisexuality*, 5(1): 39–77.

Dodge, B. 2014, 'Scientific Research on Bisexual Men: What Do We Know, and Why Don't We Know More?' in R. Ochs & S.H. Williams Eds *Rec.og.nize: the Voices of Bisexual Men*, Boston: Bisexual Resource Center.

Dodge, B. & Sandfort, T.G.M. 2007, 'A Review of Mental Health Research on Bisexual Individuals When Compared to Homosexual and Heterosexual Individuals', in B.A. Firestein Ed. *Becoming Visible: Counseling Bisexuals Across the Lifespan*, New York: Columbia University Press.

Dodge, B., Reece, M. and Gebhard, P.H. 2008, 'Kinsey and Beyond: Past, Present, and Future Considerations for Research on Male Bisexuality', *Journal of Bisexuality*, 8(3/4): 177–191.

Dodge, B., Schnarrs, P.W., Reece, M., Goncalves, G., Martinez, O., Nix, R., Malebranche, D., Van Der Pol, B., Murray, M. & Fortenberry, J.D. 2012, 'Community Involvement Among Behaviourally Bisexual Men in the Midwestern USA: Experiences and Perceptions Across Communities', *Culture, Health and Sexuality*, 14(9): 1095–1110.

Doll, L.S., Petersen, L.R., White, C.R., Johnson, E.S., Ward, J.W. & The Blood Donor Study Group 1992, 'Homosexually and Nonhomosexually Identified Men Who Have Sex with Men: A Behavioural Comparison', *The Journal of Sex Research*, 29(1): 1–14.

Douglas, M. 1966, *Purity and Danger: An Analysis of Concepts of Pollution and Taboo*, New York: Ark.

Douglas, A. 1931, *The Autobiography of Lord Alfred Douglas*. London: Martin Secker.

Dowsett, G. 1997, *Practising Desire: Homosexual Sex in the Era of AIDS*, Stanford: Stanford University Press.

Dunstan, D. 1991a, 'Letter to Tony Mordini' October 3rd 1991, FUSA DC Correspondence Personal Box 39. Courtesy of Dr Dino Hodge.

Dunstan, D. 1991b, 'Letter to Tony' n.d. [ca early 1991], FUSA DC Undated Correspondence Box 39. Courtesy of Dr Dino Hodge.

Dworkin, S.H. 2002, 'Biracial, Bicultural, Bisexual: Bisexuality and Multiple Identities', *Journal of Bisexuality*, 2(4): 93–107.

Easterling, B., Knox, D. & Brackett, A. 2012, 'Secrets in Romantic Relationships: Does Sexual Orientation Matter?', *Journal of GLBT Family Studies*, 8(2): 196–208.

Easton, D. & Liszt, C.A. 1997, *The Ethical Slut*, San Francisco: Greenery Press.

Ebin, J. 2012, 'Why Bisexual Health?', *Journal of Bisexuality*, 12(2): 168–177.

Ebsworth, M. & Lalumière, M. 2012, 'Viewing Time as a Measure of Bisexual Sexual Interest', *Archives of Sexual Behavior*, 41(1): 161–172.

Edser, S.J. & Shea, J.D. 2002, 'An Exploratory Investigation of Bisexual Men in Monogamous, Heterosexual Marriages', *Journal of Bisexuality*, 2(4): 5–43.

Eisner, S. 2013, *Bi: Notes for a Bisexual Revolution*. Berkeley, CA: Seal Press.

Ekstrand, M.L., Coates, T.J., Guydish, J.K., Hauck, W.W., Collette, L. & Hulley, S.B. 1994, 'Are Bisexually Identified Men in San Francisco a Common Vector for Spreading HIV Infection to Women?', *American Journal of Public Health*, 84(6): 915–919.

Elia, J.P. 2010, 'Bisexuality and School Culture: School as a Prime Site for Bi-Intervention', *Journal of Bisexuality*, 10(4): 452–471.

Eliason, M. 1997, 'The Prevalence and Nature of Biphobia in Heterosexual Undergraduate Students', *Archives of Sexual Behaviour*, 26(3): 3–17.

Eliason, M. 2001, 'Bi-Negativity: the Stigma Facing Bisexual Men', in B. Beemyn & E. Steinman Eds *Bisexuality in the Lives of Men: Facts and Fictions*, New York: Haworth Press.

Epstein, B.J. 2012, 'We're Here, We're Not? Queer: GLBTQ Characters in Children's Books', *Journal of GLBT Family Studies*, 8(3): 287–300.

Erera, P. 2002, *Family Diversity: Continuity and Change in the Contemporary Family*, Thousand Oaks, CA: Sage.

Erickson-Schroth, L. & Mitchell, J. 2009, 'Queering Queer Theory, or Why Bisexuality Matters', *Journal of Bisexuality*, 9(3–4): 297–315.

Evans, T. 2003, 'Bisexuality: Negotiating Lives Between Two Cultures', *Journal of Bisexuality*, 3(2): 93–108.
Fahs, B. 2009, 'Compulsory Bisexuality?: The Challenges of Modern Sexual Fluidity', *Journal of Bisexuality*, 9(3): 431–449.
Feinstein, B.A., Dyar, C., Bhatia, V., Latack, J.A., Davila, J. 2014, 'Willingness to Engage in Romantic and Sexual Activities with Bisexual Partners: Gender and Sexual Orientation Differences', *Psychology of Sexual Orientation and Gender Diversity*, 1(3): 255–262.
Filipe, E.M., Batistella, E., Pine, A., Santos, N.J., Paiva, V., Seurado, A. 2005, 'Sexual Orientation, Use of Drugs and Risk Perception Among HIV-positive Men in Sao Paolo, Brazil', *International Journal of STD and AIDS*, 16(1): 56–60.
Finkenauer, C. & Hazam, H. 2000, 'Disclosure and Secrecy in Marriage: Do Both Contribute to Marital Satisfaction?', *Journal of Social and Personal Relationships*, 17(2): 245–263.
Firestein, B.A. Ed. 2007, *Becoming Visible: Counseling Bisexuals Across the Lifespan*, New York: Columbia University Press.
Fitzpatrick, R., Hart, G., Boulton, M., McLean, J. & Dawson, J. 1989, 'Heterosexual Sexual Behaviour in a Sample of Homosexually Active Men', *Genitourinary Medicine*, 65: 259–262.
Fleckenstein, J.R. & Cox II, D.W. 2015, 'The Association of an Open Relationship Orientation with Health and Happiness in a Sample of Older US Adults', *Sexual and Relationship Therapy*, 30(1): 94–116.
Fletcher, J. & Wassmer, T. 1970, *Hello Lovers! An Introduction to Situation Ethics*, Washington: Corpus Books.
Fonow, M. & Cook, J. Eds 1991, *Beyond Methodology: Feminist Scholarship as Lived Research*, Bloomington: Indiana University Press.
Foster, B., Foster, M. & Hadady, L. 1997, *Three In Love: Ménages à Trois From Ancient To Modern Times*, San Francisco: Harper.
Foucault, M. 1977, *Discipline and Punish: The Birth Of The Prison*, New York: Vintage Books.
Foucault, M. 1984, 'What is Enlightenment? and On the Genealogy of Ethics: an Overview of Work in Progress', in P. Rabinow Ed. *The Foucault Reader*, Harmondsworth: Peregrine.
Foucault, M. 1985, 'Truth, Power and Sexuality', in V. Beechey & J. Donald Eds *Subjectivity and Social Relations*, Philadelphia: Open University Press.
Foucault, M. 1986, 'Of Other Spaces', *Diacritics*, 16: 22–27.
Foucault, M. 1988, 'Power and Sex', in L. Kritzman Ed. *Michel Foucault: Politics, Philosophy, Culture: Interviews & Other Writings 1977–1984*, London: Routledge.
Fox, R. Ed. 2004, *Current Research on Bisexuality*, New York: Harrington Park Press.
Frieden, L. 2002, 'Invisible Lives: Addressing Black Male Bisexuality in the Novels of E. Lynn Harris', in B. Beemyn & E. Steinman Eds *Bisexual Men in Culture and Society*, New York: Harrington Park Press.
Fukuyama, M. & Ferguson, A.D. 2000, 'Lesbian, Gay, and Bisexual People of Color: Understanding Cultural Complexity and Multiple Oppressions,' in R.M. Perez; K.A. DeBord & R.J. Bieschke Eds *Handbook of Counseling and Psychotherapy with Lesbian, Gay, and Bisexual Clients,* Washington, DC: American Psychological Association.

Galtung, J. 1990, 'Cultural Violence', *Journal of Peace Research*, 27(3): 291–305.
Galupo, M.P. 2008, *Bisexuality and Same-sex Marriage*, New York Routledge.
Game, A. & Metcalfe, A. 1996, *Passionate Sociology*, London: Sage Publications.
Garber, M. 1995, *Vice Versa: Bisexuality and the Eroticism of Everyday Life*, New York: Simon & Schuster.
Garner, A. 2003, *Families Like Mine*, <http://www.familieslikemine.com/advice/0312.php>.
Garner, A. 2004, *Families Like Mine: Children of Gay Parents Tell It Like It Is*, New York: HarperCollins.
Garofalo, R., Wolf, R.C., Kessel, S., Palfrey, J. & DuRant, R.H. 1998, 'The Association Between Health Risk Behaviours and Sexual Orientation Among a School-based Sample of Adolescents', *Paediatrics*, 101(5): 895–902.
George, S. 1992, *Women and Bisexuality*, London: Scarlet Press.
Gerbner, G., Gross, L., Morgan, M. & Signorielli, N. 2002, 'Growing Up With Television: The Cultivation Perspective', in M. Morgan Ed. *Against the Mainstream: The Selected Works of George Gerbner*. New York: Peter Lang.
Gibian, R. 1992, 'Refusing Certainty: Toward a Bisexuality of Wholeness', in E.R. Weise Ed. *Closer To Home: Bisexuality and Feminism*, Seattle: Seal Press.
Glendinning, V. 1983, *Vita: The Life of V. Sackville-West*, London: Penguin.
Gochros, J.S. 1985, 'Wives' Reactions to Learning That Their Husbands Are Bisexual', *Journal Of Homosexuality*, 11(1/2): 101–113.
Gochros, J.S. 1989, *When Husbands Come Out of the Closet*, New York: Haworth Press.
Goetstouwers, L. 2006, 'Affirmative Psychotherapy with Bisexual Men', *Journal of Bisexuality*, 6(1/2): 27–49.
Goffman, E. 1963, *Stigma: Notes On The Management Of Spoiled Identity*, Harmondsworth: Penguin.
Goldberg, A.E & Allen, K.R. Eds 2013, *LGBT-Parent Families: Innovations in Research and Implications for Practice*, New York: Springer.
Goldfeder, M. & Sheff, E. 2013, 'Children in Polyamorous Families: A First Empirical Look', *The Journal of Law and Social Deviance*, 5: 150–243.
Goodenow, C., Netherland, J. & Szalacha, L. 2002, 'AIDS-Related Risk Among Adolescent Males Who Have Sex With Males, Females or Both: Evidence From a Statewide Survey', *American Journal of Public Health*, 92(2): 203–210.
Goodfellow, J. 1998, 'Analysing Data in Narrative Inquiry Research', in J. Higgs Ed. *Writing Qualitative Research*, Centre for Professional Education Advancement, University of Sydney: Hampden Press.
Goodman, P. 1977, *Drawing The Line: The Political Essays of Paul Goodman*, New York: Free Life Editions.
Goparaju, L. & Warren-Jeanpiere, L. 2012, 'African American Women's Perspectives on 'Down Low/DL' Men: Implications for HIV Prevention', *Culture, Health and Sexuality*, 14(8): 879–893.
GOSSIP, 1996, 'Gossip Column', *Sydney Star Observer*, 12.
Grace, A.P. & Benson, F.J. 2000, 'Using Autobiographical Queer Life Narratives of Teachers to Connect Personal, Political and Pedagogical Spaces', *International Journal of Inclusive Education*, 4(2): 89–109.
Grant, C. 2008–2013, *The Courtland Chronicles* <http://catgrant.com/bookshelf/the-courtland-chronicles/>

Green, B., Payne, N.R., Green, J. 2011, 'Working Bi: Preliminary Findings from a Survey on Workplace Experiences of Bisexual People' *Journal of Bisexuality*, 11(2–3): 300–316.

Grever, C. 2001, *My Husband Is Gay: A Woman's Guide to Surviving the Crisis*, Freedom, CA: Crossing Press.

Grever, C. 2012, 'Unintended Consequences: Unique Issues of Female Straight Spouses', *Journal of GLBT Family Studies*, 8(1): 67–84.

Grosz, E. 1995, *Space, Time, and Perversion: Essays on the Politics of Bodies*, New York: Routledge.

Haag, P. 2011, *Marriage Confidential*, New York: Harper Collins.

Hashimoto, M. 2007. 'Visual Kei Otaku Identity—An Intercultural Analysis', *Intercultural Communication Studies*, 16(1): 87–99.

Halperin, D.M. 2009, 'Thirteen Ways of Looking at a Bisexual', *Journal of Bisexuality*, 9(3): 451–455.

Hardy, J. 2012, *Girlfag: A Life Told in Sex and Musicals*, Eugene, OR: Beyond Binary Books.

Hart, Kylo-Patrick, R. 2005, 'Cinematic Trash or Cultural Treasure? Conflicting Viewer Reactions to the Extremely Violent World of Bisexual Men in Gregg Araki's 'Heterosexual Movie' The Doom Generation,' *Journal of Bisexuality*, 7(1/2): 52–69.

Hartman-Linck, J.E. 2014, 'Keeping Bisexuality Alive: Maintaining Bisexual Visibility in Monogamous Relationships', *Journal of Bisexuality*, 14(2): 177–193.

Hatterer, L.J. 1970, *Changing Homosexuality in the Male: Treatment for Men Troubled by Homosexuality* New York: McGraw-Hill.

Hatterer, M.S. 1974, 'The Problems of Women Married to Homosexual Men', *American Journal of Psychiatry*, 13(13): 275–278.

Hatzenbuehler, M.L., Corbin, W.R. & Fromme, K. 2008, 'Trajectories and Determinants of Alcohol Use Among LGB Young Adults and their Heterosexual Peers: Results from a Prospective Study', *Developmental Psychology*, 44(1): 81–90.

Hawley, J. 2005, 'Good Golly, Miss Olley', *The Age 'Good Weekend'* September 24th.

Hays, D. & Samuels, A. 1989, 'Heterosexual Women's Perceptions of their Marriages to Bisexual or Homosexual Men', *Journal of Homosexuality*, 18(1–2): 81–100.

Heath, M. 2005, 'Pronouncing the Silent 'B' in GLBTTIQ', *Health in Difference 5 Conference*, January 20th–22nd, Melbourne Australia.

Heath, M., 2010, 'Who's Afraid Of Bisexuality?' *Gay & Lesbian Issues & Psychology Review*, 6(3): 118–121.

Heckert, J. 2005, *Resisting Orientation: On the Complexities of Desire and the Limits of Identity Politics,* Sociology PhD, University of Edinburgh, <http://sexualorientation.info/thesis/index.html>.

Heckert, J. 2010, 'Intimacy with Strangers/Intimacy with Self: Queer Experiences of Social Research', in K. Browne & C.J. Nash. Eds *Queer Methods and Methodologies: Intersecting Queer Theories and Social Science Research*, Surrey, UK: Ashgate.

Herek, G.M. 2002, 'Heterosexuals' Attitudes Toward Bisexual Men and Women in the United States', *Journal of Sex Research*, 39(4): 264–274.

Hernandez, B.C. & Wilson, C.M., 2007 'Another Kind of Ambiguous Loss: Seventh-Day Adventist Women in Mixed-Orientation Marriages', *Family Relations*, 56(2): 184–195.

Hidalgo, D.A., Barker, K. & Hunter, E. 2008, 'The Dyadic Imaginary: Troubling the Perception of Love as Dyadic', *Journal of Bisexuality*, 7(3): 171–189.

Higgins, D. 2002, 'Gay Men from Heterosexual Marriages: Attitudes, Behaviours, Childhood Experiences, and Reasons for Marriage', *Journal of Homosexuality*, 42(4): 15–34.

Higgins, D., 2006, 'Same-sex Attraction in Heterosexually Partnered Men: Reasons, Rationales and Reflections', *Sexual and Relationship Therapy*, 21(2): 217–228.

Hill, D.B. 2006, "'Feminine' Heterosexual Men: Subverting Heteropatriarchal Sexual Scripts?', *The Journal of Men's Studies*, 14(2): 145–159.

Hill, I. Ed. 1987, *The Bisexual Spouse*, New York: Harper & Row.

Hills, M. 2010, 'Torchwood' in D. Lavery Ed. *The Essential Cult TV Reader*. Lexington, KY: University Press of Kentucky Press.

Hochschild, A.R. 1983, *The Managed Heart: Commercialization of Human Feeling*. Berkeley, CA: University of California Press.

Hodge, D. 2014. *Don Dunstan: Intimacy & Liberty*. Adelaide: Wakefield Press.

Hooks, B. 1994, *Teaching To Transgress: Education as the Practice of Freedom*, New York: Routledge.

Hou, C. & Lu, H. 2013, 'Online Networks as a Venue for Social Support: A Qualitative Study of Married Bisexual Men in Taiwan', *Journal of Homosexuality*, 60(9): 1280–1296.

Hosie, A. 2010, 'Column', *Sydney Morning Herald*, 11.

House, S. 2006, *Just Like That*, Playscript courtesy of Stephen House.

Hudson, J.H., 2013, 'Comprehensive Literature Review Pertaining to Married Men Who Have Sex With Men (MMSM)', *Journal of Bisexuality*, 13(4): 417–601.

Hughes, T.L. & Eliason, M. 2002, 'Substance Use and Abuse in Lesbian, Gay Bisexual and Transgender Populations', *Journal of Primary Prevention*, 22(3): 263–298.

Hutchings, J. & Aspin, C. 2007, *Sexuality and the Stories of Indigenous People*, Wellington: Huia Publishers.

Hutchins, L. & Ka'ahumanu, L. Eds 1991, *Bi Any Other Name*, Boston: Alyson.

Iantaffi A. 2010, 'A Personal Reflection on the Next 25 Years of Sex and Relationship Therapy, Research and Theory, *Sexual and Relationship Therapy*, 25(4): 369–371.

Iantaffi, A. Grey, J.A. & Rosser, B.R. 2015, 'Characteristics of Bi-Attracted Men Who Have Sex with Men: Findings from Three Internet-Based Studies on HIV', *Journal of Bisexuality*, 15(3): 435–451.

Imielinsky, K. 1969, 'Homosexuality in Males With Particular Attention to Marriage', *Psychotherapy and Psychosomatics*, 17: 126–132.

Isay, R.A. 1998, 'Heterosexually Married Homosexual Men: Clinical and Developmental Issues', *American Journal of Orthopsychiatry*, 48(3): 424–432.

Israel, T. 2004, 'Conversations, Not Categories: The Intersection of Biracial and Bisexual Identities', *Women and Therapy*, 27: 173–84.

Israel, T. & Mohr, J.J. 2004, 'Attitudes Toward Bisexual Women and Men: Current Research, Future Directions', *Journal of Bisexuality*, 4(1–2): 117–134.

Izod, J. & Dovalis, J. 2015, *Cinema as Therapy: Grief and Transformational Film*, London: Routledge.

James, S.D. 2009, 'Calvin Klein Ad Taps Foursome Sex', *ABCNews.com* <http://polyinthemedia.blogspot.com/2009/06/calvin-klein-foursome-ad-and-its.html>.

Jaspal, R. 2014, 'Arranged Marriage, Identity, and Well-being Among British Asian Gay Men', *Journal of GLBT Family Studies,* 10(5): 425–448.

Jeffreys, S. 1999, 'Bisexual Politics: A Superior Form Of Feminism?' *Women's Studies International Forum,* 22(3): 273–285.

Jeffries, W.L. 2010, 'HIV Testing Among Bisexual Men in the United States', *AIDS Education and Prevention,* 22(4): 356–370.

Jeffries, W.L. 2011, 'The Number of Recent Sex Partners Among Bisexual Men in the United States', *Perspectives on Sexual and Reproductive Health,* 43(3): 151–157.

Jeffries, W.L., Dodge, B., 2007, 'Male Bisexuality and Condom Use at Last Sexual Encounter: Results from a National Survey', *Journal of Sex Research,* 44(3): 278–289.

Jeffries, W.L., Dodge, B. & Sandfort, T.G.M. 2008, 'Religion and Spirituality Among Bisexual Black Men in the USA', *Culture, Health and Sexuality,* 10(5): 463–477.

Jenn, K. 2007, 'Men 'Rather Die' Than Admit Gay Affairs', *News.Com* <www.news.com.au/story/0.23599.215373558–1702.00.html>.

Jensen, M. 2007, 'Readers' Choice: The Top 25 Gay TV Characters revealed', *AfterElton* <http://www/afterelton.com/people/2007/11/top25gayTVcharacters?page=0. AfterElton.com2008-01-20>.

Jenkins, H., Jenkins, C. & Green, S. 1998. '"The Normal Female Interest in Men Bonking": Selections from Terra Nostra Underground and Strange Bedfellows," in C. Harris & A. Alexander Eds *Theorizing Fandom: Fans, Subculture, and Identity,* New Jersey: Hampton Press.

Jesdale, B. 2013, 'Data Unicorns', *Bill and Tuna* <http://billandtuna.blogspot.com.au/2013/05/data-unicorns.html>

Johnson, S. 1987, *Going Out Of Our Minds: The Metaphysics Of Liberation,* Freedom, CA: The Crossing Press.

Jones, D. 2000, 'The Dance King and I', *The Weekend Australian Arts Review,* May 6–7, 16–18.

Jones, G., Kamper, A. & Haynes, R. 2010, 'Minister David Campbell Lived His Secret Gay Life for 25 years', *The Daily Telegraph,* May 21.

Jones, G. 2000, 'Coming Clean About Bisexuality: A Male Perspective', <http://www.garrett.jones.care4free.net.bisexEDIT.html>.

Jones, S.R. & McEwen, M.K. 2000, 'A Conceptual Model of Multiple Dimensions of Identity', *Journal of College Student Development,* 41(1): 405–414.

Jorm, A.F., Korten, A.E., Rodgers, B., Jacomb, P.A. & Christensen, H. 2002, 'Sexual Orientation and Mental Health: Results from a Community Survey of Young and Middle-aged Adults', *The British Journal of Psychiatry,* 180(5): 423–427.

Joseph, S. 1997, *She's My Wife, He's Just Sex,* Sydney: Australian Centre for Independent Journalism, University of Technology.

Julz, 2005, 'Magic Man', *Journal of Bisexuality,* 5(2): 213–220.

Kaestle, C.E. & Ivory, H.A. 2012, 'A Forgotten Sexuality: Content Analysis of Bisexuality in the Medical Literature over Two Decades', *Journal of Bisexuality,* 12(1): 35–48.

Kahaleole Chang Hall, L. & Kauanui, L.J. 1996, 'Same-Sex Sexuality in Pacific Literature', in R. Leong Ed. *Asian American Sexualities,* New York: Routledge.

Kamuf, P. Ed. 1991, *A Derrida Reader: Between The Blinds*, New York: Harvester Wheatsheaf.

Karlson, M. 2007, 'Bisexuals Exist- and So Do Bisexual Parents', *Bi-Victoria Newsletter*, August/September: 1–4.

Kaye, B. 2000, *Is he Straight? The Checklist for Women Who Wonder*, San Jose: to Excel.

Kaye, B, 2001, 'Living La Vida Limbo', *Straight Talk Newsletter*, 1(3). <http://www.gayhusbands.com/newsletter.html>

Kaye, B. 2002a, 'Do You Really Want To Know – The 'Other Man'', *Straight Talk Newsletter*, 2(11). <http://www.gayhusbands.com/newsletter.html>

Kaye, B. 2002b, 'Closed Loop – What Every Straight Wife Should Know', *Straight Talk Newsletter*, 2(15). <http://www.gayhusbands.com/newsletter.html>

Kaye, B. 2002c, 'The Excuse For Abuse Straight Gay Husbands', *Straight Talk Newsletter*, 2(11). <http://www.gayhusbands.com/newsletter.html>

Kaye, B. 2002d, 'Women Who Want to Debate or Confront Me', *Straight Talk Newsletter*, 2(17). <http://www.gayhusbands.com/newsletter.html>

Kaye, B. 2003a, 'Limbo Women', *Straight Talk Newsletter*, 3(33). <http://www.gayhusbands.com/newsletter.html>

Kaye, B. 2003b, 'A Tribute to Children', *Straight Talk Newsletter*, 3(25). <http://www.gayhusbands.com/newsletter.html>

Kaye, B. 2004, *Doomed Grooms: Gay Husbands of Straight Wives*, New York: iUniverse.

Kaye, B. 2008, *Straight Wives: Shattered Lives*, http://www.gayhusbands.com.

Kaye, B. 2008, *Bonnie Kaye's Straight Talk: A Collection of Her Best Newsletters About Gay Husbands*, British Columbia, Canada: CCB Publishing.

Kays, J.L. & Yarhouse, M.A. 2010, 'Resilient Factors in Mixed Orientation Couples: Current State of the Research', *The American Journal of Family Therapy*, 38(4): 334–343.

Kazmi, Y. 1993, 'Panopticon: a World Order Through Education or Education's Encounter With the Other/Difference', *Philosophy and Social Criticism*, 19(2): 195–213.

Keating, A. 2005, 'Shifting Worlds, Una Entrada' in A.L. Keating Ed. *EntreMundos/Among Worlds: New Perspectives on Gloria E, Anzaldua*, New York: Palgrave Macmillan.

Kent, S. & Morreau, J. 1990, *Women's Images of Men*, London: Pandora.

Kentlyn, S. 2008, 'The Radically Subversive Space of the Queer Home: 'Safety House' and 'Neighbourhood Watch', *Australian Geographer*, 39(3): 327–337.

Kich, G. 1996, 'In the Margins of Sex and Race: Difference, Marginality, and Flexibility' in M.M. Root Ed. *The Multiracial Experience: Racial Borders as the New Frontier*, Newbury Park, CA: Sage Publications.

King, A.R. 2011, 'Are We Coming of Age? A Critique of Collins's Proposed Model of Biracial–Bisexual Identity Development', *Journal of Bisexuality*, 11(1): 98–120.

King, J.L. 2004, *On the Down Low: A Journey Into the Lives of 'Straight' Black Men Who Sleep With Men*, New York: Broadway Books.

King, M. & McKeown, E. 2003, *Mental Health and Social Wellbeing of Gay Men, Lesbians and Bisexuals in England and Wales*, London: Mind National Association for Mental Health.

Kingma, D.R. 1998, *The Future of Love*, New York: Doubleday Books.

Kinsey, A., Pomeroy, W., Martin, C. 1948, *Sexual Behavior in the Human Male*, Philadelphia: Saunders.

Kinsey, A., Pomeroy, W., Martin, C. & Gebhard, P. 1953, *Sexual Behavior in the Human Female*, Philadelphia: Saunders.

Klaar, C.M. 2012, 'Straight Wives of HIV-Positive Husbands Who Contracted the Virus Through Male-to-Male Sexual Contact', *Journal of GLBT Family Studies*, 8(1): 99–120.

Klein, F. 1993, *The Bisexual Option*, New York: Harrington Park Press.

Klein, F., Sepekoff, B. & Wolf, T.J. 1985, 'Sexual Orientation: A Multi-Variable Dynamic Process', *Journal of Homosexuality*, 11(1–2): 35–49.

Klein, F. & Schwartz, T. 2001, *Bisexual and Gay Husbands: Their Stories, Their Words*, New York: Harrington Park Press.

Klesse, C. 2007, *The Spectre of Promiscuity: Gay Male and Bisexual Non-monogamies*, Hampshire: Ashgate.

Klesse, C. 2011, 'Shady Characters, Untrustworthy Partners, and Promiscuous Sluts: Creating Bisexual Intimacies in the Face of Heteronormativity and Biphobia', *Journal of Bisexuality*, 11(2–3): 227–244.

Kohn, B. & Matusow, A. 1980, *Barry and Alice: Portrait of a Bisexual Marriage*. Prentice-Hall.

Kollen, T. 2007, 'Part of the Whole? Homosexuality in Companies' Diversity Policies and in Business Research: Focus on Germany', *International Journal of Diversity in Organisations, Communities and Nations*, 7(5): 315–322.

Kollen, T. 2012, 'Just a Private Affair and Irrelevant for Companies? The State of the Art in Human Resource Research Regarding "Sexual Orientation"', *Journal of Human Research*, 26(2): 143–166.

Kollen, T. 2013, 'Bisexuality and Diversity Management—Addressing the B in LGBT as a Relevant 'Sexual Orientation' in the Workplace', *Journal of Bisexuality*, 13(1): 122–137.

Kolodny, D. 2000, *Blessed Bi Spirit: Bisexual People of Faith*, Michigan: Continuum.

Kort, J. 2007, 'Gay Guise: What to do When your Client has Sex with Men and is not Gay', *Psychotherapy Networker Magazine* July/August <www.straightguise.com/default.asp?id=1345>.

Kort, J. 2012a, 'Why We Care About John Travolta's Sexuality' <http://www.huffingtonpost.com/joe-kort-phd/jobn-travolta-sexuality_>.

Kort, J. 2012b, E-mail Correspondence with the Author on Sexual Addiction.

Kort, J. 2013, 'Why some Straight Men are Romantically or Sexually Attracted to Other Men', *Huffington Post*, <http://www.huffingtonpost.com/joe-kort-phd/why-some-straight-men-are-romantically-or-sexually-attracted-to-other-men_b_3670740.html>

Kort, J. 2014a, *Is My Husband Gay, Straight or Bi?: A Guide for Women Concerned About Their Men*. Lanham, MD: Rowman & Littlefield.

Kort, J. 2014b, 'Are 'Heteroflexible' and 'Homoflexible' Shades of 'Bisexual'?' *Huffington Post* <http://www.huffingtonpost.com/joe-kort-phd/are-heteroflexible-and-homoflexible-shades-of-bisexual_b_4549126.html>

Kosky, M. 1989, *Women and AIDS Project Report*, Perth. Western Australia: Western Australia AIDS Council.

Kowalewski, M.R. 1988, 'Double Stigma and Boundary Maintenance: How Gay Men Deal With AIDS', *Journal of Contemporary Ethnography*, 17(2): 211–228.

Kroeger, B. 2003, *Passing: When People Can't be Who They Are*, New York: Public Affairs.

Kubler-Ross, E. & Kessler, D. 2005, *On Grief and Grieving: Finding the Meaning of Grief Through the Five Stages of Loss*. New York: Scribner.

Lambert, S. 2010, '12 Reasons Why I Love Dating Bi Men', *Bisexual Examiner*, <http://www.examiner.com/bisexual-in-national/12-reasons-why-i-love-dating-bi-men>.

Lambert, S. 2011, 'Find Plenty of Bisexual Films at the New York LGBT Film Festival', *Bisexual Examiner* <http://www.examiner.com/bisexual-in-national/find-plenty-of-bisexual-films-at-the-new-york-LGBT-film-festival>.

Lambert, S. Ed. 2014, *Best Bi Short Stories: Bisexual Fiction*, Cambridge, MA: Gressive Press.

Lamey, A. 2003, 'Why Everyone Should be Able to Marry Anyone: The Case for Polygamy is Similar to the Case for Gay Marriage', *National Post*, <www.nationalpost.com/home/story.html?id=A05E507E-01B1-43E8-88EC-859591991D7F>.

Lamont, A. 2008, 'Drag Icon Prepares to Hang Her Heels in the Closet for the Last Time', *Sydney Star Observer*, February 28th: 5.

Larkin, S. 2005, 'Bisexual MP Threat to Expose Others', *Herald Sun*, <www.heraldsun.news.com.au/common/story_page/0.5478.16203100%255E1702,00.html>

Latham, J.D. & White, G.D. 1978, 'Coping with Homosexual Expression Within Heterosexual Marriages: Five Case Studies', *Journal of Sex and Marital Therapy*, 4(3): 198–212.

Laumann E.O., Gagnon J.H., Michael R.T. & Michaels S. 1994, *The Social Organization of Sexuality: Sexual Practices in the United States*, Chicago: University of Chicago Press.

Le Compte, M.D. 1993, 'A Framework for Hearing Silence: What Does Telling Stories Mean When We are Supposed to be Doing Science?' in D. McLaughlin & W.G. Tierney Eds *Naming Silenced Lives: Personal Narratives and Processes of Educational Change*, New York: Routledge.

Leavitt, D. 2013, *The Two Hotel Francforts*, London: Bloomsbury.

Leavitt, L.J. 2006, *Forbidden Fruits: Memoirs of a Mixed Orientation Marriage*, Victoria, Canada: Trafford Publishing.

Leddick, D. 2003, *The Secret Lives of Married Men*, Los Angeles: Alyson Books.

Letherby, G. 2003, *Feminist Research in Theory and Practice*, Buckingham: Open University Press.

Letts, W. & Sears, J. 1999, *Queering Elementary Education: Advancing the Dialogue About Sexualities and Schooling*, Lanham, MD: Rowman & Littlefield

Levi, A., McHarry, M. & Pagliassotti, D. Ed. 2010, *Boys' Love Manga: Essays on the Sexual Ambiguity and Cross-Cultural Fandom of the Genre*, Jefferson, N.C.: McFarland & Co.

Lewis, F. 2009, 'Sexual Occidentation: The Politics of Conversion, Christian-love and Boy-love in 'Attār', *Iranian Studies*, 42(5): 693–723.

Ley, D. 2009, *Insatiable Wives: Women Who Stray and the Men Who Love Them*, New York: Rowman & Littlefield.

Li, T., Dobinson, C., Scheim, A.I. & Ross, L.E. 2013, 'Unique Issues Bisexual People Face in Intimate Relationships: A Descriptive Exploration of Lived Experience', *Journal of Gay and Lesbian Mental Health,* 17(1): 21–39.

Lippa, R.A. 2012, 'Men and Women with Bisexual Identities Show Bisexual Patterns of Sexual Attraction to Male and Female 'Swimsuit Models'', *Archives of Sexual Behaviour,* 42: 187–196.

Livholts, M. Ed. 2012, *Emergent Writing Methodologies In Feminist Studies,* New York: Routledge.

Lizarraga, S.S. 1993, 'The Gift?' in T.D. Rebolledo & E.S. Rivero Eds *Infinite Divisions: An Anthology Of Chicana Literature*, Tucson: University of Arizona Press.

Llama, B. 2010, 'A Double Life', *Bruce Llama,That's One Crazy Llama* Saturday, May 22, <http://brucellama.wordpress.com/2010/05/22/a-double-life/>.

Low, L. & Pallotta-Chiarolli, M. 2015, '"And Yet We Are Still Excluded": Reclaiming Multicultural Queer Histories and Engaging with Contemporary Multicultural Queer Realities' in F. Mansouri Ed. *Cultural, Religious and Political Contestations: The Multicultural Challenge,* Basel, Switzerland: Springer.

Lubowitz, S. 1995a, *The Wife, The Husband, His Boyfriend . . . Her Story,* Canberra: AIDS/Communicable Diseases Branch of the Commonwealth Department of Human Services and Health.

Lubowitz, S. 1995b, 'Women Partners of Bisexual Men', *National AIDS Bulletin,* 9(3): 38–39.

Lubowitz, S. 1997, *'Three in a Marriage' Video and Booklet Training Package for Health Care Workers,* Sydney: AIDS Council of NSW.

Lugones, M. 1990, 'Playfulness, "World"-Travelling, and Loving Perception' in G, Anzaldua Ed. *Making Face, Making Soul Haciendo Caras,* San Francisco: Aunt Lute Books.

Lugones, M. 1994, 'Purity, Impurity, and Separation', *Signs: Journal Of Women In Culture and Society,* 19(2): 458–479.

Lynn Harris, E. 1994, *Invisible Life,* New York: Anchor.

Lynn Harris, E. 1994, *Just As I Am,* New York: Doubleday.

Lynn Harris, E. 1996, *And This Too Shall Pass,* New York: Anchor.

Madison, D.S. 2007, 'Co-performative Witnessing', *Cultural Studies,* 21(6): 826–831.

Malcolm, J.P. 2000, 'Sexual Identity Development in Behaviourally Bisexual Married Men: Implications for Essentialist Theories of Sexual Orientation Psychology', *Evolution and Gender,* 2(3): 263–299.

Malebranche, D.J. 2008, 'Bisexually Active Black Men in the United States and HIV: Acknowledging More than the "Down Low"', *Archives of Sexual Behavior,* 37: 810–816.

Malebranche, D.J., Peterson, J.L., Fullilove, R.E. & Stackhouse, R.W. 2004, 'Race and Sexual Identity: Perceptions About Medical Culture and Healthcare Among Black Men Who Have Sex With Men', *Journal of the National Medical Association,* 96(1): 97–107.

Malebranche, D.J.; Arriola, K.; Jenkins, T.R; Dauria, E.; & Patel, S.N. 2010, 'Exploring the "Bisexual Bridge": A Qualitative Study of Risk Behavior and Disclosure of Same-sex Behavior Among Black Bisexual Men', *American Journal of Public Health*, 100(1): 159–164.

Malinsky, K.P. 1997, 'Learning to be Invisible: Female Sexual Minority Students in America's Public High Schools' in M.B. Harris Ed, *School Experiences of Gay and Lesbian Youth*, New York: Harrington Park Press.

Mallon, G.P. 2011, 'The Home Study Assessment Process for Gay, Lesbian, Bisexual, and Transgender Prospective Foster and Adoptive Families', *Journal of GLBT Family Studies*, 7(1–2): 9–29.

Malone, J. 1980, *Straight Women/Gay Men: A Special Relationship*, New York: Dial Press.

Mann, C. & Stewart, F. 2000, *Internet Communication and Qualitative Research*, London: Sage.

Mark, K; Rosenkrantz, D; Kerner, I. 2014, 'Bi'ing into Monogamy: Attitudes Toward Monogamy in a Sample of Bisexual-identified Adults'. *Psychology of Sexual Orientation and Gender Diversity*, 1(3): 263–269.

Marotta, V. 2002, 'Zygmunt Bauman: Order, Strangerhood and Freedom', *Thesis Eleven*, 70(1): 36–54.

Marotta, V. (in press, 2016), *Theories of the Stranger: Debates on Cosmopolitanism, Identity and Cross-Cultural Encounters*, Surrey, UK: Ashgate.

Marsh, V. Ed. 2011, *Speak Now: Australian Perspectives on Same-Sex Marriage*, Melbourne: Clouds of Magellan.

Martin, E. & Pallotta-Chiarolli, M. 2009, 'Exclusion By Inclusion: Bisexual Young People, Marginalisation and Mental Health in Relation to Substance Abuse' in A.Taket, B.R. Crisp, A. Nevill, C. Lamaro, M. Graham & S. Barter-Godfrey Eds *Theorising Social Exclusion*, London: Routledge.

Martin, F. 2012, 'Girls Who Love Boys' Love: Japanese Homoerotic Manga as Trans-national Taiwan Culture', *Inter-Asia Cultural Studies*, 13(3): 365–383.

Martinez, O., Dodge, B., Goncalves, G., Schnarrs, P.W., Muñoz-Laboy, M., Reece, M., Malebranche, D., Van Der Pol, B., Kelle, G., Nix, R. & Fortenberry, J.D. 2012a, 'Sexual Behaviours and Experiences Among Behaviourally Bisexual Latino Men in the Midwestern United States: Implications for Sexual Health Interventions', *Journal of Bisexuality*, 12(2): 283–310.

Martinez, O., Dodge, B., Reece, M., Schnarrs, P.W., Rhodes, S.D., Goncalves, G., Muñoz-Laboy, M., Malebranche, D., Van Der Pol, B., Nix, R., Guadalupe K. & Fortenberry, J.D. 2012b, 'Sexual Health and Life Experiences: Voices From Behaviourally Bisexual Latino Men in the Midwestern USA', *Culture, Health and Sexuality*, 13(9): 1073–1089.

Martino, W. & Pallotta-Chiarolli, M. 2003, *So What's A Boy?: Addressing Issues of Masculinity in Education,* London: Open University Press.

Mason, G. 1995, 'OutLaws: Acts of Proscription in the Sexual Order' in M. Thornton Ed. *Public and Private- Feminist Legal Debates*, London: Oxford University Press.

Matteson, D.R. 1996, 'Counselling and Psychotherapy with Bisexual and Exploring Clients' in B.A. Firestein Ed. *Bisexuality: The Psychology and Politics of an Invisible*, Thousand Oaks, CA: Sage.

McAuley, S. 2010, *Insignificant Others*, New York: Simon and Schuster.

McCormack, M., Anderson, E. & Adams, A. 2014, 'Cohort Effect on the Coming Out Experiences of Bisexual Men', *Sociology*, 48(6): 1207–1223.

McCormack, M., Wignall, L. & Anderson, E. 2015, 'Identities and Identifications: Changes in Metropolitan Bisexual Men's Attitudes and Experiences', *Journal of Bisexuality*, 15(13): 3–20.

McKirnan, D.J., Doll, L., Burzette, R.G. 1995, 'Bisexually Active men: Social Charcteristsics and Sexual behaviour', *The Journal of Sex Research*, 32(1): 65–76.

McLean, K. 2003, *Identifying as Bisexual: Life Stories of Australian Bisexual Men and Women,* PhD Thesis, *Melbourne:* School of Political and Social Inquiry, Monash University.

McLean, K. 2004, 'Negotiating NonMonogamy: Bisexuality and Intimate Relationships' in R. Fox Ed, *Current Research on Bisexuality*, New York: Harrington Park Press.

McLean, K. 2008, 'Coming Out, Again: Boundaries, Identities and Spaces of Belonging' *Australian Geographer*, 39(3): 303–313.

McLean, K. 2011, 'Bisexuality and Nonmonogamy: A Reflection', *Journal of Bisexuality*, 11(4): 513–517.

McLelland, M. 2006, 'Why are Japanese Girls' Comics Full of Boys Bonking?' *Refractory: A Journal of Entertainment Media,* <http://refractory.unimelb.edu.au/2006/12/04/why-are-japanese-girls%E2%80%99-comics-full-of-boys-bonking1-mark-mclelland/>.

McLelland, M., Nagaike, K., Suganuma, K. & Welker, J. 2015, Eds *Boys' Love Manga and Beyond: History, Culture and Community,* Jackson: University of Mississipi Press.

Messinger, J.L. 2012, 'Antibisexual Violence and Practitioners' Roles in Prevention and Intervention: An Ecological and Empowerment-Based Approach in Public Health Social Work', *Journal of Bisexuality,* 12(3): 360–375.

Meyer, M.D.E. 2010, 'Representing Bisexuality on Television: The Case for Intersectional Hybrids', *Journal of Bisexuality,* 10(4): 366–387.

Meyer, U. 2010, 'Hidden in Straight Sight: Trans*gressing Gender and Sexuality Via BL', in Levi, A., McHarry, M. & Pagliassotti, D. Ed. 2010, *Boys' Love Manga: Essays on the Sexual Ambiguity and Cross-Cultural Fandom of the Genre*, Jefferson, N.C.: McFarland & Co.

Meyer, U. 2013, 'Drawing From the Body- the Self, the Gaze and the Other in Boys' Love Manga', *Journal of Graphic Novels and Comics*, 4(1): 64–81.

Miller, M. 2002, 'Ethically Questionable?' Popular Media Reports on Bisexual Men and AIDS', in B. Beemyn & E. Steinman Eds *Bisexual Men in Culture and Society*, New York: Harrington Park Press.

Miller, M., Andre, A., Ebin, J. & Bessonova, L. Eds 2007, *Bisexual Health: An Introduction and Model Practices for HIV/STI Prevention Programming,* New York: National Gay and Lesbian Task Force Policy Institute, Fenway Community Health and BiNet, USA.

Millett, G., Malebranche, D., Mason, B. & Spikes, P. 2005, 'Focusing "Down Low": Bisexual Black Men, HIV Risk and Heterosexual Transmission', *Journal of the National Medical Association*, 97(7): 52S-59S.

Mizoguchi, A. 2003. "Male-Male Romance By and For Women in Japan: A History and the Subgenres of Yaoi Fictions', *U.S. Japan Women's Journal*, 25: 49–75.

Molina, M.L. 1994, 'Fragmentations: Meditations on Separatism', *Signs: Journal Of Women In Culture and Society*, 19(2): 449–457.
Moore, D.L. & Norris, F.H. 2005, 'Empirical Investigation of the Conflict and Flexibility Models of Bisexuality', *Journal of Bisexuality*, 5(1): 5–25.
Moore, H. 2008, *The Bishop's Daughter*, New York: W,W Norton & Co.
Moraga, C. 1981, 'The Welder' in C. Moraga & G. Anzaldua Eds *This Bridge Called My Back: Writings By Radical Women of Colour*, Watertown, MA: Persephone Press.
Morris, J.F., Balsam, K.F. & Rothblum, E.D. 2002, 'Lesbian and Bisexual Mothers and Nonmothers: Demographics and the Coming-out Process', *Journal of Family Psychology*, 16: 144–156.
Mosher, W.D., Chandra, A. & Jones, J. 2005, *Sexual Behaviour and Selected Health Measures: Men and Women 15–44 Years of Age, United States, 2002*, U.S. Department of Health and Human Services, Centers for Disease Control and Prevention <www.cdc.gov/nchs/data/ad/ad362.pdf>.
Mulick, P.S. & Wright, L.W. Jr, 2002, 'Examining the Existence of Biphobia in the Heterosexual and Homosexual Populations', *Journal of Bisexuality*, 2(4): 45–64.
Munoz-Laboy, M.A. 2004, 'Beyond 'MSM': Sexual Desire Among Bisexually-Active Latino Men in New York City', *Sexualities*, 7(1): 55–80.
Muñoz-Laboy, M. & Dodge, B. 2007, 'Which Bisexual Latino Men are at Highest HIV/STI Risk? An Exploratory Analysis', *American Journal of Public Health*, 97(6): 1102–1106.
Muñoz-Laboy, M. 2008, 'Familism, Sexual Regulation and Risk Among Bisexual Latino Men', *Archives of Sexual Behavior*, 37(5): 773–782.
Muñoz-Laboy, M., Sririam, V., Weinstein, H. & Vasquez del Aguila, E. 2009, 'Negotiating Bisexual Desire and Familism: The Case of Latino/a Bisexual Young Men and Women in New York City', *Culture, Health and Sexuality*, 11(3): 331–344.
Murphy, M. 1990, 'Thinking About Bisexuality', *Resources For Feminist Research*, 19(3–4): 87–88.
Nadal, K.L. 2008, 'Preventing Racial, Ethnic, Gender, Sexual Minority, Disability, and Religious Microaggressions: Recommendations for Promoting Positive Mental Health', *Prevention in Counselling Psychology: Theory, Research, Practice and Training*, 2(1): 22–27.
Nadal, K.L., Issa, J.L., Meterko, V., Wideman, M. & Wong, Y. 2011, 'Sexual Orientation Microaggressions: 'Death by a Thousand Cuts' for Lesbian, Gay, and Bisexual Youth', *Journal of LGBT Youth*, 8(3): 234–259.
Nahas, R. & Turley, M. 1979, *The New Couple: Women and Gay Men*, New York: Seaview Books.
Naples, N. 2004, 'The Outsider Phenomenon' in S.N. Hesse-Biber & M.L. Yaiser Eds *Feminist Perspectives on Social Research*, Oxford: Oxford University Press.
Nicolson, N. 1973, *Portrait of a Marriage*, London: Weidenfeld & Nicolson.
Noel, M.J. 2006, 'Progressive Polyamory: Considering Issues of Diversity' *Sexualities*, 9(5): 602–620.
O'Brien, J. 2007, 'Queer Tensions: The Cultural Politics of Belonging and Exclusion in Same Gender Marriage Debates' in N. Rumens & A. Cervantes-Carson Eds *Sexual Politics of Desire and Belonging*, Amsterdam: Rodopi.

O'Rourke, M. 2005, 'On the Eve of a Queer-Straight Future: Notes Toward an Antinormative Heteroerotic', *Feminism and Psychology*, 15(1): 111–116.

Oakley, A. 1981, 'Interviewing Women: A Contradiction in Terms' in H. Roberts Ed *Doing Feminist Research*, London: Routledge.

Ocean, M. 2008, 'Bisexuals are Bad for the Same Sex Marriage Business', *Journal of Bisexuality*, 7(3/4): 303–311.

Ochs, R & Williams, S.H. Eds 2014, *Rec.og.nize: the Voices of Bisexual Men*. Boston: Bisexual Resource Centre.

Orlando, L. 1991, 'Loving Whom We Choose' in L. Hutchins and L. Ka'ahumanu Eds *Bi Any Other Name: Bisexual People Speak Out*, Boston: Alyson Publications.

Page, E.H. 2004, 'Mental Health Services' Experiences of Bisexual Women and Bisexual Men: an Empirical Study', *Journal of Bisexuality*, 3(3–4): 137–160.

Pallotta-Chiarolli, M. 1995, "A Rainbow in My Heart': Negotiating Sexuality and Ethnicity' in C. Guerra & R. White Eds *Ethnic Minority Youth in Australia: Challenges and Myths*, Hobart: National Clearinghouse on Youth Studies.

Pallotta-Chiarolli, M. 1999, "Multicultural Does Not Mean Multisexual': Social Justice and the Interweaving of Ethnicity and Sexuality in Australian Schooling', in D. Epstein & J.T. Sears Eds *A Dangerous Knowing: Sexual Pedagogies and the Master Narrative*, London: Cassell.

Pallotta-Chiarolli, M. 2005a, *When Our Children Come Out: How to Support Gay, Lesbian, Bisexual and Transgender Young People*, Sydney: Finch Publishing.

Pallotta-Chiarolli, M. 2005b, "We're the X-Files': Bisexual Students 'Messing Up Tidy Sex Files'" in K. Gilbert Ed. *Sexuality, Sport and the Culture of Risk*, Oxford: Meyer & Meyer.

Pallotta-Chiarolli, M. 2005c, 'Ethnic Identity' in J.T. Sears Ed. *Youth, Education, and Sexualities: An International Encyclopedia*, Westport, CT: Greenwood Publishing Group.

Pallotta-Chiarolli, M. 2006a, 'Polyparents Having Children, Raising Children, Schooling Children', *Lesbian and Gay Psychology Review*, 7(1): 48–53.

Pallotta-Chiarolli, M. 2006b, 'On the Borders of Sexuality Research: Young People Who Have Sex With Both Males and Females', *Journal of Gay and Lesbian Issues in Education*, 3(2–3): 79–86.

Pallotta-Chiarolli, M. 2008, *Love You Two*, Sydney: Random House.

Pallotta-Chiarolli, M. 2010a, *Border Sexualities, Border Families in Schools*, New York: Rowman & Littlefield.

Pallotta-Chiarolli, M. 2010b, '"To Pass, Border or Pollute": Polyfamilies Go to School' in M. Barker and D. Langdridge Eds *Understanding Non-Monogamies*, London: Routledge.

Pallotta-Chiarolli, M. 2011, "Messing Up the Couples' Cabinet': On the 'Queerly Mixed' Borders of the 'Residual' and the 'Emergent' in the Marriage Debates' in V. Marsh Ed. *Speak Now: Australian Perspectives on Same-Sex Marriage* , Melbourne: Clouds of Magellan

Pallotta-Chiarolli, M. 2014, '"New Rules, No Rules, Old Rules or Our Rules": Women Designing Mixed-Orientation Marriages with Bisexual Men' in M.

Pallotta-Chiarolli & B. Pease Eds. *The Politics of Recognition and Social Justice: Transforming Subjectivities and New Forms of Resistance,* London: Routledge.

Pallotta-Chiarolli, M. 2015a Ed. *Bisexuality in Education: Erasure, Exclusion and the Absence of Intersectionality,* New York: Routledge.

Pallotta-Chiarolli, M. 2015b, '"The Problem Is That He's A Man, Not That He's Bisexual": Women discussing bi-masculinities and bi-misogyny' in M. Flood & R. Howson Eds *Engaging Men in Building Gender Equality,* London: Cambridge Scholars Publishing

Pallotta-Chiarolli, M. & Lubowitz, S. 2003, 'Outside Belonging: Multi-Sexual Relationships as Border Existence' in S. D'Onofrio-Anderlini Ed. *Women and Bisexuality: A Global Perspective,* New York: Haworth Press.

Pallotta-Chiarolli, M. & Martin, E. 2009, '"Which Sexuality? Which Service?' Bisexual Young People's Experiences with Youth, Queer and Mental Health Services', *Journal of LGBT Youth,* 6(2–3): 199–222.

Pallotta-Chiarolli, M., Haydon, P. & Hunter, A. 2013, '"These Are *Our* Children": Polyamorous parenting' in A. Goldberg & K. Allen Eds. *LGBT-Parent Families: Innovations in Research and Implications for Practice,* New York: Springer.

Pallotta-Chiarolli, M. & Pease, B. Eds 2014, *The Politics of Recognition and Social Justice: Transforming Subjectivities and New Forms of Resistance,* London: Routledge.

Palmer, W.A. 1991, 'Female Partners of Bisexual Men', in *A Report on the GAMMALine* Melbourne: Telephone Counselling Service.

Parker, S. 2011, '"A Girl's Love': Lord Alfred Douglas as Homoerotic Muse in the Poetry of Olive Custance', *Women: A Cultural Review,* 22(2–3): 220–240.

Parrini, R., Castañeda, X., Magis-Rodríguez, C., Ruiz, J. & Lemp, G. 2011, 'Identity, Desire and Truth: Homosociality and Homoeroticism in Mexican Migrant Communities in the USA', *Culture, Health and Sexuality,* 13(4): 415–428.

Parsons, J.T., Kelly, B.C. & Wells, B.C., 2006, 'Differences in Club Drug use Between Heterosexual and Lesbian/Bisexual Females', *Addictive Behaviours,* 31(12): 2344–2349.

Paul, J.P. 1984, 'The Bisexual Identity: An Idea Without Social Recognition', *Journal of Homosexuality,* 92(3): 45–63.

Paul, J.P. 1996, 'Bisexuality: Exploring/Exploding the Boundaries' in R. Savin-Williams & K. Cohen Eds *The Lives of Lesbians, Gays, and Bisexuals: Children to Adults,* Belmont, CA: Thomson/Wadsworth.

Paul, J.P., Catania, J., Pollack, L., Moskowitz, J., Canchola, J., Mills, T., Binson, D. & Stall, R. 2002, 'Suicide Attempts Among Gay and Bisexual Men: Lifetime Prevalence and Antecedents', *American Journal of Public Health,* 92(8): 1338–1345.

Pearcey, M. & Olson, M. 2009, 'Understanding Heterosexual Women Married to Gay Men', *Gay & Lesbian Issues and Psychology Review,* 5(1): 35–44.

Pease, B. 2010, *Undoing Privilege: Unearned Advantage in a Divided World,* New York: Zed Books.

Persson, A. & Richards, W. 2008, 'From Closet to Heterotopia: a Conceptual Exploration of Disclosure and 'Passing' Among Heterosexuals Living With HIV' *Culture, Health and Sexuality,* 10(1): 73–86.

Persson, T.J. & Pfaus, J.G. 2015, 'Bisexuality and Mental Health: Future Research Directions, *Journal of Bisexuality*, 15(1): 82–98.
Peterson, L.W. 2001, 'The Married Man On-Line', *Journal of Bisexuality,* 1(2–3): 191–209.
Petronio, S. 1991, 'Communication Boundary Management: A Theoretical Model of Managing Disclosure of Private Information Between Married Couples', *Communication Theory*, 1(4): 311–335.
Petronio, S. 1994, 'Privacy Binds in Family Interactions: The Case of Parental Privacy Invasion', in W.R. Cupach & B.H. Spitzberg Eds *The Dark Side of Interpersonal Communication,* Hillsdale, England: Lawrence Erlbaum Associates.
Petronio, S. 2002, *Boundaries of Privacy: Dialectics of Disclosure.* Albany, NY: SUNY Press.
Petronio, S. 2010, 'Communication Privacy Management Theory: What Do We Know About Family Privacy Regulation?' *Journal of Family Theory & Review*, 2(3): 175–196.
Petronio, S. & Caughlin, J.P. 2005, 'Communication Privacy Management Theory: Understanding Families', in D. Braithwaite & L. Baxter Eds *Engaging Theories in Family Communication Multiple Perspectives*, Thousand Oaks, CA: SAGE Publications.
Pettaway, L., Bryant, L., Keane, F. & Craig, S. 2014, 'Becoming Down Low: A Review of the Literature on Black Men who have Sex with Men and Women', *Journal of Bisexuality*, 14(2): 209–221.
Pew Research Center 2013, *A Survey of LGBT Americans: Attitudes, Experiences and Values in Changing Times,* Washington, D.C: Pew Research Center.
Phelan, S. 1994, *Getting Specific: Postmodern Lesbian Politics,* Minneapolis: University of Minnesota Press.
Phellas, C. & Coxon, A.P.M. 2012, 'An Overview of Developments in Research Methods Applied to Non-Heterosexual Men', in C. Phellas Ed. *Researching Non-heterosexual Sexualities*, Surrey, UK: Ashgate.
Pitt, R. Jr. 2006, 'Downlow Mountain? De/stigmatizing Bisexuality Through Pitying and Pejorative Discourses in the Media', *Journal of Men's Studies*, 14(20): 254–258.
Poston W.S.C. 1990, 'The Biracial Identity Development Model: a Needed Addition', *Journal of Counseling and Development*, 69(2): 152–155.
Potoczniak, D.J. 2007, 'Development of Bisexual Men's Identities and Relationships' in K.L. Bieschke, R.M. Perez & K.A. DeBord Eds *Handbook of Counselling and Psychotherapy with Lesbian, Gay, Bisexual and Transgender Clients,* Washington: American Psychological Association.
Poulos, C.N. 2009, *Accidental Ethnography: An Inquiry into Family Secrecy,* Walnut Creek, CA: Left Coast Press.
Power, J., Perlesz, A., Brown, R., Schofield, M.J., Pitts, M.K., McNair, R. & Bickerdike, A. 2012, 'Bisexual Parents and Family Diversity: Findings From the Work, Love, Play Study', *Journal of Bisexuality,* 12(4): 519–538.
Pritchard, M. 1999, 'Penetration' in *Too Beautiful*, Gardena, CA: First Masquerade.
Probyn, E. 1996, *Outside Belongings*, New York: Routledge.

Prout, R. 2005, 'Confessions of a Congressman' in A. Mira Ed, *The Cinema of Spain and Portugal*, London: Wallflower Press.

Queen, C.A. 1991, 'The Queer in Me' in L. Hutchins & L. Ka'ahumanu Ed. *Bi Any Other Name*, Boston: Alyson Publications.

Rabinow, P. 1984, *The Foucault Reader*, London: Penguin.

Rambukkana, N. 2010, 'Sex, Space and Discourse: Non/monogamy and Intimate Privilege in the Public Sphere' in M. Barker & D. Langdridge Eds *Understanding Non-monogamies*, London: Routledge.

Rankin, S, Morton, J. & Bell, M. 2015, *Complicated? Bisexual People's Experiences of and Ideas for Improving Services*, Edinburgh: Equality Network.

Rasmussen, M.L. 2004, 'Wounded Identities, Sex and Pleasure: 'Doing It' at School, NOT!' *Discourse: Studies in the Cultural Politics of Education*, 25(4): 445–458.

Reece M., & Dodge B. 2003, 'Exploring the Physical, Mental, and Social Well-being Among Gay and Bisexual Men Who Cruise for Sex on a College Campus', *Journal of Homosexuality*, 46(1–2): 111–136.

Reece, M., Herbenick, D., Schick, V., Sanders, S.A., Dodge, B. & Fortenberry, J.D. 2010, 'Sexual behaviors, Relationships, and Perceived Health among Adult Men in the United States: Results from a National Probability Sample', *Journal of Sexual Medicine*, 7(suppl 5): 291–304.

Reid, A., Hughes, T., Worth, H., Saxton, P., Robinson, E., Segedin, R. & Aspin, C. 1997, *Male Call/Waea Mai, Tane Ma: Report Four: Casual Sex Between Men*, Auckland: New Zealand AIDS Foundation.

Reiger, G., Chivers, M.L. & Bailey, J.M. 2005, 'Sexual Arousal Patterns of Bisexual Men', *Psychological Science*,16(8): 574–584.

Reisen, C.A., Zea, M.C., Bianchi, F.T., Poppen, P.J., Shedlin, M.G. & Penha, M.M. 2010, 'Latino Gay & Bisexual Men's Relationships with Non-Gay-Identified Men Who have Sex with Men', *Journal of Homosexuality*, 57(8): 1004–1021.

Reynolds, R. 2000, 'Revisiting Bisexuality', *Sydney Star Observer*, 11th May: 12.

Reynolds, A.L. & Pope, R.L. 1991, 'The Complexities of Diversity: Exploring Multiple Oppressions', *Journal of Counseling & Development*, 70(1): 174–180.

Rich, A. 1979, *On Lies, Secrets, and Silence, Selected Prose 1966–1978*, New York: W.W. Norton.

Richards, C. & Barker, M. 2013, *Sexuality and Gender for Mental Health Professionals*, London: Sage.

Richardson, L. 1985, *The New Other Woman*, New York: The Free Press.

Richters, J., Bergin, S., Lubowitz, S. & Prestage, G., 2002, 'Women in Contact with Sydney's Gay and Lesbian Community: Sexual Identity, Practice and HIV Risks', *AIDS Care*, 14(2): 193–202.

Rieger G. & Savin-Williams R.C. 2012, 'The Eyes Have It: Sex and Sexual Orientation Differences in Pupil Dilation Patterns', *plosone.org*, <http://www.plosone.org/article/info%3Adoi%2F10.1371%2Fjournal.pone.0040256>

Riggs, D.W. 2007, 'Psychology, Liberalism, and Activism: Challenging Discourses of Equality Within the Same-sex Marriage Debate', *Gay and Lesbian Issues in Psychology Review*, 3(3): 185–194.

Ripley, M., Anderson, E., McCormack, M., Adams, A. & Pitts, R. 2011, 'The Decreasing Significance of Stigma in the Lives of Bisexual Men', Keynote

Address, Bisexual Research Convention, London', *Journal of Bisexuality*, 11(2–3): 195–206.

Ritchie, A. & Barker, M. 2006, 'There Aren't Words for What We Do or How We Feel So We Have to Make Them Up: Constructing Polyamorous Languages in a Culture of Compulsory Monogamy' *Sexualities*, 9(5): 584–601.

Roberts, B.C. 2015, 'Not What You (Want To) Think: *Boulevard* (2014)', *Journal of Bisexuality*, 15(3): 361–366.

Robinson, M. 2014, '"A Hope to Lift Both My Spirits": Preventing Bisexual Erasure in Aboriginal Schools', *Journal of Bisexuality*, 14/1: 18–35.

Robinson, B.A. & Moskowitz, D.A. 2013, 'The Eroticism of Internet Cruising as a Self-contained Behaviour: A Multivariate Analysis of Men Seeking Men Demographics and Getting Off Online', *Culture, Health & Sexuality*, 15(5): 555–569.

Rodriguez, E.M. 2009, 'At the Intersection of Church and Gay: A Review of the Psychological Research on Gay and Lesbian Christians', *Journal of Homosexuality*, 57(1): 5–38.

Rodriguez, E.M., Lytle, M.C. & Vaughan, M.D. 2013, 'Exploring the Intersectionality of Bisexual, Religious/Spiritual, and Political Identities from a Feminist Perspective", *Journal of Bisexuality*, 13(3): 285–309.

Roiphe, K. 2007, *Uncommon Arrangements: Seven Portraits of Married Life in London Literary Circles, 1910–1939,* New York: The Dial Press.

Rosaldo R. 1994, *Culture and Truth: The Remaking of Social Analysis,* Boston, MA: Beacon Press.

Roseneil, S. & Budgeon, S. 2004, 'Cultures of Intimacy and Care Beyond 'The Family': Personal Life and Social Change in the Early 21st Century', *Current Sociology*, 52(2): 135–159.

Rosenthal, A.M., Sylva, D., Safron, A. & Bailey, J.M. 2011, 'Sexual Arousal Patterns of Bisexual Men Revisited' *Biological Psychology,* 88(1): 11–24.

Ross, M.W. 1983, *The Married Homosexual Man*, London: Routledge & Kegan Paul.

Ross, M.W. & Paul, J.P. 1992, 'Beyond Gender: The Basis of Sexual Attraction in Bisexual Men and Women', *Psychological Reports* 71: 1283–1290.

Ross, L.E. & Dobinson, C. 2013, 'Where is the 'B' in LGBT Parenting? A Call for Research on Bisexual Parenting' in A.E. Goldberg & K.R. Allen Ed, *LGBT-Parent Families: Innovations in Research and Implications for Practice*, New York: Springer.

Ross, L.E., Siegel, A., Dobinson, C., Epstein, R. & Steele, L.S. 2012, 'I Don't Want to Turn Totally Invisible: Mental Health, Stressors, and Supports Among Bisexual Women During the Perinatal Period', *Journal of GLBT Family Studies*, 8(2): 137–154.

Ross L.E., Bauer G.R., MacLeod M.A., Robinson M., & MacKay J. 2014, 'Mental Health and Substance Use among Bisexual Youth and Non-Youth in Ontario, Canada', *PLoS ONE* 9(8) <e101604. doi: 10.1371/journal.pone.0101604>

Rostosky, S.S., Riggle, E.D.B., Pascale-Hague, D. & McCants, L.E., 2010, 'The Positive Aspects of a Bisexual Self-identification', *Psychology & Sexuality*, 1(2): 131–144.

Roughton, R. 2014, "The Significance of Brokeback Mountain", *Journal of Gay and Lesbian Health*, 18(1): 83–94.

Rudy, K. 1997, "Where Two or More Are Gathered': Using Gay Communities as a Model for Christian Sexual Ethics' in R. Goss. & A. Adams Squire Stronghart Eds *Our Families, Our Values: Snapshots of Queer Kinship*, New York: Harrington Park Press.

Russell, S.T. & Seif, H. 2002, 'Bisexual Female Adolescents: A Critical Analysis of Past Research and Results from a National Survey', *Journal of Bisexuality*, 2(2–3): 73–94.

Russo, V. 1987, *The Celluloid Closet: Homosexuality in the Movies*. New York: Harper & Row.

Rust P.C. 1992, 'The Politics of Sexual Identity: Sexual Attraction and Behavior Among Lesbian and Bisexual Women', *Social Problems*, 39(4): 366–386.

Rust, P.C. 1995, *Bisexuality and the Challenge To Lesbian Politics: Sex, Loyalty and Revolution*, New York: New York University Press.

Rust, P.C. 1996a, 'Monogamy and Polyamory: Relationship Issues for Bisexuals' in B.A. Firestein Ed, *Bisexuality: The Psychology and Politics Of An Invisible Minority*, London: Sage.

Rust, P.C. 1996b, 'Managing Multiple Identities: Diversity Among Bisexual Men and Women' in B.A. Firestein Ed, *Bisexuality: The Psychology and Politics Of An Invisible Minority*, London: Sage.

Rust, P.C. 2000, 'Bisexuality: A Contemporary Paradox for Women', *Journal of Social Issues*, 56(2): 205–221.

Rust, P.C. 2001, 'Make Me a Map: Bisexual Men's Images of Bisexual Community', *Journal of Bisexuality*, 1(2–3): 47–108.

Rust, P.C. 2007, 'The Construction and Reconstruction of Bisexuality: Inventing and Reinventing the Self' in B.A. Firestein Ed. *Becoming Visible: Counselling Bisexuals Across the Lifespan*, New York: Columbia University Press.

Ruthstrom, E. 2010, 'Much More Than Just a Threesome: 3', *Journal of Bisexuality*, 13(4): 602–605.

Ryan, A. 2000, 'Feminism and Sexual Freedom in an Age of AIDS', *Sexualities*, 4(1): 91–107.

Ryan, C. & Rivers, I. 2003, 'Lesbian, Gay, Bisexual And Transgender Youth Victimization And Its Correlates In The USA And UK', *Culture, Health And Sexuality*, 5(2): 103–119.

Ryan, M. 2007, 'Spike from 'Buffy' and 'Torchwood's' Captain Jack Harkness- Youza', *Chicago Tribune* <http://featuresblogs.chicagotribune.com/entertainment-tv/2007/07/spike-fr>.

Samuels, E. 2003, 'My Body, My Closet: Invisible Disability and the Limits of Coming-Out Discourse', *GLQ: A Journal of Lesbian and Gay Studies*, 9(1–2): 233–255.

Sandfort, T.G. M. & Dodge, B. 2008, 'And Then There Was the Down Low: Introduction to Black and Latino Male Bisexualities', *Archives of Sexual Behavior*, 37(5), 675–682.

Sandfort, T.G.M. & Dodge, B. 2009, 'Homosexual and Bisexual Labels and Behaviors Among Men: The Need for Clear Conceptualizations, Accurate Operationalizations, and Appropriate Methodological Designs', in V. Reddy, T.G.M. Sandfort

& R. Rispel Eds *Perspectives on Same-sex Sexuality, Gender and HIV/AIDS in South Africa: From Social Silence to the Social Science,* Pretoria: Human Sciences Research Council.

San Filippo, M. 2013, *The B Word: Bisexuality in Contemporary Film and Television,* Bloomington, Indiana: Indiana University Press.

San Francisco Human Rights Commission, 2011, *Bisexual Invisibility: Impacts and Recommendations,* San Francisco Human Rights Commission LGBT Advisory Committee, <http://www.sf-hrc.org/modules/showdocument.aspx?documentid=989>.

Satcher, A.J., Durant, T., Hu, X. & Dean, H.D. 2007, 'AIDS Cases Among Women Who Reported Sex with a Bisexual Man, 2000–2004, United States', *Women and Health,* 46(2–3): 23–40.

Savage, D. 2011, 'Case Closed: Bisexual Men Exist!' *thestranger.com* <http://slog.thestranger.com/slog/archives/2011/08/16/9534403-case-closed-bisexual-men-exist>

Savin-Williams, R. 2005, *The New Gay Teenager,* Cambridge, MA: Harvard University Press.

Savin-Williams, R.G. 2008, 'Then and Now: Recruitment, Definition, Diversity, and Positive Attributes of Same-Sex Populations', *Developmental Psychology,* 44(1): 135–138.

Scarduzio, J.A. & Geist-Martin, P. 2008, 'Making Sense of Fractured Identities: Male Professors' Narratives of Sexaul Harassment', *Communication Monographs,* 75(4): 369–395.

Schnarrs, P.W., Dodge, B., Reece, M., Goncalves, G., Martinez, O., Van Der Pol, B., Malebranche, D., Murray, M., Nix, R. & Fortenberry, J.D. 2012, 'Subjective Sexual Experiences of Behaviourally Bisexual Men in the Midwestern United States: Sexual Attraction, Sexual Behaviours and Condom Use', *Journal of Bisexuality,* 12(2): 246–282.

Schneider, J. & Schneider, B. 1990, *Sex, Lies, And Forgiveness: Couples Speaking Out On Healing From Sex Addiction,* New York: HarperCollins.

Schrimshaw, E.W., Downing, M.J., Jr, & Siegel, K. 2013a, 'Sexual Venue Selection and Strategies for Concealment of Same-Sex Behavior Among Non-Disclosing Men Who Have Sex with Men and Women', *Journal of Homosexuality,* 60(1): 120–145.

Schrimshaw, E.W., Siegel, K., Downing Jr, M.J. and Parsons, J.T. 2013b, 'Disclosure and Concealment of Sexual Orientation and the Mental Health of Non-Gay-Identified Behaviorally Bisexual Men', *Journal of Consulting and Clinical Psychology,* 81(1): 141–153.

Schrimshaw, E.W., Downing Jr. M.J., Cohn, D.J. & Siegel, K. 2014, 'Conceptions of Privacy and the Non-disclosure of Same-sex Behaviour by Behaviourally Bisexual Men in Heterosexual Relationships', *Culture, Health & Sexuality,* 16: 4, 351–365.

Schutz, A. 1944, 'The Stranger: An Essay in Social Psychology', *American Journal Of Sociology,* 49(6): 499–507.

Schwartz, L.B. 2012, 'Mixed-Orientation Marriages: Coming Out, Staying Together', *Journal of GLBT Family Studies,* 8(1): 121–136.

Scott-Blanton, J. 2005, *My Husband is on the Downlow . . . and I Know It,* Triangle, VA: JaRon Publishing Group.

Shallenberger, D. 1996, 'Reclaiming the Spirit: The Journeys of Gay Men and Lesbian Women Toward Integration', *Qualitative Sociology,* 19(2): 195–215.
Sheff, E. 2005, 'Polyamorous Women, Sexual Subjectivity And Power', *Journal of Contemporary Ethnography,* 20(10): 1–34.
Sheff, E. 2006, 'Poly-Hegemonic Masculinities', *Sexualities,* 9(5): 621–642.
Sheff, E. 2010, 'Strategies in Polyamorous Parenting' in M.Barker & D. Langdridge Eds *Understanding Non-monogamies,* London: Routledge.
Sheff, E. 2014. *The Polyamorists Next Door: Inside Multiple-Partner Relationships and Families,* Lanham, MD: Rowman & Littlefield.
Sheff, E. & Hammers, C. 2011, 'The Privilege of Perversities: Race, Class and Education Among Polyamorists and Kinksters', *Psychology & Sexuality,* 2(3): 198–223.
Shippee, N.D. 2011, 'Gay, Straight, and Who I Am: Interpreting Passing Within the Frames for Everyday Life', *Deviant Behavior,* 32(2): 115–157.
Silenzio, V.M., Duberstein, P.R., Tang, W., Lu, N.T. X. & Homan, C.M. 2009, 'Connecting the Invisible Dots: Reaching Lesbian, Gay, and Bisexual Adolescents and Young Adults at Risk for Suicide Through Online Social Networks', *Social Science and Medicine,* 69(3): 469–474.
Simmel, G. 1971, *On Individuality and Social Forms: Selected Writings,* Chicago: University of Chicago Press.
Simpson, M. 2006, 'Curiouser and Curiouser: The Strange 'Disappearance' Of Male Bisexuality' <http://www.marksimpson.com/blog/2006/04/26/curiouser-and-curiouser-the-strange-disappearance-of-male-bisexuality/ Retrieved October 26th, 2009.
Smith, R. 1997, *Physique: the Life of John Barrington,* London: Serpent's Tail.
Solot, D. & Miller, M. 2001, 'Unmarried Bisexuals: Distinct Voices on Marriage and Family', *Journal of Bisexuality,* 1(4): 83–90.
Som, I. 1991, 'The Queer Kitchen' in M. Silvera Ed. *Piece Of My Heart: A Lesbian Of Color Anthology,* Toronto: SisterVision.
Spears, B. & Lowen, L. 2010, *Beyond Monogamy: Lessons from Long-Term Male Couples in Non-Monogamous Relationships,* <http://thecouplesstudy.com/wp-content/uploads/BeyondMonogamy_1_01.pdf>.
Stanley, J.L. 2004, 'Biracial Lesbian and Bisexual Women: Understanding the Unique Aspects and Interactional Processes of Multiple Minority Identities', *Women & Therapy,* 21(1–2): 159–171.
Stein, A. 1997, *Sex and Sensibility: Stories of a Lesbian Generation,* San Francisco: University of California Press.
Steinman, E. 2011, 'Revisiting the Invisibility of Male Bisexuality: Grounding Queer Theory, Centering Bisexual Absences and Examining Masculinities', *Journal of Bisexuality,* 11(4): 399–411.
Steinman, E. & Beemyn, B. Eds 2001a, *Bisexuality in the Lives of Men: Facts & Fiction,* New York: Harrington Park Press.
Steinman, E. & Beemyn, B. 2001b, *Bisexual Men in Culture and Society,* New York: Haworth Press.
Stewart, F., Mischewski, A. & Smith, A.M.A. 2000, 'I Want To Do What I Want To Do: Young Adults Resisting Sexual Identities', *Critical Public Health,* 10(4): 409–422.

References

Stiles, B.L. & Clark, R.E. 2011, 'BDSM, A Subcultural Analysis of Sacrifices and Delights', *Deviant Behaviour*, 32(2): 158–189.

Stokes, J.P., McKirnan, D.J. & Burzette, R.G. 1993, 'Sexual behaviour, Condom Use, Disclosure of Sexuality, and Stability of Sexual Orientation in Bisexual Men', *Journal of Sex Research*, 30(3): 203–313.

Stokes, J.P., Taywaditep, K., Vanable, P. & McKirnan, D.J. 1996, 'Bisexual Men, Sexual Behaviour and HIV/AIDS' in B.A. Firestein Ed. *Bisexuality: The Psychology and Politics Of An Invisible Minority*, London: Sage.

Sue, D.W., Capodilupo, C.M., Torino, G.C., Bucceri, J.M., Holder, A.M.B., Nadal, K.L., Esquilin, M. 2007, 'Racial Microaggressions in Everyday Life: Implications for Clinical Practice', *American Psychologist*, 62(4): 271–286.

Sulak, J. 2013, *The Wizard and the Witch: Seven Decades of Counter-Culture, Magic and Paganism*. Woodbury, MN: Llewellyn Publications.

Suresha, R. 2013, 'Where's the 'B' in National LGBTQ Organizations? The Bisexual Representation Report Card' *Huffington Post* <http://www.huffingtonpost.com/ron-suresha/bisexual-representation-report-card_b_2748342.html?view=print&comm_ref=false>.

Suresha, R.J. & Chvany, P. Eds 2005, *Bi men: Coming Out Every Which Way*, New York: Harrington Park Press.

Suzuki, K. 1999, 'Pornography or Therapy? Japanese Girls Creating the Yaoi Phenomenon', in S. Inness Ed. *Millennium Girls: Today's Girls Around the World*. London: Rowman & Littlefield.

Swan, T.B. & Benack, S. 2012, 'Renegotiating Identity in Unscripted Territory: The Predicament of Queer Men in Heterosexual Marriages', *Journal of GLBT Family Studies*, 8(1): 46–66.

Szymanski, M. 2012, 'A Review of 'The Staircase' ', *Journal of Bisexuality*, 12(3): 442–443.

Szymanski, M. 2014, 'Angels of Sex Reveals the Perfect Bisexual Triad', *Journal of Bisexuality*, 14(2): 300–302.

Tan, C. 2015, 'A Look at Bisexuality in Science Fiction', *Lambda Literary* <www.lambdaliterary.org/features/01/18/a-look-at-bisexuality-in-science-fiction/?utm_source=+Lambda+Literary+Review+January+23rd%2C+2015&utm_campaign=Newsletters&utm_medium=email>

Taormino, T.T. 2008, 'Straight Men Who Have Sex With Men: Inside the Secret World of the Straight Guise', *Village Voice Newspaper*, July 29th.

Te Awekotuku, N. 1991, *Mana wahine Maori: Selected Writings on Maori Women's Art, Culture and Politics*, Auckland, N.Z.: New Women's Press.

Te Awekotuku, N. 1996, "Maori: People and Culture." *Maori Art and Culture* 1: 14–46.

Te Awekotuku, N. 2001, "Hinemoa: Retelling a Famous Romance", *Lesbian Studies in Aotearoa/New Zealand*, 5(1–2): 1–11.

Te Awekotuku, N. 2003, *Ruahine: Mythic Women*, Wellington: Huia

Thompson, B.Y. 2012, 'The Price of 'Community' from Bisexual/Biracial Women's Perspectives', *Journal of Bisexuality*, 12(3): 417–428.

Thorn, M. 2004, 'Girls and Women Getting Out of Hand: The Pleasure and Politics of Japan's Amateur Comics Community', in W.W. Kelly Ed. *Fanning the Flames:*

Fans and Consumer Culture in Contemporary Japan, New York: State University of New York Press.

Thorson, A.R. 2009, 'Adult Children's Experiences With Their Parent's Infidelity: Communicative Protection and Access Rules in the Absence of Divorce', *Communication Studies*, 60(1): 32–48.

Toft, A. 2009, 'Bisexual Christians: The Life-Stories of a Marginalised Community' in S. Hunt Ed. *Contemporary Christianity and LGBT Sexualities*, Surrey, UK: Ashgate.

Toft, A. 2012, 'Researching Bisexuality and Christianity: Locating a Hidden Population and the Use of Reflexivity" in C.N. Phellas Ed. *Researching Non-Heterosexual Sexualities*. Surrey, UK: Ashgate.

Tornstam, L. 2005, *Gerotranscendence: A Developmental Theory of Positive Aging*. New York: Springer.

Towle, C. 2011, 'Highlighting the B in LGBT: The Experiences of One U.K. Trade Union' *Journal of Bisexuality*, 11(2–3): 317–319.

Trahan, H.A. 2014, *Relationship Literacy And Polyamory: A Queer Approach*. PhD Dissertation, Graduate College of Bowling Green State University.

Treyger, S.E., Zajicek, L., Trepper, T. 2008, 'Helping Spouses Cope With Partners Coming Out: A Solution-Focused Approach', *The American Journal of Family Therapy*, 36(1): 30–47.

Trinh, T. Minh-ha. 1990a, 'Cotton and Iron' in R. Ferguson, M. Gever, M.T. Trinh, & C. West Eds *Out There: Marginalization & Contemporary Cultures*, Cambridge, Massachusetts: MIT Press.

Trinh, T. Minh-ha. 1990b, 'Not You/Like You: Post-Colonial Women and the Interlocking Questions of Identity and Difference' in G. Anzaldua Ed, *Making Faces, Making Soul/Haciendo Caras*, San Francisco: Aunt Lute.

Trinh, T. Minh-ha. 1991, *When The Moon Waxes Red*, New York: Routledge.

Trinh, T. Minh-ha. 1992, *Framer Framed*, New York: Routledge.

Tuller, D. 2011, 'No Surprise for Bisexual Men: Report Indicates They Exist' *New York Times* <www.nytimes.com/2011/08/23/health/23/bisexual.html>.

Tye, M.C. 2003, 'Lesbian, Gay, Bisexual, and Transgender Parents: Special Considerations for the Custody and Adoption Evaluator', *Family Court Review*, 41(1): 92–103.

Udis-Kessler, A. 1990, 'Bisexuality in an Essentialist World: Toward an Understanding of Biphobia' in T. Geller Ed. *Bisexuality: A Reader and Sourcebook*, Ojai, CA: Times Change Press.

Udis-Kessler, A. 1996, 'Identity/Politics: Historical Sources of the Bisexual Movement' in B. Beemyn & M. Eliason Eds *Queer Studies: A Lesbian, Gay, Bisexual, and Transgender Anthology*. New York: New York University Press.

Vaid, U. 2012, *Irresistible Revolution: Confronting Race, Class and the Assumptions of Lesbian, Gay, Bisexual and Transgender Politics*, New York: Magnus Books.

Valadez, G. & Elsbree, A.R. 2005, 'Queer Coyotes: Transforming Education to be More Accepting, Affirming, & Supportive of Queer Individuals' *Journal of Latinos and Education*, 4(3): 171–192.

Vangelisti, A.L. 1994, 'Family Secrets: Forms, Functions, and Correlates', *Journal of Social and Personal Relationships*,11(1): 113–135.

Vangelisti, A.L., Caughlin, J., Timmerman, L. 2001, 'Criteria for Revealing Family Secrets' *Communication Monographs*, 68(1): 1–27.

Vassallo, G. 2002, 'Bisexual Activism in Australia', Paper given at *7th International Conference on Bisexuality*, 25th–28th October, University of Technology, Sydney.

Vicari, J. 2011, *Male Bisexuality in Current Cinema: Images of Growth, Rebellion and Survival*, Jefferson, NC: McFarland & Co.

Voetsch, A.C., Thomas, P.E., Satcher Johnson, A., Millett, G.A., Mundey, L., Goode, C., Nobles, J., Sly, K., Smith, M.R., Shiloh, M. 2010, 'Sex with Bisexual Men Among Black Female Students at Historically Black Colleges and Universities', *Journal of the National Medical Association*, 102(12): 1198–1205.

Volpp, S.Y. 2010, 'What About the "B" in LGB: Are Bisexual Women's Mental Health Issues Same or Different?' *Journal of Gay & Lesbian Mental Health*, 14(1): 41–51.

Walters, K.L., Evans-Campbell, T., Simoni, J., Ronquillo, T. & Bhuyan, R. 2006, '"My Spirit in My Heart": Identity Experiences and Challenges Among American Indian Two-Spirited Women', *Journal of Lesbian Studies*, 10(1–2): 125–149.

Ward, J. 2015, *Not Gay: Sex Between Straight White Men*, New York: New York University Press.

Wark, McK. 1997, 'Bisexual Mediations: Beyond the Third Term' in J.J. Matthews Ed. *Sex in Public: Australian Sexual Cultures*, Sydney: Allen & Unwin.

Warner, J., McKeown, E., Griffin, M., Johnson, K., Ramsay, A., Cort, C. & King, M. 2004, 'Rates and Predictors of Mental Health in Gay Men, Lesbians, and Bisexual Men and Women: Results From a Survey Based in England and Wales', *British Journal of Psychiatry*, 18(5): 479–485.

Watson, J. 2008, 'Representations of Bisexuality in Australian Film', *Journal of Bisexuality*, 8(1–2): 97–114.

Weeks, J. 1987, 'Questions of Identity' in P. Caplan Ed. *The Cultural Construction Of Sexuality*, London: Tavistock.

Weeks, J. 1995, 'History, Desire, Identities' in R.G. Parker and J.H. Gagnon Eds *Conceiving Sexuality: Approaches to Sex Research in a Postmodern World*, New York: Routledge.

Weeks, J. 1998, 'The Sexual Citizen', *Theory, Culture and Society*, 15(3–4): 35–52.

Weinberg, M.S., Williams, C.J. & Pryor, D.W.1994, *Dual Attraction: Understanding Bisexuality*. New York: Oxford University Press.

Weinberg, M.S., Williams, C.J. & Pryor, D.W. 2001, 'Bisexuals at Midlife: Commitment, Salience, and Identity', *Journal of Contemporary Ethnography*, 30(2): 180–208.

Weinrich, J.D. 2014, 'Multidimensional Measurement of Sexual Orientation: Ideal', *Journal of Bisexuality*, 14(3–4): 544–546.

Weitzman, G.D. 2006, 'Therapy With Clients Who Are Bisexual and Polyamorous', *Journal of Bisexuality*, 6(1/2): 138–164.

Weitzman, G. 2007, 'Counselling Bisexuals in Polyamorous Relationships' in B.A. Firestein Ed. *Becoming Visible: Counselling Bisexuals Across the Lifespan*, New York: Columbia University Press.

Wellman, B. & Giulia, M. 1999, 'Net Surfers Don't Ride Alone: Virtual Communities as Communities', in B.Wellman Ed. *Networks in the Global Village*, Boulder, CO: Westview Press.

Wheatley, J. 2000, 'Two Of Us: Neal Blewett & Robert Brain', *The Age Good Weekend*, May 27th: 14.

Whitney, C. 1990, *Uncommon Lives: Gay Men And Straight Women*, New York: Plume.

Wickman, F. 2014, 'Was the Hero of Dallas Buyers Club Actually Bisexual?' *Slate's Culture Blog* <http://www.slate.com/blogs/browbeat/2014/01/17/was_dallas_buyers_club_s_ron_woodroof_gay_or_bisexual_friends_and_doctor.html>

Whyte, J. IV, Whyte, M.D. & Cormier, E. 2008, 'Down-Low Sex, Older African American Women and HIV Infection', *Journal of the Association of Nurses in AIDS Care*, 19(6): 423–31.

Wojtowicz, J. 1977, 'Real Dog Day Hero Tells His Story', *Jump Cut*, 15: 31–32 <http://www.ejumpcut.org/archive/onlinessays/JC15folder/RealDogDay.html>.

Wold, C., Seage III, G.R., Lenderking, W.R., Mayer, K.H., Cai, B., Heeren, T. & Goldstein, R. 1998, 'Unsafe Sex in Men Who Have Sex With Both Men and Women', *Journal of Acquired Immune Deficiency Syndromes & Human Retrovirology*, 17(4): 361–367.

Wolf, T. 1985, 'Marriages of Bisexual Men', *Journal of Homosexuality*, 11(1–2): 135–148.

Wood, A. 2006, '"Straight" Women, Queer Texts: Boy-Love Manga and the Rise of a Global Counterpublic', *Women's Studies Quarterly*, 34(1/2): 394–414.

Wood, M.M. 1934, *The Stranger: A Study In Social Relationships*, New York: Columbia University Press.

Worth, H. 2003, 'The Myth of the Bisexual Infector? HIV Risk and Men Who Have Sex With Men', *Journal of Bisexuality*, 3(2): 71–88.

Wosick-Correa, K. 2010, 'Agreements, Rules And Agentic Fidelity In Polyamorous Relationships', *Psychology & Sexuality*, 1(1): 44–61.

Wright, J.M. 2001, '"Aside from One Little, Tiny Detail, We are so Incredibly Normal': Perspectives of Children in Lesbian Step Families' in M. Bernstein & R. Reimann Eds *Queer Families, Queer Politics: Challenging Culture and the State*, New York: Columbia University Press.

Wright, L.W. Jr, Bonita, A.G. & Mulick, P.S. 2011, 'An Update and Reflections on Fear of and Discrimination Against Bisexuals, Homosexuals, and Individuals with AIDS', *Journal of Bisexuality*, 11(4): 458–464.

Yarhouse, M.A., Pawlowski, L.M. & Tan, E.S.N. 2003, 'Intact Marriages in Which One Partner Disidentifies with Experiences of Same-Sex Attraction', *The American Journal of Family Therapy*, 31(5): 375–394.

Yarhouse, M.A. & Pawlowski, L.M. 2003, 'Working Responsibly with 'Gay' Married Men and Their Spouses', *Marriage and Family: A Christian Journal*, 6(4): 459–470.

Yarhouse, M.A. & Seymore, R.L. 2006, 'Intact Marriages in Which One Partner Dis-identifies with Experiences of Same-sex Attraction: A Follow-up Study', *The American Journal of Family Therapy*, 34(2): 151–161.

Yescavage, K. & Alexander, J. 2003, 'Seeing What We Want to See: Searching for Bisexual Representation in 'Threesome' Films', *Journal of Bisexuality*, 3(2): 109–127.

Yip, A.K.T. 2003, 'Spirituality and Sexuality: An Exploration of the Religious Beliefs of Non-heterosexual Christians in Great Britain', *Theology and Sexuality*, 9(2): 137–154.

Yip, A.K.T. 2008, 'Researching Lesbian, Gay and Bisexual Christians and Muslims: Some Thematic Reflections', *Sociological Research Online* <www.socresonline.org.uk/13/1/5.html>.

Yip, A.K.T. 2010, 'Coming Home from the Wilderness: An Overview of Recent Scholarly Research on LGBTQI Religiosity/Spirituality in the West' in K. Browne; S.R. Munt & A.K.T. Yip Eds *Queer Spiritual Spaces: Sexuality and Sacred Places*, Surrey, UK: Ashgate.

Yoshino, K. 2000, 'The Epistemic Contract of Bisexual Erasure', *Stanford Law Review*, 52(2): 353–461.

Yuk, K.S.C. & Singh, A.A. 2010, 'The Bisexual Youth of Color Intersecting Identities Development Model: A Contextual Approach to Understanding Multiple Marginalization Experiences', *Journal of Bisexuality*, 10(4): 429–451.

Zanghellini, A. 2009, ''Boys Love' in Anime and Manga: Japanese Subcultural Production and its End Users', *Continuum: Journal of Media & Cultural Studies*, 23(3): 279–294.

Zell, M.G. 1992, 'A Bouquet of Lovers' in D.M. Anapol Ed. *Love Without Limits*, San Rafael, CA: Internet Resource Centre.

Zerubavel, E. 1991, *The Fine Line: Making Distinctions In Everyday Life*, Chicago: University of Chicago Press.

Ziegler, A., Matsick, J.L., Moors A.C., Rubin, J.D., & Conley, T.D. 2014, 'Does Monogamy Harm Women? Deconstructing Monogamy with a Feminist Lens', *Journal für Psychologie*, 22(1): 1–18.

Zimmerman, K.J. 2012, 'Clients in Sexually Open Relationships: Considerations for Therapists', *Journal of Feminist Family Therapy*, 24(3): 272–289.

Zinik, G. 1985, 'Identity Conflict or Adaptive Flexibility? Bisexuality Reconsidered', *Journal Of Homosexuality*, 11(1–2): 7–19.

Zipkin, D. 1992, 'Why Bi?' in E.R. Weise Ed. *Closer To Home: Bisexuality and Feminism*, Seattle: Seal Press.

Zivony, A. & Lobel, T. 2014, 'The Invisible Stereotypes of Bisexual Men', *Archives of Sexual Behaviour*, 43(6): 1165–1176.

Index

Abbott, Alicia, 129
absolute concealment, 325
access rules, 328
ACON (AIDS Council of New South Wales), 22
acted self, 154
activity equity, 228
adultery agreements, 222
advantage-seeking, 154
adventurers, 54
The Advertiser, 367
Advise and Consent (film), 359
The Age (film), 366
ageing factor:
 and ending relationship, 203;
 and staying in relationship, 197–99
agentic fidelity, 215
AIB. *See* American Institute of Bisexuality (AIB)
AIDS Council of New South Wales (ACON), 22
AIDS Councils, 319
Allen, Peter, 153
ambiguous loss, 156
American Gigolo (film), 361
American Institute of Bisexuality (AIB), 60
American Psychiatric Association, 62
"American yaoi," 121

anal sex, 70, 76, 78, 86, 91, 98, 108, 111, 117, 220, 222, 297–98, 300–3, 308–9, 314
Anatomy of Hell (film), 101
And This Too Shall Pass (film), 425
Angels of Sex (film), 486
Araki, Greg, 86, 121
Atta, Farid ud-Din, 416
Australian Bisexual Network, 366
avoiders, 54

bad bisexuals, 361
Bank Robber (film), 360
Barrington, John, 69
Barrowman, John, 363
barsexuality. *See* public performative bisexuality
battered wife syndromes, 448
Beach Boys, 116
bearable life, 194
beats, 77, 99, 118, 139, 296, 308, 352, 377, 432, 438
Bend Over Boyfriend, 117
Bennett, Pam, 367
Bernstein, Leonard, 353
Beyond Therapy (film), 440
bi-affectionate emotional intimacy, 120
bi-curiousness, 88–89
bi-furiosity, 51, 327, 348, 482

525

bimisogyny, of bisexual men, 239–48
bimonogamy, 51
bi-negativity, 6, 325
biological essentialism, 82
bipatriarchal masculinist domination, 475–79
bipatriarchy, of bisexual men, 239–48
biphobia, 6, 12, 156, 240, 332, 345, 375–77, 379, 388, 393, 433, 467
biracial-bisexual identity model, 417
bisexual-behaving people, 58
bisexual display, 50
bisexual erasure, 6
bisexual FTM partners, 15
bisexual/gay-heterosexual couples, 62–63
bisexual genital arousal patterns, 59–61
bisexual-identifying people, 58
bisexuality:
  and bipatriarchal masculinist domination, 475–79;
  bisexual men denying/repressing sexualities, 431–33;
  chic. *See* heteroflexibility;
  concurrent, 54;
  cop-out, 53;
  experimental, 54;
  and friendship networks, 338–44;
  and gendernormativity, 78–79;
  and gender roles, 65;
  historic, 53;
  homotropic, 54;
  and limbo men, 51–58;
  and local communities/neighborhoods/small towns, 349–51;
  navigating and negotiating multiple identities, 433–35;
  and ongoing negotiations and/or concerns, 143–49;
  patterns of, 52–53;
  petrotropic, 54;
  and potential ramifications, 136–43;
  queering, 51–58;
  and recognition that negotiations, 230–32;
  and relationship services. *See* health services, and women with bisexual partners;
  sequential, 54;
  silence and denial of one's MORE, 427–31;
  situational, 53;
  spatial models of, 55;
  technical, 53;
  transitional, 53;
  trendy, 53;
  wider culture and society, 351–71;
  working definition of, 5–6;
  and workplaces, 344–49.
  See also mixed-orientation relationships (MOREs)
bisexual marginalization, 51
bisexual masculinities:
  and bimisogyny and bipatriarchy, 239–48;
  vs. heterosexual masculinities, 252–55;
  overview, 235–38;
  positive factors of, 248–52
bisexual men:
  and absence/erasure of religion, 413–14;
  and ageing factor, 197–99, 203;
  at beats, 77;
  bimisogyny and bipatriarchy of, 239–48;
  and bipatriarchal masculinist domination, 475–79;
  denying/repressing sexualities, 431–33;
  disenfranchisement of, 324–25;
  either/orness of, 42;
  and friendship networks, 338–44;
  gay long-term lovers of, 385;
  vs. heterosexual masculinities, 252–55;
  and HIV/AIDS. *See* sexual health negotiations;
  as HIV/AIDS carriers, 295–96, 301, 312–13;

identification of, 73–80;
inclusive masculinity of, 85;
and local communities/
    neighborhoods/small towns,
    349–51;
in MOREs, 62–70;
navigating and negotiating multiple
    identities, 433–35;
negative impact of religion on,
    400–4;
and new sexual confidence of
    women spouse, 105–12;
orthodox masculinity of, 85;
positive factors of, 248–52;
positive impact of religion on,
    404–10;
and potential ramifications, 136–43;
representations and reporting of,
    58–62;
self-identified, 59, 62;
self-reported, 61;
and sexual inadequacy of women
    spouse, 94–105;
sexual patriarchy of, 247–48;
in sexual research, 58–62;
silence and denial of one's MORE,
    427–31;
and spirituality *vs.* religion, 411–13;
women seeking and/or attracted to,
    133–36;
and workplaces, 344–49
bisexual politics, 236
bisexual polyamorous women, 258
bisexual polyamory, 355
Bisexual Psychological Services, 156
bisexual virtual community, 468
bisexual women, 7, 48, 111, 115, 303,
    325, 384, 388–89, 482;
and nonnormative and/or
    nonheterosexual sexualities of,
    112–22
Bisexual Youth of Color (BYOC), 418
bishonen (beautiful boys), 6
bi-specific social and support groups,
    464–65

Blessed Bi Spirit (Kolodny), 396
Blewett, Neal, 369
Blier, Bertrand, 360
Blue Velvet (film), 361
bordering and negotiation strategy, 50
borderland theory, and bisexual men,
    42–45
Boulevard (film), 81
"boy on boy action," 120
"boys love" (BL), 121, 122
Brain, Robert, 369
Breillat, Catherine, 101
Brindal, Mark, 367
Brokeback Mountain (film), 153, 261,
    362, 376, 424
Brosnan, Pierce, 236
Burglar (film), 359
Burne-Jones, Edward, 9, 488
BYOC. *See* Bisexual Youth of Color
    (BYOC)

Cabaret (film), 153, 360
Caine, Michael, 359, 361
camouflaging, 327
Campbell, David, 368
Carmen, Mary, 296
case-by-case approach, 85
"*Catch Him*" section, 171
Center for Disease Control and
    Prevention, 61–62, 85, 299
central-within-the-marginal
    homosexual group, 10
Change of Heart (film), 81
Cheng, Steven, 370
chic bisexuality. *See* heteroflexibility
children, and bisexual fathers:
    and concerns of mothers, 271–75;
    necessity to disclose to, 291–92;
    overview, 259–66;
    and public disclosure, 275–84;
    and sexual diversity, 266–71;
    and strategic disclosure, 284–91
Children of Earth (TV episode), 364
Cho, Margaret, 379
Chuck & Buck (film), 72

cinema as therapy theory, 357
city-dwelling, 350
clinical traps, 14
closeted gay men, 376
CNM. *See* consensual nonmonogamy (CNM)
Cock (Bartlett), 42, 376
cognitive dissonance, 328
"cognitive leap," 75
colonial value transmission, 426
commitment-phobic bisexuals, 215
Communication Privacy Management (CPM), 153, 222, 277, 328
community, and bisexuality:
   bisexual men denying/repressing sexualities, 431–33;
   navigating and negotiating multiple identities, 433–35;
   overview, 415–26;
   silence and denial of one's MORE, 427–31
compersion, 217
complicated grief, 156
complicit masculinity, 236
compulsory monosexuality, 375
concurrent bisexuality, 54
Confessions of a Bisexual Husband (Cohen), 106
Confessions of a Congressman (film), 360
conflict (either/or) model, 55
confrontational and shocking disclosure, 159–63
Confused Generation, 67
consensual nonmonogamy (CNM), 217
conventional secrets, 154
co-performative witnessing, 473
cop-out bisexuality, 53
counseling services, and women:
   couples counseling, 455–59;
   for their partners, 452–54;
   for themselves, 446–52
countertransitions, 334
Courtland Chronicles (Grant), 122
Cover (film), 399, 420

CPM. *See* Communication Privacy Management (CPM)
Craig, Larry, 77
Craigslist, 86
'cream-pies,' 119
creative intervals, 488
Criminal Lovers, 362
"crossvoyeurism," 122
crucial counter-narrative, 14
cuckolding, 86, 119
cultivation theory, 356–57
Cumming, Alan, 358
Curiouser and Curiouser: The Strange 'Disappearance' Of Male Bisexuality, 60
Custance, Olive, 249
cyberfamilies, 392
cyberfriendships, 392

DADT. *See* Don't Ask, Don't Tell (DADT) rule
The Dallas Buyers Club (film), 72
Dark Blue, Almost Black (film), 262, 263
Davies, Russell T., 364
Davis, Clive, 353
Death at a Funeral (film), 262, 263
Deathtrap (film), 359, 361
deception and betrayal of trust, 185–86
deep acting, 154
"defense theory," 75
defensives, 54
Delany, Samuel, 425
De-Lovely (film), 128
Dempsey, Patrick, 360
Depardieu, Gerard, 360
Derridean difference, 44, 51, 484
Diagnostic and Statistical Manual of Mental Disorders, 62
Dictionary of the Maori Language (Williams), 8
disclosure, of bisexuality:
   confrontational and shocking, 159–63;
   deception and betrayal of trust, 185–86;

experiential, 175–77;
and experiential disclosure, 175–77;
followed discovery, 170–74;
gradual growing, 163–69;
initial. *See* early disclosure, of bisexuality;
initiated by woman partners, 177–78;
negotiations and re-navigations, 186–91;
shifting sexuality and intimacy, 178–85
discourse of silence, 328
discrete divulgences, 155
"discursive silence," 75
divorce, and women with bisexual partners, 207–8
doctors and general practitioners (GPs), 442–46
Doctor Who (film), 363
Dog Day Afternoon (film), 361
domestication, and lesbians, 10
dominant hegemonic masculinity, 237
Don't Ask, Don't Tell (DADT) rule, 222–23
The Doom Generation, 358
Douglas, Alfred, 249
The Down Low Chronicles, 420
'down low' partners, 299
Dry Cleaning (film), 260, 359
dualists, 54
Dunstan, Don, 369–70
dyadic dissonance theory, 154–55
dyadic imaginary, 228
The Dying Gaul (film), 170, 387

early disclosure, of bisexuality:
and ongoing negotiations and/or concerns, 143–49;
and openness toward nonheteronormative relationship, 131–33;
overview, 127–31;
and potential ramifications, 136–43;
women seeking and/or attracted to bisexual men, 133–36

Eating Out 1 (film), 116
Eating Out 2 (film), 116
effeminacy, 253
ego-integrity, 198
"Eight Metrics of Bisexual Representation and Leadership," 384
El Diputado (film), 360
elevated heterosexism, 237
emancipated innocence, 198
emotional and mental health issues, 318, 438
emotional labor. *See* emotion work
emotional monogamy, 220
emotional preparation, 222
emotion management, 154, 220
emotion work, 48, 154
The Empty Child (film), 363
ending relationship, women with bisexual partners, 202–9;
and ageing factor, 203;
and divorce, 207–8;
health and financial situations of, 205–6;
and personal growth of, 206–7;
positive outcomes and opportunities, 209;
and regretful feelings of, 204–5;
and sense of independence and freedom, 203–4;
trauma of, 208–9;
and uncertainty about future, 205–6
energy management, 221
entrenchment, 90
Episcopal Church, 396
epistemic injustice, 5
"erotic plasticity," 121
ethnicity:
and gay men, 426;
and lesbians, 426
ethnicity, and bisexuality:
bisexual men denying/repressing sexualities, 431–33;
navigating and negotiating multiple identities, 433–35;

overview, 415–26;
silence and denial of one's MORE, 427–31
experiential disclosure, of bisexuality, 175–77
experimental bisexuality, 54
extended families, and heteronormativity, 329–38
external partners genders, and MOREs, 218–19
extradyadic sex, 78

Facebook, 467
fairytale marriage, 366
falling apart, 157
false self, 154
Fassbender, Michael, 72
"female fetishism," 122
femantasy, 6, 120–22
Forty Deuce (film), 360
fractional concealment, 326
friendship networks, and heteronormativity, 338–44
fudanshi (rotten boys), 6
fugitive knowledge, 13
fujoshi (naughty or rotten girls), 6, 122

GAMMA. *See* Gay and Married Men's Group (GAMMA)
The Garden of Pan (painting), 9, 25, 488
Gay and Married Men's Group (GAMMA), 460
Gayanoia, 160
gay cowboys, 376
gay-for-pay adolescent, 360
Gay Husband Check List, 83
gay lifestyle, 382
gay magnets, 160
gay men, 57–58, 303, 325, 345, 378, 388–92;
being acceptable to family, 333;
and ethnicity, 426;
and health services, 439;
and heterosexuals, 377;

identities and families, 3, 10–11, 42, 289, 356, 375, 381, 384, 400, 419, 468;
negativity/biphobia/misogyny from, 379–88;
population, 350;
sexuality, 99.
See also lesbians
Gay Men's Health Services, 319
gay porn publication, 139
Gay Pride events, 377
gay time, 221
"gei comi," 121
gendered monogamy, 216
gendernormativity, 78–79, 235, 237, 242
gender roles:
and bisexuality, 65;
socially mandated, 122
gender-scripting, 244
genders of external partners, and MOREs, 218–19
general practitioners (GPs), 442–46
gerotranscendence, 197–98, 202, 475
Gesch/echt in Fesse/n (Sex in Bondage) (film), 359
Gestalt therapy movement, 440
girlfags, 6, 116–17, 119, 121, 122
"girl-on-girl action," 120
Going Places (film), 360
Goldberg, Whoopi, 359
good bisexuals, 361
Goodman, Paul, 440
Good Weekend (magazine), 366, 370
GPs. *See* general practitioners (GPs)
Grant, Cat, 122
"Guilt-Free Generation," 67

Habana Muda (documentary), 362
haciendo caras (making faces), 48, 415
Hacker, Marilyn, 425
halekon, 423
Harris, E. Lynn, 425
health services, and women with bisexual partners:

bi-specific social and support
groups, 464–65;
counseling for their partners,
452–54;
counseling for themselves, 446–52;
couples counseling, 455–59;
doctors and general practitioners
(GPs), 442–46;
and gay men, 439;
groups for married gay and bisexual
men, 459–64;
and lesbians, 439;
and LGBTQ, 466;
need for information and resources,
467–69;
other health services, 465–67;
overview, 437–42;
and self-perceptions, 447
hegemonic gayness, 377
hegemonic masculinities, 236
hermeneutical injustice, 5
hetero-exceptionalism, 52, 87
heteroflexibility, 6, 53, 73, 85–89, 91
heteromonogamous family, 49
heteromonogamous marriage, 428, 483
heteromonosexuality, 323, 333
heteronormative misogynist sex/gender
system, 115
heteronormativity, 10, 45, 53, 78, 351;
and binegativity, 325;
and extended families, 329–38;
and friendship networks, 338–44;
and local communities/
neighborhoods/small towns,
349–51;
overview, 323–29;
and wider culture and society,
351–71;
and workplaces, 344–49
heteropatriarchy, 10, 60, 76, 78, 79,
93, 102, 107, 108, 113, 121, 203,
227, 238–40, 242, 247, 248, 257,
260, 264, 411, 420, 427, 431,
432, 488
heterosexual friendship networks, 338

heterosexual-identifying men, 86–87
heterosexuality:
'dominant' drama of, 49;
and sexual orientations, 56
heterosexually married gay men, 65
heterosexual men/masculinities:
vs. bisexual masculinities, 252–55;
and concept of being closet, 324;
sexual orientations of, 86–87
heterosexual privilege, 375
"The Hidden Generation," 67
historic bisexuality, 53
HIV/AIDS, 4, 302, 420, 424;
and bisexual men. *See* sexual health
negotiations;
carriers, bisexual men as, 295–96,
301, 312–13;
period, 142;
pre- and post-, 305;
transmission, knowledge of, 64,
358, 422
A Home at The End of the World (film),
260
homoflexibility, 6, 91
homomonosexuality, 333
homonormative hierarchy, 10
homonormative sexual duality
Margin, 43
homonormativity:
and negativity/biphobia/misandry
from lesbians, 388–90;
and negativity/biphobia/misogyny
from gay men, 379–88;
positive and supportive
relationships, 390–92
homophobia, 11, 67, 105, 156, 240,
272, 368, 375, 376, 378, 383,
400, 420, 448
homosexuality:
as evolutionary mistake, 59;
negative views of, 62;
one-time rule of, 52, 57;
in 1960s, 128
homosexualization, 376
homotropic bisexuality, 54

"honeymoon phase," 183
Hot Child in the City (film), 359
hot wife phenomenon, 119
House of Bishops, 395
House of Sable Locks (Schechter), 116
Hughes, Sam, 370
Humpday (film), 111

identityplus, 56
The Ignorant Fairies (film), 363, 484–85
immutability defense, 376
inclusive masculinity, 85
information ownership, 277
information protection and access rules, 277
initial disclosure. *See* early disclosure, of bisexuality
Insatiable Wives (Ley), 119
Inside Daisy Clover (film), 152
Inside Monkey Zetterlandland (film), 359
Insignificant Others (McAuley), 385
institutional hazing, 87
interior exclusion, 326
Interview With A Vampire (film), 72
Investigation of a Citizen Above Suspicion (movie), 361
Invisible Life (film), 425

Just As I Am (film), 425
Just One Time (film), 358

Kafavis' Syndrome, 423
Kaye, Bonnie, 12, 57, 481
Kent, Sarah, 121
kinky/queer/polyamorous/BDSM relationships, 14
Kinsey, Alfred, 188
Kinseyan continuum of sexuality, 55
Kinsey (film), 188
Kinsey/Klein scale, 72, 73, 81
Kinsey scale, 58
"Kirk/Spock" stories, 121
Klein scale, 71

Klein Sexual Orientation Grid (KSOG), 52, 63
Koh, Adele, 370
KSOG. *See* Klein Sexual Orientation Grid (KSOG)

Lambda Literary Awards, 22
The Last of Sheila (film), 358
Laughton, Charles, 353
Lawrence, D. H., 25, 488
The Leather Boys (film), 361
Leaving Metropolis (film), 359, 387
lesbian lover, 111
lesbians, 63, 303, 325, 345, 378, 388–92:
 bed death, 109;
 and domestication, 10;
 and ethnicity, 426;
 and health services, 439;
 and heterosexuals, 377;
 identities and families, 3, 10–11, 42, 48, 104, 263–64, 289, 356, 375, 381, 384, 400, 419, 468;
 and monogamy, 215;
 negativity/biphobia/misandry from, 388–90;
 population, 350.
 See also gay men
lesbian sex, 121
LGBTQ, 8, 408, 419, 453;
 health services, 466;
 parenting/families, 277;
 population, 324;
 specific activities, 377;
 workplace networks, 345
L'Homme Blesse (film), 358–60
liberation ethics, 240
limbo men, 51–58
limbo women, 102
Lindsey, Ben, 222
livable life, 194
The Living End (film), 359
local communities/neighborhoods/small towns, and heteronormativity, 349–51

Long-Term Relationship Energy (LTRE), 229
The Lost Language of Cranes (film), 261
Love You Two (Pallotta-Chiarolli), 22, 282
LTRE. *See* Long-Term Relationship Energy (LTRE)

male bisexual behavior, 54;
  adventurers, 54;
  avoiders, 54;
  defensives, 54;
  repressors, 54
male chauvinism, 240
Maori sexual minorities, 9, 488
Maori society, 426
masculine overcompensation, 237
masculine traits, 100
The Matador (film), 236
Ménage (film), 360
mental and emotional health issues, 318, 438
men who had sex with men and women (MSMW), 5
mestizaje models, 55
mestizaje persons, 43
Metamor, 70
Metropolitan Gay and Lesbian Church, 408
metrosexuality, 88
Michael's Death (movie), 361
microaggressions, 328
microassaults, 328
microinsults, 328
microinvalidations, 328
MIM. *See* Multidimensional Identity Model (MIM)
mindful bi-furiosity, 51
Minelli, Liza, 153
13 Minutes or So (film), 73
mismarriages, 12
misogyny, 12, 24
mixed-orientation relationships (MOREs):
  absence/erasure of religion, 413–14;
  and bipatriarchal masculinist domination, 475–79;
  and bisexual fathers. *See* children, and bisexual fathers;
  bisexual men denying/repressing sexualities, 431–33;
  and bi-specific social and support groups, 464–65;
  and DADT rule, 222–23;
  and emotion management, 220;
  and energy management, 221;
  and genders of external partners, 218–19;
  and gerotranscendence, 197–98, 202, 475;
  handling mistakes and cheating, 225;
  and monogamy, 215–16;
  navigating and negotiating multiple identities in, 433–35;
  negetive impact of religion on, 400–4;
  and new sexual confidence of women, 105–12;
  and nonnormative and/or nonheterosexual sexualities of women, 112–22;
  positive impact of religion on, 404–10;
  and recognition that negotiations, 230–32;
  and relationship myths, 227–28;
  and "sacred bed" rule, 223;
  and separate or shared partners, 224;
  and sexual dissatisfaction of women, 94–105;
  and sexual health negotiations, 219–20;
  sexual research on, 62–70;
  silence and denial of one's, 427–31;
  and socializing rules, 224–25;
  societal forces and expectations of relationships, 479–88;
  spirituality *vs.* religion, 411–13;

and TMI rule, 222–23;
and wider culture and society, 351–71;
women ending relationship, 202–9;
women staying in relationship, 195–202;
and women veto power, 225–27. *See also* bisexuality
m/m/f ménage, 122
monoamory, 213
monogamous family, 270, 292
monogamous parents, 265
monogamous relationships, 3, 10, 50, 68, 112, 142, 155, 185, 195, 215–16, 228, 263–64, 291, 305, 312, 425, 445, 466, 467;
heterosexual, 43;
homosexual, 43
monogamy script, 49
mononormativity, 10, 12, 45
monosexism, 6, 9, 44, 45, 55, 82, 111, 213, 281, 282, 358, 376, 393, 467, 484, 486, 488
monosexual to multisexual model, 55
Moore, Honor, 287
Moore, Paul, 287, 396
MOREs. *See* mixed-orientation relationships (MOREs)
MSMW. *See* men who had sex with men and women (MSMW)
MSWM, 51
MSWMW, 51
Multidimensional Identity Model (MIM), 417
Murphy, Graeme, 367
mutual dare, 111
My Addiction (film), 360
Mysteries of Pittsburgh (film), 128
The Mysteries of Pittsburgh (movie), 361

The Naked Face (film), 260
Naked Lunch (movie), 361
narcissism, 87
National Center for Health Statistics, 62

National Survey of Family Growth, 62
negativity/biphobia/misandry from lesbians, 388–90
negativity/biphobia/misogyny from gay men, 379–88
nepantla, 50
nepantleras, 50, 123
New Relationship Energy (NRE), 140, 229
new sexual confidence, of women, 105–12
New York Times, 59, 60, 361
Nicolson, Harold, 354
Nicolson, Nigel, 354
nomadic exclusivities, 214
non-agenda agenda, 364
nonmonogamous family, 273, 292
nonmonogamous parents, 265
nonmonogamous relationships, 11, 43, 54, 70, 112, 132, 136, 195, 217, 225, 229, 277, 308, 337, 395, 466
nonmonogamous sexual experimentations, 106
nonnormative femininity, 100
non-normative intimacies, 12
nonpreferred sex arousal, 60
normalization, and passing, 48–50
Nowhere (film), 121
NRE. *See* New Relationship Energy (NRE)

Olivier, Sir Lawrence, 353
Olley, Margaret, 370
one-drop theory, 52
one-time rule of homosexuality, 52, 57, 340
On the Downlow (film), 420
oral sex, 58, 70, 76, 78, 85, 89, 114, 116, 119, 123, 186, 221, 298, 308, 309, 311, 314
Orbea, Roberto, 360
Oreo marriages, 325
organizational bisexual inclusivity, 467
organizational citizenship behavior, 345

orientation script, 49
orthodox masculinity, 85
OSO. *See* other significant other (OSO)
other significant other (OSO), 70
"Out and About Generation," 67
Ozpetek, Ferzan, 363, 484

Pacino, Al, 361
pain avoidance, 154
panopticonic self-monitoring, 281
panopticon model, 328
pansexuality, 56
parallel exploration phase, 418
Parents & Friends of Lesbians and
    Gays (PFLAG), 463–64
partial concealment, 325
Pasolini, Pier Paolo, 260
passing, 326–27;
    and normalization, 48–50
passionate sociology, 12–17
Pastel, Cindy, 261, 379
"patriarchal opprobrium," 122
Paul Goodman Changed My Life
    (documentary), 440
pegging, 108, 117
Period Privacy, 99
personal growth, of women:
    ending relationship, 206–7;
    staying in relationship, 200
Peterson, Mike, 245
petrotropic bisexuality, 54
Petulia (film), 361
Pew Research Centre, 324, 345, 377
PFLAG. *See* Parents & Friends of
    Lesbians and Gays (PFLAG)
The Pillow Book (film), 287
The Politics of Being Queer
    (Goodman), 440
pollution and non-compliance, 50–51
polyaffectivity, 70
"poly-affirming" counselor, 455
polyamorous bisexual parents, 265
polyamorous families, 17, 22, 292
polyamorous heterosexual men, 236
polyamorous possibility, 70

polyamorous relationships, 3, 11,
    14, 43, 54, 64, 70, 79, 84, 93,
    111–12, 115, 122, 132, 136, 217,
    227–28, 231, 309–10, 354, 401,
    455–56, 464
polyamory, 6, 70, 130, 133, 140, 213,
    225, 228, 231, 234, 342, 347,
    355, 365, 369, 401, 455–56,
    468–69
polyhegemonic heterosexual
    masculinities, 236
polyphobia, 12
polysex, 213
poly subordinate and resistant
    masculinities, 237
pomosexuality, 56
Porter, Cole, 128
positive bimasculinity, 248–52
Possible Loves (film), 45, 100
preferred sex arousal, 60, 61
primary relationship, 228
Priscilla, Queen of the Desert (film),
    261, 379
privacy boundary rule coordination,
    328
privacy rule foundations, 328
privacy rule management, 328
privacy turbulence, 328
public disclosure, and bisexual fathers,
    275–84
public performative bisexuality, 111

queer coyotes, 12–17, 90, 473
queer feminists, 94, 112–14, 122
queer heterofeminist, 124
queer heterosexuality theory, 116
queering bisexuality, 51–58
quirkily heterosexual, 116

racial identities, and bisexuality:
    bisexual men denying/repressing
        sexualities, 431–33;
    navigating and negotiating multiple
        identities, 433–35;
    overview, 415–26;

silence and denial of one's MORE, 427–31
relationship literacy, 213
relationship myths, and MOREs, 227–28
religious values, and bisexuality: absence/erasure of, 413–14; negative impact of, 400–4; overview, 395–400; positive impact of, 404–10; *vs.* spirituality, 411–13
repressors, 54
resonance, 357
re-think normative relationship, 201–2
Richardson, Tony, 353
Robertson, Kathleen, 121
Robinson, Tom, 42
Rock and Roll Hall of Fame, 353
The Rocky Horror Picture Show (film), 72, 359
Romance (film), 359
rule violations, 154
Rumi, Jelaluddin, 416

Sackville-West, Vita, 354
"sacred bed" rule, 223
safe sex practices and rules, 308–11
same-sex monogamous relationships, 346
same-sex rule, 218
San Francisco Department of Public Health HIV/AIDS Epidemiology Annual Report, 301
San Francisco Human Rights Commission, 62, 299, 442
Savage Nights (film), 296
school-based sexuality education, 279, 282
scrupulous concealers, 325
secondary relationship, 228
Second Skin (film), 359
secret male sexual friendships, 99
secret unsafe sex, 295
self-confrontation, 198
self-identified bisexual men, 59, 62

self-perceptions, and health services, 447
self-reported bisexual men, 61
self-reported sexual orientations, 61
sequential bisexuality, 54
Seventh International Bisexuality Conference, 391
sexless wastelands, 99
Sexual Alternatives for Men (Barrington), 69
sexual confidence and assertiveness, 105–12
sexual diversity, and children, 266–71
sexual fluidity, 6, 56, 86, 88, 90, 109, 150, 419, 424
sexual health negotiations, 219–20; mental and emotional health issues, 318; overview, 295–304; safe sex practices and rules, 308–11; and trust, 304–8; and unprotected sex, 311–18
sexual inadequacy, 94–105
sexual intimacy, 4, 64, 93–95, 97–98, 102, 105, 139, 158, 178, 181
sexual labelling, 90
Sexual Limbo, 102
"sexual monogamy," 220
sexual orientations: and heterosexuality, 56; of heterosexual men, 86–87; of nonheterosexual partner, 64; self-reported, 61
sexual patriarchy, of bisexual men, 247–48
sexual research: bisexual men in, 58–62; media reactions to, 59–60; on MOREs, 62–70
SFBT. *See* Solution-Focused Brief Therapy (SFBT)
The Shadow Side of Polyamory, 455
shaky/wobbly, 217
Shame (film), 72
shared-partner monogamy, 216

shocking and confrontational disclosure, 159–63
"shounen-ai," 121
situational bisexuality, 53
Skins (TV show), 86
slashart, 121
slash fiction, 121
slashvidding, 121
snowball sampling strategy, 15
social cognitive theory, 357
socializing rules, and MOREs, 224–25
socially ascriptive performances. *See* emotion work
"socially mandated" gender roles, 122
social sexual identity validation, 56
sociocentric, other-directed self, 154
Solution-Focused Brief Therapy (SFBT), 447–48
Something For Everyone (film), 260
The Soundtrack of My Life (Davis), 353
sourcing sex, 99
spirituality, and bisexuality:
 absence/erasure of, 413–14;
 negative impact of, 400–4;
 overview, 395–400;
 positive impact of, 404–10;
 vs. religion, 411–13
Splendor (film), 120–21
Stage Beauty (film), 119
The Staircase (documentary), 245
Starke, Ruth, 370
staying in relationship, women with bisexual partners, 195–202;
 as advisers and supporters, 197;
 and ageing factor, 197–99;
 personal growth of, 200;
 and re-think normative relationship, 201–2;
 and rewards of relationship, 199–200;
 support from family and friends, 196–97
Steam (film), 363, 484–85
Steiger, Rod, 260
STI. *See* HIV/AIDS
stigma management, 278

Straight for the Heart (film), 360
straight gay husbands, 57
straight–gay marriages, 80–84
Straight Guise (website), 87
Straight Leaning bisexuals, 69
"straight men's girl-on-girl fantasies," 121
straight men with gay interests, 6
Straight Spouse Network, 64, 460
strategic disclosure, and bisexual fathers, 284–91
Sunday, Bloody Sunday (film), 44–45
superfluous social interaction, 198
surface acting, 154
Sydney Gay and Lesbian Mardi Gras, 377–78
symbolic oppressor, 240
synthesis (both/and) model, 55

taboo secrets, 154
Take a Bishop Like Me, 288, 396
"Talk Test Test Trust," 311
Te Arawa, 8, 9, 25, 488
Te Awekotuku, 8
technical bisexuality, 53
Teorema (film), 260, 359
tertiary relationship, 228
testimonial injustice, 5
thorough concealment, 325
3 (film), 363, 487
Three Parent Syndrome, 283
Threesome (film), 358
Tiki, 488
TMI. *See* Too Much Information (TMI) rule
Todd, Mark, 367
Together Alone, 376
Too Much Information (TMI) rule, 222–23
Torchwood (TV program), 363–64
Total Eclipse (film), 153, 361
To the Extreme (film), 264
Touché (film), 359
traditional feminine role, 245
traditional type relationships, 474;

and bipatriarchal masculinist domination, 475–79;
overview, 473–75;
societal forces and expectations of relationships, 479–88
transgendered MTF women, 15
transitional bisexuality, 53
transitioning to safety phase, 418
Travolta, John, 88
trendy bisexuality, 53
The Trio (film), 236
true self, 154
trust, and sexual health negotiations, 304–8
trust, deception and betrayal of, 185–86
12 reasons why I love dating bi men (Lambert), 390
The Twenty-fourth Day (film), 296
Two Girls for Every Boy (song), 116
Two Guys for Every Girl (song), 116
The Two Hotel Francforts (Leavitt), 129
The Two Krishnas (Dhalla), 415
Tykwer, Tom, 487
Tyler, Raymond Winston, Junior, 425

Ultimate Guide to Anal Sex for Women 2 (Taormino), 117
unbearable life, 194
Undertow (film), 387
unlivable life, 194
unprotected sex, and sexual health negotiations, 311–18
unsatisfactory sexual relationships, 94–105
U.S. Department of Health and Human Services, 299

Vassallo, Glenn, 366, 391
The Velocity of Gary (Not His Real Name) (film), 296
Vernon, Janet, 367
Verver, Andrew, 288, 397
veto power, and MOREs, 225–27
Victim (film), 128

virtual communities, 392

Waterdrops on Burning Rocks (film), 361
Weaver, Jackie, 367
Wedin, William, 156
Weller, Peter, 361
Wernick, Sandra, 45
Wes (film), 420
West Side Story (Bernstein), 353
We Think the World of You (Ackerley), 385
Wherrett, Richard, 367
"white/black" marriages, 12
white hetero-masculine logics, 52
Wilde, Oscar, 249
Williams, Herbert, 8
Williams, Robin, 81
The Witnesses (film), 261, 424
wobbly/shaky, 217
Wojtowicz, John Stanley, 361
Women in Love (Lawrence), 25
Women Partners of Bisexual Men support group, 22
women with bisexual partners:
and absence/erasure of religion, 413–14;
as advisers and supporters, 197;
and ageing factor, 197–99, 203;
and bimisogyny and bipatriarchy, 239–48;
and bipatriarchal masculinist domination, 475–79;
bisexual men denying/repressing sexualities, 431–33;
and bisexual *vs.* heterosexual masculinities, 252–55;
bordering and negotiation strategy, 50;
and borderland theory, 42–45;
and circumstances of relationship, 178–85;
and community relations, 45–47;
and confessions of same-sex attraction, 177–78;

and confrontational disclosure, 159–63;
considering quality of relationship, 138;
and DADT rule, 222–23;
deception and betrayal of trust, 185–86;
and Derridean difference, 44, 51, 348;
disclosing to children. *See* children, and bisexual fathers;
disclosure followed discovery, 170–74;
and divorce, 207–8;
and emotion management, 220;
ending relationship, 202–9;
and energy management, 221;
and experiential disclosure, 175–77;
exploitation and disempowering of, 255–58;
and extended families, 329–38;
and friendship networks, 338–44;
and genders of external partners rule, 218–19;
and gradual growing disclosure, 163–69;
handling mistakes and cheating, 225;
health and financial situations of, 205–6;
and local communities/neighborhoods/small towns, 349–51;
mental and emotional health issues, 318;
and mestizaje persons, 43;
and monogamy, 215–16;
mystery and frustration of, 80–84;
navigating and negotiating multiple identities, 433–35;
negative impact of religion on, 400–4;
and negativity/biphobia/misandry from lesbians, 388–90;
and negativity/biphobia/misogyny from gay men, 379–88;
negotiations and re-navigations, 186–91;
new kind of sexual confidence, 105–12;
nonnormative and/or nonheterosexual sexualities of, 112–22;
and ongoing negotiations and/or concerns, 143–49;
and openness toward nonheteronormative relationship, 131–33;
passing and normalization, 48–50;
and personal growth of, 200, 206–7;
pollution and non-compliance, 50–51;
positive and supportive relationships of homonormativity, 390–92;
positive impact of religion on, 404–10;
positive outcomes and opportunities, 209;
and potential ramifications, 136–43;
regretful feelings of, 204–5;
and relationship myths, 227–28;
and relationship services. *See* health services, and women with bisexual partners;
and re-think normative relationship, 201–2;
and rewards of relationship, 199–200;
and "sacred bed" rule, 223;
safe sex practices and rules, 308–11;
seeking and/or attracted to bisexual men, 133–36;
and sense of independence and freedom, 203–4;
and separate or shared partners, 224;
and sexual health negotiations, 219–20;
and sexual inadequacy, 94–105;
shifting sexuality and intimacy, 178–85;
silence and denial of one's MORE, 427–31;

and socializing rules, 224–25;
and social relations, 45–47;
societal forces and expectations of
    relationships, 479–88;
and spirituality *vs.* religion,
    411–13;
staying in relationship, 195–202;
support from family and friends,
    196–97;
and TMI rule, 222–23;
trauma of, 208–9;
trust and sexual practices, 304–8;
uncertainty and fear about future,
    205–6;
and unprotected sex, 311–18;
unsatisfactory sexual relationships
    of, 94–105;

and veto power, 225–27;
and wider culture and society,
    351–71;
and workplaces, 344–49.
See also bisexuality
Women with Bisexual Partners
    Network, 366
Woodroof, Ron, 72
workplaces, and heteronormativity,
    344–49
wounded identities, 14
www.Gayhusbands.com (website), 171

"yaoi," 121–22
Y Tu Mama Tambien (film), 72

Zafar, Mohammed Nasem, 423

About the Author

Maria Pallotta-Chiarolli, PhD, is Senior Lecturer in the School of Health and Social Development, Deakin University, researching in gender diversity, cultural diversity, family diversity and sexual diversity. Author and editor of 13 academic and nonacademic books, Maria has won two Lambda (GLBTIQ) Literary Awards in the United States. She has also gained international recognition for writing Australia's first AIDS biography, publishing Australia's first research into ethnic minority GLBTIQ Australians, and publishing Australia's first book on bisexuality in education and polyamorous families. Maria is also a Founding Member of the Australian GLBTIQ Multicultural Council Inc. (AGMC).

Webpage: http://mariapallottachiarolli.com.au/